Crusades
Volume 10, 2011

Crusades

Edited by
Benjamin Z. Kedar, Jonathan Phillips
and Jonathan S. C. Riley-Smith with William J. Purkis

Crusades is published annually for the Society for the Study of the Crusades and the Latin East by Ashgate. A statement of the aims of the Society and details of membership can be found following the Bulletin at the end of the volume.

Manuscripts should be sent to either of the Editors in accordance with the guidelines for submission of papers on p. 295.

Subscriptions: Crusades (ISSN 1476–5276) is published annually.

Subscriptions are available on an annual basis and are £65 for institutions and non-members, and £25 for members of the Society. Prices include postage by surface mail. Enquiries concerning members' subscriptions should be addressed to the Treasurer, Professor James D. Ryan (see p. 222). All orders and enquiries should be addressed to: Subscription Department, Ashgate Publishing Ltd, Wey Court East, Union Road, Farnham, Surrey, GU9 7PT, U.K.; tel.: +44 (0)1252 331600; fax: +44 (0)1252 736736; email: journals@ashgatepublishing.com

Requests for Permissions and Copying: requests should be addressed to the Publishers: Permissions Department, Ashgate Publishing Ltd, Wey Court East, Union Road, Farnham, Surrey, GU9 7PT, U.K.; tel.: +44 (0)1252 331600; fax: +44 (0)1252 736736; email: journals@ashgatepublishing.com. The journal is also registered in the U.S.A. with the Copyright Clearance Center, 222 Rosewood Drive, Danvers MA 01923, U.S.A.; tel.: +1 (978) 750 8400; fax: +1 (978) 750 4470; email: rreader@copyright.com and in the U.K. with the Copyright Licensing Agency, 90 Tottenham Court Road, London, W1P 9HE; tel.: +44 (0)207 436 5931; fax: +44 (0)207 631 5500.

Crusades

Volume 10, 2011

Published by ASHGATE *for the*
Society for the Study of the Crusades
and the Latin East

Published by
Ashgate Publishing Limited
Wey Court East
Union Road
Farnham
Surrey GU9 7PT
England

Ashgate Publishing Company
Suite 420
101 Cherry Street
Burlington, VT 05401–4405
USA

Ashgate website: http://ashgate.com

ISBN: 978-1-4094-2813-3

ISSN 1476–5276

Typeset by N²productions

The paper used in this publication meets the minimum requirements of the American National Standard for Information Sciences – Permanence of Paper for Printed Library Materials, ANSI Z39.48-1984

Printed and bound in Great Britain by the MPG Books Group, UK

CONTENTS

R<small>EVIEWS</small>

Abbreviations

AA	Albert of Aachen, *Historia Ierosolimitana. History of the Journey to Jerusalem*, ed. and trans. Susan B. Edgington. Oxford, 2007
AOL	*Archives de l'Orient latin*
Autour	*Autour de la Première Croisade. Actes du colloque de la Society for the Study of the Crusades and the Latin East: Clermont-Ferrand, 22–25 juin 1995*, ed. Michel Balard. Paris, 1996
Cart Hosp	*Cartulaire général de l'ordre des Hospitaliers de Saint-Jean de Jérusalem, 1100–1310*, ed. Joseph Delaville Le Roulx. 4 vols. Paris, 1884–1906
Cart St Sép	*Le Cartulaire du chapitre du Saint-Sépulcre de Jérusalem*, ed. Geneviève Bresc-Bautier, Documents relatifs à l'histoire des croisades 15. Paris, 1984
Cart Tem	*Cartulaire général de l'ordre du Temple 1119?–1150. Recueil des chartes et des bulles relatives à l'ordre du Temple*, ed. Guigue A.M.J.A., (marquis) d'Albon. Paris, 1913
CCCM	Corpus Christianorum. Continuatio Mediaevalis
Chartes Josaphat	*Chartes de la Terre Sainte provenant de l'abbaye de Notre-Dame de Josaphat*, ed. Henri F. Delaborde, Bibliothèque des Écoles françaises d'Athènes et de Rome 19. Paris, 1880
Clermont	*From Clermont to Jerusalem: The Crusades and Crusader Societies 1095–1500. Selected Proceedings of the International Medieval Congress, University of Leeds, 10–13 July 1995*, ed. Alan V. Murray. International Medieval Research 3. Turnhout, 1998
Crusade Sources	*The Crusades and their Sources: Essays Presented to Bernard Hamilton*, ed. John France and William G. Zajac. Aldershot, 1998
CS	*Crusade and Settlement: Papers read at the First Conference of the Society for the Study of the Crusades and the Latin East and Presented to R.C. Smail*, ed. Peter W. Edbury. Cardiff, 1985
CSEL	Corpus Scriptorum Ecclesiasticorum Latinorum
EC, 1	*The Experience of Crusading 1: Western Approaches*, ed. Marcus G. Bull and Norman J. Housley. Cambridge, 2003
EC, 2	*The Experience of Crusading 2: Defining the Crusader Kingdom*, ed. Peter W. Edbury and Jonathan P. Phillips. Cambridge, 2003

FC	Fulcher of Chartres, *Historia Hierosolymitana (1095–1127)*, ed. Heinrich Hagenmeyer. Heidelberg, 1913
GF	*Gesta Francorum et aliorum Hierosolimitanorum*, ed. and trans. Rosalind M.T. Hill and Roger Mynors. London, 1962
GN	Guibert of Nogent, *Dei gesta per Francos*, ed. Robert B.C. Huygens CCCM 127A. Turnhout, 1996
Horns	*The Horns of Hattin*, ed. Benjamin Z. Kedar. Jerusalem and London, 1992
Kreuzfahrerstaaten	*Die Kreuzfahrerstaaten als multikulturelle Gesellschaft. Einwanderer und Minderheiten im 12. und 13. Jahrhundert*, ed. Hans Eberhard Mayer with Elisabeth Müller-Luckner. Schriften des Historischen Kollegs, Kolloquien 37. Munich, 1997
Mansi. *Concilia*	Giovanni D. Mansi, *Sacrorum conciliorum nova et amplissima collectio*
MGH	Monumenta Germaniae Historica
MO, 1	*The Military Orders: Fighting for the Faith and Caring for the Sick*, ed. Malcolm Barber. Aldershot, 1994
MO, 2	*The Military Orders, vol. 2: Welfare and Warfare*, ed. Helen Nicholson. Aldershot, 1998
MO, 3	*The Military Orders, vol. 3: History and Heritage*, ed. Victor Mallia-Milanes. Aldershot, 2008
Montjoie	*Montjoie: Studies in Crusade History in Honour of Hans Eberhard Mayer*, ed. Benjamin Z. Kedar, Jonathan Riley-Smith and Rudolf Hiestand. Aldershot, 1997
Outremer	*Outremer. Studies in the History of the Crusading Kingdom of Jerusalem Presented to Joshua Prawer*, ed. Benjamin Z. Kedar, Hans E. Mayer and Raymond C. Smail. Jerusalem, 1982
PG	Patrologia Graeca
PL	Patrologia Latina
PPTS	Palestine Pilgrims' Text Society Library
RHC	*Recueil des Historiens des Croisades*
Darm	*Documents arméniens*
Lois	*Les assises de Jérusalem*
Oc	*Historiens occidentaux*
Or	*Historiens orientaux*
RHGF	Recueil des Historiens des Gaules et de la France
RIS	Rerum Italicarum Scriptores
NS	New Series
ROL	*Revue de l'Orient latin*
RRH	Reinhold Röhricht, comp., *Regesta regni hierosolymitani*. Innsbruck, 1893

RRH Add	Reinhold Röhricht, comp., *Additamentum*. Innsbruck, 1904
RS	Rolls Series
Setton, *Crusades*	*A History of the Crusades*, general editor Kenneth M. Setton, 2nd edn., 6 vols. Madison, 1969–89
SRG	Scriptores Rerum Germanicarum
WT	William of Tyre, *Chronicon*, ed. Robert B.C. Huygens, with Hans E. Mayer and Gerhard Rösch, CCCM 63–63A. Turnhout, 1986

The Guide of MS Beinecke 481.77 and the Intertwining of Christian, Jewish and Muslim Traditions in Twelfth-Century Jerusalem

Iris Shagrir

The Open University of Israel
irissh@openu.ac.il

The short anonymous text at the centre of this article was probably written in the first decades of the Frankish kingdom of Jerusalem, sometime after the conquest of Jerusalem by the first crusaders. It was written by a not particularly well-educated author, whose Latin is unrefined and whose grammar is often inadequate. It is probable that the text dates to the first half of the twelfth century, before the completion of the Church of the Holy Sepulchre.[1] It is possible, however, as I will argue later, to date its composition with greater accuracy. The text, which addresses the city of Jerusalem and other places in the Holy Land, has received scant mention in the literature on pilgrimage to the Holy Land, and in the research on the Frankish kingdom of Jerusalem it has been largely overlooked.[2] In what follows I will attempt to explore and explain this short text's unique traits.

The only known manuscript of the text is kept in the Beinecke Collection in the Yale University Library.[3] The text is written in a firm hand, in brown ink, on both

---

I would like to thank friends and colleagues for their valuable advice while this paper was in progress, especially Ora Limor, Robert Huygens, B. Z. Kedar, Yossi Ziegler, Effie Shoham-Steiner, Gideon Bohak and Anna Gutgarts-Weinberger. This paper is part of a research project on Jerusalem in the twelfth century, supported by the Israel Science Foundation.

[1] See Denys Pringle, *The Churches of the Crusader Kingdom of Jerusalem*, vol. 3 (Cambridge, 2007), esp. pp. 20–21. For a helpful review of the state of completion of the church, see Amnon Linder, "Like Purest Gold Resplendent: The Fiftieth Anniversary of the Liberation of Jerusalem," *Crusades* 8 (2009), 31–51.

[2] The manuscript was published, with a brief critical survey, in Lisa F. Davis, "A Twelfth-Century Pilgrim's Guide to the Holy Land: Beinecke MS 481.77," *Yale University Library Gazette* 65 (1990), 11–19. The guide is mentioned also in Debra J. Birch, *Pilgrimage to Rome in the Middle Ages: Continuity and Change* (Woodbridge, 1998), p. 222 (bibliography).

[3] Beinecke MS 481.77 (henceforth: Beinecke guide). Prior to its inclusion in the Beinecke Collection (established in 1963), the manuscript was in the possession of Hans P. Kraus, the renowned Austrian-American collector and dealer in rare books and manuscripts. In the 1950s the manuscript was examined by Bernhard Bischoff, who commented in the margin "15 Juli 1099" and "Wegweiser für Jerusalem." The manuscript is part of a collection of about 400 pieces, mostly fragments. See Davis, "Pilgrim's Guide," pp. 11–14; and *Catalogue of Medieval and Renaissance Manuscripts in the Beinecke Rare Book and Manuscript Library, Yale University*, vol. 4, ed. Robert G. Babcock, Lisa F. Davis and Philip G. Rusche (Tempe, Ariz., 2004), p. 134. The library's catalogue from 1987 only mentions "Five collections of fragments that will be published separately"; see *Catalogue of Medieval and Renaissance Manuscripts in the Beinecke Rare Book and Manuscript Library, Yale University*, vol. 2, ed. Barbara A. Shailor (New York, 1987), p. 459.

sides of a small piece of parchment (118 × 184 mm.), a scrap that may originally have been intended for another codex, since the lines drawn on the parchment are vertical to the text.[4] On the recto there are twenty lines and on the verso eight lines, of which seven belong to the pilgrim's description.

The condition of the manuscript is quite good and the text is legible. It has a few worm holes and is cut off slightly at the lower edge, which caused the loss of a small portion of the text. The marks of folding into four make reading difficult along the fold lines, and some faded words may indicate the spots where the parchment was held, as just below the horizontal folding-line on the right; these are signs that the manuscript has been in use. The text is written in a well-formed and clear hand. The author or copyist of the manuscript knew the common abbreviations and used them frequently. At the same time, there are grammatical mistakes in the usage of Latin cases and declensions, and some orthographic distortions. The text is not illuminated, apart from an ornamented cross, in the same brown ink and beside it an initial A, which forms the beginning of the phrase *Ab occidente*.

The account seems to be one of the earliest descriptions of the Frankish kingdom of Jerusalem. Moreover, the text in the Beinecke manuscript is probably a copy,[5] but one made close to the time of the original writing, which may testify to its usefulness or popularity. The account mentions several pilgrimage sites and traditions that were not common in contemporary descriptions.

Text: Yale University Library, Beinecke MS 481.77[6]

[Recto] [1] AB occidente est introitus Ierusalem per Portam David. Intra c<iv>itate<m> est Sepulchrum [2] domini, foris in capite ipsius est medium mundi, ultra est carcer, ligacio, flagella(la)cio [3], locus ubi coronatus fuit, vestimenta divisa, mons Calvarie ubi fuit crucifixus; [4] subtus est Golgatha, ubi sanguis domini cecidit per petram <s>cissam, super quem monte<m> invenit [5] sancta Elena crucem domini.

Hinc prope est Sancta Maria Latina iu<x>sta est hospitale.

Ab oriente [6] est Templum Domini, in quo sunt IIII introitus, ab oriente, ab occidente, a meridie, ab aquilone.

[7] Ibi est presentacio domini, ibi fuit archa federis domini et due tabule testamenti et virga Aaron [8] et septem candelabra aurea et confessio apostolorum et ibi Iacob dormivit et hic [9] Iacobus fuit mactatus.

In angulo civitatis est cunabulum Christi et balneum et lectum [10] sue genitricis.

---

[4] Davis, "Pilgrim's Guide," p. 11.

[5] According to the library catalogue from 2004, "the script resembles early 12th century Italian hands": *Catalogue*, vol. 4, ed. Babcock et al., p. 134; Davis, "Pilgrim's Guide," p. 15, notes that the script dates the manuscript to the 1120s or earlier.

[6] I thank Professor Robert Huygens for his generous help in editing the text.

Sub Templo Domini est Porta Aurea, per qua<m> dominus intravit cu<m> ramis palmarum.

[11] A sinistra[m] parte est ecclesia Sanctae Annae et probatica piscina.

Superius est Sancta ^Maria Macdalena.

[12] Extra civitate<m> ab aquilone fuit lapidatus sanctus Stephanus.

Extra civitate<m> ab oriente [13] est Vallis Iosaphat, ubi sancta Maria sepulta fuit ab[a] apostoli<s> . Ibi est Iessemani ubi Iudas [14] Christum tradidit, prope est locus ubi [Iudas Christum]⁷ oravit Christus.

Superius est Mons Oliveti ubi [15] dominus ascendit in celum, ibi fecit *Pater Noster*.

Subtus est Bethania, ubi dominus suscitavit Lazarum.

[16] A meridie est mons Syon, ubi migravit sancta Maria. Ibi est tabu<la> ubi dominus cenavit cum [17] discipulis et lavit pedes eorum et ibi est Galilea, ubi dominus ap<p> aruit ^discipulis , ibi venit Spiritus sanctus super eos in die [18] Pentecosten.

Subtus natatoria Syloe, Acheldemac.

Betleem longe ab⁸ Ierusalem duas leugas [19], ubi natus fuit Christus, et presepe ubi positus fuit et puteus ubi stel<l>a requievit et tabula ubi reges co[20]mederunt. ***<ibi Sancta Paula et> sanctus Ieronimus iacent.

De Ierusalem ad Sanctum Abraam X leu<gas>; [Verso] [1] Ibi iacent Abraam, Ysaac, et Iacob, Sarra, Rebecca, Lia et Iosep.

De Ierusalem ad flumen Iordanis [2] X leugas. In orto Abrae est Iericho.

Superius est Quarantena, ubi dominus <ieiuna>vit XL dies [3] et XL noctibus.

Superius est mons excelsus,⁹ ubi dominus a diabolo temptatus fuit.

De Ierusalem [4] ad montem Tabor dies III, ibi est transfiguracio domini. Hinc Nazaret duas leugas, ubi dominus [5] nunciatus fuit per angelum atque nutritus.

Mare Galilea<e> hinc longe V leugas, prope est [6] locus ubi dominus saciavit V milia homines de V panibus et duobus piscibus, quod dominus benedi<xi>t.

[7] Idus Iulii capta est civitas sancta Ierusalem <a>Franci<s>. Eodem die Divisio Apostolorum.

Fur di vallunt suth scribe an ain zedel

Translation

[Recto] From the west is the entrance to Jerusalem through David's Gate. Within the city is the Tomb of the Lord, outside at its end is the middle of the world, further is the prison, the place of the binding, flagellation, where [he] was crowned and the garments were divided, Mount of Calvary where he was crucified; below is Golgotha where the blood of the Lord dropped though the slit rock. On this

---

⁷ Words erroneously repeated.
⁸ MS ad.
⁹ MS excelsum.

mountain Saint Helen found the Lord's cross. Close by is Saint Mary the Latin, next is the hospital.

To the east is the Lord's Temple in which there are four doorways, in the east, west, south, north. There is the Presentation of the Lord, there the Lord's Ark of the Covenant was and the two Tables of the Covenant, and Aaron's rod, and the seven golden lamps and the Confession of the Apostles, and there Jacob slept and there James was killed. In the corner of the city is the cradle of Christ, and the bath and the bed of his mother.

Below the Lord's Temple is the Golden Gate through which the Lord entered with palm branches. To the left side is the Church of Saint Anne and the Probatic Pool. Beyond is Saint Mary Magdalene.

Outside the city to the north Saint Stephen was stoned.

Outside the city to the east is the valley of Josaphat where Saint Mary was entombed by the apostles. There is Gethsemane where Judas betrayed Christ nearby is the place where Christ prayed.

Above is the Mount of Olives where the Lord ascended to Heaven, there he composed *Pater Noster*. Below is Bethany where the Lord raised Lazarus from the dead.

In the south is Mount Zion where Saint Mary migrated. There is the table where the Lord had supper with the disciples and washed their feet, and there is the Galilee where the Lord appeared to the disciples, there the Holy Ghost came on them in Pentecost. Below is the Pool of Siloam, Aceldama.

Bethlehem is two leagues away from Jerusalem, where Christ was born and the stable where he was put, and the well where the star rested, and the table where the kings ate. There lie Saint Paula and Saint Jerome.

From Jerusalem to Saint Abraham ten leagues. [Verso] There lie Abraham, Isaac and Jacob, Sarah, Rebecca, Leah and Joseph.

From Jerusalem to the River Jordan ten leagues. Jericho is in the Garden of Abraham. Above is the Quarantine where the Lord fasted for forty days and forty nights. Above is the High Mountain where the Lord was tempted by the devil.

From Jerusalem to Mount Tabor three days, there is the transfiguration of the Lord. From there Nazareth is two leagues, where the Lord was announced by the angel and nourished. The Sea of Galilee is five leagues farther away. Nearby is the place where the Lord fed 5,000 people with five loaves of bread and two fish which he blessed.

On the Ides of July the holy city of Jerusalem was conquered by the Franks. The day of the Dispersion of the Apostles.

The guide mentions some places in the south and north of Palestine, from Hebron to the Sea of Galilee, but in the main it deals with Jerusalem. It provides simple walking directions, designed, it seems, to assist those already present in the city. Often the writer uses words that indicate direction such as: out of, at the fringe of, on top of, beyond.

Unlike texts that open with a description of arriving in Jerusalem from a faraway place, a description of the voyage to the East or of landing at a port in the Holy Land, the starting point of this guide is at the actual entrance to the city, the present-day Jaffa Gate (*Porta David*). The content of the guide is simple and concise, and does not expand on traditions or practices connected to the places mentioned; in comparison with similar guides, it is fairly succinct even with directions and distances.

The eighth line on the *verso* is written in a slightly darker Gothic script, in middle-high German: "fur di vallunt such (suth?) – scribe an ain zedel," which probably means: "against epilepsy, write on a piece of paper."[10] The German language and the Gothic script indicate that this piece of parchment was taken back to western Europe and served an additional use. Amulet writing in the margins of non-magical texts is common in medieval manuscripts. One might assume that, due to the scarcity of writing material, any remaining empty spaces were used to keep information that might come in handy whenever needed. It is possible that the formula was kept in a private home. Yet the connection between the description of Jerusalem and this formula is not necessarily random: it is possible that the text, being related to the Holy Land, was attributed with holiness considered conducive to healing. A less likely possibility is that the Latin text itself was intended to serve as a magic charm to ward off evil, in spite of its contents not being such. The lines where the parchment has been folded show that it was kept either in a case or among someone's belongings during a journey or preserved for years in the hope that it might afford magical protection.[11]

Pilgrimage to Jerusalem at the Beginning of the Twelfth Century

The establishment of the Frankish kingdom of Jerusalem paved the way for many pilgrims to visit the holy sites and celebrate the liturgy at the original locations. The Russian pilgrim Abbot Daniel, who visited Jerusalem in 1106–7, testifies explicitly

---

[10] In transcription to modern German: "für die fallende Sucht schreibe an einen Zettel." I am grateful to Professor Joseph Ziegler for this suggestion.

[11] For further information on this matter see Sarah L. Keefer and Rolf H. Bremmer, Jr., eds., *Signs on the Edge: Space, Text and Margin in Medieval Manuscripts*, Mediaevalia Groningana n.s. 10 (Leuven, 2007), and Giuseppe Veltri, "Watermarks in the MS 'Munich, Hebr. 95': Magical Recipes in Historical Contexts," in *Jewish Studies between the Disciplines/Judaistik zwischen den Disziplinen: Papers in Honor of Peter Schäfer on the Occasion of his 60th Birthday*, ed. Klaus Herrmann, Margarete Schlüter and Giuseppe Veltri (Leiden, 2003), pp. 243–56. Also printed in Shaul Shaked, ed., *Officina Magica: Essays on the Practice of Magic in Antiquity*, IJS Studies in Judaica 4 (Leiden, 2005), pp. 255–68.

on the necessity for guidance in the city: "It is not possible without a good guide [who accompanies you] and without knowledge of the language to find and see all the holy places."[12] For the sake of the large number of Latin visitors in the early twelfth century, short descriptions were composed in a simple and functional style. The Beinecke guide and those similar to it lack an emotional or spiritual dimension, and it is hard to learn from them about the realities of the country.[13] Their often arid style does not reflect the rich literary creativity that characterized western Europe during the twelfth-century Renaissance, yet it met the immediate needs in the Holy Land.

Most of the information provided by the writers of these guides, including the linking of a certain tradition to a certain site, was gathered through conversation with the local population. In other words, choosing the sites and obtaining information was not necessarily a result of thorough investigation on the part of the authors, but often a result of information offered to them on the spot, in conjunction with other guides and oral traditions, which did not always tally with one another.

The best-known description of this period was that written by Saewulf, who made his journey from the British Isles in 1102–3. His narrative is outstanding in comparison with the other contemporary Latin guides. With a vivid and lively narrative skill, Saewulf describes a journey that lasted over a year, including a perilous sea voyage from Italy, anchoring at the port of Jaffa, and then traversing the route from Jaffa to Jerusalem, a route beset with dangers. In Jerusalem his style becomes drier and more matter-of-fact. Saewulf entered Jerusalem through *Porta David* and went directly to the Church of the Holy Sepulchre: "First one should go to the Church of the Holy Sepulchre, which is called Martyrium, not only because of the arrangement of the streets, but because it is more celebrated than all other churches."[14] From there he went on to the *Templum Domini* and to the sacred places on the Temple Mount, the Church of Saint Anne, the Valley of Jehoshaphat, the Mount of Olives and Mount Zion. Outside Jerusalem, Saewulf mentions Mount Tabor, Tiberias and the Galilee, and returns to a description of Jerusalem and its surroundings: Mount Zion, the site where Stephen was stoned, Bethlehem, the Jordan River and Hebron.

There are several other well-known but anonymous texts from the first half of the twelfth century. The First Anonymous Guide was written in 1101–4. This guide accompanied the anonymous *Gesta Francorum et aliorum Hierosolimitanorum*, appearing at the end of the chronicle as an addendum.[15] Because this short guide

---

[12] *Biblioteka literatury Drevnei Rusi*, ed. Dmitrii S. Likhachev, Library of Ancient Russian Literature 4 (St. Petersburg, 1997), p. 28. I thank Anna Gutgarts-Weinberger for all the translations from Russian.

[13] On the various types of pilgrim itinerary and travel literature, see Ora Limor, "'Holy Journey': Pilgrimage and Christian Sacred Landscape," in *Christians and Christianity in the Holy Land*, ed. Ora Limor and Guy G. Stroumsa (Turnhout, 2006), pp. 321–53.

[14] *Peregrinationes tres: Saewulf, John of Würzburg, Theodericus*, ed. Robert B. C. Huygens, CCCM 139 (Turnhout, 1994), p. 64.

[15] The First Anonymous Guide, in *GF*, pp. 98–101.

was appended to every twelfth-century manuscript of the *Gesta Francorum* it is assumed that it was attached to the original version. Both were written in a similar simple style, and their similarity may indicate a circumstantial proximity, resulting from the need to indicate those sites that crusaders should visit before returning to their homeland, as many did. Thus the juxtaposition of the two texts served to publicize the holy places liberated through the glorious *gesta* of the first crusaders. The description opens with these words:

> Here begins a description of the holy places of Jerusalem. If anyone, coming from the western lands, wishes to go to Jerusalem, let him direct his course due eastwards, and in this way he will find the stations for prayer in the lands in and around Jerusalem, as they are noted here.[16]

The description in the First Anonymous Guide has a slightly confused order of sites, starting at the Temple Mount, going towards the Damascus Gate, to the Church of the Holy Sepulchre and back to the Temple Mount. In the description of the Temple Mount, the writer has inserted the well-known excerpt from the account of the Bordeaux pilgrim (A.D. 333), describing the Jews who arrive there every year, mourning the destruction of the Temple and anointing a stone.[17] Having relied on the Bordeaux pilgrim, the First Anonymous Guide initially identifies the place as the ruins of the Jewish Temple, but further on identifies it as *Templum Domini*, the name used by the Franks. In addition to the holy places of Jerusalem, the First Anonymous Guide refers also to the River Jordan, Mount Tabor, Bethlehem and Hebron; but it is hard to know whether the writer himself actually visited those places.

Another short description dating from 1099–1103, is known as the *Qualiter* for its opening words: *Qualiter sita est civitas Ierusalem*. Like the First Anonymous Guide it opens with the words: "Anyone who may wish to go to Jerusalem, the Holy City, should continue to travel eastwards, and this is how, with God's guidance, he will reach Holy Jerusalem."[18] The pilgrim set off on his tour of Jerusalem at *Monjoie*, entering through *Porta David*, and continuing to the Holy Sepulchre and to other sites to the east, the *Templum Domini*, the Sheep Pool, Gethsemane, and the Mount of Olives. The author of the *Qualiter* ends with the statement that he himself saw everything with his own eyes. The text is also probably connected

---

[16]   Ibid., p. 98.

[17]   Ibid.; the Pilgrim of Bordeaux, ed. P. Geyer and O. Cuntz, *Itineraria et alia geographica*, Corpus Christianorum Series Latina 175 (Turnhout, 1965), p. 16.

[18]   Titus Tobler, *Itinera et descriptiones Terrae Sanctae* (Geneva, 1877), p. 415. Tobler dated it to the end of the eleventh century, as did the editors of the PPTS, who dated it to 1096. Wilkinson classifies it as an early guide that was circulating at about the same time as the First Anonymous Guide. However, the dating of the guide to the end of the eleventh century is not likely, as it was only after the crusader conquest that the Dome of the Rock started to be called "Temple of the Lord."

to a chronicle of the First Crusade, that of Baldric of Bourgueil, since the two manuscripts were found bundled together.[19]

An additional anonymous guide, also short and concise, is known as the Ottobonian guide.[20] This guide, dated 1101–3, consists mainly of a description of Jerusalem. It has much in common with the Beinecke guide, including very similar wording in some passages. The Ottobonian guide sets off at the Tower of David, goes on to the Church of the Holy Sepulchre, *Templum Domini*, the Sheep Pool, the Valley of Jehoshaphat, the Mount of Olives and Mount Zion. Outside Jerusalem, it briefly mentions Bethlehem and the Jordan River area.

Of the texts discussed above, the closest textual affinity exists between the Beinecke guide on the one hand and Saewulf's narrative and the Ottobonian guide, especially the latter, on the other.

Saewulf's narrative is the most didactic and detailed of the three, expanding on traditions of the *loca sancta* and on their scriptural context. The conciseness of the two shorter guides is better suited to their destined readership. Saewulf's description, surviving in only a single manuscript, seems intended for Christians living far from the Holy Land, those who wanted to read in detail about the holy sites and learn of their appearance and significance. By contrast, readers of the short guides needed only simple instructions and brief explanations that could be referred to in the course of touring the holy city.

The Beinecke and Ottobonian guides not only scrimped on descriptions of the sites, they also skipped many biblical traditions. In the Temple Mount area, for example, Saewulf recalls several New Testament traditions not mentioned in the other texts, such as the presentation of Jesus in the Temple (Luke 2.22–40), Jesus's debate with the Jewish Sages (Luke 2.41–52), the casting out of the vendors (Matt. 21.12–17), the healing of the paralysed man by Peter, and the arrival of Peter and John to pray in the Temple (Acts 3.1–8). Nonetheless, it should be noted that all the traditions mentioned in the Beinecke and Ottobonian guides are also mentioned by Saewulf, except for two: the Golden Candelabrum and the murder of James the Less on the Temple Mount; the latter (which will be discussed below) appears only in the Beinecke.

The opening passages of the Beinecke and Ottobonian manuscripts are almost identical.

---

[19]   Tobler, *Itinera et descriptiones*, p. LII. The *Historia* of Baldric of Bourgueil has recently been dated to 1105–7: see Steven J. Biddlecombe, "The *Historia Ierosolimitana* of Baldric of Bourgueil: A New Edition in Latin and an Analysis" (PhD thesis, University of Bristol, 2010), pp. 23–28. For the chronicle, see *RHC Oc* 4:1–111.

[20]   This guide was appended at the end of codex Ottobonianus Latinus 169, a codex that contains, among other works, a catalogue of the relics and sanctuaries of Constantinople, ascribed to an English friar who visited the East in the twelfth century. The codex was published by Silvio G. Mercati, "Santuari e reliquie Costantinopolitane secondo il codice Ottoboniano latino 169 prima della conquista latina (1204)," *Rendiconti della Pontificia Accademia Romana di Archeologia* 12 (1936), 133–54. The description of Jerusalem appears after the catalogue, at pp. 153–54. For an English translation, see John Wilkinson, ed. and trans., *Jerusalem Pilgrimage 1099–1185* (London, 1988), pp. 92–93.

The Beinecke guide

Ab occidente est introitus Ierusalem per Portam David. Intra c<iv>itate<m> est Sepulchrum domini, foris in capite ipsius est medium mundi, ultra est carcer, ligacio, flagella(la)cio, locus ubi coronatus fuit, vestimenta divisa.

The Ottobonian guide

In occidentali parte est introitus Ierusalem iuxta turre David. Infra civitatem est sepulchrum domini. In capite cuius, de foris est mundi medium. Inde, ex parte septentrionali carcer domini, iuxta ligatio, flagellatio, coronatio, despoliatio, ibique vestimenta sua fuerunt divisa.[21]

A comparison between these two opening sections demonstrates that the Latin language of the Ottobonian is of a higher, more classical standard; that the Beinecke guide is niggardly with words, especially relative pronouns and verbs; and that it is carelessly written: in the word *c<iv>itate<m>* the letters in brackets were left out, and in the word *flagella(la)cio*, a syllable is doubled. There are also obvious grammatical mistakes, *intra civitate* being just one among many others in the text.

The relationship between the two texts is difficult to determine. Perhaps the Ottobonian guide corrected an earlier text or, more likely, both authors depended on the same original work. As noted, the walking route in the two texts is similar, the entrance to the city and the tour inside the Church of the Holy Sepulchre being almost identical. But the Ottobonian guide omits two significant sites: the Church of Saint Mary the Latin and the Hospital, items that could have been omitted in copying from a common original source. Both guides continue to the Temple Mount and mention the four doors of the *Templum Domini*, citing the four cardinal directions but in a different sequence: east, west, south (*a meridie*), north in the Beinecke; east, west, north, south (*ab austro*) in the Ottobonian. Almost identical passages follow, that describe the Valley of Jehoshaphat, the Mount of Olives, Mount Zion, the Pool of Siloam and Aceldama. The descriptions of the Dead Sea and the Mount of Temptation are also very similar. The passage to Bethlehem is identical in the two texts but the reference to the traditions there differs. At this point the Ottobonian guide ends, while the Beinecke continues to Hebron and other sites.

---

[21] Mercati, "Santuari e reliquie Costantinopolitane," p. 153; Wilkinson, *Jerusalem Pilgrimage*, p. 92.

Author and Time of Composition

The text provides no direct information on the identity of Beinecke guide's author; the grammatical mistakes would suggest a not very erudite pilgrim or crusader.[22] But it is not known whether the mistakes were made by the original author or whether they crept in later. On the basis of some orthographic distortions – *iusta* instead of *iuxta*, and *iessemani* for Gethsemane (a spelling that appears in Latin only in the description of the sixth-century Anonymous of Piacenza, and is reminiscent of the Arabic *Jismāniyya*) – it has been suggested that the writer was of Italian origin. But this too cannot be convincingly ascertained.[23]

One historical event is mentioned, at the end of the text: "On the fifteenth of July, the Holy City of Jerusalem was captured by the Franks, the day of the Dispersion of the Apostles (*Divisio Apostolorum*)." The indication of the feast of the Dispersion of the Apostles is noteworthy. This feast, which commemorates the day on which the apostles left Jerusalem in their mission to spread Christianity (Mark 16.15), was not widely celebrated in western Europe before the eleventh century. At the time of the conquest of Jerusalem it was fairly new.[24] Allusion to the feast is rare in pilgrim writings of the time; it may suggest a temporal proximity between the conquest and the writing, and it must have seemed significant to the author, as it associates the personal achievement of pilgrimage with the collective Christian triumph. The import of the feast of the Dispersion of the Apostles for the crusaders is clear: it upholds the centrality of Jerusalem to Christianity and emphasizes the spiritual unity of the Christian world, despite its geographical division. From the conquerors' point of view the events celebrated by the feast meshed well to embody the fulfilment of the divine scheme, and it symbolized the closing of a circle, with the Christians now returning victorious to the cradle of Christianity.[25] As Raymond of Aguilers wrote:

> This day, I say, marks the abolition of all paganism, the confirmation of Christianity, and the renewal of our faith ... On this day, moreover, the apostles were expelled from Jerusalem and dispersed throughout the whole world. On this same day the sons of the

[22] This was first suggested by Bernhard Bischoff, who commented on the manuscript on an unknown occasion, probably at the request of Hans P. Kraus. My search for this comment in Arno Mentzel-Reuters, ed., *Handschriftenarchiv Bernhard Bischoff*, Bibliothek der MGH Hilfsmittel 16 (Munich, 1997), yielded no result. Bischoff's comment is recorded by Davis, "Pilgrim's Guide," p. 15.

[23] Davis, "Pilgrim's Guide," pp. 14–15.

[24] Colin Morris, *The Sepulchre of Christ and the Medieval West: From the Beginning to 1600* (Oxford, 2005), p. 149; Adolf Katzenellenbogen, "The Separation of the Apostles," *Gazette des Beaux-Arts* 35 (1949), 81–98; Jean Leclercq, "Sermon sur la divisio apostolorum attribuable à Gottschalk de Limburg," *Sacris Erudiri* 7 (1955), 219–28; Kaspar Elm, "Die Eroberung Jerusalems im Jahre 1099. Ihre Darstellung, Beurteilung und Deutung in den Quellen zur Geschichte des Ersten Kreuzzugs," in *Jerusalem im Hoch- und Spätmittelalter*, ed. Dieter Bauer, Klaus Herbers and Nikolas Jaspert (Frankfurt am Main, 2001), p. 47.

[25] On the association of ideas of pilgrimage and the liberation of Jerusalem, see Amnon Linder, "The Liturgy of the Liberation of Jerusalem," *Mediaeval Studies* 52 (1990), 129–30.

apostles regained the city and homeland (*patriam*) for God and for the fathers. This day, the Ides of July, is celebrated to the praise and glory of the name of God, who gave to the prayers of his Church the city and the homeland which he promised to their ancestors in faith and benediction. On this day we chanted the office of the Resurrection, since on this day he, who by his virtue arose from the dead, revived us through his grace.[26]

Allusions to the feast of the Dispersion of the Apostles appear here and there in the sources relating to the conquest of Jerusalem. The earliest seems to be in the letter sent in September 1099 by Daimbert, patriarch of Jerusalem, to Pope Paschal II, conveying the news of the conquest. The feast is not mentioned in pilgrim accounts.[27] Although allusion to the feast adds a liturgical aspect to the Beinecke guide, the feast itself did not feature prominently in the liturgy of the Frankish kingdom; its appearance on the fifteenth of July in the calendar of the Psalter of Queen Melisende may indicate that it had some importance, but this assumption should be qualified since the provenance of the calendar is uncertain.[28]

A few details may indicate that the Beinecke guide originates from the first half of the twelfth century. Its close relationship with the Ottobonian guide may suggest a temporal proximity. Moreover, from the description of the Church of the Holy Sepulchre, it seems clear that at the time of composition the church was not yet an enclosed structure; the writer goes out from the *Anastasis* to the navel of the world and continues through what seems to be the court, recognizable from earlier descriptions, to the three chapels built in the eleventh century and dedicated to the crown of thorns, the distribution of the clothes and the flagellation.

The indication that the tomb of Joseph was located in Hebron (as opposed to the better-known tradition of his tomb in Nablus) may also hint at the date of the guide's composition. Since the time of the discovery of the tombs of the patriarchs in Hebron by the Augustinian canons in 1119,[29] the place has been known to Latin visitors as the burial site of Abraham, Isaac, Jacob, Sarah, Rebecca and Leah – but not Joseph. It is possible therefore that the composition predates 1120, since Joseph's tomb in Hebron appears only in Latin texts from the early twelfth century, and it disappears later on.

---

[26] John H. Hill and Laurita L. Hill, eds., *Le Liber de Raymond d'Aguilers* (Paris, 1969), p. 151.

[27] For the letter and editor's notes, as well as additional references, see Heinrich Hagenmeyer, *Die Kreuzzugsbriefe aus den Jahren 1088–1100* (Innsbruck, 1901; repr. Hildesheim 1973), pp. 171, 388.

[28] Francis Wormald, "The Calendars of the Church of the Holy Sepulchre in Jerusalem" and "The Litanies of Saints," in Hugo Buchthal, *Miniature Painting in the Latin Kingdom of Jerusalem* (Oxford, 1957), pp. 122–23; Jaroslav Folda, "A Twelfth Century Prayerbook for the Queen of Jerusalem," *Medieval Perspectives* 8 (1993), 1–14; Bianca Kühnel, "The Bookcovers of Queen Melisende's Psalter," in *Crusader Art of the 12th Century – A Geographical, an Historical, or an Art Historical Notion?* (Berlin, 1994), pp. 67–125, esp. pp. 80–82; Barbara Zeitler, "The Distorting Mirror: Reflections on the Queen Melisende Psalter (London, B.L., Egerton 1139)," in *Through the Looking Glass: Byzantium through British Eyes*, ed. Robin Cormack and Elizabeth Jeffreys (Aldershot, 2000), pp. 69–83; Cristina Dondi, *The Liturgy of the Canons Regular of the Holy Sepulchre of Jerusalem* (Turnhout, 2004), pp. 63–64, 162–66.

[29] Robert B. C. Huygens, "Inventio Patriarcharum," *Crusades* 4 (2005), 131–55.

Traditions Mentioned in the Beinecke Guide

A closer look at a few traditions mentioned in the Beinecke guide will serve to illustrate some of its unique aspects and traditions.

Joseph's Tomb in Hebron

> From Jerusalem to Saint Abraham ten leagues. There lie Abraham, Isaac and Jacob, Sarah, Rebecca, Leah and Joseph.[30]

A sporadic tradition in Judaism and Christianity, and a more persistent one in Islam, may help explain the unusual location of Joseph's tomb in Hebron. It seems, in fact, that a local tradition has developed in Hebron, with traces of inter-religious influence. But before focusing on the twelfth century, it would be useful to review briefly the possible sources for this tradition.

The Bible says: "And the bones of Joseph, which the children of Israel brought up out of Egypt, buried they in Shechem, in the parcel of ground which Jacob bought of the sons of Hamor the father of Shechem for a hundred pieces of money; and they became the inheritance of the children of Joseph" (Joshua 24.32). However, according to a different Jewish tradition, which appears in the "Testaments of the Twelve Patriarchs" (ca. second century B.C.), Joseph was buried in Hebron: "And when the children of Israel went out of Egypt, they took with them the bones of Joseph, and they buried him in Hebron with his fathers, and the years of his life were one hundred and ten years."[31] By contrast, another longstanding tradition insists that Joseph knew he would not be buried with his forefathers and told the children of Israel: "But you should bring me up (whenever possible), even (if only my) bones! And when you bring me up, bury me in any place you desire! It is acceptable to me that only the three Patriarchs and three Matriarchs enter the grave of the forefathers."[32]

During the Byzantine period, Christians were also familiar with the parallel traditions. The majority of pilgrims, such as Theodosius at the end of the fifth century, the map of Madaba from the end of the sixth century and Arculf at the close of the seventh century, indicated the location of Joseph's tomb as being near

---

[30] The Beinecke guide: "De Ierusalem ad sanctum Abraam X leugas, ibi iacent Abraam, Ysaac et Iacob, Sarra, Rebecca, Lia et Iosep."

[31] "Testament of Joseph," in *The Testaments of the Twelve Patriarchs*, trans. R. H. Charles (London, 1908), pp. 196–97. See Elchanan Reiner, "From Joshua to Jesus – The Transformation of a Biblical Story to a Local Myth (A Chapter in the Religious Life of the Galilean Jew)," *Zion* 61 (1996), 281–317 [in Hebrew]. According to a different Christian tradition, all the patriarchs were buried in Nablus (Shechem): "So Jacob went down into Egypt, and died, he, and our fathers, And were carried over into Sychem, and laid in the sepulchre that Abraham bought for a sum of money of the sons of Emmor [the father] of Sychem" (Acts 7.15–16).

[32] *Mekhilta de-Rabbi Shimon bar Yoḥai*, trans. W. David Nelson (Philadelphia, 2006), p. 84. Written ca. fifth century A.D.

Nablus. But the Anonymous of Piacenza, who visited around 570, describes the tombs in the Cave of the Machpelah in Hebron and adds: "And there the bones of Joseph."[33]

In the early Muslim period there is more frequent and consistent evidence of the tradition of Joseph's burial in Hebron, near the Tombs of the Patriarchs. Amikam Elad notes that the Muslim tradition is a fragmentary one, probably an amalgam of several earlier traditions.[34] From the ninth century, Muslim geographers called the place identified as the tomb of Joseph the *Masjid* (= Mosque). The culmination of this tradition was the invention of Joseph's tomb in the tenth century and the establishment of a *Qubba* in his honour during the reign of the Abbasid Caliph al-Muqtadir (908–32).[35]

Several Muslim writers mentioned the site in the eleventh century. Ibn al-Murajjā, in the 1030s, described the course of Muslim prayer at the Cave of the Machpelah; it goes first to the Tombs of the Patriarchs and their wives, then turns toward Joseph's tomb, which is at some distance from the others, at the bottom of the valley.[36] The Persian traveller Nāser-e Khosraw (1047) also mentions Joseph's tomb in Hebron,[37] as does Ibn al-ʿArabi of Seville, who visited the place a year before the crusader conquest: "In the wing to the south of it, outside this sanctuary (*haram*) lays Joseph's tomb, standing alone. … The design of the tomb of Joseph, may God's prayer and blessing be upon him, is like that of the other [ancestors'] graves. This is the most trustworthy reference to his burial-place …"[38]

The Hebronite tradition lasted through the Frankish period and for centuries after. But the competing tradition was not altogether forgotten. ʿAli b. Abi-Bakr al-Harawī (who died in 1215) writes: "The tomb of Joseph the Righteous is outside

---

[33]   Theodosius, ed. P. Geyer, *Itineraria et alia geographica*, p. 115; Arculf, ed. L. Bieler, *Itineraria et alia geographica*, p. 217; the Piacenza Pilgrim, ed. P. Geyer, *Itineraria et alia geographica*, pp. 144, 168.

[34]   Amikam Elad, "Pilgrims and Pilgrimage to Hebron (al-Khalil) during the Early Muslim Period," in *Pilgrims and Travelers to the Holy Land*, ed. Bryan F. LeBeau and Menachem Mor (Omaha, 1996), p. 23. For the Muslim tradition, see also Ofer Livne-Kafri, "The Sanctity of Jerusalem in Islam According to the Arabic Genre of 'The Merits of Jerusalem,' accompanied by a Scientific Edition of a Manuscript in Classical Arabic: Abū al-Maʾālī al-Musharraf b. al-Murajjā b. Ibrāhīm al-Maqdisī, Kitāb Fadāʾil Bayt al-Maqdis wa-al-Khalīl wa-Fadāʾil al-Shām" (PhD thesis, The Hebrew University of Jerusalem, 1985), part 1, p. 319, n. 99 [in Hebrew]; Reiner, "From Joshua to Jesus," pp. 290–95.

[35]   Mujir al-Din in the fifteenth century recounts the story of the discovery of Joseph's tomb in Hebron in the tenth century initiated by the caliph al-Muktadir: Guy Le Strange, *Palestine under the Muslims: A Description of Syria and the Holy Land from A.D. 650 to 1500* (London, 1890), p. 325; Moudjir ed-dyn, *Histoire de Jérusalem et d'Hébron depuis Abraham jusqu'à la fin du XVe siècle de J.-C.*, trans. Henry Sauvaire (Paris, 1876), pp. 22–23. See also Wheeler M. Thackston, trans., *The Tales of the Prophets of al-Kisaʾi* (Boston, 1978), pp. 191–92; on the dating of the work, see pp. xix, xxxiii.

[36]   Elad, "Pilgrims and Pilgrimage to Hebron," pp. 43–44.

[37]   "Outside these walls is a hill where the tomb of Joseph son of Jacob is located under a nicely built dome with a stone tomb": *Nāser-e-Khosraw's Book of Travels (Safarnāma)*, trans. Wheeler M. Thackston, Persian Heritage Series 36 (New York, 1986), p. 36.

[38]   Joseph Drory, "Some Observations during a Visit to Palestine by Ibn al-ʿArabi of Seville in 1092–1095," *Crusades* 3 (2004), 117.

the Grotto there [that is, in Hebron]"; but he adds a reservation: "The truth is what we first mentioned [that is, that Joseph was buried in Nablus]."[39]

The crusaders conquered Hebron in 1100 and named it Saint Abraham. Not many of the pilgrims who came to the Holy Land visited Hebron, but those who came in the early twelfth century mentioned Joseph's tomb as being there. Saewulf mentions it in the passages about the Church of the Holy Sepulchre in Jerusalem, and again when describing Hebron: "But the bones of Joseph ... are buried humbly in the other outermost parts of the castle."[40] Abbot Daniel, who visited the place a few years later, describes the Tombs of the Patriarchs and the matriarchs surrounded by a stone wall, adding: "The tomb of Joseph the Beautiful is outside this enclosure, external to the cave itself, a stone's throw from that enclosure and this place is now (called) Holy Abraham."[41]

Whether the author of the Beinecke guide actually visited Hebron cannot be ascertained. It is possible that he relied on Saewulf's description, on a local tradition or on a combination of sources. Other Latin writers during the twelfth century either were not familiar with that tradition or chose to disregard it. The First Anonymous Guide states, for example: "Twelve miles further on is the castle of Abraham, called Tocor, where Abraham, Isaac and Jacob are buried with their wives."[42] The grave of Joseph is not mentioned either in Hebron or in Nablus.

Fretellus, a chaplain in the cathedral of Nazareth, who wrote in the middle of the twelfth century,[43] begins his description of the holy places in Hebron. He cites many biblical traditions related to the site and mentions the Tombs of the Patriarchs and their wives, and the graves of Adam and Eve; Joseph's tomb is not mentioned.[44] The rich and detailed narratives written in the second half of the twelfth century by John of Würzburg and Theoderich, based partly on Fretellus's text,[45] locate the traditions of Joseph in the areas of Nablus and Dothan, but not in Hebron. In Hebron, they mention the Tombs of the Patriarchs, the matriarchs and Adam. Their

---

[39] Al-Harawī, *Kitāb al-ishārāt ilā maʿrifat al-ziyārāt*, trans. Joseph W. Meri (Princeton, 2004), p. 78 n. 59, and p. 66.

[40] *Peregrinationes tres*, pp. 66, 73.

[41] *Biblioteka literatury Drevnei Rusi*, p. 74.

[42] *GF*, p. 101.

[43] On the somewhat enigmatic figure of Rorgo Fretellus and his career, see Rudolf Hiestand, "Un centre intellectuel en Syrie du Nord? Notes sur la personnalité d'Aimery d'Antioche, Albert de Tarse, et Rorgo Frotellus," *Moyen Âge* 100 (1994), 7–36, esp. pp. 35–36.

[44] This work was titled by Wilkinson "Work on Geography" (Wilkinson, *Jerusalem Pilgrimage*, pp. 181–211), a proposal harshly criticized by Hans E. Mayer in his review of Wilkinson's book in *Deutsches Archiv* 45 (1989), 204–5, and in *Al-Masaq* 2 (1989), 56–58. For the critical edition of Fretellus, see Petrus C. Boeren, *Rorgo Fretellus de Nazareth et sa description de la Terre Sainte: Histoire et édition du texte* (Amsterdam, 1980); see also Hans E. Mayer's review of Boeren's edition in *Deutsches Archiv* 38 (1982), 632.

[45] *Peregrinationes tres*, pp. 18–19.

contemporary, Benjamin of Tudela, also mentions the graves of the patriarchs and matriarchs in Hebron, without Joseph.[46]

To sum up, Joseph's tomb in Hebron appears in the Beinecke guide and in two other early twelfth-century texts, a Latin and a Russian; it then disappears for the rest of the century. That there is no further mention in Latin texts of the later twelfth century may perhaps be related to the invention of the Tombs of the Patriarchs in 1119, which did not include Joseph.[47]

"The Well of the Star" in Bethlehem

Bethlehem is two leagues away from Jerusalem, where Christ was born and the stable where he was put, and the well where the star rested.[48]

The Well of the Star is seldom mentioned in pilgrim descriptions before the crusades and appears only a few times in the twelfth century. This tradition is partly based on the Scripture – namely, that the star guided the Wise Men from the East to the place of Jesus's birth (Matt. 2.1–12). The tradition of the well is apparently a later one, and it refers to a local object that could be seen on the ground. The story appears for the first time in Gregory of Tours's "Glory of the Martyrs," dated ca. 585:

Indeed, there is in Bethlehem a large well from which the glorious Mary is said to have drawn water. Often a famous miracle is demonstrated to onlookers: that is, the star that appeared to the wise men is there revealed to the pure in heart. The pious cover their heads with linen cloths, and come and lean over the mouth of the well. Then the man whose merit will have prevailed sees the star move from one wall of the well over the waters to the opposite wall in the same way as stars are customarily moved above the orbit of the heavens. And although many look, such a miracle is seen only by those whose mind is more blameless. I have met some people who claimed that they had seen the star. Recently however my deacon reported that he, with five other men, had looked, but the star only appeared to two of them.[49]

The story related by Gregory of Tours, who was fond of miracles, does not appear in any other Latin description of the place. Gregory's main sources of information about events occurring far away from Gaul were people who returned from their journeys, such as the deacon, mentioned in the passage above, who visited Bethlehem

---

[46]   *The Itinerary of Benjamin of Tudela*, ed. and trans. Marcus N. Adler (London, 1907), p. 25. See also Elchanan Reiner, "A Jewish Response to the Crusades: The Dispute over Sacred Places in the Holy Land," in *Juden und Christen zur Zeit der Kreuzzüge*, ed. Alfred Haverkamp (Sigmaringen, 1999), pp. 223–24.

[47]   Huygens, "Inventio Patriarcharum," pp. 131–55.

[48]   Beinecke Guide: "Betleem longe ab Ierusalem duas leugas, ubi natus fuit Christus, et presepe ubi positus fuit et puteus ubi stel<l>a requievit."

[49]   Gregorius Turonensis, *Liber in Gloria Martyrum*, ed. Bruno Krusch, MGH SRM 1, part 2 (Hannover, 1885; repr. 1969), p. 38; Gregory of Tours, *Glory of the Martyrs*, trans. Raymond van Dam (Liverpool, 1988), p. 3.

and the River Jordan.[50] But none of the western pilgrims of the Byzantine period repeated the story. The tradition is mentioned only by Epiphanius, a Greek monk who visited the Holy Land in the seventh century and wrote the earliest surviving Greek description of the Holy Land; Epiphanius mentions the magical well and the star floating in its water: "And to the north of the cave is the well which was not dug. And in the water of the well is the Star that journeyed with the Magi."[51] Yet now it seems as if the star shows itself to anyone who looks into the well, and this somewhat compromises the miracle. The story of the well and the star floating on its waters may represent a local, eastern tradition whose spread was assisted by the adoration of the Magi and the Star of the East (or Star of Bethlehem) in eastern Christianity.[52] In the West, apart from the work of Gregory of Tours, it seems the story did not resonate much among Latin writers.

The Well of the Star appears for the first time in descriptions of western eleventh-century pilgrims. Jachintus, a Spanish pilgrim, tells that he saw the star above the well inside the Church of the Nativity.[53] At the beginning of the twelfth century the well and the star appear in Saewulf's account, the Beinecke guide and the *Qualiter* (1103).[54] But what remained of the wondrous tale in the twelfth century was but a faint echo – it was the well into which the star had fallen, but it could no longer be seen in its waters. Saewulf says that "the cistern is there in the church, next to the cave of the Lord's birth, into which the star is said to have fallen." Fretellus mentions the star but not the well.[55] According to the Seventh Anonymous Guide: "In Bethlehem Christ was born ... and the Well into which the star fell ..."[56] The echo becomes ever fainter through the twelfth century. Theoderich mentions only a star that decorated the church: "Also over this church a copper star shines ...

---

[50] On John the Deacon, see the editor's note in MGH SRM 1, part 2, pp. 8–9. Some parts of Gregory's work were based on the Anonymous of Piacenza. Cf. Massimo Oldoni, "Gregorio di Tours e i 'Libri Historiarum': letture e fonti, metodi e ragioni," *Studi Medievali* 13/2 (1972), 691–93. The Anonymous of Piacenza did not mention the well or the star in his account.

[51] John Wilkinson, ed. and trans., *Jerusalem Pilgrims before the Crusades* (Warminster, 2002), p. 209.

[52] The travels of the Magi and the star that guided them on their way to the east were extensively described in eastern Christian literature: Ugo Monneret de Villard, *Le leggende orientali sui Magi Evangelici* (Rome, 1952), pp. 38–39; see also the chronicle of Zuqnin (the chronicle of Pseudo-Dionysius of Tell-Mahre): *Incerti Auctoris Chronicon Pseudo Dionysianum vulgo dictum*, ed. Jean-Baptiste Chabot, vol. 1 (Louvain, 1949), pp. 47, 58–59.

[53] The manuscript is kept in the Leon Cathedral library in Spain. See Zacarías Garcia Villada, "Descripciones Desconocidas de Tierra Santa en códices españoles – II: Descripción del Presbitero Jacinto," *Estudios Eclesiásticos* 4 (1925), 322–32; and Wilkinson, *Jerusalem Pilgrims*, pp. 270–71.

[54] *Peregrinationes tres*, p. 72. In some instances the sources mention in the environs of Bethlehem the well from which King David longed to drink (2 Samuel 23.15); see, for example, the account of Abbot Daniel as well as that of John Phocas, although there is no reference to a star there: Wilkinson, *Jerusalem Pilgrimage*, pp. 144 and 333, respectively.

[55] Boeren, *Rorgo Fretellus de Nazareth*, pp. 29–30; PPTS 5 (London, 1896), p. 5; the translation of "Fetellus" in PPTS is of the related, apparently earlier text known as the *Descriptio locorum*.

[56] Titus Tobler, *Descriptiones Terrae Sanctae* (Leipzig, 1874), p. 105.

which means that the Three Magi came there, as one reads in the Gospel."[57] Thus it seems that, during the course of the twelfth century, what remained from the early miraculous story was only the textual element, the star, while all the rest was gradually forgotten.

Traditions on the Temple Mount: Jacob, James and the Confession of the Apostles

A significant process of reframing sanctity took place on the Temple Mount in the wake of the crusader conquest. That Jerusalem did not have an immediate Christian past was most keenly felt in this central compound, a new ground for Christian pilgrimage and worship. Adorning the area and investing it with power, which had begun under the Muslims with the intention of rivalling the main Christian site, the Holy Sepulchre, continued, somewhat ironically, under the Franks. The process included shifting ancient traditions back to the Temple Mount as well as the appearance there of new ones.[58] The Beinecke guide has two such traditions: "There Jacob (*Iacob*) slept and there James (*Iacobus*) was sacrificed," differentiating clearly between Jacob and James the Less.

An explicit allusion to Jacob's dream on the Temple Mount is unknown in Christian tradition before the twelfth century. The main Christian tradition, following the main Jewish tradition, links Jacob to the area of Nablus as the site of his dream and the building of the altar, and to Hebron as his burial site. When and why did Jacob make an appearance on the Temple Mount? Several explanations can be offered, though it must be admitted that they do not form a solid or consistent tradition.

The biblical story locates Jacob's dream in Beth El, or Luz (Genesis 28.18–19).[59] The Jewish midrash *Pirqe de-Rabbi Eliezer*, written probably in the eighth century, introduces a different tradition, according to which the dream, the anointing of the stone and the building of the altar all took place in Jerusalem, on Mount Moriah.[60] A thematic logic can be discerned in developing a tradition that links Jacob to the Temple Mount, as if to compensate for an absence, since he is the only patriarch who does not have a place there. It is also possible that *Pirke De-Rabbi Eliezer*,

---

[57] *Peregrinationes tres*, p. 180.

[58] Heribert Busse, "Vom Felsendom zum Templum Domini," in *Das Heilige Land im Mittelalter: Begegnungsraum zwischen Orient und Okzident*, ed. Wolfdietrich Fischer and Jürgen Schneider (Neustadt, 1982), pp. 19–32; Sylvia Schein, "The Temple between Mount Moriah and the Holy Sepulchre: The Changing Traditions of the Temple in the Middle Ages," *Traditio* 50 (1984), 175–95; Benjamin Z. Kedar and Denys Pringle, "1099–1187: The Lord's Temple (*Templum Domini*) and Solomon's Palace (*Palatium Salomonis*)," in *Where Heaven and Earth Meet: Jerusalem's Sacred Esplanade*, ed. Oleg Grabar and Benjamin Z. Kedar (Jerusalem, 2009), pp. 133–51.

[59] Luz is usually identified as Bethel: see, for example, Genesis 35.6.

[60] *Pirke de-Rabbi Eliezer*, trans. Gerald Friedlander (New York, 1981), ch. 35. On the polemical contexts of this identification, see Rachel Adelman, "Midrash, Myth, and Bakhtin's Chronotope: The Itinerant Well and the Foundation Stone in *Pirqe de-Rabbi Eliezer*," *Journal of Jewish Thought and Philosophy* 17/2 (2009), 143–76; Isaiah M. Gafni, "'Pre-Histories' of Jerusalem in Hellenistic Jewish and Christian Literature," *Journal for the Study of the Pseudepigrapha* 1 (1987), 5–22.

presumably written in a Muslim milieu, may reflect earlier Jewish stories in this vein or could have assimilated local Muslim or Christian traditions.[61]

Although there is no clear Christian tradition connecting Jacob to the Temple Mount, the anointing of the stone may be seen as a link between the two. The stone that Jacob anointed with oil is the only case of an anointed stone in the Bible, and the testimony of the Bordeaux pilgrim from A.D. 333 describing the Jews anointing a perforated stone on the Temple Mount may represent a remnant of a tradition that, in his eyes, linked Jacob's act to the Temple Mount. It is a tenuous conjecture but not an altogether refutable one,[62] and evidence of the continuous Christian awareness of the description of the anointed stone there is found in the First Anonymous Guide of the early twelfth century, which quotes the Bordeaux pilgrim: "And there, between the Temple and the altar ... is a stone to which the Jews come every year, and they anoint it and make lamentation, and so go away wailing."[63]

Muslim tradition may also provide a context for the appearance of Jacob on the Temple Mount, given that at the beginning of the twelfth century the local Muslim tradition was probably the dominant one. How the Muslim tradition itself was established is yet to be explored, but in the Abbasid period reference was made to a *mihrab* named after Jacob, and in the Fatimid period of *Qubbat Yaqub*. Nāser-e Khosraw and Ibn al-Murajjā mention the site at the northern wall of the compound.[64]

Shortly after the crusader conquest, Saewulf identified Beth El on the Temple Mount and located Jacob's dream there;[65] the Russian Abbot Daniel in 1106–8 did likewise.[66] The pilgrims Theoderich and John of Würzburg also emphasized this tradition.[67] The Franks were apparently aware of the duplication of traditions in Beth El and Jerusalem. Yet, since they considered themselves the spiritual successors of Jacob-Israel, they recognized the powerful linkage between the foundation story of Jacob building the house of God and their own *Templum Domini*.

---

[61]   Louis Ginzberg, *Legends of the Jews*, 7 vols. (Philadelphia, 1967–69), 5:292, nn. 138–41, alludes to older sources, such as Genesis Rabba.

[62]   Oded Irshai, "The Christian Appropriation of Jerusalem in the Fourth Century: The Case of the Bordeaux Pilgrim," *Jewish Quarterly Review* 99 (2009), 465–86, at p. 484, esp. n. 50.

[63]   *GF*, p. 98.

[64]   Nāser-e-Khosraw, ed. Thackston, p. 25: "It is called Jacob's Dome, as it is supposed to have been his place of prayer." Al-Murajjā mentions the Dome of Jacob located in front of the throne of Suleiman/Solomon, and tells of Jacob's dream and of God's promise to return Jacob to the place where he will build the house and where his descendants will worship God, "which is Jerusalem ... before Moses and David." See Abū al-Maʾālī al-Musharraf b. al-Murajjā b. Ibrāhīm al-Maqdisī, *Kitāb Fadāʾil Bayt al-Maqdis wa-al-Khalīl wa-Fadāʾil al-Shām*, ed. Ofer Livne-Kafri (Shfarʿam, 1995), pp. 9, 127. See also Amikam Elad, *Medieval Jerusalem and Islamic Worship: Holy Places, Ceremonies, Pilgrimage* (Leiden, 1994), p. 87. Mujir al-Din in the fifteenth century mentions traditions that link Jacob to the Temple Mount, as the place where he prayed, had his dream and built a house for God. See Moudjir ed-dyn, *Histoire de Jérusalem*, trans. Sauvaire, p. 23.

[65]   *Peregrinationes tres*, p. 67. See also Linder, "Like Purest Gold Resplendent," pp. 35–36.

[66]   *Biblioteka literatury Drevnei Rusi*, p. 44.

[67]   *Peregrinationes tres*, pp. 90–91, 162–63, 188, 194. See also the discussion in Pringle, *Churches*, vol. 3, p. 404.

Now to James the Less. According to tradition, James was the first bishop of the early Christian community in Jerusalem. His martyrdom is not narrated in the New Testament[68] but only told later by Josephus, Origen and Eusebius.[69] Some of the Christian pilgrims during the Byzantine period mentioned the pinnacle of the Temple, from which James was thrown to his death. His tomb is mentioned as being in the Valley of Kidron and on the Mount of Olives.[70] Surprisingly, the Bordeaux pilgrim, although aiming in the fourth century to drape the Temple Mount in a Christian garb, ignored the story of the martyrdom of James the Less.[71]

From the middle of the twelfth century, Latin writers mention the story of James the Less being thrown from the pinnacle of the Temple. The earliest, probably, was Achard of Arrouaise who came to the Holy Land around 1108 and served as a prior of the *Templum Domini* between 1112 and 1123. Achard composed a long poem in praise of the *Templum Domini*, emphasizing the apostolic status of Jerusalem; he mentions there the martyrdom of James, "the first bishop of the Lord's Temple."[72] Around 1137, Fretellus tells of the throwing of James from the pinnacle of the Temple,[73] and sometime in the twelfth century the Dome of the Chain, which existed from the ninth century, was sanctified as a memorial to James the Less.[74] That the story of James was firmly attached to the Lord's Temple is reflected in the inscriptions that decorated the building, copied by John of Würzburg from the Dome of the Chain.[75] James was also mentioned there by other pilgrims of the second half of the twelfth century, among them Theoderich, the Seventh Anonymous Guide and Joannes Phocas.[76] The mention of the murder of James the Less on the Temple

---

[68]   The murder of James, brother of John (both were Jesus's disciples), is mentioned in Acts 12.1–2.

[69]   Josephus, *Jewish Antiquities*, 20.199–200, trans. Louis E. Feldman, vol. 9 (London and Cambridge, 1965), pp. 495–97. Many scholars assert that the mention of this event in Josephus is a Christian interpolation: see Origen, *Contra Celsum*, 1.47, trans. Henry Chadwick (Cambridge, 1965), p. 43; Eusebius, *The Ecclesiastical History*, trans. Kirsopp Lake, vol. 2 (London and Cambridge, 1949), p. 169. Eusebius placed James's martyrdom in the south-eastern corner of the Temple Mount. In 351 James's tomb was discovered in the valley of Kidron and a monument was erected to mark this location, which attracted many pilgrims. On this tradition, see Felix M. Abel, "La Sépulture de saint Jacques le Mineur," *Revue Biblique* 28 (1919), 480–99; Yaron Z. Eliav, "The Tomb of James, Brother of Jesus, as Locus Memoriae," *Harvard Theological Review* 97 (2004), 33–59; Oded Irshai, "Jews and Judaism in Early Church Historiography: The Case of Eusebius of Caesarea (Preliminary Observations and Examples)" (forthcoming).

[70]   See, for example, Theodosius (530), *Itineraria et alia geographica*, p. 119: "Saint James … was thrown from the Pinnacle of the Temple after the ascension of the Lord, and it did him no harm, but he was killed by a fuller with the stick in which he used to carry things. He is buried on the Mount of Olives." CCSL 175, p. 119. See also Pringle, *Churches*, vol. 3, pp. 185–89.

[71]   Irshai, "Christian Appropriation," pp. 465–86.

[72]   Paul Lehmann, "Die mittellateinischen Dichtungen der Prioren des Tempels von Jerusalem Acardus und Gaufridus," in *Corona Quernea: Festgabe Karl Strecker zum 80 Geburtstage dargebracht*, MGH Schriften 6 (Leipzig, 1941), pp. 296–330, at p. 328.

[73]   Boeren, *Rorgo Fretellus de Nazareth*, p. 33.

[74]   Miryam Rosen-Ayalon, *The Early Islamic Monuments of Al-Haram Al-Sharif: An Iconographic Study*, Qedem Monographs of the Institute of Archaeology 28 (Jerusalem, 1989), pp. 25–29.

[75]   *Peregrinationes tres*, p. 92, and Pringle, *Churches*, vol. 3, pp. 182–85.

[76]   Wilkinson, *Jerusalem Pilgrimage*, pp. 19–21.

Mount in the Beinecke guide, which could have been written at the beginning of the twelfth century, might be the earliest reference to this tradition there in Frankish Jerusalem.

The Confessio *of the Apostles*

Another unique tradition in the Beinecke guide is the *confessio apostolorum*, meaning either the crypt or the confession of the apostles.[77] This seems to be a new tradition that appeared on the Temple Mount after the crusader conquest. The Beinecke guide mentions the *confessio* as part of a sequence of traditions in the *Templum Domini*: "There is the Presentation of the Lord, there the Lord's Ark of the Covenant was and the two Tables of the Covenant, and Aaron's rod, and the seven golden lamps and the Confession of the Apostles." Other twelfth-century pilgrims also mention it. Saewulf adds a short explanation: "There is the place of confession where his disciples used to confess to him."[78] John of Würzburg writes: "In the Temple our Lord set the adulterous woman free from those who accused her … The place of that event is represented in the small crypt of the Temple, the entry to which is on the left side of the Temple, and it is called 'The Confession'."[79]

Further allusion to the *confessio* appears in the Seventh Anonymous Guide of the second half of the twelfth century: "Below there is a sanctuary, in old time the Holy of Holies, where the Lord sent away the sinner taken in adultery."[80] And in the Second Anonymous Guide dating from ca. 1170 and related to the Seventh Anonymous Guide: "Under the choir to the south is a cave dug in the rock, which is called 'The Place of Confession.' This is the reason. Christ was there presented with the woman, and said to her, 'No one has condemned thee' (John 8.10) and so on."[81]

The picture that emerges from these references is not particularly clear. It seems to convey the memory of a cave on the Temple Mount and an attempt to form a story around it. The existence of the cave had been mentioned earlier in the anonymous description *Breviarius de Hierosolyma*: "But there is nothing left there apart from a single cave."[82] However, any attempt to link this cave to the apostles on the basis of the Scripture (Acts 15.1–21, 3.2, 5.21) is unhelpful.

---

[77] The word *confessio* can mean both a confession and a location. The location can be an altar, a church or a crypt with a staircase leading to it (Du Cange, *Glossarium mediae latinitatis*, s.v. "Confessio", pp. 1275–76). The meaning of *confessio* according to the context of Saewulf's account is confession; however, *confessio* can also be found in its other meaning of a crypt or a cave, such as in the description of this place in John of Würzburg's account.

[78] *Peregrinationes tres*, p. 68: "ibi est locus confessionis, ubi discipuli sui sibi confessi sunt"; Wilkinson, *Jerusalem Pilgrimage*, p. 104.

[79] *Peregrinationes tres*, p. 91; Wilkinson, *Jerusalem Pilgrimage*, p. 247.

[80] Tobler, *Descriptiones Terrae Sanctae*, p. 102; Wilkinson, *Jerusalem Pilgrimage*, p. 234.

[81] Wilkinson, *Jerusalem Pilgrimage*, p. 240.

[82] Ibid., p. 121. "Breviarius de Hierosolyma," ed. R. Weber, *Itineraria et alia geographica*, pp. 107–12.

Conclusion

The Beinecke guide shows that the route of the tour of the holy sites in Jerusalem was formed early on according to a straightforward logic of sanctity, in a route similar to the pre-crusade one, with the addition of the Temple Mount. The guide also attests to the local discourse on the holy sites and to a flow of information among the members of different religions and sects. The profusion of traditions about the holy sites, as for instance on Joseph's tomb in Hebron or on the Temple Mount, is evidence of the persistence of local traditions, preserved through indigenous, interreligious and intersectarian lore. For a western pilgrim, flooded with information, there might have been little opportunity, or possibly little interest, to challenge this information in a critical way. Thus in this very short text there are two allusions to the place of Christ's birth, in Bethlehem and on the Temple Mount.[83] It seems that, alongside the well-known map of the holy places explicitly outlined in many guides, there was also a less-defined map, of which it is possible to learn from the differences among various guides of the early twelfth century. The guides reflect the attempt to attach as many sacred traditions as possible to the holy sites. This can be seen clearly on the "new site" of the Temple Mount. There, invented traditions included either the ambiguous reference to the "confession of the apostles," or to traditions reminiscent of older, non-Christian, lore, such as the cradle of Jesus, Jacob's dream or, a third option, relocating the martyrdom of James the Less to the immediate vicinity of the *Templum Domini*.

Within the flourishing pilgrimage movement of the twelfth century, Jerusalem had an immense power of attraction. The pilgrims who came from all parts of the Christian world might have visited other holy centres on their way. Such pilgrimage centres as Constantinople and Rome, renowned for their immense array of relics and splendid churches, or smaller centres popular for pardons, healing and miracles, could have given rise to inflated expectations of the holiest city, in addition to expectations fed by biblical stories and the heroic tales of the crusaders. Clearly competition existed among the various holy places, and in the twelfth century the competition grew.[84] The inhabitants of the Holy Land knew this well and were naturally interested in increasing its attraction and strengthening the ties with their European homelands.

---

[83] The Beinecke guide says: "In the corner of the city is the cradle of Christ, and the bath and the bed of his mother." Muslim tradition tells of the birth and the infancy of Jesus in Jerusalem. Ofer Livne-Kafri has suggested that the tradition placing Jesus's cradle (Mahd ʾIssa) on the Temple Mount stemmed from the need to divert Muslim pilgrims from the site of the birth in Bethlehem, and that the cult of Mary that developed on the Temple Mount may have developed to counter Muslims visiting Mary's tomb in the Valley of Jehoshaphat: see Ofer Livne-Kafri, *The Sanctity of Jerusalem in Islam* [in Hebrew], p. 299; Elad, *Medieval Jerusalem and Islamic Worship*, pp. 93–94. For the cradle of Christ in the Koran, see Heribert Busse, *Islam, Judaism and Christianity: Theological and Historical Affiliations*, trans. Allison Brown (Princeton, 1988), pp. 117–18, 123–24; and Pringle, *Churches*, vol. 3, pp. 310–14.

[84] Debra J. Birch, "Selling the Saints: Competition among Pilgrimage Centres in the Twelfth Century," *Medieval History* 2/2 (1992), 20–34.

The beginning of the twelfth century was a crucial time for the construction of Latin Jerusalem as the capital of the Frankish kingdom. But the city the crusaders seized in 1099 was poor and politically peripheral. As part of the attempt to turn it into a teeming and attractive capital, the holy places were accorded an important religious role, with economic and demographic ramifications. The marketing of the holy places was set in motion within the city itself, by living tour guides or by written guides, while around the Christian world it was carried by the stories of the travellers who had returned and the texts that described the land.

The project of the glorifying of the city necessarily entailed glorification of its past, with a special emphasis on foundation stories, such as locating the tradition of Jacob, founder of the first house of God, on the Temple Mount. Also essential were traditions emphasizing the apostolic past of Jerusalem which alluded to the status the city deserved; among these were the traditions of James the Less, the first bishop of the city, and the confession of the apostles on the Temple Mount. Also important was linking the day of the conquest of the city to the Dispersion of the Apostles.

The Beinecke guide provides additional evidence of this project and of the endeavour to establish traditions linked to the sites that were now in Latin hands. Though short and simple, the Beinecke guide, like other guides and travel narratives from the twelfth century, does not merely describe a reality but comprises an important link between historical memory and the process of its construction. The first crusaders could not have known that this entire endeavour would come to an end in less than a century.

The Illnesses of King Richard and King Philippe on the Third Crusade: An Understanding of *arnaldia* and *leonardie*

Thomas Gregor Wagner
(Uppsala University, Sweden; thomas.wagner@idehist.uu.se)
and *Piers D. Mitchell*
(University of Cambridge; pdm39@cam.ac.uk)

Introduction

The crusade of King Richard I of England and Philippe Augustus II of France was ill-fated. In 1191, after just a few days of intense fighting before the walls of Acre, both kings fell ill from an enigmatic illness known in Latin as *arnaldia* and in French as *leonardie*. For weeks both Richard and Philippe were close to the brink of death, before they finally recovered. In the summer of 1192 another epidemic struck the crusader army and Richard again became dangerously ill – this time with a malady referred to as *febris emitritea*. For nearly three months his condition was so serious that once again his men feared for his life. At this point Richard had to abandon his plan to capture the Christian holy sites, for Jerusalem was out of the reach of a king lying on a sickbed. After he had made peace with Saladin, Richard immediately returned to Haifa to receive medical treatment. He left the Holy Land in October 1192 and it is likely that his impaired health had been a major factor influencing his return to Europe at that time. The present article describes Richard and Philippe's crusade in terms of the diseases and the medical treatment received. This approach shows how campaigning, especially during long sieges, predisposed the crusaders to sickness. In particular, the illness known as *arnaldia* or *leonardie* is investigated in an attempt to identify its place in twelfth-century medical thought. These two terms have intrigued historians, who have been attempting to identify their meaning for over three hundred years.[1]

The chronicles and the poetry of the Third Crusade (1189–92) record the repeated episodes of disease that befell the army and its leaders. There are two main approaches that might be employed in their modern interpretation.[2] One technique is to interpret what they might have meant to people living at the time of the event – for example, by determining the views of medieval medical practitioners and other scholars. This may be referred to as the social diagnosis.

---

[1] Joannes Georgius Koenig, *Disquisitio medica de Arnaldia, quam sub praesidio viri praenobilissimi, amplissimi, excellentissimi atque experientissimi domini Jacobi Pancratii Brunonis ... publicae placidaeque philiatrorum censurae subjiciet Johannes Georgius Koenig* (Altdorf, 1706).

[2] Piers D. Mitchell, "The Use of Historical Texts for Investigating Disease in the Past," *International Journal of Paleopathology* (DOI: 10.1016/j.ijpp.2011.04.002).

Another technique is to attempt to identify the cause of the disease from a modern perspective, sometimes referred to as the modern biological diagnosis. The degree to which either of these approaches will be successful depends upon whether the authors were eyewitnesses, the details recorded by the chroniclers, and whether they mention specific symptoms of the disease. This process is often difficult as the detailed symptoms of epidemics are seldom described in medieval sources. In many cases those brief statements follow stereotypical descriptions that do not allow for an accurate modern biological diagnosis. For these reasons, a retrospective analysis can often only suggest possibilities and estimate their plausibility.[3]

Bearing this in mind, the study of diseases in the past can nevertheless highlight hitherto neglected aspects of medieval life on campaign. The long siege of Acre (1189–91) shows quite plainly the logistical problems, particularly in terms of food supplies and the unhygienic conditions in the crowded encampment. In the light of these circumstances it is no wonder that crusaders of any social rank became victims of disease. Past analysis of mortality in the Third Crusade suggests that about 16 per cent of clergy named in the sources died during the campaign, and about 30 per cent of named nobles.[4] This is despite the innovative work of the mobile army field hospital of the Order of St. John, and the hospitals formed spontaneously at the siege of Acre by both English and German troops.[5] It is presumed that infectious diseases and malnutrition might have been the main causes of death among the clergy, while the knights would have died from weapon injuries as well, explaining the higher mortality. A good deal of supportive archaeological research is now available that has demonstrated evidence for infectious diseases, parasites, malnutrition and weapon injuries in the Latin East at the time of the crusades.[6] Military expeditions

---

[3] Thomas G. Wagner, *Die Seuchen der Kreuzzüge. Krankheit und Krankenpflege auf den bewaffneten Pilgerfahrten ins Heilige Land*, Würzburger medizinhistorische Untersuchungen Beiheft 7 (Würzburg, 2009), pp. 9–13; see also Susan Edgington, "Medical Knowledge in the Crusading Armies: The Evidence of Albert of Aachen and Others," in *MO*, *1*, p. 321; Karl-Heinz Leven, *Die Geschichte der Infektionskrankheiten. Von der Antike bis ins 20. Jahrhundert*, in *Fortschritte in der Präventiv- und Arbeitsmedizin*, ed. F. Hofmann (Landsberg and Lech, 1997), p. 14.

[4] Piers D. Mitchell, *Medicine in the Crusades: Warfare, Wounds and the Medieval Surgeon* (Cambridge, 2004), p. 143.

[5] Susan Edgington, "Medical Care in the Hospital of St. John in Jerusalem," in *MO*, *2*, pp. 27–33; Benjamin Z. Kedar, "A Twelfth-Century Description of the Jerusalem Hospital," in *MO*, *2*, pp. 3–26; Mitchell, *Medicine in the Crusades*, pp. 90–95.

[6] Piers D. Mitchell, "Child Health in the Crusader Period Inhabitants of Tel Jezreel, Israel," *Levant* 38 (2006), 37–44; Piers D. Mitchell, Yossi Nagar and Ronnie Ellenblum, "Weapon Injuries in the 12th century Crusader Garrison of Vadum Iacob Castle, Galilee," *International Journal of Osteoarchaeology* 16 (2006), 145–55; Piers D. Mitchell and Yotam Tepper, "Intestinal Parasitic Worm Eggs from a Crusader Period Cesspool in the City of Acre (Israel)," *Levant* 39 (2007), 91–95; Piers D. Mitchell, Eliezer Stern and Yotam Tepper, "Dysentery in the Crusader Kingdom of Jerusalem: An ELISA Analysis of Two Medieval Latrines in the City of Acre (Israel)," *Journal of Archaeological Science* 35 (2008), 1849–53.

such as crusades also had the potential to spread disease, on both the outward and return journeys.[7]

Analysis of medieval epidemics also provides insight into the medical terminology used in the contemporary chronicles. Examining the disease that the English and the French kings contracted, we encounter the terms *arnaldia*, *leonardie* and *l'ennaudie*.[8] In the medieval period, these terms appear to be unique to chronicles that describe the Third Crusade. In each medieval language dictionary we have been able to consult that includes these terms, the only examples are from the Third Crusade.[9] Other terms applied to illness in the Third Crusade such as *doble terceine*[10] and *major hemitritaeus*,[11] were well attested to in the medical literature of the age.

The Siege of Acre

The story of the severe illnesses of Richard and Philippe begins almost two years before their arrival in the Holy Land, in the summer of 1189, when the titular king of Jerusalem, Guy de Lusignan, laid siege to the city of Acre.[12] Initially commanding only about 600 men, his army was gradually reinforced by crusaders from the West: Frisians, Flemings, Germans and Bretons. However, the Christians were not strong enough to take the well-fortified city by storm. Advancing with a strong relieving force, Saladin was blocking their lines of communication. All the signs indicated that a long-lasting siege would take place, along with famine and epidemics. Enclosed by Saladin's nearby encampment, the crusaders were running out of supplies, particularly in the winter when sea travel in the Mediterranean stopped

---

[7]   Piers D. Mitchell, "Spread of Disease with the Crusades," in *Between Text and Patient: The Medical Enterprise in Medieval and Early Modern Europe*, ed. Brian Nance and Florence Eliza Glaze (Florence, 2011), pp. 309–30.

[8]   Roger of Howden, *Chronica*, ed. William Stubbs, RS 51 (London, 1870), p. 113; see Thomas G. Wagner, "Rex incidit in aegritudinem, quam Arnaldiam vocant. Untersuchungen zur '*aegritudo Arnaldia*' – der rätselhaften Erkrankung, welche die Könige Richard Löwenherz und Philipp II. August während der Belagerung von Akkon im Jahre 1191 befiel," *Fachprosaforschung – Grenzüberschreitungen* 2/3 (2006/2007), 45–57; Ambroise, *The History of the Holy War: Ambroise's Estoire de la Guerre Sainte*, ed. Marianne Ailes and Malcolm Barber, 2 vols. (Woodbridge, 2003), 1:155 and 2:162.

[9]   *Arnaldia*: W.-H. Maigne D'Armis, *Lexicon Manuale ad Scriptores Mediae et Infimae Latinitatis* (Paris, 1858), col. 207; Charles Du Fresne, *Glossarium Mediae et Infimae Latinitatis*, 2 vols. (Niort, 1883), 1:396; R. E. Latham, *Revised Medieval Latin Wordlist from British and Irish Sources* (London, 1965), p. 31. *Leonardie*: Alan Hindley, Frederick W. Langley and Brian J. Levy, *Old French–English Dictionary* (Cambridge, 2000), p. 392.

[10]   *L'estoire de Eracles empereur et la conqueste de la terre d'outremer*, RHC Oc 2:179.

[11]   Richard of Devizes, *Chronicon*, ed. Richard Howlett, RS 82 (London, 1882–86), p. 444.

[12]   *L'estoire de Eracles*, pp. 128–29; Peter W. Edbury, *The Conquest of Jerusalem and the Third Crusade* (Aldershot, 1996), pp. 80–82; Ibn al-Athīr, *RHC Or* 2:6–8; Bahā al-Dīn, *RHC Or* 3:134; Abū Shāmah, *RHC Or* 4:408; Imād al-Dīn, *Conquête de la Syrie et de la Palestine par Saladin*, trans. Henri Massé, Documents relatifs à l'histoire des croisades publiés par l'Académie des Inscriptions et Belles-Lettres 10 (Paris, 1972), pp. 168–70.

due to the bad weather. The price of food rose immensely in the Christian camp. Knights had to eat their horses and other beasts of burden.[13] Foot soldiers were said to have gnawed on the rotting bones of dogs.[14] In the search for sustenance, starving crusaders attacked the Muslim camp several times, but were repulsed sustaining heavy casualties.

The ditches beneath the city walls were repeatedly filled with new corpses. Similarly the nearby river was said to have turned red with the blood of the dead. The stench of rotting bodies was in the air, and there were so many flies that "nobody in the camp could stand it."[15] In the Muslim camp the sultan's advisers became worried about the hygienic conditions too. Referring to the smell of the corpses and corruption of the air, known in Europe as *miasma*,[16] Saladin's entourage advised him to withdraw with his baggage train to the healthier site of Kharruba.[17]

The accounts in western medieval chronicles discussed above record a number of predisposing factors associated with disease during wartime. First, malnutrition leads to weakness, vitamin deficiency diseases, and suppression of the immune system.[18] Second, overcrowding and poor hygiene was present, which would be particularly relevant to sanitation. Third, the water supplies were contaminated with corpses and there was a large number of flies, which play an important role as vectors of gastrointestinal diseases.[19]

In the late summer of 1190, a year before Richard or Philippe Augustus arrived, a severe illness developed among the crusader troops. Ambroise gave a detailed account of this in his *Estoire de la guerre sainte*:

> Then a disease ran through the army – wait while I tell you about it – it was the result of rains that poured down such as have never been before, so that the whole army was half-drowned. Everyone coughed and sounded hoarse; their legs and faces swelled up. On one day there were a thousand [men on] biers; they had such swelling in their faces that the teeth fell from their mouths.[20]

---

[13] *L'estoire de Eracles*, p. 150.

[14] *De expugnatione Terrae Sanctae per Saladinum libellus*, ed. Joseph Stevenson, RS 66 (London, 1875), p. 256.

[15] *L'estoire de Eracles*, p. 151.

[16] For the classical Greek Hippocratic view of contagion, namely through the medium of air by so-called *miasma*, a kind of foul-smelling mist or vapours that ascend out of swampland, corpses or even sick people, see Gundolf Keil, "Miasma," in *Lexikon des Mittelalters*, 9 vols. (Munich, 2002), 6:593.

[17] Ibn al-Athīr, *The Chronicle of Ibn al-Athir for the Crusading Period from al-Kamil fi'l-ta'rikh. Part 2. The Years 541–589/1146–1193*, ed. and trans. D. S. Richards (Aldershot, 2007), p. 369; Abū Shāmah, *The Rare and Excellent History of Saladin*, ed. and trans. D. S. Richards (Aldershot, 2001), p. 105.

[18] R. K. Chandra, "Nutritional Regulation of Immunity and Infection," *Journal of Pediatric Gastroenterology and Nutrition* 5 (1986), 844–52; R. L. Gross and P. M. Newberne, "Role of Nutrition and Immunologic Function," *Physiological Reviews* 60 (1980), 188–251; R. R. Watson, ed., *Nutrition, Disease Resistance and Immune Function* (New York, 1984).

[19] Valerie Curtis, Sandy Cairncross and Raymond Yonli, "Domestic Hygiene and Diarrhoea – Pinpointing the Problem," *Tropical Medicine and International Health* 5 (2000), 22–32.

[20] Ambroise, *The History of the Holy War*, 1:69 and 2:90.

Due to the mention of distinctive symptoms such as the loss of teeth, the illness can be given the modern biological diagnosis of scurvy, which is a deficiency of vitamin C.[21] In this condition the legs may swell, bruising develops in the skin, gum tissue proliferates and overgrows, teeth fall out.[22] Regarding his explanation for the illness, Ambroise opts for secular medical reasoning, following the philosophy of the classical Greek physician Hippocrates,[23] rather than religious theory such as punishment for sin.[24] The wording Ambroise chose suggests he felt the heavy rain was literally absorbed by the soldiers' bodies, hence leading to their swelling up. In modern times the effects of wet weather and flooding on siege-stressed armies are known to have a significant impact upon health, even in the recent past.[25]

However, while malnutrition was clearly present it may well not have been the worst killer. Haymar the Monk indicates this when he uses the words "various illnesses" in his description.[26] The mortality in the host peaked in the autumn and winter of 1190–91, after the crusaders had been reinforced in summer by English and French troops. Muslim historians suspected the humid winter[27] and frequent variations in temperature[28] to be the cause of ill health. Crusaders of high nobility fell victim to the diseases in the camp, among them Frederick of Swabia, son of Emperor Frederick Barbarossa.[29] Uncountable nobles (*alii innummerabiles*) perished "due to the all too corrupted air" (*ex aeris nimia corruptione*), as Matthew Paris states,[30] referring to the abovementioned *miasma* theory. The situation in both the city of Acre and Saladin's camp was similar. The sultan suffered from a "bilious fever" and again he retreated towards Kharruba.[31] Even though the chroniclers may have guessed or exaggerated the figures, the casualties appear to have been significant. The Latin sources wrote of 200,000 to 400,000 deceased,[32] whereas the Arabic-written accounts provide a more modest calculation of about 100–200

---

[21] Mitchell, *Medicine in the Crusades*, p. 2; Wagner, *Die Seuchen der Kreuzzüge*, pp. 220–26.

[22] Laura Pimentel, "Scurvy: Historical Review and Current Diagnostic Approach," *American Journal of Emergency Medicine* 21 (2003), 328–32.

[23] Hippocrates, Περί ἀέρων ὑδάτων τοπων [On airs, waters, places], ed. T. E. Page, trans. W. H. S. Jones, The Loeb Classical Library 147 (London, 1962), pp. 99–101; he considered weather conditions and climate to be the cause of illness.

[24] And so did others, for instance Haymarus Monachus, *De expugnata Accone. Liber tetrastichus seu Rithmus de expeditione Ierosolimitana*, ed. Paul E. Riant (Paris, 1866), p. 12: "Imbris, torrens validus, terram inundabat …"

[25] John Haller, "Trench Foot – A Study in Military-Medical Responsiveness in the Great War, 1914–1918," *The Western Journal of Medicine* 152 (1990), 729–33.

[26] Haymarus Monachus, *De expugnata Accone*, p. 14: "Qui praesentes aderant, poterant videre variis languoribus homines tabere."

[27] Imād al-Dīn, p. 271.

[28] Bahā al-Dīn, p. 208.

[29] Ibid.

[30] Matthew Paris, *Chronica Maiora*, ed. Henry Luard, RS 57 (London, 1874), p. 370.

[31] Bahā al-Dīn, p. 208.

[32] Reinhold Röhricht, *Die Geschichte des Königreiches Jerusalem, 1100–1291* (Innsbruck, 1898), p. 553.

every day.[33] These were the challenging conditions which the two western kings faced upon their arrival at Acre.

Descriptions of *arnaldia* and *leonardie* in 1191

A number of sources describe the illnesses sustained by Richard and Philippe shortly after their arrival at Acre. Some describe the symptoms of each king, and some write about both. In understanding the relative reliability of each source regarding the personal disease symptoms of the king, it is important to bear in mind the likelihood whether this evidence was from the direct experience of the author, from others who were eyewitnesses but written at the same time or shortly after events, or written much later when eyewitnesses were unlikely to have been alive to comment.

Richard I of England landed on 8 June 1191. Not even a week after his arrival he fell ill. Ambroise was a jongleur in the English army camp, but is not thought to have been part of the royal entourage. However, since Richard was recorded as being carried about the army camp on a stretcher while ill, it is quite possible that the author would have seen him. Ambroise wrote: "But the king was ill, his mouth and lips pale, because of an illness – may God curse it – called leonardie."[34] Ambroise also mentioned that within a few days King Phillippe also fell ill and could not ride.[35] No symptoms were given for the French king, and this may reflect the fact that Ambroise may well not have had the opportunity to see him close-up. A few days later King Richard's illness was recorded as making him tremble.[36] Ambroise also recorded that King Philippe recovered from his illness before the English king.[37] Ambroise refers back to the disease later on in the expedition, this time spelling it *l'ennaudie*.[38] These are all the symptoms of *leonardie* recorded by Ambroise, who only uses the term to refer to Richard.

On 6 August 1191, King Richard dictated a letter in the camp at Acre to William Longchamp, the bishop of Ely. In this he referred to his recent illness: "You know that we have suffered much from illness since we undertook our journey, but by the mercy of God, we are restored to full health."[39] Since he arrived at Acre on 8 June and became ill about a week later, this would place the onset of illness in mid-June. It is not clear exactly when Richard regarded himself as fully recovered, but he does appear to have been better by the beginning of August. This suggests an illness duration of several weeks, and perhaps as long as seven weeks.

---

[33] Bahā al-Dīn, p. 208.

[34] Ambroise, *The History of the Holy War*, 1:74 and 2:95: "Mais li reis [Richardz] iert malades e aveit boche e levres fades d'un enfermeté que Deu maudie ou'en apele leonardie."

[35] Ibid., 1:76 and 2:96.

[36] Ibid., 1:77 and 2:99: "que li mals qui li feseit trembler."

[37] Ibid., 1:76 and 2:98.

[38] Ibid., 1:155 and 2:162.

[39] *Epistolae Cantuarienses*, ed. William Stubbs, RS 38, 2 vols. (London, 1865), 2:347.

A French source of the Third Crusade provides much more information about the illness of King Philippe. William the Breton was the French king's chaplain, so we have good reason to assume his description of the symptoms was accurate. William thought that the illness was a result of an attempted assassination with poison. He wrote: "For, as some say, he [Philippe] had drunk the poisoned chalice handed to him by the traitors, by which he was so badly afflicted with illness, so that he lost the nails of his hands and feet as well as the hair and most of the surface of the skin."[40] In his poem about the Third Crusade called *Philippeis* the same author added more symptoms such as fever, sweating and shivering.[41] In order to explain the cause William asserted that poison made the French king sick in the first place by unbalancing the humours. According to Galen's humoural pathology the human body was imagined as a closed system of fluids containing four humours of antithetic qualities: blood, phlegm, yellow and black bile. An imbalance of these humors resulted in illness, as did their corruption by other elements such as unnatural black bile.[42] William the Breton demonstrates that he believed humoural imbalance led to the consequences such as loss of hair, nails and skin because he refers to the hot quality (*calor*) of the king's body. William the Breton does not give a label to this illness in the way Ambroise referred to King Richard's disease as *leonardie*, nor does he comment as to whether it was the same illness as Richard suffered.

Roger of Howden was a royal clerk in the English court who accompanied King Richard on the crusade.[43] He returned to Europe with King Phillippe in August 1191, so would have had access to those in the French court as well as his own. As an eyewitness writing contemporaneously, he noted at the siege of Acre that "the kings were affected by an illness, which is commonly called *arnaldia*; they suffered to the brink of death and lost in the course of the illness all their hair. But by God's grace it happened that both recovered from that illness and that they were made even stronger and more dauntless in the service of God."[44] Roger seems to have been the first to use the term *arnaldia*. Since he wrote in Latin and not French, he could not have used Ambroise's term *leonardie*, even if he had heard the word

---

[40] William the Breton, *De Gestis Philippi Augusti*, ed. Michel-Jean Joseph Brial, RHGF 17 (Paris, 1878), p. 70: "Nam, ut quidam dicunt, venenum a proditoribus porrectum hauserat, unde et tanta infirmitate gravatus est, quod et ungues manum et pedum et capillos et fere omnem cutis superficiem amisit"; T. A. Archer, *The Crusade of Richard I* (London, 1889; repr. 1978), pp. 84, 117.

[41] William the Breton, *Philippeis*, ed. Michel-Jean Joseph Brial, RHGF 17 (Paris, 1878), p. 165: "Solus cum paucis haec inter agenda Philippus, febre gravi tactus, cebroque tremore fatiscens, infirmabatur, Acharonque iacebat in urbe; tantaque scaturies, tantus calor illius ossa totaque membra fuit ita depopulatus, ut omnes a digitis ungues caderent, a fronte capilli. Unde putabatur, et nondum fama quiescit illum mortiferi gustum sensisse veneni ..."

[42] Erich Schöner, *Das Viererschema in der antiken Humoralpathologie* (Wiesbaden, 1964); Rudolph E. Siegel, *Galen's System of Physiology and Medicine: An Analysis of his Doctrines and Observations on Bloodflow, Respiration, Humors and Internal Diseases* (Basel/New York, 1968).

[43] John Gillingham, "Roger of Howden on Crusade," in *Medieval Historical Writing in the Christian and Islamic Worlds*, ed. D. O. Morgan (London, 1982), pp. 60–75.

[44] Roger of Howden, *Chronica*, p. 113.

spoken or seen the jongleur's text. Describing the illness, Roger applies the same term and the same symptoms to both kings. It is clear that Roger believed they suffered from the same condition.

The *Lyon Eracles* version of the continuation of William of Tyre's chronicle was written in French and belongs to a group of manuscripts probably copied in Acre in the second half of the thirteenth century.[45] The section covering the time of the Third Crusade mentions the French king's illness. After the supposed conspiracy had been revealed to King Philippe, we again hear that his physical condition changed for the worse: "The king took the words to heart and became anxious and annoyed, so that he severely fell from double tertian (*doble terceine*)."[46] This text does not give symptoms, but does allocate a medieval diagnostic label to the illness.

Richard de Templo wrote the *Itinerarium Peregrinorum* in England, possibly between 1217 and 1222.[47] Writing in Latin, he followed Roger of Howden's lead and refers to King Richard's illness as *arnaldia*: "When he had been there some days he contracted a very serious illness, commonly called Arnoldia. This was due to the climate of that unfamiliar region, which did not agree with his natural constitution."[48] From the *Itinerarium Peregrinorum* we know that Richard was confined to his bed also suffering from bouts of severe fever.[49]

Later English chroniclers that cover the crusade continue to use the term *arnaldia*. For example, in the early fourteenth century Nicolaus Triveth wrote his annals of six kings of England covering 1136–1307. Clearly not an eyewitness, and with all eyewitnesses long deceased by then, he used earlier sources to recreate the story of the Third Crusade. The marked similarity of his wording for Richard's illness suggests that he relied heavily on Richard de Templo's account.[50]

Major hemitritaeus in 1192

Unlike his cousin Philippe, Richard I of England remained in the Holy Land for another year. The campaign of 1191–92 was directed towards Jerusalem, which Richard approached and saw at a distance of several miles. However, he never reached it, in part due to his ill health. Autumn and winter had been extremely

---

[45] Peter W. Edbury, "The French Translation of William of Tyre's *Historia*: The Manuscript Tradition," *Crusades* 6 (2007), 69–105, at pp. 86, 93; Edbury, *The Conquest of Jerusalem*, pp. 3–7.

[46] *L'estoire de Eracles*, p. 179: "une maladie grant de doble terceine"; the term had already been used by WT, 22.17, p. 1030, to describe the illness of Raymond III of Tripoli. For a more detailed description of this illness, see Wagner, *Die Seuchen der Kreuzzüge*, pp. 227–34.

[47] Helen J. Nicholson, trans., *The Chronicle of the Third Crusade* (Aldershot, 1997), p. 10.

[48] *Itinerarium Peregrinorum et Gesta Regis Ricardi*, ed. William Stubbs, RS 38 (London, 1864), p. 214: "Cum autem per aliquot dies ibi moram fecisset, gravissimam incurrit aegritudinem, quae vulgo Arnoldia vocatur, ex ignotae regionis constitutione, cum eius naturali complexioni minus concordante."

[49] *Itinerarium Peregrinorum*, p. 220.

[50] Nicolaus Triveth, *Annales sex regum Angliae*, ed. Antonius Hall (Oxford, 1719), p. 106: "quae vulgo arvoldia vocatur."

cold and rainy. Moreover, the provisions were meagre. For eight days no supplies reached the army so that the weakest fell behind and were killed by the Saracens, who were constantly pressing and attacking. In spring there was a menace of biting insects.[51] Again an epidemic was about to emerge. It came in the summer of 1192 after a major battle with Saladin at Jaffa.

The king's biographer, Ralph of Coggeshall, wrote shortly after the crusade, but in England. He described the disease very generally:

> After this unbelievable victory of King Richard, while the same was resting at Jaffa for six weeks, a deadly disease arose by reason of polluted air; that illness afflicted the king himself and almost all of his men; and whoever was seized with infection of this illness died quickly, except for the king, for God accorded his protection to him.[52]

This quote does not provide a medieval diagnostic term, but again the *miasma* theory is applied to explain the spread of disease. Here, it is combined with a positive religious thought. God did not send this scourge; instead he provided the power to recover from it.

Richard de Templo wrote in a similar manner in his *Itinerarium Peregrinorum*: "Moreover, for King Richard and our host were battered by reason of the hardship of that day, he contracted a disease, due to both the ferocity of combat and to the stench of the corpses the camp was polluted with, so that almost everybody died."[53] Here, in addition to the *miasma* theory, the author refers to physical factors as causing disease.

Bahā al-Dīn was a Muslim nobleman who recorded the views of Richard's illness from the perspective of the Muslim camp. Saladin was informed about Richard's condition, even though the Arabic historiography did not hand down symptoms or contemporary diagnostic labels. Bahā al-Dīn wrote of a "very serious illness," which confined the king to his bed.[54] Stressing the chivalry of his master on the one hand and the helplessness of the English king on the other, we are given an account of several English legations to Saladin applying for fruits and rose-snow.[55]

A more specific account of Richard's suffering at Jaffa, in terms of terminology and symptoms, was handed down by Richard of Devizes. Richard wrote in England shortly after the crusade, "it was a continuous, undulating fever, and the physicians suspected it to be a major hemitritean fever."[56]

---

[51] *Itinerarium Peregrinorum*, pp. 304, 313, 361: "ut universi quos punxissent, viderentur leprosi ..."

[52] Ralph of Coggeshall, *Chronicon Anglicanum*, ed. Joseph Stevenson, RS 66 (London, 1875), p. 51.

[53] *Itinerarium Peregrinorum*, p. 425.

[54] Bahā al-Dīn, p. 224.

[55] Ibid., p. 341.

[56] Richard of Devizes, *Chronicon*, p. 444: "typhus erat continuus, medici majorem hemitritaeum mussitabant ..."; see Wagner, *Die Seuchen der Kreuzzüge*, pp. 234–39.

The Medieval Diagnosis for the King's Illness

Since in medieval times the terms *arnaldia* and *leonardie* appear to have been used only in the context of the Third Crusade, it is helpful to assess what this collection of symptoms might have meant to a twelfth-century physician on that crusade. A study of medical texts written around the time of the Third Crusade allows an assessment to see which disease descriptions most closely matched those of King Richard and King Philippe. In the eleventh century, Constantinus Africanus translated a number of Arabic medical texts into Latin at the monastery of Montecassino. Perhaps his most famous translation was entitled *Liber Pantegni*, from the medical text entitled *Complete Book of the Medical Art* (*kitab al-malaki*) by the tenth-century Persian physician Ali ibn al-ʿAbbas al-Majusi.[57] The *Liber Pantegni* is divided into two parts, the *Practica* and the *Theorica*. There is an important section on skin diseases in the half of the book known as the *Practica*, entitled *De cura lepre et eius significatione*.[58] The term did not translate as leprosy as we understand it today, although one subsection of *De cura lepre* probably did include leprosy. Skin diseases were divided into four main types depending upon their symptoms, the perceived underlying humoural imbalance causing the disease, and the animal felt to most closely resemble the type. One type was termed *alopicia*, and the disease was believed to be due to corruption of the blood by unnatural black bile. The term alopecia comes from the Greek for a fox (*alopex*). The signs of the disease were red, hot swellings that were corrupt. It was probably the disease of the lion (*leonina*) that Kühn referred to as a suggestive interpretation of *leonardie*.[59] However, the symptoms of the disease of the lion were completely different to those of the kings, as the patient went yellow.[60] The later section specifically on alopecia in the *Theorica* half of the book specifically refers to alopecia as the fox disease (*allopicia id est vulpes*).[61] The fox disease shares many of the key symptoms recorded for the two kings (loss of hair, red skin, fever). Copies of the *Liber Pantegni* had plenty of time to circulate in Europe before the time of the Third Crusade a century later, so it is quite likely that the highly educated doctors in the royal court of the two kings would have had access to read the content during their training. Furthermore,

---

[57] *Constantine the African and ʿAli ibn al-ʾAbbas al-Maǧusi: The Pantegni and Related Texts*, ed. Charles Burnett and Danielle Jacquart (Leiden, 1994).

[58] Constantine the African, *Liber Pantegni*, *Practica* 4.2 (London, 1515), fol. 93r. We are grateful to Michael McVaugh, University of North Carolina, for sharing his expertise on these early surgical texts.

[59] Oscar Kühn, *Medizinisches aus der altfranzösischen Dichtung*, Abhandlungen zur Geschichte der Medizin 8 (Breslau, 1904), pp. 130–32.

[60] Constantine the African, *Liber Pantegni*, *Practica* 4.2, fol. 93r.

[61] Constantine the African, *Liber Pantegni*, *Theorica* 8.24, fol. 39r: "Allopicia et tyria sunt due passiones, capillos a capite et pilos a barba et superciliis evellentes; suntque hec nomina a simili sumpta. Allopicia id est vulpes plurimum patiuntur ut pili sibi cadant et cutis vulneretur"; Stephen of Antioch, *Liber regalis*, *Practica* 4.12 (Venice, 1492), fol. 117r, covers alopecia as alopitie and recommends bloodletting, pills and purges to treat the condition. His *Theorica* 8.18, fol. 57r, equates to Constantine the African, *Liber Pantegni*, *Theorica* 8.24, fol. 39r. It discusses alopitia and the fox disease vulpi.

in 1127 Stephen of Pisa also translated the *Complete Book of the Medical Art* into Latin in Antioch, giving it the title *Regalis Dispositio* ("the royal arrangement").[62]

A century after Constantinus, Roger Frugard (ca. 1140–ca. 1195) was teaching medicine in Parma, Italy. His ideas were written down in 1180 by Guido of Arezzo the Younger.[63] In consequence, they were disseminated just before the Third Crusade. This late twelfth-century text shows influence from the *Pantegni* of Constantinus Africanus, with a section devoted to lepra.[64] Here the section on lepra states that the alopecia form was known as the fox disease (*vulpibus*). He again described how hair falling out (*cilia depilant*) was an important symptom of the alopecia form of lepra. The treatment recommended by Roger of Parma for alopecia was electuaries (sweet, sticky medicines), bloodletting, scarification and cautery. This book by Roger Frugard was written a decade before the Third Crusade. However, it is not entirely clear whether the doctors in the royal entourage of the kings participating on the Third Crusade would have read it before the crusade began, as new books would have taken time to circulate around Europe. Similar descriptions written after the Third Crusade, referring to alopecia as the fox disease, are given by Bartholomaeus Anglicus (ca. 1203–72) in *De proprietatibus rerum* ("On the properties of things")[65] and the surgical work of Guy de Chauliac (1300–68).[66]

Modern veterinary research has noted that all members of the dog family are known to suffer with hair loss and mange, but the European red fox is particularly prone to this. The cause is sarcoptic mange, an infestation by the skin parasite *Sarcoptes scabei*.[67] This is a burrowing mite that lives on species of the dog family, and is easily spread from one to another during any kind of physical contact. Clinical signs of the disease are intense itching, red crusty skin and hair loss. In longstanding cases large patches of the skin become thickened, scarred and hairless. A significant proportion of infected animals can die from the infestation. The propensity of foxes to lose their hair and develop red peeling skin may well explain why the collection

---

[62] Charles Burnett, "Antioch as a Link between Arabic and Latin Culture in the Twelfth and Thirteenth Centuries," in *Occident et Proche-Orient: Contacts Scientifiques au Temps des Croisades*, ed. Isabelle Draelants, Anne Tihon and Baudouin van den Abeele (Louvain, 2000), pp. 1–78; Charles Burnett, "Stephen, the Disciple of Philosophy, and the Exchange of Medieval Learning in Antioch," *Crusades* 5 (2006), 113–29.

[63] Tony Hunt, *Anglo-Norman Medicine: Roger Frugard's Chirurgia and the Practica Brevis of Platearius* (Cambridge, 1994), p. 5.

[64] Roger of Parma, *Incipit Practica Magistri Rogerii*, in *Cyrurgia Guidonis de Cauliaco et Cyrurgia Bruni, Theodorici, Rogerii, Rolandi, Bertopalie, Lanfranc*, ed. Bernardus Locatellus (Venice, 1498), fol. 226v.

[65] Bartholomaeus Anglicus, *De proprietatibus rerum* 7.64, ed. Anthonius Koburger (Nuremberg, 1492).

[66] Guy de Chauliac, *Inventarium sive chirurgica magna* 2.1.6, ed. Michael McVaugh, 2 vols. (Leiden, 1997) 1:313: "Allopicia enim dicitur secundum Galienum a vulpibus ..."

[67] Suzanne Kennedy-Stoskopf, "Canidae," in *Zoo and Wild Animal Medicine*, ed. Murray E. Fowler and R. Eric Miller, 5th ed. (St. Louis, 2003), pp. 482–90.

of symptoms known in the medieval period as alopecia was linked with foxes rather than any other animal.

The Medieval Meaning of *arnaldia*

In 1706, Johannes Koenig published a short book on the meaning of *arnaldia*.[68] He was unable to find any examples outside the context of the Third Crusade. In view of the symptoms given by English chroniclers covering this expedition, he suggested the term might just be an English word for hair loss. Peter Herde pointed out the similarity of the *arnaldia* to another historical disease called *febris Romana*, Roman fever.[69] Abbot Wibald of Stablo had written about the Roman fever from his own experience, as he fell ill with it in the summer of 1156. Wibald stated that it was associated with fever, hair loss and pale complexion.[70] However, the modern biological diagnosis for Roman fever has never been identified. Stefan Winkle suggested typhoid/enteric fever as a possible interpretation for *arnaldia*.[71]

While the Latin medical texts of Constantinus Africanus and Roger Frugard use the term for fox, neither Constantinus, Roger, nor other medical texts of the time use the Latin term *arnaldia* as found in English histories of the crusade.[72] If the term *arnaldia* was not borrowed from medieval medical texts, where did it come from? In fact, the term *arnaldia* does not seem to have any roots in Anglo-Saxon, Anglo-Norman, or Middle English that might explain the unique use of the term in English texts.[73] Rather than looking for English or Latin origins for this word, one possibility is that we should look to the Greek. In 1809, Bartholomew Parr published a medical dictionary that mentions *arnaldia*. He seems unaware of the use of the word in Third Crusade texts, as these are not mentioned in his entry. The entry states how the word originates from the Greek words *arnos*, for a lamb, and *algia*, for pain: "It is so called because lambs are subject to it. A malignant slow disease of the chronical kind, attended with alopecia; it was formerly very common in England."[74] Here we may have the missing link. Bearing in mind the medieval

---

[68]   Koenig, *Disquisitio medica de Arnaldia*.

[69]   Peter Herde, "*Mortalis Pestilentia*: Some Observations on Epidemics in Medieval Italy," in *Gesammelte Abhandlungen und Aufsätze, II/1. Studien zur Papst- und Reichsgeschichte, zur Geschichte des Mittelmeerraumes und zum kanonischen Recht im Mittelalter* (Stuttgart, 2002), p. 51.

[70]   *Monumenta Corbeiensia*, ed. Philipp Jaffé, *Bibliotheca rerum Germanicarum* 1 (Berlin, 1864), p. 233: "quoniam febre Romana quinque ebdomanibus apud Viterbum decubueramus et, vi non naturalis caloris cute et omnibus piliis amissis, fauces mortis vix evaseramus."

[71]   Stefan Winkle, *Kulturgeschichte der Seuchen* (Düsseldorf, 1997), p. 442.

[72]   Roger of Parma, *Incipit Practica Magistri Rogerii*, fol. 226v.

[73]   We are most grateful to the following for sharing their linguistic expertise on this point: Debbie Banham, University of Cambridge; Luke Demaitre, University of Virginia; Juhani Norri, University of Tampere, Finland; Linda Voights, University of Kansas-Missouri.

[74]   Bartholomew Parr, *The London Medical Dictionary. Including under Distinct Heads Every Branch of Medicine*, 3 vols. (London, 1809), 1:180. We are much indebted to Juhanni Norri for bringing this reference to our attention.

propensity for variable spelling, the minor variation between the Greek *arnalgia* and the Third Crusade term *arnaldia* is quite understandable. It is appreciated that there is a considerable time gap between 1809 and 1191, and it would be reassuring for this argument to find some other examples of arnaldia referring to sheep during that intervening period. However, since this dictionary entry does not mention the Third Crusade at all, and does describe the same hair loss in sheep as occurred in the two kings, we do have some evidence for this potential interpretation. At this point we still need to determine whether there were any diseases of sheep in medieval England that caused loss of hair similar to the king's on the Third Crusade, and why a chronicler might choose to compare his king to a sheep.

A number of sheep diseases of which hair loss and peeling skin are the main symptoms are currently present in Europe and known to modern veterinary medicine.[75] Sheep scab (psoroptic mange) is caused by the mite *Psoroptes ovis*, which makes the skin intensely itchy. An infected sheep then rubs its body against posts, the wool falls out, and the skin becomes pink and peels due to the inflammation. Occasionally such infestations can lead to the death of the sheep. Another disease to consider is cutaneous myiasis (fly strike). Diptera flies lay eggs on soiled areas of fleece. The eggs hatch out and the larvae eat the faeces, wool and skin, especially around the anus. This can lead to marked fleece loss at the back of the sheep and a proportion of sheep can die. Lice (*pediculosis*) cause itching which triggers rubbing against posts but generally leads to less fleece loss than does sheep scab. Sheep keds (*Melophagus ovinus*) is a wingless sucking fly. This ectoparasite also causes itchy skin, which again is rubbed against posts. Clearly, there are several diseases that can cause a sheep to lose patches of its fleece, develop red, peeling skin, and look mangy and unhealthy.

It has been suggested that there may have been about seven million sheep in Britain in 1100,[76] and by the thirteenth century over ten million sheep were being reared for their wool.[77] Indeed, Hurst has argued that the intensification of wool production at that time contributed to an increase in disease. Sheep scab and superficially similar diseases affecting the fleece of sheep apparently became a widespread problem in thirteenth- and fourteenth-century England.[78] England was a major sheep-farming nation during the medieval period, and it is likely that most people would have been familiar with sheep. In this context, it would not be so surprising for a twelfth-century English author to use the term for a disease of mangy sheep to describe the hair loss of the English king, rather than allude to foxes which would not have been as socially important to the population.

---

[75] Philip R. Scott, *Sheep Medicine* (London, 2007), p. 253–62; I. D. Aitken, *Diseases of Sheep*, 4th ed. (Oxford, 2007), pp. 321–37.

[76] W. G. Hoskins, *Sheep Farming in Saxon and Medieval England* (London, 1955), p. 6.

[77] Derek Hurst, *Sheep in the Cotswolds: The Medieval Wool Trade* (Stroud, 2005), p. 57.

[78] T. H. Lloyd, "Husbandry Practices and Disease in Medieval Sheep Flocks," *Veterinary History* 10 (1977–78), 3–14; Hurst, *Sheep in the Cotswolds*, p. 62.

It appears that the origins and meaning of the enigmatic word *arnaldia* can tentatively now be proposed. It does not have its origins in medical texts, but the term may instead have been constructed from the Greek, used in a veterinary rather than medical context. It remains unclear whether Roger of Howden created the word *arnaldia* himself, or if it was already in use but never written down prior to his chronicle. However, the fact that it was a term still in use in England in 1809 to describe sheep mange is highly illuminating.

The Medieval Meaning of *leonardie* and *l'ennaudie*

A considerable number of past authors have attempted an interpretation of the term *leonardie*. Some have based their suggestions on the symptoms, and others on the structure of the word itself.

At the beginning of the twentieth century, historians from Germany and France tended to interpret it as *Schweißfieber* – presumably allusion to the fifteenth-century sweating sickness (*sudor anglicus*).[79] A special form called *Frieselfieber*, *suette miliaire* or *trousse-galant* resulted in hair loss and a peeling skin similar to the description of William the Breton.[80] Gillingham proposed that *leonardie* was either scurvy or trench mouth,[81] perhaps due to the changes to the mouth and lips described by Ambroise.[82] The crusading army at Acre does appear to have suffered with scurvy, but the term *leonardie* is never applied to describe the disease of 1190 widespread in the Christian army; instead, it is used exclusively for the febrile disease of King Richard. Moreover, it seems highly unlikely that the two rulers came down with a vitamin deficiency almost simultaneously so soon after arriving. Kühn interpreted the Old French *leonardie* as *facies leonina* ("face like a lion") and called it "an affliction that cannot be qualified."[83]

In contrast to those attempting to match the symptoms of *leonardie* with other diseases with better-known names, Gaston Paris employed an etymological approach. He suggested that *leonardie* might be a contracted form of the words *le renardie*.[84] He had looked in Godefroy's medieval French dictionary, which mentions that *renardie* was a word for alopecia in the fourteenth century.[85] The source

---

[79] Auguste Brachet, *Pathologie mentale des rois de France: Louis XI et ses ascendants. Une vie humaine etudiée à travers six siècles d'hérédité, 852–1483* (Paris, 1903), pp. 243–47; Alexander Cartellieri, *Philipp II. August. König von Frankreich. Band 2: Der Kreuzzug* (Leipzig/Paris, 1906), pp. 203–8.

[80] J. F. C. Hecker, *Die grossen Volkskrankheiten des Mittelalters. Historisch-pathologische Untersuchungen* (Berlin, 1865), pp. 193–98.

[81] John Gillingham, *Richard I* (London, 1999), p. 160.

[82] Ambroise, *The History of the Holy War*, 1:74 and 2:95.

[83] Kühn, *Medizinisches aus der altfranzösischen Dichtung*, pp. 130–32.

[84] Gaston Paris, *L'Estoire de la guerre sainte. Histoire en vers de la troisième croisade (1190–92) par Ambroise*, Collection de documents inédits sur l'histoire de France 11 (Paris, 1897), p. LXXIII.

[85] Frédéric Godefroy, *Dictionnaire de l'ancienne langue française et de tous ses dialectes du IXe au XVe siècle*, 20 vols. (Paris, 1890–92), 7/1:18.

was actually Corbichon, who translated the Latin medical text of Bartholomaeus Anglicus into French in 1372.[86] Modern dictionaries of medieval French interpret *renart* as a medieval term for the fox, following from the eponymous hero of the popular beast epic *Roman de Renart*.[87] However, since the epic was only started in 1174 it could be argued that there was not enough time for this term to become the dominant word for a fox, instead of *goupil*, by the time of the Third Crusade.[88]

Another possibility is based on a philological argument. From a philological viewpoint, the French terms *l'ennaudie* and *leonardie* could potentially be vernacular forms of *arnaldia*. In medieval French "al" and "au" could be interchangeable (diphthongization), and "r" and "l" are sometimes interchangeable. In such circumstances, it could be that the words *l'ennaudie* and *leonardie* were derived from the Latin word used in England by other crusaders on the same expedition, including Roger of Howden. The different spelling for *leonardie* and *l'ennaudie* may just reflect the variability in spelling many words that was commonplace at that time. Some scribes might spell the same word differently even on the same page, for example. It may also be that, since the word would quite probably have been new to the scribe (it has not been noted in manuscripts that pre-date the Third Crusade), they may have just reinterpreted the *le* at the beginning of *leonardie* as an article, leading to *l'ennaudie*.[89]

One might wonder whether *leonardie* might stem from the medieval French word for a lion, which could be spelt either as *lion* or *leon*. Richard I was already known as the Lionheart by this time. For example, Ambroise describes Richard as *le quor de lion* when he first sees the coast of the Holy Land from his ship.[90] This might explain why the term was not used for other people with similar symptoms,

---

[86] Jean Corbichon, *Cestuy livre des proprietez des choses fut translate de latin [of Bartholomaeus Anglicus] en francois* (Lyon, 1482). In book 7, chapter 64, *De lepra*, Corbichon actually uses the word "renardine."

[87] *Old French–English Dictionary*, ed. Alan Hindly, Frederick W. Langley and Brian Levy (Cambridge, 2000), p. 524.

[88] Early written monuments of the *Renart*-cycle stem from the middle of the twelfth century; the first episodes of the Roman de Renart were composed from 1174–77. See John Flinn, *Le Roman de Renart dans la littérature française et dans les littératures étrangères au moyen âge*, 6th ed. (Paris, 1963), pp. 1–6; Lucien Foulet, *Le Roman de Renard*, Bibliothèque de l'école des hautes études 211, 2nd ed. (Paris, 1968), pp. 1–17. In a folkloristic approach Gaston Paris, *La poésie au moyen âge* (Paris, 1885), p. 245, assumed that literary antagonism of the wolf and the fox was anticipated long before in oral tradition. As a jongleur Ambroise might have known stories and tales such as Renard. With that in mind, it is possible that he knew one particular episode, which deals with the "illness of the lion" (written down presumably between 1180 and 1190). This branch is called "Renard médicin" and tells the story of the fox curing the lion, who is ill with fever – according to the poem a *fièvre quartaine*. One might wonder if Ambroise's leonardie/l'ennaudie could allude to this animal legend of a sick king.

[89] We are grateful to those French historians and romance philologists who shared their thoughts on those possibilities with us, including Sophie Marnette and Tony Hunt, both University of Oxford, and Sylvia Huot, University of Cambridge. However, we should stress that not all experts consulted for this article shared the same viewpoint, and all agreed that this is a complex issue with more than one possible interpretation.

[90] Ambroise, *The History of the Holy War*, 1:37 and 2:65.

such as King Philippe. The Ambroise text has the spelling *quor de lion*, but has *leonardie* rather than *lionardie* as we might expect if this were the explanation. However, this might be accounted for by the variability in spelling at that time. Similarly, *leonardie* might potentially reflect the name Leonard, being Leonard's disease. However, there were no renowned medical authors of the time with the name Leonard writing on alopecia, which might explain the disease being named after them. In consequence, we think such a suggestion unlikely.

A further option to consider that would explain the unique occurrence of this word is that *leonardie* and *l'ennaudie* might be ghost words that do not really exist. It is theoretically possible that the term *leonardie* was created by a scribe struggling to read an earlier version of the manuscript. A word that is only found in one document is sometimes referred to as a *hapax legomenon*. Such words can be very difficult to interpret, as it may be unclear whether they are genuine words that were just used occasionally, or ghost words that were mistranscribed from a poorly written or illegible original. If the latter was the case for *leonardie*, then it would be futile to try to find out what the word meant. Only if an earlier manuscript can be found that uses the true word for that disease can the genuine meaning be identified.

A Modern Biological Diagnosis for *arnaldia* and *leonardie*

Having now explored the possible origins and meaning for *arnaldia* and *leonardie* to people in the medieval period, it is tempting to attempt a modern biological diagnosis of the disease. Others have already made suggestions, such as when Gillingham proposed scurvy or trench mouth.[91] In modern times, loss of hair, nails and peeling skin are known to occur in a range of severe illnesses, including febrile infectious diseases.[92] In some cases this occurrence is due to toxins produced by the infective micro-organism. However, in most cases the body appears to focus all its efforts on fighting the life-threatening illness at the expense of maintaining nonessential tissues, such as hair and nails, which can grow back in due course. The medical term used to describe hair loss in this manner is *anagen effluvium*.[93] In our opinion there is not enough information in the sources to allow any kind of guess as to which infectious disease caused the two kings to develop fever and become so ill that their hair and nails fell out. However, at least modern medicine can explain why the hair and nails were lost.

---

[91] Gillingham, *Richard I*, p. 160.

[92] Marcia Ramos-e-Silva, Melissa Azevedo-e-Silva and Sueli Coclho-Carneiro, "Hair, Nail and Pigment Changes in Major Systemic Disease," *Clinics in Dermatology* 26 (2008), 296–305.

[93] L. C. Sperling, "Hair and Systemic Disease," *Dermatology Clinics* 19 (2001), 711–26; Hans R. Eichelbaum, "Über Veränderungen des Blutbilds beim Haarausfall nach allgemeinen Krankheiten," *Archiv für Dermatologie* 139 (1922), 235–59; M. Amagai, "Toxin in Bullous Impetigo and Staphylococcal Scalded-Skin Syndrome Targets Desmoglein," *Nature Medicine* 6 (2000), 1275–77.

The Meaning of *major hemitritaeus*

Richard of Devizes used this term to refer to the illness of King Richard at Jaffa.[94] Unlike *leonardie* and *arnaldia*, this *major hemitritaeus* was employed in many other medieval writings. The term hemitritean had been in medical use for fevers since classical times, and understandably over the next thousand years its meaning was refined and evolved.[95] By the twelfth century teachings of those associated with Salerno in Italy, such as Archimatheus Salernitanus, described hemitritean as a composite fever, which combined elements of a continuous and an intermittent fever.[96] If the fever was preceded by the adjective *major*, that characterized a sub group of the hemitritean fevers with eighteen hours of fever *in summo labore* and a six-hour afebrile phase *in falsa quiete*.[97] In between, there were stages of continuous fever lasting several days. In his *Glossae in Isagogas Johannitii*, Archimatheus Salernitanus stated that "hemitritean (fever) is called the double of a tertian (fever)."[98] A double tertian fever is also the phrase used in the continuation of William of Tyre to describe the febrile illness experienced by King Philippe during the siege of Acre.[99]

A precise description of a *medius hemitritaeus* was handed down by Peter of Blois, a twelfth-century physician, who studied in Tours, Bologna and Paris. About 1170–75 he had a written medical dialogue with his friend Peter Medicus concerning the case of a French knight called Geldewin. Peter of Blois states that, if the fever were a major hemitritean, "the patient would suffer non-remittent prostration because of the putrefaction of the black bile, inside and outside, in the movement of the interior matter, and his teeth would chatter."[100] In agreement with the Salernitan text composed by Archimatheus (*maior comparatus quartane habeat*

---

[94] Richard of Devizes, *Chronicon*, p. 444.

[95] Hippocrates, *Επιδημιων* [Epidemics], ed. T. E. Page, trans. W. H. S. Jones, The Loeb Classical Library 147 (London, 1962), p. 149, classifies the hemitritean for the first time stressing the continuous element: "*πυρετοί συνεχέες* (…) *ό δέ τρόπος ήμιτριταϊος* …"; however, Celsus, *De medicina* 1–4, ed. E. H. Warmington, trans. W. G. Spencer, The Loeb Classical Library 292 (London, 1971), p. 226, describes it as a special, fatal form of the tertian fever: "Alterum longe perniciosius, quod tertio quidem die revertitur, ex quadraginta autem et octo horis fere triginta et sex per accessionem occupat (interdum etiam vel minus vel plus), neque ex toto in remissione desistit, sed tantum levius est. Id genus plerique medici ήμιτριταῖον appellant."

[96] Archimatheus Salernitanus, *Glossae in Isagogas Johannitii*, ed. Hermann Grensemann (Hamburg, 2004), p. 63: "Emitriteus dicitur ab emi, quod est medium, et triteus tertiana eo, quod omnis emitriteus habet unam materiam sui, materiam tertiane et iterum aliam."

[97] Ibid., p. 64: "Emitritei tres sunt species, minor, medius et maior …"; he also states, upon the authority of Galen, that the affliction results from an abundance of black bile.

[98] Ibid., p. 63: "Vel emitriteus dicitur duplum tritei."

[99] *L'estoire de Eracles*, p. 179.

[100] Urban T. Holmes and Frederick R. Weedon, "Peter of Blois as a Physician," *Speculum* 37 (1962), 252–56. For a collection of Peter of Blois's letters see PL 207:2–560. PL 207:126: "Quod si major hemitritaeus esset, propter putrefactionem melancholiae intus et extra in motu materiae interioris, aeger enim motum et aptitudinem membrorum amitteret: dentes etiam ipsius ad se invicem clauderentur."

melancoliam extra),[101] Peter ascribes an abundance of black bile to the *major* form. His patient, however, showed these symptoms "to a very small degree" and was therefore diagnosed as having *medius hemitritaeus*.[102]

A number of suggestions have been proposed for the modern biological diagnosis of hemitritean, double tertian, or semitertian fever.[103] However, this is a very complicated issue to interpret. The periodic nature of some fevers described in medieval medical texts does suggest a modern biological diagnosis of malaria to be plausible. For example, quartan fever (peaking every third day) and tertian fever (peaking on alternate days),[104] do sound compatible with a modern biological diagnosis of quartan malaria (*Plasmodium malariae*) and tertian malaria (*Plasmodium vivax*) as it is extremely rare for any other diseases to cause fevers with such periodicity. In contrast, it is the more complex, more frequent and often unpredictable nature of hemitritean or semitertian fever that fails to have a character unique to any one disease known today. It is quite possible that some cases were due to a mixed infection by different species of malaria, while others were caused by any of a wide range of other infectious diseases.

While such discussion highlights the difficulty in attributing a modern diagnostic label to the medieval social diagnosis of hemitritean and double tertian fever as found in the medical texts of the time, we must be very careful not to assume that every individual documented as having one of these fevers really did so. Even discounting incorrect diagnoses by those actually attending a case, if the author of a text was not one of those medical attendants it is quite possible that he simply guessed what the disease might be. Since so many infectious diseases, and a few non-infectious ones, cause a fever, we do not believe it is wise to label King Richard's illness at Jaffa with a modern biological diagnosis. As no symptoms were given, it may be wise to restrict comment to the medieval social diagnosis of hemitritean fever and leave it at that.

Social Consequences of Disease on Crusade

The sources for the Third Crusade that we have studied here generally propose secular, rather than religious, explanations for the cause of disease. In the twelfth and thirteenth centuries, medical science drew attention to the body and humoural balance, despite the idea that its flesh and blood were the creation of God (*homo*

---

[101] Archimatheus Salernitanus, *Glossae in Isagogas Johannitii*, p. 64, also writes: "Item maior est afflictio, quando uterque humor putrefit cotidie quam si de tertio in tertium putrefit, unde in medio debet colera putrefieri intus et flegmate [*sic*] extra, ut cotidie de utroque affligantur."

[102] PL 207:126: "Quae omnia quia in hac febre minime accident, constat medium esse hemitritaeum …"

[103] Saul Jarcho, "A History of Semitertian Fever," *Bulletin of the History of Medicine* 61 (1984), 411–30; Holmes and Weedon, "Peter of Blois," p. 255.

[104] In classical and therefore medieval fever terminology, today counts as day one.

omnis creatura est).[105] Due to that demystification of the human body, illness had lost a great part of its negativism, and suffering and death are less frequently described as a punishment from an avenging God.[106] In fact, physical disease and its symptoms were generally considered to be caused by an unhealthy environment, by foul-smelling vapours, by hunger, stress, anger and grief; reasons which all related to classical medical humoural theory. But still illness was deemed an ordeal that had to be endured, particularly in the era of the crusades.

In the holy wars against non-Christians, casualties were declared by the clergy to be martyrs, even though death might be caused by epidemics or starvation. Therefore, illness was sometimes depicted by religious authors as a joyful experience, the hour of death as a moment of "praying and rejoicing" (*orans et exsultans*).[107] For Gunther of Pairis, a Cistercian monk who described an epidemic in Acre in 1203, dying from disease was a short cut to heavenly salvation. The afterlife is eternal, he writes; on the other hand, illness is only a "brief calamity that quickly passes."[108] In this perception, illness was understood as a form of mental cleansing or "a spiritual purgative" – it meant suffering for the sake of God. In this context, it is not difficult to understand that bodily distress could not be used as an excuse for retreat from a holy war, even though an excuse on grounds of ill health was used in other areas of life.

In the service of God disease was no excuse to retreat. During the First Crusade, for instance, Count Stephen of Blois, even though elected a commander of the crusader army, left the siege of Antioch on grounds of illness. He might indeed have been ill. However, he was criticized harshly by his contemporaries for what was perceived as dishonourable behaviour.[109] When King Philippe left the Holy Land, setting sail for his homelands in August 1191, there was even more disapproval. While the French chroniclers try to exculpate their king by referring to his "very severe illness,"[110] the English *Itinerarium Peregrinorum* states that he was "cursed instead of blessed" by those who were left behind.[111] In satirical songs (for instance *Maugré tous sainz et maugré Dieu aussi*), even those who followed Philippe back to France were sneered at.[112] The Norman poet Ambroise broached the issue of Philippe's half-hearted commitment in great detail, complaining:

---

[105] Hildegard of Bingen, *Causae et curae*, ed. Laurence Moulinier (Berlin, 2003), p. 76.

[106] Wolf von Siebenthal, *Krankheit als Folge der Sünde* (Hanover, 1950), pp. 42–58.

[107] Jacques de Vitry, *Epistolae*, ed. R. B. C. Huygens, CCCM 171 (Turnhout, 2000), pp. 491–652, at p. 578.

[108] Gunther of Pairis, *Hystoria Constantinopolitana*, ed. Peter Orth (Hildesheim and Zürich, 1994), p. 132: "brevis illa et cito transitura calamitas …"

[109] *GF*, p. 63. See also James A. Brundage, "An Errant Crusader: Stephen of Blois," *Traditio* 16 (1960), 380–95.

[110] Rigordus, *Gesta Philippi II. Augusti*, MGH SS 26:292: "Gravabatur enim rex tunc morbo gravissimo …"; Radulph Niger, *Chronica*, MGH SS 27:339: "Capta Acaron dedicione facta, metu infirmitatis rediit rex Francie in terram suam …"; Wilhelm of Andres, *Chronica*, MGH SS 24:720: "intemperiem transmarine aeris sustinere non valens, quia valde infirmabatur …"

[111] *Itinerarium Peregrinorum*, p. 238.

[112] Cartellieri, *Philipp II. August*, pp. 238–39.

He was going back because of his illness, so the king said, whatever is said about him, but there is no witness that illness gives a dispensation from going with the army of the Almighty King, who directs the paths of all kings. I do not say that he was never there, nor that he had not spent iron and wood, lead and pewter, gold and silver, and helped many people, as the greatest of earthly kings among the Christians, but for this reason he should have remained to do what he could, without failing, in the poor, lost land that has cost us so dear.[113]

As Philippe's example shows, the religious ideas behind a crusade did contrast with those secular concepts about the body, for to the pope a crusade was a spiritual experience. Ideally, campaigning in divine service demanded a steadfast, saint-like leader, an almost supernatural figure, willing to sacrifice himself if necessary. In contrast, the physical perception of illness reduced the idealized image of a crusading prince to its very core, as merely human. As life (in our cultural perception) is the final and most valuable possession of all individuals, the desire to save it is a natural one. The same can be assumed for Richard I. It is plain to see, especially in the second year of his campaign (1192), that his bellicosity towards Saladin was dependent upon his actual state of health. Even in negotiations with Saladin, when the Angevin felt better, he firmly insisted on his conditions and he did not accept the final terms until he was too weak to read the treaty word by word.[114]

The difference between Richard and Philippe, in terms of a historiographical judgment, was simply that Richard was seen quite clearly to act in the sense of the crusading spirit demanded by Ambroise and others. Regardless of his fevers, he put his suffering body to work. In July 1191, for instance, he was carried to the front line in his litter made of silk (*in culcitra serica*), in order to strengthen and motivate his fighting men with his presence.[115] Later, during the march toward Jerusalem at the end of May 1192, he heard rumours concerning a conspiracy allegedly conducted by Richard's brother John and Philippe Augustus, threatening to throw his kingdom into confusion. Deeply worried, the king of England took to his bed. He had already decided to return home, when a chaplain, William by name, refreshed his fighting spirit stating that, if he would return to England now, he would lose all his fame and show a lack of faith in God.[116] Finally in 1192, he was struck by illness again and suffered together with his men.[117] Despite these setbacks, he was willing to go on to the brink of death. Not least the approval of exactly this crusading spirit made him the "Lionheart" and Philippe August the "cursed one."

It might be argued that King Richard's eventual withdrawal from the kingdom of Jerusalem was a combination of many factors, including dwindling manpower and finances, a military stalemate with a skilful military tactician (Saladin), a

---

[113] Ambroise, *The History of the Holy War*, 1:85 and 2:105.

[114] Bahā al-Dīn, pp. 346–48.

[115] *Itinerarium Peregrinorum*, p. 224.

[116] Ibid., pp. 362–63.

[117] Ibid., p. 425. Röhricht, *Die Geschichte des Königreiches Jerusalem*, pp. 606–54, covers most of the sources for this episode of his campaign.

disloyal brother in England, as well as his poor health. However, his first action on concluding a truce with Saladin was to travel directly to Haifa in order to receive medical treatment there.[118] This does suggest that he had accepted that his physical health would not allow further campaigning. The ever-presence of illness during his military campaign is an important factor that should not be underestimated. The contemporary chroniclers knew the justification of retreat on grounds of ill health, but they did not accept this excuse during a crusade. To plead illness was not a suitable excuse for release from a crusader's vow. It was rather perceived as desertion, not from an ordinary army, but from the army of Christ. If death from illness on crusade led the soul to heaven, then there was no need to leave that crusade to seek medical attention for the physical body.

Conclusion

This study of disease on the Third Crusade has highlighted a number of important points relevant to the wider crusading movement and medieval warfare as a whole. There was a significant mortality on military expeditions, due not only to weapon injuries but also to infectious disease and malnutrition. Unlike other military campaigns, the special nature of a crusade meant that becoming sick was no excuse to retreat. Death in the service of God was perceived to have been a great honour. To bring medical care to the troops was perfectly acceptable, but for a soldier to return to Europe in order to receive medical care before the crusade was over was regarded as desertion.

The disease suffered by both kings at the siege of Acre seems to closely match descriptions of alopecia in medical texts of the time, the fox disease. This medieval diagnostic label is distinct from the modern use of the word. In the medieval period the term alopecia implied not just hair loss, but also fever and red peeling skin, with the patient often becoming very unwell. The origins of the words *arnaldia* and *leonardie* have been investigated in order to improve our understanding of social attitudes to the illness of the two kings leading the Third Crusade. These neologisms, perhaps created around the time of that crusade, have been fascinating scholars for at least three centuries. The suggestions here are merely that, possible explanations for their meaning. The variability in spelling at the time means that more than one interpretation can always be argued, and in the future experts in medieval French and Latin philology may highlight parallels of which we are currently unaware that may modify this interpretation. The Latin term *arnaldia* could well have originated from the Greek for the sheep disease. It appears to be found only in English chronicles and that of Roger of Howden is the earliest surviving manuscript to use the term. Sheep mange with hair loss and red skin was well attested to in medieval Europe, and the importance of sheep and wool to medieval English life may explain why

---

[118] Ambroise, *The History of the Holy War*, 1:191 and 2:187.

the English chroniclers used the term for sheep mange to describe the illness of the kings. The origins of *l'ennaudie* and *leonardie* are not entirely clear. Possibilities include that they were French versions of the Latin *arnaldia*, that they were derived from the French term for the fox, that *leonardie* came from Richard's nickname as the Lionheart, or were merely ghost words created by a scribe struggling with difficult handwriting in an earlier manuscript that no longer survives.

The modern biological interpretation of *leonardie* and *arnaldia* is that both kings suffered with a severe febrile illness, quite possibly an infectious disease, which then resulted in the loss of hair, nails and superficial layers of skin. Regardless of the microbiological cause, the diseases these kings suffered had major implications for their actions, the outcome of the crusade, and the manner in which they were subsequently regarded back in Europe.

A Genoese Perspective of the Third Crusade

Merav Mack

The Van Leer Jerusalem Institute
merav.mack@vanleer.org.il

The Genoese author of *The Short History of the Kingdom of Jerusalem* relates the story of a Genoese ship that sailed into the harbour of Acre in the summer of 1187. It was not long after the battle of Hattin and rumours had already spread about the devastating results of the battle for the Christians: the deaths of hundreds of knights and the capture of the Holy Cross and the king of Jerusalem. As the ship entered the harbour, the sailors sensed that things were not as usual. They quickly realised that Acre, too, had been seized by Saladin. They feared for their fate but, luckily, a great nobleman, Marquis Conrad of Montferrat, was among the passengers.[1] When he saw a Muslim patrol boat approaching their ship, he warned the crew and his fellow passengers that no one should speak but him. He instructed the Muslim guards to sail back to shore and tell Saladin that the ship was full of Christians, "and specifically Genoese merchants." He then added that "as soon as we heard of Saladin's victory, we came to his land safely and with trust; we pray and ask that he [Saladin] present us an arrow, as a token of trust."[2] Conrad cunningly obtained Saladin's permission and saved the ship, which quickly turned back and sailed to Tyre in time to save the last Latin stronghold of the kingdom of Jerusalem. Conrad assumed command of the remaining forces and some of his Genoese companions stayed on to help him in the battle against Saladin.

Conrad's arrival signalled the beginning of the Frankish resistance and the establishment of a new leadership in the Latin kingdom of Jerusalem. It also presented exciting opportunities for the adventurous knights who came to help. The limited forces that arrived joined the survivors of Hattin and refugees from Jerusalem and other cities; together, they were to hold on for three more years until the arrival of the main contingents of the Third Crusade.

While the author of the chronicle clearly enjoyed telling the story of Conrad's first encounter with Saladin's forces, today's historians can appreciate an additional aspect of this episode. The battle between the Muslims and the Christians was a kind of medieval warfare in which merchants were able to play two roles

---

[1] *Regni hierosolymitani brevis historia*, in Caffaro, *Annali genovesi di Caffaro e de' suoi continuatori: dal MXCIX al MCCXCIII*, ed. Luigi T. Belgrano and Cesare Imperiale di Sant'Angelo, Fonti per la storia d'Italia, 5 vols. (Genoa and Rome, 1890–1929) (hereafter cited as *Ann. Ian.*), 1:145. On Conrad of Montferrat and his family ties with the Latin East, see David Jacoby, "Conrad, Marquis of Montferrat, and the Kingdom of Jerusalem (1187–1192)," in *Dai feudi monferrini e dal Piemonte ai nuovi mondi oltre gli Oceani*, ed. Laura Balletto, Biblioteca della società di storia, arte e archeologia per le province di Alessandria e Asti 27 (Alessandria, 1993), pp. 187–238.

[2] *Regni hierosolymitani brevis historia*, *Ann. Ian.*, 1:145.

simultaneously – trading with the Muslims while fighting them. Saladin authorized merchants' access to his territory and the continuation of trade. Did the Genoese merchants capitalize on this commercial opportunity? How did it reflect on their loyalties to the crusade and to the sustainability of the kingdom of Jerusalem? This paper focuses on the Genoese community during an unusual period in the history of western European and Mediterranean societies. It makes particular use of a surprising number of commercial contracts that provide new perspectives on the Third Crusade as they emerge from the accounts of the people who were positioned at the backstage of the crusades.

Thousands of such documents exist in the archives of Genoa and they enrich the historical sources of the Third Crusade. Among them are contracts and wills that were registered by the local notaries in their cartularies and later deposited in the city's archives. They provide an incomparable wealth of information about life at the time of the Third Crusade. While these documents are usually short, and rarely provide background information or explain the circumstances for each deed, when studied in large numbers and in the context of Genoa's general commercial activities, they provide a detailed picture. Furthermore, as they tell the stories of individuals, they reveal, between the lines of their wills and other legal documents, the fears and hopes of these crusaders and merchants. Three cartularies survive from the time of the Third Crusade, containing documents from January 1190 to April 1192. The documents were registered by the notaries Oberto Scriba da Mercato, Guglielmo Cassinese and Guglielmo di Sori.[3] Hundreds of deeds from this period mention the kingdom of Jerusalem, or *Ultramare* as they called it.[4] Many documents in which *Ultramare* is not mentioned are also relevant to this study because they provide information about the preparations for the crusade in Genoa during this period. Through them, we may better understand Genoa's policies and plans, including those not specified in its official documents. For example, it will be demonstrated that, as part of its involvement in the planning of the crusade, in the year 1190, Genoa established a precedent – later followed by the Venetians during the Fourth Crusade – by committing its entire fleet to the purpose of the crusade. The popular reaction in Genoa to Saladin's defeat of the Latin forces was remarkably strong, and encompassed all social strata; all usual activities in politics and business were interrupted to come to the aid of the Latin kingdom.

---

[3]   *Oberto Scriba de Mercato (1190)*, ed. Mario Chiaudano and Raimondo Morozzo della Rocca, *Notai Liguri del secolo XII*, 2 vols. (Turin, 1938) (hereafter cited as OS); *Guglielmo Cassinese (1190–1192)*, ed. Margaret W. Hall, Hilmar C. Krueger and Robert L. Reynolds, *Notai Liguri del secolo XII*, 2 vols. (Turin, 1938) (hereafter cited as GC); Guglielmo di Sori, mss. in the Archivio di Stato di Genova, *Cartolare notarile* 3/ii and *MS Diversorum* 102 (hereafter cited as GS).

[4]   While *Ultramare* means "beyond the sea" and may apply to all regions from Alexandria to Antioch, several documents confirm that Genoese notaries used this term specifically in relation to the Latin kingdom of Jerusalem. In all the documents written during the 25-year period studied in this research, the notaries never employed this term to refer to cities outside the kingdom of Jerusalem. Moreover, wills written at the time of the crusades include bequests for the aid of *Ultramare* leaving no doubt as to the meaning of the term in Genoese writings.

It will be demonstrated that the charitable activities of individual Genoese formed part of their crusading activities, thus revealing a personal devotion that far surpassed mere compliance with the city's political agenda. While many benefited from the commercial opportunities that opened on both sides of the battlefield, any attempt to polarize the motivations of the Genoese into either piety or profit would be a misinterpretation of the real nature of their conduct.

Diplomatic Efforts and Military Preparations for the Crusade

Genoa received early news of the Frankish defeat at the battle of Hattin in 1187.[5] Initial reports did not convey the full scale of what had happened, including the loss of Jerusalem and the Church of the Holy Sepulchre. The Genoese were determined and motivated "for the sake of God and piety not to let the land be subjugated by the Saracens," and they assumed leading positions in the diplomatic activities necessary to organise aid and to plan a wide military response.[6] Among the first actions taken by the commune was to send Rosso della Volta to England to discuss the reaction to the fall of Jerusalem.[7] Based on the annals and chronicles of the time it is apparent that Rosso was one of Genoa's most experienced diplomats in eastern Mediterranean matters. He even met Saladin in Alexandria in 1177, when they concluded the terms of peace between Genoa and Egypt.[8] Rosso's embassy to England was successful and was followed by another mission, in which two other senior diplomats were sent to France to attend the summit between the kings of England and France at the end of 1189. This was the first of a trio of meetings in which the terms of the crusade were designed and finalised.[9] Rosso, who is mentioned in the French chronicles as the captain of King Philip's ships, continued to play a central role in this matter the following year.[10]

---

[5] *Epistola Januensium ad Urbanum papam*, in Roger of Howden, *Gesta regis Henrici secundi, The Chronicle of the Reigns of Henry II and Richard I, A.D. 1169–1192*, ed. William Stubbs, 2 (London, 1867), p. 11.

[6] "pro Deo et intuitu [*sic*] pietatis terram non permitterent subiugari a Sarracenis," *Regni Iherosolymitani brevis historia, Ann. Ian.*, 1:143.

[7] *Ann. Ian.*, 2:29.

[8] *Ann. Ian.*, 2:11.

[9] These meetings are mentioned in the French, English and Genoese sources. The first took place shortly after Christmas 1189, followed by another on 13 January 1190 and again in March 1190. See *Ann. Ian.*, 2:30–31; Rigord, *Gesta Philippi Augusti*, in *Oeuvres de Rigord et de Guillaume le Breton*, ed. Henri-François Delaborde, Société de l'Histoire de France (Paris, 1882), pp. 30–31, 105; Guillaume le Breton, *Gesta Philippi Augusti*, in *Oeuvres de Rigord et de Guillaume Le Breton*, p. 41; Rigord, *Histoire de Philippe Auguste*, ed. Élisabeth Carpentier, Georges Pon and Yves Chauvin (Paris, 2006), 62, pp. 244–45. In the diplomatic archives of Genoa, the earliest record in which the shipping terms were concluded between France and the consuls of Genoa is from February 1190. See Cesare Imperiale di Sant'Angelo, ed., *Codice diplomatico della repubblica di Genova*, Fonti per la storia d'Italia, 3 vols. (Rome, 1942) (hereafter cited as CDG), 2.192, pp. 366–68.

[10] *Ann. Ian.*, 2:11. Rigord, *Histoire de Philippe Auguste*, 88, pp. 306–7.

In Genoa, the preparations for the crusade lasted from 1187 until the departure of the first Genoese contingent in 1189, while cooperation with the French and the English forces continued until they sailed in 1190. As the management of commerce and shipping played a significant part in the preparations, evidence of commercial activities opens a small window onto this busy time. The notarial evidence, derived from intensive study of the cartularies, shows that Genoa secured its entire fleet for the crusade and withheld all major commercial activities, including ventures to all long-distance destinations.[11] Every year between March and May merchants registered their investments in planned commercial journeys, mainly to North African destinations – Ceuta, Bougie and Tunisia.[12] In the first half of 1190, no such commercial or military ventures were planned to any long-distance destinations. The ships were kept in harbour or sent out on short circular routes to nearby destinations, such as Sardinia, Sicily, Marittima (south of Livorno, on the Maremma coast), Marseilles and even to Genoa's longstanding rival Pisa, following a temporary peace concluded for the sake of the crusade. This important success was credited to Pope Clement III who, as part of his own crusading efforts, pressured the maritime cities to put their conflict on hold. This aim was achieved, however, only after the Genoese destroyed Pisa's newly built stronghold at Bonifacio in Corsica.[13]

Genoa saved its navy for the shipping of the French crusaders in the spring of 1190. The first wave of Genoese crusaders, however, sailed out in the autumn of 1189 and brought military help and supplies to the East in advance of the French and the English.[14] The early departure was perhaps also intended to free more space on the ships for the transportation of the French the following spring. These Genoese

---

[11] There are many studies on the patterns of commerce of this period in the Mediterranean in general and in Genoa in particular, as well as on shipping and on naval transportation. Some of the major works include monumental works applying wide perspectives, while some are more detailed. Adolf Schaube, *Handelsgeschichte der romanischen Völker des Mittelmeergebiets bis zum Ende der Kreuzzüge* (Munich, 1906); Wilhelm von Heyd, *Histoire du commerce du Levant au moyen-âge*, 2 vols. (Leipzig, 1885–86); Robert S. Lopez and Irving W. Raymond, *Medieval Trade in the Mediterranean World: Illustrative Documents Translated with Introduction and Notes* (London, 1955); Geo Pistarino, "Genova e il Vicino Oriente nell'epoca del regno latino di Gerusalemme," in *I comuni italiani nel regno crociato di Gerusalemme*, ed. Gabriella Airaldi and Benjamin Z. Kedar (Genoa, 1986), pp. 57–139. John H. Pryor, *Geography, Technology and War: Studies in the Maritime History of the Mediterranean, 649–1571* (Cambridge, 1988). The following works relate more specifically to the Genoese: Eugene H. Byrne, *Genoese Shipping in the Twelfth and Thirteenth Centuries* (Cambridge, Mass., 1930); Michel Balard, "Le film des navigations orientales de Gênes au XIIIe siècle," in *Horizons marins: Itinéraires spirituels*, ed. Henri Dubois, Jean-Claude Hocquet and André Vauchez, 2 (Paris, 1987), pp. 99–122.

[12] Oberto Scriba da Mercato, cartolare notarile, 1, 2, 4 from 1182, 1184, as well as 1186 (the documents from 1182 and 1184 are not yet published).

[13] The battle between the two cities continued in 1187 and at the beginning of 1188. The final truce was achieved only under massive pressure. Two cardinals were sent to mediate between the enemies. When the pact was eventually concluded they asked one thousand Genoese citizens whose names were recorded in the document to take a personal oath to keep the peace: *Ann. Ian.*, 2:26; CDG 2.171–73, pp. 320–33.

[14] *Ann. Ian.*, 2:32–33.

contingents were headed by some of the city's leading figures, including the troop commander and acting consul Guido Spinola, who later remained in the Latin East to re-establish and govern the local Genoese community, and to acquire vast legal and commercial rights for the commune. In addition to Guido Spinola, the annals mention six other nobles who formed the Genoese leadership of the crusade: Nicola Embriaco, Fulcone da Castello, Simone Doria, Baldovino Guercio, Spezzapietra and Rosso della Volta. This very impressive list consisted of former consuls of the commune, highly respected diplomats and naval commanders. Their commercial activities are well recorded in the notarial archives and they often appear in the Genoese annals and in diplomatic acts. In addition to Rosso della Volta, whose activities in Egypt and England have already been mentioned, the former consul Fulcone da Castello was Rosso's brother-in-law and the commander of the Genoese fleet that fought the Pisans off the shores of Corsica in 1188.[15] Baldovino Guercio was another naval commander who acted as a senior diplomat in Constantinople on several occasions, before and after the Third Crusade.[16]

Many other citizens of Genoa – nobles, soldiers and infantry – joined the Genoese leadership and took part in the military efforts in the Latin East. They were praised by Conrad of Montferrat in his charters of 1190 and 1192 in which he rewarded the commune with privileges and possessions in Tyre, a city in which Genoa had never before possessed property.[17] Similar commendations were repeated in letters of concession granted by Guy of Lusignan and Henry of Champagne.[18] This period was one of constant fighting under severe weather conditions and famine. Many nobles died, especially during the arduous siege of Acre, which lasted from the summer of 1189 to 1191.[19] Roger of Howden listed many of them by name but he did not include the Genoese nobles in his records, and we learn about the price they paid only indirectly. Two of the leaders noted above seem to have perished or perhaps were captured by the enemy. Nicola Embriaco and Spezzapietra, often mentioned in documents and annals prior to the crusade, were clearly absent in the years that followed it. Spezzapietra was a consul in 1182 and 1188, and Nicola Embriaco served as consul four times.[20] Another Genoese noble, an important merchant by the name of Rubaldo di Buontommaso, was in an Egyptian prison

---

[15] *Ann. Ian.*, 2:25. On the family relationship, see OS: 26, 24 September 1186, and Diane Owen Hughes, "Urban Growth and Family Structure in Medieval Genoa," *Past and Present* 66 (1975), 3–28.

[16] *Ann. Ian.*, 2:12–14, and Pasquale Lisciandrelli, ed., *Trattati e negoziazioni politiche della repubblica di Genova (958–1797)*, Atti della Società Ligure di Storia Patria [hereafter cited as ASLSP] n.s. 75 (Genoa, 1960), no. 161, p. 37. See also Paul Magdalino, *The Empire of Manuel I Komnenos, 1143–1180* (Cambridge, 1994), p. 222.

[17] On the location and history of the Genoese quarter in Tyre, see Merav Mack, "The Italian Quarters of Frankish Tyre: Mapping a Medieval City," *Journal of Medieval History* 33 (2007), 147–65.

[18] Dino Puncuh, ed., *I Libri iurium della repubblica di Genova*, I/2, 331–36 (Rome, 1996), pp. 137–52.

[19] Roger of Howden, *Gesta regis Ricardi*, pp. 147–50.

[20] Nicola Embriaco was consul in 1176, 1179, 1185 and 1188. Unlike the consuls Nicola Embriaco and Spezzapietra, we find that Rosso della Volta and Baldovino Guercio continued to be engaged in commercial and diplomatic activities for many more years.

during the same period. The notarial documents show that his wife, Leona, had learnt about his imprisonment at the beginning of 1192 and hastened to ransom him while the war was still being fought. She empowered a messenger to pay a large sum of money for her husband's release.[21] Rubaldo's name is absent from the records in later years, which suggests that the mission was most likely unsuccessful. When, a few years later, his grand-daughter Mabilia married Filippo Spezzapietra the contract gives details of the investment made with her dowry but says nothing about the crusade in which their relatives seem to have perished.[22] We see how the legal nature of most of the remaining sources from medieval Genoa left no room for storytelling or for the display of emotions.

Under the leadership of Guido Spinola the Genoese continued fighting in Acre and established a permanent base for the Genoese in Tyre, a community which enjoyed many commercial and legal privileges. At the same time preparations continued in Genoa for the transportation of several thousand crusaders the following spring. In February 1190, at a ceremony attended by all six consuls of the commune in Genoa, as well as the city judges and another three dozen Genoese nobles, a contract was signed between Genoa and France.[23] King Philip of France, represented by Duke Hugh III of Burgundy, his closest ally in the organization and launching of the crusade, agreed to a fee of nine marks of Troyes for the transportation of each knight with his two horses, escorted by two squires. Provisions included food for eight months and wine for four months. The consuls were paid 2,000 silver marks in advance of the total fee of 5,850 marks. The value of the mark was between 45s and 48s Genoese in this period, so that the advance payment for the 650 French knights they expected to come was between £4,500 and £4,800 Genoese.[24] This was a substantial amount of money,[25] but the investments required of the Genoese were sizable as well. For example, evidence shows that the value of one large ship built in Genoa on the eve of the Third Crusade amounted to £1,920 Genoese.[26] It is not surprising to find in the French chronicles of the crusade praise for the Genoese for their hard work in preparation.[27]

For common people, nine marks or £20 5s Genoese was a large amount of money, well beyond their annual salary. The wages of professional people had not been much more than 2s a day, which is what Baudizio da Ripa, a professional caulker

---

[21]   GC: 1504, 22 January 1192.

[22]   Guglielmo di Sori MS., fol. 158r.

[23]   CDG 2.192, pp. 366–68.

[24]   In most documents from the years 1190–91, the exchange rate between the Genoese pound and the silver mark was 45s Genoese to a silver marc. Between July and September 1191 there were slight fluctuations in the mark's value, between 45s Genoese and 48s. See GC: 275, 423, 588, 828, 936, 963, 979, 1044.

[25]   The transportation fee was much higher in comparison with later crusades: see Michel Balard, "Genova e il Levante (secc. XI–XII)," in *Comuni e memoria storica alle origini del comune di Genova*, ed. Dino Puncuh, ASLSP n.s. 42/1 (Genoa, 2002), p. 534.

[26]   OS: 355, 8 April 1190. A quarter of this ship was sold for £480.

[27]   Rigord, *Histoire de Philippe Auguste*, 76, pp. 274–75.

– a skilled and dangerous occupation – received in 1191 to complete the work on a large crusader ship.[28] The mariners and sailors who went to the battle zone in Acre in 1191 were paid between £2 10s and £7 for the return journey, except for the captain who received £15 for navigating the ship.[29] The knights had many other expenses to take into account, such as the wages of their squires, their weapons and horses, and many other additional travel costs. Some wealthy crusaders were escorted by a large number of people. The bishop of Liège, for example, brought with him an entourage of at least eight people, including his seneschal, chaplain, chamberlain, nephew and personal butler. By the end of his journey he was in such deep debt that he was forced to borrow 200 marks in Genoa to help him get back home, asking his staff to pledge for him as guarantors.[30]

We have additional evidence of preparations for the expedition in the winter of 1190: many Genoese crusaders had sailed ahead of the French, and yet more ships were required. Groups of investors had signed detailed contracts with shipbuilders in which deadlines were specified to ensure that the vessels would be ready for the summer. For example, three ship owners had ordered 54 beams of beech wood (*serras de fago*) and an additional 20 oak plates (*quadrales quercus*) for their ship. Another contract detailed the work expected of the contracted carpenter.[31] The largest ship contracted was under construction in April 1190 in Finale Ligure, 52 kilometres west of Genoa. A quarter of this vessel was sold for £480. The ship had two castles and other features that resemble the specifications made for crusader ships.[32] Other arrangements made by the French representatives included the order of a large amount of local wine for the king. The cartularies contain a contract signed with Mabilia Leccavella, a Genoese businesswoman, who promised to supply 13 barrels (*vegetes*) – thousands of litres of wine, which she sold for a handsome profit.[33] Interestingly, although the crusade is not mentioned in the

---

[28]   GC: 1427, 19 December 1191. Caulking was a skilled profession involving some risk in handling highly flammable material in proximity to the newly built wooden ships. See Hilmar Krueger, *Navi e proprietà navale a Genova seconda metà del sec. XII*, ASLSP n.s. 25 (99) (Genoa, 1985), p. 164. Furthermore, in the year 1213, the Genoese annals describe a major caulking accident in which the *Contesa*, a large ship, was burnt to ashes together with two neighbouring ships. See *Ann. Ian.*, 2:128–29.

[29]   GC: 37, 7 January 1191; GC: 178, 4 February 1191; GC: 205, 12 February 1191; GC: 210, 13 February 1191; GC: 215–16, 15 February 1191.

[30]   GC: 761, 21 June 1191, and GC: 828, 13 July 1191. The terms of the loan specify that it would be paid back in a secular location in Liège.

[31]   OS: 224 and 229, 7–8 March 1190.

[32]   OS: 355, 8 April 1190; CDG 2.192, pp. 366–68. See also Krueger, *Navi e proprietà navale a Genova*, pp. 76–78.

[33]   OS: 271, 20 March 1190. Mabilia charged the king's messengers 7s Genoese for each *meçarolia (mezzarola)* of wine. In total she sold him 13 *vegetes*. This measure is not very commonly used in the sources. John Pryor finds evidence that each *veges* contained either 6 or 12 *meçaroliae*. Each *meçarolia* of wine equals two *barili* of 100 pints each, a total of 148.86 litres. According to these figures, King Philip ordered from Mabilia a total of either 11,611 litres or 23,222 litres of wine and paid £27.30 or £54.60. See Pryor, *Geography, Technology and War*, pp. 77–78. In the estimation of the *meçarolia*, Pryor followed Horace Doursther, *Dictionnaire universal des poids et mesures anciens et modernes* (Brussels, 1840), pp. 69, 432. Eugene Byrne followed Pietro Rocca's nineteenth-century dictionary

document itself, the contract was obviously related to it. Why else would the king of France buy Ligurian wine, and ask it to be ready for the time of his departure?

The Delay in the Embarkation on the Crusade

The bustling atmosphere in Genoa during these months of preparations was interrupted when it became clear that the proposed departure date was slipping. On 1 August 1190, King Philip Augustus finally entered Genoa escorted by the duke of Burgundy and other barons and knights. He had already missed the favourable spring winds, and because he was taken ill he decided to remain in the city to recover until St. Bartholomew's day on 24 August. King Richard I arrived even later, two weeks after Philip, his fleet entering the port of Genoa on 13 August. A ceremony was held in the city on that day, but King Richard did not stay in Genoa itself, preferring to rest at the picturesque Ligurian village at the Portofino bay.[34] Another month would pass before the kings met again in Messina. Shortly afterwards they decided that it was better to wait until the following spring to set sail, a decision that had great repercussions for business in Genoa. One such consequence was the unexpected registration of approximately thirty private contracts. Starting in July 1190, citizens of Genoa and other travellers and crusaders ventured to the kingdom of Jerusalem independent of the kings' fleet. It is not easy to distinguish between the roles that the Genoese assumed on these ventures when they travelled as merchants, ship owners, diplomats and crusaders, which were often combined. As we will see below, sons and relatives of the Genoese leaders of the crusade were among the investors and travellers in the late summer of 1190.

The Role of the Genoese during the Crusade: Crusaders, Suppliers, Negotiators and Mediators

The contracts signed in Genoa on the eve of the crusade in 1190 reflect the preparations required for such a complex venture involving a diverse group of travellers. They were written to protect the various interests of the individuals and groups taking part – namely, the crusaders, the merchants and the mariners, as well as the bankers, investors and ship owners. In the following paragraphs an attempt will be made to explain their respective perspectives, interests and concerns.

Few contracts were drawn by the crusaders themselves, but several records dictated by crusader travellers are of particular interest. Anselmo Burone (or Buxono), one of the Genoese crusaders in the expedition of 1190, drew up his last will prior to the departure. Amongst other things, he wrote that in the event

---

of Genoese measures in which one *mezzarola* equals 91.480 litres. See Byrne, *Genoese Shipping*, pp. 41–42; Pietro C. Rocca, *Pesi e misure antiche di Genova e del Genovesato* (Genoa, 1871), p. 108.

[34] *Ann. Ian.*, 2:35; Roger of Howden, *Gesta regis Ricardi*, p. 113.

that he should die before embarking from Genoa, £10 Genoese be bequeathed to Simone Vento to support Simone's travel to the Latin East (*ad suum pasare* [*sic*] *de Ultramare*).[35] Since Simone was one of the two commanders of the Genoese forces, this money was actually bequeathed for the crusade.[36]

From the crusaders' point of view, one positive outcome of the delay was that they were able to reduce the price of their journey. Thus, several days after the arrival of King Philip Augustus, two Genoese ship owners, Lanfranco Malfigliastro and Ansaldo Mallone agreed to transport Gaucher, lord of Salins, and his thirteen knights for the reduced fee of 8½ marks per knight.[37] The contract repeated the conditions of the general contract between France and Genoa, with one important addition: the destination was spelled out more precisely, being either Acre or Tyre, depending on the crusaders' decision. This clause was added to reduce misunderstandings or potential tensions between the crusaders and the captain or the travelling merchants. Sixty years later, in 1250, an argument between ship owners and crusaders concerning the route and the ports of destination was adjudicated in the court of Messina.[38]

The ship owners Lanfranco Malfigliastro and Ansaldo Mallone also signed a contract with the mariners who joined this venture.[39] Here, we find another unusual clause, which specified, presumably at the crew's request, that the return trip from the Latin East be limited to ports in Christian territory. Did the mariners have a particular concern in mind? It seems unlikely that they should have been worried about travelling to destinations in the Almohad realm because Ceuta, Bougie and Tunisia maintained their popularity among the Genoese as commercial destinations even at the time of the crusades. More likely, they preferred to avoid the Egyptian port of Alexandria, as many, though not all, Genoese merchants did for as long as the war lasted. In previous years we find about a dozen contracts to Alexandria in each cartulary. Twice in 1184, in March and September, merchants set out from Genoa to Alexandria; some went via Sicily, while others sailed first to Ceuta or Tunisia or to the kingdom of Jerusalem.[40] The ship owner Enrico Nepitella was a frequent visitor in Alexandria. In September 1184, he warned the merchants on his ship that he might sell the vessel in Alexandria.[41] In 1186, a merchant who travelled to Ceuta

---

[35] OS: 609, 10 August 1190.

[36] This will may thus be added to Steven Epstein's list of crusaders' wills: Steven Epstein, *Wills and Wealth in Medieval Genoa, 1150–1250* (Cambridge, Mass., and London, 1984), pp. 187–88.

[37] OS: 599, 6 August 1190. Jean Richard lists the lord of Salins in the contingent from Franche-Comté, along with the archbishop of Besançon and the lord of Champlitte: Jean Richard, *The Crusades, c.1071–c.1291*, trans. Jean Birrell (Cambridge, 1999), p. 222. Donald Queller and Thomas Madden used an old reference to this document, and thus wrongly dated this contract to 1184: Donald E. Queller and Thomas F. Madden, *The Fourth Crusade: The Conquest of Constantinople*, 2nd ed. (Philadelphia, 1997), p. 12. David Jacoby, "Conrad Marquis of Montferrat," pp. 219–20.

[38] Benjamin Z. Kedar, "The Passenger List of a Crusader Ship, 1250: Towards the History of the Popular Element on the Seventh Crusade," *Studi medievali* 13 (1972), 267–78.

[39] OS: 640, 16 August 1190.

[40] Oberto Scriba da Mercato, cartolare notarile 2 (1184), 137v–143r; 189v.

[41] Oberto Scriba da Mercato, cartolare notarile 2 (12 September 1184), 143r.

planned to meet Enrico in Alexandria.[42] Interestingly, between 1190 and 1192 there are no records of Enrico's own international ventures. Enrico Napitella and other Genoese merchants who left their destinations unspecified in the contracts may, however, have travelled to Alexandria without making it a binding commitment in their legal contracts. There is only one document from 1190 in which a returning merchant mentions his visit to Alexandria, post factum, and several documents of 1191 explicitly excluded Alexandria, suggesting that it may have still been visited by others. News coming from captives in Alexandria and evidence of the first merchant who was sent there from Genoa in 1192 are further evidence of continued communication and commercial interaction, as will be discussed below.

Supplies

In addition to human resources, the Genoese ships that sailed to Acre and Tyre between 1189 and 1192 brought supplies on board. There was, in fact, particular urgency in getting food to the crusaders following a period of famine in the Levant. The first evidence of Genoese food sent to Franks and crusaders is found in the cartulary of Oberto Scriba from January 1190. At the beginning of that winter, after the first wave of Genoese crusaders had been transported to Tyre, returning ships brought news of the food shortage. There are many detailed and lengthy descriptions of the hunger and suffering of the Christians in the *Itinerarium*. The titles of some of the chapters described the harsh situation: "perishing with hunger, our people devour the corpses of their horses" (ch. 67); "even noblemen steal when they cannot afford to buy bread" (ch. 73); "the starving … die from drinking wine" (ch. 76).[43] The full description of the grave circumstances covered several pages, and also mentioned the arrival of Italian supply-ships, including one full of grain that provided some relief.[44] There is a story in the same narrative about an avaricious Pisan merchant who hid large quantities of grain in his house in expectation of greater profit later on in the year. The merchant was miraculously punished when fire burnt down his house.[45] The Genoese cartularies from the years 1190 to 1192 repeatedly noted merchants who purchased wheat and barley and shipped it to *Ultramare*. In the case of the first supply ship, whose venture was planned in January 1190, the Genoese ship owner Bernardo Riccio had drafted a contract with two mariners from the neighbouring communities of Noli and Camogli.[46] The ship

---

[42] OS: 171, 20 October 1186.

[43] "Nostri, fame pereuntes, cadavera equorum …"; "Nobiles etiam viri, cum non haberent unde panem emerent, furabantur"; "Famelici … vinum potantes moriuntur": *Itinerarium peregrinorum et gesta regis Ricardi*, ed. William Stubbs, *Chronicles and Memorials of the Reign of Richard I*, 2 vols. (London, 1864), 1:124–33. Translated by Helen J. Nicholson, *The Chronicle of the Third Crusade: A Translation of the Itinerarium peregrinorum et gesta regis Ricardi* (Aldershot, 1997), pp. 126–37.

[44] Ibid, ch. 79.

[45] Ibid, ch. 80.

[46] OS: 17, 16 January 1190.

itself was berthed not in Genoa, but in the port of Gaeta, possibly because Genoa sought to keep its own ships for the French crusaders. The entire crew had agreed to assemble in Gaeta and thence sail to Sardinia to buy grain and ship it to the Levant. Each mariner was promised wages of 14 besants (nearly £5 Genoese) and the right to ship 10 *minas* of wheat or barley. Bernardo promised to pay part of the salary in Sardinia, presumably so that they could purchase the grain they wanted to ship. Bernardo signed a similar contract with Ansaldo di Sori, a more professional seaman, possibly even the captain, judging by his wages. Bernardo promised to pay him 20 besants and allow him to carry 20 *minas* of wheat or barley. Finally, Bernardo also agreed that, if for any reason the ship remain in *Ultramare* during the summer, Ansaldo would be allowed to take his leave and depart on another ship.[47] Both contracts include the condition discussed previously, that the return journey would be to whatever Christian land the ships' captains selected. This specification of "Christian land" in the terms of the contracts was the only indication that the planned journey took place under exceptional conditions.

Seamen were often paid half their wages before departing from Genoa, probably so that they could invest the money in commodities.[48] This particular allocation of space on the ship for grain, however, can be understood in light of the severe food shortage in the kingdom of Jerusalem. It was an opportunity for the seamen to achieve both goals: assist the crusaders and make extra profit. This is an example of how crusade and commerce could be integrated. Indeed, there is evidence that other Genoese merchants invested a large amount of money in the purchase of grain at that time, some explicitly to ship it to the Latin East. One such case involved two women, Ricomanna and her daughter Agnese, who invested £20 each in the shipping of grain.[49] As there is no evidence that either of them was otherwise engaged in this trade, it is quite likely that this may have been their way of providing help and support for the crusaders. This hypothesis is supported by a will written at the time by Agnese's newly wed husband, Guglielmo Gallo, who bequeathed £7 10s "for the service of God and *Ultramare*," thus revealing his concern for the fate of the kingdom of Jerusalem.[50]

There are several other cases of Genoese merchants who allocated profit or commodities to help the crusade. For example, in 1191 the Genoese merchant Guido Bonaventura carried with him a substantial amount of money – £411 Genoese – to Sicily. Guido was given various instructions concerning this investment but he

---

[47] OS: 49, 25 January 1190. "Si navis … staencaverit Ultramare in hac proxima estate … Ansaldus si voluerit possit as cendere in aliam navem et esse scapulus." According to Augustin Jal, *scapolo* is a nautical term referring exactly to such cases of termination of contract, in which the mariner is freed from his contracted engagement on naval matters: Augustin Jal, *Nouveau glossaire nautique*, ed. Michel Mollat (Paris, 1988).

[48] Eugene H. Byrne, "Commercial Contracts of the Genoese in the Syrian Trade of the Twelfth Century," *The Quarterly Journal of Economics* 31:1 (1916), 150.

[49] GC: 1526, 27 January 1192.

[50] GC: 334, 21 March 1191. On the previous day, Guglielmo received a dowry of £150 from Ricomanna, Agnese's mother.

could also make his own choices, especially with respect to his travel route and destinations. One explicit request of his business associate Ruggero Noxenzio was that £20 should be used "for the service of God and *Ultramare*."[51] As mentioned above, in several cases, people mentioned the kingdom of Jerusalem in their wills and the notaries employed standard phrases to this effect. A similar formula used in such bequests was that the money be used *in recuperare Terram Ultramaris*.[52] Such phrases and bequests are commonly found in wills written during later crusades in the thirteenth century,[53] and appear alongside other charitable bequests, such as donations to hospitals and the building of bridges and churches. The wide range of donations to the Third Crusade, and especially the shipping of supplies, demonstrates the heightened public concern for crusading goals, as expressed through their involvement in the preparation and progress of the campaign.

Numerous Genoese citizens, including merchants, travellers, seamen and crusaders, benefited from the Third Crusade. Mabilia, the wine merchant, was one of many. Other examples included relatives of the crusade leaders who engaged in trade in Tyre between the years 1190 and 1192. For example, three brothers of the Spinola family sailed to the Levant in August 1190 carrying an investment of £897 Genoese.[54] The extensive privileges secured for the Genoese in Tyre by Guido Spinola must have played a considerable role in their commercial plans.[55] The rivalry between Conrad of Montferrat and Guy of Lusignan allowed some Genoese nobles and businessmen to create and capitalize on new opportunities.[56] The most remarkable case was that of Ansaldo Bonvicino, who accompanied Conrad of Montferrat from Constantinople in 1187 and stayed on to assist him in the defence of Tyre. Conrad appointed him castellan of Tyre and granted him property.[57] Another Genoese noble who benefited from the situation was Marino Rocia whom Conrad granted a house in Tyre in recompense for his "good service and great fidelity."[58] Both men linked their future with that of the kingdom of Jerusalem when they decided to permanently settle in Tyre.[59]

---

[51] GC: 320, 20 March 1191, quoting: "in servicio Dei et de Ultramare, vel mittat."

[52] OS: 609, 10 August 1190.

[53] Epstein, *Wills and Wealth in Medieval Genoa*, pp. 186–88.

[54] OS: 642, 647,655.

[55] *I Libri iurium*, I/2, 331–32, pp. 137–42.

[56] Jacoby, "Conrad, Marquis of Montferrat," pp. 193–211.

[57] Ansaldo is mentioned as Conrad's *privato* in *Regni Iherosolymitani brevis historia*, *Ann. Ian.*, 1:144. According to a Venetian document from the thirteenth century, Conrad of Montferrat granted Ansaldo a house that previously belonged to the Venetian commune. It is mentioned in a thirteenth-century inventory by the Venetian official Marsilio Zorzi. See Oliver Berggötz, ed., *Der Bericht des Marsilio Zorzi* (Frankfurt am Main, 1991), p. 168. Ansaldo witnessed one of Conrad's concessions to Genoa as the castellan of Tyre, signed on 11 April 1190, CDG 2.194, p. 371.

[58] "Pro bono servicio et maxima fidelitate, quam mihi in Tyro Martinus Rocia nobilis Ianuensis civis exibuit." Ernest Strehlke, ed., *Tabulae ordinis Theutonici ex tabularii regii Berolinensis codice potissimum* 24 (Berlin, 1869; repr. Toronto, 1975), p. 21.

[59] For the location of their properties in Tyre, see Mack, "The Italian Quarters of Frankish Tyre," pp. 153–55, 162; David Jacoby, "Mercanti genovesi e veneziani e le loro merci nel Levante crociato," in *Genova, Venezia, il Levante nei secoli XII–XIV*, ed. Dino Puncuh (Genoa, 2001), p. 226.

Mediators and Negotiators

Genoese also played a significant role during the crusade as negotiators or mediators, especially in the case of ransom and exchange of captives. An interesting anecdote found in *The Continuation of William of Tyre* mentions that, in 1187, Latins who surrendered in Gaza, Ascalon and Jerusalem were brought to Alexandria under Saladin's special protection and were given his word that they would not be sold into slavery. According to the chronicler, they were fed and carefully protected by the governor of Alexandria throughout the following winter. At that time, 38 foreign ships were berthed in Alexandria, most of them Italian: Venetian, Pisan and Genoese. In March 1188, when the captains were about to depart, the governor of Alexandria summoned them and proposed that they took the poorer captives with them. They declined at first, claiming that these people were too impoverished to pay for their own provisions, let alone the transport fee. The governor, appalled by their merciless attitude towards their Christian brothers, insisted and in the end he even agreed to provide the food for these passengers on condition that they be taken care of and brought to safety in Christian land. He further threatened the captains that if he should learn that they did not honour their word, he would "seize the merchants of your land who come to this country."[60]

Evidence of refugee presence in Genoa is almost non-existent in the sources. One exception is a contract registered by a family who were either travellers or refugees. In this deed, of 8 April 1190, a certain *Magdala* of Jerusalem and her son *Wuilielmus* appointed another son named *Martinus* to travel to the Latin East and deliver a large sum of money, £370 Genoese, to his three siblings: his sister *Adalaxia* and his two brothers *Iohannes* and *Symon* in *Ultramare*.[61] He presumably hoped to find his brothers and sister amongst the refugees that Balian of Ibelin had managed to rescue at the end of the siege of Jerusalem in 1187, and whom he later escorted to Tyre and Tripoli.[62] As we will see in the following paragraphs, this sum would have sufficed to ransom them.

In the spring of 1191, Genoa's merchants resumed their travels on some of the peace-time trade routes including the North African Almohad cities. Alexandria, however, was explicitly excluded from many merchants' destination-lists, including those on ships departing for Sicily, Naples and Bougie, as well as the kingdom of Jerusalem. While the travel instructions of this period often included permission for ships to continue their ventures in all destinations, these contracts specifically excluded Alexandria.[63] Alexandria reappeared as an explicit destination in travellers'

---

[60] Margaret Ruth Morgan, ed., *La Continuation de Guillaume de Tyr (1184–1197)*, Documents relatifs à l'histoire des Croisades 14 (Paris, 1982), chs. 60–61, pp. 74–75; translation in Peter Edbury, *The Conquest of Jerusalem and the Third Crusade: Sources in Translation* (Aldershot, 1996), pp. 65–66.

[61] OS: 356, 8 April 1190.

[62] Morgan, *La Continuation de Guillaume de Tyr*, trans. Edbury, *Conquest of Jerusalem*, chs. 56–58.

[63] Ten documents repeating this prohibition, applying this standard formula, are found in the cartulary of Guglielmo Cassinese: GC: 8, 438, 601, 605, 920, 1197, 1198, 1200, 1310, 1313. The date range is from April to September 1191.

contracts only in January 1192; the crusade would not end for another eight months, yet exceptional circumstances led to this revival of contact:[64] Leona, the wife of Rubaldo di Buontommaso, acting under emergency conditions, had sought to rescue her husband from Egyptian imprisonment. This unique document begins with an explanatory statement, a rare phenomenon in such contracts, explaining that it was written "because it is believed that Rubaldo di Buontommaso is in prison in the region of Alexandria." While this may be an apologetic note, the contract elaborates no further. It is also not known who brought Leona this news from her husband. Leona then commissioned Ansaldo da Castello to pay 200 besants, a very substantial sum, to ransom her husband, authorizing him to double it if her husband should instruct him to do so. She also promised to pay Ansaldo's travel expenses to Alexandria, apparently via Marseille.[65] There are no means to estimate how many other Genoese were able to cross the lines and transfer information and money between the Christians and the Muslims. The restrictions in the contract on travel to Alexandria do not suggest that all merchants avoided the Egyptian seaport; if so, no preclusion would have been needed. Rather, it would seem that, in times of war, merchants were granted even greater freedom of action and trusted to make the right decision in the best interest of their investors and their commercial partners.

The Aftermath of the Crusade and Its Impact

On 2 September 1192, a truce was signed between Saladin and Richard I that officially ended the Third Crusade.[66] One month later, King Richard, together with his knights and soldiers, embarked on their ships and began their long journey home.[67] From Genoa's perspective, the departure of King Philip II in the summer of 1191 held more significance than the date of the truce for two reasons: first, the liberation of Acre implied the restoration of Genoa's commercial privileges in this important city; and, second, because they were in charge of the transportation of King Philip's army back to Europe.

Genoese merchants and crusaders at the time of the Third Crusade were at the heart of great changes that affected life in the Mediterranean in many ways. It has been long demonstrated that these were critical years for the commercial and technological revolution of the Middle Ages.[68] As a result of the crusade, Genoa

---

[64] This volume of the cartulary by Guglielmo Cassinese ends in the early part of 1192 – too early for the registration of the usual commercial contracts to the Latin East or Alexandria.

[65] GC: 1503–1504, 22 January 1192. The former document reveals Ansaldo's plan to travel first to Marseille.

[66] *La Continuation de Guillaume de Tyr*, p. 142.

[67] Rigord, *Histoire de Philippe Auguste*, 88, pp. 307–8.

[68] See, for example, Robert S. Lopez, *The Commercial Revolution of the Middle Ages, 950–1350* (Cambridge, 1976); Eugene Byrne, "Genoese Trade with Syria in the Twelfth Century," *American Historical Review* 25 (1920), 191–219; Michel Balard, *La Romanie génoise: xiie–début du xve siècle*, 2 (Rome, 1978), pp. 505–31.

underwent major political transformations while its commercial world changed and expanded.

With the absence of many leading figures, including the city's consuls, on crusade the commune resolved to appoint its first *podestà*. This individual was an elected governor, a citizen of another city, who was invited to rule Genoa for a limited period of time in exchange for a substantial salary. At the height of civil strife in the city, this solution proved to be very effective. The *podesteria* was one of the main reasons for Genoa's economic prosperity in the years that followed.[69] The first *podestà*, Manigoldo Tetocio of Brescia, who governed during the time of the Third Crusade, was highly commended in the Annals for his efficient governance of the city and his ability to maintain order. In the year 1192 the consular system was re-introduced, but it was not easy for these men to keep the peace and both internal and external conflicts quickly resumed after the crusade. The renewed hostility between Genoa and Pisa demanded much attention, while in the streets of Genoa itself internal fights became even more violent and more devastating as a result of the introduction of a new war-machine, the *bolzone*, a powerful wooden bow, which was now used to fight at home. The della Volta family led a series of attacks on the Bellobruno clan, while the two families set fire to each other's compounds, using such machines to destroy their enemies' houses and towers.[70]

Naval commanders who excelled during the Third Crusade were acknowledged and rewarded. Margarito of Brindisi, admiral of the Sicilian fleet, who came to rescue the Latin East in 1187 with 200 galleys, later became the first count of Malta.[71] His own successor was the Genoese pirate, Guglielmo Grasso; he, in turn, was succeeded by Enrico Pescatore, also known as Count Henry of Malta.[72] In both medieval and modern literature we find an ambiguous treatment of pirates, who on some occasions were valiant heroes, while on others they were feared and despised.[73]

---

[69] Avner Greif discusses in detail the economic benefits of the *podesteria*, but mentions the role of the Third Crusade in the initiation of this position only in passing: "On the Political Foundations of the Late Medieval Commercial Revolution: Genoa during the Twelfth and Thirteenth Centuries," *Journal of Economic History* 54 (1989), 271–87.

[70] *Ann. Ian.*, 2:44–45, and Tav. VI, fig. XXXIII.

[71] Hiroshi Takayama, "Familiares Regis and the Royal Inner Council in Twelfth-Century Sicily," *English Historical Review* 104 (1989), 369; Roger of Howden, *Gesta regis Henrici secundi*, p. 54. See also Marie-Louise Favreau-Lilie, *Die Italiener im Heiligen Land, vom ersten Kreuzzug zum Tode Heinrichs von Champagne (1098–1197)* (Amsterdam, 1989), pp. 254–55; *La Continuation de Guillaume de Tyr*, ch. 73; in a charter of 1194, Margarito is described in the following words: "Margaritus de Brundusio, dei et Regia gratia Comes *Malte* et *Regij* uictoriosi storij amiratus ac domini Regis familiaris," Gennaro Maria Monti, ed., *Codice diplomatico Brindisino* (Trani, 1940), no. 31, pp. 55–56.

[72] On Guilelmo Grasso see J. K. Fotheringham, "Genoa and the Fourth Crusade," *English Historical Review* 25 (1910), 28. On Henry of Malta, see David Abulafia, "Henry Count of Malta and his Mediterranean Activities: 1203–1230," in *Studies on Malta before the Knights*, ed. Anthony T. Luttrell (London, 1975), pp. 104–25; Balard, *La Romanie génoise*, pp. 589–90.

[73] Fotheringham portrays these pirates and corsairs in a darker, contemptuous light. While detailing their activities based on the sources, he does not attempt to explain their official appointments, honorary titles and the fiefs granted to them. See Fotheringham, "Genoa and the Fourth Crusade," pp.

At the time of the Third Crusade, and in the decade that followed it, piracy entered its "Golden Age" and began to play a dominant role in the international world of power and prestige.[74] The pirates, with their small independent fleets, were able to provide faster assistance to the Latin East than many institutionalized powers. Guglielmo Grasso, for example, had collaborated with a Pisan pirate during the Third Crusade. Together they launched an attack on the ship in which Saladin sent a fragment of the Holy Cross to Constantinople. Bringing the Holy Cross to Genoa was perceived as a heroic moment for the whole city.[75] The Third Crusade proved that these ferocious pirates were also faithful Christians and Genoese patriots who could be relied on in moments of crisis. For them, it was a unique opportunity to jump up the social ladder from its very bottom to the top ranks of the nobility.

While, for the most part, life returned to normal, the Third Crusade did create a lasting legacy. New commercial relations formed between Genoa and England that would prosper for centuries afterwards. Aboard the crusader ships from England were English merchants with their merchandise, including some Jewish merchants. One of them, Abram *de Stanforti*, was a particularly interesting case, as a large number of the Jews of Stamford had been massacred in the spring of 1190 by the English crusaders on the eve of their departure.[76] In the absence of any other documentation one can only wonder how they ended up sailing together on the same ships. Certain English commodities, especially Stamford threads, are often mentioned in the Genoese documents from the time of the Third Crusade onwards. There is evidence of professional exchange during the years of the crusade, exchange which evolved further in the next century when the Genoese were given the right to an independent quarter in Southampton.[77]

It is interesting to consider who profited most from the crusade. It has been claimed that every aspect of Genoa's commercial activity profited from St. Louis's

---

28–30. Charles M. Brand, "The Byzantines and Saladin, 1185–1192: Opponents of the Third Crusade," *Speculum* 37 (1962), 178. See also Pinuccia F. Simbula, "Îles, corsaires et pirates dans la Méditerranée médiévale," *Médiévales* 47 (2004), 19.

[74] Balard, *La Romanie génoise*, pp. 587–98.

[75] *Regni hierosolymitani brevis historia*, *Ann. Ian.*, 1:141. See Fotheringham, "Genoa and the Fourth Crusade," pp. 28–30; Brand, "The Byzantines and Saladin," p. 178.

[76] Abram is mentioned with a fellow merchant named Simon of Stamford. GC: 675, 3 June 1191. On the Jews of Stamford, see Robin R. Mundill, *England's Jewish Solution: Experiment and Expulsion, 1262–1290* (Cambridge, 1998), pp. 19–20. William of Newburgh describes the massacre: *William of Newburgh* (liber 4), ed. Richard Howlett, in *Chronicles of the Reigns of Stephen, Henry II and Richard I*, 1 (London, 1884, repr. 1964), pp. 310–11, 322. See also Christoph Cluse, "Stories of Breaking and Taking the Cross: A Possible Context for the Oxford Incident of 1268," *Revue d'histoire ecclésiastique* 90 (1995), 433.

[77] Edward Miller, "The Fortunes of the English Textile Industry during the Thirteenth Century," *Economic History Review*, n.s. 18 (1965), 68; Robert L. Reynolds, "The Market for Northern Textiles in Genoa, 1179–1200," *Revue belge de philologie et d'histoire* 8 (1929), 495–533. For the Genoese community in Southampton, see David Abulafia, "Cittadino e 'denizen': mercanti mediterranei a Southampton e a Londra," in *Sistema di rapporti ed élites economiche in Europa (secoli XII–XVII)*, ed. Mario Del Treppo (Naples, 1994), pp. 273–92.

crusade in 1248 to 1254.[78] The same may be said about the Third Crusade. Genoa as a city, as well as its individual merchants, benefited from the growing demand for its commodities and leading to expansion of its commercial horizons; for example, in its trade with England. Ship owners and even sailors were able to draw significant profit from trade in a large variety of goods, including grain, alcohol and weapons in addition to the usual merchandise. Some of the Genoese warriors and settlers obtained property and fame, and the commune acquired unprecedented privileges in the major cities along the shorelines of the Latin East. While wars often provided opportunities for the Italian merchants seeking privileges in commercial seaport cities in the Mediterranean, it seems that the Third Crusade was especially rewarding for the Genoese.[79] The greatest profits were made by the bankers who were able to lend money to the crusaders and the pilgrims on their way east, as well as to some of the unfortunate individuals who lost all they had and needed financial help on their journey home. Bishop Raoul of Liège was among those who had to borrow money on his way back to cover his "great expenses and loss of money" overseas.[80] In June 1191, the Genoese banker Nicola Blondo lent the poor bishop a large amount of money for his travel – 200 silver marks. It may be useful to compare this sum with the 9 marks that the Genoese asked for the transportation and provisions of a knight accompanied by two squires and a pair of horses. One of the clauses of the contract between them specified that this loan was to be repaid by August in the land of the count of Flanders *in seculare loco*. Sea-loans were given to all destinations, and the bankers and merchants accepted all the usual currencies.[81]

While the bishop of Liège returned from his journey much poorer than when he left, it is impossible to estimate how much other people lost as a result of the Third Crusade. Did the collection of the Saladin tithe make the lives of people in western Europe 10 per cent worse than it was previously? Can one estimate how much was gained due to the absence of the kings from Europe and from the peace imposed in western Europe during the crusade?

Genoa was one of the Third Crusade's main crossroads for moving crusaders, merchants, supplies and substantial sums of money. The city had benefited greatly from this expedition. Some of these advantages cannot be easily substantiated because they included matters such as the form of citizens' identity, the experience gained and the lessons learnt from the encounter with different cultures, languages, religions and customs. In other words, the profit is the sum of what people gain from travels under extreme situations of war, death, captivity, illness and hunger.

[78] Michel Balard, "Notes on the Economic Consequences of the Crusades," in *EC, 2*, p. 237.
[79] Balard, "Genova e il Levante," pp. 527–49; Pistarino, "Genova e il vicino oriente nell'epoca del regno latino di Gerusalemme," pp. 98–107. On the Genoese privileges in Tyre, see Mack, "The Italian Quarters of Frankish Tyre," pp. 161–64.
[80] GC: 761, 21 June 1191.
[81] For example, see GC: 1134, 25 September 1191. Baldovino Scoto received from Ogerio Porco a sum of £19 2s Genoese and promised to pay 2¾ hyperperon to the pound in Constantinople, or, alternatively, a golden ounce in Sicily for every S42 Genoese, or, if they end up in *Ultramare*, at the ratio of 3 besants to the Genoese pound.

These experiences influenced their identities and redefined their hopes and fears. Some of the Genoese encountered in this paper found new homes in the Latin East, making new alliances and rising to power. The leaders of the kingdom of Jerusalem encouraged their enthusiasm and offered a variety of exciting opportunities, perhaps similar to those that so attracted the first crusaders who had settled in the Holy Land after fulfilling their vows. Higher social status, wealth and, perhaps, the joy of risk and adventure that could only be weighed against what they had been familiar with back home. Some met the challenge and faced it willingly, while others turned back to tell their stories from the safety of their daily routines at home. Through this study of scattered evidence found in numerous notarial documents from Genoa of the time of the Third Crusade, we have obtained some insight into the meaning of this crusade to many such people of various nationalities and social ranks who lived in Genoa or passed through the city during those years – those who risked their lives and wealth in order to save the Latin East.

"Scandalia … tam in oriente quam in occidente": The Briennes in East and West, 1213–1221

Guy Perry

University of Leeds
G.J.M.Perry@leeds.ac.uk

John of Brienne (king of Jerusalem, 1210–25) was the last king of Jerusalem to habitually reside in any part of the Latin East until the Lusignans of Cyprus succeeded the Hohenstaufen in 1269. By then, the kingdom would be tottering towards its final elimination, and the kingship, especially, would be but a shadow of its former self. And no king of Jerusalem after John would ever again regard that kingdom as his primary base: the Hohenstaufen and Charles of Anjou were based in the West, the Lusignans on Cyprus. If these are principal reasons for taking an interest in John's reign, then we can narrow down the period in which we are most concerned still further. John spent almost two-thirds of his reign outside his kingdom proper, thereby initiating a trend which was to reach the level of absentee kingship in the next generation. He spent most of 1218–21 in Egypt, trying to lead the Fifth Crusade; he then passed almost all the remainder of his reign, 1222–25, in the Latin West, trying to drum up support for a new crusade once the Fifth Crusade had failed. Thus, the final lengthy period of rule by any king of Jerusalem essentially based and resident in that kingdom was the opening seven years of King John's reign, 1210–17. This, then, is a time well worth examining in detail.

Despite its significance, this is a very neglected age in the history of the kingdom of Jerusalem. Such detailed analyses as we have in fact struggle to find very much to say.[1] The main reason for this is the scarcity of extant source material for this particular period of Jerusalemite history. Comparatively speaking, a fair number of the Jerusalemite *acta* issued at this time have survived; but, as Peter Edbury has noted, "it is unfortunate that the narrative accounts [we have] shed almost no light at all on the politics of the kingdom of Jerusalem between [John's] accession in 1210 and the beginning of the Fifth Crusade in 1217."[2] The narrative accounts that Edbury is referring to here are what he now labels as "Ernoul-Bernard" and "Colbert-Fontainebleau": both these naratives pass swiftly from John's coronation through to the Fifth Crusade.[3] Relatively recently, however, some notable efforts have been made to fill this gap. Hans Mayer eased the task by exposing forgeries

---

[1] For an obvious example of this, see Ludwig Böhm's *Johann von Brienne, König von Jerusalem, Kaiser von Konstantinopel* (Heidelberg, 1938), pp. 29–41; but see below, n. 7.

[2] Peter W. Edbury, *John of Ibelin and the Kingdom of Jerusalem* (Woodbridge, 1997), pp. 32–34.

[3] Ernoul-Bernard, *Chronique d'Ernoul et de Bernard le Trésorier*, ed. Louis de Mas Latrie (Paris, 1871), pp. 409–11; Colbert-Fontainebleau (the main text in *RHC Oc* 2), pp. 311–21.

in Röhricht's register of the Jerusalemite *acta*.[4] Closely analysing the remaining corpus, Edbury then led the way with pioneering work on King John's rupture with the Ibelins (ca. 1210–13). Focusing on other matters, though, Edbury has barely re-examined John's rule beyond 1213.[5] Mayer's up-to-date, authoritative study of the Jerusalemite chancellery has added some depth to scholarly appreciation of John's difficulties in the early years of his reign (above all, concerning the break with the Ibelins).[6] Yet, even taken together, the work of Edbury and Mayer is very far from constituting a comprehensive reappraisal of the period 1210–17 in the kingdom of Jerusalem.[7]

One of the most damaging consequences of this comparative neglect is that several significant events that took place in the kingdom of Jerusalem during this period can end up unduly minimized, and hence seriously misread. This article will refer to several such events in passing – such as the early death of John's queen, Maria, which provoked a dramatic crisis amongst the kingdom's elites; and the murder of the papal legate and patriarch, the future saint Albert of Vercelli, in 1214. The present article dwells on just one such noteworthy event: an episode of considerable consequence, which I have labelled the "Erard of Brienne affair." It should be made absolutely clear at the outset, however, that this article focuses on that affair's impact within a specifically Jerusalemite and Latin Eastern context; and that means, above all, on the then-king of Jerusalem, Erard's cousin, King John.

The family tree (Fig. 1) should make the following far more readily comprehensible. The "Erard of Brienne affair" had its origins in the events of 1190, when Count Henry II of Champagne had set out to participate in the Third Crusade. Before departure, Henry had stipulated that, should he himself never return, his county was to pass to his brother, Theobald (III), and thence to Theobald's descendants. In the event, Henry did not return; he died, as ruler of the kingdom of Jerusalem, following a fall from a window in 1197. By then, though – through his marriage to Queen Isabella I of Jerusalem – Henry had sired two daughters in the East, Alice and Philippa. The kingdom of Jerusalem passed to other hands – to Isabella's eldest daughter by a previous husband – leaving Alice and Philippa, relatively speaking, landless. Yet, as direct descendants of the senior line of the house of Champagne, they had (it could be plausibly argued) a prior claim to their father's county. Champagne passed, as Henry had wished, first to his brother, Theobald III, and then, in May 1201, into the hands of Theobald's widow, Countess Blanche, who served as regent for her own and Theobald III's posthumous son, Theobald IV.

---

[4]   Hans Eberhard Mayer, *Marseilles Levantehandel und ein akkonensisches Fälscheratelier des 13. Jahrhunderts* (Tübingen, 1972).

[5]   Peter W. Edbury, *The Kingdom of Cyprus and the Crusades, 1191–1374* (Cambridge, 1991), pp. 41–48; also Edbury, *John of Ibelin*, pp. 32–34.

[6]   Hans Eberhard Mayer, *Die Kanzlei der lateinischen Könige von Jerusalem*, 2 vols. (Hanover, 1996), esp. 1:304–23 and 2:697–704, 738–62.

[7]   But see Guy Perry, "The Career and Significance of John of Brienne, King of Jerusalem, Emperor of Constantinople" (DPhil thesis, University of Oxford, 2009), ch. 2, pp. 74–126. It is expected that a monograph, based substantially on this thesis, will soon be published.

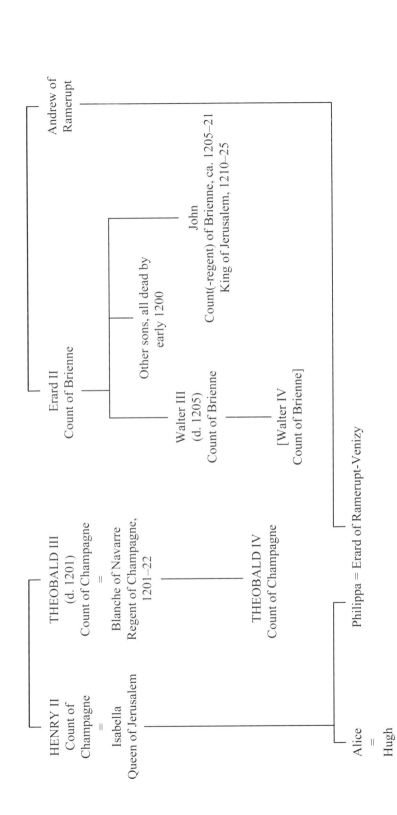

Fig. 1   The Brienne claim to Champagne, 1215–21

The posthumous nature of Theobald IV's birth complicated the matter. Evergates summarizes as follows: "[from the time of Theobald III's death, then,] the question was fairly posed: did not the daughters of Count Henry II, born whilst he was still count, have a better claim to Champagne than his brother's posthumous son?"[8]

It is now clear just how feverishly Blanche worked to ward off this prospective, truly dangerous, challenge to her infant son's inheritance. Above all, she pressed hard for the implementation of an earlier scheme, by which Alice and Philippa would be married, in the Latin East, to men of royal blood.[9] The calculation was presumably that the sisters (and their husbands) would then be less likely to come west to cause trouble for Blanche and her son. Alice, the elder sister (and therefore, presumably, the greater threat), married King Hugh of Cyprus in 1210. At around the same time, Blanche scored another notable success that clearly bears the marks of her handiwork. Her trusty *fidelis* John, count(-regent) of Brienne within Champagne, became king of Jerusalem through marriage, and, as a consequence, at least the *de facto* guardian of the as-yet unmarried Philippa, in the East.[10] A couple of years later, however, this particular achievement of Blanche's began to unravel. John's cousin in Champagne, Erard of Brienne, publicized his intention of seeking Philippa's hand in marriage. As lord of Ramerupt and Venizy, Erard was ultimately a *fidelis* of Blanche's for his "great holdings," in much the same way as King John still was for his western lands. But these ties did not prevent Erard from moving against the countess and her young son. It was plain that, having married Philippa, Erard would then try to advance her (rather debatable) claim to the county of Champagne.

Erard placed himself under ecclesiastical protection by taking the cross. He then outlined his marriage scheme to the French king, Philip Augustus. Philip had effectively established himself as chief protector of Blanche and young Theobald, yet it was obviously in his interests to keep Blanche feeling somewhat insecure. Thus, Philip's response to Erard was – in some ways – studiedly non-committal. For her own part, exploiting what pretexts she could, Blanche seized Erard's fiefs in Champagne, and even had him imprisoned for a time whilst he was en route to the East. Meanwhile, she obtained various papal rulings: among them that Count Henry II's marriage had been invalid (and his daughters were therefore illegitimate); and that, equally, the projected marriage between Erard and Philippa would not be lawful, since the couple were too closely related, within the prohibited degrees.[11] A papal bull was dispatched to the Latin East, threatening excommunication if the illicit "marriage" were performed.

---

[8] Theodore Evergates, *The Aristocracy in the County of Champagne, 1100–1300* (Philadelphia, 2007), p. 37.

[9] For Blanche's efforts, see esp. Perry, "The Career and Significance of John of Brienne," pp. 59–65. No. 823 in Röhricht's *RRH* is particularly noteworthy. In 1207, Blanche offered a substantial bribe to several leading Jerusalemite figures, essentially to keep Philippa in the East – so showing clearly how important this was to her.

[10] See Perry, "The Career and Significance of John of Brienne," pp. 57–65.

[11] For more on the ruling concerning Henry's marriage, see below, n. 31.

Nevertheless – shockingly – the marriage took place. By mid-1215, Erard and his bride were sailing back to France. He was arrested twice further en route, finally arriving in Champagne with Philippa, after a round trip of two and a half years. Calling largely on what may be described as the Brienne "affinity" and connections within Champagne, Erard soon rallied a surprisingly substantial number of disaffected lords and knights to his cause. The Champenois "civil war" – feared for some fifteen years – finally broke out, around the start of the year 1216.

In the short term, the war proved disastrous for Erard. He and his supporters were repeatedly castigated by several of the greatest authorities in Latin Christendom, as disloyal, ambitious vassals and sacrilegious disturbers of the peace. Erard and Philippa were excommunicated, on several grounds; and salvoes of similar ecclesiastical sanctions were also fired off against their *coadjutores* and *fautores*. Matters reached a climax in 1218 when Erard's most powerful ally, the duke of Lorraine, was forced out of the war by the combined forces of Blanche and her allies (the emperor-elect Frederick (II), the duke of Burgundy and the count of Bar). It was not until November 1221, however, that Erard and Philippa began to relinquish their claim to Champagne. And when they finally did so, not only did Erard formally receive back his fiefs, but the couple's marriage was acknowledged, and they obtained a down-payment of 4,000 *l.* and a lifetime rent of 1,200 *l.* This was (as Evergates puts it) a "handsome reward for … persistence, sufficient to place [Erard] amongst the wealthiest barons of [Champagne]." In the end, he had done rather well out of it all.[12]

Because the "Erard of Brienne affair" impacted far more on Champagne than it did anywhere else, its influence on other parts of the Latin world has tended to be ignored until now. This is quite surprising, since even a cursory examination of the subject, as attempted above, shows some of its wider ramifications. The crux of the affair – Erard's marriage – occurred, of course, in John's kingdom of Jerusalem itself. Even so, the episode has barely been looked at from any Latin Eastern angle, let alone from the perspective of the leading Latin Eastern figure most obviously concerned – namely, King John himself. The best lengthy account of the affair remains d'Arbois de Jubainville's, but he does not seriously address the actual context of the marriage in the Latin East, and has very little to suggest about John's reactions to it in the aftermath.[13] More startlingly, the German Ludwig Böhm –

---

[12] The above summary is derived chiefly from Henri d'Arbois de Jubainville's detailed treatment of the same subject in his *Histoire des ducs et des comtes de Champagne*, 7 vols. (Paris, 1859–69), 4:107–87; and Evergates's recent outlines in *The Aristocracy in the County of Champagne*, pp. 36–42, and in his *The Cartulary of Countess Blanche of Champagne* (Toronto, 2010), pp. 3–10. Philippa lived as Erard's wife in Champagne until he died in the mid-1240s. She did not long survive him. Queen Blanche of France then had her buried with honour in Blanche's new foundation of Maubuisson (see Henri d'Arbois de Jubainville, "Les premiers seigneurs de Ramerupt," *Bibliothèque de l'École des Chartes* 22 (1861), 440–58, at p. 449).

[13] D'Arbois de Jubainville, *Histoire des ducs et des comtes de Champagne*, 4:111–87.

John's twentieth-century "biographer" – simply omits all mention of the affair in his section on John as king of Jerusalem before the Fifth Crusade.[14]

The present article argues two principal points. First, King John was intimately involved in the affair. Second, it had a noteworthy, detrimental effect on John for an admittedly fairly short period in the mid-1210s, during which it tainted his relations with the key western powers on whom he was particularly dependent. Moreover, simply by pursuing the above two points as comprehensively as is feasible, it is possible to show that the whole situation did indeed loom up significantly in the Latin East as well as in the West. In short, Innocent III was basically right when he wrote that the affair had given rise to "scandalia ... *tam in oriente* quam in occidente."[15]

John's involvement in this is best examined by seeking to answer three questions. First, did John support his cousin's marriage scheme? Second, what actually took place following Erard's arrival in the kingdom of Jerusalem? Third, how, and how successfully, did John salvage his own reputation and standing – and, to a lesser extent, that of the wider Brienne family – after Erard's marriage had taken place?

Erard's bid for Champagne should plainly be sited within the context of the Brienne family's sudden success in significantly advancing itself and its interests in the early thirteenth century – a momentous shift in gear spearheaded, of course, both by John's eldest brother, Count Walter III (the dominant figure in southern Italy, 1201–1205) and, shortly after that, by John himself, who became king of Jerusalem in 1210. Both these developments, like Erard's projected scheme soon afterwards, were facilitated through the medium of marriage. Unlike Erard's, though, the earlier two were widely approved of by the leading interested western powers – and this is a key difference. John's achievement in becoming king of Jerusalem was very much more than being simply, as we might guess, the greatest single inspiration to Erard. Erard could underline that he himself hailed from what was now a royal dynasty, and hence that he was of suitable stature to marry Philippa and, with her, claim Champagne.[16] Furthermore, John's royal situation probably appeared key to the realization of Erard's scheme. As king of Jerusalem and hence head of the Jerusalemite royal family, John seemed to be in a position to choose or approve Philippa's husband.[17] Erard himself drew attention to this

---

[14] Cf., however, a summary of the present article in Perry, "The Career and Significance of John of Brienne," pp. 115–26.

[15] My italics; cited in Theodore Evergates, *Feudal Society in the Bailliage of Troyes under the Counts of Champagne, 1152–1284* (Baltimore, 1975), p. 198. "Scandalia" is a word often used to signify sex or marriage "scandals."

[16] Given the extensive and complex interconnections between the branches of the Brienne dynasty at this time, it may well appear somewhat overstated to argue that Erard was not really a Brienne (see Evergates, *The Aristocracy in Champagne*, pp. 135, 139).

[17] Though, as we have seen, Erard proved too closely related to Philippa for the marriage to be licit.

point when he first outlined his marriage scheme to the French king, Philip Augustus.[18]

John's actual attitude to Erard and his plan is, unfortunately, not clear. Erard himself, of course, was by no means an unknown quantity to John; he was head of the main cadet branch of the Brienne dynasty until John himself founded a replacement. As count(-regent) of Brienne, John had certainly had some – perhaps many – dealings with Erard, before travelling east in 1210 to become king of Jerusalem. A comparatively little-known "Brienne" *actum* (one of the few overlooked by d'Arbois de Jubainville, but printed by Lalore) records John's assent, in 1208, to a donation made by Erard to the monastery of Saint Pierre in Troyes.[19] Since Erard was, at around that time, the most senior mature Brienne male in northern France after John himself, John may well have left Erard as his proxy ("procurator") in the county of Brienne, when he (John) departed to take up the crown of Jerusalem.[20]

At first sight, it appears common sense to suppose that John supported his cousin's scheme for familial-dynastic motives. Against this, though, may conceivably be set the notion that John was not in a position to do much to support the interests of his wider family, given the weakness of his own position as king of Jerusalem. An anecdote in *Lignages* might appear to confirm this. When a vassal in the king's presence and in his court perpetrated a killing of a relative of the king, John apparently let the murderer escape untried and unpunished to Tripoli.[21] I have argued at length elsewhere, though, that the cumulative weight of evidence strongly suggests that John was nowhere near such a *roi fainéant* as this (in fact, rather isolated) anecdote would have us believe.[22]

I would suggest that it was most advisable for John either not to support Erard at all; or – if he could not resist the temptation to do it – then to do so only covertly. As regent and then as count(-regent) of Brienne (1201–10), John had grown into a role as one of Blanche's leading supporters within Champagne, though not as a principal prop always at her side. (Rumour, indeed, later grew up around this support, mushrooming into the highly diverting notion of a love-triangle involving John, Blanche, and the French king Philip himself.[23]) John was present at the French royal court in 1209, when Philip had declared that the young Theobald IV's inheritance was not legally challengeable until the child came of age (at twenty-one, in this case).[24] John certainly acted in a capacity supportive of Blanche in 1209–10.

---

[18] *Layettes du Trésor des chartes*, ed. Alexandre Teulet et al., 5 vols. (Paris, 1863–1909), vol. 1, no. 1474.

[19] *Collection des principaux cartulaires du diocèse de Troyes*, ed. Charles Lalore, 7 vols. (Troyes, 1875–90), vol. 5, no. 123.

[20] See Perry, "The Career and Significance of John of Brienne," pp. 72–73.

[21] *Lignages d'Outremer*, ed. Marie-Adélaïde Nielen (Paris, 2003), pp. 73–74.

[22] See Perry, "The Career and Significance of John of Brienne," esp. ch. 2, and above all pp. 91–102.

[23] Colbert-Fontainebleau, p. 307.

[24] See esp. *Littere baronum: The Earliest Cartulary of the Counts of Champagne*, ed. Theodore Evergates (Toronto, 2003), no. *88; and d'Arbois de Jubainville, *Histoire des ducs et des comtes de Champagne*, 4:108–9.

During that period, John and another Champenois count loyal to Blanche, William of Joigny, formally affirmed that, in their presence, Count William of Sancerre had acknowledged all the fiefs that the latter held from Countess Blanche.[25] It was, we may infer, precisely to protect herself from adventurers such as Erard that Blanche had vigorously promoted her trusty John's candidacy for the throne of Jerusalem in ca. 1208. If later, as king of Jerusalem, John let Blanche down, then it would be all too obvious that he was doing so out of crude opportunism, to advance his family's dynastic goals.

Although plainly not a "first-rank" figure, John had been accepted as king of Jerusalem largely because his candidature had swiftly acquired the backing of leading key powers in the West (including King Philip, Innocent III, and Blanche herself). It was hoped that this would translate into strong mobilization in support of the beleaguered kingdom. For a king of Jerusalem like John, then, it would be an extremely serious matter to risk this backing, whether in support of Erard or for any other reason.[26] The "Erard of Brienne affair" in fact began soon after the "crisis of 1212–13" in the kingdom of Jerusalem, a brief but dramatic period precipitated by the early death of John's queen, Maria. This event called into question John's position as king, since he had only become so through marriage to her. Calling, notably, on the Church's support, John succeeded in retaining his crown – although it could be argued that he was doing so, fundamentally, only as "crowned regent" for his and his late queen's infant daughter, the "right heir" to the kingdom.[27]

That kingdom, though, remained acutely vulnerable to Ayyubid attack. Part of John's solution may well have been, as we shall see, a proposed marriage alliance with the powerful, northern Latin Christian kingdom of Cilician Armenia.[28] The security of Acre had undoubtedly been compromised still further by the recent Ayyubid fortification of Mount Tabor, which overlooks parts of the strategically significant Jezreel Valley to its south. Shortly after helping John through the crisis of 1212–13, Innocent III responded to the new threat by formally launching a great new crusade to the East (the later Fifth).[29] Just as the "Erard of Brienne affair" was getting underway, John may well have been doing all he could to keep his own nose clean – to help garner as much support as was possible in the West for the forthcoming crusade. In this situation, it would evidently have been folly for John to give open assistance or support to Erard, if the upshot would be to risk alienation of precisely those western backers on whom he and his kingdom placed the greatest hopes.

---

[25] See Henri d'Arbois de Jubainville, ed., "Catalogue d'actes des comtes de Brienne, 950–1356," *Bibliothèque de l'École des Chartes* 33 (1872), no. 138.

[26] See esp. Perry, "The Career and Significance of John of Brienne," pp. 57–73.

[27] Ibid., pp. 97–102, 105–6.

[28] See below, p. 72.

[29] See *Quia maior*, PL 216, cols. 817–22; and Perry, "The Career and Significance of John of Brienne," pp. 82–85.

It is worth underlining a further reason for John not to risk alienating them. John had become the first *de jure* king of Jerusalem to rule in the East whilst also formally retaining, for the present, a great western lordship (that is, his ancestral county of Brienne) in his own hands. This is his marker on the road that would lead to the "cross-Mediterranean empires" of his successor as king of Jerusalem, Frederick II, and later of Charles of Anjou.[30] To maintain that position from the distant Latin East, John depended ultimately on the goodwill of Blanche in Champagne, of King Philip in France, and of Innocent III in Latin Christendom as a whole.[31]

Against all this must be set the obvious, glittering attractions of Erard's scheme. It must have seemed to present the Briennes with an admittedly somewhat risky, but nevertheless breathtaking, opportunity to make a huge dynastic advance in their rich homeland of Champagne through exploiting their present, quite brief phase in possession of the crown of Jerusalem. (This phase was destined to end in the medium-term at best, since John had sired no male line, of Brienne kings of Jerusalem, through his late wife, Queen Maria.) It is plausible to suggest, then, that on some level at least, Erard's scheme would have appealed to the intensely ambitious, risk-taking side of an individual like King John.

It is clear that, at some point in 1213–14, John had a new "proxy" back in Brienne – namely, his kinsman, the Champenois Jacques of Durnay, whom he had appointed marshal of the kingdom of Jerusalem.[32] Mayer has suggested that Jacques was sent back to the county of Brienne in consequence of the crisis of 1212–13. He argues that since John feared, at that time, that he himself might soon be effectively deposed, Jacques's function in Brienne was to prepare for the possibility that John might return there very soon.[33] This argument is perfectly plausible, since it is not clear either when exactly Jacques was sent back, or what it was that he was instructed to do. However, it may be that Mayer has here underestimated the impact of the "Erard of Brienne affair" on John. Even though John was far away in the Latin East, it is quite possible that, for him, the most alarming development of late

---

[30] The phrase is derived from Christopher Tyerman, *God's War: A New History of the Crusades* (London, 2006), p. 197; see also Perry, "The Career and Significance of John of Brienne," pp. 7, 72.

[31] Bernard Hamilton has identified another reason why John, if aware of it, would not have been comfortable about the way that the "Erard of Brienne affair" unfolded. In response to Erard's challenge, as we have seen, Blanche sought to undermine Philippa's right to inherit Champagne by questioning whether she and her sister were legitimately born. Alice and Philippa would certainly be illegitimate if their mother's preceding marriage had not been properly annulled. But if Blanche was right about this – and she did get some backing from a papal commission of inquiry – then, logically, the bar of illegitimacy would descend not only on Alice and Philippa, but also on their half-sister, Queen Maria of Jerusalem. In short: this argument, if made good, could have the effect of de-legitimizing John's right to the crown which he had recently fought so hard to retain. In the event, this threat to John's kingship never properly materialized. See Bernard Hamilton, "King Consorts of Jerusalem and their Entourages from the West from 1186 to 1250," in *Die Kreuzfahrerstaaten als multikulturelle Gesellschaft*, ed. Hans Eberhard Mayer (Munich, 1997), p. 20.

[32] "Catalogue d'actes des comtes de Brienne," no. 145; and Perry, "The Career and Significance of John of Brienne," esp. pp. 31, 71, 95.

[33] Mayer, *Die Kanzlei der lateinischen Könige von Jerusalem*, 2:739.

1213 was Blanche's seizure of the fiefs that Erard held from her in Champagne.[34] John may have been particularly apprehensive about this because of the obvious difficulties of trying to manage his new cross-Mediterranean lordship: he could not help but be aware that he was not "on the pulse" with events back in Champagne. It may well have appeared to him that it was better to be safe than sorry; and hence to conclude that he must act as if all of the Briennes' ancestral holdings were in serious danger. And, if Erard had indeed been running the county of Brienne as John's proxy over the course of the last few years, then that county (as Erard's present main powerbase) could well have appeared much more in danger of confiscation than would otherwise have been the case. John may thus have sent Jacques of Durnay back to the West for the purpose of protecting his own vulnerable ancestral lands, by loudly disassociating John himself from Erard and his activities, and to garner first-hand information on the current situation in Champagne. Having imperilled the Brienne lands – and also because he was now coming out to the East – in ca. 1213–14 Erard was no longer a suitable figure to remain John's proxy for Brienne (if, indeed, he had earlier fulfilled that role). It may thus be suggested that Jacques was also sent back to replace Erard as proxy, at least until the dust there had settled.

Having arrived in the Latin East under the shadow of the papal bull against him, Erard seems to have been obliged to loiter, for some time, in the kingdom of Jerusalem. During the months following his arrival, two noteworthy events occurred – though it is extremely difficult to tease out their precise impact on Erard and his scheme. Arguably, the more significant of the two was the murder of the papal legate and patriarch of Jerusalem, Albert of Vercelli – apparently, by a disgruntled clerk. John, though, appears to have moved swiftly to derive what advantage he could from this. He may well have had a directing hand in the process by which his own close associate, the Champenois Ralph of Merencourt – bishop of Sidon and royal chancellor – succeeded Albert as patriarch-elect.[35] Erard was surely in touch with King John during this period. If John was indeed countenancing Erard's scheme, then perhaps they both could have hoped for a rather more cooperative attitude from John's ally Ralph than they would have had from the saintly Albert. (In view of the papal bull, though, even Ralph would have to move circumspectly.) Also, in 1214, John married Stephanie (sometimes called "Rita"), a plausible heiress to the reigning king, Leo, of Cilician Armenia. This marriage held out the prospect of resurrecting John's long-term dynastic ambitions for his own issue (ambitions that had earlier perished, in the kingdom of Jerusalem, along with his first wife, Queen Maria). Marriage to Stephanie reopened the possibility, now firmly closed off in the kingdom of Jerusalem, of establishing a line of Brienne kings in the Latin East.[36]

---

[34] For this, see esp. d'Arbois de Jubainville, *Histoire des ducs et des comtes de Champagne*, 4:113.

[35] See Perry, "The Career and Significance of John of Brienne," pp. 103–4.

[36] Ibid., pp. 113–14.

Erard's marriage finally took place at the end of this rather mysterious pause. Although the marriage's legality and consequences were much discussed afterwards, few surviving sources look closely at its immediate surrounding circumstances. For these, we have to fall back on the two main narrative accounts of John's reign, those of Ernoul-Bernard and Colbert-Fontainebleau. Both accounts have serious shortcomings. Ernoul-Bernard suggests that Queen Maria of Jerusalem gave her half-sister, Philippa, to Erard. This certainly did not happen, since Maria had died more than a year before Erard himself came out to the Latin East.[37] Whilst Ernoul-Bernard can thus be read as placing the marriage too early, Colbert-Fontainebleau appears to place it too late – apparently after the Fourth Lateran Council, which is plainly incorrect.[38] Interestingly, Colbert-Fontainebleau underlines the prospect that Philippa was proactive in bringing the marriage about – secretly leaving the castle at Acre at night before marrying Erard the next day.[39] However, the two accounts do agree on one fundamental point: namely, that the marriage took place at Acre, behind John's back, whilst the king was away at Tyre.[40] Colbert-Fontainebleau then emphasizes that although John was actually delighted with the match, he had to pretend otherwise in public.[41] The newly-weds may well have stayed on in the kingdom of Jerusalem, apparently without too much difficulty, for another couple of months after their marriage. If so, then this provides a further indication that King John was not as "corrocez" with them as he pretended, since he might otherwise have taken action against them (such as, for instance, forcibly separating the couple, or expelling or imprisoning Erard).[42]

It may be suggested that, in his capacity as Philippa's effective guardian, John could have prevented the marriage if he had really been determined to do so. Given that Erard had publicized his intention to marry Philippa, and the greatest authorities in the West had spoken out against this, John would surely have been justified, in the eyes of his kingdom's elites, in taking action to make sure that Philippa was effectively inaccessible to Erard (confined, say, in a royal fortress such as the castle at Acre, or in a secure religious establishment). The fact that, by hook or by crook, Philippa eventually married Erard may provide an indication that John did not, in fact, carry out any such action decisively. It may appear best, then, to agree with Colbert-Fontainebleau (and therefore with d'Arbois de Jubainville). In the last analysis, we may guess, John actually made the marriage possible – when his back was ostentatiously turned.

---

[37] Ernoul-Bernard, pp. 409–11.

[38] Colbert-Fontainebleau, p. 319; and below, p. 74.

[39] Colbert-Fontainebleau, p. 319.

[40] Ibid., p. 319; Ernoul-Bernard, p. 409.

[41] Colbert-Fontainebleau, pp. 319–20.

[42] For this, see esp. the detailed chronology proposed by d'Arbois de Jubainville, in *Histoire des ducs et des comtes de Champagne*, 4:114–17.

Reinterpreting evidence that has long been available suggests that, in the aftermath of the marriage, John did act against what appear to be well-founded suspicions that there had been a Brienne stitch-up. It would seem that he made substantial efforts to publicly disavow any hand in the marriage, as well as continuing to disassociate himself from Erard's designs on Champagne. Like many other Latin rulers, John sent a proctor to the Fourth Lateran Council – in his case, the Jerusalemite baron John Le Tor.[43] At the council, this John, and the king's clerical allies (chiefly, Ralph of Merencourt), were surely involved in at least informal discussions concerning the "Erard of Brienne affair." Whilst it is impossible to ascertain what these involved, what is plain is that at the council the canons prohibiting consanguineous marriage were altered (which in the end would have the effect of making it easier for the Church to formally recognize Erard's marriage to Philippa).[44] Quite possibly, King John's allies played a leading part pushing for this change.

By the time of the council, the French monarchy had come out far more robustly than before against Erard. Back in mid-1215, the heir to the French crown, the future Louis VIII, had written to King John of Jerusalem. Louis's letter restates the basics of the case, as the French crown then saw it. Young Theobald's right to inherit could not be challenged until he was of age. Indeed, it was highly unlikely that he ever could be ousted by either Alice or Philippa, since it was well known that their father had earlier relinquished any rights that they might otherwise have had to Champagne. And Erard and Philippa could not marry in any case, since the pair were too closely related. This "fraternal" but stern warning to King John was unmistakable.[45] Quite possibly, it was on receipt of this letter that John decided that he must send an envoy to France, to explain away the awkward fact that the marriage had recently taken place under his very nose. This, then, may well be at least a substantial part of the explanation why John Le Tor went on to France after the Fourth Lateran Council.[46]

John appears to have given no support of any kind to Erard in the Champenois civil war that followed. It is difficult to assess how much damage was done to Erard's cause there by the absence of any such backing whatsoever. But, had it been available to him, Erard would surely have wanted at least the formal endorsement of a figure who was both a king, and still the effective head of the Brienne dynasty. John's lack of support for Erard, at this critical stage, may well have been decisive in reassuring John's own, powerful, long-term western backers that the king himself was no longer out of line with them (if, indeed, he ever had been). Since Innocent III and Philip Augustus were quite shrewd enough to harbour strong suspicions concerning John's involvement in the marriage, it might appear remarkable that

---

[43]   Colbert-Fontainebleau, p. 319.

[44]   See esp. d'Arbois de Jubainville, *Histoire des ducs et des comtes de Champagne*, 4:116, n.b.

[45]   A printed copy of this letter is readily available in PL 216, cols. 975–76, and now in Evergates, ed., *The Cartulary of Countess Blanche of Champagne*, no. 12 (pp. 41–42). Unfortunately, the letter has been misread in the past, as having been sent by King John to Louis, and not vice versa.

[46]   See Colbert-Fontainebleau, p. 319.

both seem to have proved ready to accept John's protestations and move on. The best explanation for this is probably the simplest – and, maybe, enhances respect for John's political judgement. The course adopted by both Innocent and Philip was much the easiest one open to them and politically expedient, once it was plain that John would not flout them (further?) to assist his notorious cousin.

In the aftermath of the marriage, the papacy set the machinery in motion for ecclesiastical sanctions against both Erard and Philippa, and their *fautores* and *coadjutores*. It was at least arguable that the greatest of the latter was, in fact, John himself, but no such sanctions were ever employed against him, even though they were duly utilized against Erard and his allies in the Champenois civil war. In fact, in all the voluminous papal correspondence on the subject of Erard's marriage, there is no clear statement, or even suggestion, that the papacy held John substantially responsible for it. It seems likely that the acceptable conduct of the king's associates at the Fourth Lateran Council, followed shortly afterwards by John's abstention from the Champenois civil war, sufficed to put an end to any period of real tension between John and the papacy. And renewed papal support for John soon showed its usefulness to him, yet again, in the run-up to the Fifth Crusade.[47]

In a similar manner, John appears to have contrived to quickly mend his relationship with the French crown. And where King Philip led, the weaker Blanche may well have felt obliged to follow. Certainly, there is no clear sign of any tensions concerning the "Erard of Brienne affair" between King John and either Philip or Blanche, when John returned to the West in 1222 (that is, shortly after Erard and Philippa had begun to formally relinquish their claim to Champagne).

Although Erard's design on Champagne ultimately failed, he was not the only member of the Brienne family who, in the end, derived substantial advantage from it. Despite denying Erard any formal endorsement in the civil war, John too gained quite notably. As has already been said, many of Erard's leading supporters in that war hailed from what could be labelled as the Brienne "affinity," strongly connected to the dynasty.[48] And several of them eventually "took an honourable exit from a hopeless situation by coming out East to take part in the Fifth Crusade" (an enterprise headed, of course, by John himself). There is no sign that they held a grudge against the king for not formally endorsing Erard's cause earlier. On the contrary, several of the chief "Erardians" – such as John's close kinsmen Simon of Joinville and Erard of Chacenay – stalwartly backed John during that crusade, when his own leadership of it came under challenge.[49] A hitherto-neglected *actum* even appears to show that a good relationship was soon restored between John and Erard

---

[47] See esp. *Regesta pontificorum Romanorum inde ab anno post Christo nato 1198 ad annum 1304*, ed. August Potthast, 2 vols. (Berlin, 1874–75), vol. 1, nos. 5178–79, 5180, 5209; and Perry, "The Career and Significance of John of Brienne," pp. 111, 114.

[48] See esp. d'Arbois de Jubainville, *Histoire des ducs et des comtes de Champagne*, 4:128–31.

[49] See Perry, "The Career and Significance of John of Brienne," pp. 149–53; and Guy Perry, "From John, King of Jerusalem, to the Emperor-elect Frederick II: A Hitherto-neglected Letter from the Fifth Crusade" (forthcoming).

himself (if, indeed, such a relationship had ever been lost). In early 1224, King John mediated peace in a dispute between Erard and Albert, abbot of Vauluisant.[50]

The implications of the above reconstruction can, of course, be utilized to revivify discussion concerning various broader nexus questions and themes. The "Erard of Brienne affair" underscores the continuing weaknesses, as well as the strengths, of Latin Christendom's great powers at certain local and regional levels, both in the West and in the East. Despite the relatively firm concordance of those great powers against Erard and his scheme, the "marriage" still happened, and civil war followed in Champagne, before all was settled and the great powers got what was basically their way. It is in the combination of such strengths and weaknesses, at a local-regional level, that we may discern something of the situation and opportunities for what we may term "adventurer-figures" on the make – figures like John himself, as well as Erard. The differing outcomes that emerged, as various Briennes (and, of course, others) strove to advance themselves and their dynasty, indicate how the very nature of that combination could vary according to a plethora of differing circumstances.

That there is a need for this article indicates that the relationship between the Latin West and East – certainly in this period – still requires careful, and detailed, analysis. In the "Erard of Brienne affair," we witness Erard himself (with John, it seems, covertly co-operating) essentially trying to harness the Brienne family's temporary clout in the Latin East to impact back on its homeland in the Latin West. Whilst not entirely new, this may still appear as a somewhat novel development. Perhaps, then, the key point to re-emphasize here is that it was only now, from the late twelfth century onwards, that it was becoming possible – for the first time since the pioneer days of the Latin East – for one individual to be a Latin Eastern ruler whilst also formally remaining the lord of a great seigneury back in the West. This development – well underway, it should be stressed, before the epoch of Frederick II – plainly had the potential to problematize relations between the Latin Eastern rulers in question, and at least some powers back in the West.

A final suggestion to bring this article full circle. For dynastic reasons (including his continuing retention of the county of Brienne), John was intimately bound up in this "Erard of Brienne affair," both in a manner, and to a degree, that no-one else, even amongst the great in his kingdom, could really share with him. Might this be part of the beginning of a process of "alienation" (which of course accelerated dramatically under the Hohenstaufen), by which the outlook of the kings of Jerusalem, and those of their kingdom's elite, came to critically diverge? And might this help explain those elites' future readiness to accept a regent (*bailli*) in place of the absent king – fulfilling many of the functions that were needed, yet not fixating,

---

[50] Bibliothèque nationale de France, MS Lat. 5468, fol. 141r. Noted in Perry, "The Career and Significance of John of Brienne," Appendix 1 ("Catalogue of little-known *acta* closely concerning John of Brienne"), no. 11.

as an actual king might well have done, largely on a political *schema* that was "alien" to those elites? In short, are we approaching here the classic case of the rejection of the ruler whose interests do not coincide sufficiently with those of the ruling class in the polity in question? Such, at least, is a good starting-point for further discussion.

Pope Gregory IX and the Grant of Indulgences for Military Campaigns in Europe in the 1230s: A Study in Papal Rhetoric

Rebecca Rist

University of Reading
r.a.c.rist@reading.ac.uk

Gregory IX (1227–41), born at Agnani in ca. 1170, was probably fifty-seven when he became pope and enjoyed a long pontificate of fourteen years. Like his predecessors Innocent III (1198–1216) and Honorius III (1216–27), throughout his time as pope he was deeply involved in complex diplomatic relations with the Holy Roman Emperor Frederick II (1220–50), against whom he finally took the decision to authorize a crusade in 1239, a move which would sour relations between the papal curia and Hohenstaufen emperors for decades.[1] Yet, despite his preoccupation with imperial politics, during his time in office Gregory also set a precedent in authorizing several new crusades against groups living in Christian Europe who were accused of heresy.[2] His authorization of such crusades was influenced by the wishes of local political leaders and prelates who looked to the papacy for support and endorsement of such military campaigns against suspected heretics.

---

[1] In my recent book, *The Papacy and Crusading in Europe, 1198–1245* (Continuum, 2009), I suggested that Gregory IX was much older than 57 when he became pope and that he was from the Conti family. These ideas have been repeatedly aired in recent secondary literature, but for a revised opinion of his age and family background see Burkhard Roberg, in *Lexikon des Mittelalters*, vol. 4: *Erkanzler bis Hiddensee* (Münich and Zürich, 1989), col. 1671; Theo Kölzer, in *Lexikon für Theologie und Kirche*, ed. M. Buchberger and K. Hofmann, 10 vols. (Freiburg im Breisgau, 1930–38), vol. 4, col. 1019; Sandro Carocci, *Baroni di Roma: dominazioni signorili e lignaggi aristocratici nel duecento e nel primo trecento* (Rome, 1993), p. 373. For Gregory IX's letters calling for a crusade against Frederick II, see, for example, Gregory IX, *Ascendit de mari* (21 May 1239), *Epistolae selectae saeculi XIII e regestis pontificum Romanorum*, ed. Carolus Rodenberg, MGH, 3 vols. (Berlin, 1883–94) [henceforward: Rodenberg], 1:646–54. The intention in this article is not to discuss exhaustively every letter issued by Gregory IX concerned with crusading in Europe in the 1230s, but rather, by analysing a number in detail, to show the power of papal rhetoric, in particular with regard to the grant of indulgences.

[2] Elizabeth Kennan, "Innocent III, Gregory IX and Political Crusades: A Study in the Disintegration of Papal Power," in *Reform and Authority in the Medieval and Reformation Church*, ed. Guy F. Lytle (Washington, D.C., 1981), p. 15; Christoph Maier, *Preaching the Crusades: Mendicant Friars and the Cross in the Thirteenth Century* (Cambridge, 1994), pp. 32–62; Nikolaus Paulus, *Geschichte des Ablasses im Mittelalter*, vol. 2 (Paderborn, 1923; repr. Darmstadt, 2000), pp. 19–39, esp. pp. 26 and 28. Recently, the historian Mark Pegg has questioned whether there was an established Cathar Church in the south of France; see Mark Pegg, *A Most Holy War: The Battle for Christendom* (Oxford, 2008), passim. Although I do not agree with Pegg's position, nevertheless my use of the term "heretic" throughout this article reflects the contemporary papal documents and implies no judgement on the actual beliefs of the accused.

Nevertheless, despite setting a precedent in calling for crusades in Europe, Gregory was cautious about their implementation. Although he was careful to endorse his predecessor Honorius III, who at the beginning of his pontificate had renewed the plenary indulgence for taking part in the Albigensian Crusade, Gregory became eager to end crusading in the south of France and to explore alternative means of dealing with heresy. The caution which he showed in approving clerical appointments and issuing the crusade indulgence for military ventures in Europe other than the south of France, showed that he was fully aware that the prestige of the papacy could be seriously undermined and the crusading ideal brought into disrepute if a crusade served merely to enhance the power of the local clergy. Indeed, his call for a crusade in 1238 against the Bulgarian king John Asen (1218–41) was intended to remind all Christians, including the clergy, that the papacy alone had the authority to authorize crusading campaigns.[3] Yet, on the other hand, Gregory was sensitive to criticism of papal authorization of crusading and for this reason supported the establishment of inquisitorial processes to deal with heretics, alongside, and sometimes instead of, crusades.

Since a number of different temporal and ecclesiastical powers asked for papal approval of crusades in diverse parts of Europe, Gregory was confronted with a whole host of complex choices and decisions. He had to keep in constant communication with his legates in countries and territories far from Rome. Through these men he attempted to ensure not only that crusades were efficiently preached and organized, but that both crusaders and the local clergy would continue to implement his directives once they were underway. Yet, despite Gregory's apparently cautious approach, his authorization of crusades in Europe was actually an extremely bold decision, and since he was fully aware that he was creating a precedent he was most careful in all his correspondence to the Christian faithful to maintain continuity with the pronouncements of his predecessors. Not only did he promote ideas of holy war and military service for God – themes by now traditionally associated with crusading – but he also ensured that when granting the plenary indulgence he used similar language and images to that employed by previous popes in their calls for crusades to the East. By strategic use of analogy and formulaic language, his authorization of crusades in Europe was thereby made more familiar and so more acceptable to the Christian faithful.

So Gregory's correspondence shows awareness of the need for continuity with the approach of his predecessors. From the beginning of his pontificate he already had an ongoing campaign in Europe to oversee – the Albigensian Crusade. In a letter of March 1228, responding to an appeal of Louis IX of France (1226–70), he prolonged the legation of Cardinal Romano Bonaventura of Sant' Angelo in Peschiera, whom Honorius III had originally appointed as his legate for the south of France. Gregory exhorted Louis's mother Blanche of Castile, widow of the crusader Louis VIII (1223–26), to resume the crusade there against those suspected

---

[3] Maier, *Preaching the Crusades*, pp. 37–38.

of heresy.[4] He also sent two further letters of 1228 to the south of France: to Cardinal Romano, emphasizing that the legate was to continue to fulfil his mandate and to the French clergy, renewing Honorius's grant of the plenary indulgence for crusading:[5]

> We grant to all those submitting to the labour, personally or at their own expense, full forgiveness of their sins, of which they freely make oral confession with contrite hearts, and as the reward of the just we promise them a greater share of eternal salvation ....[6]

In fact, this re-issue proved unnecessary since the following year all crusading activity in the south of France came to an end.[7] At the Council of Paris (1229) Romano formally accepted Raymond VII, the southern French nobleman against whom the crusade had recently been targeted, back into communion with the Church; Raymond was then formally pardoned by Louis IX.

Elsewhere in Europe Gregory was also actively involved in authorizing military ventures. In 1228, he sent to Hungary four letters regarding a campaign against the Cumans, a nomadic and pagan tribe of Asian origin whom local lords often employed as mercenaries and against whom King Bela IV of Hungary (1235–70) had recently campaigned.[8] Since there is no evidence that vows were taken, the campaign was not a crusade. Yet Gregory signalled his approval of military action and granted a limited indulgence for those who fought. His correspondence reveals how he developed a combined strategy of encouraging both missionizing and military activity. In a letter of March 1228 to the king of Hungary, Gregory urged him to continue to work to convert the pagan Cumans.[9] In another, he likewise congratulated his legate Robert, archbishop of Esztergom, on his missionary efforts, but also now promised that those who fought to recover Christian territory,

---

[4] Gregory IX, *Negotium quod agitur* (21 March 1228), *Bullarium Franciscanum romanorum pontificum*, vol. 1, ed. Johannis H. Sbaralea (Rome, 1759), pp. 37–38; Paulus, *Geschichte des Ablasses im Mittelalter*, p. 27.

[5] Gregory IX, *Licet alia vice* (June/July 1228), *Les Registres de Grégoire IX*, ed. Lucien Auvray, 4 vols., Bibliothèque des écoles françaises d'Athènes et de Rome, 2nd ser. (Paris, 1890–1955) [henceforward: Auvray], vol. 1, cols. 143–44; *Ardenti desiderio aspirantes* (21 October 1228), Auvray 1, cols. 141–43.

[6] Gregory IX, *Ardenti desiderio aspirantes*, col. 142: "plenam suorum peccaminum, de quibus veraciter fuerint corde contriti et ore confessi, veniam indulgemus, et in retributione justorum salutis eterne policemur augmentum ..."

[7] Ibid., cols. 141–43.

[8] Nora Berend, *At the Gates of Christendom: Jews, Muslims and "Pagans" in Medieval Hungary, c.1000–c.1300* (Cambridge, 2001), p. 31; Paulus, *Geschichte des Ablasses im Mittelalter*, pp. 23–24, for examples of the papacy's grant of different levels of indulgences; on the campaign against the Cumans, see ibid., p. 31.

[9] Gregory IX, *Immensas gratiarum actiones* (21 March 1228), *Vetera monumenta historica Hungariam sacram illustrantia*, ed. Augustin Theiner, 2 vols. (Rome, 1859–60) [henceforward: Theiner], 1:87. See Berend, *At the Gates of Christendom*, pp. 68–73; Nora Berend, "How Many Medieval Europes? The 'Pagans' of Hungary and Regional Diversity in Christendom," in *The Medieval World*, ed. Peter Linehan and Janet L. Nelson (London, 2001), pp. 79–90.

or who took up arms against those opposed to the Cumans' conversion, should be granted a limited indulgence of two years.[10] He also took pains to supervise the newly founded Cuman bishopric. In a letter to its canons, Gregory declared their recent episcopal elections void because they had not been conducted in accordance with canon law, and stated that he intended to install his own candidate as bishop.[11] And he ordered the provincial prior of the Dominicans in Hungary to allow certain friars deemed suitable by the legate Robert and a Dominican, Theoderic, whom he appointed as the new bishop of the Cumans, to be sent to aid their conversion.[12]

Preaching missions followed but had little immediate success. The Cuman bishopric was short-lived and the Mongol conquest of 1241 made its planned re-establishment impossible. Nevertheless, Gregory's grant of indulgences for both missionizing and campaigning was highly significant and his correspondence merits close attention. So, in his letter congratulating his legate Robert on his missionary work among the Cumans, he promised a small indulgence of a hundred days for those who helped construct churches and other buildings in Hungary for the use of new converts. Furthermore, he promised that those who fought to recover lands held by Christians adjacent to Cuman territory which had been overrun by the Seljuk Turks of Iconium, or who fought those who opposed the conversion of the Cumans, should be granted a larger indulgence of two years:[13]

> We concede, that for the faithful, who personally shall have gone or shall have sent aid for the constructing there of churches and suitable buildings, an indulgence for sins which, however, shall not exceed a length of a hundred days. And for those setting out to recover the lands of Christians near the Cumans, which the sultan of Konya or other infidels have occupied, and for those men who take action both against those who fight converted Cumans and those who prohibit others from acceptance of the Christian faith, you may bestow a two-year remission – not, however, exceeding it, and in accordance with the disposition of the devotion, the amount of help and the labour which they shall have sustained on this account – and you may announce and cause to be announced an indulgence and remission of this kind, where you think it useful.[14]

---

[10]   Gregory IX, *Gaudemus in Domino* (21 March 1228), Theiner 1:87–88.

[11]   Gregory IX, *Cumana ecclesia pastoris* (21 March 1228), Auvray 1, col. 107; *Degli annali sacri della citta di Como decade*, ed. Primo Luigi Tatti, 3 vols. (Como, Milan, 1663–1735), 2:934–35; X 1.6.50, *Corpus iuris canonici*, ed. Emil Friedberg, vol. 2 (Leipzig, 1881), col. 91; see also *Corpus iuris canonici*, ed. Aemilius Ludwig Richter, 2 parts (Leipzig, 1839), part 2, col. 88.

[12]   Gregory IX, *Cum venerabili fratre* (21 March 1228), Theiner 1:87.

[13]   For the territorial ambitions of the Seljukids see, for example, Claude Cahen, *Pre-Ottoman Turkey: A General Survey of the Material and Spiritual Culture and History c.1071–1330*, trans. J. Jones-Williams (London, 1968), pp. 119–37.

[14]   Gregory IX, *Gaudemus in Domino*, pp. 87–88: "concedimus, ut fidelibus, qui personaliter ierint vel miserint subsidium ad construendum ibidem ecclesias et edificia opportuna, peccatorum indulgentiam, que tamen centum dierum spatium non excedat, et proficiscentibus ad recuperandam christianorum terras Cumanis vicinas, quas Soldanus de Iconio vel infideles alii occuparunt, ac euntibus contra illos, qui Cumanos conversos impugnant, et prohibent alios ad fidem christianam venire, remissionem, biennium tamen non excedentem, iuxta devotionis affectum, quantitatem subsidii et laborem, quem propter hoc sustinuerint, largioris, et indulgentiam et remissionem huiusmodi denunties et denuntiari, facias ubi videris expedire."

It is clear from this statement that Gregory believed that the major aim of Hungarian military action against the Cumans ought to be the recovery of Christian territory. As in his call to renew crusading in the south of France, he described the campaign as a defensive operation.[15] Yet he stressed that the indulgence granted was not to exceed two years, thereby making clear that the campaign was not of equal status to the Albigensian Crusade. His caution may have been due in part to the fact that – again in contrast to the crusade in the south of France – in granting a plenary indulgence against the Cumans he had no precedent to follow. He probably also wished to emphasize that, although the papacy regarded all conflicts against the enemies of the Church as meritorious, they were not all of equal merit, nor were they all crusades.

By contrast to Hungary, Gregory did eventually authorize crusades against heretics in Germany. In 1230, a synod at Bremen condemned as heretics the Stedinger, a group of peasants who for many years had been in conflict with their lord, Gerhard II, archbishop of Bremen.[16] This condemnation followed the murder in 1229 of the German noble Hermann II of Lippe, Gerhard's brother.[17] Six months later the archbishop had travelled to Rome to seek the pope's permission to preach a crusade against the Stedinger.[18] Yet, Gregory was cautious about authorizing a crusade. His first response was to ask the provost of Münster to attest that they had indeed been excommunicated and that the charges levied against them were indeed valid.[19] Once satisfied of their validity, Gregory wrote to Bishop John of Lübeck and to two prominent Dominicans in the archdiocese of Bremen, asking them to intervene and recall the Stedinger from heresy.[20] Indeed, even when peaceful initiatives failed he made no quick decision in favour of a crusade. Instead, he requested Bishops John of Lübeck, Gottschalk of Ratzeburg and Conrad of Minden to reinvestigate the charges.[21]

In October 1232, however, Gregory decided that he should delay no longer in authorizing military action,[22] and he ordered the bishops of Minden, Lübeck and

---

[15] For example, Gregory IX, *Ardenti desiderio aspirantes* (21 October 1228), Auvray 1, cols. 141–43.

[16] Maier, *Preaching the Crusades*, p. 52; Paulus, *Geschichte des Ablasses im Mittelalter*, p. 27. For the German nobility of the area around Bremen and the counts of Lippe, see *Urkundenbuch zur Geschichte der Stadt Bremerhaven I. Lehe und Vieland im Mittelalter 1072–1500*, ed. Jürgen Bohmbach and Bernd-Ulrich Hucker (Bremerhaven, 1982), pp. 21–26.

[17] Maier, *Preaching the Crusades*, p. 52.

[18] *Historia monasterii Rastedensis*, MGH SS 25:506.

[19] Christian Krollmann, "Der Deutsche Orden und die Stedinger," in *Alt-Preussiche Forschungen*, Historische Kommission für Ost-und-West-Preussiche Landesforschung 14 (Königsberg, 1937), p. 5.

[20] Gregory IX, *Si ea que* (26 July 1231), in *Bremisches Urkundenbuch*, ed. D. R. Ehmck and W. von Bippen (1873), 1:196–97.

[21] Krollmann, "Der Deutsche Orden und die Stedinger," p. 5; Kennan, "Innocent III, Gregory IX, and Political Crusades: A Study in the Disintegration of Papal Power," p. 25.

[22] Gregory IX was already in communication with the archdiocese of Bremen for other reasons besides the problem of heresy. In 1233, for example, he wrote a letter informing the bishop and *scholasticus* of Hildesheim that Cardinal Otto of San Nicolas in Carcere Tulliano, papal legate to Germany and Denmark, had appointed the Dominican prior and the dean and *scholasticus* of Bremen

Ratzeburg to preach a campaign to the faithful in Paderborn, Hildesheim, Verden, Münster, Osnabrück, Minden and Bremen.[23] In January 1233, he instructed Bishops Conrad of Paderborn, Conrad II of Hildesheim, Luderus of Verden, Ludulfus of Münster, and Conrad of Osnabrück to give whatever help they could to aid the bishops of Ratzeburg, Minden and Lübeck in their preaching.[24] In June, he granted the bishops of Minden, Lübeck and Ratzeburg the same indulgence for those who took part in crusading against the Stedinger as bestowed on those who went on crusade to the Holy Land.[25]

Following this grant, the recruitment of crusaders peaked in early 1234 with the support of Dominicans who travelled throughout the Rhineland, Westphalia, Holland, Flanders and Brabant urging men to take the cross.[26] *The Annals of Stade* recorded that the Germans responded enthusiastically to the idea of a crusade, that fighting ensued and that many Stedinger were killed.[27] *The Chronicle of Emo*, however, suggested that the response of northern Germans was less impressive and that concern over whether preachers had the requisite authority to preach the crusade discouraged many from joining the campaign.[28] Whether or not Gregory was aware of this dissatisfaction, his correspondence suggests that he hoped for a peaceful end to the conflict. In 1234, he urged his legate William of Modena to do all in his power to end the discord which had arisen between the archbishop, clergy and people of Bremen and the Stedinger.[29] William seems to have had some diplomatic success and, in August 1235, Gregory instructed the archbishop and chapter of Bremen to absolve the Stedinger from the sentence of excommunication which the archbishop had imposed in 1229, provided that they fully obeyed the Church's mandates in the future.[30] It is clear that Gregory was keen for the crusade to end and the dispute to be settled by diplomatic means.

This study of Gregory's correspondence reveals that his grant of indulgences for the campaign developed gradually. In his general letter to the bishops of Linden,

---

as general visitors in the diocese of Bremen to set up an inquiry into the provost of the church of Reepsholt concerning charges of simony. See Gregory IX, *Cum dilectus filius* (4 June 1233), Auvray 1, cols. 764–65.

[23] Gregory IX, *Lucis eterne lumine* (29 October 1232), Rodenberg 1:393–94.

[24] Gregory IX, *Clamante ad nos* (19 January 1233), *Regesta pontificum Romanorum*, ed. August Potthast, 2 vols. (Berlin, 1874) [henceforward: Potthast], vol. 1, no. 9076; Nicolaus Staphorst, *Historia ecclesiae Hamburgensis diplomatica, das ist: Hamburgisches Kirchen-geschichte*, vol. 1, part 2 (Hamburg, 1725), p. 18.

[25] Gregory IX, *Littere vestre nobis* (17 June 1233), Rodenberg, 1:436–37. See Paulus, *Geschichte des Ablasses im Mittelalter*, pp. 31–32.

[26] Maier, *Preaching the Crusades*, p. 55.

[27] *Annales Stadenses*, MGH SS 16:361.

[28] *Emonis chronica*, MGH SS 23:515–16.

[29] Gregory IX, *Grandis et gravis* (18 March 1234), *Bremisches Urkundenbuch*,1:215. For a comprehensive account of the German mission of William of Modena see Gustav Donnar, *Kardinal Willhelm von Sabina, Bischof von Modena 1222–1234. Päpstlicher Legat in den Nordischen Ländern (+1251)* (Helsingfors, 1929).

[30] Gregory IX, *Ex parte universitatis* (21 August 1235), Potthast vol. 1, no. 9992; Staphorst, *Historia ecclesiae Hamburgensis*, p. 21. See Maier, *Preaching the Crusades*, p. 52.

Lübeck and Ratzeburg of 1232, he enjoined them for the remission of their sins ("in remissionem peccatorum iniungentes") to lead the faithful of Paderborn, Hildesheim, Verdun, Münster, Osnabrück, Minden and Bremen in a campaign to exterminate heretics, and gave specific instructions about the granting of spiritual indulgences to campaigners:

> To all who shall have come to your solemn preaching, we relax for them twenty days, and for the others who shall have undertaken that journey in their own person and at their own expense, and also those who shall have come there at others' expense, we relax a period of three years; indeed we relax a period of five years of their enjoined penance for those about to remain there, according to the need of the business and your foresight. But for others, who shall provide from their own means to help the faithful, we grant an indulgence of the remission of their sins according to the quantity of subsidy and the degree of devotion. We concede pardon for all their sins, of which indeed they shall have been contrite and confessed, for all who shall have died in the prosecution of that business.[31]

It is clear that this statement advocated a "hierarchy" of indulgences for those who took part in different capacities in the Stedinger campaign, with the grant of different indulgences of twenty days, three years and five years; for those who died, having been sorry for and having confessed their sins, there was full remission of sins. As we have already seen, for the Albigensian Crusade Gregory had granted the same plenary indulgence as had previously been granted by his predecessors Innocent III and Honorius III. In the case of the Stedinger, a plenary indulgence was only granted for those who *died* fighting, rather than simply for those who took part. This again confirms that in 1232 Gregory did not regard the campaign as of equal importance to the Albigensian Crusade which had only recently ended.

Yet, in 1233, Gregory changed his mind about the status of the Stedinger campaign. He now made a distinction between those who fought in campaigns against heretics and those who did so after having vowed to take the cross. The latter were to be awarded the same plenary indulgence as those going to the Holy Land: "Indeed catholics, who, having taken up the sign of the cross, shall have girded themselves to exterminate the same heretics, let them rejoice in that indulgence and be armed with that privilege, which are conceded to those going to the aid of the Holy Land."[32] It is likely that Gregory's response to the victories of the

---

[31] Gregory IX, *Lucis eterne lumine*, p. 394: "omnibus qui ad sollempnem praedicationem vestram accesserint, viginti dies, et aliis qui laborem istum in propriis personis subierint et expensis, nec non et illis qui in expensis illic accesserint alienis, triennium, ibi vero iuxta exigentiam negotii et vestram providentiam moraturis quinquennium de iniuncta sibi penitentia relaxamus. Aliis autem, qui de suis facultatibus ad subventionem fidelium ministrabunt, iuxta quantitatum subsidii et devotionis affectum remissionem suorum peccaminum indulgemus; universis qui decesserint in huius prosecutione negotii, omnium peccatorum, de quibus vere contriti et confessi fuerint, veniam concedentes." See Paulus, *Geschichte des Ablasses im Mittelalter*, p. 31.

[32] Gregory IX, *Littere vestre nobis*, p. 437: "Catholici vero, qui crucis assumpto caractere ad eorundem hereticorum exterminium se accinxerint, illa gaudeant indulgentia illoque privilegio sint muniti, que accedentibus in Terre Sancte subsidium conceduntur."

Stedinger in the winter of 1232–33 and their capture of the archbishop of Bremen's fortress at Slutter caused him to make this change in policy.[33] He may also have wished to signal that the campaign was of equal importance to that which was also contemporaneously being preached against other heretical groups in Germany, thereby avoiding any diversion of resources from the Stedinger campaign.[34]

For, besides crusading against the Stedinger, in the 1230s Gregory had authorized yet another crusade against German heretics. Alongside papal pronouncements, an increasing number of imperial statutes and decrees against heresy had been promulgated in Germany in the 1220s and 1230s.[35] Writing to the archbishop of Marburg in 1224, Frederick II had ordered that a new imperial decree against heresy, which prescribed burning or the loss of his tongue for the guilty, should be published throughout Lombardy. Using this decree as a basis, Gregory promulgated new anti-heretical statutes with the same penalties both in Lombardy and in Rome. In June 1231, he authorized *Excommunicamus*, a general letter to the German archbishops, which decreed that all heretics be excommunicated and their property confiscated, thereby reaffirming Constitution 3 of Lateran IV (1215).[36] Gregory hoped that, although Frederick's powers were not strong enough to create a legal framework which would allow for the establishment of inquisitors in northern Italy, the imperial decree would nevertheless enable the secular authorities to operate voluntarily to combat heresy in towns throughout the country.[37]

It is therefore clear from Gregory's correspondence that he continued to endorse his predecessor Innocent III's policy of advocating both spiritual and secular punishment for heretics. As early as 1199, Innocent had argued in *Vergentis in senium*, addressed to the town of Viterbo, that, just as under Roman law traitors were punished for their treachery by confiscation of their possessions, so those convicted of heresy should have their property confiscated for betraying the majesty of God Himself.[38] Gregory's interest in tackling heresy by establishing inquisitorial

---

[33] *Annales Stadenses*, p. 361. See Maier, *Preaching the Crusades*, p. 55.

[34] Maier, *Preaching the Crusades*, p. 55.

[35] For a comprehensive list of these statutes and decrees, see Hans Köhler, *Die Ketzerpolitik der Deutschen Kaiser und Könige in den Jahren 1152–1254*, Jenaer Historische Arbeiten 6 (Bonn, 1913), pp. 73–74. For Gregory IX's call for crusades against German heretics, see also Paulus, *Geschichte des Ablasses im Mittelalter*, p. 27.

[36] Frederick II, *Cum ad conservandum* (March 1224), Rodenberg 1:174. See *Monumenta Germaniae Historica. Leges*, vol. 2, ed. Georg Heinrich Pertz (Hannover, 1837), pp. 252–53; Edict of Annabaldus, senator of the city of Rome, *Omnes heretici* (February 1231), Auvray 1, cols. 352–53; Gregory IX, *Excommunicamus* (February 1231), Auvray 1, cols. 351–52.

[37] Maier, *Preaching the Crusades*, p. 168.

[38] Innocent III, *Vergentis in senium* (29 March 1199), *Die Register Innocenz' III, Publikationen des Österreichischen Kulturinstituts in Rom*, ed. Othmar Hageneder, Anton Haidacher and Alfred A. Strnad (Graz, Vienna, Cologne, 1964–), vol. 2, pp. 3–5. See Albert Shannon, *The Medieval Inquisition* (Washington, D.C, 1983), pp. 128–29; Helen Nickerson, *The Inquisition: A Political and Military Study of its Establishment*, 2nd ed. (London, 1932), p. 206. For the use of inquisitorial records as a source for heresy, see Caterina Bruschi and Peter Biller, "Texts and the Repression of Heresy: Introduction," in *Texts and the Repression of Medieval Heresy*, ed. Caterina Bruschi and Peter Biller, York Studies in Medieval Theology 4 (Woodbridge, 2003), pp. 3–22.

proceedings was not confined to Italy. From early in his pontificate he advocated the use of such processes in Germany. Conrad of Marburg, formerly the confessor of St. Elizabeth of Thuringia and probably a secular priest rather than a Dominican, persuaded Gregory that there were organized groups of devil-worshippers in Germany who had sold their souls to Lucifer.[39] It is difficult to gauge from the sources the political context in which these heretics were believed to operate, but they were suspected of links with the nobility of north-west Germany. In response to these allegations, Gregory instructed Conrad in 1227 to proceed diligently with an investigation into their activities.[40] This signalled only the beginning of his interest. In 1231 he sent *Ille humani generis* to the prior and sub-priors of the Dominican convent at Friesach. In this letter he linked the spread of heresy directly to the malice of Satan, complained that heretics were openly and contemptuously teaching errors, and declared that, acting in a new capacity as inquisitors, the Dominicans must take action against both heretics and their supporters.[41] The same letter was later sent to Duke Henry I of Brabant and Duke Otto II of Bayern.[42] Then in 1232 Gregory ordered Siegfried, archbishop of Mainz, to send religious men to all parts of his diocese to make enquiries concerning those suspected of heresy.[43] If they should find any suspect guilty they were to proceed in accordance with *Excommunicamus*.[44]

In that year too, Gregory had promised a series of partial indulgences to those who took part in a military campaign against the same heretics in Germany.[45] It was only in 1233, however, that he began to consider calling for a crusade in response to the clergy's continuing concern. In June, he informed Conrad of Marburg that he was much disturbed that he had received petitioning letters from the archbishop of Mainz and the bishop of Hildesheim, ordering him to advocate the use not only of the spiritual but also the material sword, and promising the same plenary indulgence

---

[39]   Bernard Hamilton, *The Medieval Inquisition* (London, 1981), pp. 75–76; Wolfgang Stürner, *Friederich II, Vol. 2: Der Kaiser 1220–1250* (Darmstadt, 2000; repr. 2009), pp. 297–99.

[40]   Gregory IX, *Sollicitudinem tuam quam* (12 June 1227), Rodenberg 1:277. For the career of Conrad of Marburg, see Alexander Patschovsky, "Zur Ketzerverfolgung Konrads von Marburg," *Deutsches Archiv für die Erforschung des Mittelalters* 37.2 (1981), 641–93.

[41]   Gregory IX, *Ille humani generis* (27 November 1231), *Acta imperii inedita*, vol. 1, ed. Eduard August Winkelmann (Innsbruck, 1880), pp. 499–501. See Peters, *Inquisition*, p. 55; Dietrich Kurze, "Anfänge der Inquisition in Deutschland," in *Die Anfänge der Inquisition im Mittelalter mit einem Ausblick auf das 20. Jahrhundert und einem Beitrag über religiöse Intoleranz im nichtchristlichen Bereich*, ed. Peter Segl (Cologne, 1993), p. 159.

[42]   Gregory IX, *Ille humani generis* (3 February 1232), *Bullarium ordinis praedicatorum*, ed. Thomás Ripoll and Antonin Brémond, 8 vols. (Rome, 1729–40) [henceforward: *Bullarium*], 1:37; Gregory IX, *Ille humani generis* (4 February 1232), in Ludwig Förg, *Die Ketzerverfolgung in Deutschland unter Gregor IX. Ihre Herkunft, ihre Bedeutung und ihre rechtlichen Grundlagen*, Historische Studien 218 (Berlin, 1932), pp. 96–98.

[43]   Gregory IX, *Ille humani generis* (29 October 1232), Rodenberg, 1:394–96.

[44]   Ibid., pp. 394–96; *Solent heretici ad* (25 June 1231), *Acta imperii selecta. Urkunden Deutscher Könige und Kaiser 928-1398*, ed. Johann Friedrich Böhmer (Innsbruck, 1870), pp. 665–67.

[45]   Gregory IX, *Cum de summo* (11 October 1231), *Analecta Hassiaca* 2, ed. Johann Philipp Kuchenbecker, *Collectio* 3 (Marburg, 1730), pp. 73–75.

for those who should take up the cross as was granted to those who went on crusade to the Holy Land.[46] This message was repeated a few days later in letters to Conrad of Marburg, the archbishop of Mainz and the bishop of Hildesheim, as also to the bishops of the province of Mainz, to Frederick II and to his son Henry.[47] In October, Gregory placed Landgrave Conrad of Thuringia under his protection in return for his devotion to the Apostolic See in defence of the catholic faith – which suggests that the count had already responded to the pope's authorization of a crusade.[48] Indeed, Gregory notified the bishop of Hildesheim of the landgrave's action and ordered him to ensure Conrad was not molested while on campaign.[49]

Following the Diet of Mainz in July that same year, the archbishop of Mainz and a certain Bernard, a Dominican, reported to Gregory that Conrad of Marburg and the Franciscan Gerard of Lutzelkolb had been murdered by a faction of German noblemen.[50] Conrad, zealous and fanatical about his cause, had made the tactical mistake of impugning the count of Seyn, a man powerful enough to force him to resign; indeed, it was probably supporters of the count who soon afterwards had him murdered.[51] Although Gregory appointed no new inquisitors in Germany, Conrad's death propelled him to reiterate the commitment which he had already made to a crusade against heretics.[52] In October, he instructed Archbishop Siegfried III of Mainz, the bishop of Hildesheim and the Dominican prior of Germany to proceed in accordance with Constitution 3 of Lateran IV and recent imperial statutes,[53] expressed indignation at the cruel killings not only of Conrad but also of Gerard, and ordered the prelates to prepare for a crusade.[54]

Gregory's dismay at the death of Conrad of Marburg recalled Innocent III's anger at the murder in 1208 of his legate to the south of France, Peter of Castelnau, which had precipitated the Albigensian Crusade. Shortly after both murders both popes sent letters advocating a crusade, although, like Innocent, Gregory had in fact already granted the plenary indulgence for crusading before the death of his legate.[55] Gregory wrote letters to the crusader Count Henry of Thuringia, to the bishop of Hildesheim and to the bishop-elect of Magdeberg, to Count Henry of Aschersleben, to Conrad Count Palatine of Saxony, to Duke Otto of Brunswick, to Margrave Henry of Minden and Margraves John and Otto of Brandenburg. In

---

[46] Gregory IX, *O altitudo divitiarum* (10 June 1233), Rodenberg 1:429–30.

[47] Gregory IX, *Vox in Rama* (11–14 June 1233), Rodenberg 1:432–35.

[48] Gregory IX, *Dignum est et* (20 October 1233), Rodenberg 1:450–51.

[49] Ibid., p. 451.

[50] Aubrey of Trois Fontaines, *Chronica Albrici monachi Trium Fontium*, MGH SS 23:931–32.

[51] Hamilton, *The Medieval Inquisition*, p. 76.

[52] Ibid., p. 76.

[53] Gregory IX, *Dolemus et vehementi* (21 October 1233), Rodenberg 1:451–52. See Maier, *Preaching the Crusades*, p. 57.

[54] Gregory IX, *Querit assidue perfidia* (31 October 1233), Rodenberg 1:455–56.

[55] A letter of Innocent III to King Philip Augustus of France issued before the death of Peter of Castelnau promised the same indulgence for those who took up arms against heretics as granted to crusaders going to the Holy Land: see Innocent III, *Inveterata pravitatis heretice* (17 November 1207), *Die Register Innocenz III*, 10:254–57.

all these letters he promised papal immunity for those who took the cross against heretics in Germany and placed crusaders' possessions under the protection of the Holy See.[56] Yet although, according to *The Annals of the Brother Preachers of Erfurt*, Bishop Conrad of Hildesheim carried out the papal orders, the crusade never got under way.[57] Rather, another diet at Frankfurt in February 1234 settled the problem peacefully.[58]

It is clear from a close reading of these letters that as early as 1231 Gregory had promised a series of indulgences to those who took part in this campaign against heresy in northern Germany. In one letter he stated:

> To all in each area who have gone to hear your preaching we relax twenty days; to those indeed who, in order to fight against heretics and their favourers, receivers and defenders in fortifications and castles and those who rebel otherwise against the Church, have spiritedly shown advice and help or favour, having trusted to the mercy of almighty God and the authority of the blessed Peter and Paul His apostles, we relax three years of the penalty enjoined on them; and if someone of these people by chance shall have died for the prosecution of that business, we grant as an indulgence to them full pardon for all sins of which they shall have been contrite.[59]

And, in another letter of 1232, he again promised a series of indulgences for those who helped in enquiries which he had ordered the archbishop of Mainz to undertake into suspected heretical activity.[60] In this letter, as in his letter of 1232 concerned with the Stedinger campaign, he presented the faithful with a "hierarchy" of indulgences: those who listened to the sermons of preachers against heresy were to receive an indulgence of twenty days. Others, who gave help, advice or favour to combat heretics and their supporters, were to receive an indulgence of three years:

> Indeed for those men who shall have boldly offered advice, council or favour to fight heretics, their favourers, receivers and defenders, in fortifications and castles or others rebelling against the Church – for these, having trusted to the mercy of almighty God and to the authority of blessed Peter and Paul His apostles, we relax three years from the penance enjoined on them.[61]

---

[56] Gregory IX, *Tam sinceritatis affectum* (11 February 1234), Rodenberg 1:466–67.

[57] *Annales Erphordenses fratrum praedicatorum*, MGH SS 42:84.

[58] Maier, *Preaching the Crusades*, p. 57.

[59] Gregory IX, *Cum de summo*, pp. 74–75: "omnibus qui ad praedicationem tuam accesserunt in singulis civitatibus XX. dies, illis vero qui ad impugnandum haereticos nec non fautores, receptatores et defensores eorum in munitionibus et castellis vel aliis contra Ecclesiam rebellantes tibi ex animo consilium et auxilium praestiterunt vel fauorem de Omnipotentis Dei misericordia et beatorum Petri et Pauli Apostolorum eius auctoriate confisi, tres annos de iniuncta sibi poenitentia relaxamus, et si qui ex his pro prosecutione huius negotii forte decesserint, eis omnium peccatorum de quibus corde contriti fuerint plenam veniam indulgemus."

[60] Gregory IX, *Ille humani generis*, pp. 394–96.

[61] Gregory IX, *Ille humani generis*, p. 395: "illis vero qui ad impugnandum hereticos, fautores, receptatores et defensores eorum in munitionibus et castellis vel alias contra ecclesiam rebellantes ipsis ex animo auxilium, consilium prestiterint vel favorem, de omnipotentis Dei misericordia et beatorum Petri et Pauli apostolorum eius auctoritate confisi, tres annos de iniuncta sibi penitentia relaxamus."

And to encourage armed conflict, a full indulgence was again granted for those who died fighting against heretics provided that they first repented of and confessed their sins.

Furthermore, as with the Stedinger campaign, in 1233 the pope increased the status of the campaign against the German heretics. In June of that year he enjoined the papal inquisitor Conrad of Marburg to do all he could to counter heresy for the remission of his sins and promised that those who took up the cross should receive the same indulgence as that granted crusaders to the East: "On those who, having assumed the character of the cross, shall have girded themselves to exterminate the same heretics, we bestow that indulgence and that privilege, which are conceded for those going to aid the Holy Land."[62] Therefore, as also in the case of the Stedinger campaign, Gregory made a careful distinction between those who merely fought in a military campaign against heretics and those who actually vowed to go on crusade. Whereas previously only those soldiers who died merited the plenary indulgence, now all who took the cross automatically received it. So, in 1233, Gregory emphasized that he now regarded the campaigns against both the Stedinger and other German heretics as full-blown crusades for which crusaders were to be granted the same plenary indulgence as those who travelled to the East.

Gregory repeated this grant of the indulgence in letters to the archbishop of Mainz, the bishop of Hildesheim, Conrad of Marburg, the bishops of the province of Mainz, Frederick II and his son Henry.[63] In his letter to the archbishop of Mainz, the bishop of Hildesheim and the prior of the Dominicans concerning the death of Conrad of Marburg he also granted the same plenary indulgence for those who took part in the crusade. But by describing it as the same indulgence as granted for the crusade to *Jerusalem* rather than to the Holy Land, he employed a slightly different formulation:

> To all those truly penitent and confessed, who ... shall have undertaken the labour in their own persons or at their own expense, we grant an indulgence of pardon for all their sins just as for those going to Jerusalem ...[64]

So, as with the Stedinger campaign, although Gregory did not at first regard the campaign against German heretics as a crusade, later, in order to encourage the

---

[62] Gregory IX, *O altitudo divitiarum*, p. 430: "qui crucis assumpto caractere ad eorundem hereticorum exterminium se accinxerint, illam indulgentiam idque privilegium elargimur, que accedentibus in Terre Sancte subsidium conceduntur." For the role of Gregory IX in the complex gestation of the Barons' Crusade during the 1230s, which may cast light on the pope's handling of the Stedinger campaign, see Michael Lower, *The Barons' Crusade: A Call to Arms and Its Consequences* (Philadelphia, 2005), pp. 13–36 and 37–57. It is also interesting to note that in terms of the extension of the scope of the Stedinger campaign there are intimations of the genesis of the Second Crusade of 1145; see Lower, *The Barons' Crusade*, pp. 14 and 47.

[63] Gregory IX, *Vox in Rama*, pp. 432–35.

[64] Gregory IX, *Querit assidue perfidia*, p. 456: "omnibus vere penitentibus et confessis, qui ... laborem subierint in personis propriis vel expensis, omnium peccatorum suorum veniam sicut euntibus Ierosolimam indulgemus."

faithful to participate, he decided to grant the plenary indulgence for those who formally took the cross.

Several years before these campaigns took place in Germany, Willbrand of Oldenburg, bishop of Utrecht, preached a military campaign with papal approval in Frisia in the late summer and autumn of 1228 and in the summer and winter of 1230. This crusade was directed against Drenther peasants who had murdered Bishop Otto II, Willbrand's predecessor.[65] The thirteenth-century chronicle, *The Deeds of the Bishops of Utrecht*, our only source for the campaign, states that at the time of his election to the see, Willbrand was in Italy at the court of Frederick II, that he had previously acted as imperial envoy to the curia and that he had earlier crusaded in the East.[66] Willbrand's distinguished political record meant that he was in a strong position to request and obtain powers to preach the cross and he may have petitioned Gregory for these powers before returning to his bishopric in 1228. It still seems strange, however, that, in contrast to the cases of reported heretical activity in Germany, there is no evidence that Gregory had Willbrand's allegations against the Drenther investigated.[67] Possibly the long-standing reputation of his family as crusaders was a sufficient guarantee of his credentials, since his family had participated enthusiastically in crusades to the Holy Land and his father, Count Henry II of Oldenburg-Wildeshausen, had died in Syria in 1197.[68] Since there are no extant papal letters relating to the Drenther we cannot be sure that the bishop received papal authorization. What we do know from *The Deeds of the Bishops of Utrecht* was that the campaign's success was limited, that it ended in September 1232 and that it was not renewed.[69]

Yet, by comparison to crusades organized against heretics in Germany, the absence of papal letters concerned with this "crusade" against the Drenther means that we do not know what kind of indulgence Gregory granted those who fought – if indeed he did grant an indulgence. *The Deeds of the Bishops of Utrecht* recorded that those who gathered to take part in military action were spurred on by the exhortation of Willbrand, bishop of Utrecht, but also that the pope had granted an indulgence: "and in another part of the land certain Frisians from Friesland have come, roused through the indulgence of the lord pope and the exhortation of the lord bishop."[70]

---

[65] *Gesta episcoporum Traiectensium*, MGH SS 23:417, 421 and 422–23. See Maier, *Preaching the Crusades*, p. 167.

[66] *Gesta episcoporum Traiectensium*, pp. 415–16. Willbrand wrote a famous *Itinerarum* about his experiences in the East; see *Wilbrandi de Oldenborg Peregrinatio*, in *Peregrinatores medii aevi quatuor*, ed. J. C. M. Laurent, 2nd ed. (Leipzig, 1873), pp. 159–90.

[67] Maier, *Preaching the Cusades*, p. 168.

[68] *Gesta episcoporum Traiectensium*, p. 416. See Maier, *Preaching the Crusades*, p. 168; Dieter Rüdebusch, *Der Anteil Niedersachsens an den Kreuzzügen und Heidenfahrten*, Quellen und Darstellungen zur Geschichte Niedersachsens 80 (Hildesheim, 1972), p. 45.

[69] *Gesta episcoporum Traiectensium*, p. 416.

[70] Ibid., p. 417: "et in alia parte terre accesserunt quidam Frisones de Westergo, per indulgenciam domni pape et exhortacionem domni episcopi evocati."

This description did not elaborate on whether or not the indulgence was the same as that conceded for crusading in the Holy Land. Yet, *The Deeds of the Bishops of Utrecht* described the bishop as preaching that those who took part would receive a "certain" – which would seem to suggest a plenary – remission of their sins:

> And finally, after it had been much discussed by all, it was agreed on that the bishop personally should hurry to the Frisians, proclaim an indulgence and preach and should enjoin on them a journey against the Drenther ... for the certain remission of their sins.[71]

So, according to *The Deeds of the Bishops of Utrecht*, whether or not Bishop Willbrand of Utrecht received authority from Rome to do so, he granted a full indulgence for the campaign. Constitution 3 of Lateran IV, the great ecumenical council of 1215, had stated that those who took part in a crusade against heretics were eligible for plenary indulgences, while Constitution 62 of the same council recognized the power of bishops to grant indulgences for a limited period of one year in certain circumstances. Yet, although the bishop may have cited such legislation in claiming the power to make the grant, it is unclear whether this would have been enough to persuade others that he had the authority to call for a crusade.[72] Furthermore, the fact that Constitution 62 referred to short-term penances for jubilees or consecrations of new churches, rather than to plenary indulgences for military campaigns, implied that the bishop's canonical basis for a claim of authority was weak.[73] Nevertheless, it seems probable that those who listened to his sermons were persuaded that the indulgence promised for fighting was equal to that which popes traditionally conceded to crusaders to the Holy Land.

By contrast to this campaign, the authorization of crusades against heretics in Bosnia is well documented in papal correspondence. Gregory IX's predecessor Honorius III had issued a number of letters concerned with both heresy and ignorance of catholic beliefs in Bosnia.[74] In the later years of his pontificate, Honorius had called on the archbishop of Kalocsa to preach a crusade, urging John III Doukas Vatatzes of Nicaea (1222–54), the son of the exiled Nicaean emperor Theodore II

---

[71] Ibid., p. 421: "Et tandem post multum tractatum ab omnibus in eo convenitur, ut episcopus personaliter ad Frisones discurrat, indulgentiam clamet et predicet et eis iter contra Drentos ... in quandam certam remissionem peccatorum suorum iniungat." See also pp. 422–23, passim.

[72] *Constitutiones Concilii quarti Lateranensis cum Commentariis glossatorum*, ed. Antonius García y García, *Monumenta iuris canonici*, Series A, vol. 2 (Vatican City, 1981), pp. 47–51 and 101–103. See also *Decrees of the Ecumenical Councils, Vol. 1: Nicaea I to Lateran V*, ed. Norman P. Tanner (London, 1990), pp. 233–35 and 263–64. The *Gesta episcoporum Traiectensium* never referred to the Drenther as heretics.

[73] Although Spanish bishops issued crusade-type indulgences for fighting in the 1160s; see Peter Linehan, "The Synod of Segovia (1166)," *Bulletin of Medieval Canon Law* 10 (1980), 35–36.

[74] For his letters to Bosnia, see Honorius III, *Inter alias sollicitudinis* (3 December 1221), *Honorii III romani pontificis opera omnia quae extant*, ed. César Auguste Horoy, 5 vols. (Paris, 1879–82) [henceforward: Horoy], vol. 4, cols. 36–37; *Si zelus vos* (5 December 1221), Horoy 4, cols. 40–41; *Super gregem dominicum* (12 March 1222), Horoy 4, cols. 110–11; *Per G. Spalatensem* (27 July 1223), Horoy 4, cols. 401–402.

Laskaris (1254–58), to take part.[75] It is difficult to assess from Gregory IX's letters to Bosnia, written in response to information supplied to him by the local clergy, whether most Bosnians were genuinely heretical, espousing some form of dualism, or merely *bona fide* catholics ignorant of basic Church doctrines and practices.[76] Even more difficult to determine was Gregory's own views on this issue. Certainly, Gregory gave no immediate attention to the Bosnian Church on becoming pope: its needs were not his first priority. He only became concerned in 1232 after reports from Bosnia that its missionary bishop was the brother of a heresiarch, and, even more serious, that his own ordination was uncanonical. In a letter to Archbishop Ugrinus of Kalocsa, Bishop Stephen of Zagreb and the provost of the church of Saint Laurence in the diocese of Kalocsa, Gregory ordered an enquiry into the bishop of Bosnia and a report on its findings to be sent to Rome.[77] The next year he informed the Dominican John of Palestrina, his legate in Bosnia, that, since the enquiry had established that the bishop held heretical doctrines, he was to be deposed and replaced.[78] Following this decision, Gregory wrote to Matej Ninoslav, the Ban of Bosnia, stating that, as a reward for having abjured heresy, he and all his possessions were to be placed under the papacy's protection.[79] He ordered the Dominicans of Bosnia to ensure that the son of a certain Ubanus – named Priezdan – a relative of Ban Ninoslav, and held as a hostage for the latter's acceptance of catholicism, should be released.[80] Gregory also informed Coloman, duke of Croatia and brother of the king of Hungary, that Ninoslav's reaffirmation of his faith meant that he was to be allowed to pursue his policies against heretics unhindered.[81]

These letters demonstrate that Gregory wanted the problem of heresy to be tackled within Bosnia by the local Bosnian clergy. But, between October 1233 and February 1234, under the influence of Duke Coloman of Croatia, who wished to overrun Bosnia and proposed a crusade against Bosnian heretics, Gregory changed his mind. He now decided that he was not content that heresy be tackled internally,[82] and ordered the archbishops, bishops, abbots and other prelates, as well as the Christian faithful in Carneola, Istria, Dalmatia, Bosnia, Croatia, Serbia and other parts of the Slavic world, to show kindness to his new legate, the Carthusian

---

[75] Honorius III, *Gratum gerimus et* (15 May 1225), Horoy 4, cols. 851–52; *Significavit nobis venerabilis* (15 January 1227), Horoy 5, col. 175.

[76] John Fine, *The Bosnian Church: A New Interpretation. A Study of the Bosnian Church and Its Place in State and Society from the 13th to the 15th Centuries*, East European Monographs 10 (Boulder and New York, 1975), p. 136; Franjo Sanjek, *Les Chrétiens bosniques et le mouvement cathaire, XIIe–XIVe siècles* (Brussels and Paris, 1976), p. 68; Raoul Manselli, "Les 'Chrétiens' de Bosnie: le Catharisme en Europe orientale," *Revue d'histoire ecclésiastique* 72 (1977), 613–14; Paulus, *Geschichte des Ablasses im Mittelalter*, p. 27.

[77] Gregory IX, *Graves et enormes* (5 June 1232), *Acta Honorii et Gregorii IX*, ed. Aloysius Tautu (Vatican City, 1950) [henceforward: Tautu], pp. 233–34.

[78] Gregory IX, *Humanae conditionis miseriam* (30 May 1233), Tautu, pp. 268–69.

[79] Gregory IX, *Quos prosequitur Domini* (10 October 1233), Tautu, p. 271.

[80] Gregory IX, *Dilectus filius nobilis* (10 October 1233), Tautu, p. 273.

[81] Gregory IX, *Dilecto filio nobili* (10 October 1233), Tautu, p. 272.

[82] Fine, *The Bosnian Church*, p. 139.

prior of the monastery of St. Bartholomew of Trisulti, whom he dispatched with a specific mandate to preach the cross against heretics as the Bosnians requested.[83] He also urged Coloman of Croatia to gird himself for action in parts of Slavonia so that those infected by the stain of heresy might be converted,[84] and he conceded to Coloman and his wife that, despite the interdict placed on Bosnia, their clergy should be allowed to celebrate mass in areas overrun by their army, provided the service was conducted quietly behind closed doors.[85]

Six further letters of 17 October 1234 show that Gregory was now determined to continue with the idea of a Bosnian crusade. He granted powers to the new bishop, John of Wildeshausen, also provincial of the Dominicans in Hungary, to facilitate his preaching against heretics,[86] and he placed Hungarians signed with the cross and their possessions under the Church's protection.[87] He ordered the bishop of Zagreb to ensure that crusaders were protected,[88] placed the duke of Croatia under his protection and instructed the bishop to ensure that the duke and his possessions should not be harmed.[89] He expressed his joy to John of Wildeshausen that he had been chosen by the legate John of Palestrina to be bishop of Bosnia and encouraged him to continue his zealous persecution of heretics.[90] Yet the Bosnians were resentful of the appointment of a foreigner as their spiritual leader and John's attempts to reform the Bosnian Church proved unsuccessful.[91]

After these letters, there seems to have been no further papal correspondence with Bosnia until late 1235. That August, however, Gregory approved the concession made by Andrew II king of Hungary and Croatia (1205–35) to his son Duke Coloman of the territory of Bosnia, thereby signalling that the papacy was prepared to accept the duke's disputed claim to the throne of Croatia and Hungary.[92] In fact, it was Bela IV, not Coloman, who in 1235 succeeded Andrew II on the throne.[93] Gregory sought to persuade John of Wildeshausen, who wished to resign his bishopric, to withdraw his resignation,[94] and in August 1236 put Sibislav, the knez of Usora, a son of Stephen, former Ban of Bosnia, and all his goods under papal protection: a reward for having stood alone among the chieftains of Bosnia

---

[83]   Gregory IX, *Miserias et erumpnas* (13 February 1234), Rodenberg 1:467–69.

[84]   Gregory IX, *Si tue serenitatis* (14 October 1234), Theiner 1:128–29. It is generally assumed that by "Slavonia" the pope meant Bosnia and the surrounding area. But "Slavonia" could also have referred to Slavdom in general or even in particular to Slavonia, north of the Sava. See Fine, *The Bosnian Church: A New Interpretation*, p. 139.

[85]   Gregory IX, *Ut pro regis* (16 October 1234), Theiner 1:129.

[86]   Gregory IX, *Quod maius in* (17 October 1234), Tautu, p. 283.

[87]   Gregory IX, *Sacrosancta Romana Ecclesia* (17 October 1234), Theiner 1:129–30.

[88]   Gregory IX, *Cum dilectos filios* (17 October 1234), Theiner 1:129–30.

[89]   Gregory IX, *Pro fidei meritis* (17 October 1234), Theiner 1:30; *Cum illustrissimum in* (17 October 1234), Theiner 1:30; see also under the incipit *Cum karissimum in*, Auvray 1, col. 1143.

[90]   Gregory IX, *Exultamus in Domino* (17 October 1234), Theiner 1:130.

[91]   Maier, *Preaching the Crusades*, p. 58.

[92]   Gregory IX, *Licet apostolice sedis* (9 August 1235), Theiner 1:133.

[93]   Berend, *At the Gates of Christendom*, p. 120.

[94]   Gregory IX, *Deputatus Iesu Christi* (20 September 1235), Theiner 1:137.

in remaining true to the catholic faith.[95] Gregory notified Robert, archbishop of Esztergom, Bartholomew, bishop of Pécs, and the provost of Esztergom of this favour,[96] and also at the same time placed Ban Stephen's widow under the Church's protection.[97]

Following these letters, a new crusade began in 1237–38 which allowed Duke Coloman of Croatia to occupy major parts of Bosnia and Herzegovina.[98] Gregory's letter announcing Coloman's victory and granting the bishop of the Cumans power to establish and consecrate the Dominican Ponsa as the new bishop for Bosnia, with added jurisdiction over the province of Hum, suggests that his earlier attempt to persuade John of Wildeshausen to continue as bishop had been unsuccessful.[99] In December, Gregory urged the archbishop of Esztergom, the archbishop of Kalocsa and their suffragans to use whatever money they could spare to help the bishop of Bosnia tackle heresy.[100] He praised Coloman for his success and encouraged him to continue the crusade.[101]

Gregory continued to issue such letters concerned with crusading. He ordered the abbot of Várad to collect money from crusaders who had redeemed their vows for the use of the bishop of Bosnia,[102] urging him to make sure that money, which a certain Jula, a ban of Coloman's, had deposited with the Dominicans at Pécs to help the crusade, be assigned to the bishop.[103] He instructed the prior and Dominican brothers of Pécs to send money, deposited with them by Ban Ninolav for the construction of a cathedral in Bosnia, to the same bishop.[104] Ponsa was entrusted with all legatine powers in the Bosnian diocese, securing him the same powers to combat heresy as had been awarded to his predecessor John of Wildeshausen.[105] And, in December 1239, Gregory ordered Ponsa, in his capacity as prior of the Dominicans in Hungary, to despatch friars to preach the Gospel in Bosnia, confirming to him and to the chapter of St. Peter in Bosnia (the bishop's see) the right to church possessions granted by Coloman and the crusaders – presumably goods seized during the campaign.[106] In the same month, Gregory again urged

---

[95] Gregory IX, *Quos in medio* (8 August 1236), Theiner 1:147.

[96] Gregory IX, *Cum dilectum filium* (8 August 1236), Theiner 1:147.

[97] Gregory IX, *Quos in medio* (8 August 1236), Theiner 1:147; *Cum dilectam in* (8 August 1236), Theiner 1:147.

[98] Sanjek, *Les Chrétiens bosniques et le mouvement cathaire, XIIe–XIVe siècles*, p. 72.

[99] Gregory IX, *Inspirationis divine gratia* (26 April 1238), Theiner 1:162–63.

[100] Gregory IX, *Ecclesiarum regimini presidentes* (22/23 December 1238), Theiner 1:168; *Ecclesiarum regimini presidentes* (22 December 1238), Auvray 2, col. 1198.

[101] Gregory IX, *De superni regis* (22 December 1238), Theiner 1:168.

[102] Gregory IX, *Gerentes in desideriis* (22 December 1238), Theiner 1:169.

[103] Gregory IX, *Apud dilectos filios* (22 December 1238), Theiner 1:169.

[104] Gregory IX, *Indignum se gratia* (22 December 1238), Theiner 1:169; see in Potthast 1 as *Dux Bosniae indignum*, no. 10691.

[105] Gregory IX, *Sedi apostolice presidentis* (23 December 1238), Theiner 1:169–70.

[106] Gregory IX, *Cum sicut ex* (6/7 December 1239), Theiner 1:170; *Iustis petentium desideriis* (7 December 1239), Theiner 1:172. The first of these letters may have been 6 August 1239; see in Potthast 1, no. 10823.

the prior and Dominican brothers of Bosnia to send Ban Ninoslav's deposit to the Bosnian bishop and repeated his request to Ponsa to send brothers to preach the Gospel.[107] Both the pope and Dominicans were careful to ensure that crusading was followed by preaching and long-term pastoral care for the Bosnians.

By contrast to the Drenther campaign, in the case of Bosnia there was no doubt of the pope's eventual authorization of a crusade indulgence. At first, in 1233, he ordered his legate John of Palestrina to depose the bishop of Bosnia and then enjoined him for the remission of his sins to ordain as bishops for the dioceses of Bosnia two, three or four suitable men learned in the law.[108] The following year he conceded an indulgence of ten days for those who listened once a week to the preaching against heretics of the new bishop of Bosnia, John of Wildeshausen.[109] He also granted the bishop power to bestow *in extremis* the last rites and to absolve those who had been excommunicated for violent crimes against the clergy if they died while fighting:

> For those who have incurred the noose of excommunication for arson and the violent laying on of hands against clerics or other religious persons, and go against the heretics settled in parts of Slavonia for the defence of the Faith and are about to die at a fitting time in so happy a work, you may impose, according to the rite of the Church, the favour of absolution.[110]

These concessions showed the relative importance Gregory now attached to the campaign in Bosnia and reflected a concern that insufficient numbers would be willing to take part. Nevertheless, Gregory did not yet grant the plenary indulgence as a reward for the living.

Later in 1234, however, Gregory finally decided to give the Bosnian campaign the full status of a crusade by granting the plenary indulgence to those who took the cross – just as he had done in the case of the Stedinger and other German heretics. In February, he conceded to prelates and other Christian faithful the same indulgence as for those who went on crusade to the East: "For those who ... having assumed the character of the cross, shall have girded themselves to exterminate heretics, we bestow that indulgence and that privilege, which are conceded for those going to aid the Holy Land."[111] And in October he also conceded to the bishop of Bosnia the

---

[107] Gregory IX, *Indignum se gratia* (27 December 1239), Theiner 1:173; *Cum sicut ex* (6/7 December 1239), Theiner 1:172–73.

[108] Gregory IX, *Humanae conditionis miseriam*, pp. 268–69.

[109] Gregory IX, *Quod maius in*, p. 283.

[110] Ibid., p. 283: "ut illis qui, pro incendiis et iniectione manuum violentia in clericos vel alias religiosas personas, excommunicationis laqueum incurrerunt, contra haereticos in Slavoniae partibus constitutos pro defensione fidei accedentibus, et ad tempus congruum in tam felici opere moraturis, iuxta formam Ecclesiae beneficium absolutionis impendas."

[111] Gregory IX, *Miserias et erumpnas*, p. 469: "qui ... crucis assumpto caractere ad hereticorum exterminium se accinxerint, illam indulgentiam illudque privilegium elargimur, que accedentibus in Terre Sancte subsidium conceduntur."

power of granting this same plenary indulgence for those who crusaded in Bosnia.[112] After this, the pope's letters made no further reference to the plenary indulgence for Bosnia until 1238. But in December of that year Gregory renewed his call for men to take up arms against heretics and conceded to the recently-elected Bishop Ponsa the same power to grant the indulgence as had been previously granted to John of Wildeshausen: "and finally on behalf of this business ... we concede to you that power which our dear son brother John, your predecessor, is known to have held from the Apostolic See."[113] This letter showed more caution than previous correspondence, emphasizing that the degree of mercy for sins was to be dependent on the amount of help given and making no reference to the Holy Land. Yet, the very fact that Gregory had stated that he conceded the same powers as he had previously granted to John of Wildeshausen – and we know from his letters to John that these were plenary – strongly suggests that he intended and expected Ponsa to grant the plenary indulgence.

In 1238, Gregory also sent letters to Hungary to preach a crusade against John Asen, king of the Vlachs and Bulgars and ruler of Bulgaria from 1218 to 1241. Although nominally a catholic, John Asen, like the exiled Byzantine emperors in Epiros and Nicaea, had designs on Latin Constantinople.[114] The pope authorized this crusade after Asen's renewal of his alliance with the exiled Greek emperor in Nicaea, John III Doukos Vatatzes (1221–54).[115] As early as 1235 Gregory had asked King Bela IV of Hungary, who some time before had taken the cross for the Holy Land, to crusade instead on behalf of the Latin Empire, which was still threatened by exiled Byzantines seeking to re-establish Greek rule.[116] In 1238, Gregory came to believe that an alliance between Asen and Vatatzes would threaten to thwart Bela's proposed crusade in aid of John of Brienne (d. 1237), the new regent emperor of Constantinople.[117] Gregory was already in frequent communication with the Hungarian clergy – as in 1232 when he had ordered an enquiry into the missionary bishop of Bosnia.[118] In November 1235, he had granted the archbishop of Esztergom the privilege that he, or anyone acting on his behalf, might promulgate a sentence of excommunication or suspension without first acquiring a special mandate from the Apostolic See.[119] He had also urged the bishops and other prelates of the province of Esztergom to welcome and receive with kindness its visiting archbishop.[120]

Three years later, in January 1238, Gregory wrote a long general letter to the archbishops of Esztergom and Kalocsa, to the bishop of Perugia, the pope's legate

---

[112] Gregory IX, *Exultamus in Domino*, p. 130.

[113] Gregory IX, *Sedi apostolice presidentis*, p. 170: "tibi super ipso illam, quam dilectus filius frater Iohannes predecessor tuus ab apostolica sede habuisse dignoscitur, concedimus."

[114] Michael Angold, "Byzantium in Exile," in *The New Cambridge Medieval History, Vol. 5. c.1198–1300*, ed. David Abulafia (Cambridge, 1999), p. 548.

[115] Maier, *Preaching the Crusades*, p. 37.

[116] Ibid., p. 37; Lower, *The Barons' Crusade*, p. 60.

[117] Maier, *Preaching the Crusades*, pp. 37–38.

[118] See p. 93 for details.

[119] Gregory IX, *Fidem et devotionem* (20 November 1235), Theiner 1:139.

[120] Gregory IX, *Ad obedientiam et* (20 November 1235), Theiner 1:140.

in Hungary, and to all the Hungarian bishops, promising a full indulgence for sins to those who crusaded against Asen.[121] In a separate missive he urged the legate to encourage the king of Hungary to take such action.[122] And in a number of letters he exhorted all the bishops of Hungary, his legate the bishop of Perugia (a former bishop of Bosnia), the bishop of Raab (Hungary), the bishop of Zagreb, the archbishop of Kalocsa and the archbishop of Esztergom to join the campaign.[123]

There was no further correspondence between the papal curia and royal or ecclesiastical dignitaries in Hungary until the summer. But, in June 1238, Bela IV invaded Bulgaria and sought to establish ecclesiastical privileges for the regions of Bulgaria-Walachia and Severia.[124] In response, Gregory called on the prelates of Hungary to organize a solemn procession and beseech God to help the Hungarian king;[125] he also urged Bela himself to carry the sign of the cross before his army when going into battle and promised that he would concede a conquered Bulgarian kingdom to no other than the king himself.[126] He placed Bela, his kingdom and all his possessions under the protection of the Apostolic See, and announced this privilege to the archbishop of Esztergom and to the bishop of Vác;[127] he also conceded to the king various canonical privileges with respect to the kingdom of Bulgaria and informed his legate of the concession.[128] He then ordered the Dominicans and Franciscans to preach a crusade against Asen throughout Hungary,[129] repeating this in a general letter to Hungary's archbishops and bishops.[130] Yet, despite Gregory's authorization, the crusade never took place. It seems that the mere threat of a campaign had the desired effect of forcing Asen back into an alliance with Bela – which allowed a Bulgaro-Hungarian force to muster in support of the Latin Empire which in 1239 was being threatened by the exiled emperors of Nicaea.[131]

So, in contrast to earlier Hungarian campaigns against the Cumans, in 1238 Gregory granted the plenary crusading indulgence for Hungarians and other Christian faithful who took up arms against the Bulgarian John Asen: "For those who with you shall have undertaken that labour in their own person and at their own expense, we grant as an indulgence full pardon for their sins."[132] He also clarified

---

[121] Gregory IX, *Supremus opifex qui* (27 January 1238), Theiner 1:159–60.

[122] Gregory IX, *Devotionis tue litteras* (27 January 1238), Theiner 1:161.

[123] Gregory IX, *Sacratissimam Petri sedem* (27 January 1238), Theiner 1:161; *Sacratissimam Petri sedem* (27 January 1238), Auvray 2, cols. 876–77.

[124] Theiner 1:170–71.

[125] Gregory IX, *Et sibi karissimus* (8 August 1238), Theiner 1:164–65.

[126] Gregory IX, *In celorum rege* (8 August 1238), Theiner 1:164; *Cum sicut nobis* (9 August 1238), Theiner 1:166.

[127] Gregory IX, *Cum de superni* (9 August 1238), Theiner 1:166–67.

[128] Gregory IX, *Litteras quas nobis* (9 August 1238), Tautu, pp. 325–26; *Cum carissimus in* (9 August 1238), Tautu, p. 326.

[129] Gregory IX, *Sicut littere karissimi* (9 August 1238), Theiner 1:167.

[130] Gregory IX, *Sicut littere karissimi* (11 August 1238), Theiner 1:167.

[131] Maier, *Preaching the Crusades*, p. 38.

[132] Gregory IX, *Supremus opifex qui*, p. 160: "qui tecum laborem istum in propriis personis subierint et expensis, plenam peccaminum veniam indulgemus."

to his legate, the bishop of Perugia, that the indulgence to be conceded was the same plenary indulgence as that which, since Innocent III's pontificate onwards, had been granted for those going to the aid of the Holy Land: "We bestow the indulgence, which was conceded to those going across the sea to aid the Holy Land, and we state that the land of that Asen is to be occupied by the aforementioned king and other catholics …"[133] Gregory too emphasized in letters to the bishops of Hungary, including the archbishop of Esztergom, his legate the bishop of Perugia, the bishop of Raab, the bishop of Zagreb and the archbishop of Kalocsa, that he was granting the same indulgence as for those crusading in the East.[134] And he granted a similar indulgence in letters of 9 August to Bela IV, to the provincial prior of the Dominicans and the minister of the Franciscans of Esztergom, as well as to the archbishops and bishops of Hungary.[135] Indeed on 8 August he conceded to Hungarian prelates who were helping to further Bela's campaign that, in order to encourage the faithful, they should even be allowed, when preaching to the army, to grant a small indulgence of a few days to those who listened to their sermons.[136]

Meanwhile, his correspondence also reveals that Gregory was authorizing military campaigns against heretics in Italy. In the 1230s and 1240s, anti-heretical fraternities began to surface in many northern Italian towns.[137] As early as 1227, Gregory IX contacted the Order of the Militia of Jesus Christ, a quasi-military Order recently founded in Italy to fight heretics; he granted full remission of all sins for those who faced danger of death from campaigning.[138] Then, in 1231, he granted the people of Padua an indulgence of three years if they would embark on military activity against Ezzelino III da Romano (1194–1259), Frederick II's lieutenant in Lombardy.[139] Although Frederick was hostile to heresy in his own

---

[133] Gregory IX, *Devotionis tue litteras*, p. 161: "indulgentiam elargimur, que conceditur transeuntibus in subsidium terre sancte, ac terram ipsius Assani expomimus predicto Regi et aliis catholicis occupandam." See also the letters *Sacratissimam Petri sedem*, p. 161; *Sacratissimam Petri sedem*, cols. 876–77.

[134] Gregory IX, *Sacratissimam Petri sedem*, cols. 876–77.

[135] Gregory IX, *Litteras quas nobis*, pp. 325–26; *Sicut littere karissimi*, p. 167.

[136] Gregory IX, *Et sibi karissimus*, pp. 164–65.

[137] Maier, *Preaching the Crusades*, p. 76. There are numerous recent publications on the rise of heresy in the thirteenth century, not only in the south of France, but also in Italy and Germany; see in particular Wolfgang Stürner, *Friedrich II*, vol. 1: *Die Königsherrschaft in Sizilien und Deutschland 1194–1220* (Darmstadt, 1992; repr. 2009), pp. 71–73, 75, 146, 178 and 238; Stürner, *Friedrich II*, vol. 2: *Der Kaiser 1220–1250*, pp. 112 and 367.

[138] Gregory IX, *Egrediens hereticorum ab* (22 December 1227), *Bullarium* 1:25.

[139] Gregory IX, *Cum de summo* (2 September 1231), *Italia Sacra*, vol. 5, ed. Ferdinando Ughelli and Nicola Coleti (Venice, 1720), pp. 445–46. See Otto Volk, *Die abendländisch-hierarchische Kreuzzugsidee* (Halle, 1911), p. 116; Paulus, *Geschichte des Ablasses im Mittelalter*, p. 31. For a recent detailed examination of the career of Ezzelino III da Romano, see Stürner, *Friedrich II*, vol. 1: *Die Königsherrschaft in Sizilien und Deutschland 1194–1220*, pp. 147 and 241; Stürner, *Friedrich II*, vol. 2: *Der Kaiser 1220–1250*, pp. 99, 106, 269, 273, 275, 292, 310, 317, 331, 461, 463, 480, 511, 530, 572–73, 579, 582 and 593.

lands, Ezzelino supported local heretics in territories under his control.[140] The pope warned him that he must renounce his evil heresy, crush the heretics and return to the true Church, ordering him to appear personally in Rome within two months of receiving the letter.[141]

Four years later, in 1235, Gregory again granted the brothers of the Militia of Jesus Christ in Parma a plenary indulgence for fighting against heretics, thereby according them crusader-like status.[142] He ordered the bishop of Parma to ensure that the Militia was protected,[143] and instructed the Master General of the Dominican Order and his friars to lend it encouragement and support.[144] He placed the Militia under the special protection of the Holy See,[145] and granted members and their wives a special dispensation that, although Parma was at this point under interdict, they might receive the Sacraments in certain exempted churches.[146] He also approved and confirmed the statutes and regulations of the Militia.[147] Yet, despite such papal attempts to encourage military action and curtail his power, both Ezzelino and Frederick II occupied Vicenza in 1236 and Padua in 1237. Indeed, even after Frederick's death Ezzelino remained the papacy's implacable enemy. As a continuing supporter of Frederick II's heir Manfred, Ezzelino became a prime target of the papal campaign against the emperor in northern Italy – and from 1256 on the papacy would organize a crusade against him.[148]

Again, a detailed look at Gregory's correspondence is invaluable for understanding papal policy. It is clear that, as early as 1227, Gregory had granted the brothers of the Militia of Jesus Christ in Italy a plenary indulgence for fighting against heretics:

> For all the faithful and for those who persist in true penitence, who shall have faced danger of death for the catholic faith and the freedom of the Church, we grant as an indulgence a pardon for all their sins which the Lord conceded to us through St. Peter …[149]

---

[140]   David Abulafia, "The Kingdom of Sicily under the Hohenstaufen and Angevins," in *The New Cambridge Medieval History, Vol. 5*, p. 504.

[141]   Gregory IX, *Utinam inspiceres nec* (1 September 1231), *Acta imperii inedita* 1:499; *Tentare volumus varias* (1 September 1231), Potthast 1, no. 8792; Gianbatista Verci, *Storia degli Ecelini*, vol. 3 (Bassano, 1779), pp. 234–35.

[142]   Gregory IX, *Est angelis ad* (18 May 1235), *Bullarium* 7:11. See Volk, *Die abendländisch-hierarchische Kreuzzugsidee*, p. 116. For the complex political and regional issues behind Ezzelino de Romano's antagonism towards Gregory IX and the specific case of Parma see Luigi Canetti, *Invenzione della memoria. Il culto e l'immagine di Domenico nella storia dei primi fratri predicatori* (Spoleto, 1996), pp. 69–82.

[143]   Gregory IX, *Quos pietate sua* (18 May 1235), *Bullarium* 7:11.

[144]   Gregory IX, *Experimentis multiplicibus informati* (18 May 1235), *Bullarium* 7:10.

[145]   Gregory IX, *Sacrosancta Romana Ecclesia* (18 May 1235), *Bullarium* 7:10.

[146]   Gregory IX, *Devotionis vestrae precibus* (18 May 1235), *Bullarium* 7:10.

[147]   Gregory IX, *Quae omnium conditoris* (24 May 1235), *Bullarium* 7:11–13.

[148]   Trevor Dean, "The Rise of the Signori," in *The New Cambridge Medieval History, Vol. 5*, p. 460.

[149]   Gregory IX, *Egrediens hereticorum ab*, p. 25: "omnibus …, et in vera penitentia persistentibus, qui mortis periculum pro Fide Catholica et Ecclesie libertate subierint, ea, quam Nobis Dominus in D. Petro concessit auctoritate confisi, peccatorum omnium veniam indulgemus."

In 1231, he also granted the citizens of Padua an indulgence of three years to fight against Ezzelino da Romano: "To all who shall have genuinely proceeded against him shall be granted an indulgence of three years," while those who *died* merited the plenary indulgence.[150] And, in 1235, he reiterated to the brothers of the Militia his grant of a plenary indulgence for campaigning: "For those who take up that labour for the defence of the catholic faith and the freedom of the Church ... we grant an indulgence of all their sins of which they are truly contrite and confessed."[151] So, although Gregory was willing to grant a plenary indulgence to members of a military confraternity for fighting against heretics, he was careful to grant only a limited indulgence of three years to the people of Padua unless they actually *died* fighting. He was not willing to grant the latter the full crusading indulgence because at this point he had no wish to authorize a crusade in Italy. The papacy would not grant the plenary crusade indulgence to Italians taking the cross against Ezzelino da Romano until 1256.[152]

This study of Gregory's correspondence allows us to make a number of important inferences about papal authorization of military campaigns and crusades in Europe in the 1230s. When granting indulgences, Gregory IX never made direct comparisons between crusades against groups accused of heresy in Europe and crusades against Muslims in the East. Nor did his letters concerned with the former mention any former or ongoing crusades in Spain or the Baltic. It is therefore difficult to determine just how important Gregory considered crusades against heretics to be in relation to other crusading enterprises. What is certain, however, is that most of his letters granting a plenary indulgence for crusading within Europe deliberately used the same formulas as those of Innocent III and Honorius III – stating that it was the same indulgence as that granted for crusades to the Holy Land. There was therefore no change in the papal position, which had always regarded the Holy Land crusade as a standard by which other crusades were to be judged.[153] Indeed, that Gregory bestowed the "Holy Land indulgence" when he wished to signal the importance of a military campaign strongly suggests that he wished it to be recognized as a crusade not only by campaigners but also by theologians and canon lawyers who made detailed studies of papal decretals.

Gregory IX had realized that, once he had taken the highly significant step of authorizing new crusades within Europe, the best way to encourage them was to evoke images of the Holy Land.[154] Like his predecessors, he regarded crusades to the Holy Land as a model for other crusades. His correspondence suggests that he also conceived of a "hierarchy" of European campaigns. Although he employed

---

[150] Gregory IX, *Cum de summo*, p. 446: "omnibus qui ex animo processerint contra illum, tres annos sibi de injuncta penitentia relaxamus."

[151] Gregory IX, *Est angelis ad*, p. 11: "qui laborem pro defensione Catholice fidei, et Ecclesiastice libertatis, ... omnium peccatorum suorum, de quibus vere contriti, et confessi fuerint, veniam indulgemus."

[152] Dean, "The Rise of the Signori," p. 460.

[153] For example, Gregory IX, *Sicut littere karissimi*, p. 167.

[154] For example, Gregory IX, *Miserias et erumpnas*, pp. 467–69.

similar language to describe these campaigns, the type of indulgence which he originally granted for fighting varied, albeit often eventually upgraded to the full crusade indulgence. Letters to the south of France promised the plenary indulgence for those who took part in the crusade against heretics there, and it was similarly granted for the crusade of 1238 against John Asen. By contrast, Gregory only granted an indulgence of two years for the campaign against the Cumans. For combating the Stedinger, German and Bosnian heretics, he increased the spiritual rewards for campaigning, until he finally granted for those who took the cross the same plenary indulgence as was granted for the Holy Land. On the other hand, for combating heretics in Italy, Gregory only granted the plenary indulgence for fighting to one specific quasi-military fraternity. The plenary indulgence was not issued lightly for campaigns in the 1230s and the precedent for its issue was the Albigensian Crusade. Yet, unlike Innocent III and Honorius III who, once they had decided to authorize military action in the south of France, granted it without hesitation, Gregory IX was much more cautious about doing so elsewhere in Europe.

A Cypriot Royal Mission
to the Kingdom of Poland in 1432

Łukasz Burkiewicz

Jesuit University, Cracow
lukasz.burkiewicz@uj.edu.pl

Despite the fact that Polish contacts with Cyprus were never as extensive or as intensive as with the remaining parts of the Greek world in the later Middle Ages, the very position of the island on a pilgrimage route made it a customary stop for Poles travelling to the Holy Land. Moreover, Poland's important role on the later medieval European stage contributed to the fact that the kings of Cyprus showed interest at least twice in bringing Mediterranean affairs to the attention of the rulers of Poland.[1]

The Poles who arrived in Cyprus were crusaders and pilgrims on their way to Jerusalem. We have no information of any specific connections between Poles and Cyprus before the fourteenth century. The oldest testimony dates back to 1347 – it was then, in the Church of the Holy Sepulchre in Jerusalem, that Philippe de Mézières, future chancellor of the king of Cyprus Peter I of Lusignan, encountered Albert de Pachost, voivode of Brześć and later of Kujawy, who was considered a hero for defending Kujawy against the Teutonic knights in 1332. He made a great impression on Philippe owing to his ascetic practices connected with his pilgrimage vows.[2]

---

[1] Polish literature about the crusades is generally based on the translations of Steven Runciman, *A History of the Crusades*, 3 vols. (Cambridge, 1951–54), and Jonathan Riley-Smith, ed., *The Oxford Illustrated History of the Crusades* (Oxford, 1995). Research concerning the medieval history of Cyprus is at a comparatively early stage of development and based on the works of Łukasz Burkiewicz, *Na styku chrześcijaństwa i islamu. Krucjaty i Cypr w latach 1191–1291* [On the point of contact of Christianity and Islam. The Crusades and Cyprus, 1191–1291] (Cracow, 2008); "Templariusze i ich wpływ na politykę wewnętrzną Królestwa Cypru w przededniu kasaty zakonu" [The Knights Templar and their influence on the internal politics of the kingdom of Cyprus on the eve of the Order's dissolution], *Studia Historyczne* 205 (2009), 3–18; "Polityka Wschodnia Fryderyka II Hohenstaufa ze szczególnym uwzględnieniem jego stosunku do Królestwa Cypru (w świetle kroniki Filipa z Novary)" [The eastern policy of Frederick II Hohenstaufen with special emphasis on his attitude to the kingdom of Cyprus (in the light of the *Chronicle* of Philip of Novara)], *Prace Historyczne Uniwersytetu Jagiellońskiego* 133 (2006), 7–29; "Podróż króla Cypru Piotra I z Lusignan po Europie w latach 1362–1365 i jego plany krucjatowe" [King Peter I of Cyprus's journeys in Europe in 1362–1365 and his crusading plans], *Studia Historyczne* 197 (2007), 3–29; "The Cypriot Jews under the Venetian rule (1489–1571)," *Scripta Judaica Cracoviensia* 6 (2008), 49–61; "Królestwa Cypru jako obiekt zainteresowań państw śródziemnomorskich w latach 1192–1489. Próba zarysowania problemu" [The kingdom of Cyprus as an object of interest to Mediterranean countries between 1192–1489. A sketch of the problem], *Prace Historyczne Uniwersytetu Jagiellońskiego* 137 (2010), 27–41.

[2] Marzena Głodek, *Utopia Europy zjednoczonej. Życie i idee Filipa de Mézières (1327–1405)* [Utopia of United Europe. Life and ideas of Philippe de Mézières] (Słupsk, 1997), pp. 122, 133–35.

At the turn of the fourteenth and fifteenth centuries Cyprus was already being visited by Polish pilgrims heading to Jerusalem, among whom were the ensign of Sieradz Jan Łaski,[3] the West Pomeranian prince Bogislaw X the Great,[4] the bishop and poet Johannes Dantiscus, a son of the castellan of Sącz Stanislav Odrowąż-Pieniążek,[5] the castellan of Cracow and grand Crown *hetman* John Tarnowski,[6] a nobleman from Greater Poland John Goryński,[7] Duke Nicolas Christopher Radziwiłł,[8] and Maurycy Paul Henik.[9]

Certainly, the visit of King Peter I of Lusignan to Cracow in 1364 and the Cypriot diplomatic mission that arrived at the court of Ladislaus Jagiello in 1432 played the most vital role for Polish–Cypriot contacts. The sojourn of King Peter I of Cyprus in Cracow is well-known. Peter I arrived in Cracow in September 1364 along with Emperor Charles IV of Luxembourg. At that time Peter I was travelling across Europe to gain support for a new crusade. He hurried to Cracow to a grand meeting of monarchs and princes from central Europe in 1364. King Casimir III the Great of Poland played the role of a mediator in the conflict between Emperor Charles IV and King Louis I of Hungary. King Peter, during his visit to Cracow, raised the issue of the situation of Christians in the East and called for the initiation of a new crusade against the Muslims. Emperor Charles IV officially repeated his declaration of support for this cause, promising to call a meeting of princes and electors of the Reich and to summon his vassals by letter to take part in the crusade.

---

[3] *Spominki o Łaskich 1392–1515* [Reminiscences on the Łaski family 1392–1515], ed. Aleksander Hieschberg, Monumenta Poloniae Historica 3 (Lvov, 1878), pp. 265–66 (see Appendix 4). Jan Łaski stayed in the island around 1450 and lost his sight during his sojourn in Nicosia.

[4] Edward Rymar, *Wielka podróż wielkiego księcia. Wyprawa Bogusława X Pomorskiego na niemiecki dwór królewski, do Ziemi Świętej i Rzymu (1496–1498)* [Great journey of a great king. The expedition of Bogusław X the Pomeranian to the German court, Holy Land and Rome] (Stettin, 2004), pp. 119–20. Prince Bogislav reached Cyprus in July 1496 and stayed on the island for six days.

[5] Jacek Knopka, *Polacy w Grecji. Historia i współczesność* [The Poles in Greece. A history to the present day] (Bydgoszcz, 1997), p. 5. Stanislav Odrowąż-Pieniążek, a son of the castellan of Sącz, born in Krużlowa, died while travelling by sea to the Levant and was buried in Cyprus in 1509.

[6] Kazimierz Hartleb, "Najstarszy dziennik podróży do Ziemi Św. i Syrii Jana Tarnowskiego" [The oldest travel journal to the Holy Land and Syria of Jan Tarnowski], *Kwartalnik Historyczny* 44 (1930), 26–44. In his paper the author published fragments of *Ad ingenuum adolescentem Constantem Alliopagum carmen: Terminatio ex itinerario*. John Tarnowski visited Cyprus in 1517.

[7] Waldemar Baranowski, *Prace do badań nad historią literatury i oświaty: Peregrynacja do Ziemi Świętej Jana Goryńskiego* [Works for the research on the history of literature and education: Jan Goryński's peregrination to the Holy Land], 1 (Warsaw, 1914), p. 263. John Goryński stayed on the island in around 1560.

[8] Mikołaj Krzysztof Radziwiłł, *Podróż do Ziemi Świętej, Syrii i Egiptu (1582–84)* [Journey to the Holy Land, Syria and Egypt] (Warsaw, 1962), pp. 51–52. Nicolas Christopher Radziwiłł set off from Poland in 1582 on a pilgrimage to the Holy Land and during it he stayed in Cyprus twice.

[9] Knopka, *Polacy w Grecji. Historia i współczesność*, p. 5. Maurycy Paul Henik, having visited Italy in April 1585 headed for Venice through Zante, Crete, Cyprus and Tripoli to Palestine. For many years he was a courtier to Martin Cromer.

King Louis I of Hungary, King of Poland Casimir III the Great and all dukes taking part in the congress also expressed support for the crusade.[10]

A result of the crusade policy of Peter I and his journey across Europe was the sacking of Alexandria in October 1365. After a few days of pillaging and plundering, Christian troops, loaded with rich loot, departed from the totally devastated city. The successive rulers of Egypt could not forget the insult committed by the king of Cyprus and could not forgive the cruelty done to the citizens of Alexandria by the crusaders.[11]

In the following years the Mamluks' major problem was a pirate fleet operating from Cyprus, made up of Catalonians and supported by the ruler of the island. In response to its operations in 1426 the Mamluks attacked Cyprus and after the battle of Chirokitia on 7 July, Janus of Lusignan, the ruler of the island, was taken captive. Sultan Barsbay granted the act of pardon and made peace with Janus and agreed, on certain conditions, to give him his freedom for the price of 200,000 ducats. A half of this sum was to be paid before setting Janus free, the other half after he made it to the island. The kingdom of Cyprus was additionally obliged to pay an annual tribute of 5,000 ducats and made to submit to the command of the sultan who was officially made vice-king of Cyprus. Apart from that, Cyprus was obliged to deliver wheat and barley to Egypt annually. Catalan pirates were also forbidden from using the island as their base of operations.[12] However, King Janus was determined to get back his sovereignty. He decided to seek support against the Mamluks among his co-religionists in western Europe. Unfortunately, the envoys sent to the pope, emperor and various Italian rulers failed to secure a positive outcome for their efforts. But the most unusual Cypriot mission in this period was a delegation that arrived at the

[10] Joannes Dlugossii, *Annales seu Cronicae incliti Regni Poloniae*, 9 (Warsaw, 1978), p. 318; Stanisław Szczur, "Krakowski zjazd monarchów w 1364 roku" [Cracow convention of monarchs in 1364], *Roczniki Historyczne* 64 (1998), 36, 55; Roman Grodecki, *Kongres krakowski w roku 1364* [Cracow congress in 1364] (Cracow, 1995), pp. 20–21, 56, 60–67, 69; Henryk Pachoński, *Dwa zjazdy krakowskie za Kazimierza Wielkiego* [Two Cracow conventions during the ruling of Casimir the Great] (Cracow, 1914), pp. 13–20; Guillaume de Machaut, *The Capture of Alexandria*, trans. Janet Shirley, introduction and notes by Peter W. Edbury (Aldershot, 2001), pp. 43–47; Jan Szlachtowski, *Joannis de Czarnkow Chronicon Polonorum, 1333–1384*, ed. Adam Bielowski, Monumenta Poloniae Historica 2 (Lvov, 1872), pp. 630–31; *Rocznik świętokrzyski* [Świętokrzyski Annals], ed. Adam Bielowski, Monumenta Poloniae Historica 3, p. 80.

[11] See on all this most recently Peter W. Edbury, "The Crusading Policy of King Peter I of Cyprus, 1359–1369," in *The Eastern Mediterranean Lands in the Period of the Crusades*, ed. P. M. Holt (Warminster, 1977), p. 99; Peter W. Edbury, *The Kingdom of Cyprus and the Crusades, 1191–1374* (Cambridge, 1991), pp. 170–71.

[12] See on all this most recently Peter W. Edbury, *The Lusignan Kingdom of Cyprus and its Muslim Neighbours* (Nicosia, 1993), pp. 7–8; Edbury, "The Crusading Policy," p. 99; Edbury, *The Kingdom of Cyprus*, pp. 170–71; Nicholas Coureas, "Trade between Cyprus and the Mamluk Lands in the Fifteenth Century, with special reference to Nicosia and Famagusta," in *Egypt and Syria in the Fatimid, Ayyubid and Mamluk Eras*, 5, ed. Urbain Vermeulen and Karl d'Hulster, Orientalia Lovaniensia Analecta 169 (Leuven, 2007), p. 421; Nicholas Coureas, "Apple of Concord: The Great Powers and Cyprus, 400–1960," Κυπριακαί Σπουδαί 67–68 (Nicosia, 2005), 452–53; Nicholas Coureas, "The Influence of the Kingdom of Aragon in Cyprus, Rhodes, Latin Greece and Mamluk Egypt during the Later Middle Ages, 1276–1479," in Κυπριακαί Σπουδαί, Τόμος ΞΒ´-ΞΓ´ 1998–1999, (Nicosia, 2000), 221.

court of Ladislaus Jagiello in 1432. It is still a comparatively unknown episode in the history of Polish–Cypriot contacts.[13]

In March 1432, a group of envoys from the king of Cyprus, Janus of Lusignan, reached Wiślica, a town situated half way between the capital of Poland – Cracow – and Sandomierz.[14] At the time King Ladislaus Jagiello resided in Wiślica. The group comprised 200 people and its leaders were the titular marshal of the kingdom of Jerusalem and a participant of the battle of Chirokitia, Baldwin (Badin) of Norès[15] – *Regni Cypri Marsalcus*[16] – and his two sons. Baldwin was a member of the Norès family who had been royal vassals in Cyprus from 1217 onwards. His ancestors had a very important position in the Cypriot court and were marshals of Cyprus and titular marshals of the kingdom of Jerusalem; he was thus regarded as a trusted (and trustworthy) king's man. Among the envoys was also Peter of Bnin, a knight of Polish origin, who had settled in Cyprus while on his journey across the Levant. Thanks to his skills and, as Jan Dlugosz reports, his wit, he was held in high regard by King Janus.[17] The powers given by King Janus suggested that the person who was supposed to be the leader of the envoys was Marcellus – *sacrae theologiae doctor dominus magister Marcellus, confessor et secretarius noster*[18] – a doctor of theology and the king's confessor and secretary.[19] However, Johannes Dlugossius does not mention him among the envoys from Cyprus that arrived in Wiślica. Marcellus may not have reached Poland or else our source did not distinguish him from the other delegates.

[13] Sir George Hill mentioned this episode in his monumental work *A History of Cyprus*, 2 (Cambridge, 1948), p. 494, but he described only the fact that the Cypriot mission was sent to the Polish kingdom without any explanation. Moreover, he mentioned only some of the Polish sources.

[14] Joannes Dlugossii, *Historiae Polonicae*, 11, in *Opera Omnia*, ed. Adam Przeździecki, 13 (Cracow, 1867), p. 477; Joannes Dlugossii, *Annales seu Cronicae incliti regni poloniae liber undecimus et liber duodecimos 1431–1444* (Warsaw, 2001), pp. 62–63 (see Appendix 3); Matthias de Mechovia, *Chronica Polonorum* (Cracow, 1521), 4.52, p. 299.

[15] Martin Cromer, *Polonia: siue de origine et rebus gestis Polonorum libri XXX* (Cologne, 1586), pp. 306–7; Maciej Stryjkowski, *Kronika Macieja Stryjkowskiego niegdyś w Królewcu drukowana* [Chronicles of Maciej Stryjkowski printed in Konigsberg] (Warsaw, 1766), ch. 16, p. 543; Matthias de Mechovia, *Chronica Polonorum*, 4.52, p. 299; Hill, *History of Cyprus*, 2:494. On 13 January 1433, Baldwin of Norès, writing to Rome to Amadeus of Sabaudia, mentioned the fact that he was earlier in Poland.

[16] Joannes Dlugossii, *Historiae Polonicae*, 11, p. 477.

[17] Joannes Dlugossii, *Historiae Polonicae*, 11, p. 477; Matthias de Mechovia, *Chronica Polonorum*, 4.52, p. 299; Stryjkowski, *Kronika Macieja Stryjkowskiego*, p. 543; Cromer, *Polonia*, pp. 306–7; Łukasz Gołębiewski, *Panowanie Władysława Jagiełły* [The Reign of Ladislaus Jagiello] (Warsaw, 1846), p. 380; *Herbarz Polski Kaspra Niesieckiego S.J., powiększony dodatkami z późniejszych autorów, rękopisów, dowodów urzędowych i wydany przez Jana Nep. Bobrowicza* [Armorial of Poland by Kasper Niesiecki S.J., expanded by later authors, manuscripts, official documents and published by Jan Nep. Bobrowicz], 2 (Lipsk, 1839), p. 257.

[18] *Codex epistolaris saeculi decimi quinti, tomus I: 1384–1492*, ed. August Sokołowski and Joseph Szujski, pars 1, 1384–1444, Monumenta Medii Ævi Historica res Gestas Poloniae Illustrantia 2 (Cracow, 1876), letter 76, p. 72 (see Appendix 1).

[19] Leontios Makhairas, *Recital Concerning the Sweet Land of Cyprus Entitled "Chronicle"*, ed. and trans. R. M. Dawkins, 2 vols. (Oxford, 1932), 1:§705; Hill, *History of Cyprus*, 2:494.

The letter of 2 January 1432 from the king of Cyprus to the Polish king contains several essential details. First of all, Janus of Lusignan underlines his position by calling himself the king of Armenia, Jerusalem and Cyprus. He wanted to present the importance of his position and, furthermore, he made reference in his letter to the king of Denmark, who already enjoyed a close relationship with the king of Poland. These statements served to enhance the position of the kingdom of Cyprus at the Polish court.

The envoys of King Janus, having left Cyprus and probably stopping in Rhodes, and crossing *Mare Leontium*, the Black Sea, reached the port of *Alba Regalis* – Białogród[20] – in Wallachia. Immediately after disembarking they bought the horses necessary to cover the route further into Poland. The journey through Wallachia and Moldavia, a wild and hostile country, was not easy. The envoys suffered a lot of adversity but, owing to the Wallachians' fear of revenge from the king of Poland, evaded death.[21] Finally, by travelling through Russia, they reached Wiślica, where Jagiello was in residence.[22]

In Wiślica, the Cypriot delegation was given a warm welcome by King Ladislaus Jagiello of Poland. The marshal of the kingdom of Jerusalem, Baldwin of Norès, handed over gifts on behalf of his ruler to King Ladislaus and Queen Sophia and other high-ranking royal dignitaries. Among them were cloths in various colours, an aloe tree, perfumes and, as reported by Johannes Dlugossius, some aromatic twigs emitting a pleasant fragrance. The marshal presented them with a report on the situation of the kingdom of Cyprus after the invasion of the Mamluk sultan in 1426.[23] He described the defeat and capture of King Janus and his son by the sultan of Egypt in great detail. The king had only regained his freedom after he declared his dependence on Egypt and obliged himself to pay an annual tribute of, as stated by Johannes Dlugossius, 50,000 florins.[24]

On behalf of his king, Baldwin of Norès passed a request to King Ladislaus Jagiello to grant a loan of 200,000 florins. With this loan, the king of Cyprus would be able to hire an army and clear his name of the shame caused to Christendom by the sultan. In exchange for this, King Janus of Lusignan offered the whole kingdom

---

[20] Andrzej Dziubiński, *Na szlakach Orientu. Handel między Polską a Imperium Osmańskim w XVI–XVIII wieku* [On the Oriental route. Trade between Poland and the Ottoman Empire] (Wroclaw, 1998), p. 11. There are also some remarks in the bibliography suggesting Polish commercial relations with Cyprus in the fourteenth and fifteenth century through the port in Białogród in the Black Sea.

[21] Joannes Dlugossii, *Historiae Polonicae*, 11, p. 477; Cromer, *Polonia*, pp. 306–7; Stanisław Sroka, "Historia Europy Środkowo-Wschodniej od XIII do połowy XV wieku" [The history of central and eastern Europe from the thirteenth to the fifteenth century], in *Wielka Historia Świata* [The great history of the world], ed. Krzysztof Baczkowski, 5 (Cracow, 2005), p. 474. In 1387, Moldavian *hospodar* Peter I paid liege homage to Hedwig and Jagiello, their successors, and the crown of Poland.

[22] Joannes Dlugossii, *Historiae Polonicae*, 11, p. 477; Makhairas, *Chronicle*, 1:§705; Hill, *History of Cyprus*, 2:494.

[23] Joannes Dlugossii, *Historiae Polonicae*, 11, pp. 477–78; Hill, *History of Cyprus*, 2:494; Makhairas, *Chronicle*, 1:§705.

[24] Joannes Dlugossii, *Historiae Polonicae*, 11, p. 478; Matthias de Mechovia, *Chronica Polonorum*, 4.52, p. 299.

of Cyprus as a pledge. Ladislaus Jagiello, before the loan had been repaid, was to have two out of three votes in all questions concerning the island and receive two-thirds of all the profit made in the kingdom of Cyprus. To cement the agreement King Janus asked for his only son John[25] to marry Jagiello's daughter, Hedwig.[26]

The king of Poland conferred with his advisers on the proposal of the ruler of Cyprus. As reported by Johannes Dlugossius, Ladislaus Jagiello answered that he would be eager to help King Janus, and not only with his army, but also with financial support, were it not that his country was in such close proximity to the Tatars, who he claimed were the most barbaric of all the nations that the world had seen and he had to constantly fight with them. He also said that he could not give the hand of his daughter to the son of Janus of Lusignan because his daughter had died some months earlier.[27] He added, however, that had she been alive, she would definitely have agreed to marry such a magnificent heir to the throne. Jagiello also expressed regret as to the events that had befallen the island and King Janus himself. He also asked for the king of Cyprus not to bear a grudge against him for not granting him the loan as he himself had had to make considerable financial outlays to pay for the war with the Tatars. He added that it would be wrong to support a foreign kingdom while not satisfying the needs of one's own.[28]

Marshal Baldwin accepted Jagiello's answer. At the same time, he did not hide the joy of having received so many precious gifts, expensive vessels and furs. Moreover, all the envoys were also given generous gifts, including drinking vessels, clothes and horses. Delighted, they decided not to take the shorter, more dangerous route through Wallachia and headed for Venice where they departed for Cyprus.[29]

Jagiello was unable to undertake the long and dangerous journey to Cyprus owing to serious problems in Lithuania. The brother of the Polish king, Świdrygiello, who was grand duke of Lithuania, and aspired toward complete independence, made an alliance in the summer of 1431, supported by Sigismund of Luxembourg, with the Teutonic knights and Moldavia against Poland. Though the danger of conflict was avoided in 1434, Jagiello could not leave his country before then.[30]

The news of the visit of the Cypriot delegation in Wiślica reached Rome from where, on 8 May 1432, a prosecutor of the Teutonic Order sent information to the

---

[25] Sir George Hill, *A History of Cyprus*, 3 (Cambridge, 1948), pp. 497–547.

[26] Joannes Dlugossii, *Historiae Polonicae*, 11, p. 478; Hill, *History of Cyprus*, 2:494; Cromer, *Polonia*, pp. 306–7; Stryjkowski, *Kronika Macieja Stryjkowskiego*, p. 543; Matthias de Mechovia, *Chronica Polonorum*, 4.52, p. 299; Makhairas, *Chronicle*, 1:§705; *Herbarz Polski*, 2, p. 257; Gołębiewski, *Panowanie*, p. 381.

[27] Krzysztof Baczkowski, "Dzieje Polski późnośredniowiecznej (1370–1506)" [History of Poland in the late Middle Ages], in *Wielka Historia Polski* [The great history of Poland], ed. Stanisław Grodziski, Jerzy Wyrozumski and Marian Zgórniak, 2 (Cracow, 2003), pp. 121, 126–28. Hedwig died on 8 December 1431.

[28] Joannes Dlugossii, *Historiae Polonicae*, 11, p. 478; Stryjkowski, *Kronika Macieja Stryjkowskiego*, p. 543; Hill, *History of Cyprus*, 2:494; Makhairas, *Chronicle*, 1:§705; Gołębiewski, *Panowanie*, p. 381.

[29] Joannes Dlugossii, *Historiae Polonicae*, 11, pp. 478–79; Hill, *History of Cyprus*, 2:494; Makhairas, *Chronicle*, 1:§705; Gołębiewski, *Panowanie*, pp. 381–82.

[30] Baczkowski, *Dzieje Polski*, pp. 135–37; Gołębiewski, *Panowanie*, p. 382.

grand master, inaccurately reporting that the Poles had made a pact with Venice and the kingdom of Cyprus.[31]

In 1431, Janus had suffered a stroke which resulted in his complete paralysis. On 10 June 1432, he had another stroke from which he never recovered and he died on 28 or 29 June and probably never saw the return of the envoys from Poland. He was buried on 29 June in a Dominican church in Nicosia.[32]

The most important question that needs to be addressed about this episode is why the kingdom of Cyprus decided to send a mission to Poland in the first place. Was the position of Poland in the second decade of the fifteenth century so important that it was seen to offer a suitable ally for the Cypriots?

The reasons why the king of Cyprus chose Poland as his potential ally and decided to send his delegation are interesting. Peter of Bnin, mentioned earlier, who was one of the envoys and probably served as a guide and translator, came from the Bniński family, who were arms-bearing Łodzia and had properties mostly in Bnin – a place from which his house took its name – and in Łódź Poznańska.[33] Boniecki's *Armorial of Poland* mentions Peter of Bnin who was castellan of Gniezno and gave rise to numerous noble houses.[34] On the other hand, Żychliński reports that, apart from the office of castellan of Gniezno, from 1439 he was also castellan of Poznań, which suggests that he returned from Cyprus to Poland.[35] A curious copy of a document from *Wyciąg z Ksiąg Sądu Głównego Gubernji Wołyńskiej Departamentu Cywilnego* [Excerpt from the Books of Major Court of Wołyń Province of the Civil Department] (original spelling) issued by King Casimir III the Great to Peter of Bnin, son of King John of Cyprus (*sic*), is mentioned by Bobrowicz in *Polish Armorial by Kasper Niesiecki*.[36] At the same time, he adds that Niesiecki mentions Peter of Bnin elsewhere in his work and he is not mentioned as the son of the ruler of Cyprus but "being called not his son, but also someone being with great graces with Janus." Further, he describes Peter as castellan of Gniezno in 1433 and adds that he later became castellan of Poznań. He also emphasizes the fact that he was a Polish envoy during Emperor Sigismund's clash with the Teutonic Order.[37]

---

[31] *Codex epistolaris saeculi decimi quinti, tomus III: 1392–1501*, ed. Anatol Lewicki, Monumenta Medii Ævi Historica res Gestas Poloniae Illustrantia 14 (Cracow, 1894), letter 12, p. 518 (see Appendix 2).

[32] Hill, *History of Cyprus*, 2:491, 495.

[33] *Polska Encyklopedia Szlachecka* [Polish gentry encyclopaedia], ed. Stefan J. Starykoń-Kasprzycki and Michał Dmowski, 8 (Warsaw, 1937), p. 66.

[34] *Herbarz Polski. Wiadomości historyczno-genealogiczne o rodach szlacheckich* [Armorial of Poland. Historical and genealogical information on noble families], ed. Adam Boniecki (Warsaw, 1899), pp. 294–95.

[35] *Złota księga Szlachty Polskiej przez T. Żychlińskiego* [Golden book of the Polish gentry by T. Żychliński] (Posen, 1879), pp. 2–3.

[36] *Herbarz Polski*, pp. 171–72 (see Appendix 5). Any information about Piotr of Bnin that is contained in the work of Niesiecki is the result of misunderstanding. It is impossible that Piotr of Bnin was a son of the king of Cyprus.

[37] *Herbarz Polski*, pp. 256–57.

It is most likely that Peter of Bnin travelled through the Levant and settled in Cyprus at some point in the late 1420s. He was probably influential within the royal court at Nicosia, which enabled him to persuade King Janus to address his request to King Ladislaus Jagiello, who, having defeated the Teutonic Order in 1410, had become one of the most powerful rulers in Europe.

The council of Constance (1414–18) that discussed numerous international conflicts may have been the place where members of the Polish delegation met with representatives of the king of Cyprus, since they were present during the deliberations. At that time, the Cypriot envoys may have heard about the Polish and Teutonic diplomatic and propaganda struggle which echoed anew in the surroundings of the ruler of Cyprus late in the 1420s.[38] The Polish direction could be prompted by the brother of Janus, Hugh of Lusignan, archbishop of Nicosia and generally known as the cardinal of Cyprus. Hugh was made cardinal in May 1426 and received the deaconry of S. Adriano. He was the regent of Cyprus during the Egyptian captivity of his brother from July 1426 until May 1427. In 1431, Janus had a stroke and was paralyzed from head to foot. At that time the cardinal of Cyprus, Hugh of Lusignan, sent several envoys to the pope, the emperor and the various Italian rulers, asking for a loan.[39] During his search for help he chose Poland as a destination for one of his envoys. Probably, he did it because of his experience at the council in Constance and the position of Poland, which was a strong kingdom in Europe after the victory at Grunwald in 1410. The cardinal of Cyprus sent a letter, dated August 1434 in Basle, to King Ladislaus III of Varna in which the clergyman expressed condolences for Jagiello's death.[40]

On the other hand, between 1424 and 1425 the king of the Kalmar Union (Denmark, Norway, Sweden), Eric VII, made a pilgrimage to the Holy Land, and on his way visited Cyprus. During his visit he probably passed on to Janus information about the ruler of Poland and the alliance they had entered into in 1419. It is likely that the subject of the talks was also the Grunwald victory of King Jagiello. Moreover, in the letter of King Janus to the Polish king dated 2 January 1432 where he offers his mission, he mentions being acquainted with the king of Denmark, though it was Eric whom he had in mind.[41]

---

[38]   Danuta Quirini-Popławska, "Italia i basen Morza Śródziemnego w latach 1204–1453" [Italy and the Mediterranean area], in *Wielka Historia Świata* 5:163; Baczkowski, *Dzieje Polski*, p. 111; Krzysztof Baczkowski, "Cesarstwo rzymsko-niemieckie od początków XIII do połowy XV wieku" [The Roman and German Empire from the beginnings of the thirteenth until the middle of the fifteenth century], in *Wielka Historia Świata* 5:398.

[39]   Hill, *History of Cyprus*, 2:482–83, 486, 493.

[40]   *Codex epistolaris saeculi decimi quinti, tomus II: 1382–1445*, ed. Anatol Lewicki, Monumenta Medii Ævi Historica res Gestas Poloniae Illustrantia 12 (Cracow, 1891), letter 223, pp. 332–33 (Copy in Kórnik code 194, 11.68, pp. 386–87. Inscription: Cardinalis Cipri Regi Polonie).

[41]   Anna Waśko, "Region bałtycki od XIII do połowy XV wieku" [The Baltic area from the thirteenth until the mid-fifteenth century], in *Wielka Historia Świata* 5:518; Baczkowski, *Dzieje Polski*, pp. 117, 126–28. See Heinz Barüske, *Erich von Pommern: ein nordischer König aus dem Greifengeschlecht* (Rostock, 1997); Janus Møller Jensen, *Denmark and the Crusades, 1400–1650* (Leiden, 2007). The pilgrimage of Eric to the Holy Land happened in the following stages: he left Denmark in August 1423,

Hedwig (1408–31), the daughter of Ladislaus Jagiello and Anna of Celje, was meant to be married to Frederick Hohenzollern, son of the margrave of Brandenburg.[42] In 1413, she was accepted as heir to the Polish crown. In 1421, an arrangement in Cracow was made which stated that, if Jagiello died without leaving a son, Frederick, as Hedwig's husband, should ascend to the throne of Poland.[43] There were also other stipulations for marrying the heiress to Prince Bogislaw IX of Słupsk who was designated to become the heir to the throne of Denmark, Sweden and Norway after the death of Eric VII (ca. 1382–1459).[44]

On the other hand, in Cyprus, especially among the advisers who surrounded the king, the memory of the visit of King Peter I of Lusignan in 1364 was particularly vivid. The chancellor of King Peter, Philippe de Mézières himself, the founder of the Order of Knighthood of the Passion of Christ, was certain of Poland's mission to defend Christian civilization.[45]

What did the king of Cyprus expect to get by his mission to Poland, which was surely very expensive for his kingdom? To anticipate military assistance from Poland was fantasy, but some kind of loan was more likely, because from the Cypriot point of view the kingdom of Poland was a strong state with a well-filled treasury. The king of Cyprus had heard about the Grunwald victory, but he did not know that Poland had problems with the Tatars and in Lithuania. However, the most significant aspect of the Cypriot mission to the Polish court was in relation to a matrimonial matter. The Cypriot–Polish marriage could have raised the international position of Cyprus. It was no secret that the rulers of the kingdom of Cyprus were looking for a good matrimonial candidate in a European royal house, and in making overtures to Poland Janus of Lusignan was trying to connect his state with one of the most powerful kingdoms in Europe.

The important source of knowledge of the Polish situation was the king of the Kalmar Union, Eric VII, who was in Cyprus between 1424 and 1425 during his pilgrimage to the Holy Land. He talked the situation in Europe over with the king of Cyprus and told him about negotiations with the kingdom of Poland for marrying his cousin, the prince of Słupsk Bogislaw IX, with Hedwig, daughter of the Polish king. This union failed, because Hedwig was later betrothed with Frederick of Hohenzollern, but the information that she was a successor to the Polish throne was

---

and travelled through Gorzów Wlkp. (Landsberg), Szczecin, Stargard and Słupsk (Stolpe), reaching Cracow in January 1424; from there he went to Budapest and then to Venice whence he sailed to Palestine via Cyprus.

[42] Marceli Kosman, *Władysław Jagiełło* [Ladislaus Jagiello] (Warsaw, 1968), pp. 278–80: Frederick I Hohenzollern (1371–1440), originally the burgrave of Nuremberg, for supporting Sigismund of Luxembourg he was granted Brandenburg to hold in fee, in 1417 the title of elector, his son was to become Hedwig Jagiełłówna's husband and in the future the king of Poland.

[43] Jerzy Krzyżaniakowa and Jadwiga Ochmański, *Władysław II Jagiełło* [Ladislaus II Jagiello] (Wrocław, 1990), pp. 259–61.

[44] Kosman, *Władysław Jagiełło*, p. 278; Krzyżaniakowa and Ochmański, *Władysław II Jagiełło*, pp. 277–78.

[45] Głodek, *Utopia Europy*, pp. 122, 133–35.

remembered by the king of Cyprus. Though she lost her position as successor after the birth of Ladislaus Jagiello's sons, she was still a very attractive candidate as a wife for the heir of the Cypriot throne. The confirmation of a familiarity between the rulers of Denmark and Cyprus is found in the letter of 2 January 1432, in which Janus of Lusignan mentioned his acquaintance with Eric VII.

Appendix 1

Codex epistolaris saeculi decimi quinti, tomus I: 1384–1492, ed. August Sokołowski and Joseph Szujski, pars 1: ab anno 1384 ad annum 1444, Monumenta Medii Ævi Historica res Gestas Poloniae Illustrantia 2 (Cracow, 1876), letter 76, p. 72.

Ianus Dei gratia Armeniae, Ierusalem et Cipri rex scribit domino regi Poloniae.[1]

Illustrissime et excelse princeps, domine maior et frater inclite. Satis et multum dudum cum ad nostram frequentem devenisset notitiam, quantis qualibusque virtutum oraculis vestram summus omnipotens decoravit regiam dignitatem, totis conatibus anhelamus in vestrae amicitiae necessitudinem devenire, si quando fata ex superis comodum et facultatem nostris optatibus contribuerunt, ut tanto ingenti spatio remotos aliqua causa contingerit opportuna. Audiveramus namque vestram excellentiam regiam ad sancti sepulcri limina navigaturam, quam galleris et navibus et maxima ex regno nostro navali classe honoraturam sperantes, iuxta condecenciam vestrae regiae maiestatis volebamus summo cum desiderio vobis letissime obviare atque occurrere. Sed cum ad has partes vidimus illustrissimum fratrem nostrum, dominum Henricum Daciae regem adventurum frustratos nos esse desiderio nostro persensimus. Verum quia nuper de nostro mandato pro executione apostolicae bullae in subsidium terrae sanctae emanatae, cum quibusdam sacratissimis reliquiis ad praesentiam V. S.. praeclarus et honorandus artium liberalium et sacrae theologiae doctor dominus magister Marcellus, confessor et secretarius noster in partibus Ierosolimitanis, sedis apostolicae commissarius destinatur, statuimus pro nostri desiderii executione ipsum et vestram illustritatem cum deportatione ambasiatae nostrae constituere nostri parte publice et occulte referendum vestrae maiestati cui universa, quae duxerit requirendum sincere et fideliter propalare poteritis. Sciendum nos totis praecordiis paratos esse et intentos ad omnia, quae vestrae excellentiae grata fore sciverimus pariter et accepta. Datum Nychoszije Cipri die secunda Ianuarii millesimo CCCCXXXII.

---

[1] After the death of the last king of Armenia, Leo V of Lusignan (d. 1393), his title was claimed by his distant cousin James of Lusignan, the king of Cyprus. The territory then controlled by Cypriots and Armenians was limited to the fortress of Korykos, which was finally captured by the Turks in 1448. This title was alive until the reign of Charlotte of Lusignan (r. 1458–64) and it was used by King Janus in his letter to the king of Poland.

Appendix 2

Codex epistolaris saeculi decimi quinti, tomus III: 1392–1501, ed. Anatol Lewicki, Monumenta Medii Ævi Historica res Gestas Poloniae Illustrantia 14 (Cracow, 1894), letter 12, p. 518.

Meinen demutigen willigen gehorsam czuvor. Erwirdiger gnediger liber herre homeister. Als ich euwern gnoden vor geschreiben habe by Kale Iacob, wy dy Polen fruntschafft suchen wo sy mogen, unde vorumme das sy sich mit den Venedigern haben vorbunden etc., nu haben sy ouch fruntschafft gesucht mit dem konige von Cypry, welches sone der konig us Polen seine tochtir hat vorloubet; unde der konig us Cypry alreit eine galeie hat gesant wol angericht kein Venedic, in der man des konigs tochtir us Polen brengen solde, als mir denne der cardinal us Cypry selbis hat gesaget. Unde wy dy Polen haben vorgegeben, wy das konigreich von Polen mit derselben tochtir entlich komen mochte an des koniges son von Cypry, wenne sy ein recht erbe czum konigreiche were, grose gobin unde kostlichkeit sy mit yr haben geloubet. Nuwelich so hat Lanczisky dem obgenanten cardinal us Cypry alhir vorkundiget den tot des konigis tochtir us Polen, den der konig us Cypry noch nicht weis. Sunder der cardinal us Cypry hat an suwmen brife geschreiben noch der galeie kein Venedic, ab sy noch do were, das sy wedir keren solle. Ich habe den obgenanten cardinal alhir undirrichtet, wy dy selbe konigis tochtir us Polen were vorloubet des margkraffen son von Brandeburg, der manch ior in dem konigreich czu Polen ist vorhalden; ouch wy sy were vorloubet gewest dem herczoge us Pomern; unde dese hinderlist der Polen misseful sere dem obgenanten cardinal us Cypry, wenne her des selben konigs bruder ist us Cypry. Euwer gnode bevele ich dem almechtigen gote, der sy geruche langeczeit czu enthalden. Gegeben czu Rome, am VIII. tage maii, anno domini etc. XXXII.

Obirster procurator
dutsches ordens.

Appendix 3

Joannis Dlugossii seu Longini canonici Cracoviensis Historiae Polonicae, 11, in *Joannis Długosz canonici Cracoviensis Opera Omnia*, ed. Adam Przeździecki, 13 (Cracow, 1867), pp. 477–79 [or Joannes Dlugossii, *Annales seu Cronicae incliti regni Poloniae liber undecimus et liber duodecimus 1431–1444* (Warsaw, 2001), pp. 62–63].[46]

Ianus Hierusalem, Cyprique Rex, apud Wladislaum Poloniae Regem per legatos cladem Cypri per Soldanum factam exponit, petens sub certis conditionibus subsidium.

Stante Wladislao Rege in Vislicia, venit ad suam Serenitatem ambasiata notabilis Iani, Hierusalem, Cypri et Armeniae Regis, Baldwinus de Noris Regni Cypri Marsalcus, miles insignis, habens in comitiva sua ducentos equites; inter quos erant duo filii sui, adolescentes pulcherrimi, et Petrus de Bnino Polonus natione, miles, qui maiori animo, quam fortunae suae conveniebat, usurus, in Cyprum perveniens et incolatum suum illic figens, celebris et favore regio propter altius ingenium et factivitatem habebatur. Ambasiata ipsa, galea propria per mare Leoninum vecta, in Alba Rogali, in Valachia portum cepit; exinde equis coemptis, per Valachiam (ubi multa horrenda sustinuit a populo scelerato et inculto facinora, et nisi Wladislaum Regem expavisset, prope caedes aderat) in Russiam et Poloniam pervenit. Excepta est cum omni maiestate et honore per Wladislaum Regem, et omnia necessaria copiose administrata. Ipse Baldwinus Marsalcus, praesentatis Wladislao Regi, Sophiae Reginae, Praelatis, Principibus et optimatibus suis, nomine Iani Regis Cypri, satis notabilibus muneribus, flaminibus videlicet subtilibus varii coloris de Czamletho, lignum aloes, aromata pretiosa et virgulas quasdam odoriferas, fumum suavem spirantes, legationem suam, obtenta audientia, orditus, commemoravit vulnus gravissimum Regni Cypri et cladem per Soldanum Babyloniae habitam, qui Anno Domini Millesimo quadringentesimo vicesimo sexto, cum magna suorum potentia Regnum Cypri irrumpens, ipsum Ianum sibi cum dimicatione occurrentem conflixit, et desertum a suis, cum filio captivavit. Nec aliter liberatio sua et filii sui haberi poterat, donec Rex spopondit esse Soldani tributarius, et penderet sibi pro annuo tributo florenorum millia quinquaginta. Petebat itaque: ut Wladislaus Poloniae Rex mutuaretur Iano Cypri Regi ducenta aureorum millia, cum quibus, comparatis gentibus, posset et ignominiam illatam Christianitati excutere et tributum; offerens, quasi pro vadio, Regnum universum Cypri, ita videlicet, ut Wladislaus Rex duas in illo haberet voces et duas omnium introituum portiones, tertia ipsi Iano Regi Cypri

---

[46] Jan Długosz [Joannes Dlugossii] (1415–80) was a Polish priest, chronicler, diplomat, soldier and secretary of Bishop Zbigniew Oleśnicki of Cracow. He is best known for his *Annales*, covering events in eastern Europe from 980 to 1480, which were summarized by later chroniclers such as Prince-Bishop of Warmia Martin Cromer (1512–89), Professor of Jagiellonian University Matthias de Mechovia (1457–1523) and Maciej Stryjskowski (1547–93).

relicta. Item: ut filiam suam Hedvigim, quam adhuc existimabat vivere, Wladislaus Rex Poloniae filio unico Iani Regis Cypri desponsaret in uxorem. Wladislaus autem Rex, habita super huiusmodi propositis cum Praelatis et baronibus suis deliberatione, ipsi Baldwino respondit: se quidem amplissime de omni casu et infortunio, qui Iano Regi Cypri et suo Regno, imo toti Christianitati accidit, moestum esse, et non solum pecuniis, sed et gentibus suis, ipsum relevaturum fore, pro reparando casu tam foedo et gravi, si Regnum ipsius Thartaris, fortioribus, quos habet Orbis, barbaris, confrontatum non esset, quibus resistentiam continuam suorum militum opponere cogitur, et quotidiano Marte belli ferre fortunam. Rogabat sibi non succenseri, si petitum non praestaret mutuum: magnis sibi impensis pro sustinendo bello Thartarico opus esse; neque aequum, nec iustum, Regno proprio indigente, alterius necessitatem, suo deserto et periculis exposito, supplere. Matrimonium filiae frustra peti pridem fatis exceptae; si tamen viveret, non abnuere se affinitatem tam optimi et clari Regis, et tale daturum se responsum, quo merito laetatus fuisset. Benigne Regis Wladislai responsio a Baldwino Marsalco excepta est: quippe et ipsemet intelligebat prudenter et formaliter responsum. Remissa sunt Iano Cypri Regi et filio suo in vasis pretiosis, in Schubis et pellibus, notabilia munera. Sed et ipse Baldwinus cum filiis, et omnes potioressui, liberaliter remunerati vasis, vestibus et equis, laeti in Venetias regrediebantur, exinde freto in Cyprum traiecturi, horrentes iter brevius, propter Valachorum crudelem immanitatem.

Appendix 4

Spominki o Łaskich 1392–1515 [Reminiscences on the Łaski Family 1392–1515], ed. Aleksander Hieschberg, Monumenta Poloniae Historica 3 (Lvov, 1878), pp. 265–66.

Anno vero M. quadringentesimo quinquagesimo primo, post mortem vero sue consortis mortuus est Magnificus vir Dominus Iohannes, heres in Laszko, infra Rogaciones, dominica Vocem iucunditatis. Sepultus est in sua ecclesia Laszko, ante aram maiorem sancti Michaelis, per filios suos Andream, Iohannem, Mathiam, Peregrinum, suos successores. Miles Ierosolimitanus erat; redeundo ex Ierusalem in Cipris regno, civitate Nicomedia [*sic*], ob egritudinem corporis aliquamdiu commoratus, ibidem visum oculorum morbi dolore correptus ammisit et in Laszko visu ammisso adductus, breviter mortuus atque sepultus.

Appendix 5

Herbarz Polski Kaspra Niesieckiego S.J., powiększony dodatkami z późniejszych autorów, rękopisów, dowodów urzędowych i wydany przez Jana Nep. Bobrowicza [Armorial of Poland by Kasper Niesiecki S.J., expanded by later authors, manuscripts, official documents and published by Jan Nep. Bobrowicz], 2 (Lipsk, 1839), pp. 171–72.

Actum in Castro Pyzdry feria Secunda ante festum trium Regum Anno Domini Millesimo Quadrigentesimo Secundo – Reverendus in Christo pater Joannes Roman Celsissimi Reverendissimi Commitis [sic] in Bnin Episcopi Poznaniesis Cappellanus, Officio praesenti ad acticandum Diploma Serenissimi Casimiri Tertii, communiter dicti Magnus, Regis Poloniae, in pargamine conscriptum et Sigillo Regni Munitum obtulit, tenoris sequentis:

Casimirus Tertius Dei Gratia Rex Poloniae, Dux Silesiae, Masoviae, Cujaviae, Prusiae, terrarumque Russiae Dominus, post extinctam Illustrissimam familiam Navitorum Comitum de Bnin licet hic Comitatus ad nostram voluntatem et dispositionem est adventus tamen nostrorum Comitum, Baronorum et aliorum tam spiritualis, quam secularis conditionis Magnatorum Usi Consilio hunc Comitatum Bnin cum toto illius Districtu Serenissimo Petro Joannis Regis Cypriae filio Coronae [here follows an illegible word] vero pretendenti illi et ejus Successoribus damus, et in perpetuum condonavimus, volentes ut ab omnibus redittibus Regni sit liber, tempore tamen belli (utinam nunquam incidenti) Centum pedestres armatos ad Castra nostra statuere tenebitur concedimus, etiam Serenissimo Petro modum Cudendae Pecuniae sed ut sit in valore et pondere conformus, monetae Regni nostri magnopere illum obstringimus, ad finem volumus, ut Serenissimo Petro ob omnibus Civibus incolis Regni nostri congrua exhibeatur reverentia, non tamen obedientia imo Serenissimus Petrus spondet et tenebitur ad leges Regni nostri se omnino conformare. – Datum in Residentia Civitatis nostrae Koło, feria tertia ipso die Conversionis S.. Pauli, Anno Domini Millesimo Trecentesimo Sexagesimo Quinto

Kazimierz Trzeci Król – Andreas Wilczek praepositus Cracoviensis Praefectus Cancellariae Regni. – Ex protoculo Castrensi Pyzdrensi Extractum. Cyprian Mroczyński mp.

"A poor island and an orphaned realm …, built upon a rock in the midst of the sea …, surrounded by the infidel Turks and Saracens": The Crusader Ideology in Leontios Makhairas's Greek *Chronicle* of Cyprus

Angel Nicolaou-Konnari

University of Cyprus
an.konnaris@cytanet.com.cy

Literary production in medieval and early modern Cyprus is characterized by a rich historiographical tradition, the amazing continuity, variety, and volume of which constitute a unique case in the literary history of the Latin and Ottoman-ruled Greek world. One could suggest a number of complex historical and social factors that contributed to the creation of this historiographical tradition, especially when the Cypriot case is compared to that of Venetian Crete, a comparative examination of literary production in Cyprus and Crete under Latin rule and of their respective social, cultural, and ideological context still lacking.[1] For the purpose of this study it is important to stress that the change in the languages used for the composition of these "histories" of Cyprus reflects cultural relations and linguistic evolution on the island as well as the process of the formation of ethnic identity (or identities). This "school" of history writers may be extended to encompass a corpus stretching from Neophytos the Recluse in the late twelfth–early thirteenth century to Archimandrite

---

A first version of the present study, under the title "The Crusader Ideology in the Greek Cypriot *Chronicle* of Leontios Makhairas: Holy War or National War?" was presented at the joint research conference of the Institute for Advanced Studies at the Hebrew University of Jerusalem and the Israel Science Foundation *Holy War: Past and Present. The Crusader Phenomenon and its Relevance Today*, which was organised by Sophia Menache, Judith Bronstein, and Adrian Boas (Jerusalem, 1–6 June 2008). I am grateful to the editor and two reviewers for their constructive comments, to Laura Minervini for her valuable suggestions, and to Despina Ariantzi for providing material. For the quotation in the title, see below n. 64.

[1] A comprehensive study of medieval and early modern Cypriot historiography is also still lacking. The best synthesis for the Cypriot literary production during the Frankish and Venetian periods remains Gilles Grivaud, "Ὁ πνευματικὸς βίος καὶ ἡ γραμματολογία κατὰ τὴν περίοδο τῆς Φραγκοκρατίας" ["Intellectual life and letters during the Frankish period"], in Ἱστορία τῆς Κύπρου [History of Cyprus], ed. Theodoros Papadopoullos, 5: Μεσαιωνικὸν βασίλειον – Ἐνετοκρατία [Medieval kingdom – Venetian period], part 2 (Nicosia, 1996), pp. 836–1207; and Gilles Grivaud, *Entrelacs chiprois. Essai sur les lettres et la vie intellectuelle dans le royaume de Chypre 1191–1570* (Nicosia, 2009) (revised French version); also Gilles Grivaud, "Literature," in *Cyprus. Society and Culture 1191–1374*, ed. Angel Nicolaou-Konnari and Chris Schabel, The Medieval Mediterranean 58 (Leiden and Boston, 2005), pp. 219–84 (English version for the period up to 1374). For early modern writers, see prosopographical entries in Paschalis M. Kitromilides, *Κυπριακή λογιοσύνη 1571–1878. Προσωπογραφική Θεώρηση* [Cypriot men of letters 1571–1878. A prosopographical approach], Cyprus Research Centre, Texts and Studies in the History of Cyprus 42 (Nicosia, 2002).

Kyprianos in the eighteenth, including Latin Eastern chroniclers of the thirteenth century and Cypriots of the diaspora in the seventeenth.[2] In the fifteenth century, the composition of the important chronicle attributed to Leontios Makhairas, a dynastic history of the Lusignan rule of Cyprus written in the local Greek dialect, constitutes a major landmark in the island's historiographical production.[3] I have argued elsewhere that Makhairas's text reveals a "Cypriot" and not a "Latin Eastern crusader" ideology.[4] This article aims at investigating further the way the notion of the crusades and holy war is perceived in the chronicle, something which inevitably raises many issues related to the expression of political ideology, ethnic identity, and culture conflict in the text.

The chronicle recounts the history of Cyprus from the fourth-century visit of St. Helena to the island to the death of King John II of Lusignan (1432–58) in 1458, its focus lying on the reigns of Peter I (1359–69) and Peter II (1369–82). It survives in three manuscripts that were copied in the sixteenth century and preserve two recensions: the codex of the Biblioteca Nazionale Marciana in Venice (= MS Ven. Marc. gr. VII, 16, 1080, hereafter cited as V), datable to after 1523, contains the oldest and longest text and the only one that includes first-person references to Makhairas and his family; the manuscripts of the Bodleian Library in Oxford (= MS

---

[2] On the necessity to study medieval Cypriot literature in a global way to include works in Greek, French, and Italian and reveal literary exchanges, see generally Grivaud, "Intellectual Life and Letters," pp. 866–68, 947–49, 960–61, and Angel Nicolaou-Konnari, "Literary Languages in the Lusignan Kingdom of Cyprus in the Thirteenth Century," Μολυβδο-κονδυλο-πελεκητής [Molyvdo-kondylo-pelekitis] 7 (2000), 7–27. For the historicity of Neophytos's theological works, see Catia Galatariotou, *The Making of a Saint. The Life, Times and Sanctification of Neophytos the Recluse* (Cambridge, 1991), part 3, passim, and Angel Nicolaou-Konnari, "The Conquest of Cyprus by Richard the Lionheart and Its Aftermath: A Study of Sources and Legend, Politics and Attitudes in the Year 1191–1192," Επετηρίδα Κέντρου Επιστημονικών Ερευνών (Κύπρου) [Cyprus Research Centre Annual Review] 26 (2000), 25–123, passim; for Latin Eastern chroniclers, see below; for Kyprianos, see Kitromilides, *Cypriot Men of Letters*, pp. 174–77; for seventeenth and eighteenth-century authors, see ibid., passim, and below, n. 7, on Pietro and Giorgio de Nores.

[3] For a useful annotated bibliography of the chronicle, see Michalis Pieris and Angel Nicolaou-Konnari, "Λεοντίου Μαχαιρά, Εξήγησις της γλυκείας χώρας Κύπρου η ποία λέγεται κρόνικα τουτέστιν χρονικόν. Βιβλιογραφικός Οδηγός" ["Leontios Makhairas, *Recital Concerning the Sweet Land of Cyprus Entitled 'Chronicle'*. An Annotated Bibliography"], Επετηρίδα Κέντρου Επιστημονικών Ερευνών (Κύπρου) [Cyprus Research Centre Annual Review] 23 (1997), 75–114; for more recent bibliography, see Michalis Pieris, "Λογοτεχνία και λογοτεχνικότητα κατά το πέρασμα της Κύπρου από τον Μεσαίωνα στην Αναγέννηση" ["Literature and literality in Cyprus in the passage from the Middle Ages to the Renaissance"], in *"La Serenissima" and "La Nobilissima": Venice in Cyprus and Cyprus in Venice*, Proceedings of the Symposium held at the Bank of Cyprus Cultural Foundation (Nicosia, 21 October 2006), ed. Angel Nicolaou-Konnari, Bank of Cyprus Cultural Foundation (Nicosia, 2009), notes 1–25 at pp. 137–40.

[4] See Angel Nicolaou-Konnari, "Diplomatics and Historiography: The Use of Documents in the *Chronicle* of Leontios Makhairas," in *Diplomatics in the Eastern Mediterranean 1000–1500: Aspects of Cross-Cultural Communication*, ed. Alexander D. Beihammer, Maria G. Parani, and Christopher D. Schabel, The Medieval Mediterranean 74 (Leiden and Boston, 2008), p. 293; see also Angel Nicolaou-Konnari, "La *Chronique* de Léontios Machéras: Historicité et identité nationale," in *Matériaux pour une histoire de Chypre (IVe–XXe s.)*, ed. Paolo Odorico, *Études Balkaniques. Cahiers Pierre Belon* 5 (1998), 55–80.

Oxon. Bodl. Selden, supra 14, hereafter cited as O), dated to the year 1555, and the Biblioteca Classense in Ravenna (= MS Raven. Class. gr. 187, hereafter cited as R), datable to ca. 1600, preserve a very similar shorter version; there also exists an Italian translation of the Ravenna text at the Biblioteca Apostolica Vaticana, commonly attributed to Diomedes Strambali (= MS Vat. lat. 3941).[5] Although complex issues concerning the authorship of and relationship between the recensions are not yet resolved, Makhairas's involvement in an early phase of the process of the creation of the chronicle is undeniable; to the extent he may be credited with the paternity of the original text (or, more likely, the V version), its composition may be placed in the second quarter of the fifteenth century, more precisely between sometime after 1426 (the last mention of Leontios and his brother Peter in the V version is in relation to the July 1426 battle of Khirokitia and its aftermath) and ca. 1432 (last known mention of Leontios in the sources), with later annalistic additions (most probably by another writer).[6]

The reconstruction of Makhairas's life and career from the sparse evidence provided mostly by the V version as well as the study of his cultural and ethnic awareness as revealed in the chronicle suggest that these were factors that had a great impact on the literary nature and ideological identity of the text. Leontios was probably born ca. 1380 (or, for some scholars, ca. 1360) and died sometime after 1432. He came from a family milieu with an apparently long tradition of serving the Frankish royal and seigneurial administration, in particular the important Nores (or

---

[5] The best critical edition remains Leontios Makhairas, *Recital Concerning the Sweet Land of Cyprus Entitled "Chronicle"*, ed. and trans. R. M. Dawkins, 2 vols. (Oxford, 1932) (hereafter cited as Makhairas, *Chronicle*), which uses only V and O; a parallel diplomatic edition of all three manuscript texts has recently been made available, see Leontios Makhairas, Χρονικό της Κύπρου. Παράλληλη διπλωματική έκδοση των χειρογράφων [Chronicle of Cyprus. Parallel diplomatic edition of the manuscripts], ed. Michalis Pieris and Angel Nicolaou-Konnari, Cyprus Research Centre, Texts and Studies in the History of Cyprus 48 (Nicosia, 2003) (hereafter cited as Makhairas, *Diplomatic Edition*). The only edition of Strambali's translation is still *Chronique de Strambaldi*, in *Chroniques d'Amadi et de Strambaldi*, 2e partie, ed. René de Mas Latrie (Paris, 1893).

[6] For the dating of the chronicle and the manuscripts, see Makhairas, *Diplomatic Edition*, pp. 26, 29, 33–34, 37; Michalis Pieris, "Γύρω από τη χρονολόγηση του Λεοντίου Μαχαιρά" ["Dating the *Chronicle* of Leontios Makhairas"], Αφιέρωμα στον Στυλιανό Αλεξίου, Αριάδνη, Επιστημονική Επετηρίδα Φιλοσοφικής Σχολής Πανεπιστημίου Κρήτης [Volume in honour of Stylianos Alexiou, Ariadne, Annual Review of the School of Letters at the University of Crete] 5 (1989), 229–54; and Angel Nicolaou-Konnari, "Η διασκευή του χειρογράφου της Ραβέννας της *Εξήγησης* του Λεοντίου Μαχαιρά και η *Narratione* του Διομήδη Strambali" ["The Ravenna Recension of the *Exegesis* of Leontios Makhairas and the *Narratione* of Diomedes Strambali"], in *"Τ' άδόνιν κείνον πού γλυκά θλιβᾶται", Εκδοτικά και ερμηνευτικά ζητήματα της δημώδους ελληνικής λογοτεχνίας στο πέρασμα από τον Μεσαίωνα στην Αναγέννηση (1400–1600)* ["That sweet-grieving nightingale," Editing and interpreting vernacular Greek literature in the passage from the Middle Ages to the Renaissance (1400–1600)], Proceedings of the Fourth International Conference *Neograeca Medii Aevi* (Nicosia, November 1997), ed. Panayiotis Agapetos and Michalis Pieris (Herakleion, 2002), pp. 287–315. On the authorship problems, see generally Grivaud, "Intellectual Life and Letters," pp. 1067–69, and Nicolaou-Konnari, "Diplomatics and Historiography," pp. 294–95. Despite the unresolved paternity issue, for reasons of convenience and understanding, Makhairas will be referred to as the author of the chronicle in this study. For references to Leontios and his family, see below, n. 8.

Norès) family.[7] Leontios was a secretary of John de Nores in 1402 and participated in the battle of Khirokitia during the Mamluk invasion in 1426, appointed by Badin de Nores as the person in charge of the wine distribution to the army; he also seems to have served the Lusignans on diplomatic missions, as attested by the French traveller Bertrandon de La Broquière who met "Lyon Maschere" in 1432 on one of his trips to Asia Minor and who says that Makhairas spoke "assés bon françois."[8] We may thus consider Leontios to have been a member of that group of bilingual or multilingual civil servants and administrators who belonged to the Greek and Syrian burgesses, had access to both the Greek and the Latin worlds participating in both cultures, and acquired social and economic prominence in virtue of their education and linguistic abilities. It seems that by the end of the fourteenth century, and following the political, social, and economic changes that resulted from Peter I's wars, his murder, and the 1373–74 Genoese invasion, feelings of ethnic identity in relation to Cyprus as a geographical and political entity had emerged amongst the particular milieu to which Makhairas belonged and the circles in which he moved, namely the wealthy educated Greek burgesses and the Frankish ruling class. This common group consciousness was also the product of two centuries of cultural interaction between Greeks and Franks and is expressed in the chronicle by the ethnic name "Κυπριώτης" (*Kypriotis*/"Cypriot"), used extensively to denote the entire population of the island, regardless of rite, origin, or social status, while language in the form of the Greek Cypriot dialect seems to have been a condition of ethnic affiliation associated with it.[9]

---

[7] For the family, see Angel Nicolaou-Konnari, "L'identité dans la diaspora: travaux et jours de Pierre (avant 1570 (?) – après 1646) et Georges de Nores (1619–1638)," in *Identités croisées en un milieu méditerranéen: le cas de Chypre (Antiquité – Moyen Âge)*, ed. Sabine Fourrier and Gilles Grivaud (Rouen, 2006), pp. 329–53; Angel Nicolaou-Konnari, "Κύπριοι της διασποράς στην Ιταλία μετά το 1570/1: η περίπτωση της οικογένειας Δενόρες" ["Cypriots of the Diaspora in Italy after 1570/1: The case of the Nores family"], in *"La Serenissima" and "La Nobilissima"*, pp. 218–39; and Angel Nicolaou-Konnari, *Two Cypriots of the Diaspora: Works and Days of Pietro (before 1570 (?) – after 1646/8) and Giorgio de Nores (1619–1638)*, 2 vols. (forthcoming), 1: ch. 1. See below, n. 79.

[8] References to Makhairas and his family are to be found in V39v, 195r, 195v, 203r, 213v, 216r, 248r, 249r, 252v(?), 264v, 266v, 281v(?), 282r, 282v, 283r, 296r, 303r, 303v; O218v, 221v, 269v, 285r, 288r, 295v, 296v, 317v, 324v, 325r, R137v, 138v, 158v, 165v, 167r, 170r, 170v, 178v, 182r: see Makhairas, *Diplomatic Edition*, pp. 121–22, 324–25, 335, 348–49, 351–52, 393, 394, 398–99, 414, 423, 424, 425, 448, 456–57, and in Bertrandon de La Broquière, *Le Voyage d'Outremer de Bertrandon de la Broquière*, ed. Charles Schefer (Paris, 1892), p. 106, extract also in Louis de Mas Latrie, ed., *Histoire de l'île de Chypre sous le règne des princes de la maison de Lusignan*, vols. 2–3 (Paris, 1852–55; repr. Famagusta, 1970), 3:3–4; also see below, n. 34. For a full account of the available information, see Pieris and Nicolaou-Konnari, "Makhairas, *Recital*. An Annotated Bibliography," pp. 83–85, and Nicolaou-Konnari, "Diplomatics and Historiography," pp. 294–96 and n. 6.

[9] See Gilles Grivaud, "Éveil de la nation *chyproise* (XIIe–XVe siècles)," *"Kyprios character." Quelle identité chypriote? Sources travaux historiques* 43–44 (1995), 105–16, esp. pp. 111, 112–13; Nicolaou-Konnari, "Chronique," pp. 62–66, 75–77; Nicolaou-Konnari, "Literary Languages," pp. 9–10, 16; Angel Nicolaou-Konnari, "Ethnic Names and the Construction of Group Identity in Medieval and Early Modern Cyprus: The Case of *Kypriotis*," *Κυπριακαὶ Σπουδαί* [Cypriot Studies] 64–65 (2000–2001), 260–65; Angel Nicolaou-Konnari, "Η ονοματολογία στα χειρόγραφα του Χρονικού του Λεοντίου Μαχαιρά" ["Onomatology in the manuscripts of the *Chronicle* of Leontios Makhairas"], in

Makhairas's narrative borrows from many literary genres, but it may be considered to be primarily a kind of memoirs (the history of a period that is contemporary or almost to the time he lived and of which he is not a simple compiler but a first or second-hand witness) and a dynastic history (in which historical time is organized according to genealogical time and which mainly consists of the encomium of Peter I of Lusignan, the king's reign occupying approximately 24 per cent of the text). Accordingly, wherever he does not draw on personal recollection, he makes a point of specifying his written and oral sources. There can be little doubt that Makhairas's career influenced his concept of history-writing, the style of his narrative, and, most importantly, the nature of the sources he used – namely, material and documents from the Lusignan state archives and perhaps from private archives. The extensive use of archival sources, which at times makes the text resemble an epistolary narrative, endows his history with credibility and documentary realism and, together with the use of prose and the Greek vernacular spoken on the island as well as the orality of his narrative technique, also serving as marks of authenticity, furnishes the text with vividness and rhythm.

It is, therefore, not surprising that Makhairas's chronicle does not fit well into any of the conventional history-writing categories of the western or Byzantine traditions; in fact, it embodies the fusion of the Byzantine and Latin Eastern worlds, transforming the crusader tradition of William of Tyre's continuators and "Ernoul," Philip of Novara, and the anonymous compiler of *Les Gestes des Chiprois* (perhaps Gerard of Monréal who put together a short annalistic text and the chronicles of Philip of Novara and the Templar of Tyre and may also have been the author of the first and third parts of the compilation) into a Greco-Frankish tradition proper to the socio-cultural reality of fifteenth-century Cyprus. In other words, Makhairas outlines the borders of late medieval Cypriot history-writing placing it at the fringe of crusader, western, and Byzantine historiography.[10] Chronologically, he is the immediate continuator of Latin Eastern chroniclers[11] and, thematically, he

---

Αναδρομικά και Προδρομικά. Approaches to Texts in Early Modern Greek, Papers from the Conference *Neograeca Medii Aevi V* (Exeter College, University of Oxford, September 2000), ed. Elizabeth Jeffreys and Michael Jeffreys (Oxford, 2005), pp. 333–36, 351–52, 357–58; Angel Nicolaou-Konnari, "Greeks," in *Cyprus. Society and Culture*, pp. 53–57, esp. p. 54; Alexander Beihammer, "Gruppenidentität und Selbstwahrnehmung im zyprischen Griechentum der frühen Frankenzeit. Ein Interpretationsversuch anhand von zeitgenössischen Briefen und Urkunden," *Jahrbuch der Österreichischen Byzantinistik* 56 (2006), 205–37; and Nicolaou-Konnari, "Diplomatics and Historiography," pp. 296–97; for *Kypriotis*, see below, n. 57.

[10] On the nature and sources of Makhairas's chronicle, see Grivaud, "Intellectual Life and Letters," pp. 1066–84; Nicolaou-Konnari, "Chronique," pp. 69–71 and passim; and Nicolaou-Konnari, "Diplomatics and Historiography," pp. 297–301 and passim with earlier bibliography.

[11] In between Latin Eastern narrative sources and Makhairas's text we may place a lost account by John of Mimars of at least some of the events surrounding the 1373 Genoese invasion of Cyprus and its aftermath, which our chronicler explicitly states that he used: Makhairas, *Chronicle*, 1:§548, and *Diplomatic Edition*, p. 385 (only in V241v); a certain Aimery of Mimars commissioned the only manuscript (completed in 1343) that preserves *Les Gestes des Chiprois*, see Filippo da Novara, *Guerra di Federico II in Oriente (1223–1242)*, ed. and trans. Silvio Melani (Naples, 1994), pp. 5–6, and *Cronaca*

may have used annalistic lists of the kings of Jerusalem, the *Continuations*, and the chronicle of the Templar of Tyre for the introductory matter of his chronicle concerning the First Crusade, the kingdom of Jerusalem, and the foundation of the Lusignan kingdom of Cyprus as well as for the events surrounding the usurpation of government by Amaury of Lusignan, lord of Tyre, in 1306 and the suppression of the Templars in 1307.[12] Stylistically, he shares many traits with Latin Eastern chroniclers, especially with Philip of Novara and Gerard of Monréal who also belonged to the educated circles of statesmen and jurists, wrote in prose and in the vernacular, and were witnesses and often essential participants of the events they describe; in fact, one could see in their works, written from a Latin Eastern and often Cypro-centered perspective, the traces of a subtle evolution of the crusader Levantine ideology, the former composing the apology of his lord John of Ibelin, with a more limited and more outwardly partial scope than that of Leontios's, and the latter compiling the "Deeds of the Cypriots."[13]

Consequently, not only does Makhairas's text not constitute a *mimesis* of Latin Eastern or Byzantine models, but Leontios is the first Cypriot historiographer

---

del Templare di Tiro (1243–1314). La caduta degli Stati Crociati nel racconto di un testimone oculare, ed. and trans. Laura Minervini (Naples, 2000), pp. 2–3.

[12]   Makhairas, *Chronicle*, 1:§§9–12, 18–29, 41, 99, 13–17, and *Diplomatic Edition*, pp. 69–70, 74–81, 88–89, 116–17, 89–100, 70–74. For the complex manuscript tradition and the editions of the *Continuations* of William of Tyre's *History*, see Peter W. Edbury, "The French Translation of William of Tyre's *Historia*: The Manuscript Tradition," *Crusades* 6 (2007), 69–105. Particularly for the 1306 and 1307 events, Makhairas may have used the chronicle of the Templar of Tyre (a different copy, though, from the unique extant manuscript that preserves the text, which is mutilated at this point), see *Cronaca del Templare di Tiro*, §§424–32, 463–66 and 459–62 respectively (a different copy, though, from the unique extant manuscript that preserves the text, which is mutilated at this point); see discussion in Aneta P. Ilieva, "The Suppression of the Templars in Cyprus according to the Chronicle of Leontios Makhairas," in *MO, 1*, pp. 212–19; Nicolaou-Konnari, "Diplomatics and Historiography," pp. 317–19, 304–5; Chris Schabel and Laura Minervini, "The French and Latin Dossier on the Institution of the Government of Amaury of Lusignan, Lord of Tyre, Brother of King Henry II of Cyprus," *Επετηρίδα Κέντρου Επιστημονικών Ερευνών (Κύπρου)* [Cyprus Research Centre Annual Review] 34 (2008), 75–119, and Peter W. Edbury, "New Perspectives of the Old French Continuations of William of Tyre," *Crusades* 9 (2010), 107–13. In their introductions, the editors of the *Guerra di Federico II in Oriente*, pp. 7–36, and the *Cronaca del Templare di Tiro*, pp. 5–20, discuss the relationship between these texts, earlier Latin Eastern narrative sources, and sixteenth-century Cypriot chronicles ("Amadi" and Florio Bustron) but not with Makhairas's text.

[13]   For the continuity between Latin Eastern and Cypriot historiography, see generally Grivaud, "Intellectual Life and Letters," pp. 957–82 (pp. 961–67 on the *Continuations* and pp. 970–82 on Gerard), 1017–29 and 1038–39 (Philip); Nicolaou-Konnari, "Chronique," pp. 61, 67–69 and passim, who inscribes Makhairas's text within a historiographical tradition divided between the Byzantine and the Latin Eastern ones; and Aneta P. Ilieva, "Crusading Images in Cypriot History Writing," in *Cyprus and the Crusades*, Papers Given at the International Conference "Cyprus and the Crusades" (Nicosia, 1994), ed. Nicholas Coureas and Jonathan Riley-Smith (Nicosia, 1995), pp. 295–309, who notes the ideological continuity between the texts of Philip of Novara and the Templar of Tyre and Makhairas's chronicle. Especially on Philip, see Michel Zink, *La Subjectivité littéraire. Autour du siècle de saint Louis* (Paris, 1985) pp. 205, 207–21, and Grivaud, "Literature," pp. 258–61, with more recent bibliography. See Nadia Anaxagorou, *Narrative and Stylistic Structures in the Chronicle of Leontios Makhairas* (Nicosia, 1998), ch. 5, who surprisingly compares Makhairas's text with Byzantine and western but not with Latin Eastern or other Cypriot chronicles in Old French or Italian.

who chooses to write the history of the "sweet land of Cyprus" ("γλυκείας χώρας Κύπρου") under Lusignan rule.[14] Nothing indicates in the chronicle that it was commissioned. On the contrary, motivated by violent emotions provoked by the dire situation of Cyprus after the 1426 Mamluk invasion, Makhairas intends his text to be didactic and moralising and this intention is explicitely stated in the *prooimion*: the destiny of the "well-beloved land of Cyprus" ("ἀκριβῆς χώρας Κύπρου") is in God's hands, but people should remember and learn from "the histories of old times" ("παλαιὰς ἱστορίας"); he has thus "resolved" ("ἐβουλεύτηκα") to write the "recital" ("ἐξήγησις", literally *exegesis* or *narratio*) of the glory and fall of the Lusignan dynasty because people should "consider the end of the matters, and from the end judge truly the nature of the beginning" ("σκοπᾶτε τὰ τέλη τῶν πραγμάτων, καὶ ἀπὸ τὸ τέλος τὴν ἀρχὴν") so that the kingdom might "come safely through" ("μήπως καὶ γλυτώσουν") the threats it faces.[15] In short, thematically, stylistically, and ideologically Makhairas invents a *Kypriotike* tradition of history writing.

In doing so, he does not reject the Byzantine heritage of his identity neither does he express ethnic and cultural antipathy between Greeks and Franks, a dear theme in both Byzantine and crusader historiography.[16] On the contrary, he has a balanced sense of his wider Greek identity, that allows him to participate in the

---

[14] The expression "the sweet land of Cyprus" copies the commonplace *la douce France* or *le doux pays de France*, attested in French literature from the twelfth century onwards. See indicatively, for the twelfth century, "France dulce" in *La Chanson de Roland*, ed. and trans. Pierre Jonin (Paris, 1979), II.16 (p. 52); and "dulcia Francia" in Peter of Blois, *Epistolae*, PL 207:293B; for later examples, Colette Beaune, *Naissance de la nation France* (Paris, 1985), pp. 418–20, 429–30. See discussion in Grivaud, "Intellectual Life and Letters," p. 1188, who notes the use of the expression in a lament in verse for the 1570/1 Turkish conquest of Cyprus: see Theodoros Papadopoullos, "Ὁ Θρῆνος τῆς Κύπρου" ["The Lament of Cyprus"], *Κυπριακαὶ Σπουδαί* [Cypriot Studies] 44 (1980), 30, line 321; Gilles Grivaud, "A propos des influences franques dans l'oeuvre de Leontios Machairas," in *Editing and Interpreting Vernacular Greek Literature*, pp. 321–22; Nicolaou-Konnari, "Chronique," p. 60 and n. 10; Nicolaou-Konnari, "Onomatology," pp. 348–49 and n. 47; and Teresa Shawcross, *The Chronicle of Morea. Historiography in Crusader Greece* (Oxford, 2009), pp. 228–29, who cites the verse "Chipre, douce terre et douce isle" from a work by a thirteenth-century *trouvère*, see Rutebeuf, "La Complainte de Constantinople," in *Oeuvres complètes*, ed. Michel Zink (Paris, 1989–90), pp. 402–16, line 38.

[15] Makhairas, *Chronicle*, 1:§§1–2, 11, and *Diplomatic Edition*, pp. 65, 75. For the chronicle's *prooimion*, see Grivaud, "Intellectual Life and Letters," pp. 1073, 1080, and passim, and Nicolaou-Konnari, "Chronique," pp. 58–61.

[16] See indicatively, from a rich bibliography, Donald M. Nicol, "The Byzantine View of Western Europe," *Greek, Roman and Byzantine Studies* 8 (1967), 315–39; Catherine Asdracha, "L'image de l'homme occidental à Byzance: le témoignage de Kinnamos et de Choniatès," *Byzantinoslavica* 44/1 (1982), 31–40; Paris Gounaridis, "Η εικόνα των Λατίνων την εποχή των Κομνηνών" ["The image of the Latins in the Comnenian period"], *Μνήμη Δ. Α. Ζακυθηνού, Σύμμεικτα* [In memory of D. A. Zakythinos, Symmeikta] 9/1 (1994), 157–71; Bunna Ebels-Hoving, *Byzantium in westerse Ogen, 1096–1204* (Assen, 1971); A.-D. van den Brincken, *Die "Nationes Christianorum Orientalium" im Verständnis der Lateinischen Historiographie* (Cologne and Vienna, 1973), pp. 16–76; Angel Nicolaou-Konnari, "Strategies of Distinction: The Construction of the Ethnic Name *Griffon* and the Western Perception of the Greeks (Twelfth – Fourteenth Centuries)," *Byzantinistica. Rivista di Studi Bizantini e Slavi* 2nd Series 4 (2002), 181–96, esp. pp. 181–83, 189–93; and Marc Carrier, *L'image des Byzantins et les systèmes de représentation selon les chroniqueurs occidentaux des croisades (1096–1261)* (Unpublished PhD thesis, Université de Paris I, 2006). See more specifically for Outremer chroniclers, Peter W. Edbury and

Byzantine *oecumene*, and of his particular Cypriot identity as a loyal subject of the Lusignan kingdom.[17] In a frequently quoted passage, Leontios sets the margins of the Cypriots' oecumenical Greekness or "Romanity" and clearly adheres to the threefold Byzantine ideology of imperial supremacy, Orthodox Christianity, and Greek learning, stating that "because there are two natural rulers in the world, the one lay and the other spiritual, so there were in this little island: the emperor of Constantinople and the patriarch of Antioch the Great" and deploring the state of the Greek language on the island, which "became barbarous" after the Lusignans took Cyprus.[18] On the other hand, Makhairas does not adopt the standard anti-Latin outlook of Byzantine chroniclers and he actually condemns the "old hatred of the Franks for the Greeks" ("τὴν παλαιὰν μισιτείαν τοὺς Φράνγγους μὲ τοὺς Ρωμαίους").[19] Thence, the Latins are not rejected in their capacity as members of a particular religious group, even though religious affiliation remains in the chronicle the main differentiating trait between Greeks and Franks. His concept of religious tolerance is admirably summed up in this passage:

> I am not condemning the Latins, but what is the need for a Greek to become a Latin? For should a good Christian despise the one faith and betake himself to the other? And why should you despise the former faith? He was no heretic who became a good Christian: the Latins derive from the Apostle and the Greeks are an independent Church.[20]

Thus, although he writes the history of the last crusader kingdom in the Levant, his text in fact reflects this kingdom's evolving character – from a French crusader society with Greek subjects and a vested interest in the kingdom of Jerusalem in the thirteenth century to a Cypriot society of Franks and Greeks in the fifteenth century. It is within this Cypro-centred context that we must view the way military expeditions undertaken by the Lusignan kings or directed against the kingdom are perceived in the chronicle. In this respect, the study of the concept of holy war in the text should not involve complex discussions as to whether this reflects a Byzantine or western

---

John Gordon Rowe, *William of Tyre. Historian of the Latin East* (Cambridge, 1988), ch. 8, and Ilieva, "Crusading Images," pp. 297, 299, 300–1, 303.

[17] His claim to participation in the Byzantine *oecumene* is predominantly present throughout the chronicle: see discussion in Costas P. Kyrris, "Some Aspects of Leontios Makhairas' Ethnoreligious Ideology, Cultural Identity and Historiographic Method," *Στασῖνος* [Stasinos] 10 (1989–93), 167–281, passim; and Nicolaou-Konnari, "Onomatology," pp. 328–31, 340–41, 344, 351–55.

[18] "And (when the Latin period began) men began to learn French, and their Greek became barbarous, just as it is today, when we write both French and Greek, in such a way that no one in the world can say what our language is" ("καὶ ἀπὸ τότες ἀρκέψα νὰ μαθάνουν φράγγικα, καὶ 'βαρβαρίσαν τὰ ρωμαῖκα, ὡς γοιὸν καὶ σήμερον, καὶ γράφομεν φράγκικα καὶ ρωμαῖκα, ὅτι εἰς τὸν κόσμον δὲν ἠξεύρουν ἵντα συντυχάννομεν"), Makhairas, *Chronicle*, 1:§158, and *Diplomatic Edition*, p. 148; also see Nicolaou-Konnari, "Onomatology," pp. 351–53.

[19] Makhairas, *Chronicle*, 1:§348, and *Diplomatic Edition*, p. 259 (only in V144v–145r. Half a century later, R94v gives the milder version "the old habit the Franks had for the Greeks" / "τὶν παλεαν σινιθιαν τουσ φρανκουσ με τουσ ρομεουσ"); see Nicolaou-Konnari, "Onomatology," p. 355.

[20] Makhairas, *Chronicle*, 1:§579, and *Diplomatic Edition*, p. 403. See generally Nicolaou-Konnari, "Onomatology," pp. 353–55.

tradition but should be investigated in relation to the chronicle's particular nature as the product of a frontier society.[21]

A closer analysis of the text itself illustrates and supports the above theoretical considerations. It is, however, essential to state at the beginning that the omission of an event in the chronicle as well as the varied importance attributed to the events that are included may be the result of the availability of information but are also significant insofar as they represent a deliberate choice, thus indicating the author's ideological intentions.[22] Consequently, given the chronicle's purely Cypriot contents and aims, the crusades as military expeditions with a concrete political significance for the Levant are practically ignored. Makhairas mentions very briefly the capture of the Holy Land by the crusading troops during the First Crusade, significantly associating in the leadership of the expedition "the most holy pope" ("ὁ ἁγιώτατος πάπας"), the king of France, and the emperor of Constantinople, only because he wants to "come down to narrate ("νὰ ξηγηθοῦμεν") about the Latin kings who were crowned in Jerusalem" and thence to Guy of Lusignan (1192–94). But this "narrative" consists in fact of an enumeration of the names of the kings of Jerusalem, followed by a confused reference to the Latin conquest of Cyprus during the Third Crusade. The crusader nature of the conquest and Richard the Lionheart's 1191 campaign on the island are entirely omitted while the events surrounding the sale of the island to Guy of Lusignan are presented as a simple transaction between the Templars and Guy; the latter is said to have taken the island "with the aid of God and of the Genoese" ("μὲ τὴν βοήθειαν τοῦ θεοῦ καὶ τῶν Γενουβίσων"), the association of these two "patrons" hardly allowing for any illusions of crusading heroics.[23] Despite Makhairas's effort to mark meticulously the date of an event, it is noteworthy that a number of the dates supplied in the text for the aforementioned events are wrong.[24] Guy's initial apprehensions for his Greek subjects are not

---

[21]   For the notion of war in Byzantium, often explained and justified in religious terms but remaining essentially an imperial affair, see Hélène Ahrweiler, *Ἡ πολιτικὴ ἰδεολογία τῆς Βυζαντινῆς Αὐτοκρατορίας* [The political ideology of the Byzantine empire], trans. Toula Drakopoulou (Athens, 1977), passim, and esp. pp. 27, 37–43, 118–22; Athina Kolia-Dermitzaki, *Ὁ βυζαντινὸς "ἱερός πόλεμος". Ἡ ἔννοια καί ἡ προβολὴ τοῦ θρησκευτικοῦ πολέμου στό Βυζάντιο* [The Byzantine "Holy War." The notion and propagation of religious war in Byzantium] (Athens, 1991); and Timothy S. Miller and John Nesbitt, eds., *Peace and War in Byzantium. Essays in Honor of George T. Dennis, S.J.* (Washington, D.C., 1995). For the western concept of holy war, see below, n. 29.

[22]   For Makhairas's "silences," see Aneta P. Ilieva, "Franks and Greeks: Patterns of Initial Co-Existence in Morea and in Cyprus after the Chronicle of the Morea and Leontios Makhairas," in *Πρακτικὰ τοῦ Δ΄ Διεθνοῦς Συνεδρίου Πελοποννησιακῶν Σπουδῶν* [Proceedings of the Fourth International Conference of Peloponnesian Studies] (Corinth, 1990) (Athens, 1992), 1:145–62; Kyrris, "Some Aspects of Leontios Makhairas' Ethnoreligious Ideology," passim; and Nicolaou-Konnari, "Greeks," p. 42.

[23]   Makhairas, *Chronicle*, 1:§§10, 18–21, and *Diplomatic Edition*, pp. 65, 74–76. For the long, detailed accounts of the 1191 events in western and Latin Eastern sources, which clearly present the conquest as a crusading expedition, see a comparative study in Nicolaou-Konnari, "The Conquest of Cyprus," passim, esp. pp. 89–92.

[24]   See Makhairas, *Chronicle*, 1:§18, line 1, §19, lines 1, 3, 5, 8, 52, §21, lines 1, 2 and commentary in ibid., 2:50–52. For the great number of wrong dates in the chronicle and date discrepancies amongst

presented in terms of ethnic antagonism but of fear of their demographic superiority and of possible expeditions undertaken by the Byzantine emperor in order to recover the island. Makhairas's account of Guy asking Saladin for his advice on the best way to control the island follows closely the one in the *Continuations* of William of Tyre; the Latin Eastern narrative, however, does not include the Greek chronicler's allegation that the crusader king actually sought the sultan's alliance against a Christian ruler, the emperor of Constantinople.[25] Moreover, the settlement of the Latins and the establishment of the Latin Church in Cyprus are described in very concrete social and economic terms, despite the text's implication that one of the main attractions for the new settlers lay in the holy relics preserved on the island and its proximity to Jerusalem.[26]

The awareness that the Lusignan king of Cyprus was also by rights "the heir of the kingdom of Jerusalem" ("κληρονόμον ... τοῦ ρηγάτου Ἱεροσολύμου") is present in the chronicle and is consistently expressed in the formulaic addresses in the interpolated documents: "Peter de Lusignan, by the grace of God king of Jerusalem and Cyprus" ("Πέτρος τε Λουζουνίας διὰ τῆς χάριτος τοῦ θεοῦ ρήγας Ἱεροσολύμων καὶ Κύπρου").[27] The legitimacy of the dynasty, however, is thought to be achieved with regards to the existence of the kingdom of Cyprus and not the recovery of that of Jerusalem as the Lusignans' ancestral kingdom. Thus, no other major crusading expeditions are mentioned, not even the Fourth Crusade and the fall of Constantinople into the hands of the Latins in 1204, or that of Emperor Frederick II in 1228–29 that had such a great impact on Cypriot politics, or that of Saint Louis who sojourned in Cyprus for eight months in 1248–49. Similarly, the Cypriot involvement in the defence of Latin Syria in the thirteenth century, the fall of Acre in 1291, and the participation of King Hugh IV (1324–59) in the leagues against the Turks in the 1330s to 1350s are ignored. With the exception of two vague mentions of the "Smyrna galleys," only on one occasion does Makhairas refer to "the armed expeditions which, as you have heard, were made in Turkey" in order to explain in an almost disapproving way that King Hugh's great wealth had been spent in these campaigns. Despite his claim, he had not spoken previously about these expeditions.[28] Although these omissions may reflect the contents of

---

the three manuscript texts, a fact first pointed out by the text's editor R. M. Dawkins with regards to V, see ibid., 2:14; *Diplomatic Edition*, p. 41; Grivaud, "Intellectual Life and Letters," p. 1073 and n. 23; and Nicolaou-Konnari, "Diplomatics and Historiography," p. 299 and n. 16.

[25] Makhairas, *Chronicle*, 1:§§22–25, 348, and *Diplomatic Edition*, pp. 76–78, 259; *La Continuation de Guillaume de Tyr (1184–1197)*, ed. Margaret Ruth Morgan (Paris, 1982), pp. 138–39.

[26] Makhairas, *Chronicle*, 1:§§26–29, 99, and *Diplomatic Edition*, pp. 78–81, 116–17.

[27] See, for example, Makhairas, *Chronicle*, 1:§§87, 89–90, 104, 217, 251, 320–24 (320 for the quotation) and, particularly for addresses, 251, 346, 512, 515, 516, 616, etc., and *Diplomatic Edition*, pp. 111, 112, 119, 182 (only in O108v), 200, 244–46 (244 for the quotation) and, particularly for addresses, 200, 258, 359, 362, 363, 418–19, etc.; see also Nicolaou-Konnari, "Onomatology," p. 345, and Nicolaou-Konnari, "Diplomatics and Historiography," pp. 312–13.

[28] Makhairas, *Chronicle*, 1:§§64–86, and 113 (reign of Hugh IV), 114 and 119 (Smyrna galleys), 157 (Cypriot contribution to the leagues), and *Diplomatic Edition*, pp. 100–111, and 123 (reign of Hugh IV), 123 and 126 (Smyrna galleys), 147 (Cypriot contribution to the leagues). For all these crusading

the texts the chonicler had at his disposal, they also suggest that in the first half of the fifteenth century the earlier crusades seemed futile from a Cypriot perspective. Instead, the text discusses at length the expeditions of Peter I against the Turkish controlled southern coastlands of Asia Minor in the 1360s and his capture of Alexandria in 1365 as well as the Mamluk invasion of Cyprus in 1426.

Viewed from the contemporary western standpoint, Peter's wars conformed to the criteria according to which an expedition could be considered to be a crusade, in the sense that they were waged against the infidel, they were condoned or sanctioned by the pope, and they aimed at the liberation or defence of Christian land or at expansion into Muslim lands; they were thus justifiable wars because they had a just cause, were approved or authorized by a legitimate authority, and their participants had pure motives.[29] Peter's campaign against Alexandria, in particular, was presented by contemporary propaganda designed for consumption in the West as having traditional crusader goals, namely the recovery of the Holy Land by a Christian army fighting with the aid of God, Alexandria being only a *primum passagium* inscribed within the larger scheme of the crusade proclaimed and preached by the pope in 1363. Extant texts include Pope Urban V's letters and bulls, and the king's own correspondence with western rulers, as well as literary texts of a varied nature.[30] This fourteenth-century western attitude contrasts sharply

---

expeditions, see generally Peter W. Edbury, *The Kingdom of Cyprus and the Crusades 1191–1374* (Cambridge, 1991; repr. Cambridge, 2000), chs. 3–5, passim, and ch. 7, pp. 141–61, esp. 150–51, 156–61, and Nicholas Coureas, "Cyprus and the Naval Leagues, 1333–1358," in *Cyprus and the Crusades*, pp. 107–24.

[29] From a rich bibliography on the definition of the crusade, see Carl Erdmann, *Die Entstehung des Kreuzzugsgedankens* (Stuttgart, 1935), English trans. Marshall W. Baldwin and Walter Goffart as *The Origin of the Idea of Crusade* (Princeton, N.J., 1977); Paul Rousset, *Les origines et les charactères de la première croisade* (Geneva, 1945); Paul Alphandéry and Alphonse Dupront, *La chrétienté et l'idée de croisade*, 2 vols. (Paris, 1954–59); Franco Cardini, *Le crociate tra il mito e la storia* (Rome, 1971); Frederick H. Russell, *The Just War in the Middle Ages* (Cambridge, 1975); Jonathan Riley-Smith, *What Were the Crusades?* (London, 1977); Jonathan Riley-Smith, *The First Crusade and the Idea of Crusading* (Philadelphia, 1986); Norman Housley, *The Later Crusades. From Lyons to Alcazar, 1274–1580* (Oxford, 1992), pp. 1–6; Peter Partner, *God of Battles. Holy Wars of Christianity and Islam* (London, 1997), esp. introduction and chs. 4–5; Jean Flori, *Pierre l'Ermite et la première croisade* (Paris, 1999); Christoph T. Maier, *Crusade and Propaganda: Model Sermons for the Preaching of the Cross* (Cambridge, 2000); Thomas Asbridge, *The First Crusade. A New History* (New York, 2004); Christopher Tyerman, *Fighting for Christendom: Holy War and the Crusades* (Oxford, 2004); and Norman Housley, *Contesting the Crusades* (Oxford, 2006). For the Byzantine notion of holy war, see above, n. 21.

[30] See *Annales ecclesiastici*, ed. Caesar Baronius and Odoricus Raynaldus, new ed. Augustin Theiner, 37 vols. (Bar-le-Duc and Paris, 1864–82), 1363, §§15–19; Pope Urban V, *Lettres secrètes et curiales se rapportant à la France*, ed. Paul Lecacheux and G. Mollat, Bibliothèque des Écoles françaises d'Athènes et de Rome (Paris, 1902–55), nos. 476–89; Peter's letters to the rulers of Florence and the seneschal of the kingdom of Naples in Mas Latrie, *Histoire de l'île de Chypre*, 2:236–37 (in 1362), and in J. A. C. Buchon, *Nouvelles recherches historiques sur la principauté française de Morée et ses hautes baronnies*, 2 vols. (Paris, 1843), 2:134–35; Philippe de Mézières, *The Life of Saint Peter Thomas by Philippe de Mézières*, ed. Joachim Smet, O. Carm. (Rome, 1954), passim, esp. pp. 102, 103, 105, 128, 131, 134, and later works by Mézières; Guillaume de Machaut, *La Prise d'Alixandre* (*The Taking of Alexandria*), ed. and trans. R. Barton Palmer (New York and London, 2002), and *The*

with the chronicle's fifteenth-century Cypriot outlook: Makhairas does not justify Peter's expeditions in terms of war sanctioned by God for the restoration of Christian jurisdiction, neither does he demonize his adversary by attributing to the Mamluks intentions of launching a holy war for expansion of Islam when they invade Cyprus; of course, the kingdom of Cyprus was a Christian polity protected by God, but wars waged by the kingdom did not have a spiritual character or entirely pure motives. Only indirectly does the text allude to Peter's crusader intentions, even though the rightfulness of the cause of his wars is not openly questioned. Interestingly, one of the rare cases where a crusader goal is explicitly ascribed to the king is connected with the queen's marital indiscretions. The king attributes his wife's unfaithfulness to divine punishment for his vain ambitions and pride because "I sought to win what my ancestors had not … God made me king of Cyprus and gave me also the title of Jerusalem and before the time appointed I pressed on and was zealous to win the kingdom of Jerusalem."[31]

The picture of a king who questions his crusader call constitutes an excellent stylistic device used by Makhairas to criticize indirectly the outcome of Peter's wars for Cyprus. Indeed, our chronicler proposes a more complex interpretation of the king's policy and motives. His analysis of the economic and political causes and results of Peter's wars, often implicit but easily deduced by the careful reader, is pragmatic and realistic and is supported by abundant information on logistics (lists of the names of the nobles participating in the campaigns, numbers and types of vessels, types of arms and siege machines, ways of financing and supplying expeditions, and so on), something which betrays his intentions and the nature of his sources:[32] because of the embargo, imposed by "the most holy pope" in his effort to assist "the poor Cypriots" ("οἱ πτωχοὶ οἱ Κυπριῶτες") who were surrounded by Muslim people, merchants from the West conducted their trade with the East and particularly Egypt only in Cyprus and, as a result, the whole island became very rich; this prosperity was threatened by Turkish piracy and the growing

Capture of Alexandria, trans. Janet Shirley, introduction and notes Peter W. Edbury, Crusade Texts in Translation 8 (Aldershot, 2001). For a discussion about these and other writers, see: Mas Latrie, *Histoire de l'île de Chypre*, 2:245–46, 337, n. 2; Nicolas Jorga, *Philippe de Mézières (1327–1405) et la croisade au XIVe siècle* (Paris, 1896; repr. London, 1973), pp. 80–82, 306, 378–79, 392–93, and passim; Sir George Hill, *A History of Cyprus*, 4 vols. (Cambridge, 1940–52), 2:327, n. 2 (reference at p. 328), 335, n. 3, 368; Edbury's introduction to Machaut, *The Capture of Alexandria*, pp. 8–16; Palmer's introduction to Machaut, *La Prise d'Alixandre*, pp. 11–33. See generally Edbury, *The Kingdom of Cyprus*, pp. 162–64; Grivaud, "Literature," p. 228; Peter W. Edbury, "Machaut, Mézières, Makhairas, and *Amadi*: Constructing the Reign of Peter I (1359–1369)," in *Philippe de Mézières and His Age: Piety and Politics in the Fourteenth-Century*, ed. Renate Blumenfeld-Kosinski and Kiril Petkov, The Medieval Mediterranean 91 (Leiden – Boston, 2012), pp. 349–58; Angel Nicolaou-Konnari, "Apologists or Critics? The Reign of Peter I of Lusignan (1359–1369) Viewed by Philippe de Mézières and Leontios Makhairas," in the same volume, pp. 359–401.

[31] Makhairas, *Chronicle*, 1:§§243, 251, and *Diplomatic Edition*, pp. 196, 200.

[32] See Makhairas, *Chronicle*, 1:§§157, 215, and *Diplomatic Edition*, pp. 147–48, 180–81 (the way Peter financed his crusades), *Chronicle*, 2:328, 329, 330 (entries "perpiriarii," "ships and shipping," "siege engines," "taxes"), and Nicolaou-Konnari, "Onomatology," pp. 337, 340–48, esp. 346, and Nicolaou-Konnari, "Diplomatics and Historiography," pp. 299–300 (references to lists of officers of the crown, lists of names of nobles, and information about taxes).

Venetian presence in Alexandria following the relaxation of the papal embargo on Christian trade with Egypt in 1344, which meant that Famagusta was bypassed; the kingdom's economy would be destroyed by the Genoese invasion in 1373 and the Mamluk one in 1426.[33]

Accordingly, Peter's first military and naval exploits are presented in the chronicle as intended to contain Turkish aggression and curb piracy. Makhairas describes how the Armenian inhabitants of Gorhigos handed over their town to Peter in 1360 because of their king's inabilitiy to defend them against the advances of the Turks. Although he interpolates in the narrative the miracles worked by the picture of the Virgin of Gorhigos, which blinded one of the Turkish leaders, the Lusignan king's motives are said to be his wish "to possess land in Turkey" and the Cypriot guard of the town swear that they will hold this strategic port in the name of King Peter and the Holy Cross so that the Turks should not take it and be in position to harass the kingdom of Cyprus.[34] Similarly, the 1361 campaign against Satalia is clearly presented as conducted both for the defence of the kingdom, since the Turkish rulers might use the coastal town as a base to attack Cyprus, and because of its considerable commercial potential; the king's men advise him to hold the place for his own benefit and there are even negotiations between the emir of Satalia and the Cypriots regarding the selling and buying of land.[35] Interestingly, the participation in the expedition of Philippe de Mézières (1327–1405), the king's chancellor, and the papal legate Peter Thomas (ca. 1305–66), the two most ardent exponents of Peter's crusading politics, is completely ignored in the text.[36] The Cypriot guard at Satalia do not seem to have been particularly motivated by high crusader ideals either, as they conspire in 1367 to hand the castle back to the Turks because provisions and their salaries from Cyprus were delayed. Subsequent Turkish counter-attacks on Cyprus, Satalia, and Gorighos and Cypriot raids in retaliation on other places along the coast of Anatolia, including Myra, Anamur, Siq, and Alaya, are described either in terms of pillaging and piracy (the verb "κουρσεύγω", "to pillage" or "to ravage", consistently used),[37] or as expeditions intended to relieve the two Cypriot outposts

---

[33]   Makhairas, *Chronicle*, 1:§91 (quotation) and passim, and *Diplomatic Edition*, pp. 112–13 (quotation) and passim. See discussion in Edbury, *The Kingdom of Cyprus*, pp. 150–53, and David Jacoby, "The Venetians in Byzantine and Lusignan Cyprus: Trade, Settlement, and Politics," in *"La Serenissima" and "La Nobilissima"*, p. 73 and passim.

[34]   Makhairas, *Chronicle*, 1:§§112–15, and *Diplomatic Edition*, pp. 122–24; for date discrepancies between V and O (and R), see *Chronicle*, 2:98. See Jorga, *Philippe de Mézières*, pp. 110–15, and Edbury, *The Kingdom of Cyprus*, pp. 163–64 for the events. The detailed way in which Leontios describes the topography of Gorhigos suggests that he may have visited the area; thanks to La Broquière, *Le Voyage d'Outremer*, p. 106, we know that in 1432 he was on a diplomatic mission in Laranda, a town north of Taurus which he may have reached through the port of Gorhigos.

[35]   Makhairas, *Chronicle*, 1:§§117–25 (123, "hold the place for yourself"), 128 (sell and buy land), and *Diplomatic Edition*, pp. 125–29 (128, "hold the place for yourself"), 131 (sell and buy land). See Jorga, *Philippe de Mézières*, pp. 119–28, and Edbury, *The Kingdom of Cyprus*, p. 163 for the events.

[36]   See Nicolaou-Konnari, "Apologists or Critics?," pp. 387–88.

[37]   For "κουρσεύγω" and "κουρσάρης", see Makhairas, *Chronicle*, 1:§§95, 127, 143, 318, etc. (Cypriot raids), 139, 140, 152, etc. (Turkish raids), and *Diplomatic Edition*, pp. 114 (only in O39v and R26r), 130 (only in V45v and R35r), 137–38, 243 (only in V122v), etc. (Cypriot raids), 135–36, 136,

in Asia Minor or to suppress the 1367 mutiny of the garrison stationed in Satalia. The raid against Myra, though, is associated with the transfer of the icon of St. Nicholas to the Latin cathedral of Famagusta, which bears the name of the saint.[38]

The crusader purpose of Peter's first trip to Europe in 1362–65, intended to rally support for his military ambitions, is downplayed in favour of his dynastic dispute with Hugh of Lusignan, prince of Galilee; Makhairas claims that the king was summoned to appear before Pope Innocent VI for the settlement of the problem, something which is not corroborated in papal letters. The text provides only a vague reference to the king's envoys recruiting mercenaries in Italy and an even vaguer mention of other envoys (including our chronicler's brother Paul) who travelled widely in the West "on the king's business" ("διὰ δουλεῖες τοῦ ρηγός"), both references placed before Peter's journey. Makhairas mentions the king visiting Rhodes, Venice, the papal court in Avignon, France, Genoa, and the German emperor but in a confused order and a very fragmentary way.[39] Peter's crusading policy is mentioned in a single passing phrase ("and the king begged the rulers of the West to send a force to go against the men of false belief, to win back the kingdom of Jerusalem, the house of Christ") and so is the preaching of the expedition by the legate in Rhodes ("everyone with zeal and faith should assemble speedily, every Christian to go to attack the men of alien faith"). These are in fact the only instances in the text where the description of an expedition corresponds to the definition of a crusade, but there is no mention of Peter taking the cross or

---

143 (only in V53v), etc. (Turkish raids). See below notes 46 and 52 for more examples. In Byzantine Greek, the word κουρσάρης derives from medieval Latin cursarius (Italian corsaro) and has a very strong and often negative connotation, indicating the pirate or the ravager; it is first attested in tenth and eleventh-century texts while κοῦρσος ("pillaging") in ninth-century texts. In Cypriot texts, it is first attested in the Greek translation of the Assizes of the Court of Burgesses – see Ἀσῑζαι τοῦ βασιλείου τῶν Ἱεροσολύμων καὶ τῆς Κύπρου, in Bibliotheca graeca medii aevi, ed. Constaninos Sathas, 7 vols. (Venice and Paris, 1872–94), 6:49–50, 298 ("κουρσάροι"), 89 ("κουρσάριδες") – and could be a direct loanword from Old French coursaire, see for example Philippe de Mézières (Chancellor of Cyprus), Le Songe du vieil pelerin, ed. G. W. Coopland, 2 vols. (Cambridge, 1969), 1:254, 261 ("coursayres"), and Makhairas, Chronicle, 2:251. See Charles du Fresne Du Cange, Glossarium ad scriptores mediae et infimae graecitatis, 2 vols. (Lyons, 1688; repr. Graz, 1958), 1:cols. 740–41; Emmanuel Kriaras, Λεξικὸν τῆς μεσαιωνικῆς ἑλληνικῆς δημώδους γραμματείας [Dictionary of medieval Greek vernacular literature], 15 vols. so far (Thessalonike, 1968–), 8:340–3; and Dikaios V. Vayiakakos, "Πειρατεία καὶ γλῶσσα" ["Piracy and language"], in Πειρατές καὶ κουρσάροι [Pirates and corsairs], ed. Charis Kalliga and Alexis Malliaris (Athens, 2004), pp. 243–45.

38 Makhairas, Chronicle, 1:§§116, 124, 126–28 (127 for St. Nicholas), 132–35, 137–44, 150–52, 194–95, 200–1 (Satalia mutiny), 317–18, and Diplomatic Edition, pp. 124–25, 128–31 (130 for St. Nicholas), 133–35, 135–38, 140–43, 167–69, 171–72 (Satalia mutiny), 242–44.

39 Makhairas, Chronicle, 1:§§105–8, 129 and 131 (dispute), 109 (mercenaries), 110 (the king's business), 129, 131, 136–37, 149, 153, 159–61, and 164–69 (Peter's journey), and Diplomatic Edition, pp. 119–21 and 131–32 (dispute), 121 (mercenaries), 121–22 (only in V39v, the king's business), 131–33, 134–35, 140, 143, 149–50 and 151–53 (Peter's journey). For Peter's first journey to Europe, see documents in Mas Latrie, Histoire de l'île de Chypre, 2:237–73, and discussion in Jorga, Philippe de Mézières, pp. 142–201, Hill, A History of Cyprus, 2:324–28, and Edbury, The Kingdom of Cyprus, pp. 164–66.

of the proclamation of the crusade in 1363.[40] Instead, Makhairas does not hesitate to promptly demystify its causes and implications: Peter's "desire to go to destroy the miscreant Saracens" made him grant privileges to the Genoese with the 1365 treaty so "that there might be peace between them, and he be not hindered in his expedition," the western lords are said to have been seized with great anger at the Muslim threats against the island, expressing their eagerness to come "to Syria to spoil and ravage all the land of the sultan of Cairo," while the people of Famagusta reacted to the news of the expedition in a clearly more pragmatic and self-interested way, "bitterly vexed" ("ἐπικράνθησαν πολλά") because of the negative impact Peter's plans would have on their trade.[41]

The narrative of the military events surrounding the capture of Alexandria on 10 October 1365 is very brief (only three paragraphs in R. M. Dawkins's edition as opposed, for example, to roughly thirty or more dedicated to Peter's love affairs) and is given in a matter-of-fact way, this time the text providing correct dates. Ample emphasis is put on the way the spoils were divided, the king taking nothing because he would keep the town for himself, and on the decision of the king and his council to abandon the town because, after they had taken all the things of value and riches they could, "there was no advantage / profit / benefit" (the Greek word "διάφορος" allowing for all three possible interpretations).[42] Significantly, the presence and role in the events of Peter's chancellor Philippe de Mézières is entirely effaced while the papal legate Peter Thomas is duly given his religious part (he is said to have made prayers of thanks to God and said mass in memory of those who had been killed) but is also specifically mentioned as one of the members of the king's council who unanimously agreed to abandon Alexandria.[43]

The text does refer to the fact that when the news of the victory reached the West the pope "rejoiced greatly and all Rome with him" and the rulers of the West, envious of the Cypriot king's glory, promised to accompany Peter with a great host on an expedition to destroy the "miscreant Saracens," only to explain immediately afterwards that they had changed their minds after they had heard

---

[40] Makhairas, *Chronicle*, 1:§§131, 169, and *Diplomatic Edition*, pp. 132–33 (first quotation in O58r and R36r, V46v giving the less elaborate "the king asked that the westerners go against the Saracens"), 153 (second quotation in O80v, V60v and R48v giving the more neutral "everyone with zeal and faith should assemble speedily to go to attack their enemies").

[41] Makhairas, *Chronicle*, 1:§§153, 160, 170, and *Diplomatic Edition*, pp. 143, 149, 153.

[42] Makhairas, *Chronicle*, 1:§§160–70 (preparations for the expedition), 171–73 (the expedition), 130, 216, 233–49, 251–59, and 280–81 (love affairs), and *Diplomatic Edition*, pp. 149–53 (preparations for the expedition), 153–55 (the expedition), 132, 181, 191–99, 200–5, and 220–22 (love affairs). For the Alexandria campaign, also see Mézières, *Life*, pp. 125–41, and Machaut, *La Prise d'Alixandre*, pp. 111–91; generally, Jorga, *Philippe de Mézières*, pp. 277–304; Edbury, *The Kingdom of Cyprus*, pp. 167–68; Edbury, "Machaut, Mézières, Makhairas, and *Amadi*"; and Nicolaou-Konnari, "Apologists or Critics?," pp. 384–88, with a comparison of the different accounts.

[43] The legate is mentioned in Makhairas, *Chronicle*, 1:§§101, 104, 167, 169, 172–74, and *Diplomatic Edition*, pp. 117–18, 119, 152, 153, 154–55, 155–56, but the chancellor only once in Makhairas, *Chronicle*, 1:§153, and *Diplomatic Edition*, p. 144; see Nicolaou-Konnari, "Apologists or Critics?," pp. 380–81, 378.

rumours of peace negotiations, spread by the Venetians.[44] Any crusader overtones concerning Peter's subsequent efforts to capitalize on the destruction of Alexandria by further assaults against Syria and Egypt are lost in the text, which describes the events in terms of a political and economic antagonism between the interests of the Cypriots, on the one hand, and of Venetian and other western merchants, on the other.[45] The failure of Peter's campaign of January 1367, after his fleet's dispersal in a storm, is described in a matter-of-fact way, accompanied by rich information on logistics and a long list of participants. Cypriot raids on the Turkish southern Asia Minor coast and the Syrian coast in 1366, 1367, and 1369 (at the beginning of Peter II's reign) are explicitly said to have been conducted for the sole purpose of pillaging and pirating, Makhairas commenting on the lack of discipline of the Cypriots, who "for a little gain ... would go in disorder, whilst the enemy lay in ambushes and slaughtered them." After the 1367 raids, Peter decreed that anyone privateering against the Mamluks (the verb again being "κουρσεύγω") could find a base in Famagusta, the proclamation renewed at the beginning of Peter II's reign.[46] Similar to the reason given for his first trip to Europe, Peter's second trip, in 1367, is supposed to be on account of a dispute with Florimond of Lesparre, a Gascon lord, rather than because of any intention to revive the western interest in his war.[47] Peter is mentioned as having visited Rhodes, Naples, Rome, Florence, Milan, and the German emperor who was in Italy. With subtle ironic undertones Makhairas comments that "favours were shown and promises were made to the king of Cyprus by the rulers of the West, who agreed to accompany him with a great host to destroy the sultan," with the duke of Milan actually said to be "greatly delighted that the king of Jerusalem had consented to see him"; but the pope, who could not support the venture because of domestic problems with the duke of Milan and the pressure exercised by Venice and Genoa, "asked the king ... to make peace with the sultan because of the necessities of the Christians" and, despite the initial enthusiam, the promises never materialized.[48]

---

[44] Makhairas, *Chronicle*, 1:§§174–76 (175 for the quotations), 183, 185–86, and *Diplomatic Edition*, pp. 156–57 (156 for the quotations), 160–61, 161–62.

[45] See, for example, Makhairas, *Chronicle*, 1:§§176–80, 188–89, 197, etc., and *Diplomatic Edition*, pp. 157–58, 163–64, 170, etc. See generally Edbury, *The Kingdom of Cyprus*, pp. 168–69.

[46] Makhairas, *Chronicle*, 1:§§180 (Alaya in 1366), 190–91 (failed expedition of 1367, sack of Tripoli), 210–12 (210 for the quotation, raids in 1367 against Tripoli, Tortosa, Valania, Lattakia, Cilician ports of Malo and Ayas), 213 (Peter's decree), 219–22 (privateering in 1367 and 1368), 284–88 (privateering and raids against Sidon, Beirut, Giblet, Boutron, Tortosa, Lattakia, Ayas, and Alexandria in 1369), and *Diplomatic Edition*, pp. 158–59 (1366), 164–66 (1367 expedition), 177–79 (177–78 for the quotation, 1367 raids), 179 (Peter's decree), 183–85 (privateering in 1367 and 1368), 224–27 (1369 raids). For "κουρσεύγω," see above, n. 37, and below, n. 52, with more examples. See generally Edbury, *The Kingdom of Cyprus*, pp. 169–70, 197.

[47] Makhairas, *Chronicle*, 1:§§206, 214, 216, and *Diplomatic Edition*, pp. 175–76, 181–82. Lesparre's homage to Peter is one of the illustrations in the Book of Hours of Louis of Savoy, who married Anna of Lusignan (Peter's great-niece) in 1434: Paris, Bibliothèque Nationale de France, MS lat. 9473, fol. 235v; see *Chypre. D'Aphrodite à Mélusine*, ed. Matteo Campagnolo, Chantal Courtois, Marielle Martiniani-Reber, and Lefki Michaelidou (Geneva, 2006), p. 131, ill. XLII.

[48] Makhairas, *Chronicle*, 1:§§216–18 (217, 218 for the quotations), 223, 244, and *Diplomatic Edition*, pp. 181–83 (182, 183 for the quotations, only in O108v and R62r for the duke of Milan), 185,

The long account of the negotiations for peace between the Cypriots and the Mamluks that lasted from 1365 to 1370, with the Venetians acting as intermediaries and manipulators and the pope as counsellor to the king, occupies approximately 55 paragraphs and astonishes the reader with its thoroughness and amount of detail; this betrays once more the fact that Makhairas had access to documents from the royal archives. Based on these original sources, which he often cites verbatim, he can evaluate the events soberly, providing a perceptive assessment of the economic and political implications and conflicting interests, that may be summarized as follows: the pope and the western rulers were deterred from supporting Peter by the Venetians, Genoese, and Catalans, whose trade was threatened, and the Cypriot king was advised to conclude peace; if he wished to carry on hostilities, he should consider the fact that the sultan was a powerful lord and that pillaging benefited only the army, while the cost of the war was on the king's shoulders; the king acknowledged that it was better to have the Venetians as allies than profit from more pillaging ("a friend in the path is better than wealth in life"), and as a gesture of good will he diverted his fleet from a projected assault on Beirut, cynically ordering his captain to ravage Turkish lands instead; the sultan was advised that Muslim merchants also wanted trade with the westerners to resume, while many Muslim people would go on the side of the Christians if they did not feel safe; the conclusion of peace in 1370, under the reign of Peter II, is said to have been the result of the "compassion" ("ἐσπλαγχνίστην μας") shown by the sultan for the Cypriots and of the pressure exercised by the republics on the pope to tell Cyprus and Rhodes to sign the treaty (which he did "for the love of the republics and for the advantage of Christendom"); when they heard the news about the treaty the merchants of Famagusta rejoiced much.[49] Although Peter's policy of commercial protectionism and his crusading motives were not necessarily mutually exclusive, in modern terms what is implied in the chronicle – and is corroborated by the surviving draft treaty of 1367 – is that the king must have known that Jerusalem as the goal of his venture was never a feasible aim and that Alexandria was untenable without western help; however, in order to bolster the declining commercial role of Cyprus, the result of the resumption of direct Christian trade with Muslim lands by the middle of the fourteenth century, he used aggression and the threat of aggression to destroy Famagusta's rival, get the sultan to concede preferential commercial facilities to Cypriot merchants trading in his lands, and perhaps persuade the pope to reimpose the embargo.[50]

---

197. For Peter's second journey to Europe, see documents in Mas Latrie, *Histoire de l'île de Chypre*, 2:291–331, and discussion in Jorga, *Philippe de Mézières*, pp. 369–83; Hill, *A History of Cyprus*, 2:355–59; and Edbury, *The Kingdom of Cyprus*, p. 170.

[49] Makhairas, *Chronicle*, 1:§§175–86 (178 for the quotation), 187–89, 192–93, 196–98, 202–5, 217–18, 223–30, 284, 290–309 (300, 303 for the quotations), and *Diplomatic Edition*, pp. 156–62 (157–58 for the quotation), 163–64, 166–67, 169–70, 172–75, 182–83, 185–91, 224, 227–38 (232, 234 for the quotations).

[50] For the 1367 draft treaty and other relevant documents, see Mas Latrie, *Histoire de l'île de Chypre*, 2:291–302 and 302–8, 347–50. For a discussion about Peter's motifs, see Peter W. Edbury, "The Crusading Policy of King Peter I of Cyprus, 1359–1369," in *The Eastern Mediterranean Lands in the*

Whatever traits of crusader ideology may be traced in relation to Peter's military exploits disappear completely in the account of the 1426 Mamluk invasion of Cyprus, which Makhairas actually eyewitnessed and describes as a huge disaster for the kingdom of Cyprus, foretold by portents and natural phenomena.[51] The chronicler does not hesitate to accuse the Cypriots that they had provoked the wrath of the Muslims, thus causing the invasion, because of the many raids which they shamelessly made upon the sultan's lands and the support they gave to other pirates ("Καὶ διὰ τὲς πολλὲς φορὲς ὅπου ἐκουρσεῦγαν τὴν Συρίαν οἱ κουρσάριδες, ἐσυνιθίζαν καὶ οἱ Κυπριῶτες καὶ ἐκουρσεῦγαν τους πολλὰ φανερὰ καὶ ἀδιάντροπα").[52] The Cypriots were growing rich from plundering Muslim land and from slave trading while the Muslims endured patiently the mischief done them. "The foolish people and many of the knights" thought that the Muslims were afraid of them; but God was a fair judge and he punished the Cypriots because the sultan had the right on his side. The narrative includes the story of a young Christian boy from Alexandria who saw in a vision that God would withdraw his help from the Cypriots in their conflict with the Muslims because they did not put their hopes in Him but in their vain arms ("[the Cypriots] δὲν ὀρπίζουν εἰς τὸν θεόν, ἀμμὲ ὀλπίζουν εἰς τὰ ψεματινά τους ἄρματα"). And it even tells the story of a good sheikh from Damascus who sent his son to Cyprus to warn the king that the sultan, a most powerful ruler, was angry with him for breaking the agreements and could easily destroy Cyprus; but the Cypriots paid no attention to him because of their "arrogance" ("σουπέρπια").[53] The description of the defeat of the Cypriot army and the capture of King Janus (1398–1432) by the Egyptians has nothing heroic about it; Makhairas does not hesitate to admit that "the Cypriots were in disorder and ... unskilled in war" ("ἐξηγήθησαν τὴν ἀταξίαν τοὺς Κυπριῶτες, καὶ πῶς εἶνε ἄπρακτοι τῆς ἀντρείας") and to cite incidents of disgraceful behaviour by

---

Period of the Crusades, ed. P. M. Holt (Warminster, 1977), pp. 90–105; Edbury, *The Kingdom of Cyprus*, pp. 171, 177–79; Housley, *The Later Crusades*, pp. 41–43; and Antony Leopold, *How to Recover the Holy Land. The Crusade Proposals of the Late Thirteenth and Early Fourteenth Centuries* (Aldershot, 2000), pp. 191–92.

[51] Makhairas, *Chronicle*, 1:§690, and *Diplomatic Edition*, p. 454 (only in V301r).

[52] For examples of the use of the word "κουρσεύγω" and its derivatives "κοῦρσος" and "κουρσάροι"/"κουρσάριδες" in relation to the Cypriot and Mamluk raids and the 1426 invasion of Cyprus, see indicatively Makhairas, *Chronicle*, 1:§§636, 646 (quotation), 651, 661, 676, 695, etc., and *Diplomatic Edition*, pp. 426–27, 430 (quotation), 431–32, 437, 446, 455, etc.; more examples above in notes 37 and 46. Also, the word "ἀζάπιδεσ" (*azapides*) is used twice: see Makhairas, *Chronicle*, 1:§§651, 676, and *Diplomatic Edition*, pp. 431, 446 (only in V288v, 294v; O301v, 315v and R172v, 178r give the alternative "κουρσάριδες"). On this word, of Arabo-Turkish origin, see Du Cange, *Glossarium graecitatis*, 1:col. 31, Mas Latrie, *Histoire de l'île de Chypre*, 2:299, 3:885, Makhairas, *Chronicle*, 2:215, and Kriaras, *Dictionary*, 1:107–8. A "Nicollin Azapi" is mentioned in 1367 in Limassol: see Jean Richard, ed., *Chypre sous les Lusignans. Documents chypriotes des archives du Vatican (XIVe et XVe siècles)* (Paris, 1962), p. 78.

[53] Makhairas, *Chronicle*, 1:§§636, 646–47 (quotation), 651, 661–67 (story of the good sheikh), 668–70 (670 for the quotation, story of the boy), and *Diplomatic Edition*, pp. 426–27, 430–31 (quotation), 431–32, 436–42 (story of the good sheikh), 442–44 (443 for the quotation, story of the boy). For the story of the good sheikh, also see below, n. 71.

the undisciplined soldiers, rioting in order to get more wine, or to explain how the king escaped death by shouting in Arabic that he was the king.[54]

The study of the linguistic construction of ethnicity and alterity in the text yields interesting results about the way it expresses Cypriot self-perception and the perception of the "Other" and elucidates several ideological issues that are essential for the purposes of this article. It is important to stress in advance that the comparative study of language and name usage in all three manuscripts that preserve the chronicle reveals no significant differences or ideological deviations.[55] The use of ethnic names conforms in the main with the Byzantine usage,[56] allowing for some particularities which derive from the island's socio-cultural experience during the Lusignan rule. The enemy par excellence are the Muslims, mainly described in ethnic terms. Ethnic names designating the Muslims are employed in a very precise way, with a clear geographic and racial distinction between the "Σαρακηνοί" ("Saracens," the name used for the Arabs of Syria, Palestine, and Egypt as well as the Mamluks) and the "Τοῦρκοι" ("Turks," the name used for both the groups of Asia Minor and the Ottomans). For the Egyptians the ethnic "Μαμουλοῦκοι"/"Μαμουλούκιδες" ("Mamluks") is also used, while the more archaic "Ἀγαρηνοί" ("Hagarenes"), designating the Muslims in general, is encountered only twice and "Ἀράπιδες" ("Arabs," or perhaps black Africans) once. Interestingly, on one occasion the use of "Hagarenes" is attributed to Byzantine

---

[54] Makhairas, *Chronicle*, 1:§§651–59 (Mamluk raids on Limassol, Karpasia, Famagusta and the area around it, Salines and the area around it, and elsewhere), 671–95 (671 for the quotation, 679 for the riot, 683 for the king shouting in Arabic) (Mamluk invasion), and *Diplomatic Edition*, pp. 431–36 (Mamluk raids), 444–55 (444 for the quotation, 448 for the riot, 450–51 for the king speaking in Arabic) (Mamluk invasion). On these events, with a comparison with the Arabic accounts, see Robert Irwin, "Οἱ εἰσβολὲς τῶν Μαμελούκων στὴν Κύπρο" ["The raids of the Mamluks against Cyprus"], in *History of Cyprus*, 5:159–76. The incident with the king is also reported in Arabic sources: see M. Tahar Mansouri, ed., *Chypre dans les sources arabes médiévales*, with French trans., Cyprus Research Centre, Texts and Studies in the History of Cyprus 38 (Nicosia, 2001), p. 129. In *La Chronique d'Enguerran de Monstrelet*, ed. L. Douët-d'Arcq, 6 vols. (Paris, 1857–62; repr. New York, 1966), 4:263, *The Chronicles of Enguerrand de Monstrelet*, trans. Thomas Johnes, Esq., 2 vols. (London, 1840), 1:533, repr. in Theophilus A. H. Mogabgab, *Supplementary Excerpts on Cyprus, or Further Materials for a History of Cyprus*, 3 vols. (Nicosia, 1941–45), 1:63–64, the Catalan knight Carceran Suarez is the one who is said to have saved the king's life by speaking in Arabic.

[55] See Nicolaou-Konnari, "Onomatology," pp. 328, 357.

[56] For the use of ethnic names in Byzantine texts, see K. Lechner, *Hellenen und Barbaren im Weltbild der Byzantiner. Die alten Bezeichnungen als Ausdruck eines neuen Kulturbewußtseins*, Ph.D. Dissertation (Munich, 1954); H. Ditten, "Βάρβαροι, Ἕλληνες und Ῥωμαῖοι bei den letzten Byzantinischen Geschichtsschreibern," *Actes du XIIe Congrès International des Études Byzantines* (Belgrade, 1964), 2:273–99; Donald M. Nicol, *Byzantium and Greece*, Inaugural Lecture in the Korais Chair of Modern Greek and Byzantine History, Language and Literature (London, 1971), repr. in Donald M. Nicol, *Studies in Late Byzantine History and Prosopography*, Variorum Reprints (London, 1986), no. XV; Robert Browning, "Greeks and Others. From Antiquity to the Renaissance," in *History, Language and Literacy in the Byzantine World*, Variorum Reprints (Northampton, 1989), no. II; Panayiotis K. Christou, *Οἱ περιπέτειες τῶν ἐθνικῶν ὀνομάτων τῶν Ἑλλήνων* [The adventures of the ethnic names of the Greeks] (Thessalonike, 1993), pp. 85–138; and Angel Nicolaou-Konnari, "The Encounter of Greeks and Franks in Cyprus in the Late Twelfth and Thirteenth Centuries. Phenomena of Acculturation and Ethnic Awareness" (unpublished PhD thesis, Cardiff University, 1999), ch. 5.

envoys to Cyprus, whose message to King Peter II is reported seemingly verbatim in the chronicle, and this suggests that Makhairas may have used the original name found in the relevant document; similarly, in formulaic addresses the sultan of Egypt is called "the sultan of Babylon." The names "Λατῖνοι" ("Latins'") and "Φράγκοι" ("Franks") are used for the first crusaders and the Latin settlers in Syria, Palestine, and Cyprus as well as for the westerners in general; both names and especially "Latins" often also indicate religious affiliation within the Christian Church and are used in juxtaposition with the Orthodox Greeks, the Byzantines in general or the Cypriots in particular, consistently designated as the "Ρωμαῖοι" (*Romaioi*). The inclusive name "Δυσικοί" ("westerners") is also sometimes encountered, but the prevailing usage is to designate the various groups with their specific ethnic names (Venetians, Genoese, etc.); the ethnic "Λαγκουβάρδοι" ("Longobards") is used once for the crusaders of the Third Crusade. The name *Polain*, that described the second or third generation of the Latins who had settled in the crusader states in western crusader literature but also in texts from Outremer, is attested in the chronicle in relation to the name of the church of "St. George of the *Polain*" in Nicosia; the literal translation "Ἅγιος Γεώργιος τῶν Ὀρνιθίων" is meaningless in Greek and probably indicates that the name had lost its ethnic connotations by the fifteenth century. In most cases where the Muslims confront the Cypriots, either in battle or in negotiations, the ethnic names are used: "Saracens" and "Turks" as opposed to the Cypriots, generally described as *Kypriotes*.[57]

However, ethnic antagonism may occasionally be expressed with names that indicate a collective religious identity: "the Muslim people" ("τὸ γένος τῶν Μουσθλουμάνων/Μουσουλμάνων" or "τὸ Μουσθλουμάνειο"), generally referring to the subjects of the sultan of Egypt, as opposed to "the Christians" ("οἱ Χριστιανοί"), a name that includes the Cypriots (Greeks and Latins), the Byzantines, the crusaders, and generally the westerners; interestingly, the name "Muslims" is encountered a lot more rarely than "Christians." Religious names are frequently

---

[57] See indicatively Makhairas, *Chronicle*, 1:§§9, 10, 90, 91, 159, 171, 659, 661, etc. (Saracens), 33, 91, 112–14, etc. (Turks), 659, 671–73, etc. (Mamluks), 32 and 346 (Hagarenes), 672 (Arabs), 230 and 307 (sultan of Babylon), 18, 27, 72–73, 87, 101, 579–80, etc. (Latins), 33, 73, 101, 203, 348, etc. (Franks), 22, 27, 72–73, 101, 348, etc. (*Romaioi*), 131 (westerners), 22 (Longobards), 51, 65, and (195) (*Polain*), 75, 91, 166, 306, 379, 440, 454, etc. (*Kypriotes*), and *Diplomatic Edition*, pp. 69, 70, 112, 148, 153–54, 435–36, etc. (Saracens), 83–84, 112–13, 122–24, etc. (Turks), 435, 444–45, etc. (Mamluks), 83 and 258 (only in V15v, 143r, Hagarenes), 444 (Arabs), 190 and 236–37 (sultan of Babylon), 74, 79, 103–4, 111, 117, 403, etc. (Latins), 83–84, 104 (only in V28v), 118 (only in V37r), 174, 259, etc. (Franks), 76, 79, 104, 117, 259, etc. (*Romaioi*), 133 (only in V46v, westerners), 76 (Longobards), 94, 101, and (215) (*Polain*), 106, 112, 152, 236, 277, 316, 323, etc. (*Kypriotes*). For *Polain*, see Margaret Ruth Morgan, "The Meanings of Old French *Polain*, Latin *Pullanus*," *Medium Aevum*, 48/1 (1979), 40–54; for *Kypriotes*, also see above n. 9 and more examples in Nicolaou-Konnari, "Ethnic Names and the Construction of Group Identity," pp. 262–63, and Nicolaou-Konnari, "Onomatology," pp. 335–36; for messages of embassies and formulaic addresses in the chronicle, see Nicolaou-Konnari, "Diplomatics and Historiography," pp. 301–3 (303 for the Byzantine embassy), 312–13 (312, n. 57 for the sultan); for the use of ethnic names in the chronicle, see Nicolaou-Konnari, "Onomatology," pp. 328–36, 353, 366–67, 371 with more examples.

used in connection with Peter's expeditions against Asia Minor and Egypt, but only on two occasions do they appear in relation to the island's 1426 Mamluk invasion: in the good sheikh's letter to the king of Cyprus where the sultan is called "sole ruler of Islam" ("μονοκράτωρ τοῦ Μουσθλουμανείου") and in a passage which describes the Muslim invaders burning Christian churches and monasteries.[58] Ethnic antipathy also often acquires religious connotations and all Muslims are described as "ἄθεοι" ("godless"), "ἄπιστοι" ("infidel," "faithless"), "ἀλλόπιστοι" ("miscreant," "men of false belief"), "ἐχθροὶ τοῦ Θεοῦ" ("enemies of God"), or "παράνομοι" ("men of wrong belief"). There is no distinction in the scale of "Otherness" between the Arabs and the Turks, Makhairas considering both nations to be equally threatening to Cyprus and praying to the Lord to deliver the island from "the godless Hagarenes, Saracens, and Turks" ("τοὺς ἄθεους Ἀγαρηνοὺς, Σαρακηνοὺς ὁμοίως καὶ Τούρκους").[59] The sultan is "τρισκατάρατος" ("thrice-accursed"), "λύκος ἄγριος" (a "savage wolf"), and "σκύλλος" (a "dog"). In the reported treaties and letters, however, where most probably the original formulaic expressions of the notarial language are to a large extent preserved, the "most high lord the great sultan" is called a "loved friend" and a "dear brother."[60]

The study of language also reveals that the use of crusading vocabulary is very limited in the chronicle. For the expeditions against the Muslims the word "μάχη" (literally "battle" or "war") is used twice in relation to the 1365 capture of Alexandria, a common word that does not convey any crusader meaning, as well as terms which roughly mean "passage" and, thus, may have been drawn upon crusader literature:

---

[58]   See Makhairas, *Chronicle*, 1:§§10, 18, 91, etc. ("Christians" used for the first crusaders and the westerners), 113, 141, 171–72, 195, 202–3, 226, 304, 317, etc. ("Christians" used in relation to Peter's expeditions), 695 ("Christians" used in relation to the 1426 events), 196 (quotation), 226 (quotation), 202, 287, etc. ("Muslims" used in relation to Peter's expeditions), 664 (quotation) and 695 ("Muslims" used in relation to the 1426 events), and *Diplomatic Edition*, pp. 70 (only in V5r), 75, 89 (only in O14v and R14v), 112, etc. (Christians used for the first crusaders and the westerners), 122–23, 136–37, 154, 168–69, 173–74, 187 (only in O114r and R64v), 188 (only in V83v), 234, 243, etc. ("Christians" used in relation to Peter's expeditions), 454 ("Christians" used in relation to the 1426 events), 169 (quotation), 188 (quotation, only in V83v), 173 (only in V73v and R58v), 226 (only in V110v), etc. ("Muslims" used in relation to Peter's expeditions), 438 (quotation) and 454, etc. ("Muslims" used in relation to the 1426 events). For the use of religious names in the chronicle, see Nicolaou-Konnari, "Onomatology," pp. 353–54, 371.

[59]   See Makhairas, *Chronicle*, 1:§§9, 32 (quotation), and 661 (godless), 153, 188, 370, and 489 (infidel, faithless), 131, 169, 175, and 368 (miscreant, men of false belief), 91 (enemies of God), 152 and 696 (men of wrong belief), and *Diplomatic Edition*, pp. 69, 83 (quotation compiled from V15v and R11v), and 436 (godless), 143 (only in V53v), 163 (only in V68v), 271 (only in V154r and R100v), and 343 (only in V209r) (infidel, faithless), 132–33 (only in O58r and R36r), 153 (only in O80v), 156 (only in O83r), and 269 (only in O140v and R99v) (miscreant, men of false belief), 112 (only in V34v, enemies of God), 143 (only in V53v) and 456 (only in V302v) (men of wrong belief).

[60]   See Makhairas, *Chronicle*, 1:§§284, 204, 234, and *Diplomatic Edition*, pp. 224, 174 (only in V74v), 191 (only in V85r). For addresses and titles used for the sultan, see Makhairas, *Chronicle*, 1:§§230, 302, 307, etc., and *Diplomatic Edition*, pp. 190, 233, 236–37, etc.; also Nicolaou-Konnari, "Diplomatics and Historiography," p. 312, n. 57, for a comparison of these formulae with those in extant original documents. For the Muslims as the "Other" in the chronicle, see Nicolaou-Konnari, "Onomatology," pp. 355–56, 371.

for "διάβασις" (literally "crossing"), used for the First Crusade, "ταξείδιν" (literally "journey"), describing Peter's plans for a crusade, "ἄμε" (literally "going"), used for the expedition against Alexandria, and "ἔλα" (literally "coming"), referring to the 1426 Mamluk invasion, the crusading connotation is not evident in Greek; but the use of "πασάντζιν" on one occasion with regards to Peter's efforts for a new crusade after the Alexandria events constitutes a direct transliteration of *passagium*, a word which clearly belongs to the crusading lexicon.[61] However, there are no words or expressions that could correspond to *bellum sacrum/guerre sainte*, *expeditio crucis/croiserie*, or *peregrinatio*. Most importantly, the text does not use a collective name that could be considered to be the equivalent of *milites Christi* or *crucesignati*, in modern Greek σταυροφόροι, a late introduction in the Greek language, attested only since 1856. The word "πιλιγρίνοι" (and its derivative "πιλιγρίνικα"), an obvious Latin loanward employed only once, clearly means "pilgrims" in the original sense of the word.[62]

Stylistically, though, a number of expressions and images that may be considered to pertain to the crusading rhetoric are occasionally employed, even though in most cases these represent literary conventions and commonplaces attested in both western and Byzantine historiography. The conquest of southern Asia Minor and Lesser Armenia by the Turks and that of Palestine and Egypt by the Mamluks, as well as the Mamluk invasion of Cyprus, are interpreted in terms of the cause-and-effect relationship between the people's sins and divine punishment ("we pay no heed to the ills which may be coming upon us, and do much ill, and therefore deserve even more than comes to us").[63] In order to describe the extent of the defencelessness of Cyprus, the image of a rock in the midst of the sea, surrounded by the infidel

---

[61] See Makhairas, *Chronicle*, 1:§§159 and 307 ("μάχη"), 10 ("διάβασις"), 153 ("ταξείδιν"), 169 ("ἄμε"), 674 and 680 ("ἔλα»), 217 ("πασάντζιν"), and *Diplomatic Edition*, pp. 148 and 236–37 ("μάχη"), 70 (only in V5r, "διάβασις"), 144 ("ταξείδιν"), 153 ("ἄμε"), 445 and 448 (only in V296v) ("ἔλα"), 182 (only in V79v, "πασάντζιν").

[62] For σταυροφόροι, see George D. Babiniotis, *Λεξικό τῆς νέας ἑλληνικῆς γλώσσας* [Modern Greek dictionary] (Athens, 1998), p. 1667. It was only in the early thirteenth century that the word *crucesignati* was used in connection with the crusaders: see, for example, Matthew Paris, *Historia Anglorum*, ed. Frederic Madden, 3 vols., RS 44, 1:79–80 (*crucesignatorum*); and *Der Mittelenglische Versroman* über *Richard Löwenherz*, ed. K. Brunner, Wiener Beiträge zur Englischen Philologie 42 (Vienna and Leipzig, 1913), p. 195, line 2143 ("for he is crossed, and pylgrym"). For "pilgrims," see Makhairas, *Chronicle*, 1:§§688, 691, and *Diplomatic Edition*, pp. 453–54. For a study of the use of crusading vocabulary in western and Outremer sources, see Nicolaou-Konnari, *The Encounter of Greeks and Franks in Cyprus*, chapter 6, and Ilieva, "Crusading Images," passim (particularly for the *Continuations* and the texts of Philip of Novara and the Templar of Tyre); more generally, Riley-Smith, *What Were the Crusades?*, p. 12; Hans Eberhard Mayer, *The Crusades*, trans. John Gillingham (Oxford, 1972), p. 15; and Robert Bartlett, *The Making of Europe. Conquest, Colonization and Cultural Change, 950–1350* (London, 1993), pp. 101–5, 250–55.

[63] See, for example, Makhairas, *Chronicle*, 1:§§112, 230, 482, 644 (quotation), 651, and *Diplomatic Edition*, pp. 122, 190, 338, 430 (quotation), 431–32; generally, Nicolaou-Konnari, "Chronique," p. 59. For the sin and punishment pattern in the Byzantine and western traditions, it is worth citing indicatively two authors from or connected with Cyprus, Neophytos the Recluse and Philippe de Mézières; see respectively Galatariotou, *The Making of a Saint*, pp. 185, 186, 189, 207, 208, 214, n. 41, and Nicolaou-Konnari, "Apologists or Critics?," p. 368.

Turks and Saracens, is used on four occasions.[64] The Cypriots' victories against the Muslims (in relation to the expeditions against the Turks in Asia Minor and the Mamluks in Alexandria, but also Cypriot raids and privateering) are often attributed to divine intervention with expressions such as "by the power of God," "by the aid/help of God," "by the will of God," "God showed grace to the Christians," "God gave strength to the Christians," "God gave the victory to the Christians and they routed the Turks," or "the Christians rejoiced with great joy and gave much joyful thanks to God."[65] Although the Byzantine emperor is considered by Guy of Lusignan to be a potential threat to his sovereignty, the Latins and the Greeks will be united before the common Muslim enemy: the count of Savoy, Amedeo VI (1343–83), helps Emperor John V Palaiologos (1354–91) to regain Greek lands which had been occupied by the Turks (and they recover them "by the grace of Almighty God"), while the Byzantine envoys wish Peter II "may God increase your years and give you strength against the Hagarenes."[66]

Moreover, Peter's heroic side as a defender of Christendom is not underrated and he is described by a western lord as "a good and orthodox Christian" who was "zealous for the holy church, and avenged the wrongs of the Christians"; governed by "his desire to bring an army (for Syria) to go to destroy the miscreant Saracens," he challenges the sultan in a very chivalric manner: "I swear to you on my faith as the Christian I am" that "I shall come down upon you and will give you to know what kind of man I am; and my faith is in God, that he will give me the victory."[67] The fact that after the Genoese invasion the Cypriots had to return Satalia "to the miscreant Turks" is said to be "a great shame for Christendom."[68] Most importantly, the biblical comparison used for the sultan of Egypt, whose heart "God hardened … even as the heart of Pharaoh," is reminiscent of a similar image in the letter of Pope Innocent III dated ca. 20 June 1203; in the letter, which is the earliest explicit written prohibition of the diversion to Constantinople addressed to the crusaders that survives, Doge Enrico Dandolo is identified with Pharaoh of the story of Exodus, who held the children of Israel in bondage. This "biblical code" is also used by Philippe de Mézières in the 1390s to describe the enemy of the new order of crusaders.[69] Finally, the account of the execution in Egypt of

---

[64]   See Makhairas, *Chronicle*, 1:§§91, 106, 370, 489 (quotation in the title), and *Diplomatic Edition*, pp. 112, 120, 271, 343 (quotation in the title); generally, Nicolaou-Konnari, "Ethnic Names and the Construction of Group Identity," p. 263, and Nicolaou-Konnari, "Onomatology," p. 335.

[65]   Makhairas, *Chronicle*, 1:§§114, 121, 126, 133, 195, and 317 (Asia Minor), 171–72 (Alexandria), 180, 212, and 219 (Cypriot raids), 221 (raid against Cyprus), and *Diplomatic Edition*, pp. 124, 127, 130 (only in V45r), 133 (only in V47r), 169 (only in V71r), and 243 (Asia Minor), 154 (Alexandria), 159 (only in V65r), 179, (only in V77v), and 183 (only in V80r) (Cypriot raids), 184 (only in V81r, raid against Cyprus).

[66]   Makhairas, *Chronicle*, 1:§§22, 183 (quotation), 346 (quotation), and *Diplomatic Edition*, pp. 76–77, 159–61 (161 for the quotation, only in V66v), 258 (quotation, only in V143r).

[67]   Makhairas, *Chronicle*, 1:§§216, 153, 228, 230, and *Diplomatic Edition*, pp. 181, 143, 189 (only in V84r), 190–91.

[68]   Makhairas, *Chronicle*, 1:§368, and *Diplomatic Edition*, p. 269.

[69]   See Makhairas, *Chronicle*, 1:§189, and *Diplomatic Edition*, p. 164 (only in V69r); Alfred J. Andrea, *Contemporary Sources for the Fourth Crusade*, with contributions by Brett E. Whalen (Leiden,

two Christians captured in Limassol during the 1425 Mamluk raid, who according
to the chronicle were later canonized, clearly belongs to the literary topos of the
martyrdom of the soldiers of God in the hands of the infidel:

> both of them suffered death for their sweet Lord Jesus. And they chose to die in the
> faith of Christ rather than to live in lies and to turn Moslem; and they reviled the sultan
> and those who tormented them. And at the last the sergeant cut off their holy heads, and
> they rendered their holy souls into the hands of the living God, and their memory abides
> for ever.[70]

This imagery, though, cannot be considered to constitute plain anti-Islamism
inscribed within a holy war context that justifies violence against the infidel. At
times Makhairas does not even hesitate to acknowledge the positive qualities of
the Muslims, noting the valour ("ἀντρείαν") of the Turks and the patience of the
Arabs, who endured much but chivalrously never took vengeance without warning
their enemies, and citing the long story of the good sheikh mentioned above.[71] The
fact that Makhairas is capable of depicting war with the Muslims and expressing
their alterity in religious terms does not affect the way he perceives expeditions
against them: they are wars waged for the interests of the insular kingdom and
not religious conflicts. The menacing "Other" for Leontios is whoever threatened
the stability and social order of this kingdom and not only the infidel; even the

---

Boston and Cologne, 2000), pp. 60–61 for Innocent's letter; Philippe de Mézières, *La Sustance de la
Chevalerie de la Passion de Jhesu Crist en francois*, ed. Abdel Hamid Hamdy, "Philippe de Mézières
and the New Order of the Passion. Part III (Transcription of the Ashmole MS. 813)," *Bulletin of the
Faculty of Arts* (Alexandria University) 18 (1964), 46; Philippe de Mézières, *Une epistre lamentable et
consolatoire. Addressée en 1397 à Philippe le Hardi, duc de Bourgogne, sur la défaite de Nicopolis*, ed.
Philippe Contamine and Jacques Paviot with the collaboration of Céline Van Hoorebeeck (Paris, 2008),
pp. 203–4; and generally Angel Nicolaou-Konnari, "Alterity and Identity in the Work of Philippe de
Mézières (1327–1405) and Leontios Makhairas (ca. 1360/80–after 1432)," in *Identity / Identities in Late
Medieval Cyprus*, Proceedings of the Joint Newton Fellowship and Annual ICS Byzantine Colloquium,
Centre for Hellenic Studies, King's College London and Cyprus Research Centre, Nicosia (13–14 June,
London) (forthcoming). The "biblical code" of Pharaoh may be traced back to early Christian literature,
see indicatively in the fourth century Gregory of Nazianzus, *Lettres théologiques*, ed. P. Gallay, Sources
chrétiennes 208 (Paris, 1974), no. 101, sections 44.1 and 58.3, and Gregory of Nazianzus, *De theologia*,
in *Gregor von Nazianz. Die fünf theologischen Reden*, ed. G. Barbel (Düsseldorf, 1963), section 3.17.
Pietro Valderio, *La guerra di Cipro*, ed. Gilles Grivaud and Nasa Patapiou, Cyprus Research Centre,
Texts and Studies in the History of Cyprus 22 (Nicosia, 1996), pp. 33 and 192, uses the code within the
context of the conquest of Cyprus by the Ottoman Turks in 1570–71.

[70] Makhairas, *Chronicle*, 1:§§657, 660, and *Diplomatic Edition*, pp. 435 (only in V285r (bis)), 435–
36. The story is also reported in *La Chronique d'Enguerran de Monstrelet*, 4:246–47, *The Chronicles
of Enguerrand de Monstrelet*, 1:528, repr. in Mogabgab, *Supplementary Excerpts on Cyprus*, 1:61–62.

[71] Makhairas, *Chronicle*, 1:§§141, 636, 646, 661–67, and *Diplomatic Edition*, pp. 136, 426, 430,
436–42. As far as I know, the story of the good sheikh is not mentioned by Arabic sources but it is
reported in a strikingly similar but shorter version in *La Chronique d'Enguerran de Monstrelet*, 4:243–
44, *The Chronicles of Enguerrand de Monstrelet*, 1:527, repr. in Mogabgab, *Supplementary Excerpts on
Cyprus*, 1:60–61; Kyrris, "Some Aspects of Leontios Makhairas' Ethnoreligious Ideology," pp. 239–45,
discusses Makhairas's religious tolerance as demonstrated by the sheikh's story and questions the story's
authenticity.

"cursed" Greek peasants ("καταραμένοι χωργιάτες"), who took advantage of the 1426 Egyptian invasion to rise in revolt, are attributed this role[72] and, especially, the "evil" Genoese. The study of the way war against the Genoese is presented in the chronicle yields interesting analogies with the way war against the Muslims is, and clarifies further Makhairas's attitude.

The "Otherness" of the Genoese in their capacity as the kingdom's enemies is expressed in a language the violence of which equals and even surpasses at times that used for the Muslims and, most importantly, it is frequently perceived in religious terms; in fact, Makhairas does not find any excuses for the "haughty and traitorous Genoese people" ("τὸ σουπέρπιον γένος τῶν Γενουβίσων καὶ παράβουλον") precisely because they are Christians. They are said to be "godless" ("ἄθεοι"), "faithless" and "treacherous" ("ἄπιστοι"), "enemies to God" ("ὀχτροὶ τοῦ Θεοῦ"), "traitors to their oath" ("ἐφίορκοι"), "bad Christians and creatures of the devil" ("κακοὶ χριστιανοὶ, τὰ ἔργα τοῦ διαβόλου"), "cursed" ("καταραμένοι"), who had no right to lay their pestilent hands upon the body and blood of the Lord during mass because of the atrocities they had commited, including the murder of a priest. God allowed the island to be invaded by the Genoese because of the Cypriots' sins, but God also "delivered" them from the hands of their enemies many a time in battles; religious vocabulary and expressions are even used for the negotiations between the Cypriot envoys and the Genoese admiral. Although Makhairas deplores the fact that after the Genoese invasion it was impossible for the Cypriots to keep Satalia, the manpower and the money required for its maintenance being needed in Cyprus "because of the Genoese," he does not hesitate to state that "they were all agreed that they should return the said castle to the Turks rather than the Genoese should take it."[73] This assessment of the threatening "Other" illustrates perfectly the text's political ideology and echoes, *mutatis mutandis*, the oft-quoted words attributed to the Great Duke Loukas Notaras a little before the fall of Constantinople to the Ottomans in 1453: "Rather the Turkish turban than a Roman cardinal's hat."[74]

---

[72] For the 1426–27 uprising, see Makhairas, *Chronicle*, 1:§§696–97 (697 for the quotation), 700, and *Diplomatic Edition*, pp. 456–57 (457 for the quotation, only in V303v), 458; generally, Nicolaou-Konnari, "The Conquest of Cyprus," pp. 69–70, and Nicolaou-Konnari, "Greeks," p. 20.

[73] See indicatively Makhairas, *Chronicle*, 1:§§153 (quotation), 473, 474 (traitorous), 401 (godless), 421, 423, 473, 474, 545 (faithless/treacherous), 473 (enemies of God), 473 (traitors to their oath), 537 (bad Christians and creatures of the devil), 520 (cursed), 416 (pestilent hands), 421, 482, 644 (sins), 441–43 (violence committed by the Genoese), 369, 498, 545, 549 (delivered by God), 487–92 (negotiations), 366–68 (Satalia), and *Diplomatic Edition*, pp. 143 (quotation), 334, 334–35 (traitorous), 290 (godless), 302, 303 (only in V178v), 334, 334–35, 382 (only in V239r–v) (faithless/treacherous), 334 (only in O204v and R131r, enemies of God), 334 (traitors to their oath), 376 (bad Christians and creatures of the devil), 365 (only in V226r, cursed), 298 (pestilent hands), 302, 338, 430 (sins), 316–18 (violence committed by the Genoese), 270, 350–51, 382, 385 (delivered by God), 342–48 (negotiations), 268–70 (Satalia). For more examples of verbal abuse of the Genoese, see Nicolaou-Konnari, "Onomatology," p. 356.

[74] See Stephen Runciman, *The Fall of Constantinople* (Cambridge, 1969), p. 71 and note at p. 214 with sources. For an interpretation of the nature of the duke's patriotism, see Tonia Kioussopoulou, "Η έννοια της πατρίδας κατά τον 15o αιώνα" ["The notion of fatherland in the fifteenth century"], in *1453. Η άλωση της Κωνσταντινούπολης και η μετάβαση από τους μεσαιωνικούς στους νεώτερους*

It is difficult to determine to what extent Makhairas's view of war against the Muslims as a mainly Cypriot affair incorporated a social reality (the way the entire population of the island perceived the events) or simply reflected his arbitrary subjectivity and historiographical intentions, which determined the ideology and historicity of his text.[75] Even if we accept that the chronicle is to a certain extent a cultural product of the particular milieu to which its author belonged and of the sources available to him and that Makhairas construes historical events with the benefit of hindsight, evidence suggests that discontentment because of the social and economic effects of Peter's wars on the Cypriot society must have existed amongst the Frankish nobility and the burgesses. This is highlighted by the king's murder in 1369, and, interestingly, the account of Peter's last days in the chronicle has nothing heroic or flattering about it, Makhairas describing in a climactic way the king's moral degradation and abuse of power.[76] On the other hand, in both contemporary and modern literature Peter's wars are considered to be "the most famous period of Cypriot involvement in the crusading movement." Fourteenth-century literature includes the hagiographical *vita* of Peter Thomas (written in 1366) and later works by the king's chancellor and friend Philippe de Mézières and *La Prise d'Alixandre* by Guillaume de Machaut (ca. 1300–77), a verse biography of the king. Both writers have the merit of contemporaneity (Philippe had first-hand knowledge while Machaut was almost entirely dependent on what other people could tell him) and present Peter as the ideal crusader and defender of the Church. A close comparison of the way Peter's three apologists portray the Cypriot king (the epic hero of the non-Cypriot writers as opposed to Makhairas's more realistic and human picture) together with an examination of the interdependence between ideological bias and historical reliability would show their difference of perspective and would enhance our understanding of the social logic of the chronicle. An endeavour of this kind should be inscribed within the larger framework of the study of the underestimated relationship between medieval Cypriot and medieval French historiography; the connection between Makhairas's text and contemporary French chronicles, in particular, such as the *Chroniques* of Jean Froissart's continuator Enguerrand de Monstrelet (ca. 1390/5–1453), requires further investigation in order to trace affinities in form, style, and content and, most importantly, to identify common sources. This line of research would complement the present study and remains a *desideratum*.[77]

χρόνους [1453. The fall of Constantinople and the passage from medieval to modern times], ed. Tonia Kioussopoulou (Herakleion, 2005), pp. 157–58.

[75] See, generally, Zink, *La subjectivité littéraire*, pp. 5–23, and, particularly for Makhairas, Nicolaou-Konnari, "Chronique," p. 57.

[76] Makhairas, *Chronicle*, 1:§§259–81, and *Diplomatic Edition*, pp. 205–22; see discussion in Nicolaou-Konnari, "Apologists or Critics?," pp. 396–99. The illustration of the murder in the Book of Hours of Louis of Savoy, Paris, Bibliothèque Nationale de France, MS lat. 9473, fol. 64v, is not very flattering either; see *Chypre. D'Aphrodite à Mélusine*, p. 131, ill. XLIII.

[77] See generally Edbury, *The Kingdom of Cyprus*, pp. 161 (quotation), 162–63, 171–9. For a comparison of the three writers, see now Edbury, "Machaut, Mézières, Makhairas, and *Amadi*,"

Moreover, a study of the way two sixteenth-century Cypriot narrative sources, the history of Florio Bustron and the chronicle known under the name of the sole manuscript's owner Francesco Amadi, perceive the same events and the extent to which they inscribe them within the concept of the crusades and holy war might shed some light on many obscure issues concerning their relationship and common sources with Makhairas's text as well as the ideological aspects of history writing in the insular kingdom; but this study too would go beyond the scope of this article and I can only say here that the two writers adhere largely to Makhairas's *kypriotike* perception of history.[78] One would be remiss if one did not mention a revival of the crusader spirit in Cypriot historiography composed after the Ottoman conquest of the island in 1570/1, as attested in a recently discovered historical treatise written by Giorgio de Nores (1619–38) in Italy in the 1630s, a work which seems to have been influenced by the spirit of Torquato Tasso's *Gerusalemme Liberata* (1581).[79] Finally, the association of the British colonization of Cyprus (1878–1960) with Richard the Lionheart's 1191 crusader conquest ("a chain from Richard to Victoria" linking "the first coming of the English" with the "second British occupation") in nineteenth- and twentieth-century British, Greek, and French literature points to the topicality of the idea of the crusades in relation to the modern history of Cyprus.[80]

---

and Nicolaou-Konnari, "Apologists or Critics?"; see also above, n. 30. The connection between the chronicles of Makhairas and Monstrelet has been completely overlooked in secondary literature; see above, n. 54.

[78] See Grivaud, "Intellectual Life and Letters," pp. 1148–53 ("Amadi"), 1154–68 (Bustron); and Edbury, "Machaut, Mézières, Makhairas, and *Amadi*."

[79] Giorgio Denores, *Discorso sopra l'isola di Cipri con le ragioni della vera successione in quel Regno – A Discourse on the Island of Cyprus and on the Reasons of the True Succession in that Kingdom*, ed. and trans. Paschalis M. Kitromilides, Hellenic Institute of Byzantine and Post-Byzantine Studies, Graecolatinitas nostra, Sources (Venice, 2006). See Angel Nicolaou-Konnari, "Φιλίες του πνεύματος στους ιταλικούς λογοτεχνικούς κύκλους του *Cinquecento*: ο Torquato Tasso (1544–1595), ο Pietro de Nores (πριν από το 1570 (;) – μετά από το 1646/8) και οι άλλοι" ["Friendships of the mind in the Italian literary circles of the *Cinquecento*: Torquato Tasso (1544–1595), Pietro de Nores (before 1570 – after 1646/8), and the others"], in *Proceedings of the Fourth International Cyprological Conference* (Nicosia, 29 April–3 May 2008), *Medieval Section*, ed. Charalampos G. Chotzakoglou (forthcoming) and above n. 7.

[80] See indicatively Sir Garnet Wolseley, *Cyprus 1878. The Journal of Sir Garnet Wolseley*, ed. Anne Cavendish (Nicosia, 1991), p. 112; William Hepworth Dixon, *British Cyprus* (London, 1879), p. 139 (quotation); Sir Harry C. Luke, *Cyprus. A Portrait and An Appreciation* (London, 1957; revised ed. London, 1965), pp. 34, 85 (quotation); Doros Alastos, *Cyprus in History. A Survey of 5000 Years* (London, 1976), pp. 301, 318–19; Nikolaos P. Vasiliades, Ἐθνομάρτυρες τοῦ Κυπριακοῦ Ἔπους 1955–1959 [National martyrs of the Cypriot epos 1955–1959] (Athens, 1979), p. 38; (Comité de rédaction), "Chronique: Notice nécrologique pour Louis de Mas Latrie," *ROL* 4 (1896), 462–71, repr. in Evangelos Louis Louizos and Hugues Jean de Dianoux de la Perrotine, eds., *Correspondances et écrits de Louis de Mas Latrie sur Chypre*, I, Fondation A. G. Leventis (Nîmes, 1997), p. 62; H. Wallon, "Notice sur la vie et les travaux du comte Jacques-Marie-Joseph-Louis de Mas Latrie, membre libre de l'Académie des Inscriptions et Belles Lettres," *Bibliothèque de l'École des chartes* 60 (1899), 617–39, repr. in Louizos and Dianoux de la Perrotine, *Correspondances et écrits de Louis de Mas Latrie*, p. 75; generally, Nicolaou-Konnari, "The Conquest of Cyprus," p. 92.

Clio sous le regard d'Hermès:
itinéraires et œuvre de Dominique Jauna,
historien de Chypre et des croisades

Philippe Trélat

Groupe de Recherche d'Histoire de l'Université de Rouen
phil_trelat@yahoo.fr

Summary

With the publication of the Histoire générale des royaumes de Chypre, Jérusalem, d'Arménie et d'Egypte *in Leiden (1747), Dominique Jauna offered an original historical work to the readers of the Enlightenment. Condemned by positivist history and forgotten by modern historiography, Jauna's work still merits the attention of historians.*

Born in 1662 in Turin, Dominique Jauna emigrated to the Levant very early in his life and pursued a parallel career as a trader and a consular administrator. Following the looting of his warehouses at Damietta, Jauna returned to France in 1705. He met the Maurists at Saint-Germain des Prés from whom he acquired his training as a historian. Thanks to the palaeographer Bernard de Montfaucon, Dominique Jauna found employment with Charles VI in Vienna as a consultant and Inspector-General of Trade in 1730. This post allowed him to write his Histoire générale, *enabling him to reflect on readings in libraries and archives and on memories gleaned from his years of activity in Cyprus and Egypt.*

The structure of the Histoire générale *reveals the author's intent to extend the humanist historiography of the Renaissance, represented by Florio Bustron and Etienne de Lusignan, expressing the singularity of the territory and the history of medieval Cyprus. His treatment of the history of the crusades is rather classic, with a chronology faithfully observed. Well-documented, the* Histoire générale *was, until the work of François-Joseph Michaud, a key reference for historians interested in the medieval East.*

La politique et les activités diplomatiques ont bien souvent contribué à faire naître des vocations d'historiens. Ce constat se vérifie pour l'histoire des croisades et des États de l'Orient latin à l'époque moderne, si l'on songe à Jacques Bongars, au service d'Henri IV pendant près de trente ans dans des négociations avec les princes allemands et auteur de la première compilation des historiens des croisades.[1] En revanche, le commerce a plus rarement aiguillé des négociants vers l'écriture du passé. Dominique Jauna, d'abord homme d'affaires au Levant puis intendant général du commerce à la cour de Vienne, fait donc figure d'exception en publiant en 1747 à Leyde, l'*Histoire générale des royaumes de Chypre, Jérusalem, d'Arménie et d'Egypte comprenant les Croisades et les faits les plus mémorables de l'Empire ottoman.*[2]

Son œuvre a connu un destin contrasté: après quelques comptes rendus élogieux dans des revues et de nombreuses citations au XVIIIe siècle, elle est vouée aux gémonies par l'histoire positiviste du siècle suivant.[3] Aujourd'hui, Jauna mérite

---

[1] Jacques Bongars, *Gesta dei per Francos, sive orientalium expeditionum et regni Francorum Hierosolymitani historia*, 2 vols. (Hanau, 1611); Géraud Poumarède, *Pour en finir avec la Croisade. Mythes et réalités de la lutte contre les Turcs aux XVIe et XVIIe siècles* (Paris, 2004), p. 402.

[2] Titre complet: Chevalier Dominique Jauna, *Histoire générale des roïaumes de Chypre, de Jérusalem, d'Arménie, et d'Egypte, comprenant les croisades, et les faits, les plus mémorables, de l'empire ottoman, avec plus d'exactitude qu'aucun auteur moderne les a encore rapportés, et les faits les plus mémorables, de l'Empire ottoman, depuis sa fondation jusqu'à la fameuse bataille de lepante, où finit cette histoire, dans laquelle on trouve aussi l'anéantissement de l'empire des Grecs. On y a ajouté I. L'etat présent de l'Egypte. II. Dissertation sur les caractères hiéroglifiques des anciens égyptiens III. Reflexions sur les moïens de conquérir l'Egypte et la Chypre par M^r le Chevalier Dominique Jauna, conseiller de sa Majesté Impériale et Roïale, et Intendant Général du Commerce dans tous ses Etats Héréditaires*, 2 vols. (Leyde 1747, repr. 1785) (cité par la suite: Jauna). Une réédition posthume intervient donc en 1785, sous le même titre, mais sans nom d'auteur, à Leyde chez les frères Murray et à Franeker chez Romar. De manière générale, les croisades n'ont pas été un sujet prisé par les historiens et imprimeurs de la République des Provinces-Unies. On connaît également des éditions en néerlandais de l'*Histoire des Croisades* de Maimbourg en 1683 et réimprimé en 1691 et de *Versuch einer Geschichte der Kreuzzüge und ihre Folgen* de Christoph Maier en 1783 et réimprimé en 1791; voir Willem Frijhoff, "Damiette appropriée. La mémoire de croisade, instrument de concorde civique (Haarlem, XVIe–XVIIIe siècle)," *Revue du Nord* 88 (2006), 7–42 at pp. 8–9.

[3] Quelques extraits de comptes rendus: "on peut assurer, sans crainte de se tromper, que cette histoire est non seulement la meilleure, qui existe, mais encore la seule, qui soit vraiment complète d'une époque aussi intéressante. L'auteur est non-seulement consulté les meilleurs auteurs, mais, ayant passé lui-même une grande partie de sa vie sur les lieux mêmes, il a eu l'avantage de pouvoir profiter des différentes sources, inconnues à ceux qui l'avoient précédé dans cette carrière." in *L'Esprit des journaux, françois et étrangers par une société de gens de lettres*, 12 (déc. 1785), p. 425; "si Jauna s'appuyoit de quelque autorité; mais cet écrivain, qui s'annonce pour donner l'histoire des Croisades plus exactement que personne, veut être cru sur sa parole: ainsi l'on ne doit s'en servir que quand on ne trouve rien dans les anciens: cependant cet ouvrage mérite beaucoup d'attention, parce que Jauna nous assure qu'il a puisé dans une quantité de manuscrits originaux, dont la connoissance n'est pas parvenue jusqu'à nous"; in Wilhelm E. J. Wal, *Histoire de l'Ordre teutonique*, 8 vols. (Paris-Liège, 1784–90), 1:150 n. 1. "Au premier examen, l'ouvrage superficiel et faux de Dominique Jauna n'inspirait aucune confiance; il ne renferme en réalité rien qui puisse être utilisé, si on en excepte une carte de l'île, dressée autrefois par Coronelli, et reproduite par Jauna." in Louis de Mas Latrie, *Histoire de l'île de Chypre sous le règne des princes de la maison de Lusignan*, 3 vols. (Paris, 1852–61), 2:II.

mieux que l'oubli dans les bilans historiographiques des croisades;[4] quelques voix dissonantes ont pourtant montré que l'on pouvait encore glaner des informations et des analyses pertinentes dans son travail, notamment pour l'histoire de Chypre.[5] Il paraît donc opportun de procéder à une mise au point historiographique.

Produit de la formation et de la culture de son auteur, *l'Histoire générale* doit s'appréhender en tenant compte des expériences professionnelles et sociales de Dominique Jauna. Sans succomber à un déterminisme réducteur, ni à une prétention à l'exhaustivité, il est nécessaire de restituer d'abord le parcours d'un individu dans la perspective de l'éclosion de son œuvre historique au terme de sa longue existence, avant d'analyser le contenu de l'ouvrage pour terminer par l'évocation de la méthode de travail de Jauna et l'identification de sa documentation.

Les itinéraires de Dominique Jauna

Les sources permettant de connaître les origines et la formation de Jauna se limitent à peu de choses. La documentation extraite par Anna Pouradier Duteil-Loizidou des Archives Nationales françaises (séries marine et affaires étrangères) et des Archives de la Chambre de Commerce et d'Industrie de Marseille a déjà donné matière à un article de Brunehilde Imhaus retraçant les années chypriotes du négociant.[6] Des recherches complémentaires permettent d'étoffer nos connaissances sur sa carrière.

Né en 1662 à Turin, Dominique Jauna, comme les autres membres de sa famille émigrés à Chypre, ses neveux Jean et Pierre, est identifié dans la documentation

---

[4] L'absence d'une référence à l'ouvrage de Jauna est constatée chez Heinrich K. L. von Sybel, *Geschichte der ersten Kreuzzugs* (Düsseldorf, 1841), trans. Lady Duff Gordon, *The History and Literature of the Crusades* (Londres, 1861); Aziz S. Atiya, *The Crusade, Historiography and Bibliography* (Bloomington, Ind., 1962); Christopher Tyerman, *The Invention of the Crusades* (Basingstoke, 1998), pp. 99–126; Giles Constable, "The Historiography of the Crusades," in *The Crusades from the Perspective of Byzantium and the Muslim World*, ed. Angeliki E. Laiou and Roy Mottahedeh (Washington, D.C., 2001), pp. 1–22; Constable, *Crusaders and Crusading in the Twelfth Century* (Burlington, 2008), pp. 3–43. Seul un chapitre de Ronnie Ellenblum évoque la figure de l'historien ligure pour son projet de conquête de l'Égypte: Ronnie Ellenblum, *Crusader Castles and Modern Histories* (Cambridge, Eng., 2007), p. 11 n. 31. Par ailleurs, nous n'avons pas consulté Mikhail A. Zaborov, *Vvedenie v istoriografiju Krestovykh pokhodov* [Introduction à l'historiographie des croisades] (Moscou, 1966) et Zaborov, *Istoriografija Krestovykh pokhodov (XVe–XIXe vv.)* [Historiographie des croisades XVe–XIXe s.] (Moscou, 1971).

[5] Parmi les études les plus récentes: Gilles Grivaud, "Les minorités orientales à Chypre (époques médiévale et moderne)," in *Actes du colloque Chypre et la Méditerranée orientale: migrations, échanges et territoires. Identités et langue, image et mémoire (Lyon, Maison de l'Orient méditerranéen, octobre 1997)*, ed. Yannis Ioannou, Françoise Métral and Marguerite Yon (Lyon, 2000), pp. 43–70 at pp. 53, 57; Chris Schabel, "The Myth of Queen Alice and the Subjugation of the Greek Clergy on Cyprus," in *Identités croisées en un milieu méditerranéen: le cas de Chypre (Antiquité–Moyen Âge)*, ed. Sabine Fourrier and Gilles Grivaud (Mont Saint-Aignan, 2006), pp. 257–77 at pp. 269–70.

[6] Brunehilde Imhaus, "Quelques remarques à propos de Dominique Jauna," Ἐπετερίς τοῦ Κέντρου Ἐπιστημονικῶν Ἐρευνῶν [Annuaire du centre de recherches scientifiques] 27 (2001), 127–37.

consulaire par son village d'origine, Pigna en Ligurie (province d'Imperia), alors sous domination de la maison de Savoie.[7]

Son éducation et sa formation d'homme d'affaires ne sont pas éclairées par les sources. Ses demandes de postes, auprès du ministre Maurepas en 1728 à Marseille ou à Paris, trahissent une expérience acquise sur le tas, Jauna met toujours en avant ses longues années d'exercice du négoce sur les différentes places de la Méditerranée pour convaincre ses interlocuteurs de lui confier un emploi.[8] De même, sa connaissance des langues orientales doit certainement davantage à son parcours professionnel et son réseau de relations qu'à un enseignement traditionnel. À l'instar de beaucoup de marchands du Levant de cette époque, Dominique Jauna est un polyglotte accompli, ce qu'il ne manque pas de souligner dans la dédicace de son *Histoire générale* pour assurer du caractère supérieur de son œuvre sur celle d'autres historiens qui n'auraient pas des compétences aussi étendues.[9] Il connaît l'italien comme ses écrits en témoignent; il utilise le français avec ses confrères de la nation française de Larnaca et c'est la langue qu'il choisit naturellement pour rédiger son *Histoire générale*; il a également, au minimum, des notions de grec et de turc, nécessaires à la conduite de ses affaires à Chypre, d'anglais, utilisé avec les négociants des places de Venise et Livourne, et d'arabe, en raison de son mariage avec une Chypriote maronite et de sa résidence au Caire.[10]

Dominique Jauna gagne le Levant très jeune, vers vingt ans, en s'agrégeant d'abord à la petite communauté de marchands français d'Alep.[11] Son activité commerciale le conduit ensuite à Chypre où il est recensé par la documentation consulaire, pour la première fois, en 1687. Lui, dans son *Histoire générale*, affirme être témoin de l'extraction du vitriol dans le canton de Chrysochou, dès 1684.[12] Très rapidement, bénéficiant du statut de protégé de la France, il entre dans son

---

[7]   Naples, Archivio di Stato di Napoli, fondo Ministero Affari Esteri (ensuite ASN Aff. Est.), f. 6803; Marseille, Archives de la Chambre de Commerce et d'Industrie (ensuite ACCIM), B 5 fols. 541r, 746v; Anna Pouradier Duteil-Loizidou, *Consulat de France à Larnaca (1696–1699)*, Sources et études de l'histoire de Chypre 17, 2 (Nicosie, 1995), n° 64 p. 134. La réédition posthume de son *Histoire générale* comprend un portrait de l'historien alors âgé de 79 ans. Une famille "Giauna di Pigna" est connue dans les archives conservées à Turin: Turin, Archivio di Stato di Torino, Archivio di Corte, Paesi, Città e contado di Nizza, Pigna, mazzo 42, fascicolo 17. La graphie "Jauna" serait la francisation de "Giauna." Le "i" ne se prononce pas et indique seulement la palatalisation du "g". Je remercie vivement Madame Yvette Giauna pour ces renseignements.

[8]   Paris, Archives Nationales (ensuite AN) Marine, B7 295, fol. 1r.

[9]   Jauna, 1:III–IV. Jauna affirme qu'une longue résidence à Chypre "lui aurait fait presque perdre sa langue maternelle," sans doute l'italien: ibid., p. 2.

[10]   ASN Aff. Est., f. 6803; Elvira Contino, *Mire di espansione commerciale del Regno di Napoli nel secolo XVIII I progetti di compagnie con le Indie Orientali* (Naples, 1990), pp. 153–55; Pouradier Duteil-Loizidou, *Consulat de France*, 2: n° 64 p. 134, pp. 331–32.

[11]   AN Affaires étrangères, B III 132, fol. 89v; sur les marchands français à Alep: Abderrahman Moallla, "Une ville du Levant au XVIIIe siècle: Alep," in *La Méditerranée au XVIIIe siècle, Actes du Colloque international tenu à Aix-en-Provence les 4, 5, 6 septembre 1985*, ed. Société Française d'Étude du XVIIIe siècle (Aix-en-Provence, 1987), pp. 79–89.

[12]   Jauna, 1:65.

administration consulaire et exerce la charge de chancelier du consul Balthazard Sauvan, pendant 18 mois (1687–88).[13]

Les affaires du négociant ligure prospèrent sur l'île où, en 1693, il fait venir son neveu Pierre Jauna, alors âgé d'environ 18 ans.[14] Suivant l'exemple d'autres marchands français, il contracte une alliance avec une maronite chypriote, Elisabeth Vincens, de la région de Kythrea qui lui apporte une dot de 25,000 livres et peut-être un lot de trois jardins où se pratique la sériciculture.[15] De cette union naît un fils, Jean-Michel, baptisé dans l'église paroissiale de Larnaca le 30 octobre 1697.[16]

Dominique participe régulièrement aux assemblées consulaires de la nation française à Larnaca, conjuguant des missions diplomatiques auprès du pacha à Nicosie à ses activités commerciales qui se rapportent notamment au trafic de la soie.[17] Cette position pourtant enviable ne semble pas le satisfaire et être à la mesure de ses ambitions. Si l'on en croit la documentation consulaire, il aurait échoué à s'emparer du poste de consul à Chypre durant l'absence de son titulaire, François Luce, en 1699.[18] Cet échec l'incite peut-être à se tenir éloigné de l'île pour quelques mois et à rejoindre Nice où on le retrouve rédigeant, à l'intention de Victor Amédée II de Savoie, un mémoire pour l'établissement d'une société de commerce au Levant.[19] En outre, le souverain lui confie la mission d'attirer les marchands dans les ports de Nice et Villefranche.[20]

De retour sur l'île, Dominique Jauna envisage de redéployer son activité commerciale vers des régions jusqu'alors peu explorées par les marchands occidentaux, et où les profits peuvent donc être importants. Damiette, en Égypte, présente cette perspective avec la nomination, à la fin du XVIIe siècle, d'un vice-consul provisoire en la personne d'Arnaud Richard de La Ciotat. Dominique Jauna

---

[13]   AN Affaires étrangères, B III 132, fol. 89v; Anna Pouradier Duteil-Loizidou, *Consulat de France à Larnaca (1660–1696)*, Sources et études de l'histoire de Chypre 20, 1 (Nicosie, 1991), n° 43 p. 135, n° 47 pp. 140 et 142, n° 48 p. 144, n° 51 pp. 147–48, n° 52 pp. 149–52, n° 53 pp. 153–54, n° 55 pp. 155–57.

[14]   ACCIM, B 5, fol. 541; Annexe 1.

[15]   Pouradier Duteil-Loizidou, *Consulat de France*, 2: n° 9 p. 51, n° 35 p. 96, n° 64 p. 134; Duteil-Loizidou, *Consulat de France à Larnaca (1700–1702)*, Sources et études de l'histoire de Chypre 31, 3 (Nicosie, 1999), n° 67 p. 160; Duteil-Loizidou, "La communauté française à Chypre à la fin du XVIIe et au début du XVIIIe siècles," in *Actes du colloque Chypre et la Méditerranée orientale: migrations, échanges et territoires. Identités et langue, image et mémoire (Lyon, Maison de l'Orient méditerranéen, octobre 1997)*, ed. Yannis Ioannou, Françoise Métral and Marguerite Yon (Lyon, 2000), pp. 71–77 at p. 74; Brunehilde Imhaus pense avoir identifié les vestiges de la résidence de Jauna, au milieu de jardins, dans la péninsule du Carpasse, après Rizocarpasso, près de la petite église d'Aghia Mavra: Imhaus, "Quelques remarques," pp. 127–31.

[16]   ACCIM, B 8, fol. 335r; Paris, Archives du Ministère des Affaires étrangères, Mémoires et documents, Autriche 21, fol. 67r.

[17]   Imhaus, "Quelques remarques," pp. 133–35.

[18]   Pouradier Duteil-Loizidou, *Consulat de France*, 2: n° 132 p. 283.

[19]   Turin, Archivio di Stato di Torino, Archivio di Corte, Paesi, Città e contado di Nizza, Porto di Villafranca, mazzo 4 fascicolo 12: *Proggetto di Dom. co Iauna per il stabilimento d'una società regolata da' Sudditi di S. A. R. che applichi al Commercio Maritimo co Paesi stranieri*; Alain Bottaro, *Les sources de l'histoire du comté de Nice à l'Archivio di Stato di Turin* (Nice, 2008), p. 243; Pouradier Duteil-Loizidou, *Consulat de France*, 2: n° 64 p. 134.

[20]   ASN Aff. Est., f. 6803.

y envoie en 1700 son neveu, Pierre, qui enrichit la société familiale par ses activités liées au commerce du riz avec la France.[21] La bonne marche des affaires connaît un brutal coup d'arrêt, le 30 novembre 1701, lorsque la maison des Jauna, à Damiette, est pillée par des Égyptiens révoltés contre la présence grecque et occidentale dans leur ville.[22]

Lors de cet épisode malheureux, Dominique Jauna, présent alors à Damiette, est contraint de se réfugier quelques mois chez le consul français de Maillet au Caire avant de rentrer à Chypre où il est enregistré en 1702, dans des archives conservées en Angleterre, comme agent de marchands anglais à Larnaca et Tripoli.[23] En 1703, il rejoint Marseille où il entreprend de faire venir son fils mais il essuie le refus de son épouse.[24] Jean-Michel Jauna reste donc à Chypre où on le retrouve à partir de 1724, sur les traces de son père, négociant pour le compte de la maison de commerce de son oncle, Alexandre Grégoire, député de la ville de Marseille au bureau du commerce, et associé à ses cousins les Touche.[25]

De retour en France, Dominique Jauna s'établit à Marseille où il conserve ses relations avec les membres de la Chambre de Commerce et d'Industrie sur laquelle il aurait eu quelques visées. En attendant le dédommagement du pillage de Damiette, il prend la direction d'une manufacture d'amidon en 1705.[26] Trois ans plus tard, le député du commerce de Marseille refuse à Jauna le monopole de la fabrication de l'amidon au nom de la liberté du commerce.[27] Parallèlement, Dominique multiplie les démarches pour être indemnisé de ses pertes et finit par obtenir en 1706, 12,000 livres à titre de dédommagements par arrêt du Conseil du Roi, à prélever sur les navires en partance pour Alexandrie.[28]

---

[21] Raoul Clément, *Les Français d'Égypte aux XVIIe et XVIIIe siècles* (Paris, 1960), pp. 120–21; Jauna s'était rendu en Égypte avant 1700 puisqu'il rapporte le témoignage que lui a laissé, en 1697 "un vieux raïs ou capitaine de saïque" sur l'ensablement du port de Damiette: Jauna, 1:204.

[22] Clément, *Français d'Égypte*, p. 121.

[23] Jauna, 2:1204; Bruce Masters, "Trading Diasporas and Nations: The Genesis of National Identities in Ottoman Aleppo," *The International History Review* 9/3 (1987), 345–367 at p. 358.

[24] Anna Pouradier Duteil-Loizidou, *Consulat de France à Larnaca (1703–1705)*, Sources et études de l'histoire de Chypre 20, 4 (Nicosie, 2002), n° 28 pp. 80–82.

[25] ACCIM, B 8, fol. 335r; AN Affaires étrangères, B I 631, fol. 351v; B III 2, fol. 138; B III 25, pièce 62; B III 26, pièce 31; Pouradier Duteil-Loizidou, *Consulat de France*, 4: n° 38 p. 96; les archives de la chambre de commerce de Marseille conservent plusieurs autorisations de résidence délivrées à des commis employés chez Grégoire, Touche et Jauna entre 1736 et 1739. Sa mauvaise gestion de la maison de commerce à Larnaca l'aurait contraint à fuir à Venise en 1741 chez un négociant Jean-Baptiste Driuzzi: ACCIM, B 10, fols. 162v, 207v, 293, 418v; AN Affaires étrangères, B III 26, pièces 31. Par ailleurs, un registre, conservé à la Custodie de Terre Sainte à Jérusalem, mentionne Jean-Michel Jauna, procureur de la Terre Sainte, chevalier du Saint Sépulcre par procuration le 31 mai 1731: Jean-Pierre de Gennes, *Les chevaliers du Saint-Sépulcre de Jérusalem*, 2 vols. (Versailles, 1995–2004), 2/1:402.

[26] AN Marine, B 7 73, fol. 112v.

[27] Joseph Fournier, *La chambre de commerce de Marseille et ses représentants permanents à Paris (1599–1875)* (Marseille, 1920), pp. 64–65.

[28] ACCIM, B 6; un dossier volumineux sur cette affaire est conservé aux archives nationales: AN Affaires étrangères, B III 132, fols. 54r, 68r–167v; Imhaus, "Quelques remarques," p. 136–37; Pouradier Duteil-Loizidou, *Consulat de France*, 3: n° 102 pp. 225–26, n° 104 pp. 227–28; Duteil-Loizidou,

Les sources ne permettent plus de suivre de manière continue la carrière du futur historien. Il semble reprendre une activité commerciale maritime toujours sous la protection de la France mais connaît une série de revers qui lui font perdre tout crédit. En 1715, la correspondance consulaire révèle que Jauna est propriétaire d'un navire dont l'équipage se plaint auprès du consul de France à Naples, le comte de Charleval, de ne pas être payé. Ce dernier ordonne alors la saisie et la vente du bateau, ce qui n'est pas suffisant pour rembourser tous les créanciers de cet homme "sans ressource qui a abusé de la foy publique."[29]

Les années suivantes sont encore moins bien documentées et l'on doit se contenter des informations que laisse Dominique Jauna dans les différents mémoires qu'il rédige. Un premier écrit, aujourd'hui perdu, traitait du commerce méditerranéen. En 1728, Dominique est l'auteur d'un traité intitulé *Observations sur la Compagnie des Indes présentées à Monseigneur le Comte de Maurepas, ministre et secrétaire d'État* qui témoigne d'une réflexion dépassant le cadre européen. A-t-il pris part aux activités d'une compagnie maritime hors de la Méditerranée? Les sources ne permettent pas de le préciser mais elles autorisent à lier la carrière de Dominique à celle de son neveu, Pierre Jauna. Comme d'autres marchands de retour du Levant, Pierre se rend en Martinique où il occupe différents postes dans l'administration coloniale: trésorier des invalides en 1713, conseiller au conseil supérieur en 1719, conseiller honoraire en 1737.[30] Au cours de cette période, l'oncle et le neveu restent en relation selon un document daté de 1729.[31]

Si Dominique Jauna put continuer d'exercer des activités commerciales, le succès n'a pas dû suivre. Dans la lettre qui accompagne son mémoire sur le commerce des Indes, Jauna postule à un emploi "dans les affaires de commerce, soit à Paris, soit à Marseille, soit même en le chargeant de la visite des échelles du Levant."[32] Il s'interroge sur les carences de la Compagnies de Indes et dénonce notamment la mauvaise gestion du personnel administratif, attentif d'abord à ses intérêts. La critique porte également sur l'importation de produits comme les toiles de coton qui nuisent aux manufactures du royaume. Jauna se fait le chantre de la liberté de commerce en montrant l'inutilité de mesures qui visent à interdire le trafic des Indiennes et préconise plutôt l'importation de produits bruts (laine, lin) afin de donner du travail aux classes les plus pauvres du royaume.[33] Malgré l'application

---

Consulat de France à Larnaca (1706–1708), Sources et études de l'histoire de Chypre 55 (Nicosie, 2006), pp. 476–77; Clément, *Français d'Égypte*, p. 121.

[29] AN Marine, B 7 27 fol. 260r; B 7 100, fol. 127r.

[30] AN Colonies, C⁸ᴬ 20, fol. 63; AN Colonies, C⁸ᴬ 21, fol. 94; AN Colonies, C⁸ᴬ 22, fol. 428; AN Colonies, C⁸ᴬ 23, fols. 61, 64, 273; AN Colonies, C⁸ᴬ, 24 fols. 36, 237, 286; AN Colonies, C⁸ᴬ 26, fols. 44, 77, 195; AN Colonies, C⁸ᴬ 49, fol. 204.

[31] AN Colonies, C⁸ᴬ40.

[32] AN Marine, B 7 295, fol. 1v; Paul Masson, *Histoire du commerce français dans le Levant au XVIIIe siècle* (Paris, 1911), p. 433. La lettre, publiée en Annexe 2, informe également que les autorités françaises lui ont refusé peu avant 1730, le poste de consul de Naples.

[33] AN Marine, B7 295, fols. 2r–6r; Edgar Depitre, *La toile peinte en France aux XVIIe et au XVIIIe siècles* (Paris, 1912), p. 106.

à poser un diagnostic et à apporter des réponses aux problèmes soulevés par les dysfonctionnements de la Compagnie des Indes, sa demande d'emploi ne semble pas aboutir, raison pour laquelle Dominique Jauna décide de se mettre au service d'un autre protecteur: l'empereur d'Autriche.

Une lettre conservée aux archives nationales (Annexe 2) permet de mieux comprendre l'exil de Jauna à Vienne et sa vocation tardive d'historien. Il écrit de la capitale autrichienne, le 29 octobre 1730, à Bernard de Montfaucon de la congrégation de Saint-Maur, un des fondateurs de la paléographie et de l'archéologie grecque à l'abbaye de Saint-Germain des Prés. Jauna révèle qu'il a été accueilli à Paris auprès du savant peu de temps auparavant. A-t-il partagé avec son protecteur mauriste son désir d'écrire une histoire de Chypre et des croisades? La documentation ne permet pas de l'affirmer, mais Jauna a pu trouver auprès des moines une bibliothèque très fournie sur le sujet qui allait occuper ses dernières années et surtout, acquérir les méthodes de l'historien.[34] Pour l'aider à accéder à la cour de Vienne, Montfaucon recommande Jauna à l'un de ses anciens protégés, l'alsacien Jean-Christophe Bartenstein, futur vice-chancelier d'Autriche. Le discours de Jauna sait convaincre Charles VI qui le nomme conseiller et inspecteur général du commerce.[35]

En attendant de mieux connaître l'itinéraire autrichien de Dominique Jauna grâce aux archives de Vienne, un document anonyme, conservé au ministère français des Affaires étrangères, daté de 1732, dévoile le projet de l'intendant d'établir une compagnie commerciale en Méditerranée pour assurer le développement des activités économiques de l'Empire par le port de Trieste. Deux navires à destination de l'Orient, l'un vers Smyrne et l'autre vers Alexandrie et Chypre assureront le transport des draps de laine, de soie et des autres marchandises. Quatre autres navires s'occuperont du commerce avec les ports occidentaux.[36]

---

[34] De nombreux savants laïcs comme Rollin, Guillaume de Villefroy, Nicolas Fréret fréquentaient Saint-Germain des Prés: Blandine Kriegel, *L'histoire à l'âge classique 3. Les académies de l'histoire*, 2nd ed. (Paris 1996), pp. 98–101. Lors de son voyage en Italie, Montfaucon a pu repérer le livre des remembrances de la secrète du royaume de Chypre pour l'année 1468–69 qu'il intitule maladroitement dans son catalogue "Registre des lettres du roi de Chypre" (n° ccxxxi du fond Ottoboni): Louis de Mas Latrie, "Le registre des lettres du roi de Chypre," *Bibliothèque de l'École des Chartes* 55 (1894), 235.

[35] Annexe 2; Emmanuel de Broglie, *La société de l'abbaye de Saint-Germain des Prés au XVIIIe siècle. Bernard de Montfaucon et les Bernardins (1715–1750)*, 2 vols. (Paris, 1888–91), 1:304–6; sur Bartenstein et Montfaucon: Alfred Ritter von Arneth, *Johann Christoph Bartenstein und seine Zeit* (Vienne, 1871), p. 9; Dom Ignaz E. Kathrein, "Aus dem Briefverkehr deutscher Gelehrten mit den Benedictinern der Congregation von St. Maur und deren Beziehungen zu den literarischen und religiösen Bewegungen des 18. Jahrhunderts. I. Die unedierte Correspondenz des Johann Christoph Bartenstein und Dom Bernard de Montfaucon," *Studien und Mittheilungen aus dem Benedictiner- und dem Cistercienser-Orden* 23 (1902), 111–26, 386–403, 625–31; 24 (1903), 175–84, 446–66; Max von Braubach, "Johann Christoph Bartensteins Herkunft und Anfänge," *Mitteilungen des Instituts für Österreichische Geschichtsforschung* 61 (1953), 99–149 (pour sa relation avec Jauna: p. 128).

[36] Archives du Ministère des Affaires étrangères, Mémoires et documents, Autriche 21, fols. 66r–71v; sur le rôle croissant de Trieste dans la politique commerciale de l'Autriche: Romano Ruggiero *Le commerce du royaume de Naples avec la France et les pays de l'Adriatique au XVIIIe siècle* (Paris, 1951).

Son intérêt pour le commerce en Méditerranée se manifeste encore, en 1738, par la rédaction, avec le marchand anglais Jean de la Roche, d'un projet de Compagnie maritime dans le royaume de Naples.[37] Dans le mémoire soumis au secrétaire d'État, Montealegre, marquis de Salas, Jauna termine son exposé en formulant le souhait d'acquérir la charge d'inspecteur du commerce dans le jeune royaume afin de mieux servir le roi, Charles de Bourbon, vainqueur des Autrichiens en 1734. Craint-il de perdre la protection dont il bénéficie en Autriche avec la disparition de Charles VI en octobre 1740? Faut-il croire Jauna, lorsqu'il évoque dans sa correspondance, les effets néfastes du climat d'Europe centrale sur sa santé? Toujours est-il que sa demande, réitérée dans d'autres courriers, n'aboutit pas et il poursuit donc sa carrière à Vienne.[38]

Si l'historien ligure a su élargir sa réflexion à l'échelle des intérêts de l'Empire, il n'a pas pour autant abandonné les idées qui avaient mûri auprès du consul de Maillet en Égypte. En 1739, Jauna fait parvenir à Maurepas un mémoire sur la conquête de l'Égypte. Aux yeux de l'auteur, ce projet s'inscrit dans un moment favorable car les Ottomans en guerre contre l'Empire ne résisteraient pas à l'appui que pourrait apporter la France à Charles VI. Une alliance tripartite entre l'Empire, la Russie et la France permettrait de vaincre les Turcs et d'ouvrir l'accès à la mer Rouge.[39] Ce projet, semblable en de nombreux points à celui qui est formulé dans la troisième partie de l'*Histoire générale*, se différencie toutefois par l'insistance sur le gain économique d'une telle conquête.

Au cours de ces mêmes années, Jauna s'attelle à la rédaction de son œuvre historique, souhaitant la dédier à Charles de Bourbon.[40] Les autorités napolitaines, craignant que l'ouvrage ne soutienne pas suffisamment les prétentions de Charles au titre de roi de Jérusalem, refusent le projet d'épître dédicatoire. Le livre, achevé en 1740, porte finalement une dédicace à Marie-Thérèse d'Autriche, auprès de laquelle Dominique occupe toujours la charge d'intendant du commerce à Vienne.[41] Échouant dans ses tentatives de trouver un emploi sur les rives de la Méditerranée, Dominique Jauna a jeté ses dernières forces dans cette vaste entreprise intellectuelle qui, au soir de sa vie, le ramène dans son jardin de mûriers chypriote et les ruelles du Caire.

---

[37] ASN Aff. Est., f. 6803; Contino, *Mire di espansione* (voir supra n. 10), pp. 43–48; José Miguel Delgado Barrado, "Puerto y privilegio en Espana durante el siglo XVIII," in *Puertos y Sistemas Portuarios (Siglos XVI–XX): Actas del Coloquio internacional El sistema portuario español, Madrid, 19–21 octubre, 1995*, ed. Augustin Guimerá and Dolores Romero (Madrid, 1996), pp. 253–73 at p. 259.

[38] ASN Aff. Est., f. 6803; Contino, *Mire di espansione*, pp. 69–70.

[39] AN Marine, B 7 340; Masson, *Histoire du commerce* (voir supra n. 31), p. 511; Gaston Rambert, *Histoire du commerce de Marseille. VI: de 1660 à 1789. Les colonies* (Paris, 1949), p. 517.

[40] ASN Aff. Est., f. 6803.

[41] Jauna, 1:I–II; par ailleurs le dernier volume paru de la correspondance de l'érudit allemand Johan Christoph Gottsche éclaire sur les démarches entreprises par Jauna pour faire imprimer son manuscrit. En 1737, Nicolas Philippe de Lalande lui apporte son aide pour revoir et corriger le texte. Jauna se montre hésitant sur le choix de l'imprimeur, d'abord à Leipzig, puis sa préférence va à Venise. On ne connaît pas les raisons qui le poussent finalement à faire imprimer l'*Histoire générale*, dix ans plus tard à Leyde: Johann Christoph Gottsched, *Briefwechsel. Historisch-kritische Ausgabe*, ed. Franziska Menzel, Detlef Döring, Rüdiger Otto et Michael Schlott (Berlin-New York, 2010), pp. 375, 420, 497, 589.

Analyse de l'œuvre

Si la correspondance de Jauna laisse penser que la genèse de l'*Histoire générale* se situe au moment où l'auteur élabore son projet de compagnie maritime à Naples, l'examen de la composition de ce travail, l'œuvre d'une vie, révèle plutôt une lente gestation qui commence peut-être à Chypre, se poursuit près du Nil, puis à Saint-Germain des Prés avant la "délivrance" de l'ouvrage à Vienne.

Le travail de Dominique Jauna relève de plusieurs genres historiographiques. La division de l'ouvrage en quatre parties distinctes rend compte de la conscience qu'a l'auteur de la diversité des domaines qu'il souhaite aborder. La première partie est la plus volumineuse avec 1,204 pages et s'intitule *Histoire générale des roïaumes de Chypre, de Jérusalem, d'Arménie, et d'Égypte, comprenant les croisades, et les faits, les plus mémorables, de l'empire ottoman, avec plus d'exactitude qu'aucun auteur moderne les a encore rapportées, et les faits les plus mémorables, de l'Empire ottoman, depuis sa fondation jusqu'à la fameuse bataille de Lépante, où finit cette histoire, dans laquelle on trouve aussi l'anéantissement de l'empire des Grecs.* Viennent ensuite l'*État présent de l'Égypte* (p. 1205–1388) qui dresse un tableau géographique et historique de l'Égypte avec des considérations ethnographiques, puis une *Dissertation curieuse et utile sur les caractères hiéroglifiques des anciens Égyptiens* (p. 1389–1416) et enfin une *Réflexion sur les moïens de conquérir l'Égypte et la Chypre* (p. 1417–1439).

La première partie de l'œuvre appartient clairement à l'historiographie du royaume de Chypre et des croisades. Elle se divise en 24 livres selon la distribution suivante: les deux premiers livres (p. 1–88) consistent en une approche géographique de l'île de Chypre et présentent son histoire jusqu'à l'arrivée des croisés. Les onze livres suivants (p. 89–726) présentent l'histoire des croisades jusqu'à la prise d'Acre en 1291. Enfin, les onze derniers livres (p. 727–1126) s'intéressent à l'histoire de Chypre. La structure de l'*Histoire générale* dévoile la volonté de l'auteur de prolonger l'historiographie humaniste de la Renaissance, incarnée par Florio Bustron et Étienne de Lusignan, en exprimant la singularité du territoire et de l'histoire chypriote.[42]

Son traitement de l'histoire des croisades est d'une facture classique, avec une trame chronologique fidèlement respectée, interrompue par les descriptions des principales villes qui sont les théâtres des événements décrits, Jérusalem (p. 89 et suiv.), Damiette (p. 204), Tyr (p. 286–87) et Acre (p. 296). Bien que rédigée au cœur du XVIIIe siècle, dominé par les lectures rationalistes de l'histoire des croisades de Voltaire, Diderot, Hume et Gibbon, l'œuvre de Dominique Jauna

---

[42] Gilles Grivaud, "Éveil de la nation chyproise," *Sources, travaux historiques* 43–44 (1995), 105–116; Florio Bustron, *Chronique de l'île de Chypre*, ed. René de Mas Latrie (Paris, 1886); Étienne de Lusignan, *Chorograffia et breve historia universale dell'isola di Cipro principiando al tempo di Noè per il fino al 1572* (Bologna, 1573; repr. Famagusta 1973; repr. Nicosia 2004); de Lusignan, *Description de toute l'isle de Chypre* (Paris, 1580; repr. Famagusta 1968; repr. Nicosia 2004).

prolonge davantage la tradition historique du siècle précédent.[43] L'*Histoire des Croisades pour la délivrance de la Terre Sainte* publiée en 1675–76 par le père jésuite Louis Maimbourg, auquel il voue une grande admiration, a été une source d'inspiration comme peut-être, dans une moindre mesure, l'ouvrage, non cité, de Johann Daniel Schœpflin, *De Sacris Galliae Regum in Orientem Expeditionibus*, publié à Strasbourg en 1724.[44]

De manière générale, Jauna ne condamne pas la violence contenue dans la croisade mais fustige les divisions des princes chrétiens face à leur adversaire musulman, responsables de l'échec final de l'entreprise guerrière.[45] Le personnage de Saladin, dont la magnanimité est vantée au-delà du rang des historiens hostiles aux croisades, trouve à peine grâce aux yeux de Jauna qui lui reproche sa décision d'exécuter Renaud de Châtillon.[46]

L'accent mis sur les exploits des croisés autrichiens est un autre trait saillant de cette *Histoire générale*. L'intendant général du commerce de la couronne autrichienne qui dédie son livre à Marie-Thérèse, sans doute toujours à la recherche d'une plus grande reconnaissance, ne pouvait manquer l'occasion de flatter ses protecteurs. Sa description du siège d'Acre met ainsi en avant le rôle de Léopold, duc d'Autriche, qui survit en 1190 à un massacre lors d'une tentative infructueuse de prise de la Tour des mouches, et que le duc de Souabe récompense "en lui donnant pour armes un écu de gueules à la face d'argent, que les Princes de cette Auguste maison ont toujours porté depuis, comme un trophée à la gloire, que ce grand homme s'étoit acquise, au péril de sa vie, pour le recouvrement du Roïaume de Jésus Christ & la destruction des Infidèles."[47] De la même manière, les exploits d'Amédée V de Savoie contre les Ottomans en 1310 sont salués par Dominique Jauna, originaire du comté de Nice, alors sous domination savoyarde. L'historien souligne la fidélité de la maison de Savoie à la croisade jusqu'au prince Eugène qui a donné "des preuves éclatantes de son zèle & de sa valeur contre ces mêmes infidèles, dont il s'étoit rendu la terreur."[48] Ces rares excès de flagornerie ne doivent pas cependant éclipser les intentions profondes de Jauna, d'exprimer l'identité de la nation *chyproise* à travers son histoire.

Avec l'*Etat présent de l'Egypte*, l'historien cède un peu la place à l'homme politique et au marchand. Le style est beaucoup plus personnel et on ressent chez Jauna une véritable fascination pour le pays et ses habitants. Son exposé, qu'il a envisagé d'écrire sous forme épistolaire, certainement pour suivre le modèle

---

[43] Voltaire, *Histoire des croisades par M. Arouet de Voltaire* (Berlin, 1751); Denis Diderot, "croisades," *L'Encyclopédie ou Dictionnaire raisonné des sciences, des arts et des métiers* (Paris, 1754); David Hume, *The History of England*, 6 vols. (Londres, 1754–62); Edward Gibbon, *The History of the Decline and Fall of the Roman Empire*, 7 vols. (Londres, 1776–88). Ces œuvres ont été maintes fois rééditées.

[44] Jauna, 1:769.

[45] Ibid., 1:IV, 261.

[46] Ibid., 1:273.

[47] Ibid., 1:323.

[48] Ibid., 1:771–72.

du consul de Maillet, n'a pas pour but ultime de fixer les souvenirs du marchand levantin, mais plutôt de mettre à l'ordre du jour des souverains européens le projet de percement d'un canal entre la mer Rouge et la Méditerranée. Cet ouvrage permettrait le transit des marchandises depuis l'Inde jusqu'à Alexandrie, en passant par Djedda et Suez.[49] Jauna n'est pas le premier auteur à formuler une réflexion aussi audacieuse. Depuis le XVIIe siècle, existe en France un courant intellectuel favorable à cette entreprise de jonction des deux mers qui apporterait de grands bénéfices commerciaux. Colbert, puis son fils Seignelay, ambitionnaient pour la France une présence maritime et commerciale renforcée en mer Rouge, mais les nombreuses ambassades envoyées à Constantinople échouaient à convaincre le sultan.[50] Dans les milieux diplomatiques du Levant, on discute de ces idées diffusées notamment par le *Parfait négociant* de Jacques Savary.[51] Lors de son séjour en Égypte, Jauna s'est certainement entretenu de ce projet avec le consul Benoît de Maillet, fervent partisan du canal, dont les notes seront mises en forme et publiées par l'abbé Le Mascrier seulement en 1735.[52] L'abandon du projet par la France a sans doute incité Jauna à le porter ensuite à la cour de Vienne auprès de Charles VI dont l'intérêt pour le développement du commerce méditerranéen de l'Empire ne s'est jamais démenti.[53]

La dernière partie de l'œuvre au titre explicite, *Réflexion sur les moïens de conquérir l'Égypte et la Chypre*, range Dominique Jauna parmi les propagandistes de la croisade. Il prend soin de démarquer son analyse de ses réflexions sur la percée d'un canal en Égypte en affirmant que, dans cette partie, ses motivations ne relèvent que de la religion.[54] Reprenant des arguments développés dans le mémoire envoyé en 1739 à Maurepas, il préconise une union des principaux chefs d'États européens afin de préparer la conquête de l'Égypte et de Chypre. Cette entreprise ne devrait rencontrer aucune difficulté aux yeux de son auteur, car les différentes villes qui sont les verrous des deux pays sont très mal défendues; en outre, les Occidentaux peuvent compter sur la collaboration des populations chrétiennes orientales.[55] Loin de prêcher dans le désert, Jauna perpétue un courant de pensée qui s'ordonne autour de la conquête de l'Égypte. Pour des raisons différentes, R. P. Coppin, ancien consul des Français à Damiette et son *Bouclier de l'Europe ou la guerre sainte*

---

[49]   Ibid., 1:préface non paginée, 2:1357.

[50]   François Charles-Roux, "L'échelle d'Egypte II," *Revue de la Méditerranée* 13/4 (1953), 417.

[51]   Jacques Savary, *Le Parfait Négociant, ou Instruction générale pour tout ce qui regarde le commerce de France et les pays étrangers*, 7th ed. (Paris, 1713).

[52]   Abbé Jean-Baptiste Le Mascrier, *Description de l'Égypte, contenant plusieurs remarques curieuses sur la géographie ancienne et moderne de ce pais ... composée sur les Mémoires de M. de Maillet* (Paris, 1735).

[53]   François Charles-Roux, *Les origines de l'expédition d'Égypte* (Paris, 1910), pp. 20–21, 24; Charles-Roux, *Autour d'une route. L'Angleterre, l'isthme de Suez et l'Égypte au XVIIIe siècle* (Paris, 1922), pp. 10–13; Hussein Husny, *Le canal de Suez et la politique égyptienne* (Montpellier, 1923), pp. 52–55; David Kimche, "The Opening of the Red Sea to European Ships in the Late Eighteenth Century," *Middle Eastern Studies* 8/1 (1972), 63–71 at pp. 63–64.

[54]   Jauna, 2:1420.

[55]   Ibid., 2:1422–35.

en 1686, Leibniz et son mémoire de jeunesse destiné à détourner Louis XIV de ses ambitions rhénanes, redécouvert et édité seulement au début du XIXe siècle, étaient les représentants les plus éminents de ces projets.[56] Les réflexions de Jauna, celles de son *Histoire générale* comme celles de son mémoire de 1739, ont eu un écho dans les milieux diplomatiques puisque le consul Dironcourt les évoque dans sa correspondance comme des idées ridicules dont on parle à Constantinople.[57] Les activités de conseiller de Jauna, passé au service de l'Autriche, ne semblent donc pas inquiéter les autorités françaises.

Les préoccupations politiques, religieuses et économiques paraissent finalement très liées dans l'œuvre de Jauna. Partir à la conquête de l'Égypte répond autant à un appel tardif à la croisade qu'à une volonté de modernisation des circuits commerciaux ou à un désir d'affirmation des Habsbourg en Méditerranée. Jauna a dû mettre autant de cœur à sa formation d'historien et à son travail sur les sources qu'à ses entreprises commerciales et à sa charge d'intendant du commerce.

"Discours sur les sources et sources du discours"[58]

L'étude de l'historien Jauna au travail se heurte à un obstacle majeur: les archives ne livrent pas d'informations, à notre connaissance, sur l'entreprise historiographique et l'on doit se contenter des données que fournit l'œuvre elle-même.[59]

Dominique Jauna considère l'histoire comme une discipline supérieure aux autres sciences par la dimension concrète de ses objets. Elle présente aux lecteurs, des faits, des lieux et des personnages sur lesquels il doit porter des jugements. L'histoire a ainsi une vertu d'édification dans la mesure où elle permet d'exposer des actions vertueuses qui poussent à l'imitation ou, au contraire, des faits méprisables qu'il faut condamner.[60]

À côté de la vocation de l'historien centrée sur la glorification et la défense de la religion catholique, Jauna n'en reste pas moins fils du siècle des Lumières et un souci d'objectivité le conduit parfois à rejeter les présages de la nature comme ces orages qui précèdent la défaite de Hattin en 1187; il se montre toutefois beaucoup moins réservé sur l'interprétation des tremblements de terre ou des phénomènes célestes en 1569, annonciateurs de la fin de la domination latine sur l'île.[61]

---

[56] Charles-Roux, *Les origines*, pp. 22–27; Alphonse Dupront, *Le mythe de croisade*, 4 vols. (Paris, 1997), 1:413–28; Faruk Bilici, *Louis XIV et son projet de conquête d'Istanbul* (Ankara, 2004), pp. 78–79.

[57] AN, Aff. étr. B 1 329 fols. 317r–v; Masson, *Histoire du commerce*, p. 562.

[58] Nous empruntons le titre du chapitre IV de Franck Collard, *Un historien au travail à la fin du XVe siècle: Robert Gaguin* (Genève, 1996), p. 169.

[59] Il faut sans doute parier sur la destruction du manuscrit de Jauna qui prive l'historien contemporain d'un matériau de travail précieux.

[60] Jauna, 1:préface non paginée.

[61] Ibid., 1:261, 1078–79.

Suivant le plan de travail habituel d'un historien, Jauna informe son lecteur qu'il a amorcé sa recherche par une lecture assidue "de plusieurs manuscrits et mémoires" afin de collecter les informations nécessaires à la synthèse.[62] À plusieurs occasions, il fait part des difficultés qu'il a pu rencontrer pour accéder à un document, et parfois des échecs dans sa quête de manuscrits comme celui d'"Abydemus patefactus, disciple d'Aristote" (Paléphate d'Abydos), qui aurait écrit une histoire de Chypre.[63]

Il insiste particulièrement sur le recours aux sources écrites dans une langue orientale sans être davantage précis. Jauna assure que l'originalité de son travail réside dans sa méthode de "comparer ce qu'ils [plusieurs manuscrits et mémoires] en ont dit à tout ce que j'ai trouvé, & observé moi-même sur les lieux & parmi les habitants de ces différentes régions."[64] L'écrivain souhaite ainsi clairement affirmer la supériorité de son ouvrage sur ceux de ses prédécesseurs en particulier Maimbourg ou Loredano à qui il reproche de n'avoir pas connu les lieux dont ils s'entretiennent.[65] Lorsqu'il rapporte des observations personnelles, Dominique Jauna se montre souvent très pertinent et livre encore des informations intéressantes à la recherche historique contemporaine. Il localise, par exemple, au centre de Nicosie, une église de la Miséricorde transformée en mosquée en 1571 après la conquête ottomane de l'île. Cette indication permet peut-être de résoudre l'énigme que pose la dédicace "Stavro tou Missericou" de la petite mosquée, ancienne église au temps des Lusignan, située au sud de la cathédrale Sainte-Sophie.[66]

L'historien témoigne dans l'avant-propos de son travail de son souci de consulter la bibliographie la plus récente sur les questions qui l'intéressent en mentionnant au passage plusieurs historiens actifs dans la première moitié du XVIIIe siècle: Nicolas Gueudeville pour son *Atlas historique, ou Nouvelle introduction à l'histoire avec un supplément par Limiers* publié à Amsterdam en sept volumes de 1713 à 1721, les historiens allemands Jacques-Guillaume Imhof (1651–1728) et Johann Georg von Eckhart (1664–1730) et les historiens du duché de Lorraine, Dom Calmet et

---

[62] Ibid., 1:préface non paginée.

[63] Ibid., 1:10; Paléphate est un historien grec originaire d'Abydos contemporain d'Alexandre le Grand et Aristote. Il aurait rédigé une série de mémoires sur l'île de Chypre, Délos, l'Attique et l'Arabie selon l'encyclopédie *Souda* du Xe siècle: Palaephotus, *On unbelievable tales*, ed. Jacob Stern (Wauconda, Ill., 1996), pp. 1–2.

[64] Jauna, 1:préface non paginée. On déplore pourtant que l'historien utilise bien peu son expérience de commerçant sur l'île pour faire part d'observations au lecteur. Sur les 1,204 pages consacrées à Chypre et aux croisades, il évoque seulement sur trois pages les productions que l'on rencontre sur l'île avec un regard aiguisé et ajoute qu'il a envoyé du vin de Chypre à des souverains européens: ibid., 1:66–69.

[65] Giovanni Francesco Loredano, *Istoria de' re Lusignani, publicate da Henrico Giblet* (Bologne, 1647), publié et traduit en français sous le titre *Histoire des rois de Chypre de la maison de Lusignan*, 2 vols. (Paris, 1732). Chris Schabel, que je remercie pour ses remarques pertinentes, prépare une mise au point historiographique sur Loredano.

[66] Philippe Trélat, *Nicosie, une capitale de l'Orient latin, société, économie et espace urbain (1192–1474)*, Thèse de doctorat soutenue à l'université de Rouen, 2 vols. (Mont Saint-Aignan, 2009), 2:150–53.

Charles-Hyacinthe Hugo (1667–1739). Enfin il ajoute à cette liste la *Généalogie Diplomatique de la très-Auguste maison d'Autriche* parue à Vienne en 1737.[67]

L'intérêt porté à la connaissance du terrain conduit Dominique Jauna à ne pas se cantonner aux sources historiographiques mais à prendre aussi en compte les relations des voyageurs qui se sont rendus au Levant, suivant en cela le travail des cosmographes comme Olfert Dapper.[68] Malheureusement, Jauna ne signale pas les récits de voyage qu'il a consultés.

Cette approche qui rompt avec les histoires plus événementielles de Maimbourg ou Loredano, prévaut pour l'étude de l'île de Chypre dans les deux premiers livres. Il réquisitionne alors ses souvenirs d'ancien résident pour préciser l'utilisation contemporaine d'une plante comme le henné par les femmes turques, signaler sur le mont Olympe un temple dédié à Vénus devenu une chapelle Saint-Michel, dresser un tableau des villes insulaires à son époque ou énumérer les productions locales et le gibier que l'on peut encore chasser dans le pays.[69] Ces chapitres introductifs se démarquent également par la citation quasi systématique des sources qui soutiennent le récit de l'histoire antique de l'île. Le médiéviste pourra déplorer que Dominique Jauna n'ait pas fait preuve de la même rigueur méthodologique pour la suite de son récit.

Identifier les matériaux utilisés par Jauna pose de nombreuses questions: quelles éditions d'une œuvre a-t-il consultées? A-t-il lu toutes les sources auxquelles il renvoie? Quelle part faut-il attribuer aux ouvrages de compilation? La rigueur commanderait de comparer le texte de Jauna avec les sources potentielles de son œuvre; pour cette première étude, on se limitera aux indications données par l'historien dans son texte, en présentant la liste de ces sources dans l'ordre des différentes parties de son œuvre.[70]

Pour son exposé sur la géographie et l'histoire ancienne de l'île qui ouvre l'ouvrage, les principaux auteurs de l'Antiquité sont convoqués, de langue grecque (Homère, Hésiode, Strabon, Théophraste, Ptolémée, Hérodote, Eusèbe de Césarée, Pausanias, le Pseudo-Apollodore, Scylax, Isocrate, Zosime, Sozomène, Thucidide, Diodore de Sicile, Plutarque) et latine (Dion Cassius pour sa *Vie de l'Empereur Trajan*, Macrobe, Servius, Justin, saint Jérome, Tacite, Pline, Ammian Marcellin). Pour compléter les références de ces auteurs, Jauna puise également ses informations dans les compilations de sources comme la *Souda*, encyclopédie byzantine du Xe siècle ou celle de l'antiquaire et polygraphe hollandais Jean Meursius, auteur de *Creta, Cyprus, Rhodus; sive de nobilissimarum harum insularum rebus et antiquitatibus commentarii*, Amsterdam 1675.[71] À côté des

---

[67] Jauna, 1:11.

[68] Ibid., 1:72; Olfert Dapper, *Description exacte des isles de l'Archipel, et de quelques autres adjacentes: dont les principales sont Chypre, Rhodes …* (Amsterdam, 1703: 1st ed. en néerlandais, Amsterdam 1688).

[69] Jauna, 1:5–8; 66–69.

[70] Annexe 3.

[71] Jauna, 1:3, 11, 83.

sources, Jauna utilise peu la bibliographie disponible sur le sujet et se contente de citer trois figures incontournables des études antiques à l'époque moderne: le savant rouennais Samuel Bochart (1599–1667), Nicolas Coeffeteau (1574–1623) et Charles Rollin (1661–1741).[72] Ainsi Jauna, en amateur d'histoire ancienne, cite davantage les textes originaux des historiens, géographes et philosophes de l'antiquité que les compilations ou les ouvrages historiographiques mais ces allégations nc garantissent pas la fidélité à la devise humaniste *ad fontes* c'est-à-dire la consultation de la source originale.

Pour la période médiévale de son récit, Dominique Jauna renoue avec une approche traditionnelle de l'histoire des croisades et du royaume de Chypre. La primauté accordée aux événements politiques et militaires et les analyses parfois succinctes ont déjà été soulignées par l'historiographie.[73] À l'instar de synthèses trop rapides, les causes de la première croisade sont escamotées; le départ des croisés serait la conséquence de la compassion de Dieu envers "les misères de son peuple."[74] Afin de suivre le fil des événements, Jauna s'appuie pourtant sur les sources narratives les plus sûres comme Guillaume de Tyr et l'auteur anonyme qui prolonge son récit, dénommé Continuateur de la Guerre sainte, Hayton d'Arménie, Jacques de Vitry, Vincent de Beauvais et son *Miroir historique* ou encore la *Nuova Cronica* de Giovanni Villani.[75] Dans une moindre mesure, l'historiographie byzantine retient son attention avec Étienne de Byzance, Théophane et Nicétas Choniatès.[76]

Il se tourne également vers des sources moins diffusées comme les écrits de Pierre de la Palud ou le récit de "Florent, évêque de Ptolémaïde" pour la prise d'Acre en 1191.[77] Cette dernière citation doit renvoyer au poème versifié d'Aymar le moine, originaire de Florence, archevêque de Césarée depuis 1181, puis patriarche de Jérusalem dont une édition de son *De Expugnata Accone* par Jean Hérold est parue en 1549.[78] En revanche, on s'étonne de l'absence de références aux *Gesta Dei per Francos*, publiés en 1610 par Jacques Bongars et à la *Bibliothèque orientale* de

---

[72] Ibid., 1:5, 13, 31, 48; Samuel Bochart, *Geographia Sacra* (Caen, 1646); Nicolas Coeffeteau, *Histoire romaine contenant tout ce qui s'est passé de plus mémorable depuis le commencement de l'empire d'Auguste jusqu'à celui de Constantin le Grand* (Lyon, 1623); Charles Rollin, *Histoire ancienne des Égyptiens, des Carthaginois, des Assyriens, des Babyloniens, des Mèdes et des Perses, des Macédoniens, des Grecs*, 13 vols. (Paris, 1730–38); sur ces auteurs et leur usage à l'époque moderne, voir Mouza Raskolnikoff, *Histoire romaine et critique historique dans l'Europe des Lumières* (Rome, 1992), pp. 6–7.

[73] Supra n. 3.

[74] Jauna, 1:105.

[75] Annexe 3.

[76] Jauna, 1:12, 54, 205.

[77] Ibid., 1:299, 382.

[78] Autres éditions: Aymar le moine, *Haymari Monachi ... De Expugnata Accone liber tetrastichus*, ed. Paul E. D. Riant (Lyon, 1866); Aymar le moine, "Monachi Florentini ... De recuperatione Ptolemaidae liber," in *Chronica magistri Rogeri de Hovedene*, ed. William Stubbs, RS 51 (Londres, 1868–71); *Der "Rithmus de expeditione Ierosolimitana"des sogenannten Haymarus Monachus Florentinus*, ed. Antonio Placanica and Sascha Falk (Florence, 2006).

Barthélémy d'Herbelot qui mettaient à la disposition des historiens les principales sources occidentales et orientales des croisades.

Jauna n'a pas circonscrit sa recherche aux travaux imprimés et a exploré les dépôts d'archives, surtout italiens, mais aussi les bibliothèques viennoises, pour consulter des manuscrits qu'il ne permet pas toujours à son lecteur d'identifier. Derrière "les chroniques de Venise" qui évoquent le projet d'un transfert des institutions de la Sérénissime à Constantinople après 1204, on reconnaît le récit de Daniel Barbaro, auteur d'une chronique de Venise des origines à 1414, conservée à la *Marciana*.[79] Plus remarquables sont les mentions de Bustron, certainement Florio Bustron, auteur de l'*Historia overo commentarii de Cipro*, pour étayer son récit des heurts entre Génois et Vénitiens à l'occasion du couronnement de Pierre II à Famagouste en 1372 et de Georgios Boustronios, chroniqueur de langue grecque du royaume de Chypre, à propos de Charlotte de Savoie.[80] Il faut saluer la perspicacité de Dominique Jauna qui a découvert ces deux manuscrits sans doute à Venise, même s'il ne les a pas exploités complètement. Ces sources, fondamentales pour l'histoire du royaume des Lusignan, ne seront réutilisées qu'un siècle plus tard par le comte Louis de Mas Latrie qui se garde bien de rappeler qu'elles étaient déjà connues de l'historien ligure.[81]

Les documents d'archives, des lettres et des bulles pontificales, viennent compléter son récit à maintes reprises. Jauna cite et parfois reproduit ceux conservés à la bibliothèque du Vatican: deux lettres envoyées par le pape Innocent III en 1206, l'une à Geoffroy le Rat, maître des Hospitaliers et l'autre aux évêques de Paris et d'Orléans, un bref du 5 août 1211 qui enregistre le don de terres de Livon aux Hospitaliers figurant dans les registres d'Innocent III, une lettre d'Honorius III à Guérin de Montaigu, datée de 1226 constituent quelques exemples de cette documentation.[82] Il est possible que Dominique Jauna ait eu le loisir de consulter ces documents à Rome où il s'est rendu.[83] La présence aux archives du Vatican de Quirini, correspondant de Bernard de Montfaucon, a pu faciliter l'accès aux

---

[79] Jauna, 1:419; Venise, Biblioteca Nazionale Marciana, MS It. VII 126 (coll. 7442) *Historia veneta raccolta et descritta dal nobil homo ser Zuanne Bon l'anno MDCXX*; Freddy Thiriet, *La Romanie vénitienne au Moyen Age*, 2nd ed. (Paris, 1975), pp. 16, 92.

[80] Jauna, 2:866, 1048; Bustron, *Chronique* (voir supra n. 41), p. 289; George Hill, *A History of Cyprus*, 4 vols. (Cambridge, Eng., 1948–52), 2:382. La recherche dispose d'une édition diplomatique de Georgios Boustronios: Τζωρτζῆς (Μ)πουστρούς (Γεώργιος Βο(σ)τρ(υ)ηνός ἡ Βουστρώνιος) Διήγησις Κρονίκας Κύπρου [Georges Boustrous (Georges Bo(s)tr(y)enos, ou Boustrianos), Chronique narrative de Chypre], ed. Georges Kehagioglou (Nicosie, 1997) et d'une traduction réalisée par Nicolas Coureas: George Boustronios, *A Narrative of the Chronicle of Cyprus 1456–1489*, trans. Nicolas Coureas (Nicosie, 2005).

[81] Mas Latrie, *Histoire de l'île de Chypre* (voir supra n. 3), 2:VI–VII.

[82] Jauna, 1:405, 425, 428, 507. Autres exemples: pp. 455, 533, 641. Dominique Jauna a pu également consulté les *Annales ecclesiastici post Baronium a. 1198 ad. 1585* d'Odorico Raynaldi publiées à Rome de 1646 à 1677 en 10 volumes.

[83] L'historien signale encore un manuscrit, peut-être de Melchior Bandini, consulté à Rome parmi les archives de Giaccomo Bosio et l'épitaphe funéraire de la reine Charlotte dans l'église du Saint-Esprit: Jauna, 1:726, 2:1037.

documents.[84] Cependant, certaines lettres figurent déjà dans des récits antérieurs donc rien n'assure que Jauna ait consulté les originaux. On retrouve, par exemple, l'épître adressée par Frédéric II à son arrivée à Limassol en 1228 à Jean d'Ibelin, avec de légères variantes, chez Florio Bustron et Loredano.[85]

Ce que l'on appelle aujourd'hui la bibliographie est largement mis à profit par Dominique Jauna. Les textes d'Étienne de Lusignan et de Giovanni Francesco Loredano sont les plus souvent cités (17 fois pour le premier, et 18 fois pour le second) même s'il leur impute des lacunes qu'il ne manque pas de compléter.[86] Ces citations abondantes et la comparaison des récits laissent deviner combien la dette de Jauna à ces deux auteurs est grande. Solliciter les textes de Georgios Boustronios et Florio Bustron, plus proches des événements, aurait enrichi l'*Histoire générale* mais, à l'état manuscrit, ils n'ont pas été d'un usage aussi aisé que les imprimés.

Pour traiter d'événements historiques extérieurs au royaume de Chypre, Guichenon, pour l'histoire de la maison de Savoie, et le père jésuite Maimbourg, autorité pour l'histoire des croisades, remportent les suffrages de Jauna.[87] Le polygraphe Francesco Tatti da Sansovino, auteur de *Venetia città nobilissima et singolare, descritta in XIII* paru à Venise en 1581 est cité en référence pour les affaires concernant les conséquences de la quatrième croisade.[88] Jauna consulte encore Pandolfo Colenucio, auteur de l'*Historia del reyno de Napoles* paru à Séville en 1584 sur Charles d'Anjou et les travaux d'André Duchesne pour relater le procès des Templiers.[89]

Les historiens de l'ordre de Saint-Jean de Jérusalem sont largement sollicités: Heinrich Pantaleon, auteur de *Militaris Ordinis Johanitarum, Rhodiorum aut Melitensium equitum* paru à Bâle en 1581, le chevalier Frà Antoine Geuffroy, commandeur de la Vinadière (orthographié "Vinaudière" chez Jauna) et secrétaire du Grand Maître de la Sengle, auteur de *Aulae turcicae othommanicique imperii descriptio* paru à Bâle en 1573 et surtout Giacomo Bosio et son *Dell'istoria della sacra religione et illustrissima militia di san Giovanni Girosolimitano* paru à Rome en trois volumes (1594–1602).[90] Jauna précise qu'il est aussi redevable à Melchiore Bandini, un autre historien de l'ordre de Malte, pour son récit du siège d'Acre en

---

[84] Broglie, *La société de l'abbaye* (voir supra n. 34), pp. 347–50.

[85] Jauna, 1:517; Bustron, *Chronique*, p. 64; Loredano, *Histoire des rois* (voir supra n. 64), 1:54; George Hill précise que la date du 17 septembre 1228 qui figure dans la seule version de Jauna est erronée car Frédéric II a quitté l'île le 3 septembre: Hill, *A History of Cyprus*, 2:94.

[86] Jauna se montre même extrêmement critique à l'égard d'Étienne de Lusignan: "auroit été à souhaiter, que le Père Luzignan se fit aussi bien aquité de l'Histoire de ce Roïaume qu'il a composé mais il faut avouër, que ce bon Religieux étoit beaucoup plus recommandable par sa naissance, & par sa piété, que par son savoir. malgré toutes les diligences qu'il paroit avoir faites, il a rempli son livre d'un si grand nombre de Fables, & d'imaginations, qu'un Auteur moderne a dit, que c'étoit un assemblage de Blasphêmes historiques." Jauna, 1:86.

[87] Ibid., 1:135, 261, 315, 2:969, 995, 1038, 1048.

[88] Ibid., 1:419, 420, 421.

[89] Ibid., 1:669, 764; André Duchesne, *Historiae Francorum scriptores, coetanei, ab gentis origine usque ad Philippi IV tempora*, 5 vols. (Paris, 1636–49).

[90] Annexe 3.

1291. Il a eu la satisfaction de retrouver, dans un vieux manuscrit en parchemin, ce qu'il pense être un fragment de l'œuvre de Bandini, déjà perdue à l'époque de Bosio.[91] Son autre source sur la chute d'Acre en 1291 se cache sous le nom de "chevalier Toxan" qui peut être le frère castillan Juan Antonio de Foja (orthographié selon les auteurs, Foxa, Fojan ou Foxan) auteur d'une *Historia Hierosolimitana* dont des copies sont conservées à Malte, Londres et Madrid.[92]

D'autres auteurs sont mis à contribution par Jauna. Le passage de Saint Louis en Orient est décrit à travers le regard de Joinville; le portrait de Tamerlan suit le récit qui figure dans *Les œuvres mêlées de monsieur le Chevalier Temple* parues en 1694; la montée en puissance du pouvoir ottoman en Méditerranée orientale est relatée en s'appuyant sur Giovanni Sagredo, auteur d'une *Histoire de l'Empire ottoman* en 1673.[93]

D'autres historiens italiens sont cités comme Paul-Émile, humaniste de Vérone qui a travaillé en France auprès de Louis XII, Marco Antonio Sabellico et ses différents travaux sur Venise, Giovanni Tracagnota auteur du *Delle Historie del Mondo* paru à Venise en 1562.[94] Il s'inspire également d'historiens très connus et lus à l'époque comme le poète jésuite, Gabriel Daniel (1649–1728).[95]

La conquête de l'île par les Ottomans occupe une place importante dans le livre mais n'est traitée qu'à travers le regard de deux auteurs, Angelo Calepio et Antonio Maria Graziani, alors que les témoignages disponibles au XVIIIe siècle sont déjà nombreux.[96]

Bien que s'appuyant sur un large éventail de sources, parfois très pertinentes comme Georgios Boustronios et Florio Bustron, Dominique Jauna reste toutefois très dépendant d'une bibliographie (Lusignan, Loredano, Maimbourg) dont il

---

[91] Jauna, 1:726; Giaccomo Bosio, *Dell'istoria della sacra religione e illustrissima militia de San Giovanni Girosolimitano*, 3 vols. (Rome, 1594), 1:préambule: "*Affaticossi prima d'ogni'altro intorno à ciò, il Cavaliere Fra Melchionne Bandino, il quale essendo Cancelliero di quest'Ordine, in tempo del Gran Maestro Fra Giovanni di Lastic, scrisse l'Istoria della detta Religione fin a tempi suoi. Però di quanto egli scrisse, poco o nulla si trova; essendosi quell'Istoria con danno incomparabile de gli Studiosi perduta.*" Sur Giacomo Bosio et Melchiore Bandini: Anthony Luttrell, "The Hospitallers' Historical Activities: 1440–1530," *Annales de l'ordre souverain militaire de Malte* 25 (1967), 145–50, reprint in Luttrell, *Latin Greece, the Hospitallers and the Crusades 1291–1440*, Variorum Reprints (Londres, 1982), étude n° II, p. 146; Poumarède, *Pour en finir avec la croisade* (voir supra n. 1), pp. 436–38.

[92] Jauna, 1:255, 726. Sur le chevalier Foja: Anthony Luttrell, "The Hospitallers' Historical Activities: 1530–1630," *Annales de l'ordre souverain militaire de Malte* 26 (1968), 57–170, reprint in Luttrell, *Latin Greece*, étude n° II, p. 60.

[93] Jauna, 1:622, 2:910, 1065, 1109, 1174; Giovanni Sagredo, *Memorie istoriche de monarchi ottomani de 1300 a 1640* (Venise, 1673).

[94] Jauna, 1:315, 425, 641, 647, 694.

[95] Ibid., 1:587, 694.

[96] Ibid., 2:1114; Angelo Calepio, *Vera et fidelissima narratione del successo dell'espugnatione et defesione del regno di Cipro* écrit en 1572 et publié dans: Étienne de Lusignan, *Chorograffia*, fols. 92r–125r; Étienne de Lusignan, *Description*, fols. 237v–271v, trans. in Claude D. Cobham, *Excerpta Cypria: Materials for a History of Cyprus* (Cambridge, 1908, repr. 1969), pp. 125–48; Antonio M. Graziani, *De Bello Cyprio* (Rome, 1624), repr. en français: *Histoire de la guerre de Chypre* (Paris, 1685).

admet lui-même les lacunes. Le manque de temps, la dispersion des sources, les difficultés à accéder aux manuscrits ont sans doute contraint l'historien à accorder une confiance exagérée à cette tradition historiographique.

Pour l'*Etat présent de l'Egypte*, Dominique Jauna s'intéresse davantage à la géographie, aux habitants et à la culture du pays qu'à son histoire. C'est la raison pour laquelle ses observations personnelles sont nombreuses ainsi que les témoignages oraux qu'il a recueillis. Dans son introduction, il précise que R. P. Fulgence, gardien des capucins, et Benoît de Maillet, consul de la nation française au Caire, ont été ses principaux informateurs.[97] Au fil de ses rencontres avec Hadgi-Ali, évêque arménien, envoyé du roi d'Éthiopie en Égypte, il collecte des renseignements sur le pays et se contente de citer Bossuet et son *Discours sur l'histoire universelle* comme unique source écrite.[98]

La dernière partie du travail de Jauna qui a nécessité de recourir à des sources porte sur les écritures égyptiennes. Il ajoute aux auteurs de l'Antiquité, déjà cités dans son travail historique sur Chypre, les écrits de Flavius Vopiscus, un des auteurs fictifs de la collection de biographie dite *Histoire d'Auguste*, de l'orateur Philostrate l'Athénien, de Martianus Capella, d'Athénée dont les *Dépnosophistes* sont édités dès 1514, de Dictys de Crète et son *Ephéméride de la guerre de Troie*, d'Eupolème et son *Histoire des rois de Judée*, d'Hésychios d'Alexandrie.[99]

Les ouvrages d'auteurs contemporains dont Jauna a disposé pour identifier les différents types d'écriture auxquels il a été confronté, sont plus rarement mentionnés. Il note toutefois avoir consulté ceux du voyageur français D'Arvieux, du jésuite toulousain Guillaume Bonjour connu pour être auteur de plusieurs mémoires sur l'Égypte, du prêtre marseillais Arseré, auteur d'un dictionnaire turc et arabe, du cardinal Bembo et de l'intendant de marine et collectionneur Michel Bégon.[100]

Certes, l'historien regrette aujourd'hui que Jauna n'ait pas davantage évoqué les lieux où il a vécu, notamment Chypre, avec les vestiges de ses monuments médiévaux mais il n'a jamais eu l'ambition de laisser une œuvre autobiographique. Le regard qu'il porte sur l'île est avant tout celui d'un historien et l'*Histoire générale* constitue le chaînon intermédiaire qui relie les œuvres historiques d'Étienne de Lusignan et de Loredano à l'historiographie positiviste du XIXe siècle. Comme ses prédécesseurs, il cède parfois à la facilité de romancer certains événements, mais à d'autres moments, il s'efforce d'offrir au lecteur les sources les plus fiables en faisant revivre notamment les récits de Georgios Boustronios et de

---

[97] Jauna, 1:1205. Le père Fulgence de Tours, capucin mathématicien appartient à la mission d'Égypte: Édouard E. F. Descamps, *Histoire générale comparée des missions* (Paris, 1932), p. 491. En parallèle à ses activités de consul de la nation française, de Maillet a conduit plusieurs expéditions archéologiques en Égypte auxquelles a pu participer Jauna: Henri A. Omont, *Missions archéologiques françaises en Orient aux XVIIe et XVIIIe siècles*, 2 vols. (Paris, 1902), 1:282–97.

[98] Jauna, 1:12, 2:1219, 1370.

[99] Ibid., 2:1393, 1400

[100] Ibid., 2:1392, 1414.

Florio Bustron. Au siècle des Lumières, Dominique Jauna est également porteur d'une tradition historiographique de la croisade que l'*Histoire des croisades* de Voltaire a aujourd'hui tendance à éclipser. Cette épopée, largement positive à ses yeux, nourrit son désir de voir à nouveau les peuples de l'Europe chrétienne s'unir dans un élan commun contre le Turc. Bien documentée, *l'Histoire générale* reste, jusqu'aux travaux de François-Joseph Michaud, une référence incontournable chez des historiens qui s'intéressent à l'Orient médiéval. L'œuvre de Dominique Jauna résiste à un jugement tranché tant les réflexions sont multiples: prémonitoire avec son projet de canal entre la mer Rouge et la Méditerranée, il apparaît, d'un autre côté, en complet décalage avec son siècle et le contexte politique en soutenant une conquête de l'Égypte. C'est cette complexité qui rend cette œuvre encore digne d'intérêt.

Annexe 1: Généalogie des familles Jauna-Vincens

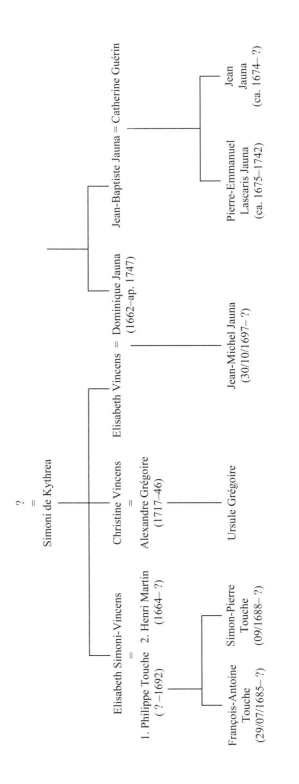

Annexe 2: Lettre de Dominique Jauna à Bernard de Montfaucon, 29 octobre 1730, Vienne

Dominique Jauna remercie Bernard de Montfaucon de l'avoir accueilli à Paris et ensuite recommandé au baron de Bartenstein. Reçu par le prince Eugène et par deux fois par l'empereur Charles VI, il obtient le titre de conseiller et la charge d'inspecteur général du commerce. Il souligne le plaisir procuré par la lettre de Montfaucon à Bartenstein et confesse avoir été invité plusieurs fois à sa table en compagnie de l'épouse de Bartenstein et de ses quatre enfants. Renouvelant son dévouement à Montfaucon, Jauna termine en lui annonçant son départ imminent pour les Pays-Bas sur ordre de Charles VI.

A: Lettre (186 × 235mm) figurant dans un volume de la correspondance de Bernard de Montfaucon: Paris, Archives Nationales, fonds français 17708, fols. 252r–253r

a. Emmanuel de Broglie, *La société de l'abbaye de Saint-Germain des Prés au XVIIIe siècle. Bernard de Montfaucon et les Bernardins (1715–1750)*, 2 vols. (Paris, 1888–91), 1:304–306 d'après A

Mon très Révérend Père,

Si je me suis si longtemps privé de l'honneur de vous écrire et de vous remercier très humblement, comme je fais, des bontés dont vous m'avez comblé pendant mon séjour à Paris, et de l'efficace recommandation dont vous m'honorâtes pour M. le baron de Bartenstein,[1] ce n'a esté que pour attendre la décision de mon sort, et pouvoir en marquer à V.(otre) Révérence quelque chose de positif.

Mgr le prince Eugène[2] eut la bonté de me recevoir fort gracieusement, les premiers ministres de S. M. I. C.[3] en firent de même et eurent tous celle de parler en ma faveur à ce monarque, qui, peu de temps après, m'honora d'une audience. Il m'écouta avec sa bénignité naturelle, et marqua tant de plaisir à m'entendre parler sur le commerce, que sa complaisance me présagea l'heureux succès de mon voyage, d'autant plus qu'il m'ordonna de me préparer à lui en raisonner plus amplement.

---

[1] Né à Strasbourg, Jean-Christophe Bartenstein (1690–1767) est le fils d'un professeur protestant. Après un passage à Paris chez les Mauristes à Saint-Germain des Prés, il entre au gouvernement autrichien en 1715 grâce à l'appui de Bernard de Montfaucon. Il est un conseiller très écouté par Charles VI puis Marie-Thérèse pour les affaires étrangères. Vice-chancelier de l'État autrichien, il est également l'auteur de plusieurs mémoires pour l'instruction de Joseph II. (voir bibliographie n. 34)

[2] François Eugène, prince de Savoie (1663–1736) a grandi à la cour de Louis XIV. Il embrasse la carrière militaire à 19 ans et passe en Autriche où il devient un fidèle de la monarchie des Habsbourg sous trois empereurs, Léopold Ier, Joseph Ier et Charles VI. Il participe aux différentes campagnes militaires contre les Turcs et conduit des activités diplomatiques contre les Bourbons: Derek McKay, *Prince Eugene of Savoy* (New York, 1977).

[3] Sa Majesté Impériale Catholique: Charles VI (1685–1740).

J'eus donc le bonheur d'une seconde audience, le 12 de ce mois; mes très humbles remontrances sur le même sujet furent reçues si favorablement que ce Grand Prince ne tarda pas à me faire ressentir les effets d'une récompense qui m'engage à son service pour le reste de mes jours, S. M. I. C. m'a honoré du titre son cons^e (eiller) (fol. 252v) et de la charge d'inspecteur général du Commerce, même fait largement payer des frais de mon voyage, ce qui me dédommage avec usure du Consulat de Naples,[4] qu'on m'a refusé en France.

Souffrez, mon Révérend Père, qu'après vous avoir rendu compte de ce qui me regarde, j'aye l'honneur de vous assurer de l'extrême plaisir que fit votre lettre à M. le Baron Bartenstein et des sensibles marques d'amitié que votre précieuse recommandation m'a attirées de ce secrétaires d'État, aussi illustre par ses rares mérites que par les éminents emplois qu'il occupe à la cour, puisque, non content d'avoir avantageusement parlé en ma faveur dans toutes les occasions il a voulu m'honorer plusieurs fois de sa table en compagnie de plusieurs seigneurs dont la plupart instruits de vos excellents ouvrages et des rares mérites de V.(otre) R.(évérence) se sont fait un grand plaisir de boire à votre santé; Madame de Bartenstein a même excité la compagnie à la redoubler; elle est d'aussi bonne humeur que belle et riche, et encore plus vertueuse, parlant fort bien quatre sortes de langues, et enfin très digne d'un si célèbre époux. Leur famille consiste en un garçon de six ans et trois filles, dont l'aînée n'en a que quatre.

Au reste, mon Révérend Père, j'espère d'avoir l'honneur de vous écrire de plus près; S. M. I. C. m'a fait celui de m'ordonner de passer aux Pays-Bas,[5] pour où je compte de partir dans une quinzaine de jours; je supplie très humblement V.(otre) Révérence de vouloir m'honorer de ses commandements despotiques (fol. 253r) partout où le destin me conduira, puisque, et par devoir et par inclination, rien ne me fera jamais tant de plaisir que les occasions de pouvoir vous donner des marques effectives de la profonde reconnaissance et du respect infini avec lequel j'ai l'honneur d'être

mon Très Révérend Père,

votre très humble et très obéissant serviteur.

Le Ch Jauna.

A Vienne le 29 octobre 1730.

---

[4] Dominique Jauna faisait déjà des affaires à Naples en 1715 et sera à l'origine d'un projet de société maritime dans le royaume de Naples en 1738 (voir n. 28 et 36).

[5] Depuis le traité d'Utrecht en 1713, les Pays-Bas méridionaux sont passés sous la domination des Habsbourg d'Autriche.

Annexe 3: Liste alphabétique des sources mentionnées dans Jauna, *Histoire générale des royaumes de Chypre, Jérusalem, d'Arménie et d'Egypte* (Leyde, 1747, repr. 1785).

Les nombres entre parenthèses correspondent à la pagination de l'*Histoire générale* où figure la référence. Les noms des auteurs ont été orthographiés comme ils figurent dans les éditions de 1747 et 1785 alors qu'ils sont relevés, sous leur forme communément admise aujourd'hui, dans le texte de l'article.

Les références non identifiées sont: Coutou (1:65); Zénon, *Medicinae Principes* (1:83); rabin Charde (2:1404).

Auteurs de l'Antiquité (–Ve siècle)	Auteurs médiévaux (Ve–XVe siècles)	Auteurs modernes (XVIe–XVIIIe siècles)
Abydemus patefactus ... avoit écrit une Histoire de l'île de Chypre (1:10)	Ayton d'Arménie (1:641, 689, 694, 701, 709, 717, 734)	père Ange Calopin, dominiquain (2:1114)
Apian/Ammian Marcellin (1:68, 2:1410, 1411)	Bocace (2:839)	Mr Arseré, prêtre de Marseille, *dictionnaire turc et arabe* (2:1392)
Apollodore (1:17)	Continuateur de la Guerre sainte (1:255, 266, 315, 386, 425, 557, 689, 694, 713, 768)	Mr d'Arvieux (2:1392)
auteur des Thébaïques (2:1400)	Etienne de Byzance (1:12)	Auteur du livre intitulé, *Militaris Ordinis Janitarum* (1:557)
Athénée (2:1400)	Florent, évêque de Ptolémaïde (1:299)	Chevalier Melchior Bandini, *Histoire Jérosolimitaine* (1:726)
chronique tyrienne (1:20)	George, patriarche de Constantinople (1:77)	Blondel (1:préambule)
Clément d'Alexandrin/Alexandran (2:1406, 1409, 1410, 1411, 1414)	Guillaume de Tyr / archevêque de Tyr (1:60, 143, 178, 179, 197, 203, 240, 248, 302, 315, 382)	Bochard (1:5, 13)
Ctésias (2:1400)	Jacques de Vitriac (1:382)	R. P. Bonjour de la compagnie de Jésus (2:1392, 1414)
Dictys cretensis (2:1400, 1409)	Jean Villani (1:480, 694, 2:800)	Bosio ... *Histoire de Malte* (1:387, 577, 698, 726, 765, 768, 2:794, 832, 866)
Diodore de Sicile (1:577, 2:1382, 1388, 1405, 1411, 1415, 1416)	sire de Joinville (1:622)	Bustron (2:866)
Dion Cassius, *Vie de l'Empereur Trajan* (1:8)		Georges Bustron (2:1048)

Auteurs de l'Antiquité (–Ve siècle)	Auteurs médiévaux (Ve–XVe siècles)	Auteurs modernes (XVIe–XVIIIe siècles)
Eratosthene … avoit écrit une histoire d'Amathunte (1:11)	Nicétas Choniatès (1:205)	le très-R. P. Calmet (1:préambule)
Eupolume *Histoire des rois de Judée* (2:1400)	Pierre de la Palu (1:382)	Coëffeteau, *Histoire romaine* (1:48)
Eusèbe (1:13, 2:1399, 1402, 1404, 1405, 1407)	Photius (1:11)	Colbert (2:1358)
Hermias Sozomene, surnommé le scholastique a écrit *Histoire ecclésiastique* (1:83)	*Régistres d'Innocent III à la bibliothèque Vaticane* (1:428)	Colenucio (1:669)
Hérodote (1:11, 13, 16, 22, 24, 26, 2:1381, 1382, 1388, 1399, 1405, 1411, 1413, 1416)	saint antonin (1:60)	père Daniel (1:587)
Hésichius (2:1400)	Saint Thomas d'Aquin, *De regimine principum* (1:698)	Duschesene (1:764)
Hésiode (1:3)	Suidas (1:11, 83, 2:1393)	Eccar (1:préambule)
Homère (1:3, 15, 16, 20, 2:1378, 1381)	Théophanes (1:54)	R. P. Fulgence, gardien des capucins … au Caire (2:1205)
Isocrate et son discours à la louange d'Evagoras (1:26, 31)	Vincent de Beauvais … dans son *Miroir historique* (1:280, 454, 600, 608)	*Généalogie Diplomatique de la très-Auguste maison d'Autriche*, à Vienne l'an 1737 (1:préambule)
Joseph (1:20, 2:1375, 1404, 1405, 1415)		Gratiani (1:68, 114)
Justin (1:11, 13, 87)		Gueudeville dans son nouvel atlas (1:préambule)
Lucain (2:1410)		Guichenon (1:135, 2:970, 995, 1038, 1048)
Macrobe (1:11)		Henri Catarin (1:85)
Martianus, Capelle (2:1393)		-historiens espagnols (2:817)
Méla (1:16, 2:1399)		-le père Hugo (1:préambule)
Nicéphore *Histoire ecclésiastique* (1:8)		-Imhof (1:préambule)
		-*In Actis Eruditiorum* (1:préambule)
		-rabin japhe (2:1404)
		Jason de Nores (1:préambule)

Auteurs de l'Antiquité (–Ve siècle)	Auteurs médiévaux (Ve–XVe siècles)	Auteurs modernes (XVIe–XVIIIe siècles)
Onesime (1:83)		Le Blond, dans son *Livre de la décadence de l'Empire romain* (1:préambule)
Pausanias (1:16, 31, 2:1408)		rabin Levi (2:1404)
Philon de Biblis (2:1406)		Loredan / Loredano (1:374, 384, 460, 563, 697, 2:795, 805, 809, 819, 839, 848, 876, 914, 930, 970, 971, 1000, 1048)
Philostrate (2:1393)		
Platon (2:1376, 1381, 1400, 1401, 1407)		
Pline (1:65, 2:1393, 1398, 1399)		
Plutarque (1:14, 15, 17, 23, 2:1400, 1411)		Lusignan (1:50, 65, 86, 383, 425, 697, 775, 2:809, 839, 866, 395, 914, 995, 1000, 1024, 1026, 1048)
Ptolémée (1:11, 65)		
Pythagore (2:1415)		
saint Augustin (2:1405)		Mr. Marcel, commissaire de la marine à Arles (2:1392)
saint Jérome (1:14, 2:1404, 1412)		
saint Luc (2:1403)		Monsieur de Meaux, dans son *histoire Universelle* (2:1370)
Scylax (1:11, 19)		
Septante (2:1398)		Paul-Emile (1:315, 425, 641, 647, 694)
Servius (1:11)		Mr de Maillet, consul au Caire (2:1205)
Strabon (1:5, 7, 47, 65, 179)		P. Maimbourg (1:261, 315, 666, 769)
Tacite (1:16, 22, 49, 299, 2:1405)		Murcius (1:3)
talmud de Babylone (2:1404)		*Nouvelles Littéraires de Ratisbonne* (1:préambule)
Théopompe (1:11)		
Tite-Live (2:1393, 1399, 1406)		relation des voyageurs (1:72)
Théophraste (1:11)		Rollin … dans le 4ème volume de son *Histoire ancienne* (1:31, 2:1370)
Théopompe (1:11)		
Thucidide (1:26)		Sagredo (2:1065, 1109, 1174)
Vopiscus (2:1393)		

Auteurs de l'Antiquité (–Ve siècle)	Auteurs médiévaux (Ve–XVe siècles)	Auteurs modernes (XVIe–XVIIIe siécles)
Zozime (1:53)		Monsieur de Seignelai (2:1325)
		Vie de St Norbert (1:préambule)
		Sansovin …, *Histoire* (1:419, 420, 421)
		Se'be'lique (1:425)
		chevalier Temple (2:910)
		chevalier Toxan (1:255, 726)
		Tracagnota (1:425, 694)
		P. Vignier (1:préambule)
		chevalier De la Vinaudière, Sécrétaire de Claude de la Sangle, Grand-Maître de Malte, … *Aureum Turcicum Imperiique Ottomanici descriptio* (1:689)

Saladin's Legacy in the Middle East before the Nineteenth Century

Diana Abouali

Dartmouth College
Diana.Abouali@Dartmouth.edu

Saladin's place in the popular and historical imagination of modern Arabs is unparalleled for any pre-modern historical figure with the exception of Muhammad, the prophet of Islam. In the twentieth and twenty-first centuries, Saladin and the major events of his military career, namely the reconquest of Jerusalem in 1187 and legendary battles like Hittin, have been used symbolically in print, film, art, and political rhetoric to forward anti-colonial, anti-Zionist, and anti-imperial agendas. His Kurdish roots are conveniently overlooked as he was moulded into the hero of Arab nationalism, and his status as a Muslim warrior and sultan rendered him a popular figure even with Muslims beyond the Arab world. Yet, despite his popularity and stature in recent times, Saladin is commonly presented by western historians of the crusades as an obscure historical figure before the nineteenth century – a forgotten sultan, overshadowed by two other legendary warriors who battled crusader armies in their lifetimes: Nur al-Din Zengi and al-Zahir Baybars. As cultural encounters heightened with Europe, where Saladin had enjoyed legendary status for centuries, Arabs and Muslims in the nineteenth century were finally reintroduced and reacquainted with the life and achievements of the great Ayyubid commander.

This commonplace narrative that credits European literary culture with Saladin's rehabilitation into the historical imagination of Arabs and Muslims is a misinformed one. On the contrary, Saladin remained very much alive in the historical imagination of Arabs and Muslims, and never receded into obscurity. Histories and literary texts from the Mamluk and Ottoman periods that contain in them accounts of the crusader era attest to Saladin's continued presence. Saladin was also a figure that inhabited the popular memories of Arab Muslims, and not just the rarified world of the ʿulamaʾ (religious scholars) who composed those Mamluk and Ottoman works. As I will show in this article, Saladin was a historical figure whose name could be

I would like to thank A. Kevin Reinhart, Dana Sajdi, and Ilham Khuri-Makdisi for reading and commenting on earlier drafts of this article, Hussein Kadhim for providing me with information on Ahamd Shawqi's poetry and related references, and William Granara for help with translation. An earlier version of this article was presented at the New England Medieval Conference, which was held at Dartmouth College, 3–4 October 2008. Many thanks to the organizers of the conference, Cecilia Gaposchkin and Chistopher MacEvitt, for the opportunity to present my work, and to the participants for their comments. Research at the Bodleian Library, Oxford was made possible by an NEH Summer Institute grant in 2008.

invoked symbolically as part of a particular political or social message. In a poem written in Jerusalem during the early seventeenth century, Saladin is mentioned in such a way that demonstrates persistence of and communal familiarity with his personality and historical context.

Misconceptions

A belief commonly held by modern historians of the crusades is that Saladin was forgotten, or overlooked, in the Muslim Middle East until his "rediscovery" in the second half of the nineteenth century. Carole Hillenbrand claimed that "Saladin, who was soon eulogized in medieval Europe in the centuries after the crusades and then eagerly cast in heroic mould by the European Enlightenment … was ignored for centuries in the Middle East."[1] Jonathan Riley-Smith forwarded several theories to explain Saladin's obscurity in Muslim communal memory, which range from his Kurdish origins to the brief time-span of the "quasi-empire" he founded.[2] But, whatever the actual reason for Saladin's absence from the historical memory of Muslims, this common belief suggests that it was symptomatic of a broader disinterest by medieval/pre-modern Muslims in Europe or "the West." In other words, Muslims cared so little about Latin Christians from western Europe that they were oblivious to the distinctions among them, even when they appeared in the eastern Mediterranean beginning with the First Crusade. According to Bernard Lewis, there was little room in the Muslim *Weltanschauung* to accommodate the varieties of non-Muslims – in this case, Latin Christians from western Europe – because it was premised on a binary system of categorizing peoples, "between believers and unbelievers."[3] Emmanuel Sivan wrote in 1972 about the failure of Muslim historians not only to recognize who the crusaders were, but also to understand the real nature of their wars.[4] These historians' inability to distinguish one crusader group from the next betrayed not only Muslim parochialism, but also the shortcomings of their craft. Their apathy and lack of curiosity ultimately led the crusades to fade from collective Muslim memory. Thus, Riley-Smith claimed that Muslims forgot about the crusades, or at least "lost interest":

> In the Islamic world the crusades almost passed out of mind … Very few writers, apart from the Ottoman historiographer, Naʿima, who drew comparisons between the central Middle Ages and the struggle in the Balkans at the turn of the seventeenth and eighteenth

---

[1] Carole Hillenbrand, *The Crusades: Islamic Perspectives* (New York, 2000), pp. 592–93.

[2] Jonathan Riley-Smith, "Islam and the Crusades in History and Imagination, 8 November 1898–11 September 2001," *Crusades* 2 (2003), 152.

[3] Bernard Lewis, *The Middle East and the West* (Bloomington, 1964), p. 116.

[4] Emmanuel Sivan, "Modern Arab Historiography of the Crusades," *Asian and African Studies* 8 (1972), 109–49.

centuries, did more than mention the crusaders in passing ... The fact is that the Muslims had lost interest.[5]

From this premise one can easily extrapolate that Muslims forgot about Saladin because they forgot about the crusades. This assumption is reinforced by a presumed absence of Saladin as a theme or subject in post-Ayyubid Arabic poetry and literature. Apart from the chronicles by his contemporaries, Baha' al-Din Yusuf ibn Shaddad and ʿImad al-Din al-Isfahani, and the courtly poems composed for him during his rule, there are no major elegies, panegyrics, or epics glorifying his various military feats and victories that have endured as a widespread popular tradition in the Arabic-speaking Middle East and North Africa.[6] Saladin's neglect contrasts even more sharply with the development of the legendary character of Saladin in European literature and culture, as Hillenbrand cogently points out above.[7] These notions of Muslim apathy to things European, the inability of Muslims to formulate a nuanced or informed understanding of non-Muslim peoples, and their lack of an historical awareness of the crusades are recycled time and again in works by European historians of the crusades. For instance, in his biography of Saladin, Hannes Möhring wrote: "Before the nineteenth century, Muslims had very little interest in the crusades or in European affairs. Their interest in Saladin was hardly any greater, despite the fact that he had reconquered Jerusalem and, from the Sunni perspective, had overthrown the heretical Fatimids."[8] Likewise, Helen J. Nicholson, in an article on Muslim reactions to the crusades, spoke not only of "a commonplace of modern crusading history that until the nineteenth century the Islamic world had very little interest in the West," but also that "[u]ntil the end of the nineteenth century ... the Muslim world had not taken a great interest in [Saladin]."[9] Saladin's descent into obscurity was deemed to be at variance with the popular attention devoted to his own commander and predecessor, Nur al-Din Zengi (1118–74), because of his commitment to Sunni revivalism and jihad, or to the thirteenth-century Mamluk sultan, al-Zahir Baybars (1223–77), for his

---

[5] Jonathan Riley-Smith, *The Crusades, Christianity, and Islam* (New York, 2008), p. 71.

[6] Baha' al-Din Yusuf ibn Rafiʿ Ibn Shaddad, *The Rare and Excellent History of Saladin, or, Al-Nawadir Al-sultaniyya waʾl-mahasin al-Yusufiyya*, trans. D. S. Richards (Aldershot, 2001); ʿImad al-Din Muhammad ibn Muhammad Katib al-Isfahani, *Al-fath al-qussiyy fi-l-fath al-Qudsi* (Cairo, 1965). See also ʿAbd al-Rahman ibn Ismaʿil Abu Shamah and Ahmad Baysumi, *ʿUyun al-rawdatayn fi akhbar al-dawlatayn al-Nuriyya wa-l-Salahiyya* (Damascus, 1991); Salih J. Altoma, *Salah al-Din fi al-shiʿr al-ʿarabi al-muʿasir*, Kitab al-shahr 9 (Riyadh, 1979).

[7] Riley-Smith also comments on Saladin's alternative career in Europe as legendary knight: see Riley-Smith, *The Crusades, Christianity, and Islam*, p. 64. See also Margaret A. Jubb, *The Legend of Saladin in Western Literature and Historiography* (Lewiston, 2000).

[8] Hannes Möhring, *Saladin: The Sultan and His Times, 1138–1193*, trans. David S. Bachrach (Baltimore, 2005), pp. 101–2.

[9] Helen J. Nicholson, "Muslim Reaction to the Crusades," in *Palgrave Advances in the Crusades*, ed. Helen J. Nicholson (Basingstoke, 2005), pp. 279–80.

uncommon skill in battle against the crusader armies that was memorialized in an eponymous folk epic.[10]

Muslim interest in Saladin, as the line of argument goes, increased during the second half of the nineteenth century because of heightened cultural encounters with Europe. Much of the credit for reacquainting the Muslims of the eastern Mediterranean with Saladin is given to the German emperor, Kaiser Wilhelm II, whose homage to and renovation of the Ayyubid commander's tomb in Damascus in 1898 is seen as the primary catalyst for his revival.[11] Indeed, the Kaiser's visit inspired Ahmad Shawqi (1868–1932), arguably the greatest Arab poet of the early twentieth century, to introspectively and shamefully "ask how it was that Saladin's greatness had been ignored by Muslim writers until they had been reminded of it by [the Kaiser]."[12] The translation efforts of European literary and historical works (mostly from French) into Arabic that began in the nineteenth century also played an important role in reviving interest in the crusades, and are credited with introducing to Arabs the concept of the crusades as a distinct phenomenon.[13] As Sivan notes, "The terms *al-hurub al-salibiyya*, or *hurub al-salib* and *al-salibiyyun* (crusaders) seem to have appeared only in modern times" – a byproduct of the translation effort that would mark the nineteenth-century Arab cultural movement known as the *Nahda*.[14] While the "Christian intelligentsia," who undertook much of the translations in the early to mid-nineteenth century, initially did so for their own particular reasons, Christian and Muslim Arab politicians, literary figures like Shawqi, and even historians soon appropriated Saladin as a symbol par excellence of Arab resistance to western imperialism and, later, Zionist/Israeli aggression.[15] The problem with this rendition of Saladin's historical legacy in the Muslim Mediterranean is that it credits Europeans not only with a realization of Saladin's historical importance, but also with the task of "reminding" Arabs (Muslim or Christians) of the Ayyubid commander and reacquainting them with their own

---

[10] Hillenbrand, *The Crusades: Islamic Perspectives*, p. 593. For more information on the Baybars folk epic, see Gamal al-Ghitani, ed., *Sirat al-Zahir Baybars* (Cairo, 1996); R. Paret, "Sīrat Baybars," *Encyclopaedia of Islam, Second Edition*, ed. P. Bearman, Th. Bianquis, C. E. Bosworth, E. van Donzel and W. P. Heinrichs (Brill, 2008), at http://www.brillonline.nl/subscriber/entry?entry=islam_SIM-1306 (accessed 29 March 2011).

[11] Hillenbrand, *The Crusades: Islamic Perspectives*, pp. 593–94; Riley-Smith, *The Crusades, Christianity, and Islam*, p. 160.

[12] Riley-Smith, *The Crusades, Christianity, and Islam*, p. 64. See, for instance, Shawqi's poem, "Tahiyyatu Ghalyum al-thani li-Salah al-Din fi-l-qabr" [Wilhelm II's homage to Saladin at his grave], in *Al-Shawqiyyat: Shi'ir al-marhum Ahmad Shawqi, al-juz' al-thalith* (Beirut, 1985), pp. 48–49. For more on Ahmad Shawqi and Salah al-Din, see Altoma, *Salah al-Din fi al-shi'r al-'arabi al-mu'asir*.

[13] Riley-Smith, *The Crusades, Christianity, and Islam*, pp. 70–73; Hillenbrand, *The Crusades: Islamic Perspectives*, pp. 591–92; Sivan, "Modern Arab Historiography," pp. 111–12.

[14] Sivan, "Modern Arab Historiography," pp. 109–10. See also Werner Ende, "Wer ist ein Glaubensheld, wer ist ein Ketzer," *Die Welt des Islams* 23–24 (1984), 80.

[15] Sivan, "Modern Arab Historiography," p. 118; Hillenbrand, *The Crusades: Islamic Perspectives*, pp. 594–614.

memory of the crusades. The rendition assigns Europeans cultural superiority, and Muslims ignorance and apathy.

A careful assessment of the historical chronicles and literary works written by the locals of Jerusalem and the Holy Land, however, can and does provide an alternative account of the legacy of Saladin and the crusades in the Middle East. References to Saladin by Muslims of the eastern Mediterranean did not cease in the period between the end of the Ayyubid state and the Kaiser's laying of the bronze wreath on Saladin's tomb at the close of the nineteenth century; and when Saladin or the crusades were mentioned, it was not necessarily "in passing." The crusades and Saladin, it turns out, were not omitted from the historical narrative as conceived by medieval Muslim historians. Indeed, quite the opposite occurred.

It is not too difficult to find references to Saladin in Arabic literary sources from the Mamluk and Ottoman period. Even a cursory look at the literature reveals that Saladin features prominently in historical chronicles privileging Jerusalem and Palestine, many of which fall into the genre "Virtues of Jerusalem" (Ar. *fada'il Bayt al-Maqdis*). Mujir al-Din al-ʿUlaymi's (1456–1522) magisterial history of Jerusalem and Hebron, *al-Uns al-jalil bi-tarikh al-Quds wa-l-Khalil*, is one example where Saladin figures prominently in the sections on the crusader period.[16] This work, "the most comprehensive and detailed source for the history of Jerusalem written during the Middle Ages," was well known in its day; there are a large number of extant manuscripts that date from the sixteenth century onward, which also makes the case for general familiarity with Saladin as a historical figure and his role in the region's history.[17] Since Mujir al-Din is concerned with the cities of Jerusalem and Hebron, his treatment of Saladin's historical record is more detailed and complete than that of Nur al-Din Zengi. For the period spanning the First Crusade to his death, Saladin is the unrivaled protagonist of Mujir al-Din's narrative.

Lesser known works on the history of Jerusalem, such as *Kitab muthir al-gharam ila ziyarat al-Quds wa-l-Sham*, written by Shihab al-Din Ahmad b. Muhammad of Jerusalem in 1351, and *Al-Mustaqsa fi fada'il al-Masjid al-Aqsa*, by Nasr al-Din Muhammad b. Muhammad al-ʿAlami (d. 1545), also make extensive reference to Saladin; the latter, based on the works of Ibn Shaddad, al-Isfahani, Abu Shama and Mujir al-Din al-ʿUlaymi, has an entire chapter devoted Saladin's reconquest of Jerusalem and other cities.[18] Muhammad al-Khalili's (d. 1734) short essay on the conditions in Jerusalem and Hebron between 1714 and 1716, entitled *Kitab tarikh al-Quds wa-l-Khalil*, also pays homage to the Ayyubid commander. While al-Khalili's

---

[16] Mujir al-Din al-Hanbali, *Al-Uns al-jalil bi-tarikh al-Quds wa-l-Khalil* (Amman, 1973). For more on al-ʿUlaymi, see H. Busse, "Mudjir al-Dīn al-ʿUlaymī," in *Encyclopaedia of Islam, Second Edition*, at http://www.brillonline.nl/subscriber/entry?entry=islam_SIM-5308 (accessed 29 March 2011).

[17] Donald P. Little, "Mudjīr Al-Din Al-ʿUlaymi's Vision of Jerusalem in the Ninth–Fifteenth Century," *Journal of the American Oriental Society* 115 (1995), 237–47; Busse, "Mudjīr."

[18] Shihab al-Din Ahmad b. Muhammad, "Kitab muthir al-gharam ila ziyarat al-Quds wa-l-Sham," in *Fada'il Bayt Al-Maqdis fi makhtutat ʿArabiyya qadima*, ed. Mahmud Ibrahim (Safat, Kuwait, 1985), pp. 329–419; Nasr al-Din Muhammad al-ʿAlami, "Al-Mustaqsa fi fada'il Masjid Al-Aqsa," in *Fada'il Bayt al-Maqdis*, pp. 489–521.

purpose in writing the text was to document the rehabilitation of various structures and foundations that was carried out in the two cities by the district governor, Rajab Pasha, the author also provides some historical background. As in Mujir al-Din's chronicle, al-Khalili's rendition of the crusader period is a laudatory account of Saladin's achievements spanning five folios in length (the entire manuscript has 69 folios).[19] It appears from even a cursory look at the historical literature, then, that neither Saladin nor his military and political achievements seem to have been forgotten. Instead, they constitute key episodes in the historical narrative of the cities and regions of late twelfth-century Syria and Palestine. The authors of these histories present Saladin as a victorious leader and conqueror who purified the city of Jerusalem after a century of desecration wrought upon it by Latin Christian rule.

If we can say, then, that the memory of Saladin was an enduring one, then so too was the memory of the crusades – not necessarily as a distinct and defined phenomenon, or series of phenomena, but certainly as a manifestation of European (western/Latin Christian) military aggression and occupation of the eastern Mediterranean coast, with Jerusalem as a target, whether or not this was the actual intent of the crusader movement. The memory of the crusades – of Latin Christian intent toward the capturing of Jerusalem as expressed in military terms – did not fade from the minds of those who lived on the Syrian/Palestinian coast, nor did fears of renewed attack ever fully subside. Mujir al-Din al-ʿUlaymi, writing on the eve of the sixteenth century, recalled how in 1060 the immense chandelier that hung under the dome of the Aqsa mosque fell from the ceiling. "The Muslim residents of the city took it to be a bad omen," Mujir al-Din wrote. "They said, 'Something tremendous will happen in the lands of Islam.' And indeed, that event was the Frankish conquest of Jerusalem." A few decades later, in 1541–42, Muhammad Nasir al-Din al-ʿAlami wrote that "the Muslims throughout the lands of Islam were extremely perturbed by the conquest of Jerusalem; its occupation by the Franks lasted for ninety-nine years, and the lands of Islam had never endured a calamity greater that."[20] Likewise, Muhammad al-Khalili noted that, even as he was writing in the early eighteenth century, the cities and regions of Palestine that suffered from crusader rule "still endure grief and loss."[21]

The fears of a possible attack against the Syrian/Palestinian coast were sometimes fueled by rumors, such as those that circulated when Fakhr al-Din Maʿan, a rebellious Druze leader who challenged Ottoman rule, fled his home in the Lebanese mountains and made his way across the Mediterranean to the shores of Tuscany in 1613. According to the Ottoman historian Mustafa Naîma (1655–1716), the Medicis agreed to harbor Fakhr al-Din in return for his help in planning

---

[19] Oxford, Bodleian Library, MS E. D. Clarke Or 33, fols. 1–69. For information on Muhammad al-Khalili, see his entry in Muhammad b. Khalil al-Muradi, *Silk al-durar fi aʾyan al-qarn al-thani ʿashar*, vol 4. (Beirut, 1997), pp. 108–11; also Muhammad al-Khalili, *Tarikh al-Quds wa-l-Khalil*, ed. Nufan Raja al-Sawariyah and Muhammad Adnan al-Bakhit (London, 2004).

[20] al-Alami, "Al-Mustaqsa fi fadaʿil Masjid al-Aqsa," p. 503.

[21] al-Khalili, "Kitab tarikh al-Quds wa-l-Khalil ʾalayhi al-salam," 27v.

a military campaign against the Ottomans, and the Tuscans were hoping to launch their own attack against the Syrian coast. Indeed, the Ottomans took the threat so seriously they sent naval reinforcements along the Syrian coast in case such an attack took place.[22] In Jerusalem, the significance and meaning of such rumors were well understood by residents of the city; a few years after the Tuscan incident, in 1621, the notables of Jerusalem pleaded with the provincial governor in Damascus against the appointment of a French consul to their city, and made their case thus: "Jerusalem," they argued, "is a place at which the infidels look with covetous eyes … their schemes and plots against it never cease. We fear lest they occupy us … as it happened several times before."[23]

Against this broader context of rumors and fears of another crusade in the early seventeenth century, a local Jerusalem affair was unfolding – an affair that demonstrated the enduring memory of the crusades and Saladin among the residents of Jerusalem, as captured in a poem that is the subject of this article. Soon after the rebel Fakhr al-Din's escape to Tuscany, a resident of Jerusalem named ʿAbd al-Samad al-ʿAlami, the son of a local and popular shaykh and Sufi mystic, Muhammad al-ʿAlami, acquired administrative control of the Salahiyya Khanqah. This khanqah (a residence-cum-prayer hall for Sufis) was one of the preeminent religious institutions in the city.[24] Founded by Saladin in 1189 after his capture of Jerusalem two years earlier, the khanqah occupies the former Latin Patriarchate's palace, which was erected in the 1120s and is adjacent to the Church of the Holy Sepulchre.[25] In a legal tug of war that lasted six months, ʿAbd al-Samad al-ʿAlami managed to wrestle control of the khanqah from the hands of the Khalwati (Sufi) shaykhs who had been associated with the institution for years. The Khalwatis argued that they were rightfully entitled to its administration and the privileges that came with it. ʿAbd al-Samad accused the Khalwati shaykhs of desecrating the site, misusing the property, and failing to fulfill the demands, purpose and spirit of the foundational deed set down by Saladin over 400 years before, which therefore rendered them in breach of the trust. (Indeed, once ʿAbd al-Samad received court-sanctioned appointment, he requested an inspection of the khanqah. This was carried out by the judge of Jerusalem at the time and the chief architect of Jerusalem, and confirmed ʿAbd al-Samad's claims of misuse, neglect and financial disarray.) When ʿAbd al-Samad took over as administrator of the khanqah and its vast collection of endowments that included land and property in Jerusalem and beyond, his father,

---

[22]   Dror Zeevi, *An Ottoman Century: Jerusalem in the 1600s* (Albany, 1996).

[23]   K. J. Asali, "Jerusalem under the Ottomans, 1516–1831 AD," in K. J. Asali, ed., *Jerusalem in History* (Brooklyn, 1990), p. 209.

[24]   Mahmud K. Hawari, *Ayyubid Jerusalem (1187–1250): An Architectural and Archaeological Study* (Oxford, 2007), p. 38. For more on the institution, see J. Chabbi, "Khānkāh," *Encyclopaedia of Islam, Second Edition*, at http://www.brillonline.nl/subscriber/entry?entry=islam_COM-0495 (accessed 29 March 2011).

[25]   Hawari, *Ayyubid Jerusalem*, pp. 38–39; Benjamin Z. Kedar, "Some New Sources on Palestinian Muslims before and during the Crusades," in *Die Kreuzfahrerstaaten als multikulturelle Gesellschaft*, ed. Hans Eberhard Mayer (Munich, 1997), pp. 130–31.

Shaykh Muhammad al-ʿAlami, composed a poem of nineteen lines commemorating the event.[26] In the poem, Muhammad al-ʿAlami portrays his son as a new Saladin, a new savior of Jerusalem in a new age.

The Poem

Muhammad al-ʿAlami's poem about the Salahiyya Khanqah (see Appendix) was found among his collected writings, all of which remain in manuscript form.[27] The majority of Muhammad al-ʿAlami's work showcases his talents as a Sufi poet and shaykh; most of the poems address mystical and devotional matters. But among his poems are those with more experiential, and sometimes autobiographical, content. The poem on the Salahiyya Khanqah is one such composition. Its importance lies partly in the fact that it records an event in the religious and social history of Jerusalem: the transfer of administrative control of a major religious institution from one group to another, and an attempt by a local Jerusalem family to ensure for itself the social and political advantages that come with the administrative control of an institution like the Salahiyya Khanqah.[28] As a text intended for public recitation before an audience of elites and commoners alike, the poem is also important because it invokes Saladin's name both directly and indirectly, thus proving that the general Jerusalem public was familiar with Saladin as a historical figure and that he was part of Jerusalem's collective memory in the early seventeenth century.

Shaykh Muhammad's poem on the Salahiyya Khanqah is partly a tribute to the khanqah's founder and Jerusalem's champion:

> Look to the *khanqah*, erected in the cause of our faith, by the hand of the righteous Salah al-Din, the high-minded one;

> By him I mean the deceased king, may God's pleasure with him increase, he who saved Jerusalem from godlessness and injustice.

Shaykh Muhammad devotes several verses to Saladin's vision for the khanqah: how he established it for the "righteous [Sufi] masters from the world over, Arabs and non-Arabs," as well as for "the poor, the righteous, the wise." As a Sufi lodge,

---

[26]   Berlin, Staatsbibliothek, MS Or. Oct. 1446, fols. 59v–60r; see also MS Jerusalem/University of Jordan, *Diwan al-shaykh Muhammad al-ʿAlami*.

[27]   There are a number manuscript works and poetry collections (*diwan*) attributed to Shaykh Muhammad al-ʿAlami: see Carl Brockelmann, *Geschichte der arabischen Litteratur: Supplementband*, 2 (Leiden, 1938). In addition to the works listed by Brockelmann, additional manuscripts exist among the private papers of the ʿAlami family (Jerusalem and Ramallah). The University of Jordan's Center for Documents and Manuscripts has a microfilm copy of a *diwan* manuscript in the hand of Muhammad Salih b. Muhammad al-ʿAlami and dated 1338H/1919–20.

[28]   For more detail on the transfer of administrative control of the Salahiyya Khanqah, see Diana Abouali, "Family and Society in a Seventeenth-Century Ottoman City: The Alamis of Jerusalem" (Ph.D. thesis, Harvard University, 2004).

it offered these pious men all that they needed and wished for, and it was a place of sanctuary where they could devote themselves to meditation and prayer. But after Saladin had established this good deed, Shaykh Muhammad writes, it was "lost" in the sense that it no longer fulfilled the purpose for which it was created:

> Our lodges weep over the departure of their lodger, having been replaced with women, children and servants.

> It is filled with foreigners and their belongings, and with grain, firewood, and beasts.

> …

> Its conditions had become nothingness, as if it had never been nor will ever endure.

On behalf of the residents of Jerusalem, Shaykh Muhammad was expressing public outrage at the unfortunate condition into which the khanqah had descended. The final verses are an enjoinder by Shaykh Muhammad for "one who strives for this kindness" ("*li-saʿin li-hadha al-khayr*") to restore the Salahiyya to its former glory. Of course, this seeker turns out to be Shaykh Muhammad's son, ʿAbd al-Samad. Like Saladin before him, ʿAbd al-Samad would restore to Jerusalem its former glory through the purification and rehabilitation of Saladin's khanqah.

Both the literal and metaphysical themes of decay, restoration and rejuvenation are addressed by Shaykh Muhammad and permeate the poem, and can be read as a lifecycle for the khanqah in which Shaykh Muhammad sees himself, and his son, playing a part. In the poem, the Salahiyya Khanqah follows a historical trajectory that is reminiscent of the one enjoyed by Jerusalem and its holy sites in the post-crusader *fadaʾil* literature. After the fall of Jerusalem, the crusaders desecrate the city, targeting the Aqsa mosque and the Dome of the Rock in particular. Once the city is liberated of crusader rule, the ruined and defiled holy sites are rehabilitated through the efforts of Salah al-Din (Saladin), the city's savior. Like the Dome of the Rock and the Aqsa mosque, Shaykh Muhammad describes the khanqah as having suffered from ruin and neglect. And, like the Dome of the Rock and the Aqsa, the khanqah was, in the eyes of Shaykh Muhammad, a symbol of the city. The association between Salah al-Din and restoration – whether it be to the khanqah, Jerusalem, the Dome of Rock/Aqsa Mosque, or religion – is strongly made in the poem, and that the Ayyubid commander's name easily lends itself to such statements is not lost on Shaykh Muhammad, either. One of the verses of the poem reads, in Arabic, *Daʿat masalihaha mudh ghaba salihuha kaʾanna salihaha lil-dini lam yaqum*. In this verse, Shaykh Muhammad is playing with various permutations of the Arabic root word *S-L-H*, from which the Arabic name, Salah al-Din, literally meaning the righteous of religion, is derived. *Salah* also means recovery or salvation; and *Salih* is one who is righteous, or who fixes things; to wit, a restorer. (*Taslih*, another form of the root, means fixing, or restitution.) A final permutation of S-L-H that appears in this verse is *masalih*, which means benefit or interest. The use of the word, *salihuha* (its restorer) is also a reference to Salah al-Din/Saladin. Hence, the verse above can be translated as: "Its benefits were lost once its good-doer was gone, as if this righteous one had not acted for the sake of our faith [i.e. Islam]." With the khanqah in the state that Shaykh Muhammad had described, it was in need of a new restorer – one who would "purify it" and restore to the khanqah to the glory it had enjoyed (*Hatta yaʿuda laha ma kana min niʿamin*). ʿAbd al-Samad was the new restorer, the new Salah al-Din. Through this association, ʿAbd al-Samad was a legitimate successor to those who had ravaged the khanqah and left it in disrepair. As Saladin had restored the sanctity and the honor of the Aqsa mosque and the Dome of the Rock, ʿAbd al-Samad would do the same for the Salahiyya Khanqah.

Shaykh Muhammad al-ʿAlami's poem clearly demonstrates that Saladin was not forgotten by Muslims – at least, not by those living in Jerusalem. It shows that the people of seventeenth century Jerusalem perceived the crusades and the personality of Saladin as familiar and recognizable symbols, and that these symbols were harnessed to serve social or political ends. Muhammad al-ʿAlami's symbolic use of Saladin in his poem reveals a clever manipulation and reassignment of symbols and meanings; not only does Muhammad al-ʿAlami seem to channel Saladin (or rather, it is his son who has channeled him through his actions), but he fashions and presents his son as a new, or as another, Saladin. In a sense, it is an example of what Stephen Greenblatt might call self-fashioning – "the cultural system of meanings that creates specific individuals by governing the passage from abstract potential to concrete historical embodiment."[29] But, at the same time, it also recalls an earlier and long-standing practice of modeling and fashioning, and one that is endemic to Muslim societies; the practice of modeling one's behavior after that of Muhammad, the prophet of Islam. Indeed, Muhammad's station in the Muslim world-view is so immense and fundamental that ʿImad al-Din al-Isfahani chose to express Saladin's greatness by refashioning the Ayyubid commander as a new Muhammad whose achievements marked a new age and a new order:

> I chose to date my history from a second Hijra ... this Hijra being the Hijra of Islam to Jerusalem, undertaken by the Sultan Salah al-Din ... History would do well to be dated from this year ... Indeed this Hijra is of more lasting significance than that first ...[30]

Shaykh Muhammad al-ʿAlami could do no better than to model his son after one whose actions were more consequential than the watershed moment of early Islamic history.

---

[29] Stephen Greenblatt, *Renaissance Self-Fashioning: From More to Shakespeare* (Chicago, 1980), pp. 3–4.

[30] From al-Isfahani's *al-Fath al-qussi*, quoted in Tarif Khalidi, *Arabic Historical Thought in the Classical Age* (Cambridge, 1994), p. 182. The *Hijra* refers to the migration of Muhammad and his followers from Mecca to Medina in 621. The event marks the first year of the Islamic (*Hijri*) calendar.

The poem on the Salahiyya Khanqah is one piece of evidence that shows how the Islamic world did not, in the words of one historian, "suddenly show signs of interest" in the crusades during the nineteenth century.[31] Rather, this poem indicates that both the memory of the crusades and Saladin were very much alive in the Arab historical memory and popular imagination before then. Together with other historical and literary works that document the period of the crusades, this poem also demonstrates that Muslims of the eastern Mediterranean had developed and expressed their own historical understandings of the crusader period and of Saladin that were separate from the historical development and treatment they received in European letters. While Arab and Muslim thinkers and writers of the late nineteenth century to the present may have been influenced by those European writings, whatever was borrowed from the West was ultimately grafted onto pre-existing Arab and Muslim conceptions of the crusader period.

Yet as much as this poem is about Saladin and Salahiyya Khanqah, and as valuable as it is in revising the historical legacy of Saladin and the crusades in the Muslim Middle East before the nineteenth century, this poem essentially memorializes a minor event that took place in Jerusalem in the early years of the seventeenth century. Perhaps because of the controversial way he and his son took administrative control of the Salahiyya Khanqah, it was essential that Shaykh Muhammad al-ʿAlami convince his fellow citizens of the legitimacy of his project, and thus he felt compelled to compose his poem. His clever use of symbols and rhetoric, which drew upon the personality or idea of Saladin and the fears of another crusade, were part of this endeavor. Shaykh Muhammad al-ʿAlami and his son saw in themselves the means to the city's salvation from ruin and moral decay, and in turn they were able to draw upon historical antecedents and to ensure for themselves a place within a certain historical narrative and tradition.

---

[31] Riley-Smith, "Islam and the Crusades in History," p. 161.

Appendix: MS Berlin Or. Oct. 1446, 59v–60r

[59v]

و قال رحمَهُ الله تعالى في الصَّلاحيّة

بِرحمةٍ شَمَلَتْ للخَلقِ كُلِّهِم   يَا ربّ بالمصطفى المبعوثِ للأمم

مِن الصلاح صلاح الدّين ذي الهِمَم   انظُرْ لِخَانقَةٍ للدينِ قَدْ جُعِلَتْ

اَلمُنقذَ القُدْس مِنْ كُفرٍ و من ظلم   اعنِي به المَلِكَ المرحُومَ زيدَ رضى

مِنْ سَايرِ¹ القُطرِ عُربٍ و من عجم   اعَدَّها مَنْزِلاً للسادة الصُّلَحَا

نَفعَ المساكين اهل الخير و الحِكَم   يَبْغى² بذاكَ لِوَجْهِ الله مُحتَسِباً

سَادُوا و شادُوا بسَيرٍ ثابت القَّدم   مَشَايخ الدّين أربابُ الفَلاح و مَنْ

حَبَاهُم اللهُ بالاحسان و النّعم   اهل النُّفُوسِ مَنْ هُم³ بالصَّفَا وُصِفُوا

يأوُونَ [مِن]⁵ مَنْزِلٍ سامٍ عن السَّلَم   كَانَتْ رِباطاً لَهُم مِنْ أَيْنَ مَا [وُجِدُوا]⁴

و كلُّ مَا عُدَّ مِنْ نُعْمَى و من نعم   لَهُمْ بهِ كُلُّ مَا يَبْغُونَ مِنْ أَرَبٍ

عَنهم ‹دعاةٌ لحال؟› البؤسِ وَ الألَم   مِنْ بَعْدِ إحْيَاء ذاكَ الخير قد ضعت

---

¹ سائر MS Jerusalem Diwan Muhammad al-'Alami al-Hasani

² يبقى MS Jerusalem

³ هم مَنْ MS Jerusalem

⁴ Unclear in MS Berlin

⁵ Does not appear in MS Berlin

[59v]

And the deceased recited [the following]
about the Salahiyya [Khanqah]:

Lord, I swear by the Chosen One who was sent to the nations with a mercy that embraced all of creation.

Look to the khanqah, erected in the cause of our faith, by the hand of the righteous Salah al-Din, the high-minded one;

By him I mean the deceased King, may God's pleasure with him increase, he who saved Jerusalem from godlessness and injustice.

He founded it as an abode for the righteous [Sufi] masters from the world over, Arabs and non-Arabs,

[an abode] with which he desired to act in God's service, protecting and helping the poor, the righteous, and the wise [Sufis]

[These, the real] masters of our religion, the most accomplished, and those who lead and build with a steady foot.

The people of the soul[?] are those described as pure, may God bestow upon them His grace and blessings.

It was a lodge for them, from where ever they came, [for them to] take shelter in this sublime house

[There] they had everything they could wish for, and everything that could be considered happiness and grace.

And after bringing to life that goodness, his message was lost to them, those who are the guardians of misery and pain,

[60r]

إذ ابدلت٦ بالنِّسَا وَ الوِلْدِ وَ الخَدِم	تَبكِي منَازِلُنَا مَنْ بُعْدِ نازِلهَا
وَ بالْغِلَالِ وَ بالأحْطَابِ و البُهُم	وَ بالأجَانَبِ و الامداد قد مُلِيت٧
للّهِ عَالِمُها مِنْ شِدَّةِ الظُّلَم	وَ بعْدَ عَالِمهَا تَشكوُا مَعَالِمُها
كأنَّ صَالِحَها للدِّينِ لم يَقُم	ضَاعَتْ مَصَالِحُها مذ غاب صَالحُها
كأنّها لَمْ تكُنْ يَوماً وَ لم تَدُم	وَ حَالُ اوْصَافِهَا أَضْحَى إلى عَدَمٍ
وَ الحقُّ يَظْهَرُ مِنْ مَعْنى و من كَلِم	وَ كلُّ ذَلكَ مُولي٨ الحقَّ يَعلَمُه
وَ حَالُهَا وَاضِحٌ كالشّمسِ في عَلَم	وَ هَا هِيَ الآنَ بَينَ النَّاسِ طاهرةٌ٩
لِكَيْ يُشَارك اَهلَ البِرِّ و الكَرِم	لَعَلَّ سَاعٍ لِهذا الخَيرِ يُظْهرُهُ
حَتَّى يَعُودَ لَهَا مَا كان من نِعَم	للّهِ مُنْتَصِراً باللّهِ مُعتصِماً

6 MS Jerusalem اذا بَدَتْ

7 MS Jerusalem مُلِئت

8 MS Jerusalem مولى

9 MS Jerusalem ظاهرة

[60r]

Our lodges weep over the departure of their lodger, having been replaced with women, children and servants.

It is filled with foreigners and their belongings, and with grain, firewood, and beasts.

After the [sufis] left, [the khanqah's] features complained to God about the grave injustice.

Its benefits were lost once its good-doer was gone, as if this righteous one had not acted for the sake of our faith

Its conditions had become nothingness, as if it had never been nor will never endure.

The Lord of Truth knows all this, and truth is apparent in every meaning and word.

And here it is now, manifest among the people, and its current state as clear is as the sun.

May one who strives for this kindness show it so that he may stand among the pious and charitable people.

Victorious in God, infallible with God, may it return to its former state of grace.

REVIEWS

Adrian J. Boas, *Domestic Settings: Sources on Domestic Architecture and Day-to-Day Activities in the Crusader States* (The Medieval Mediterranean, 84). Leiden and Boston: Brill, 2010. Pp. xxvii, 393. ISBN 978 90 04 18272 1.

In addition to his numerous articles, Boas has written two recent books particularly worthy of note: *Crusader Archaeology: The Material Culture of the Latin East* (1999), and *Archaeology of the Military Orders: A Survey of the Urban Centres, Rural Settlements, and Castles of the Military Orders in the Latin East (c. 1120–1291)* (2006). This last book I reviewed in *Crusades*, 6, pp. 181–83.

Domestic Settings, much of which is based on research for Boas's Ph.D. dissertation, is perhaps his most important contribution to crusader studies to date. Although Boas has some limited consideration of domestic architecture in the *Archaeology of the Military Orders*, the present book is comprehensive, since it summarizes all of the available archaeological research, including unpublished research, with regard to crusader domestic architecture.

The book has an introduction, 15 chapters, three appendices, a glossary of terms, a bibliography, and an index. Numerous plans, maps, tables, and black-and-white photographs provide sufficient illustrations.

The introduction emphasizes that heretofore all discussions about crusader architecture have virtually ignored the Frankish house. Yet much information actually exists on this topic, some in unpublished excavations and surveys. Most of it comes from the former kingdom of Jerusalem, in addition to some information from Cyprus, primarily from Nicosia and Famagusta. Some comparative material also exists from contemporary Byzantine, Muslim, and European houses. It should also be pointed out that, although the book is primarily focused on the Frankish house, other domestic settings of the crusaders are considered as well, including crusader palaces, castles, and monastic buildings.

The book's first three chapters consider the sources and evolution of urban and rural housing. These include the houses of merchants, tower houses, courtyard houses, hall houses, and village houses. The author concludes that the Franks were, indeed, influenced by eastern house types, especially the urban model that was closed to the outside street, its main door opening into a central courtyard. Another main type of Frankish house had a European antecedent, more suitable for business, namely the house with a shop and storage on the bottom floor, open to the street, and with domestic apartments situated above.

Subsequent chapters deal largely with various aspects common to most Frankish domestic settings. Chapter 4 deals with living rooms and bedrooms; Chapter 5 with kitchens, dining space and food; Chapter 6 with domestic work and workspace; Chapter 7 with furniture and household installations; Chapter 8 with the communal institutions of domestic life; Chapter 9 with storage space, stables and shelters for livestock; and Chapter 10 with courtyards and gardens. Chapter 11 focuses on distinctive differences with between houses in Frankish and non-Frankish villages; Chapter 12 on urban neighborhoods and streets; Chapter 13 on overcrowding and pollution; and Chapter 14 deals with property values and the cost of housing. Again, the main point that needs to be emphasized is that the book uses a variety of sources (not just archaeological evidence), including historical sources like the *Geniza* documents, in order to construct a comprehensive picture of domestic life in the crusader East.

Chapter 15 summarizes the chief conclusions. One conclusion Boas draws is that in the Frankish territories (again, the evidence is primarily from the kingdom of Jerusalem) eastern and western house designs, and building techniques, were both used, "often existing side by side in a single building" (p. 243). The Franks assimilated much from the domestic architecture of the East, most prominently the courtyard house. They also used western house plans that included Italian-styled merchant palaces, tower houses, and houses built on burgage plots. Boas compares this development to that of the "Crusader castle," which evolved into a uniquely formidable model seen at Belvoir, Crac des Chevaliers, and Saranda Kolones. In castle design, "necessity imposed originality and speeded up a process that was not dissimilar to what was happening with domestic architecture" (p. 243). However, domestic crusader architecture, which evolved at a slower rate, did not produce a unique model comparable to the "Crusader castle."

The book concludes with three useful appendices: "A Typology of Frankish Houses in the Latin East," "Gazetteer of Archaeologically Recorded Sites in the Latin East," and "Analysis of Plaster and Mortar from Frankish Sites."

Until this book modern commentary on day-to-day activities in crusader domains has been drawn selectively from literary sources and from the excavation of crusader castles. Now, for the first time, the disparate archaeological and literary evidence has been assembled, summarized, and synthesized, to the great benefit of anyone interested in daily life in the crusader East.

JOHN ROSSER
BOSTON COLLEGE

Bertrandon de la Broquère, *Le voyage d'orient: espion en Turquie*, trans. (into modern French) by Hélène Basso, with an introduction and notes by Jacques Paviot (Collection Famagouste). Toulouse: Anacharsis, 2010. Pp. 224. ISBN 978 2 914777 599.

Philip the Good, duke of Burgundy, entertained various projects for crusades against the Turks. In order to obtain intelligence about the state of the Ottoman Empire, he commissioned his *premier écuyer tranchant*, Bertrandon de la Broquère (d. 1459, often spelled Broquière with an i), to travel overland across the empire –

from Jerusalem to Vienna and home to Burgundy. After his return, Bertrandon put down in writing the narration of his travels, the *Voyage d'Oultremer.*

Bertrandon describes how, in 1431, he set off with a group of European pilgrims to Jerusalem and made the standard pilgrimage visits in the company of Franciscan friars stationed in the East. Yet instead of returning by sea with his companions, he set off for Damascus, where he found a caravan of returning Meccan pilgrims bound for Istanbul and negotiated his passage with them. For months, Bertrandon shared the life of his Turkish companions: eating cones of pita filled with yogurt, getting drunk with them on wine bought from Christian merchants. He came to look like them as well, dressed as he was in clothes he had purchased in the *souq* in Damascus: in Anatolia, onlookers kissed his hand as the caravan passed by, taking him as a returning *hajji.* He even developed the prejudices of his Turkish companions: Turks, he affirms, are trustworthy, but Greeks are liars and Arabs thieves. When he takes leave of his companion and protector, "Mehmet the Mamluke," he praises him as a true and generous friend and protector.

Bertrandon is a sharp observer, and gives detailed descriptions of, for example, the rites of the *hammam*, or how the Turkish women make pita bread. He describes how his Turkish companions perform ablutions and make prayers, without the slightest hint of polemic or disdain; they in turn express surprise and delight in seeing how Bertrandon prays. He gives a detailed account of how Ibrahim Bey of Konya receives, with pomp and ceremony, the ambassador of King John II of Cyprus. Bertrandon does occasionally address directly the purpose of this "spying" expedition, discussing the solidity of the Ottoman military forces, the defense of certain strongholds, etc. Yet these passages only seem to highlight the tone of fascination and at times delight that dominates his text. He describes a world where cultures, languages and religions are inextricably intertwined. He meets Genoese and Venetian merchants who supply Circassian slaves to the Ottomans. He meets a young Cypriot named Anthony who, having been caught in bed with a Muslim beauty, had to apostatize. He affirms that Ibrahim Bey, whose mother was Greek, had been baptized in the Greek rite and that many of the Turkish beys had themselves baptized in the Greek rite "to prevent themselves from stinking." He is moved by the tears of a Hungarian noblewoman held captive in Ottoman Serbia. At the end of his narrative, he describes, with pride, how he reached the court of Burgundy and presented himself to the duke dressed in the clothes he had bought in Damascus.

Hélène Basso provides an accurate and very readable modern French translation of Bertrandon's text, and Jacques Paviot gives a helpful introduction and informative notes. The book is attractively produced and affordable and makes this fascinating text available to a broad public.

JOHN V. TOLAN
UNIVERSITÉ DE NANTES

Bullarium Cyprium I–II: Papal Letters concerning Cyprus 1196–1261, 1261–1314,
2 vols., ed. Christopher Schabel, with an introduction by Jean Richard (Texts and
Studies in the History of Cyprus, 64). Nicosia; Cyprus Research Centre, 2010.
Pp. xvi, 516, 528. ISBN 978 9963 0 8116 5, 978 9963 0 8117 2.

Christopher D. Schabel, *Greeks, Latins, and the Church in Early Frankish Cyprus*
(Variorum Collected Studies Series, 949). Farnham and Burlington, VT: Ashgate,
2010. Pp. xii, 332. ISBN 978 1 4049 0092 9.

The publication of the first two volumes of the *Bullarium Cyprium* – a third volume
covering the years 1316–78 will follow in due course – is a major publishing
event. What Schabel has done is to collect and edit all the papal letters relating to
Cyprus from the inception of the Lusignan regime to the death of Pope Clement
V. These total just under 600. The overwhelming majority are to be found in the
papal registers, although there is also a significant number in the cartulary of
Nicosia cathedral (published by Schabel and Nicholas Coureas in 1997) as well as a
scattering of others. Schabel has published the full text of each bull except in those
instances where the material of Cypriot interest comprises only a small part of the
whole. He has also provided a full summary of each item in English, whilst keeping
notes and commentary to a reasonable minimum. Jean Richard has contributed an
extended and instructive introduction, surveying papal relations with Lusignan
Cyprus to 1378.

In many cases the letters have not previously been published in full, and scholars
have usually relied on the summaries in the printed editions of the registers. These
summaries are often inadequate and in some cases seriously misleading. So, instead
of having to plough though the various editions of the registers of individual popes,
a task not made any easier by the inadequacies of some of the indexes, we now
have all this material conveniently and reliably assembled in these volumes. Here
are riches indeed! The letters are an informative source, often giving details about
matters that are otherwise totally unknown. The value of papal correspondence
from this period is, of course, recognized for all parts of Latin Christendom,
but its importance is especially true of Cyprus for which comparatively little
material has been preserved. There is, for example, only one Latin cartulary –
that of Nicosia cathedral – surviving from the island. The Nicosia cartulary does,
as Schabel points out in his introduction, alert us to the limitations of the papal
registers: only about one-fifth of the papal letters preserved in the cartulary were
also entered in the registers, and that corroborates evidence drawn from other
parts of western Christendom which shows that, valuable though they are, the
registers contain only a small proportion of the letters that were sent. Many of the
letters are concerned with purely church matters, but there are significant numbers
that deal with international diplomacy and high politics as well as those giving
various exemptions and privileges in response to petitions from the recipients. Of
particular interest in this connection are the dispensations for marriage within the

prohibited degrees, something which became increasingly necessary in view of the comparatively small number of noble families living in what from 1291 onwards was a distant outpost of western Christendom. There is also much indispensable information about the relations between the Latin and Greek clergy which allows for a much more nuanced view of how the regime treated the indigenous population than is sometimes allowed.

This last point – relations between the Christian communities – is considered from various angles in several of the ten papers that comprise Schabel's Variorum volume. As is well known, Ashgate's Variorum series affords authors what might fairly be described as a "retrospective exhibition," although in this case there is a previously unpublished paper on the 1231 martyrdom of a group of Greek monks. What makes this volume all the more noteworthy is that, side by side with his interest in Cyprus in the thirteenth and fourteenth centuries, Schabel has published – and continues to publish – extensively on fourteenth-century European intellectual history. Several of these papers, when taken together, comprise a revisionist approach to the Latin treatment of the Greek Church on Cyprus in which the Latins, if not exactly "whitewashed" – from the 1220s onwards they insisted that the Greeks accept the authority of the Latin bishops and ultimately of the pope – are portrayed in a manner that at least gives their actions a rational context. What has gone is the view that the Latins systematically oppressed and disendowed the Greek church. Even the martyrdom of the thirteen Greek monks in 1231 by the Latins – an unprecedented event in the dismal history of East–West Church affairs – can be seen as the inevitable outcome of the Greeks' obduracy in claiming that the western practice of using unleavened bread in the eucharist was heretical. Another paper, entitled "Frankish Pyrgos and the Cistercians," which first appeared in 2000, serves as a good example of the pitfalls of relying on the summaries of the papal letters in the older printed edition, and how the examination of the full text of a papal letter – in this case one issued by Pope Honorius III in 1224 – can correct the misconceptions thus caused.

These are perceptive papers, and, together with the appearance of the *Bullarium*, they mark a significant enhancement in our understanding of the first two centuries of Lusignan rule in Cyprus. At this point in a generally favourable review, the reviewer usually has a sentence beginning: "But ..." or "However, ...". It is a tribute to the volumes under consideration that I limit myself to just one quibble: *apropos* the *Bullarium*, it is high time that the patriarch of Jerusalem in the 1190s was given his true name – Monachus – and not "Aymar," an error perpetrated in the nineteenth century as the result of a blundered reading in one of our narrative sources.

Peter W. Edbury
Cardiff University

Marie-Anna Chevalier, *Les ordres religieux-militaires en Arménie cilicienne: templiers, hospitaliers, teutoniques et Arméniens à l'époque des croisades* (Orient Chrétien Médiéval). Paris: Geuthner, 2009. Pp. iv, 890. ISBN 978 2 7053 3819 0.

As stated in the acknowledgements, this monograph represents Marie-Anna Chevalier's doctoral thesis. Her supervisor was Professor Gérard Dédéyan, one of the most outstanding authorities on the history of the Armenians in the Middle Ages, in particular during the period of the crusades.

The work of any student of Professor Dédéyan raises high expectations. These expectations are reinforced by the title of Chevalier's book. It presents itself as the first comprehensive history of the Templars, Teutonic Knights and Hospitallers in Cilician Armenia during the times of the crusades. Moreover, Chevalier expands the geographical framework of her study to the Latin crusader states, analysing the relations between the Armenians and the military orders.

It can be stated without exaggeration that the expectations raised are in no way disappointed, the more so since Chevalier delivers some excellent additional tools for the historian in the appendix of her work. This is true not only for the subject of the military orders in Cilician Armenia but also for the history of Cilician Armenia during the period of the crusades. Besides detailed genealogical data, the author provides a very useful prosopographic table which contains members of the three big military orders connected to Cilician Armenia and Armenians in general. Possibly the most valuable part of the appendix is the new French translation of significant parts of Armenian sources written during the times of the crusades. Armenian sources for the time in question are either not edited at all or only in extracts. If edited, they are – mostly due to their age – hard to obtain. In addition, older translations into European languages frequently do not meet today's academic standards.

Chevalier arranged the main body of her work in four parts. The first one is organized chronologically and describes the "formation period," i.e. the different stages of settlement of the military orders in Cilician Armenia. This comprises the mutual interaction between the orders as well as their interaction with individual Armenian rulers. At the same time the author emphasizes the orders' impact on the areas they ruled over, starting from the period of the first contacts with the Armenians until the middle of the thirteenth century.

The second part is divided by themes, describing and analysing the material situation of the military orders. On the one hand, this covers the donations and privileges which were given by the Armenian rulers; on the other, Chevalier shows the organizational structure of the each order as well as their sources of income and finance. Furthermore, the landed property of the military orders in Cilician Armenia is discussed, including its strategic importance as part of the line of defence against the hostile Muslim neighbours.

The third part is also arranged thematically. It deals with the political relations of the military orders with the Armenian rulers. In connection with this the author analyses the orders' influence on the different social classes in Cilician Armenia and the often controversial relationship with the Armenian high clergy over questions of doctrine.

In the fourth part, the author describes the decline of the institutions of the military orders in Cilician Armenia. This description is embedded in the general history from the fall of the last Latin state in Outremer until the end of the kingdom of Cilician Armenia itself. The attacks of the Mamluks against the border fortifications of the military orders, as a reaction to the Armeno-Mongolian alliance, led to the complete loss of the fortifications of the Templars and Hospitallers within three decades. Various proposals for a further crusade were advanced during the fourteenth century – e.g., by the grand masters of the military orders, Hethum of Korykos and others – but were ultimately without success. With reference to the trial of the Templars in Cyprus, the author examines the role of the Armenians involved, as well as that of the military orders in Cilician Armenia. At the end of the fourth part Chevalier analyses the reintroduction of the Hospitallers into their former Armenian commanderies in the fourteenth century.

Without wanting to diminish Chevalier's achievement, it may be noted that more frequent reference to modern editions of contemporary Arabic sources could have been of additional benefit. This may equally be true for a first-hand analysis of other Arabic and Syro-Aramaic sources used. It may also be indicated that some minor inaccuracies have crept in when quoting in the footnotes. For example, the three parts of the *Chronicon Ecclesiasticum* by Bar Hebraeus were published not in 1872 but between 1872 and 1877, each of them with a Latin translation. In this context, Chevalier mentions a translation from the Syro-Aramaic into English; unfortunately, this valuable work by Ernest W. Wallis Budge, published in 1932, is not the translation of the *Chronicon Ecclesiasticum*, the ecclesiastical history, but of the *Chronography* of Bar Hebraeus, which is a secular history. The *Chronography* is actually used and correctly quoted by Chevalier in the footnotes as well as in the bibliography.

The author has produced a splendid monograph on the history of the three big military orders in Cilician Armenia. Moreover, she has added an important new component for the history of Cilician Armenia during the times of the crusades. As Professor Jean Richard says in the foreword of the book, Dr Chevalier deserves our undivided gratitude.

DRAGAN PROKIC
UNIVERSITÄT MAINZ

The Clash of Cultures on the Medieval Baltic Frontier, ed. Alan V. Murray with Anne Huijbers and Elizabeth Warwzyniak. Aldershot and Burlington, VT: Ashgate, 2009. Pp. xxiv, 369. ISBN 978 0 7546 6483 3.

During the past twenty years a rapidly growing number of studies dedicated to the impact of the crusades in the Baltic area have come into existence. Previously, most studies on the Baltic crusades were viewed from the perspective of the Teutonic Knights. More recent studies have challenged or rather freed themselves from former Marxist-inspired or nationally biased research that had formed many of the generally held beliefs about the eastward expansion of Latin Christendom, the German "Drang nach Osten," which included the creation of Danish, Swedish, Polish empires and kingdoms during the period between 1100 and the middle of the sixteenth century. Now the clash of cultures in the region is being reinterpreted in the light of modern crusade scholarship. It has been argued that, besides a series of political, economic, or territorial motives behind the expansion, the purpose of the crusades was to christianize the indigenous peoples living along the Baltic shores. In addition, a number of studies on the impact of crusading in Scandinavia, Poland and the areas targeted by crusades have appeared. They have demonstrated how crusade ideology helped both with legitimizing the wars of conquests and politically exploiting the power struggle among the various political players in the Baltic area, thus influening an important part of royal or princely ideology. The crusades resulted in the implementation of a new faith, religious practices and structures, and, when followed up by settlement by the conquerors, new ruling elites, power structures, collecting of taxes and so on.

This collection of sixteen studies covers all of these aspects and is highly recommended to be read alongside its predecessor, and in many respects companion, *Crusade and Conversion on the Baltic Frontier 1150–1300* (2001) also edited by Alan V. Murray (and reviewed in *Crusades* 3). The present volume also focuses on the period ca. 1150–1300, but several of the authors take their studies into the sixteenth century. After a brief introduction by Alan V. Murray, which sets the stage, two articles by Marek Tamm and Eva Eihmane provide a general framework for the entire collection by describing the integration of the knowledge about the Baltic into the existing geographical and encyclopaedic literature, and how the clashes between the conquerors and indigenous peoples were viewed within the changing intellectual climates from the Middle Ages to the present respectively. This provides a very useful historiographical starting point for the rest of the volume. The next two articles discuss how the societies changed as a result of the conquests in two case studies concerning Finland and Livonia by Andris Šnē and Phillip Line. Iben Fonnesberg-Schmidt and Rasa Mažeika tackle the important – and also to contemporaries explosive – debate about the relationship between peaceful and forced conversion, crusade and mission. The former argues that papal involvement became more manifest only in the thirteenth century, whereas the latter shows how Peter of Dusburg, historiographer of the Teutonic Order, was at great pains to present the wars of the knights as a just war. The next highly interesting section describes how it was not just peoples who were converted, but also trees and the landscape, with new symbols and sounds marking the advance of Christianity into the Baltic region (Kurt Villads Jensen and Carsten Selch Jensen). Further articles by Tiina Kala and Anu Mänd try to answer the obvious but difficult question of how deeply the Baltic peoples were christianized by looking at the religious practices of the rural population and the veneration of saints. The focus then changes to the role and importance of the Orthodox church in the area and how it was presented in the sources (Torben K. Nielsen, Michael C. Paul, and Anti Selart). The last section deals with military aspects of the conflict. Alan V. Murray presents a fascinating piece on the use of music in war as an illustration of a wider cultural conflict. The use of bells and new instruments were in fact creating a new "soundscape." Together with the articles by Kurt Villads Jensen and Carsten Selch Jensen, it adds a whole new dimension to the way the clash of cultures can be viewed. Stephen Turnbull takes a fresh look at the use of siege engines and Kaspars Kļaviņš deals with the interesting topic of the use of local Baltic peoples in the defence of Livonia. The volume concludes with a selected bibliography of works in English on the East Baltic lands in the age of the crusades, demonstrating that more and more scholars, from both the areas that organized the crusades and the regions targeted by them, publish in English, thus breaking down the language barrier and providing access to fascinating and complex local historiographical traditions.

The editor is to be complimented for doing an extraordinarily good job in assuring the internal cohesion sometimes difficult to uphold in collective works. The articles taken together cover a broad range of topics serving as an excellent introduction through case-studies to the complex matter of the clash of cultures in the medieval Baltic frontier of which the crusade was but one – albeit important – aspect. Especially interesting is the focus on the areas and peoples targeted by the crusades not simply as those at the receiving end but as active players in the process of conversion and the creation of new power structures. The book thus forms an important contribution both to crusade studies and to the history of the medieval Baltic in general.

Janus Møller Jensen

Østfyns Museer, Nyborg

The Debate on the Trial of the Templars (1307–1314), ed. Jochen Burgtorf, Paul E. Crawford and Helen J. Nicholson. Farnham and Burlington, VT: Ashgate, 2010. Pp. xxiv, 399. ISBN 978 0 7546 6570 0 (hardback), 978 1 4094 1009 6 (e-book).

The volume contains twenty-eight papers read at conferences at Kalamazoo and Leeds in the summer of 2007. They are framed by a measured and informative introduction written by Malcolm Barber and by the editors' concluding remarks. Five papers (by Alan Forey on the Templars' reputation, Anthony Luttrell on the election of James of Molay, Nicholas Morton on dependence on patrons, Bernard Schotte on the Flemish rebellion of 1302 and Ignacio de la Torre on monetary fluctuations in France) deal with background events and themes before the arrest of the Templars in 1307. Eight (by Thomas Krämer on torture, Dale Streeter on the tribunals, David Bryson on individuals regarded by the Templars as "traitors," Jochen Burgtorf on commandery inventories, Alain Provost on the case of Guichard of Troyes, Paul Crawford on the involvement of members of the University of Paris, Jochen Schenk on evidence for kinship and Magdalena Satora on the transmission of news about the process) relate to events in France. Three (by Clive Porro on the policy of King Dinis of Portugal, Sebastián Salvadó on chapel inventories in Aragon and Luis García-Guijarro Ramos on the replacement of the Temple by Montesa in Valencia) concern the Iberian peninsula. Three (by Jeffrey Hamilton on the actions of the English crown, Helen Nicholson on the process in Ireland and Simon Phillips on the Hospitallers' acquisition of Templar estates) concentrate on the British Isles and five (by Peter Edbury on Cyprus, Elena Bellomo on northern Italy, Kristjan Toomaspoeg on Sicily, Filip Hooghe on Flanders and Maria Starnawska on Poland) cover events in other countries. The collection concludes with some general aspects: renegades (Christian Vogel), Templar priests (Anne Gilmour-Bryson), the acquisition of the Templar properties by the Hospital (Theresa Vann) and later myths (John Walker).

The standard is uniformly high. The papers by Anthony Luttrell and Clive Porro are outstanding. It is good to see that the inventories made of the contents of Templar commanderies are beginning to get the attention they deserve from Jochen Burgtorf and Sebastián Salvadó. The pursuit of historical comparisons with the actions of the principals in the early fourteenth century continues with interesting contributions from Nicholas Morton on the Teutonic Knights fifty years earlier, Alain Provost on the case of the bishop of Troyes and Paul Crawford on the lists of university members involved in the enquiries into Marguerite Porete and the Templars respectively. Every article contains useful insights and this volume is essential reading.

I wonder, however, whether I am alone in feeling uncomfortable with the adoption of the word "trial." Its employment – first used, I think, in the title of Malcolm Barber's standard work on the process – is now widespread. It may be justifiable in the broadest sense, but the Templar process was an inquisitorial one, as Dale Streeter makes clear in his interesting paper, being in part a series of investigations into the beliefs and actions of individual brothers and in part an enquiry into the Order itself and whether anything had gone wrong with it. There were none of the procedures that would have safeguarded defendants had they been on trial. To continue to use the term when, in fact, one is referring to tribunals that were engaged in enquiries is misleading.

The volume's title is not well chosen for another reason. It suggests a lively discussion of controversial issues, but a feature of this collection is that it is very hard to find even echoes of any "debate." Although everyone agrees that most of the accusations were false and that many Templars were innocent of all the charges, some historians, including myself, are not convinced that all of the brothers were innocent in every respect. The editors are in the other camp, but their statement that in this collection of papers they "have found no conclusive evidence that the Templars were guilty" is unconvincing, because most of the contributors have concentrated on other matters or have avoided the topic of guilt altogether. Even Malcolm Barber does not confront it. Only Alan Forey, David Bryson and Anne Gilmour-Bryson reveal something, but not much, of their feelings. There is, of course, no reason why like-minded historians who believe that an issue is so settled that it does not need discussion should waste time on it. But why then use the word "debate" in the title? At any rate, readers should be warned that they will be disappointed if they open the book in the hope of finding controversy.

JONATHAN RILEY-SMITH
EMMANUEL COLLEGE, CAMBRIDGE

Jean Flori, *Chroniqueurs et propagandistes: introduction critique aux sources de la première croisade* (Hautes Études médiévales et modernes, 98). Geneva: Droz, 2010. Pp. 353. ISBN 978 2 600 01329 1.

The discovery of the *Ur-Gesta*, the "real" text underlying our present editions of the anonymous *Gesta Francorum*, has become the Holy Grail of crusader studies. Flori's book is essentially a quest by a very learned French scholar to penetrate the secrets of this elusive enigma. That the task should attract so much attention is hardly surprising because the *Gesta* is enormously influential. Most modern historians believe it was used by almost all the other eyewitness and near-contemporary accounts, like that of Raymond of Aguilers. The *Gesta*, on the face of it, has many virtues, with its short and apparently simple and straightforward story of the crusade, which one editor has described as that of a simple knight. But a closer scrutiny reveals it to be more complex than this, in particular because it contains many literary passages which serve as skilfully-worked counterpoints to the story, and its text has a number of cruxes suggestive of a reworking. These puzzles have not prevented it from becoming the "normal" account of the First Crusade underlying almost all modern discussions of its events and the underlying attitudes of its participants. In this book Flori suggests that we can get more hints of the nature of the *Ur-Gesta* than has yet proved possible, and at the same time tries to counter the influence of the present text by arguing that it is a work altered and disseminated by Bohemond for his own propaganda purposes. Flori thinks that the original text was altered in a series of steps, but that the work of Peter Tudebode represents an early copy and the best witness, albeit imperfect, to the text actually written by the Anonymous. At the end of a long discussion of all the accounts of the First Crusade which form the "*Gesta* Family," Flori suggests that the original text, designated G1 and now clearly lost, was produced immediately after the battle of Ascalon by the author, who went on to produce a second version, G2, about 1102–3, in which he amplified the role of Bohemond, though without disparaging that of the other leaders. A third version, G3, was altered about by Bohemond to his own glory and taken to the West in 1104, where it was reworked at his command into G4 to please the pope by suppressing the role of Peter Bartholemew in the origins of the crusade (which Flori supposes was considerable). Bohemond then ordered the production of a fifth version, G5, replete with anti-Byzantine attitudes, to influence opinion in France in favour of his proposed expedition against the Eastern Empire. Flori appears to think that G1 is irrecoverable, though he suggests that it was the *libellus* seen by Ekkehard of Aura at Jerusalem in 1101. However, Flori never analyses Ekkehard's work, which is an odd omission, and, therefore, avoids the very obvious fact that Ekkehard's account of the First Crusade does not seriously resemble that of the Anonymous. His version of Godfrey's difficulties with the Emperor Alexius is actually radically different from any other. On the other hand, as Flori notes, Ekkehard does use the word *Hispania*, meaning Saracen lands, but this is found in the letter of Daimbert and the leaders dating probably from September 1099 (which may be the work of Raymond of Aguilers). However, given the extraordinary brevity and originality of Ekkehard's very short account of the First Crusade, it is very likely that this letter gave Ekkehard the skeleton of his story.

Flori thinks that Tudebode used a very early version (G2) of the *Gesta* because in his analysis this author does not repeat material unduly laudatory of Bohemond and adopts a more open attitude to the other leaders than that displayed in his hypothetical G3–5 which he thinks were the basis for the works of the Benedictines, Guibert of Nogent, Baudri of Dol and Robert the Monk. I am very sceptical of this method of reconstructing supposed originals, partly because rather simpler ideas to explain the differences between these sources spring to mind – such as the well-known tendency of medieval authors to change about the works which, in modern terms, they were plagiarizing, in the light of their own prejudices and desires. Moreover, it is hard to have a lot of confidence in such ideas when they rest on generalizations rather than on detailed textual comparison. Flori dismisses the idea that Tudebode used the work of Raymond of Aguilers, despite the evident similarity of their accounts of the march through Dalmatia and the Balkans. He seizes upon Tudebode's failure to mention the sojourn of the bishop of Le Puy at Thessalonica, but clearly does not know this information is contained in only two recensions of Raymond's work (Bib nat.lat.5511A and the Bongars edition). It is puzzling that, although he thinks Raymond's work is very early, Flori refuses to accept that he used the *Gesta*, simply brushing aside the analyses provided by Hagenmeyer and myself. Finally, it has to be said that, despite his considerable efforts, Flori can suggest only the most minor differences between the various versions of the *Gesta* which he postulates. Nobody at this stage can say that Flori's ideas are wrong, but they are, to say the least, unproven. Perhaps the *Ur-Gesta* quest will be resolved by Marcus Bull's investigation into the whole *Gesta* tradition, which, I understand, will soon lead to a new edition of that enigmatic text.

There is much of real value in Flori's book. There is much to be said for his idea that the Anonymous was a priest rather than a knight. His stress on the propagandist ideas of the various writers leads to a thorough exploration of the differences between them. It is good to have somebody of his standing stressing the limitations of the eyewitness. The work concludes with a powerful advocacy of the work of Albert of Aachen (who was distinctly not an eyewitness), the passion of which is perhaps a little surprising because over the last twenty years recognition of the value of his work has grown, notably with the publication of the Edgington edition, but perhaps this trend in crusader historiography is not so marked in France.

JOHN FRANCE
SWANSEA UNIVERSITY

Zsolt Hunyadi, *The Hospitallers in the Medieval Kingdom of Hungary, c.1150– 1387*. Budapest: METEM and Department of Medieval Studies, Central European University, 2010. Pp. xix, 354. ISBN 978 963 9662 44 5.

The fruit of many years of research, this book is a thorough study of the Hospitallers in medieval Hungary. Hunyadi studied archival sources now in the national archives of Hungary, the Order's archives in Malta and a number of other locations. The annexes contain valuable source material. Hunyadi edited hitherto unpublished texts and reedited those previously published but containing serious mistakes. Photos of the seals of the Hungarian-Slavonian priory are included, as well as a detailed bibliography. The start date for the study is self-evident, because the Order of the Hospital of St. John appeared in Hungary in the mid-twelfth century. The choice of 1387 to end the book is linked to the fundamental changes that occurred after the end of Angevin rule. For those unacquainted with previous scholarship, Hunyadi provides syntheses of western and Hungarian research on the Hospitallers, and a brief history of the Order.

He then examines in detail the establishment of the brothers in the kingdom, the spread of their preceptories – illustrated by useful maps – and their history in the thirteenth and fourteenth centuries. Hunyadi challenges the traditional view that the establishment of the Order in Hungary was linked to the armies of the second crusaders that marched through the kingdom. Queen Euphrosyne's interest in charity, rather than any idea of using the Knights in a military role, was the motive behind the settlement of the Order in Hungary. This lack of interest in the Order's military role, and emphasis on their charitable function, continued even under Béla III. Prosperity came in the thirteenth century, with Andrew II. The king gave generous grants to the Hospitallers; he also required their services in diplomacy. During the thirteenth century, the Order received new lands and immunities in the realm. The brothers played some role in the defence of the kingdom against the Mongols, but after the Mongol invasion quickly withdrew from south-eastern lands of the kingdom where the king tried to settle them in a defensive role. Perhaps as a result, royal support diminished drastically in the second half of the century. Private donations played a minor role, due to the nature of Hungarian society, where kindred held land together, and the consent of all was needed to donate a part of the estate. The fundamental significance of the early royal donations continued to be manifest through the geography of the Order in Hungary: preceptories throughout the period were almost all in western and south-western parts of the realm. In the fourteenth century, the Hospitallers took over Templar estates after the latter's condemnation, and Hunyadi enumerates these. They also fought against enemies of the king and in order to protect their priories, while their involvement in the anti-Ottoman endeavour was minimal. The Schism split loyalties in the priory, with two opposing parties backing the two popes.

A prosopographical analysis of the officials of the priory follows: throughout the period, most arrived from outside the realm. The reconstruction – as far as the sources permit – of administrative units, and a catalogue of preceptories with their personnel constitute the next chapter. Hospitallers did not hold many castles in the realm, nor did they particularly engage in castle-building activities, contrary to previous opinion. Following Karl-Georg Boroviczény, Hunyadi also disentagles references to Hospitallers from mentions of a completely separate order, the canons regular of St Stephen.

The last two chapters focus on the activities of the Order in the kingdom. Estate management and the generation of income for fighting was an important function of Hospitaller priories in Europe. Apart from grants of estates and money, exemptions from taxes, rents, leases, tolls, and market-rights contributed to Hospitaller revenues. Through the manorial system, they had seigneurial revenues. These, however, cannot be estimated because there are no account books or other surviving information. Hospitallers were also involved in serious conflict with local clerics over tithes. The taxes the Hungarian-Slavonian priory paid for financing the Order were very low compared to other priories; and the entire financial contribution of the priory to the Order was irregular and minimal.

Unique to Hungary was the Hospitallers' role in the authentication of private legal documents in the *loca credibilia*. This activity, along with the use of seals, constitutes the final chapter. These places of authentication witnessed legal transactions before public notaries appeared in the kingdom, issuing charters under their own seal (and functioned parallel to the notaries thereafter). They recorded and verified transactions, and also had judicial and administrative functions as agents of the ruler. Nine Hospitaller preceptories served as *loca credibilia*, although two-third of the known charters were issued at the most important preceptory, Székesfehérvár. Hunyadi also surveys the Hospitaller use of seals, going beyond their use in authentication. He lists the different seal types and traces the chronological changes in these types.

The book demonstrates that the role of the Hospitallers in society and their interaction with that society was in many respects different in Hungary from western Europe. Royal support was the most significant factor determining even the location of the preceptories. Private donations played a minor role. The Hospitallers did not raise significant revenues for wars against non-Christians, nor were they particularly useful in local wars against pagans. On the other hand, they were significant as royal agents and participated in the provision of places of authentication. Hunyadi has left no stone unturned, and scrutinized all the available documents. He has meticulously reconstructed the history of the Hospitallers in the kingdom of Hungary. The book will doubtless serve generations of scholars, whether their interest focuses primarily on the history of medieval Hungary or on the Hospitaller Order.

NORA BEREND
UNIVERSITY OF CAMBRIDGE

Robert Irwin, *Mamlūks and Crusaders: Men of the Sword and Men of the Pen.* Farnham and Burlington, VT: Ashgate, 2010. Pp xii, 370. ISBN 978 1 4094 0775 1.

This volume brings together 22 essays, principally on the history, culture and historiography of Mamluk Egypt, by Robert Irwin, historian, novelist and essayist. The volume is a welcome addition to the books that Irwin has produced over the years, in particular his *The Middle East in the Middle Ages: The Early Mamluk Sultanate 1250–1382* (1986) and his works on the literature of the Mamluk period (in particular on the *Arabian Nights).* He is also well known for his anti-Edward Said broadsheet, *Dangerous Knowledge: Orientalism and Its Discontents* (2006).

These essays were originally published between 1977 and 2008, so older (and at times outdated) scholarship shares the volume with recent work. His cogent and interesting piece on Usama ibn Munqidh (article X), for example, first published in 1998, has now been largely surpassed by the more recent work of Paul Cobb. The articles are varied in length, audience, purpose and (inevitably) quality, but on the whole complement his books: Irwin writes with clarity and judiciousness, and many of the essays will be of interest not only to scholars in the field (who will already be familiar with some of them), but also to students. I will content myself in this brief review with highlighting several of the studies that will most interest readers of *Crusades.*

Irwin clearly sketches out historiographical debates and brings his knowledge of primary documents to bear on attempting to resolve them – or at times to frankly admit that they cannot be resolved, as in the case of the use of *iqta*, often translated (or mistranslated) as "fief." Irwin shows (in article I) that the uses of the term *iqta* varied over time and space. While historians such as A. Poliak described the accordance of *iqta* as the instauration of "feudal" bonds between the ruler who granted and the "vassal" who received, C. Cahen rejected what was for him an inappropriate importation of European terminology. Irwin concludes that "the epithet 'feudal' cannot be decisively ruled out of court yet" (p. 73), that a closer comparative study between land ownership and use patterns between Frankish and Muslim lords would need to be undertaken first.

He shows a keen interest in issues of trade and commerce (article II deals with coinage and its circulation in thirteenth-century Syria; article IV catalogues the activities of those European (principally Italian) merchants who traded in Syria and Egypt between 1450 and 1550). Various articles offer analyses of Mamluk politics, and in particular of the role of factions. Irwin makes judicious use here of comparative history, showing how Mamluks are willing and ready to change factions when that is in their interest (contrary to, say, eighteenth-century Japanese Samurai, for whom loyalty to their lord was paramount) and hence the conflicts between factions are surprisingly bloodless (when compared with conflicts among fifteenth-century English nobility).

Several articles offer good introductory surveys to themes and texts that will be of interest to historians of the crusades and of Egypt. Article VI, "The Image of the Byzantine and the Frank in Arab popular literature of the late Middle Ages," presents a variety of fascinating and colorful snippets from the *1001 Nights*, shadow plays, and passages from the chronicle of Qirta'i: Byzantines and Franks appear most often as scheming and debauched adversaries cleverly outwitted by the common Egyptian protagonists. While historians of the crusades will not learn much new from the essay on the "impact of the early crusades on the Muslim World" (article XI), it could be assigned to students in an introductory course on the crusades: it is a clear and cogent presentation of the (limited) impact of the Frankish conquests as seen by Arab authors of the region, who were more worried by the military domination of Turks and by the rise of Nizaris than by dangers posed by al-Ifranj. Irwin also includes in this volume two useful introductory surveys of historiography: of the history of the Mamluks (roughly from Gibbon and Volney to the 1990s) and "Orientalism and the development of Crusader Studies." In both these surveys, the accent is heavily on writings in French and English at the expense of studies in other languages (in particular German).

The book also contains a number of interesting studies of Mamluk *belles lettres*, or ʿ*adab*; in several articles, Irwin makes a good case for the use of the rich and understudied literary production of the Mamluk period for the social, culture and intellectual history of Egypt and Syria between the fourteenth and sixteenth centuries; his "Mamluk Literature" (article XVI) is a good introduction to the subject. His studies of individual authors, such as Usama ibn Munqidh, Al-Maqrizi and Ibn Khaldun, are well crafted and compelling.

Let me close by taking a closer look at one of these articles, "Ibn Zunbul and the romance of history," which examines Ibn Zunbul's sixteenth-century *Kitab infisal dawlat al-awan wa ittisal dawlat bani uthman* ("The departure of the temporal dynasty and the coming of the Ottomans"). This work has often been seen by earlier scholars as a chronicle written by a nostalgic former Mamluk official in the decades following the Ottoman conquest of Egypt (1517). Irwin shows how, in fact, the text totters precariously between our categories of "chronicle" and "fiction," and indeed calls those categories into question. Ibn Zunbul was probably far too young ever to have served under the Mamluk administration. Irwin sees the *Infiṣal* as "historical fiction": his subject is indeed the fall of the Mamluks, and much of what he relates no doubt corresponds to historical events of the Ottoman conquest. Yet, Ibn Zunbul seeks to portray the events as part of a drama of a heroic but doomed Mamluk chivalry fighting valiantly against destiny. In one scene, a Moroccan adviser arrives in Cairo with a gun, which he shows to the Mamluk sultan Qanṣawh al-Ghawri: unless the Egyptians adopt such modern weapons, they are doomed, he says. Yet the sultan refuses the monstrous Christian device and vows to follow the ways of the Prophet. This scene – probably apocryphal, as Irwin argues – highlights the quixotic heroism of the Mamluks and the inevitability of their fall. Many of the speeches that Ibn Zunbul puts into the mouths of his protagonists are rhetorical gems no doubt meant to be read aloud: here, too, it is clear that Ibn Zunbul's goal is to heighten the drama of the narrative. Hence he ignores historically important subjects (such as the arrival of the Portuguese in the Indian Ocean, related by contemporary chronicler Ibn Iyas), keeping clearly focused on his plot.

Mamluk studies are undergoing something of a renaissance now, with important research projects in Chicago, Ghent, Oxford and elsewhere; while these projects are too recent to receive mention herein, students interested in the Mamluks will find useful material in this volume and should heed Irwin's call for the study of the profuse literary production of the Mamluks.

JOHN V. TOLAN
UNIVERSITÉ DE NANTES

Nicholas Edward Morton, *The Teutonic Knights in the Holy Land 1190–1291*. Woodbridge and Rochester, NY: The Boydell Press, 2009, Pp. xiv, 228 pp. ISBN 978 1 84383 477 9.

Up to the year 2009, the chapter by Indrikis Sterns on "The Teutonic Knights in the Crusader States" published in 1985 in K. M. Setton (ed.), *A History of the Crusades*, vol. 5, pp. 315–78, was the only contribution to Morton's topic available in English. Here we are dealing with a Ph.D. thesis, which was accepted at Royal Holloway, University of London, in 2008 and then printed quickly. After the Hospitallers and the Knights Templar, English research on the military orders is now also beginning to focus on the Teutonic Knights. Stern's survey on the foundation, the early history, the organization and activities of the Teutonic Knights in the Latin East was already much outdated when it first appeared. He did use the ingenious stocktaking of the Mediterranean history of the Teutonic Order by Kurt Forstreuter (*Der Deutsche Orden am Mittelmeer* [1967]) but failed to take into account the reviewer's dissertation published in 1974 (*Studien zur Frühgeschichte des Deutschen Ordens*), nor did he discuss the controversy sparked by this dissertation concerning the relations between the Teutonic Order and the Hospitallers up to the second half of the thirteenth century.

The development of the Teutonic Order in the Latin East has been one of the topics dealt with by scholars during the last forty years. By now the position and the policies of the Teutonic Order in the Holy Land, more particularly in the crusader kingdom of Jerusalem, are seen within the context of the Order's relations with the emperor and the pope as well as the Order's own interest in the Baltic region.

The book is divided into ten chapters. Its structure and contents follow recent research by Arnold, Favreau(-Lilie), Houben, Kluger, Militzer, Pacifico, Toomaspoeg. The supplement (pp. 189–206) is a product more of diligence than of the author's own research. It covers (1) the locations of the masters 1210–90 (pp. 189–96); (2) a map, not based on the author's own research and too small to be informative, showing the development of the Order's landed estates in the kingdom of Jerusalem (pp. 196–97); (3) a list of all masters of the Order of the thirteenth century based largely on the collective volume *Die Hochmeister des Deutschen Ordens*, edited in 1998 by U. Arnold (p. 198); (4) a survey of foodstuffs made available from its own possessions to the German hospital in Acre and its legal successor, the Teutonic Order, and of the mills owned by the Order (pp. 200–1); (5) a list of persons holding offices as marshals for 1208–91 (pp. 202–3) and as grand commanders, respectively, for 1215–90 (pp. 204–6). Basically, chapters 1 to 8 are structured chronologically, but this principle is not always adhered to, resulting in a partial lack of coherence. The last two chapters (pp. 144–84) follow a systematic order dealing with the military organization and points of warfare, the tasks and strategies of the Teutonic Knights in the crusader states, the internal organization of the Order, estate administration in Syria and, last but not least, the material resources available to the Order in the crusader states supplemented by the influx of money and the import of goods from the kingdom of Sicily. With his particular interest in all problems of military history, logistics and naval history the author firmly places himself in a well-established tradition of Anglo-Saxon crusading research. This last part of the book is, in my view, the most acceptable.

We are still lacking, however, an investigation of the position and the policies of the Teutonic Order in the crusader states which correctly sums up the present state of research in a considered manner and, with the help of archival and historiographical sources, provides us with a systematic and penetrating study on several topics such as (1) the volume and origins of the (monetary) resources available to the Order in Syria, and (2) the influence of internal as well as external developments on the Order's position in the Latin East. The book under review does not fulfil these expectations. In particular, the first part (chapters 1–4) leaves much to be desired. Neither the author's knowledge of the source material nor his abilities to analyse and interpret the sources (partly quoted from secondary literature) are convincing. The question of why chronicles written in the Latin East tell us so little about the Teutonic Knights and their activities in the Holy Land is not even touched upon. The complete dismissal of *Ottokars Österreichische Reimchronik* and its report about the flight of the Teutonic Knights in 1291 as a "fictional account" is unjustified. The author's knowledge of the state of research is repeatedly lacking. A few examples may suffice. The author (p. 91 and n. 39) believes in the authenticity of a charter by Pope Clement III by which the German hospital founded in Jerusalem in the early twelfth century (and transferred to Acre after 1187) is said to have been made subject to the Hospitallers a second time. Many years ago Rudolf Hiestand revealed this to be a gross forgery. The author does know the indubitably authentic privilege by Clement III of 6 February 1191 for the *fratres Theotonici ecclesie sancte Marie Ierosolimitane* (p. 26), but he is either ignorant of the scholarly debate about the addressees generated by Favreau in 1974 or else intentionally refuses to discuss this important point, which is unlikely. But without an exact knowledge and thorough discussion of this controversy it is not possible to arrive at a considered opinion as to the origins of the Teutonic Order. The author also fails to grasp the importance of the papal privilege of 21 December 1196 by Celestin III for the German hospital at Acre (pp. 16, 26), although this charter did elevate the hospital to the rank of a hospital order.

In order to deal adequately with the topic chosen here one must rely almost exclusively on German – or more recently also on Italian – research literature, and this requires a very good understanding of both languages. The rather spare references to such scholarly works, and in particular the exclusion of existing controversies in the field and their arguments, are perhaps caused by an insufficient ability to grasp fully the carefully built argumentation on which some of the opinions previously expressed were based. Be this as it may, the reader who is not an expert does not get a solid survey of the current state of research. The author provides us with much less innovative research of his own than would seem to be the case to the uninformed reader at first glance. His theories, by the way, reveal a remarkable belief, not shared by this reviewer, in rational historical developments. The author attempts to show that the position of the Order in the Latin East was decisively influenced by developments in Prussia and that the Order, after having crushed the second Prussian revolt, increasingly devoted its material resources to fighting the Mamluks; however, it remains an open question whether and to what extent the Order did in fact transfer financial means from Europe to Acre. Given the rather restricted interest of contemporary Frankish chronicles in the affairs of the Teutonic Knights in the crusader states, and the limited value of the charter evidence, it is unlikely that one should be able to arrive at more than hypothetical results. Many points advanced by the author consequently remain unproven.

Numerous references in the footnotes to standard works in English on the crusades and the military orders are in fact redundant but are perhaps included with a view to use of the volume in university courses in the English–speaking world. Occasionally, outdated editions of source material have been used. This is less irritating than the careless editing of the footnotes and the bibliography. In the bibliography, a Madrid manuscript (Biblioteca de la Real Academia de la Historia, Collecion Salazar, G 49, Sig. 9/46) is listed under the heading "manuscript sources." But only the "carta de la Orden Teutonica" on fol. 453 is of interest for this book, the letter of 1254 by the Order's marshal Peter of Koblenz to King Alfonso X of

Castile. This document was well interpreted and satisfactorily edited more than ten years ago by J. M. R. Garcia in an article listed in the bibliography ("Alfons X, la Orden Teutonica y Tierra Santa: una nueva fuente para su studio"). The author unfortunately fails to refer to this except twice (cf. pp. 107 n. 77; 111 n. 107; 129 n. 66; 183 n. 161; 203 n. 15) and when he is trying to improve Garcia's edition, it only concerns minimal changes of punctuation.

The book does not provide us with innovative new insights; it basically lacks truly new results which one might expect from a monograph. In the framework of a somewhat shorter study focusing on the topics discussed in part 2 of the book (chapters 5–10) the author's remarks on a partial aspect of his Ph.D. topic ("The Teutonic Knights during the Ibelin-Lombard conflict", in: *On Land and by Sea*, ed. J. Upton-Ward, 2008, pp. 139–43) could conveniently have been included.

MARIE-LUISE FAVREAU-LILIE
FREIE UNIVERSITÄT, BERLIN

William J. Purkis, *Crusading Spirituality in the Holy Land and Iberia, c.1095–c.1187.* Woodbridge and Rochester, NY: The Boydell Press, 2008. Pp. xii, 215. ISBN: 978 1 84383 477 9.

Crusading as an expression of faith raises knotty problems for the scholar, since religiously sanctioned violence would seem to violate the Golden Rule. Recently, historians have considered how participants understood their experiences, with several studies noting similarities between crusading and monastic reforms. William Purkis builds on this foundation in his innovative work, challenging several long-held assumptions and integrating crusading spirituality into the larger framework of Catholic piety. While he does consider participants' perceptions, he focuses mostly on themes in preaching. Here he exposes several motifs drawn directly from monastic spirituality, most notably pilgrimage. Although other scholars have undertaken similar projects, they have ended their studies early in the twelfth century or have started after the fall of Jerusalem. In extending his project to 1187, Purkis demonstrates that not all themes in crusade propaganda survived to that point. Moreover, he takes a pan-Mediterranean view, asking how crusading affected the Iberian *Reconquista*. He argues that medieval audiences did not perceive Spanish warfare as a pilgrimage until *Reconquista* propagandists began incorporating crusades motifs in the 1120s. Overall, Purkis does several things very well in this careful study. He invites us to reconsider old questions and answers regarding early crusading ideology. He reminds us that the architects of different campaigns could adapt their messages as needed, so that even before the fall of Jerusalem there were varieties of crusading. Most importantly, he situates these crusade ideologies at the center rather than the edges of spiritual reform movements in the late eleventh and twelfth centuries. Though most reform movements in this period originated in the institutional Church, they had a dramatic effect on the laity, and arguably crusading aroused the most enthusiasm. It can be all too easy for medievalists (even crusades specialists) to treat "the crusades" as sporadic events, and Purkis helps to explain why "crusading spirituality" did not die away from European consciousness until the seventeenth century.

Purkis opens with the origins of ideology, showing that crusading spirituality grew out of church reform movements in the late eleventh century, especially new approaches to monasticism. Monastic writers wanted to imitate Christ and live an apostolic life, yet the competing methods for doing so could bewilder them. Monks retained their enthusiasm for pilgrimage, however. Thus, when preachers began promoting the First Crusade, they understandably emphasized its essentially monastic nature through these themes of pilgrimage, *imitatio Christi* (giving up one's secular ties), and *vita apostolica* (uniting for a common purpose and living communally). Crusaders could temporarily pursue a monastic calling as they traveled toward Jerusalem, though the military aspect of their undertaking added a radical new element. Purkis explores monastic texts and then considers crusade chronicles and participants' accounts, noting that the latter paid far more attention to Christo-mimesis and pilgrimage than to the communal *vita apostolica*. He draws upon a diverse and extensive body of source materials, comparing papal and monastic letters to crusade narratives, participants' letters and charters, and martyr stories. While some authors referred to apostolic metaphors, far more striking was the imagery related to Christ, including scenes where lay people left their families, incurred stigmata, and died for their faith. The cross became an obvious and highly visible symbol of Christo-mimesis.

It remained so between 1099 and 1149, and the association between pilgrimage and crusading grew even stronger. Frankish sources from Outremer called for pilgrims and crusaders without differentiating between the two. When writers began promoting the Second Crusade, they had numerous models available, by now largely focused on *imitatio Christi* rather than *vita apostolica*. Eugenius III and Bernard of Clairvaux wanted to mute Christo-mimesis without losing other traditional appeals, so they elaborated on the idea of crusading predecessors. Purkis proposes that they hoped to position the cross as a sign of God's mercy and spiritual indulgence, available in any of several crusading theaters, but lay people had internalized the message of Christo-mimesis.

Purkis's explanation for this shift in preaching demonstrates the importance of close reading. He proposes that Bernard understood the crusader's temporary vows as part of a process that would ideally culminate in permanent vows to a military order. Bernard's interest in the Templars especially has long been recognized, yet Purkis compellingly re-examines Cistercian texts to make his points. The Templars would imitate Christ while serving Outremer's military needs; crusaders had not yet reached that stage in their spiritual development. Though the Second Crusade damaged lay enthusiasm, Frankish writers continued to promote crusading until 1187. They built on Bernard's themes of pilgrimage and crusader predecessors rather than *imitatio Christi* or apostolic models.

After considering the centrality of Jerusalem in crusading themes, Purkis turns to Iberia and again offers a novel thesis. *Reconquista* did not lead to crusade; instead crusading ideology came to Spain about thirty years after the Council of Clermont. Eleventh-century observers focused on the innovation of Clermont rather than connecting Urban II's message to Iberian warfare. Urban himself had little success getting crusaders to fulfill their vows in Spain, because as a pilgrimage destination it could not (yet) compete with the Holy Land. Yet by the 1120s, Iberian writers steadily applied the message of pilgrimage and *vita apostolica* to their own struggles. They proposed opening a new route to Jerusalem through Spain and North Africa. Alfonso I established Aragonese military confraternities similar to the Templars and Hospitallers. These efforts did not, however, encourage Christo-mimesis, since Jerusalem would always have the advantage in that regard. Within a decade, Spanish writers built up local traditions connected to Charlemagne and St. James so that Spanish campaigns would become equivalent to those in Outremer.

Purkis has provided provocative and persuasive answers based on nuanced analysis of the texts. Ever since Carl Erdmann considered the origins of religious violence, most scholars have relied upon his thesis: *Reconquista* helped the Church develop a theology of religious warfare and paved the way for crusading. Purkis reverses their relationship through a fresh consideration of the sources. Further research could consider crusading ideology in other regions, or how monastic themes might apply differently based on would-be participants' social rank, ethnicity, nationality, gender, and so on. His work invites favorable comparison to Caroline Bynum's "Did the Twelfth Century Discover the Individual?" because it considers diversity and adaptation in crusading appeals. Indeed, Purkis's study provides a necessary update and complement to Bynum's work by exploring crusading appeals to lay people.

DEBORAH GERISH
EMPORIA STATE UNIVERSITY

Jonathan Riley-Smith, *Templars and Hospitallers as Professed Religious in the Holy Land* (The Conway Lectures in Medieval Studies 2008). Notre Dame: University of Notre Dame Press, 2010. Pp. xii, 131. ISBN 978 0 268 04058 3.

Jonathan Riley-Smith, one of the leading experts on military-religious orders, outlines in four chapters the history of the two most important and prominent of these institutions – the Templars and the Hospitallers – in the Levant during the twelfth and thirteenth centuries. Briefly but succinctly, the much-debated origins of these two orders at Jerusalem in the first half of the twelfth century are summarized: the Templars growing out of a company of secular knights, the Hospitallers from a breakaway group of Benedictine *fratres conversi* or serving brothers. The following paragraphs concern their houses, hospitals, castles and commanderies, the recruitment and the various classes of members, including priests, sergeants and, for the Hospitallers, sisters, their governance by the master, officers and chapters, the raising of money, typical careers, family connections and finally the differences between the two orders. From their origins the Hospitallers had a much stronger dedication towards caring for the sick and poor than did the Templars who devoted themselves almost exclusively to fighting the infidel. In the end, the Templars proved to be more vulnerable to criticism and were finally dissolved in 1312, owing to their "institutional immaturity" (p. 63): apparently the Templars did not summon representatives of their western provinces to participate in decisions by the master and his convent which concerned the Order's affairs in general. Furthermore, for fear of being outnumbered by their sergeants, the Templar knights developed a caste spirit, and their superior officers became loath to visit and correct their fellow knights. A map of the Templar and Hospitaller communities in the Levant, ample notes (pp. 71–104), a bibliography (pp. 105–18) and an index with persons, places and select subjects (pp. 119–31) recommend the book as an introductory reader to all serious students of military order history in the Latin East during the crusades 1100–1300. The notes not only permit to check the sources but sometimes also include a detailed discussion of these sources; see, for example, p. 82 n. 11 dating a report about Mongol conquests to 1260 rather than 1261; or p. 83 n. 36 on the Office of the Templars and the Hospitallers. Some statements both in the notes and in the text may spark off further discussion: for example, pp. 3, 73 n. 15 the hypothesis that at least parts of the Templar central archives were still extant in Europe during the fifteenth century. At any rate, the book is an excellent introduction to the topic outlining the current state of research. Moreover, it has been written to promote future research on neglected fields of interest, especially on the religious side of the military-religious orders. Only recently Simonetta Cerrini and others have focused their attention on the military orders in their primary role as religious orders. Studies about the saints of the orders and the veneration of saints within the orders, about the prayers and the liturgies of the orders, about indulgences and the commemoration of deceased members and benefactors, about the orders' priests, the religious discipline and jurisdiction are now beginning to deepen our knowledge and understanding and to enable comparisons with other, old and new religious orders of the Middle Ages. One should be careful using the term masterpiece; yet for this short volume the phrase may well be appropriate.

KARL BORCHARDT
UNIVERSITÄT WÜRZBURG AND MONUMENTA GERMANIAE HISTORICA

Die Urkunden der lateinischen Könige von Jerusalem: Diplomata regum Latinorum Ierosolymitanorum, 4 vols., ed. Hans Eberhard Mayer, with the collaboration of Jean Richard on the Old French texts (Monumenta Germaniae Historica). Hanover; Hahn, 2010. Pp. x, 1812. ISBN 978 3 7752 2100 9.

Medieval historians hardly need reminding that good research is founded on documents which establish the skeletal structure of hard fact on which any flesh, provided by less objective sources, can be laid. Researchers must have faith in the archival materials at their disposal, which is why trustworthy editions of them are so vital. The fewer the documents, the more important this becomes. This publication will be particularly welcomed by historians of the Latin East, who have to deal with material limited by the archival losses that took place after the western settlements fell to the Muslims. Reinhold Röhricht published a calendar containing around 1,800 documents, many of them in seventeenth- and eighteenth-century publications, over a century ago. Discoveries since then would double the number available to us – fourteen of Mayer's charters do not appear in Röhricht's *Regesta* – but that it is still a relatively small number for a region covering Palestine, Syria and Cyprus in the twelfth and thirteenth centuries.

Hans Mayer, who had burst on to the scene with the publication of his massive *Bibliographie* and his edition of the first part of the *Itinerarium peregrinorum*, began this – his life's work – in 1964, in the wake of a revolution in the historiography of the Latin East pioneered by Jean Richard and Joshua Prawer. His research publications, which comprise a major contribution to the continuing revision of the history of the Latin East over the last fifty years, have few rivals as to either quality or quantity. The editions of his *Geschichte der Kreuzzüge* have run into double figures and it is time to commission a new English translation, since a revised edition of the translation of 1972 was pubished as long ago as 1988. And throughout he has been steadily preparing this edition of the charters of the Latin kings of Jerusalem, publishing at intervals books that were preliminary studies. They include *Marseilles Levantehandel und ein Akkonensisches Fälscheratelier des 13. Jahrhunderts* (1972), *Bistümer, Klöster und Stifte im Königreich Jerusalem* (1977), *Das Siegelwesen in den Kreuzfahrerstaaten* (1978), *Varia Antiochena* (1993) and *Die Kanzlei der lateinischen Könige von Jerusalem* (1996).

The extent and ambition of *Die Urkunden* amply justifies the time Mayer has spent preparing it. His long introduction is likely to remain a standard treatment of the condition of the material and of chancery practice and diplomatic, encompassing productions both within the kingdom and abroad. The 836 entries that follow comprise deperdita (including ten documents previously unknown), consents to gifts made by others and the charters themselves. The acts of the regents are included. Only one charter was previously unknown, but the complete texts of eight are published for the first time. Appendices deal with coronation oaths, post-medieval forgeries and charters from foreign rulers that related to rights in the Holy Land. Forgeries are clearly signified. There are elaborate and useful indices.

A bonus is that the entries are provided with detailed commentaries, which are minor masterpieces and are of particular value when dealing with deperdita, such as a lost treaty with Byzantium that is the subject of D. 334. A good example of Mayer's effective treatment of elderly editions is D. 806, for the complete text of which we have had to rely on an eighteenth-century publication. For a model of historical analysis, it would be difficult to find a better discussion of the background to the lost agreement reached between Frederick II and the commune of Acre in 1236 than that attached to D. 688. As one would expect, Mayer is at his most authoritative when dealing with the technical issues involving wording or dating. A good example of his careful and convincing approach can be seen in his treatment of D. 351, relating to Gilbert of Assailly's resignation and the crisis in the Hospitaller convent in Jerusalem, which he now firmly dates to the autumn of 1171.

We are all occasionally taken to task in these essays, but in relation to one of Mayer's criticisms I have to differ. D. 486 is an important gift made by Guy of Lusignan to the Hospital of St. John in Acre. This allowed the Order to enlarge its commandery and create an international headquarters. I have suggested that two apparently nonsensical phrases in the charter would, if reworded, refer to towers on the old city walls. I went on to suggest that if this was the case both the royal chancery and the Order were guilty of astonishing carelessness. This was obviously too much for Mayer, but his alternative explanation – that the charter refers to expansion on a different axis – does not justify the problems with the Latin and cannot be made to conform to Acre's topography. Modern excavation has anyway confirmed the Order's territorial expansion north from its twelfth-century commandery buildings.

But that is incidental. No future historian will be able to ignore this outstanding work and everyone who works on the history of the kingdom of Jerusalem would be well advised to read carefully Mayer's erudite and lively commentaries.

JONATHAN RILEY-SMITH
EMMANUEL COLLEGE, CAMBRIDGE

SOCIETY FOR THE
STUDY OF THE CRUSADES
AND THE LATIN EAST

BULLETIN No. 31, 2011

Editorial

Voici le nouveau Bulletin, no. 31, 2011. Il est le complément de la revue *Crusades*, son support, son vivier d'auteurs, de chercheurs ct, ne l'oublions pas, de ceux qui, à travers le monde, exercent aussi bien souvent la lourde tâche de susciter la relève auprès de plus jeunes. Enseigner. Il forme un outil essentiel pour suivre, au fil des années, les avancées et les projets, la réflexion sans cesse renouvelée autour des croisades et de l'Orient latin, pour cerner ses évolutions historiographiques: la matière du "débat" pour reprendre ici l'expression de notre collègue Christopher Tyerman et de ses éditeurs. Le reflet de la vie de notre Société, la SSCLE.

Les données rassemblées sont issues des renseignements fournis par chacun: certains ont choisi de ne les transmettre que tous les deux ans, quelques-uns oublient d'envoyer leurs fiches, d'autres enfin récapitulent l'ensemble de leur riche production. Il faut alors harmoniser, trier, ordonner. Malgré l'ampleur du travail d'édition, je dois dire le plaisir de cette mise à jour et de découverte de vos travaux. Merci à tous les membres qui font l'effort d'envoyer leurs données de bien vouloir suivre la présentation et la forme typographique ici employée ("sélection en "langue anglaise").

Le Bulletin *de la SSCLE* est un lien précieux pour la communauté des chercheurs à l'échelle internationale. Il rassemble les adresses des membres, signalant les nouveaux arrivants (*): 33 cette année! Il est aussi une base de données scientifiques, rare et appréciée. Il recense les données bibliographiques les plus récentes des adhérents, leurs conférences et communications lors des congrès, travaux en cours, thèmes de recherche, projets multiples, informations variées sur les évènements scientifiques, colloques, expositions, etc. Le site web informatique est actuellement en cours de profondes transformations: il devrait bientôt permettre une plus grande interactivité, d'accès plus immédiat pour nos membres et au-delà. Mais il n'existerait pas davantage que ce bulletin, sans vos informations, vos cotisations et abonnements. Ma précision dépend de la vôtre, parfois aussi de la lisibilité de vos manuscrits. Je reste bien sûr à votre disposition pour corriger ce qui devra l'être, malgré le soin attentif à transcrire vos données.

La "photographie" de cette année 2010–2011 marque une certaine continuité d'intérêt pour les ordres religieux militaires. Un frémissement est à relever autour de l'histoire matérielle pour laquelle l'apport de l'archéologie est en constante sollicitation. Elle montre aussi un attrait montant autour de la guerre et de la paix: les guerres et les paix. De Toruń à Jérusalem, plusieurs rencontres et publications ont déjà ponctué la réflexion sur ce thème. Ce sujet sera au centre de nos échanges l'an prochain en Espagne. Nous nous y retrouverons le plus nombreux possible pour enrichir encore nos connaissances.

François-Olivier Touati

Message from the President

Dear Fellow Members,

First may I congratulate you for the impressive number of scholarly publications which you have produced in the past year, and equally for your participation in local and international conferences and workshops and in a wide range of fieldwork.

During the year July 2010 to July 2011, the Society has sponsored, and mounted sections at, the following Conferences.

On 9 July 2010 two of our postdoctoral members, Michael Carr and Nikolaos Chrissis organized a one-day Conference at the Institute of Historical Research in London on the theme "Contact and Conflict in the Frankish East and the Aegean: Trade and Religion among Latins, Greeks and Turks, 1204–1453." This was well supported and the papers have been accepted for publication by Ashgate and should be available in 2011.

On 12–15 July 2010, the Society for the first time sponsored a section at the International Medieval Congress at Leeds, and it is our intention that this should be a regular commitment.

On 22–26 August 2010 the Twenty-First International Congress of Historical Sciences met at Amsterdam. Professor John France organized three sessions presented by eleven members of the Society on the theme: "Acre and its Falls: 1104, 1187, 1191 and 1291."

In February 2011 Dr Darius von Guettner organized a Crusade section for members of the Society at the 8th Biennial International Conference of the Australian and New Zealand Association for Medieval and Early Modern Studies which met at the University of Otago.

On 18 March 2011 Professor François-Olivier Touati, the editor of the Society's Bulletin, organized the second workshop held at Tours with CNRS (EMAM, Equipe Monde arabe et Méditerranée) on "La monnaie au Proche-Orient: numismatique et histoire."

On 8–9 July 2011 an interdisciplinary workshop and Conference is being held at the German Historical Institute in London on the theme, "The Crusades, Islam and Byzantium." This has been organized by Dr Jochen Schenk, Dr William Purkis and our Society's Postgraduate Officer, Professor Jonathan Phillips. This is designed for postgraduate and postdoctoral students, who will give the majority of the papers, there will be three keynote speakers, and sessions will be chaired by established academic members of the Society.

On 17–19 August a session on crusading studies will be mounted at the annual meeting of the Ecclesiatical History Society in Oxford. The four speakers are members of both Societies, but this is the first occasion on which a session of crusader papers has been presented at an EHS Conference.

Looking ahead, plans are well advanced for the next International Conference to be held by the Society at Caceres from 25–29 June 2012. Our Secretary, Luis García-Guijarro Ramos, and our Conference Secretary, Manuel Rojas, will be circulating you all with details and a call for papers in the near future.

The excavations at Montfort Castle which the Society has sponsored are progressing well under the direction of Professor Adrian Boas.

Members will, I am sure, be glad to know that Ashgate Publishing have launched a series of Crusading Subsidia volumes, and that Dr Christoph Maier, reviews editor of the journal *Crusades*, is editor of this new series. This series is, of course, independent of the Society, but Dr Maier and Dr John Smedley of Ashgate would welcome proposals for monographs or collections of essays to be considered for publication in this series.

Finally, it is with regret that I must inform you of the death of Professor James Powell during last winter. The Society is particularly indebted to him for organizing the Third International Conference at Syracuse, New York, in 1991. I have extended condolences on behalf of us all to his family. We shall miss his genial and learned company at our future meetings.

I thank my fellow committee members for their cooperation and support during the past year, and wish all of you happiness and success in the year ahead.

Bernard Hamilton

Practical Information

Our treasurer, **Prof. James D. Ryan, 100 West 94th Street, Apartment 26M, New York NY 10025, U.S.A., james.d.ryan@verizon.net** has again (and ever) been successful in recruiting new members. We should thank him warmly for all his efforts. If you have any queries concerning your subscriptions and payments, please contact him at the above address.

The Bulletin editor would like to remind you that, in order to avoid delays, he needs to have information for the Bulletin each year at an early date, usually in January or February. My address is: **Prof. François-Olivier Touati, La Croix Saint-Jérôme, 11 allée Émile Bouchut, 77123 Noisy-sur-École, France;** email: **francoistouati@aol.com**.

I want to thank all members who provide me with bibliographical data. In order to make the Bulletin more useful for you, it would be helpful if those members who edit proceedings or essay volumes could let me know not only about their own papers but also on the other papers in such volumes. You are encouraged to supply any information via email.

Dr Zsolt Hunyadi is **webmaster** for our official website: **http://www.sscle.org.** There you can find news about the SSCLE and its publications as well as bibliographical data and links to related sites.

Our journal entitled *Crusades*, now no. 10, 2011, allows the Society to publish articles and texts; encourages research in neglected subfields; invites a number of authors to deal with a specific problem within a comparative framework; initiates and reports on joint programmes; and offers reviews of books and articles.

Editors: Benjamin Z. Kedar and Jonathan Phillips; Associate Editor: William J. Purkis; Reviews Editor: Christoph Maier; Archaeology Editor: Denys R. Pringle.

Colleagues may submit papers for consideration to either of the editors, Professor Benjamin Z. Kedar and Professor Jonathan Phillips. A copy of the style sheet is to be found in the back of this booklet.

The journal includes a section of book reviews. In order to facilitate the reviews editor's work, could members please ask their publishers to send copies to: **PD Dr Christoph T. Maier, Reviews editor,** *Crusades*, **Sommergasse 20, 4056 Basel, Switzerland; ctmaier@ hist.uzh.ch**. Please note that *Crusades* reviews books concerned with any aspect(s) of the history of the crusades and the crusade movement, the military orders and the Latin settlements in the Eastern Mediterranean, but not books which fall outside this range.

The cost of the journal to individual members is £25, $46 or €32; the cost to institutions and non-members is £65, US$130 or €93. **Cheques in these currencies should be made payable to SSCLE. For information on other forms of payment contact the treasurer.**

Members may opt to receive the Bulletin alone at the current membership price (single £10, $20 or €15; student £6, $12 or €9; joint £15, $30 or €21). Those members who do not subscribe to the journal will receive the Bulletin from the Bulletin editor.

Contents

List of abbreviations

Avignon SSCLE 7: La Papauté et les Croisades, *The Papacy and the Crusades*, VIIe Congrès international de la SSCLE, 7th Quadrennial Conference of the SSCLE, Avignon, 27–31 August 2008, ed. Michel Balard.

DOMMA: *Prier et combattre. Dictionnaire européen des ordres militaires au Moyen Âge*, ed. Nicole Bériou and Philippe Josserand, Paris: Fayard, 2009, 1032 p.

DTT: *The Debate on the Trial of the Templars (1307–1314)*, ed. Jochen Burgtorf, Paul F. Crawford, and Helen Nicholson, Farnham, Surrey, & Burlington, VT, Ashgate, 2010, xxv–399 p.

EHR: *English Historical Review.*

ICHS: 21st International Congress of Historical Sciences, Amsterdam, Netherland, August 2010.

IMC: International Medieval Congress, Kalamazoo or Leeds.

MO5: *The Military Orders: Politics and Power*, 5th Conference on the Military Orders, Cardiff University, 3–6 September 2009, ed. Peter Edbury, Farnham, Ashgate.

OM16: Ordines militares. Colloquia Torunensia Historica, 15, Toruń, septembre 2009.

Palmella 2009: *As ordens Militares e as Ordens de cavalaria entre o Occidente e o Oriente*, ed. C. F. Fernandes, Palmela, Portugal, 2009.

Palmella 2010: *Freires, Guerreiros, Cavaleiros. VI Encontro sobre Ordens Militares*, Palmela, Portugal, 10–14 March 2010.

Studi per Franco Cardini: "Come l'orco della fiaba." Studi per Franco Cardini, a cura di M. Montesano, Firenze, 2010.

1. Recent publications

ALVIRA-CABRER, Martin, *Pedro el Católico, Rey de Aragón y Conde de Barcelona (1196–1213), Documentos, Testimonios y Memoria Histórica*, 6 vols., Zaragoza, Institución "Fernando el Católico" (CSIC)-Diputación de Zaragoza, 2010 (Colección "Fuentes Históricas Aragonesas," 52), 3058 p.; "La Croisade des Albigeois: une armée gigantesque?," *En Languedoc au XIIIᵉ siècle, le temps du sac de Béziers*, dir. Monique Bourin, Perpignan, Presses Universitaires de Perpignan, 2010, pp. 163–88; "La Croisade contre les Albigeois," *Le Royaume Oublié. La Tragédie Cathare. The Albigensian Crusade*, dir. Jordi Savall, Hespèrion XXI-La Capella Reial de Catalunya, Alia Vox, 2009, pp. 38–43 (text in English, Spanish, Occitan, Catalan, German and Italian); "On the Term *Albigensians* in 13th Century Hispanic Sources," *Imago Temporis. Medium Aevum*, 3, 2009, pp. 123–37; "La Cruzada contra los Albigenses: historia, historiografía y memoria," *Clío & Crimen*, 6, 2009, pp. 110–41.

AMITAI, Reuven, "Armies and their Economic Basis in Iran and the Surrounding Lands, ca. 1000–1500 C.E.," in David O. Morgan and Anthony Reid, ed., *The New Cambridge History of Islam, 3: The Eastern Islamic World Eleventh to Eighteenth Centuries*, Cambridge: Cambridge University Press, 2010, pp. 539–60; "Abāqā," *The Encyclopaedia of Islam*, 3rd ed., Leiden: Brill, 2010, 1, pp. 1–9.

ANDREI, Filippo, "Alberto di Aachen e la Chanson de Jérusalem," *Romance Philology*, 63, 2009, pp. 1–69, [special issue: Romania Mediterranea II].

ARBEL, Benjamin, "L'elezione dei prelati greci a Cipro durante la dominazione veneziana," in C. Maltezou, A. Tzavara, D. Vlassi, ed., *I Greci durante la Venetocrazia: uomini, spazio, idee* (XIII–XVIII sec.), Venezia, Istituto Ellenico, 2009, pp. 373–80; "The Attitude of Muslims to Animals: Renaissance Perceptions and Beyond," in *Animals and People in the Ottoman Empire*, ed. Suraiya Faroqhi, Istanbul, Eren, 2010, pp. 57–74; "Between Segregation and Integration: Cretan Jews during the Sixteenth Century," in *"Interstizi:: culture ebraico-cristiane a Venezia e nei domini veneziani tra basso medioevo e prima epoca moderna*, ed. Uwe Israel, Robert Jütte and Reinhold C. Mueller, Roma, Edizioni di Storia e Letteratura 2010, pp. 281–94.

BALARD, Michel, Co-dir., *Au Moyen Age, entre tradition et innovation*, éd. du CTHS, Paris 2009; dir., *Les ordres militaires et la mer*, Paris, éd. du CTHS, 2009; "Constantinople et les ports pontiques: topographie, liens entre le port et la ville, fonctions," in G. Fabre, D. Le Blévec, D. Menjot, ed., *Les ports et la navigation en Méditerranée au Moyen Age*, Actes du colloque de Lattes 12–14 novembre 2004, Association pour la connaissance du patrimoine en Languedoc-Roussillon, 2009, pp. 191–200; "Les controverses politico-religieuses à Caffa (1473–1475)" in I. Augé, G. Dédeyan, éd., *L'Église arménienne entre Grecs et Latins fin XIe –milieu XVe siècle*, Paris, 2009, pp. 183–92; "Conclusion du colloque" *Spazi per la memoria storica. La storia di Genova attraverso le vicende delle sedi e dei documenti dell'Archivio di Stato*, ed. A. Assini, P. Caroli, Gênes 2009, pp. 516–20; "Jihad, Holy War and Crusading," in K. Szende, J. A. Rasson, ed., *Annual of Medieval Studies at CEU*, 16, 2010, pp. 193–201; "Les sociétés coloniales à la fin du Moyen Age," *Dynamiques sociales au Moyen Age en occident et en Orient*, ed. E. Malamut, Aix-en-Provence, 2010, pp. 151–72; "De l'art d'éviter la guerre," c.r. of E. N. Luttwak, *The grand Strategy of the Byzantine Empire*, in *Sociétal*, 69, 2010, pp. 131–36.

BALLETTO, Laura, "Spigolando tra gli atti notarili del Quattrocento: brevi note in tema di nullità e/o scioglimento del matrimonio a Genova sulla fine del medioevo," in *In uno volumine. Studi in onore di Cesare Scalon*, ed. L. Pani, Udine, 2009, pp. 1–34; "In memoria di Geo Pistarino," *Nuova Rivista Storica*, XCIV.1, 2010, pp. 285–318.

BEECH, George, *The Brief Eminence and doomed Fall of Islamic Saragossa: A great Center of Jewish and Arabic Learning in the Iberian Peninsula during the 11th century*, Zaragoza: Instituto de Estudios Islamicos y del Oriente Proximo, 2008, 394 p.; "How Angleterre came to be French country name for England in the 11th century," *Beiträge zur Namenforschung*, 43/3, 2008, pp. 289–99; "How England got its name (1014–1030)," *Nouvelle Revue d'Onomastique*, 51, 2009, pp. 17–52; "Noms de personnes, noms de lieux, noms de peoples dans la Tapisserie de Bayeux: une perspective française," *Cahiers de Civilisation médiévale*, 51, 2008, pp. 201–11; "The alternation between present and past time in the telling of the Bayeux Tapestry story," *Annales de Normandie*, 58, 2008, pp. 7–23.

BELL, Gregory D., "In Starvation's Shadow: The Role of Logistics in the Strained Byzantine-European Relations during the First Crusade," *Byzantion*, LXXX, 2010, pp. 38–71.

BELLOMO Elena, "Rinaldo da Concorezzo, archbishop of Ravenna, and the Trial of the Templars in North Italy," in *DTT*, pp. 259–72; "Metodi d'indagine sulla milizia templare in Italia nord-occidentale (1142–1308)," *Rivista di Storia della Chiesa in Italia*, 64, 2010, pp. 11–37; *"Annales Ianuenses,"* "Caffaro di Caschifellone," "Oberto Cancelliere," "Ottobono Scriba," "Iacopo Doria," in *Dictionary of Medieval Chronicles*, Brill, Leiden-Boston, 2010; "Celestine V," "St. Anthony of Padua," "Peter Damian," "Arnolfo di Cambio," in *Oxford Dictionary of the Middle Ages*, Oxford UP, 2010.

BIRD, Jessalyn, "James of Vitry's Sermons to Pilgrims (*Sermones ad peregrinos*): A Recontextualization" in *Essays in Medieval Studies: Proceedings of the Illinois Medieval Association*, 25, 2008, pp. 81–113; "The Crusades: Eschatological Lemmings, Younger Sons, Papal Hegemony, and Colonialism," in *Misconceptions about the Middle Ages*, ed.

Stephen J. Harris and Bryon L. Grigsby, Routledge, 2008, pp. 85–89; "Crusaders' Rights Revisited: The Use and Abuse of Crusade Privileges in EarlyThirteenth Century France," in *Law and the Illicit in Medieval Society*, ed. R. M. Karras, J. Kaye and E. A. Matter, University of Pennsylvania Press, 2008.

BOAS, Adrian J., *Domestic Settings. Sources on Domestic Architecture and Day-to-Day Activities in the Crusader States*, Brill, 393 p.; *Acre-East Acre-East: 1999, 2000. Two Seasons of Excavations in the Possible Quarter of the Teutonic Knights in Akko, British Archaeological Reports*, 2011, (with Georg Philipp Melloni).

BONNEAUD, Pierre, "Un débouché fréquent pour les cadets des différentes aristocraties catalanes: étude sur 283 chevaliers catalans de l'Ordre de l'Hôpital au XVe siècle (1396–1472," *Bulletin de la Société du Patrimoine de l'Ordre de Malte*, 22.

BRUNDAGE, James A., "The Managerial Revolution in the English Church," in *Magna carta and the England of King John*, ed. Janet S. Loewengard, Woodbridge, Boydell Press, 2010, pp. 83–98.

BURGTORF, Jochen, co-ed. of DTT; "The Trial Inventories of the Templars' Houses in France: Select Aspects," in DTT, pp. 105–15.

CARR, Annemarie, "The Early History of the *Madonna delle Vittorie*'s Iconographic Type," in *La Madonna delle Vittorie dal Gran Conte Ruggero al Settecento*, ed. Maria Katja Guida, exhibition catalogue, Cathedral, Piazza Armerina, 21 December 2009 – 27 February 2010, Milan: Electa, 2009, pp. 32–36; "Iconography and Identity: Syrian Elements in the Art of Crusader Cyprus," in *Religious Origins of Nations? The Christian Communities of the Middle East*, ed. Bas ter Haar Romeny, *Church History and Religious Culture* 89/1–3, 2009, pp. 127–51.

CARRAZ, Damien, 38 entries for DOMMA; "*Causa defendende et extollende christianitatis.* La vocation maritime des ordres militaires en Provence (XIIᵉ–XIIIᵉ siècle)," in *Les ordres militaires et la mer, 130ᵉ Congrès national des sociétés historiques et scientifiques (La Rochelle, 2005)*, ed. M. Balard, Paris, CTHS, 2009, pp. 21–46 (online: http://cths.fr/ed/edition.php?id=4254); "Les Lengres à Marseille au XIVᵉ siècle. Les activités militaires d'une famille d'armateurs dans un port de croisade," *Revue historique*, t. CCCIX/4, n° 652, 2009, pp. 755–77; "Saint Géraud et le culte des saints guerriers en France méridionale (Xᵉ–XIIᵉ siècle)," in *Géraud d'Aurillac, l'aristocrate et le saint dans l'Auvergne post-carolingienne, actes de la journée d'étude d'Aurillac, 21 novembre 2009*, ed. D. Carraz (*Revue de la Haute-Auvergne*, tome 72, janvier–mars 2010), pp. 91–114; "L'ordre du Temple dans la Provence du XIIᵉ siècle: l'ambiguïté d'une nouvelle expérience spirituelle à l'âge des réformes," in *Monachisme et réformes dans la vallée du Rhône (XIᵉ–XIIIᵉ siècles), actes de la 7ᵉ journée d'études du Centre d'Études d'Histoire religieuse Méridionale (Saint-Michel de Frigolet, 18 novembre 2006)*, Études Vauclusiennes, no. 75–76, 2006 [published: 2010], pp. 19–26; "Military Orders and the Town (Twelfth to Early Fourteenth Centuries). Urban Commanderies Case in the Rhône River Low Valley," *Chronica. Annual of the Institute of History of the University of Szeged*, vol. 6, 2006 [published: 2010], pp. 82–99; "Les enquêtes générales de la papauté sur l'ordre de l'Hôpital (1338 et 1373). Analyse comparée dans le prieuré de Provence," in *Quand gouverner c'est enquêter. Les pratiques politiques de l'enquête princière (Occident, XIIIᵉ–XIVᵉ siècles), Actes du colloque international d'Aix-en-Provence et Marseille, 19–21 mars 2009*, ed. Th. Pécout, Paris, 2010, pp. 508–31; "Precursors and Imitators of the Military Orders: Religious Societies for Defending the Faith in the Medieval West (11th–13th c.)," *Viator. Medieval and Renaissance Studies*, 41–42, 2010, pp. 91–111; "Les ordres militaires et hospitaliers: une 'nouvelle religion'," *Structures et dynamiques religieuses dans les sociétés de l'Occident latin (1179–1449)*, ed. J.-M. Matz and M.-M. de Cévins, Rennes, 2010, pp. 179–93.

CASSIDY-WELCH, Megan, *Imprisonment in the Medieval Religious Imagination, c. 1150–1400*, London: Palgrave, 2011; "Memories of space in thirteenth-century France: displaced people after the Albigensian crusade," *Parergon: Journal of the Australian and New Zealand Association for Medieval and Early Modern Studies*, 27:2, 2010, pp. 111–31; "Medieval Practices of Space and Place," ibidem, pp. 1–12.

CHRISSIS, Nikolaos, "A diversion that never was: Thibaut IV of Champagne, Richard of Cornwall and Pope Gregory IX's crusading plans for Constantinople, 1235–1239," *Crusades* 9, 2010, pp. 123–45; Review of Christopher Tyerman's, *God's War: a New History of the Crusades*, Cambridge MA, Belknap Press, 2009, in *The Medieval Review* (online): [https:// scholarworks.iu.edu/dspace/bitstream/handle/2022/6686/10.01.01.html].

CHRIST, Georg, "Passagers clandestins? Rôle moteur des galères vénitiennes et concurrence des navires ronds à Alexandrie au début du XVe siècle," in *Espace et réseaux en méditerranée médiévale, mise en place des réseaux, les politiques d'Etat dans la formation des réseaux*, ed. Damien Coulon, Christophe Picard, and Dominique Valérian, Paris: Éditions Bouchène, 2010, pp. 275–90; with Olaf Wagener and Hubert Mara, "Altes Kapitell – neue Ansichten: Möglichkeiten des 3D-Scannings am Beispiel eines Kapitells der pfälzischen Burg Aneboş Burgen und Schlösser," *Burgen und Schlösser*, 1, 2010, pp. 51–52.

CIPOLLONE, Giulio, "*Gerusalemme è 'dove ti manda il papa'. Prendere la croce in più direzioni*," in "*Come l'orco della fiaba.*" *Studi per Franco Cardini*, ed. Marina Montesano, Firenze, SISMEL, 2010, pp. 85–95.

CLAVERIE, Pierre-Vincent, "*L'histoire parfaite* d'Ibn al-Athīr," *Le Moyen Age*, CXV, 2009, pp. 601–606.

COUREAS, Nicholas S., *The Latin Church in Cyprus 1313–1378*, Cyprus Research Centre 2010; "Genoese merchants in the Export of Grain from Cyprus to Cilician Armenia: 1300–1310," in *Hask Hayakidagan*, 11, Antelias, Lebanon, 2009, pp. 319–38; "Commerce between Mamluk Egypt and Hospitaller Rhodes in the mid-fourteenth century: The case of Sidi Galip Ripolli," in *Egypt and Syria in the Fatimid, Ayyubid and Mamluk Eras 6, Proceedings of the 14th and 15th HES*, ed. U. Vermeulen and K. D'hulster, Leuven: Peeters, 2010, pp. 207–17; "The Reception of Arabic Medicine on Latin Cyprus: 1200–1570," ibid., pp. 219–28: "Between the Latins and Native Tradition: The Armenians in Lusignan Cyprus, 1191–1473," in *L'Église arménienne entre Grecs et Latins fin XIe–milieu XVe siècle*, ed. I. Augé and G. Dédéyan, Paris: Geuthner, 2009, pp. 205–14; "A Medieval Cypriot Diaspora: Non-noble Cypriot Migration throughout the Mediterranean from the 13th to the 16th Centuries," *Epeteris Kentrou Epistemonikon Ereunon*, 35, 2009–2010, pp. 65–82; "Philippe de Mézières' portrait of Peter Thomas as a preacher," *Carmelus* 57, 2010, fasc. 1, pp. 63–80; "The French Element in the Culture of Latin Cyprus: A varied, diachronic and multifaceted relationship [in Greek]," *Epeteris tes Kypriakes Hetaireias Historikon Spoudon*, 9, 2010, pp. 41–50.

CRAWFORD, Paul F., edition of DTT; "The Involvement of the University of Paris in the Trials of Marguerite Porete and of the Templars, 1308–1310," in DTT, pp. 129–43; "Raymond of St Gilles" and "Crusades Historiography: 1245–1500" for *Medieval Warfare and Military Technology: an encyclopedia*, ed. Clifford J. Rogers, Oxford University Press, 2010.

CUSHING, Dana, "New Evidence for the Teutonic Order's Bavarian Origins: Fragments Found" [e-article], De Re Militari: The Society for Medieval Military History: http://www.

deremilitari.org/2010/06/new-evidence-for-the-teutonic-order/bavarian-origins fragments found/

DEMURGER, Alain, articles et introduction historiographique, in DOMMA; *Croisades et croisés au Moyen Age*, Paris, Flammarion, coll. Champs Histoire, 2010 (new ed.); *Moines et guerriers. Les ordres religieux militaires au Moyen Age*, Paris, Le Seuil, 2010 (new ed. of *Chevaliers du Christ. Les ordres religieux-militaires au Moyen Age*, Paris, Le Seuil, 2002); "Templiers et Hospitaliers devant le Parlement de Paris (1250–1307)," in *Un Moyen Age pour aujourd'hui. Mélanges offerts à Claude Gauvard*, J. Claustre, O. Mattéoni, N. Offenstadt,(dir.), Paris, Presses Universitaires de France, 2010, pp. 424–31; "Les ordres religieux-militaires sur la scène (Théâtre et Opéra), XVIIIᵉ–XIXᵉ siècle," in *Il revival cavalleresco dal Don Chisciotte all'Ivanhoe (e oltre)*, Convegno Internazionale del Centro europeo di studi sulla civiltà cavlleresca, (San Gimignano, 4–5 giugno 2009, 2010), ed. M. Mesirca et F. Zambon, Pise, Pacini Editore, 2010, pp. 143–58; "Manuscrit de Chinon ou Moment Chinon? Quelques remarques sur l'attitude du pape Clément V envers les Templiers à l'été 1308," in *Come l'orco per la fiaba. Studi per Franco Cardini*, M. Montesano ed., Florence, S.I.S.M.E.L, Edizione del Galluzo, 2010.

DOUROU-ELIOPOULOU, Maria, "Political and socioeconomic institutions in the crusader states if the Eastern Mediterranean," in *The Dark Medieval Ages*, Society of Moraiti School, Athens 2010, pp. 189–201; "The evidence of Latin sources of the 13th and the 14th centuries on the islands of the Aegean," in *Il ducato dell' Egeo, Atti dell'Incontro di Studio (Nasso-Atene 2007)*, Athens 2009, pp. 73–85.

EDBURY, Peter, "The Arrest of the Templars in Cyprus," in DTT, pp. 249–58; "New Perspectives on the Old French Continuations of William of Tyre," *Crusades*, 9, 2010, pp. 107–13.

EDGINGTON, Susan, "Oriental and Occidental Medicine in the Crusader States," in *The Crusades and the Near East: Cultural Histories*, ed. C. Kostick, London, Routledge, 2011, pp. 189–215; "Crusades Sources 1095–1183," in *Medieval Warfare and Military Technology: An Encyclopedia*, ed.Clifford J. Rogers, Oxford, OUP, 2010; "Crusade Chronicles," in *Encyclopedia of Medieval Chronicles*, ed. G. Dunphy *et al.*, Leiden, Brill, 2010.

FLORI, Jean, *Chroniqueurs et propagandistes. Introduction critique aux sources de la Première Croisade*, Genève, Droz, coll. Hautes Études Médiévales et Modernes, no. 98, Ecole Pratique des Hautes Études, Sciences Historiques et Philologiques-V, 2010, 353 p.; *La fine del mondo nel Medioevo*, Bologna, il Mulino, (coll. Universale Paperbacks, n° 583), 2010, 182 p.

FOLDA, Jaroslav, "The Panorama of the Crusades, 1096 to 1218, as seen in Yates Thompson MS 12 in the British Library," in *The Study of Medieval Manuscripts of England, Festschrift in Honor of Richard W. Pfaff*, ed. G. H. Brown and L. E. Voigts, Tempe, AZ: Arizona Center for Medieval and Renaissance Studies/Brepols, 2010, pp. 251–78; (Review) Denys Pringle, *The Churches of the Crusader Kingdom of Jerusalem: A Corpus, vol. IV: The Cities of Acre and Tyre with Addenda and Corrigenda to vols. I–III*, Cambridge: Cambridge University Press, 2009, for the *Catholic Historical Review*, 97, 2011, pp. 120–21.

FONSECA, Luís Adão da, *História das Ínclitas Cavalarias de Cristo, Santiago e Avis de Fr. Jerónimo Román*, (with Paula Pinto Costa, Maria Cristina Pimenta, Isabel Morgado S. Silva, Joel Mata), ed Paula Pinto Costa, Militarium Ordinum Analecta, 10, Oporto, CEPESE and Fundação Eng. António de Almeida, 2008; "Fronteiras territoriais e memórias históricas: o caso da Comenda de Noudar da Ordem de Avis," in *Comendas das Ordens Militares na Idade Média*, Militarium Ordinum Analecta, 11, Oporto, CEPESE and Civilização Editora, 2009, pp. 37–55; "Portugal e o Mediterrâneo, entre Castela e Marrocos. A formação da fronteira marítima nos séculos XIV–XV e a noção de espaço político descontínuo," in *População e Sociedade*, 17, 2009, pp. 45–60; "Vasco da Gama," "Portugal," "Atlantique," "Tristão da Cunha," "Jean II roi de Portugal," "João Infan," in DOMMA, pp. 123–24, 491, 502–503, 731–34, 935, 952.

Forey, Alan J., "Could alleged Templar Malpractices have remained undetected for decades?," in DTT, pp. 11–19.

Franke, Daniel, articles "Battle of Sarmin, 1115," "Crusades: Narrative (1180–1245)," "Crusades: Settlement," "France: Historiography (1328–1483)," "Germany: Historiography (911–1024)," "Germany: Narrative (911–1024)," "Germany: Sources (911–1024)," "Henry I, King of the East Franks" in *The Oxford Encyclopedia of Medieval Warfare and Military Technology*, ed. Clifford J. Rogers, New York and Oxford: Oxford University Press, 2010.

Friedman, Yvonne, "Peacemaking: Perceptions and Practices in the Medieval Latin East," in *The Crusades in the Near East: A Cultural History*, ed. Conor Kostick, London: Routledge, 2010, pp. 229–257; "Gestures of Conciliation in the Latin East" (Hebrew), in *War and Peace*, ed. S. Avineri, Jerusalem, Shazar, 2010, pp. 131–50; "Christian–Muslim Peacemaking in the Medieval Latin East," in *Peace, War, and Gender* ed. Jost Duellfer and Robert Frank, Klartext Verlag, 2009, pp. 45–63.

Gabriele, Matthew, *An Empire of Memory: The Legend of Charlemagne, The Franks and Jerusalem before the First Crusade*, Oxford UP, 2011, 256 pp. Done

Gaposchkin, Cecilia, "The Role of the Crusades in the Sanctification of Louis IX of France," in *Crusades: Medieval Worlds in Conflict*, ed. T. Madden, Ashgate, 2010, pp. 195–209; "Place, Status, and Experience in the Miracles of Saint Louis," *Cahiers de Recherches médiévales et humanistes*, 19, 2010, pp. 249–46; "The Monastic Office for Louis IX of France: Lauda Celectis Regio," *Revue Mabillon*, n.s. 20 (81), 2009, pp. 143–74.

Georgiou, Stavros G., "The Bishopric of Karpasia from Its Foundation to the Middle of the XIIIth Century," in *Karpasia. Praktika Protou Epistimonikou Synedriou "Eis gin ton Agion kai ton Hiroon*," Savvato 4 kai Kyriaki 5 Apriliou 2009, Xenodocheio Navarria, Lemesos, ed. P. Papageorgiou, Limassol 2010, pp. 127–46 [in Greek]; "The Revolt of Theophilos Erotikos (1042) and the 'Nation of the Cypriots'," *Byzantina*, 29, 2009 (= Afieroma sti mnimi tou Dimitriou G. Tsami), pp. 151–62 [in Greek with English summary]; "Cyprus in XIth and XIIth Centuries: Aspects of a Byzantine Province," *Epeteris Kentrou Meleton Hieras Mones Kykkou*, 9, 2010, pp. 129–48 [in Greek]; "Notes on the Byzantine Cyprus I," *Epeteris Kentrou Meleton Hieras Mones Kykkou*, 9, 2010, pp. 445–52 [in Greek].

Grasso, Christian, "Ars praedicandi e crociata nella predicazione dei magistri parigini," in *Come l'orco della fiaba. Studi per Franco Cardini*, ed. M. Montesano, Firenze, Sismel, 2010, pp. 141–50; "La memoria contesa dei Novelli Innocenti. Ritorno sulla crociata dei fanciulli," in *Un maestro insolito. Saggi per Franco Cardini*, Firenze, Vallecchi, 2010, pp. 83–100; "Folco di Neuilly sacerdos et praedicator crucis," in *Nuova Rivista Storica*, XCIV/III, 2010, pp. 741–65.

Hamilton, Bernard, "Afterwords," in *The Crusades and the Near East*, ed. C. Kostick, Abington, Toutledge, 2011, pp. 258–62.

Hosler, John D., "Henry II of England," "Robert Curthose, duke of Normndy," "William the Conqueror," "Rochester, Siege of (1088)," "Mercenaries," in *Medieval Warfare and Military Technology: an Encyclopedia*, ed. C. Rogers, Oxford UP, 2010, 2, pp. 259–60, 3, pp. 1–3, 181–82 and pp. 452–54.

IRWIN, Robert, *Mamluks and Crusaders: Men of the Sword and Men of the Pen*, Variorum Collected Studies, Farnham, Ashgate, 2010, xii+370pp.; Edition and introduction to *The New Cambridge History of Islam*, vol. 4, *Islamic Cultures and Societies to the End of the Eighteenth Century*, Cambridge UP, 201, xxii + 920pp.

JACKSON, Peter, *Studies on the Mongol Empire and Early Muslim India*, Variorum Collected Studies series, Ashgate Publishing, 2009; "Mongol khans and religious allegiance: The problems confronting a minister-historian in Ilkanid Iran," *Iran, Journal of the British Institute of Persian Studies*, 47, 2009, pp. 109–22; "The Mongol Age in Eastern Inner Asia," in *The Cambridge History of Inner Asia, I: The Chinggisid Age*, ed. Nicola di Cosmo, Allen J. Frank and Peter B. Golden, Cambridge UP, 2009, pp. 26–44; "Mongols," in *The Oxford Encyclopaedia of the Islamic World*, ed. John L Esposito, Oxford UP, 2009, IV, pp. 40–46.

JASPERT, Nikolas, "Der Zisterzienserorden in den iberischen Reichen des Hochmittelalters: Ein Sonderweg?," in *Norm und Realität: Kontinuität und Wandel der Zisterzienser im Mittelalter*, ed. Franz J. Felten / Werner Rösener (Vita Regularis. Abhandlungen 42), Münster 2010, pp. 441–74; "Zeichen und Symbole in den christlich–islamischen Beziehungen des Mittelalters," in *Religiosità e civiltà. Le comunicazioni simboliche (secoli IX–XIII)*, ed. Giancarlo Andenna, Münster 2010, pp. 293–342; "Die Kreuzzüge," in *Weltdeutungen und Weltreligionen: 600 bis 1500*, ed. Johannes Fried / Ernst-Dieter Hehl / Walter Demel (WBG-Weltgeschichte 3), Darmstadt 2010, pp. 166–178; "El perfil trascendental de los reyes aragoneses, siglos XIII al XV: Santidad, franciscanismo y profecías," in *La Corona de Aragón en el centro de su Historia (1208–1458): La monarquía aragonesa y los reinos de la Corona* (Colección actas 74), ed. José Ángel Sesma Muñoz, Zaragoza, 2009, p. 183–218; "The election of Arnau de Torroja as ninth Master of the Knights Templar (1180): An enigmatic decision reconsidered," in Palmela 2009, pp. 371–97; articles in DOMMA: "Maurice," p. 595, "Mota de los Caballeros," p. 639, "Saint George de Carinthie (Ordre du)," pp. 816–17, Saint-Sépulcre (Ordre du), pp. 825–26; "Saints (Culte des)," pp. 834–35, "Saints militaires," pp. 835–36, "Sancha, infant," p. 842 "Vierge," pp. 958–61, "Vera Cruz de Ségovie," pp. 954–55.

JAMES, Colin Wheldon, "The Miraculous crusade. The Role of the Mystical and Miraculous in the Morale and Motivation of the First Crusade," *The Historian*, The Historical Association (London), 105, 2010, pp. 24–29.

JENSEN, Carsten Selch, "Orders, Military: Northern," in *Medieval Warfare and Military Technology:* An *Encyclopedia*, Ed. Clifford J. Rogers, Oxford University Press, 2010.

JOSSERAND, Philippe, ed. with N. Bériou, *Prier et combattre. Dictionnaire européen des ordres militaires au Moyen Âge*, Paris, Fayard, 2009, 1032 p. [DOMMA]: "Présentation" (avec Nicole Bériou), pp. 17–21; Articles: "Alcántara, ordre," pp. 61–65, "Almohades," pp. 74–75, "Alonso Méndez de Guzmán," p. 77 "Alphonse XI, roi de Castille," pp. 81–82, "Blaise, saint," pp. 159–60, "Bretagne" (avec François Colin), pp. 175–76, "Castille, couronne de," pp. 198–200, "Castronuño," p. 200, "Chambre," p. 205, "Charles Quint" (avec Gregorio Salinero), pp. 211–13, "Chasse," pp. 215–16, "Chemin de Saint-Jacques," pp. 219–20, "Clavaire," pp. 236–37, "Commanderie," pp. 245–46, "Commandeur," pp. 246–47, "Couvent," pp. 266–67, "Effectifs," pp. 319–20, "Fadrique, infant," p. 349, "Fernán Rodríguez de Valbuena," p. 359, "Frontière," pp. 372–75, "García Álvarez de Toledo," pp. 378–79, "Gonzalo Martínez de Oviedo," p. 395, "Historiographie au Moyen Âge" (avec Alain Demurger), pp. 437–38, "Jacques, saint," pp. 477–78, "Jeu," pp. 500–502, "João Fernandes," p. 504, "Juan Manuel," pp. 514–15, "Lorraine" (avec Dieter Heckmann), pp. 561–62, "*Maestrazgo*" (avec Luís Filipe Oliveira), p. 572, "Martín López de Córdoba," p. 591, "Melchiore Bandini," pp. 601–602, "Mense magistrale" (avec Carlos de Ayala

Martínez), pp. 605–606, "Mérinides," p. 608, "Morimond," p. 634, "Mythe d'origine," pp. 643–44, "Pedro López de Baeza," p. 703, "Pedro Núñez," pp. 703–704, "Pierre Ier, roi de Castille," pp. 719–20, "Reconquête," pp. 765–69, "Rodrigo Yáñez," p. 801, "Saint-Georges du comté de Luna, ordre de," pp. 817–18, "Saint-Maurice, ordre de," pp. 823–24, "Séville" (avec Daniel Rodríguez Blanco), pp. 869–70, "Treize," pp. 929–30, "Valbuena, lignage," p. 949, "Varna, campagne de," pp. 951–52, "Villalcázar de Sirga," pp. 963–64. "Vientos de cambio. Las transformaciones de la orden de Calatrava a partir de finales del siglo XIII a través de la normativa cistercience," in *El nacimiento de la orden de Calatrava. Primeros tiempos de expansión (siglos XII–XIII). Actas del Congreso internacional "850 Aniversario de la fundación de la orden de Calatrava, 1158–2008" (Almagro, 14–17 de octubre de 2008)*, éd. Luis Rafael Villegas Díaz et Ángela Madrid Medina, Ciudad Real, 2009, pp. 225–37; "Entre dos frentes: aproximación a las empresas militares de los Templarios del occidente peninsular (siglos XII–XIV)," in *Hacedores de frontera. Estudios sobre el contexto social de la frontera en la España medieval*, éd. Manuel Alejandro Rodríguez de la Peña, Madrid, 2009, pp. 179–201; "*Nuestro moro que tiene a Cervera*. Un châtelain musulman au service de l'ordre de l'Hôpital au début du XIVe siècle," in *Minorités et régulations sociales en Méditerranée médiévale (Actes du colloque international de Fontevraud, 7–9 juin 2007)*, éd. Stéphane Boissellier, François Clément et John Tolan, Rennes, 2010, pp. 161–77.

JOTISCHKY, Andrew, "The Fortunes of War: An 11th century Greek Liturgical Manuscript (Sinai gr. 512) and its History," *Crusades* 9, 2010, pp. 173–84.

KEDAR, Benjamin Z., "Un Santo venuto da Gerusalemme: Ranieri Scacceri," in *I Santi venuti dal mare*, Atti del Convegno Internazionale di studio (Bari-Brindisi, 14–18 dicembre 2005), ed. Maria-Stella Calò Mariani, Bari, 2009, pp. 173–80; (with Hervé Barbé), "Dating the Subterranean Passage at the Patriarchs' Cave, Hebron," in *Israel's Land: Papers Presented to Israel Shatzman on his Jubilee*, ed. Joseph Geiger, Hannah M. Cotton and Guy D. Stiebel, Raanana, 2009, pp. 179–84; "*Civitas* and *Castellum* in the Latin Kingdom of Jerusalem: Contemporary Frankish Perceptions," *Burgen und Schlösser*, 50, 2009, pp. 199–210; (with Cyril Aslanov) "Problems in the Study of Trans-Cultural Borrowing in the Frankish Levant," in *Hybride Kulturen im mittelalterlichen Europa. Vorträge und Workshops einer internationalen Frühlingsschule*, ed Michael Borgolte and Bernd Schneidmüller, Berlin, 2010, pp. 277–85.

KOLIA-DERMITZAKI, Athina, "The Norman factor in the gradual alienation of East and West," in *The Fourth Crusade Revisited, Atti della Conferenza Internazionale nell'ottavo centenario della IV Crociata (Andros, 27–30 maggio 2004)*, Citta del Vaticano: Pontifico Comitato di Scienze Storiche, atti e Documenti 25, 2008, pp. 32–53; "Pillage and transfer of cultural wealth to the West," in *The Fourth Crusade and the Greek World*, ed. N. Moschonas, Athens: The National Hellenic Research Foundation-Institute for Byzantine Research, Byzantium Today 5, 2008, pp. 299–326 [in Greek]; "The Image of the Bulgarians in the Byzantine sources of the 11th and the 12th centuries," in *Byzantium and the Bulgarians (1018–1185)*, ed. K. Nikolaou-K. Tsiknakis, Athens: The National Hellenic Research Foundation-Institute for Byzantine Research, Intenational Symposium 18, 2008, pp. 59–89 [in Greek].

KOSTICK, Conor, *The Crusades and the Near East: Cultural Studies* (London: Routledge, 2010), editor, 262 pp.; *Medieval Italy, Medieval and Early Modern Women: Essays in Honour of Christine Meek*, Dublin, Four Courts, 2010, editor, 270 pp.; "Eleanor of Aquitaine and the women of the Second Crusade," ibidem, pp. 195–205; "Social Unrest and the Failure of Conrad III's March Through Anatolia," *German History, 28.2, 2010*, pp. 125–42; "God's Bounty: Providing for Crusaders 1096–1148," *Studies in Church History, 46, 2010, pp. 66–77*. Reviews: Jonathan Riley-Smith, *Crusaders and Settlers in the Latin East, Journal of Military History*, 73.4, 2009, pp. 1310–1311; Jean-François Nieus, Le Vassal, Le Fief et L'Écrit, *Speculum*, 2009, 84 (4), pp. 1093–94.

LAMBERT, Malcolm David, *Christians and Pagans. The Conversion of Britain from Alban to Bede*, Yale UP, 2010.

LAPINA, Elizabeth, "St. Demetrius of Thessaloniki: Patron Saint of Crusaders," *Viator: Medieval and Renaissance Studies*, 40, 2009, pp. 93–112.

LIGATO, Giuseppe, "L'araldica dell'impero latino di Costantinopoli in un brano della biografia dell'imperatore Enrico I scritta da Enrico di Valenciennes," testo presentato al convegno su Bonifacio di Monferrato (Acqui Terme, 8 settembre 2007), ed. R. Maestri, Genova, 2009, pp. 58–79; "Un cattivo consigliere: Gerardo de Ridefort, «magister» templare," in *Studi per Franco Cardini*.

※ LOWER, Michael, "Louis IX, Charles of Anjou, and the Tunis Crusade of 1270," in *The Crusades: Medieval Worlds in Conflict*, ed. Thomas F. Madden, James L. Naus and Vincent Ryan, Farnham, Ashgate, 2011, pp. 173–93; "Urban II's Call to Crusades," in *Milestone Documents of World History: Exploring the Primary Sources that shaped the World*, ed. B. Bonhomme, Dallas, Schlager Press, 2010, 2, pp. 497–512.

MADDEN, Thomas F., "Crusades" in *The Oxford Dictionary of the Middle Ages*, Oxford, Oxford University Press, 2010.

MARVIN, Laurence W., Following entries in *Medieval Warfare and Military Technology: An Encyclopedia*, ed. Clifford J. Rogers, Oxford University Press, 2010: "Annales Gandenses," I, pp. 48–49; "Bruges, Siege of (1127)," I, pp. 258–59; "Carcassonne, Siege of (1209)," I, pp. 326–27;, "Castelnaudary, Siege and Battle of (1211)," I, pp. 334–35; "Château-Gaillard, Siege of (1203, Sept.–March 1204)," I, pp. 370–71; "Galbert of Bruges," II, pp. 145–46; "Logistic and Transporetation," II, pp. 513–17;,"Monségur, Siege of (1243)," III, pp. 29–30; "Muret, Battle of (1213)," III, pp. 36–37; "Rouen, Siege of (1204)," III, p. 302; "Simon IV de Montfort," III, pp. 24–25; "Termes, Siege of (1210)," III, pp. 347–48; "Thielt, Battle of (1128, 21 June)," III, p. 355.

MAYER, Hans Eberhard, "Reinhold Röhricht (1842–1905)," in *Schlesische Lebensbilder*, 10, Insingen, 2010, pp. 151–57; "Eid und Handschlag bei den Kreuzfahrerkönigen von Jerusalem," *Mitteilungen des Instituts für österreichische Geschichtsforschung*, 118, 2010, pp. 61–81; ed., *Die Urkunden der lateinischen Könige von Jerusalem*. Altfranzösiche erstellt von Jean Richard, Monumenta Germaniae Historica. Diplomata, Hannover, Hahnsche Buchhandlung, 2010, 4 vol. 1812 p.

MENACHE, Sophia, "Orality in Chronicles: Texts and Historical Contexts," in *Homo Legens*, Turnhout, Brepols, 2009, pp. 161–93 (Russian version in *Odysseus: Man in History*, 2009); "Iglesia y Monarquia en la Edad Media Tardia: Conflictos y Semejanzas," *Acta Mediaevalia Historica et Archaeologica*, 29, 2008, pp. 497–516; "Love of God or Hatred your Enemy? The Emotional Voices of the Crusades" [O amor de Deus ou ódio ao seu inimigo? As vozes emocionais das Cruzadas], *Mirabilia*, 10, 2010 [on line].

MINERVINI, Laura, "Le français dans l'Orient latin (XIIIᵉ–XIVᵉ siècles). Éléments pour la caractérisation d'une *scripta* du Levant," *Revue de Linguistique Romane*, 74, 2010, pp. 119–98; "Da Oriente a Occidente. Il Vecchio della Montagna nella tradizione epica," in *La tradizione epica e cavalleresca in Italia (XII–XVI sec.)*, ed. Claudio Gigante, Giovanni Palumbo, Bruxelles, P.I.E. Peter Lang, 2010, pp. 121–40; (with Chis Schabel), "The French and Latin Dossier on the Institution of the Government of Amaury of Lusignan, Lord of Tyre, brother of King Henry II of Cyprus," 34, 2008, pp. 75–119.

MITCHELL, Piers D., "Military Medicine," in *Oxford Dictionary of the Middle Ages*, ed. R. E.

Bjork, Oxford, Oxford University Press, 2010, vol. 3, pp. 1142–43; "Disease," in *Medieval Warfare and Military Technology: an Encyclopedia*, ed. C. Rogers, Oxford: Oxford University Press 2010 vol. 1, pp. 540–5411; "Military Medicine: Medical treatment," ibidem, vol. 2, pp. 585–89.

MORTON, Nicholas, "Institutional Dependency upon Secular and Ecclesiastical Patrons, and the Foundations of the Trial of the Templars," in DTT, pp. 49–68; "The Defense of the Holy Land and the memory of the Maccabees," *Journal of Medieval History*, 36/3, 2010, pp. 275–93.

NICHOLSON, Helen, *A Brief History of the Knights Templar*, London, Constable and Robinson, 2010, xvi–351 pp. (new edition of *The Knights Templar: A New History*, first published 2001); edition with J. Burgtorf and P. Crawford, of DTT, including H. J. Nicholson, "The Trial of the Templars in Ireland," pp. 225–235; "At the Heart of Medieval London: The New Temple in the Middle Ages" in *The Temple Church in London: History, Architecture, Art*, ed. Robin Griffith-Jones and David Park, Woodbridge: Boydell, 2010, pp. 1–18; "The changing face of the Templars: current trends in historiography," *History Compass*, 8/7, 2010, pp. 653–67 [online journal]; "The Crusades," "Hospitallers and their Theology," "Military Orders," "Teutonic Knights," in *Cambridge Dictionary of Christianity*, ed. Daniel M. Patte, Cambridge University Press, 2010; "Military Saints," "Knighthood and Knights," "Military theory," "Noncombatants in armies," and "Military Plans" in *The Encyclopedia of Medieval Warfare and Military Technology*, ed. Clifford Rogers, Oxford University Press, 2010, vol. 2, pp. 468–70; vol. 3, pp. 65–66, 128–29, 211–12, 351–52.

NICOLAOU-KONNARI, Angel, "Anonymous Short Chronicle of Cyprus [*Chronica delli Re, et successi del Regno di Cipro di Gallico in Italiano tradutta*]," in R. G. Dunphy, ed., *Encyclopedia of the Medieval Chronicle*, Leiden-Boston, Brill, 2010, pp. 101–102; "Boustronios, Georgios," ibidem, p. 196; "Chronique de Terre Sainte," ibid., pp. 434–35; "*Gestes des Chiprois*," ibid., p. 703; "Machairas, Leontios," ibid., pp. 1054–55; "Neophytos o Enkleistos," ibid., p. 1139; Review: D. Coulon, C. Otten-Froux, P. Pagès, D. Valérian, ed., *Chemins d'outre-mer. Études d'histoire sur la Méditerranée médiévale offertes à Michel Balard*, I–II, Byzantina Sorbonensia, 20, Paris, Publications de la Sorbonne 2004, *Jahrbuch der Österreichischen Byzantinistik*, 59, 2009, pp. 259–60.

PASTORI RAMOS, Aurelio, "La Segunda Cruzada y su fracaso en De Consideratione ad Eugenium Papam de Bernardo de Claraval," in Almuneda Blasco Vallès, e Ricardo da Costa, coord., *Mirabilia*, 10, *A Idade Média e as Cruzadas. La Edad Media y las Cruzadas – The Middle Ages and the Crusades*, Jan–Jun 2010, http://www.revistamirabilia.com/.

PAVIOT, Jacques, "L'idée de croisade à la fin du Moyen Âge," in *Académie des Inscriptions et Belles-Lettres, Comptes rendus des séances de l'année 2009*, Paris, Diffusion De Boccard, 2009, pp. 865–75.

PERRA, Photeine V., "The transition from Hospitaller to Ottoman Rhodes: A note on the information by Piri Reis and Ewliya Chelebi," *Domus Byzantinus*, 16, 2007 [Greek]; "Relations between the Knight Hospitallers of Rhodes and Venice during the First Venetian–Ottoman war (1463–1479)," *Byzantiaka*, 27, 2008 [Greek]; "Review essay a propos of a new Prosopographical Lexicon of Byzantine History and Civilization," *Byzantion*, 78, 2008.

PHILLIPS, Jonathan, *Une histoire moderne des croisades*, Paris, Flammarion, 2010.

PHILLIPS, Simon D., "The Hospitallers' Acquisition of the Templar Lands in England," in DTT, pp. 237–46.

PIANA, Mathias, "From Montpèlerin to Tarabulus al-Mustajadda: The Frankish-Mamluk Succession in Old Tripoli," in *Egypt and Syria in the Fatimid, Ayyubid and Mamluk Eras,*

VI, ed. Urbain Vermeulen, Kristof D'hulster, Orientalia Lovaniensia Analecta, 183, Leuven 2010, pp. 307–54.

PIMENTA, Maria Cristina, "Calatrava em Portugal: Notas para uma revisão da questão," in *Actas do I Congreso Internacional "El nacimiento de la Orden de Calatrava. Primeros tiempos de expansión: siglos XII y XIII*," Almagro: Ayuntamiento de Almagro y Instituto de Estudios Manchegos, 2009, pp. 189–204; "A cruzada e os objectivos fundacionais das Ordens Religioso-Militares em Portugal," *Revista Portuguesa de História*, 40, Coimbra, 2009, pp. 273–84 (in collaboration).

PINTO COSTA, Paula Maria, *Os forais de Pinhel*, Câmara Municipal de Pinhel, 2010. 143 pp.; *A presença dos Hospitalários em Portugal*. Gavião: Ramiro Leão, 2010, 80 pp.; "A cruzada e os objectivos fundacionais das Ordens Religioso-Militares em Portugal," *Revista Portuguesa de História*, 40, Coimbra, 2009, pp. 273–84 (in collaboration).

POLEJOWSKI, Karol, "Krzyżackie komendy we Francji w XV wieku – przyczynek do dziejoÅLw zakonu krzyżackiego pozaniemieckim obszarem językowym w poÅLźnym średniowieczu (Teutonic Order's commanderies in France in the XVth century)," in *Z dziejoÅLw średniowiecza. Pamięci Profesora Jana Powierskiego (1940–1999)*, Gdańsk 2010, pp. 257–74; "O ustanowieniu wspoÅLlnoty między Clairvaux a Oliwą w roku 1601 (The establishment of community between Clairvaux and Oliva in the year 1601)," *Zapiski Historyczne*, LXXV, 2010, part. 3, pp. 89–97; "Brugia, Londyn, Paryż – przyczynek do dyplomatycznej działalności burmistrza Elbląga Hartwiga Beteke (Bruges, London, Paris – contribution to the diplomatic activities of the Mayor of Elbing in the XIV century)," *Komunikaty Warmińsko-Mazurskie*, Olsztyn 2009, 266/4, pp. 517–23; "Kryzys krzyżackiej komendy Beauvoir we Francji pod koniec XIV wieku (The crisis of the Teutonic Order's commandery Beauvoir at the end of the XIVth century)," in *Pielgrzymi, pogorbowcy, prebendarze, Studia z DziejoÅLw Średniowiecza*, ed. B. Śliwiński, Malbork 2009, pp. 131–46.

PRINGLE, Denys, "Notes on Some Inscriptions from Crusader Acre," in I. Shagrir, R. Ellenblum and J. Riley-Smith, ed., *In Laudem Hierosolymitani: Studies in Crusades and Medieval Culture in Honour of Benjamin Z. Kedar*, Crusades-Subsidia, vol. 1, Ashgate: Aldershot, 2007, pp. 191–209; "Castellology in the Latin East: An Overview," *Château Gaillard: Études de Castellologie médiévale*, vol. 23. *Bilan de recherches en castellologie. Actes du Colloque international de Houffalize (Belgique), 4–10 septembre 2006*, Caen, CRAHM, 2008, pp. 361–77; "Belmont Castle (Suba)," in *The New Encyclopedia of Archaeological Excavations in the Holy Land*, ed. E. Stern, 5: *Supplementary Volume*, ed. E. Stern, H. Geva and A. Paris, Israel Exploration Society: Jerusalem/Biblical Archaeology Society, Washington DC, 2008, pp. 1602–604; "Burj al-Aḥmar (The Red Tower)," ibidem, pp. 1654–55; *An Expatriate Community in Tunis, 1648–1885: St George's Protestant Cemetery and its Inscriptions*, Cardiff Studies in Archaeology/BAR International Series, vol. 1811, Oxford, 2008, x–178 pp, 75 pl., 7 fig., 5 tables; *The Churches of the Crusader Kingdom of Jerusalem: A Corpus*, 1. *A–K (excluding Acre and Jerusalem)*, paperback ed., Cambridge UP, 2008, xxiv–329 pp., 86 fig., CCVI pl.; with J. De Meulemeester, "Die Burgen am Golf von 'Aqaba," in M. Piana, ed., *Burgen und Städte der Kreuzzugzeit*, Petersberg, Michael Imhof Verlag, 2008, pp. 148–58, and "Die Burg Kerak (al-Karak) in Jordanien," ibid., pp. 336–42; "Aqaba Castle in the Ottoman Period, 1517–1917," in A. C. S. Peacock, ed., *The Frontiers of the Ottoman World*, *Proceedings of the British Academy*, 156, 2009, pp. 95–112, 10 fig.; *Secular Buildings in the Crusader Kingdom of Jerusalem: An Archaeological Gazetteer*, paperback ed., Cambridge UP, 2009, xx + 159 pp., CXIII pl., 62 fig., 10 maps.; *The Churches of the Crusader Kingdom of Jerusalem: A Corpus*, vol. 2. *L–Z (excluding Tyre)*, paperback edition, Cambridge UP,

2009, xxiv–456 pp., CCIII pl., 107 fig., 10 maps; *The Churches of the Crusader Kingdom of Jerusalem: A Corpus*, vol. 4. *The Cities of Acre and Tyre, together with Addenda and Corrigenda to Vols. 1–3*. Cambridge University Press; Cambridge 2009. [xviii + 321 pp., CXLVIII, pls., 27 fig.; [with B. Z. Kedar], "1099–1187: The Lord's Temple (*Templum Domini*) and Solomon's Palace (*Palatium Salomonis*)," in O. Grabar and B. Z. Kedar, ed., *Where Heaven and Earth Meet: Jerusalem's Sacred Esplanade*, Yad Izhak Ben-Zvi Institute: Jerusalem /University of Texas Press: Austin, 2009, pp. 132–49, 398–99; "Perceptions of the Castle in the Latin East," *Château Gaillard: Études de castellollogie médiévale*, 24: *Château et représentations. Actes du colloque international de Stirling (Écosse), 30 août–5 septembre 2008*, Caen, CRAHM, 2010, pp. 223–29.

PUJEAU, Emmanuelle, "Enjeux autour du latin dans l'Italie du seizième siècle, in *Actes du R.E.M. Le livre dans la région toulousaine et ailleurs au Moyen Age*, Toulouse, Méridiennes, 2010, pp. 135–49.

PURKIS, William J., "Eleventh- and Twelfth-Century Perspectives on State-Building in the Iberian Peninsula," *Reading Medieval Studies*, 36, 2010, pp. 57–75.

RICHARD, Jean, "Le royaume de Chypre face aux projets de croisade," *Comptes rendus de l'Académie des Inscriptions et Belles Lettres*, 2009, pp. 858–63; "Les familles féodales franques dans le comté de Tripoli," in *Le comté de Tripoli, État multiculturel et multiconfessionnel*, ed. G. Dédéyan et K. Rizk, Paris, 2010, pp. 7–30; "Papacy and the King of Cyprus," in *Bullarium Cyprium*, ed. Ch. Schabel, Nicosia, 2010.

RIST, Rebecca, "Introduction: Crusading and State Building in the Central Middle Ages," ✳ *Reading Medieval Studies*, 36, 2010, pp. 1–6; "Salvation and the Albigensian Crusade: Pope Innocent III and the Plenary Indulgence," ibidem, pp. 95–112.

SARNOWSKY, Juergen, *Die Templer*, Munich; Beck, 2009, 128 pp.; editor, with Roman Czaja, "Die Rolle der Schriftlichkeit in den geistlichen Ritterorden des Mittelalters: innere Organisation, Sozialstruktur, Politik," *Ordines militares – Colloquia Torunensia Historica*, XV, Toruń, UMK, 2009, 307 pp.; "Dominikaner und Franziskaner im Ordensland Preußen," in *Franciscan Organisation in the Mendicant Context*, ed. Michael Robson, Jens Röhrkasten, Vita regularis, 44, Berlin-Münster, LIT, 2010, pp. 43–64.

SINIBALDI, Micaela, "Villages of Crusader Transjordan: a survey of archaeological sources," *Bulletin of Council for British Research in the Levant*, 2010, pp. 60–63.

STANTCHEV, Stefan, "*Devedo*: the Venetian Response to Sultan Mehmed II in the Venetian–Ottoman Conflict of 1462–79," *Mediterranean Studies*, 19, 2010, pp. 43–66.

TAMMINEN, Miikka, "A Test of Friendship. *Amicitia* in the Crusade Ideology of the Thirteenth Century," in: Krötzl, C. and Mustakallio, K., ed., *De Amicitia. Friendship and Society in Antiquity and the Middle Ages*, Acta Instituti Romani Finlandiae, 36, Roma 2010, pp. 213–29.

TEBRUCK, Stefan, "Landesherrschaft – Adliges Selbstverständnis – Höfische Kultur. Die Ludowinger in der Forschung," in *Wartburg-Jahrbuch*, 2008, Regensburg 2010, pp. 30–77.

TESSERA, Miriam Rita, *Orientalis ecclesia. Papato, Chiesa e regno latino di Gerusalemme (1099–1187)*, Milano, Vita and Pensiero, 2010, x–660 pp.; "Orientalis Ecclesia: The Papal Schism of 1130 and the Latin Church of the Crusader States," *Crusades*, 9, 2010, pp. 1–12.

THROOP, Susanna, ed. with Paul Hyams, *Vengeance in the Middle Ages: Emotion, Religion and Feud*, Farnham, Ashgate, 2010, 232 p., including "Zeal, Anger and Vengeance: The Emotional Rhetoric of Crusading," pp. 177–201.

TYERMAN, Christopher, "Court, Crusade and City: The Cultural Milieu of Louis I, duke of

Bourbon," in *Soldiers, Nobles and Gentlemen: Essays in honor of Maurice Keen*, ed. P. Coss
and C. Tyerman, Woodbridge, Boydell Press, pp. 49–63.

VAN, Theresa, "'Our father has won a great victory': the authorship of Berenguela's account
of the battle of Las Navas de Tolosa, 1212," *Journal of Medieval Iberian Studies*, 3, 2011,
pp. 79–92; "The Assimilation of Templar Properties by the Order of the Hospital," in DTT,
pp. 339–46.

2. Recently completed theses

ABDALLA, Amer Ahmed, *Spain's Policy towards Western Islamic Countries (1492–1574
A.D)*, PhD, University of Alexandria, supervised by Prof. Mahmoud Said Omran.

ATA-ALLAH, Heba Ibrahim, *Chronicle of Evagrius: Critical Historical Study (431–594 A.D)*,
MA, University of Alexandria, supervised by Prof. Mahmoud Said Omran

BREWER, Keagan, *Prester John: Belief in the Legend*, Honours level, University of Sydney
2009, supervised by John Pryor.

CARLSSON, Christer, *The Hospitaller Commanderies in Scandinavia 1291–1536. A Study
of their Economy based on Archaeological and Historical Material*, PhD, University of
Southern Denmark, Odense, February 2010.

CLAVERIE, Pierre-Vincent, *Honorius III et la question d'Orient (1216–1227)*, Habilitation
thesis, University de Rouen, December 2010.

DEAF, Mabroka Kamel, *William Marshal in England history (1170–1219 A.D)*, MA,
University of Alexandria, supervised by Prof. Mahmoud Said Omran.

LEWIS, Kevin James, *Novi Milites Christi et Nova Militia: An Assessment and Analysis of
the Relationship between the Cistercians and the Templars*, MA, Cardiff University, 2009,
supervised by Dr Helen Nicholson.

MENDONÇA, João Manuel M. Lamas da Silveira, *A Ordem de Avis revisitada (1515–1538).
Um alheado entardecer*, PhD Lusíada University, Lisbon, 2008, supervised by Luís Adão
da Fonseca.

PACKARD, Barbara, *Remembering the First Crusade: Latin Narrative Histories 1099–c.1300*,
PhD, Royal Holloway, University of London.

PETRE, James, *Crusader Castles of Cyprus: The Fortifications of Cyprus under the Lusignans:
1191–1489*, PhD, Cardiff University, 2010, supervised by Professor Denys Pringle.

PETROVSKAIA, Natalia I., *Echoes of the Crusades in Medieval Welsh Literary Texts*, MA,
University of Cambridge, 2008.

SEABRA, Maria Teresa da Silva Diaz de, *A comarca da Aldeia Galega do Ribatejo (séculos
XV e XVI)*, PhD Lusíada University, Lisbon, 2010, supervised by Luís Adão da Fonseca.

VANDEKERCKHOVE, Dweezil, *Politieke grenzen, geografie en hun invloed op de verspreiding
van Frankische fortificaties in het Heilig Land, 1097–1193 Casestudie Ascalon*, Universiteit
Gent, 2008, 128; Analyse van het Russisch Buitenlands beleid ten aanzien van Georgië:
spanningsveld tussen retoriek en praktijk?, Universiteit Antwerpen, 2010, 77.

ZANATY, Galal Zanaty, *The Kingdom of Castille – Leon during the Reign of King Alfonso
VI (1065–1109 A.D)*, MA, University of Alexandria, supervised by Prof. Mahmoud Said
Omran.

3. Papers read by members of the Society and others

AMITAI, Reuven, "The Impact of the Mongols on the History of Syria: Short-term Effects and the *longue duree*," at: the Burdick-Vary Symposium *The Mongol World Empire and Its World*, Institute for the Research in the Humanities, University of Wisconsin-Madison, 9–10 April 2010, "Continuity and Change in the Mongol Army of the Ilkhanate," at: the Third World Congress of Middle Eastern Studies, Barcelona, 12–16 July 2010; "From a Nameless Officer Class to Identified Officers· The Mamluks in Palestine as seen from the Epigraphic Evidence," at: Deutsche Orientalistentagung, Marburg, 21 September 2010.

ANTAKI-MASSON, Patricia, "Archéologie, étude du bâti et patrimoine mobilier," "Ora est hora: un cadran solaire au monastère Notre Dame de Balamand," "Un legs des tailleurs de pierre de Belmont: que nous révèlent les marques lapidaires?" at: the seminar *Le monastère Notre Dame de Balamand*, Balamand university (Lebanon), December 2010

BALARD, Michel, "Les migrants génois vers l'Outre-mer, acteurs des transferts culturels," at: Colloque de l'Institut historique allemand de Paris, January 2010; "La garnison de Famagouste au XVe siècle," at: Université de Toulouse le Mirail, March 2010; "Les Génois dans l'empire byzantin," at: Université de Lodz, May 2010; "The Black Sea in the international Trade," at: Université de Cracovie, May 2010.

BALLETTO, Laura, "Economia e commercio a Cipro nel periodo Genovese," at: Medieval Famagusta. Workshop in memory of A. H. S. "Peter" Megav, Nicosia, 25–26 ottobre 2008; "1449–1450: la schiavitù nella Chio dei Genovesi a metà del secolo XV (dagli atti dei notai Tommaso di Recco e Bernardo de Ferrariis)," at: *Slavery and the Slave Trade in the Eastern Mediterranean 11th to 15th centuries*, Universität Trier, 7–9 September 2009.

BELLOMO, Elena, "Templari, Oriente e Crociata: percorsi di ricerca in Italia settentrionale," at: *Freires, Guerreiros, Cavaleiros. VI Encontro sobre Ordens Militares*, Palmela, 2010; "Il Tempio e l'Ospedale nell'Italia centro-settentrionale," at: *Les Ordres religieux militaires dans la ville medievale. 1150–1350*, Clermont, 23–26 May 2010; "Islands as strongholds for the defense of Christendom: The case of the Order of Our Lady of Betlehem," at: Islands and the Military Orders, Rhodes, 28–29 April 2011.

BERKOVICH, Ilya, "The Death of Marquis Conrad of Montferrat in Medieval English Historiography," IMC Leeds, 12–15 July 2010.

BISAHA, Nancy, "Borders, Boundaries, and Peoples in Aeneas Silvius Piccolomini's De Europa," at: Renaissance Society of America Conference, Venice, 10 April 2010; "'Inventing Europe' with Aeneas Silvius Piccolomini," at: *Images of Other in Medieval and Early Modern Times*, University of Heidelberg, 18 June 2010.

BISHOP, Adam, "William the Carpenter and the usefulness of the Internet," Second International Symposium on Crusade Studies, 17–20 February 2010.

BOAS, Adrian J., "*New Archaeological Evidence for the Headquarters of the Teutonic Order at Acre and Montfort Castle*," Australian and New Zealand Association for Medieval and Early Modern Studies (ANZAMEMS), Dunedin, New Zealand January 2011.

BOMBI, Barbara, "The papacy and the Teutonic Order," at: Palmela 2010; "The Papacy and Preaching to Non-Christians after the Fourth Lateran Council," IMC Leeds, 2010.

BURGTORF, Jochen, "The Templars on Ruad, 1300–1302," at: IMC Kalamazoo, 2010.

BUTTIGIEG, Emanuel, "The Hospitaller Knights of Malta and their service to the 'poor sick of Christ', c.1580–c.1700," part of a panel entitled "Praying for health in and out of the early modern hospital," the Renaissance Society of America (RSA) Annual Meeting, Venice, 8–10 April 2010.

CARLSSON, Christer, "Scandinavian Hospitallers as Travellers in Medieval Europe," at: IMC, Leeds, 2010; "The Hospitalller Commanderies in Scandinavia 1291–1536. An Archaeological Perspective," at: Institute for Historical Research, University of London, 18 October 2010.

CARRAZ, Damien, "Le Temple et l'Hôpital sur les chemins de Compostelle," at: Commanderie d'Auzon, 23 october 2010; "Templars and Hospitallers in the Cities of the West and the Latin East (Twelfth to Thirteenth Centuries)," at: Lisboa, Universidade nova, 4 november 2010; Discussion of the "Teilprojekt: Stadtklöster im Dialog. Urbane Topographie, religiöse Kultur und kommunikative Praxis im Umfeld städtischer Klöster und Konvente in Frankreich," at: *Städtische Kulturen und Topographien im Mittelalter*, Internationale Jahrestagung des Forums Mittelalter der Universität Regensburg, 19 November 2010.

CARRIER, Marc, "Les *Gesta Francorum et aliorum Hierosolimitanorum* ont-ils servi d'ouvrage de propagande pour Bohémond de Tarente au lendemain de la première croisade?" at: *Congress 2010 of the Humanities and Social Sciences: Connected Understanding / Savoir branché*, Concordia University, 30 May 2010; "L'image ambivalente de l'Autre chrétien dans l'*Historia Ierosolimitana* du chanoine Albert d'Aix," at: *'Disputatio Montis Regalis', IXᵉ Colloque de la Société des études médiévales du Québec*, Université de Montréal, 16 April 2010.

CASSIDY-WELCH, Megan, "Refugees in historical context," opening address, *Refugees, History and Human Rights symposium*, State Library of Victoria, Melbourne, Australia, 2010; "Displacement and memory after the Albigensian Crusade," at: Centre for Medieval Studies, University of York, U.K., Feb. 2010; "Images of Loss in Medieval Refugee Narratives," at: Australian and New Zealand Association for Medieval and Early Modern Studies Conference, Dunedin, New Zealand, Feb. 2011.

CHRISSIS, Nikolaos, "New frontiers: Frankish Greece and the expansion of crusading in the early thirteenth century," at: *Contact and Conflict in Frankish Greece and the Aegean: Crusade, Trade and Religion amongst Latins, Greeks and Muslims, 1204–1453*, Institute of Historical Research, London, 9 July 2010; "Charles of Anjou's anti-Byzantine 'crusade' (1267–1282): a re-examination," at: 43rd Spring Symposium of Byzantine Studies, Birmingham, 27–29 March 2010.

CHRIST, Georg, Plenartagung des DFG Schwerpunktprogramms 1173 *Integration und Desintegration der Kulturen im europäischen Mittelalter*, http://www.spp1173.uni-hd.de/, in Mühlheim an der Ruhr "Eine Stadt wandert aus. Kollaps und Kontinuität in Alexandria im Spätmittelalter," July 2010.

CHRISTIE, Niall, "Fighting on Earth to Gain Heaven: The 'Vision of Paradise' Motif in the *Kitab al-Jihad* of 'Ali ibn Tahir al-Sulami (d. 1106)," at: 39th Medieval Workshop (Quest and Conquest: Spiritual Symbols and Myths in the Indo-Mediterranean and European Worlds), University of British Columbia, Vancouver, Canada, October 2010; "A New/Old Source on the Muslim Response to the Crusades: The *Kitab al-Jihad* of 'Ali ibn Tahir al-Sulami (d. 1106)," at: 25th Congress of the Union Européenne des Arabisants et Islamisants, Naples, Italy, September 2010; "Noble Betrayers of their Faith, Families and Folk: Some Frankish Women in the Arabian Nights," 17th International Medieval Congress, University of Leeds, England, July 2010; "Editing and Translating the Book of the *Jihad* of 'Ali ibn Tahir al-Sulami (d. 1106): A Final Report," at: *Crusades: Medieval Worlds in Conflict*, Second International Symposium on Crusade Studies, Saint Louis University, Saint Louis, U.S.A., February 2010.

CHRISTOFORAKI, Ioanna, "From Byzantine Provence to Crusader Kingdom: Perspectives and

Reflections on the Art of Medieval Cyprus" at: Study Day "*Cyprus from Byzantium to the Renaissance*," Dumbarton Oaks, Washington D.C., 1 April 2011; "An unknown Cretan icon of St Martin of Tours in the Petit Palais Musuem, Paris" [in Greek] at the International Symposium *1400–1450: The artistic production in Constantinople, Venice and Crete*, Athens, Benaki Museum, 15–16 January 2011; "Saint Martin of Tours: From Roman Amiens to Venetian Crete" at Colloquium "*Espace sacré, mémoire sacrée: les saints-évêques et leurs villes*," Université François-Rabelais, Centre de Recherche sur les mondes anciens, l'histoire des villes et l'alimentation (CeRMAHVA), Tours, France, 10–12 June 2010; "Franciscans on the Go: The Ashmolean Pieta in Context" at: 42nd Spring Symposium of Byzantine Studies, King's College London and Courtauld Institute of Art, 20–22 March 2009; "Images of the Other: Western Saints in Eastern Context": Lecture delivered at the Late Antique and Byzantine seminar of the Centre of Hellenic Studies, King's College, London, 17 March 2009; "Pelendri Revisited: Between the Narrative and the Symbolic" at: IVth International Congress of Cypriot Studies, Nicosia, 29 April–3 May 2008; "Memory and Identity: Effigial Tombstones and Funerary Plaques from Hospitaller Rhodes" at: Avignon SSCLE 7; "Lusignan Cyprus, Armenian Cilicia and the Holy Land: Artistic Interchange across Frontiers" at: International Conference on *Rough Cilicia: New Historical and Archaeological Approaches*, University of Lincoln, Nebraska, U.S.A., 24–27 October 2007.

CIPOLLONE, Giulio, "La distanza di Anselmo dal 'fervore' per la crociata. Un'obiezione di coscienza?" at: Congresso internazionale *La partecipazione di Anselmo al processo di costruzione della 'nuova'Europa*, Roma, Pontificia Università Gregoriana, 25–27 November 2010; "Il *signum* dei Trinitari. Al tempo di crociate e gihad: originalità iconografica e innovazione estetica," at: Congresso internazionale *Colori e significati. Una 'croce disarmata' tra crociata e gihad*, Roma, Pontificia Università Urbaniana, 26–28 Gennaio 2011.

CLAVERIE, Pierre-Vincent, "Les tribulations orientales du seigneur Gonfroy II de Marquise (1096–1138)," at: *19th Colloquium on the History of Egypt and Syria in the Fatimid, Ayyubid and Mamluk Eras (10th–15th centuries)*, Ghent University, 7 May 2010; "Some Considerations about the Relationship Tied between the Papacy and the Military Orders in the Middle Ages," at: Universidade Nova of Lisbon, 26 November 2010.

COSGROVE, Walker Reid, "Blood Simple: Re-contextualizing Pierre de Castelnau's Assassination," at: Western Society for French History, Lafayette, Louisiana, October 2010; "Intolerable Laxity: the Cistercian Bishops in southern France during the Albigensian Crusade," at: Crusades Studies Forum, Saint Louis, April 2010; "Assassination and Clerical Violence in Twelfth-Century Southern France," at: The Humanities Forum Conference, Saint Louis, April 2010.

COUREAS, Nicholas S., "The Use of the Arabic Language in Lusignan and Venetian Cyprus: 1200–1570," at: 19th HES, 5–7 May 2010; "Cultural Brokers at the Court of Cyprus," at: Cultural Brokers between Religions: Border-Crossers and Experts at Mediterranean Courts, Ruhr University, Bochum, 28–30 October 2010.

CRAWFORD, Paul F., "Did the Templars Lose the Holy Land? The Military Orders and the Defense of Acre, 1291," at: 21st International Congress of Historical Sciences, Amsterdam, 27 August 27, 2010, in session organized by the SSCLE; "The Hospitallers and the Trial of the Templars," at: IMC, Kalamazoo, 2010, in session organized by Western Michigan University: "Gregory VII and the Idea of a Military-Religious Order," at: 2nd International Symposium on Crusade Studies, St. Louis University, Missouri, 20 February 2010.

CUSHING, Dana, "The Atlantic Approach to the Crusades, 972–1197," at: Texas Medieval

Association Session, IMC, Kalamazoo, 2010; "The Qadi of Xelb (Silves) and the Third Crusade"; at: Society for Military History Annual Conference, Lexington VA, U.S.A.; "Identifying the Real Saviors of Acre 1191: A New Database Project," at: SSCLE Session 2/3, ICHS, 2010.

DICKSON, Gary, "Charisma, Medieval and Modern," at: Medieval History Resarch Seminar, University of Birmingham, England, 18 October 2010.

EDGINGTON, Susan, "Guido da Vigevano's *Regimen Sanitatis* and Attitudes to Old Age," at: The medieval medicine discussion group, Dept. History and Philosophy of Science, University of Cambridge, 10 May 2010; "The twelfth-century hospital of St John in Jerusalem," at: *Healing sites, public health and medical therapies: research in the history of medicine at the Open University*, London OU Regional Centre, 12 July 2010; "The capture of Acre, 1104, and Baldwin I's conquest of the littoral," at: ICHS, 2010.

FOLDA, Jaroslav, "Chrysography in Thirteenth-Century Painting: East and West," at: Graduate Art History Forum, Yale University, 15 April 2010; "Crusader Holy Places and Christian Multiculturalism in the Levant," at: Spanish National Research Council (CSIC)/Center for Humanities and Social Sciences (CCHS), Madrid, 11 October 2010; "Os Santos Lugares en Belén e Xerusalén no século XII," [in English], at: XIII Congreso Internacional de Estudos Xacobeos, Santiago de Compostela, Hostal dos Reis Católicos, 15 October 2010.

FONSECA, Luís Adão da, "A memória das Ordens Militares na Idade Média portuguesa: recordações populares e intencionalidade do poder," in Palmela, 2010; "The Hospital of St. John in the context of Medieval Military Orders," in IIIrd International Meeting "The Order of Malta, its historical reality and social projection," Santiago de Compostela, 2010.

FRANKE, Daniel, "Feeding the Fight: A Comparative Approach to East Anglian Participation in Late Plantagenet Warfare," at: IMC, Kalamazoo, May 2010; "England and the Crusade in the 'Long' Fourteenth Century: Lay Response and Impact," at: *The Crusades, Islam and Byzantium: An Interdisciplinary Workshop and Conference*, London, July 2011.

FRIEDMAN, Yvonne, "The Missing Link: Gestures and Peacemaking in the Medieval Latin East," at: Dumbarton Oaks Research Library, Byzantine forum, 20 October, 2010; "Trade and Peace-Inter-faith Commerce in Medieval Times: Culture, Norms and Negotiations," at: ESSHC (European Social Science History Conference), Ghent, 13–16 April, 2010; "Captives and Captivity," at: Van Leer Institute, Jerusalem, January 2010; "Why Make Peace? Rationales for Conflict Resolution and Treaty-Signing in the Medieval Latin East," at: *Crusades: Medieval Worlds in Conflict*, St. Louis University, 17–21 February 2011.

GABRIELE, Matthew, "The Pincer of Past and Future in the Early Middle Ages: Odo of Cluny and Adso of montier-en-der Confront the End," at: 125th Annual conference of the American Historical Association, Boston, January 2011; "Apocalyptic Language and violence in the 11th Century," Westfälische Wilhelms-Universität, Münster, June 2010; "The Language of Holy war in Contemporary American Discourse," and "Charlemagne, Jerusalem and Frankish Identity before the First Crusade," Westfälische Wilhelms-Universität, Münster, May 2010; "The Life of the Mind," University of Delaware, May 2010; "How did Crusading Cgange after 9/11?" Shenandoah Un iversity, April 2010; "The Rhetoric of Reconquest: Pope Urban II and the *Populus Christianus*," at: *Crusades: Medieval Worlds in Conflict*, 2nd Symposium on Crusade Studies, Saint Louis, February 2010.

GEORGIOU, Stavros G., "The Bishopric of Karpasia from its Foundation to the middle of the XIIIth Century," at: 1st Scientific Congress for Karpasia, Limassol, Cyprus, 4–5 April 2009; "Limassol during the proto-Christian and the Byzantine Period. The Saved Testimonies for the City and the local Church," at: 5th Scientific Conference of Oral History, Limassol of

Culture: Persons, facts, Phenomena and Institutions in its cultural History, Limassol, 27–29 November 2009.

GRASSO, Christian, "Ad promovendum negotium crucis: gestione finanziaria e promozione pubblica della crociata durante il pontificato di Onorio III (1216–1227)," at: Conference Zentralität: Papsttum und Orden im Europa des 12. und 13. Jahrhunderts., Centro di studi italo-tedesco di Villa Vigoni, Loveno di Menaggio, 16–19 July 2010; "Legati papali e predicatori della Quinta Crociata, Conference: Legati, delegati e l'impresa d'Oltremare," at: Università Cattolica di Milano, 9–11 March 2011.

VON GUETTNER, Darius, "Politics of the mission to the Prussians and the military orders" at: MO5, Cardiff, 3–6 September 2009; "Memorialisation and historical awareness – aspects of the witness' testimonies in the trials between Poland and the Teutonic Order in the fourteenth and fifteenth centuries," at: the Conference *The Trials of the Teutonic Order State with its Neighbours in 14th and 15th centuries: Political Thought and its Centres of Formation*, University of Toruń, 3–4 December 2009; "Gathering the Threads of Holy and Just War: The Conquest of Pomerania," at: the Australian Early Medieval Association Sixth Annual Conference – Gathering the Threads: Weaving The Early Medieval World, 30 September–2 October 2009, Monash University, Caulfield Campus, Victoria; "Mission to the Prussians and the attempts to establish a monastic state in Prussia," at: Fellows Research Day, School of Historical Studies, The University of Melbourne, 23 July 2009; "The Crusades: An academic view," Workshop at the History Teachers Association of Victoria State Conference, 23 October 2009, Melbourne.

HALL, Martin, "The evils of war unless it's a crusade: how John of Garland's *'De triumphis Ecclesiae'* (c. 1253) approaches conflicts of the day at a low point in Western morale" at: *Second International Symposium on Crusade Studies,* February 2010, University of Saint Louis; "An Englishman in Paris: A crusading view of the world from 1252/3," at: IMC Leeds, 2010.

HAMILTON, Bernard, "Medieval Western and Byzantine Views of the Southern Hemisphere," at: Research Seminar, School of History and Cultures, University of Birmingham, May 2010; "The Latin Empire and Western Contacts with Asia," at: International Conference *Contact and Conflict in Frankish Greece and the Aegean*, Institute of Historical Resarch, London, July 2010.

HOSLER, John D., "Military Perspective in the Writigs of John of Salisbury," at: Annual Meeting of the North American Conference on British Studies, Baltimore, MD, 2010; "Identifying King Stephen's Artillery," at: *Trebuchet to Cannon: Military Technology 1000–1600*, Danish medieval Centre, Nykøbing, 2010; "Why didn't King Stephen Crusade ?" at: IMC Leeds, 2010; "The War Councils of Louis VII," at: IMC Kalamazoo, 2010.

JACKSON, Peter, "'It is as if their aim were the extermination of the species': The Mongol devastation in Western Asia in the first half of the thirteenth century," at: Symposium on *The Mongol Empire and Its World*, University of Madison, Wisconsin, 9–10 April 2010.

JOSSERAND, Philippe, "Las cruzadas de Tierra Santa y las órdenes militares en las crónicas reales latinas de Castilla y León (siglos XII–XIII)," at: *Reconquista y cruzada en la España medieval*, dir. Carlos de Ayala Martínez et Feliciano Novoa Portela, Madrid, 22–30 November, 2010; "Le procès des Templiers dans le royaume de Castille," at: Journées internationales d'études de Montpellier, dir. Marie-Anna Chevalier, 28 January 2011.

JOTISCHKY, Andrew, "St Katherine, Sinai and devotions to saints on the 'Norman Edge'," at: Centre for Byzantine, Ottoman and Modern Greek Studies, University of Birmingham, January 2011.

Kedar, Benjamin Z., "Muslime in den fränkischen Burgen des Königreichs Jerusale," at: the conference on *Die Kreuzfahrerburgen als Zeugnisse historischer und kultureller Wechselbeziehungen zwischen Okzident und Orient im Mittelalter*, Marksburg / Braubach, Germany, 24–26 September 2010; "On writing the History of the Temple Mount/al-Haram al-Sharif," at: Symposium on the book *Where Heaven and Earth Meet*, University of Wisconsin-Madison, 28 September 2010; "The Attempt of 1234 to turn Haifa into a Genoese Emporium," at: Conference on *The Italian Presence in Acre and the Holy Land. Contacts and Trade in the Mediterranean during the Crusader Period*, Haifa, 21 October 2010; "On Books and Hermits in Twelfth-Century Nazareth," at: *International conference on Nazareth: Archaeology, History and Cultural Heritage*, Nazareth, 21–24 November 2010.

Lapina, Elizabeth,"The Origins of the Narrative of the Miracle of Intervention of Saints in the Battle of Antioch," at: *Connected Understanding*, Congress of the Humanities and Social Sciences, Concordia University, Montreal, May 2010.

Ligato, Giuseppe, "Un documento della letteratura cavalleresca caro a Carducci: l 'Epistola epica' di Rambaldo de Vaqueiras," at: *Carducci e il Monferrato*, Giornata di studio, Bologna, 17 october 2009; "'Uomo a terra!' Il disarcionamento del 'miles' medievale nella tattica e nella mentalità cavalleresche," at: *Cavalli e cavalieri. Guerra, gioco, finzione,* Convegno internazionale del Centro Europeo di Studi sulla Civiltà Cavalleresca, Certaldo, 16–18 september 2010; "La crociata a Damietta tra legato papale, profezie e strategie, at: *San Francesco e il sultano*, Firenze, 25 september 2010; "Il drago nel mosaico di Bobbio: transizione di un simbolo dall'Europa romanobarbarica al movimento crociato," at: *Pellegrinaggi e monachesimo celtico. Dall'Irlanda alle sponde del Mediterraneo*, Genova, 14 ottobre 2010.

Lower, Michael, "Christian Mercenaries and Missionaries in Thirteenth-Century North Africa," at: Second Crusades Symposium, Saint Louis University, 20 February 2010; "The Papacy and the European Mercenaries of North Africa," at: American Historical Association Annual Meeting, San Diego, 8 January 2010.

Madden, Thomas F., "Streets of Blood: The Crusader Conquest of Jerusalem in 1099," invited Plenary Lecture, *Blood: Dynasty, Sacrament, Sacrifice*: A Symposium sponsored by the Claremont All-College Consortium for Medieval and Early Modern Studies, Claremont Graduate University, 27 February, 2010; "The Crusades on Trial: Medieval History vs. Modern Myths," The Inaugural Stan and Debbie Crader Endowed Lecture, Southeast Missouri State University, 12 November, 2009.

Marvin, Laurence W., "King Louis VII on Mount Cadmus during the Second Crusade: A Failure of Leadership?" Symposium on Crusades Studies, *Medieval Worlds in Conflict*, Saint Louis University, 20 February 2010.

Menache, Sophia, "Stereotypes, gender, and Politics: Isabelle of France, Queen of England," at: Cambridge International Chronicles Symposium, 2010; "Universities and the Culture of Peace," at: *For a New Culture of Peace and Development in the Middle East: The role of University Cooperation*, Rome, 2010.

Minervini, Laura, "The Construction of Frankish Identity in the Latin East: the *Tractatus de locis et statu terre sancte* (ca. 1170–1186)," at: the *World Congress for Middle Eastern Studies*, Barcelona, 19–24 July 2010.

Mitchell, Piers D., "Arnaldia and leonardie: illness suffered by kings on the Third Crusade," at: Institute of Historical Research, University of London, 25 January 2010; "Tapeworms and dysentery: intestinal parasitic diseases in the crusades and Historic Levant," International Congress of the Archaeology and the Ancient Near East, London, 12–13 April 2010;

"Medieval medical care in the crusades: stereotypes and reality," at: Symposium *Dancing with Death: Warfare, Wounds and Disease in the Middle Ages*, California University of Pennsylvania, U.S.A., 20–22 October 2010.

MYLOD, Liz, "Pilgrim Descriptions of Jerusalem in the Thirteenth Century," at: the London Medieval Society Symposium, November 2009; "Christian Pilgrimage outside Christendom?: European Travellers in the Holy Land in the Thirteenth Century," at: IMC Kalamazoo 2010; "Routes to Salvation: Travelling through the Holy Land in the 13th Century," at: IMC Leeds 2010.

NICHOLSON, Helen J., "The trial of the Templars in the British Isles," at: Crusades Seminar, Hertford College, University of Oxford, 28 January 2010; "Charity and Hospitality in the Military Orders," at: Palmela, 2010; "The military religious orders in the towns of the British Isles" at: *Les ordres militaires dans la ville*, Clermont-Ferrand, France, 27 May 2010; "The Military Orders in Wales," at: the Welsh History Society, University of Cardiff, 2 March 2010; "Images of the Military Orders," at: Instituto de Estudos Medievais of the Universitade Novo de Lisboa, Ciclo de Conferências sobre ordens militares, 17 September 2010.

NICOLAOU-KONNARI, Angel; "Melodramatic Perceptions of History: Caterina Cornaro Goes to the Opera," *Cyprus and Venice in the Era of Caterina Cornaro*, International Conference in Commemoration of the Fifth Centenary of the Death of Caterina Cornaro, Institute for Interdisciplinary Cypriot Studies of the University of Münster, Venice, German Centre for Venetian Studies, 16–18 September 2010.

NIELSEN, Torben Kjersgaard, "The Fight for Soil and Souls – Warfare in Thirteenth Century Livonia," at: *Medieval Frontiers at War*, Cáceres, Spain, 9–11 November 2010.

OMRAN, Mahmoud Said, "The River Nile conquered The Crusaders," at: Second international symposium on Crusade studies, Saint Louis University, *Crusades Medieval World in Conflict*; "The Fall of Tarsus City (965 AD) according to Leo The Deacon," at: History Department Seminar, Faculty of Arts, Alexandria University, Egypt, 22 April 2010; "Egypt Monasticism's in The Book of Palladius (390–399)," at: First International Coptic Studies Conference, Biblotheca Alexandria, *Life in Egypt during The Coptic Period*, 21–23 September 2010; "The Seljuks in The English Source Book 1095–1176," at: First International Seljuk Symposium, 27–30 September 2010, Kayes, Turkey; "Religion's Policy or Policy of War Between Constantinople, Damascus and Bagdad," at: First International Conference *World od Islam History, Society and Culture*, University of Moscow and Mardijani Foundation, 28 – 30 October 2010.

ORDMAN, Jilana, "Feeling like a Crusader: Emotion as Evidence of Combatants' Motivations for Violence," at: Loyola University's 3rd Annual Interdisciplinary Research Symposium for Graduate Students and Alumni: New Approaches to Old Challenges, Chicago, 2010.

PARK, Danielle, "Preparation for departure on Crusade: regencies and the political ramifications of absent lords," IMC Leeds, 2010.

PHILLIPS, Christopher Matthew, "The Doctrine of Redemption in Crusade Preaching," at: Crusades symposium *Medieval Worlds in Conflict*, Saint Louis University, February 2010.

PHILLIPS, Jonathan, "The Legacy of Saladin from the Medieval to the Modern Age," at: Fifth Henry Loyn Memorial Lecture, Cardiff University, March 2010; "Saladin in the Medieval and Modern Memory," at: Radboud University, Nijmigen, November 2010; "Holy Warriors: Christian and Muslim Views of the Crusades," at: St Bonifatiuscollege, Utrecht, November 2011.

PHILLIPS, Simon D., 'The Hospitallers and Concepts of Island Existence' delivered at: *Islands and the Military Orders* symposium held on Rhodes, Greece, 27–29 April 2011.

PIANA, Mathias, "Monumentalization Trends in the Medieval Fortification Architecture of the Levant: Origins and Meanings," at: 19th HES, University of Gent, 5–7 May 2010; "Die Wehrarchitektur der Kreuzfahrer zwischen Tradition und Innovation: Die Frage nach Einflüssen und Wechselbeziehungen," at: *Ex Oriente. Die Kreuzfahrerburgen als Zeugnisse historischer und kultureller Wechselbeziehungen zwischen Okzident und Orient im Mittelalter*, Tagung des Europäischen Burgeninstituts der Deutschen Burgenvereinigung e.V., Marksburg, 24–26 September 2010.

PURKIS, William J., "Crusading in a Cistercian Monastery: Caesarius of Heisterbach's *Dialogus miraculorum*, at: *Crusades: Medieval Worlds in Conflict*, Saint Louis University, 20 February 2010; "Devotion to the Humanity and Passion of Christ in Early Crusading Spirituality," at: *Imitating, Becoming, Representing: Stigmata in Medieval and Early Modern Italy*, University of Manchester, 5 May 2010; "Memories and Constructions of Crusading in Caesarius of Heisterbach's *Dialogus miraculorum*," at: Exeter Medieval Seminar, Centre for Medieval Studies, University of Exeter, 18 May 2010; "Pluralism for Undergraduates," at: *Teaching the Crusades: Encountering the Other* – A Round Table Discussion, IMC Leeds, 13 July 2010.

REYNOLDS, Burnam W., "Mission War and the Prehistory of the Crusades," at: Second International Symposium on Crusade Studies, Saint Louis University, February 20, 2010; "Righting Ancient Wrongs: a Chapter in the Prehistory of the Crusades," at: IMC, Kalamazoo, 2010.

SHATZMILLER, Maya, "The medieval Mediterranean and Global Order: Islam, Money and Markets," at: *La presencia catalane a l'espai de trobada de la Mediterrania medieval: noves fonts, recerque i perspectives*, Barcelona, 13 May 2009; "From 'Iqtā to feudalism, or was it the other way around? A new interpretation of the economic history of Crusades in the Holy Land," at: IMC Kalamazoo, 2010.

SMITH, Thomas, "Re-evaluating the actions of the papal legate Pelagius on the Fifth Crusade," at: IMC Leeds, 2010.

STAPEL, Rombert, "Writing in the periphery: the Teutonic Order's history from the bailiwicks' standpoint," at: *Between Stability and Transformation. Textual Traditions in the Medieval Netherlands*, Ghent University, 21–22 September 2010.

TOKO, Hirofumi, "John Italos and the patriarchal clergy," at: 8th Annual Conference of Japan Association for Byzantine Studies, Kwansei Gakuin University, Nishinomiya, 28 March 2010; "The Byzantine hagiography in the post-Iconoclasm era," at: 61th Annual Conference of the Society of Historical Studies of Christianity, Miyagi Gakuin University, Sendai, 10 September 2010.

TOUATI, François-Olivier, "Au ban de la société? Regards sur les malades d'Orient et d'Occident au Moyen Âge," at: Troyes, Maison du Patrimoine, 4 février 2010; "De Jérusalem à Saint-Benoît-sur-Loire, et inversement: les *Gesta Dei Francorum* de Jacques Bongars, Hanovre, 1611," at: *Écrire l'histoire des croisades* (I), Journée d'étude (EMAM-SSCLE), Université de Tours, 19 March 2010; "Mahomet, Charlemagne et la Corse: les enjeux francs de la Méditerranée," at: *La Corse et l'Islam*, Journées universitaires d'Histoire corse, Bonifacio, 25 May 2010; "'Hors de la porte, là où le Christ a souffert pour sanctifier le peuple…'. Saint-Lazare de Jérusalem et l'espace urbain (Orient-Occident)," at: Colloque International *Les ordres religieux militaires dans la ville médiévale (1100–1350)*, Université de Clermont-Ferrand 2, 26–28 May 2010; "Justices en Méditerranée, vendetta, codes d'honneur et codes écrits: la législation du royaume de Jérusalem," at: *Les Rendez-vous de l'histoire*, Table-ronde, Blois, 15 October 2010; "L'iconographie du monnayage latin en Terre sainte au XIIe siècle: réflexions sur quelques types," Journée d'Étude, *Écrire l'histoire des croisades (II): La monnaie au Proche-Orient: numismatique et histoire*, Université François-Rabelais, EMAM, Tours, 18 mars 2011; "L'iconographie du monnayage latin en Terre sainte au XIIe siècle: réflexions sur quelques types," Journée d'Étude, *Écrire l'histoire des croisades (II): La monnaie au Proche-Orient: numismatique et histoire*, Université François-Rabelais, EMAM, Tours, 18 mars 2011; "Lepers and Leprosy: Connections between East and West in the Middle Ages," Key-Lecture, at: *Leprosy, Language and Identity in the Medieval World*, King's College, Cambridge, 12–13 avril 2011.

Weber, Benjamin, "Ethipians in Rome in the Fifteenth Century: to Visit the Schrines, Discuss the Union or Organize a Crusade?" at: IMC, Leeds, 2011.

4. Forthcoming publications

Ailes, Marianne, "Tolerated Otherness: The Unconverted Saracen in the *Chansons de geste*," in *Languages of Love and Hate*, ed. Helen Nicholson and Sarah Lambert, Brepols, 2011. Forthcoming in paperback: *The History of the Holy War: Ambroise's 'Estoire de la Guerre Sainte'*), translated Marianne Ailes, notes by Marianne Ailes and Malcolm Barber, xvi–214 pp. (original hardback: Boydell and Brewer: Woodbridge, 2003).

Alvira-Cabrer, Martin, "Después de Las Navas de Tolosa y antes de Bouvines. La batalla de Muret (1213) y sus consecuencias," *1212–1214: el trienio que hizo a Europa. XXXVII Semana de Estudios Medievales de Estella (19–23 de julio de 2010)*, Pamplona, Gobierno de Navarra [2011]; "*Combatir por Cristo*: los cruzados y el arte de la guerra," *Guerra y Paz en la Edad Media. IV Seminario Multidisciplinar del Departamento de Historia Medieval (Facultad de Geografía e Historia. Universidad Complutense de Madrid, 2—4 de marzo de 2010)*, Madrid, Sílex Ediciones [2011]; Aspects militaires de la Croisade", *Commémoration de la Croisade contre les Albigeois, 1209–2009*. Table ronde "Catharisme et croisade," Carcassonne, Conseil général de l'Aude [2010]; "Historiografía de la guerra medieval: la Corona de Aragón (siglos XI–XIII)," *Actas del I Symposium Internacional La Conducción de la Guerra (950–1350): Historiografía (Cáceres, 18–20 Noviembre 2008)*, Cáceres, Universidad de Extremadura [2010]; "Guerra y caballería: utopía y realidad," *Medievo Utópico. Sueños, ideales y utopías en el imaginario medieval. II Seminario Multidisciplinar del Departamento de Historia Medieval (Facultad de Geografía e Historia. Universidad Complutense de Madrid, 10–12 de marzo de 2008)*, coord. Martín Alvira Cabrer y Jorge Díaz Ibáñez, Madrid, Sílex Ediciones, [2010].

Amitai, Reuven, *Holy War and Rapprochement: Studies in the Relations between the Mamluk Sultanate and the Mongol Ilkhanate (1260–1335)*, Brepols; "Rashīd al-Dīn as an Historian of the Mamluks," in *Rashid al-Din, Agent and Mediator of Cultural Exchanges in Ilkhanid Iran*, ed. Anna Akasoy, Charles Burnett, and Ronit Yoeli-Tlalim, London, Warburg Institute; "Dealing with Reality: Early Mamluk Military Policy and the Allocation of Resources," in *Crossroads between Latin Europe and the Near East: Frankish Presence in the Eastern Mediterranean (12th to 14th Centuries)*, ed. Stefan Leder, Istanbuler Texte und Studien, 23, Würzburg: Ergon Verlag; "Between the Slave Trade and Diplomacy: Some Aspects of Early Mamluk Policy in the Eastern Mediterranean and the Black Sea," in *Slavery and the Slave Trade in the Eastern Mediterranean, 11th to 15th Centuries*, ed. Christoph Cluse and Reuven Amitai, Turnhout, Brepols.

Andrei, Filippo, ed., Ps.-Romualdus, *Glosula super Psalmos*, in *Corpus Christianorum Continuatio Mediaevalis*, Turnhout, Brepols; "Alberto di Aachen e la Chanson de Jérusalem," in *Romance Philology*, special issue: Romania Mediterranea, 2010.

ANTAKI-MASSON, Patricia, "Les marques lapidaires de l'abbaye de Belmont," "Les linteaux en bâtière: des marqueurs chronologiques," "L'heure de la prière au cadran canonial de l'abbaye de Belmont," Université de Balamand, 2011; "Les fortifications de Tyr à travers les sources médiévales," in *Tyr dans les textes antiques et médiévaux*, ed. J. Aliquot, P.-L. Gatier et L. Nordiguian, Beyrouth, Presses de l'Université Saint-Joseph, 2011.

ARBEL, Benjamin, "Aspects of Renaissance Studies, 1985–2005: A Survey of Three Periodicals and Some General Remarks," in G. Harlaftis, ed., *The New Ways of History: Developments in Historiography*, London & New York: Tauris Publishers, 2010; "The Triumph of the Mule in Sixteenth-Century Cyprus," *Proceedings of the Fourth International Congress of Cypriot Studies*, Nicosia, Society for Cypriot Studies; "Venise et la conquête ottomane de l'Etat mamelouk," in *La conquete ottomane de l'Egypte*, ed. Benjamin Lellouch and Michel Nicolas, Peeters, Leuven; "The Renaissance Transformation of Animal Meaning: From Petrarch to Montaigne", in Linda Kalof and Georgina Montgomery, ed, *Making Animal Meaning*, Michigan State University Press, East Lansing; "Translating the Orient for the Serenissima: Michiel Membrè in the Service of Sixteenth-Century Venice," in Albrech Fuess et Bernard Heyberger, ed., *La frontière méditeranéenne*, Centre d'Études Supérieures de la Renaissance, Tours; "The *Stato da Mar*," in E. Dursteller, ed., *A Handbook of Venetian History*, Leiden, Brill; "Venetian Famagust," in G. Grivaud and C. Schabel, *Medieval and Renaissance Famagusta*.

BALARD, Michel, *La Méditerranée au Moyen Age*, Paris: Hachette, 2011.

BALLETTO, Laura, "Geo Pistarino", Atti dell'Accademia Ligure di Scienze e Lettere, 2011; "Nuovi documenti su Pera genovese a metà del Trecento," Memorie dell'Accademia Lunigianese di Scienze "G. Capellini," 2011.

BARBER, Malcolm, ed. and trans., with K. Bate, *Letters from the East in the Twelfth and Thirteenth Centuries*, Crusade Texts in Translation, Aldershot: Ashgate, 2009.

BELLOMO, Elena, new Latin edition and translation into Italian of Caffaro, *Ystoria captionis Almarie et Turtuose*, *De liberatione civitatum Orientis Liber* and anonymous *Regni Ierosolimitani brevis hystoria*, in Caffaro, *Opere*, in collaboration with Antonio Placanica, Edizione Nazionale dei Testi Mediolatini, Società Internazionale per lo Studio del Medioevo Latino (SISMEL) [2011–2012]; "Scorci di un orizzonte mediterraneo: Genova e l'Oriente latino nella storiografia italiana (1951–2001)," in Runciman Conference; "Ordini monastico militari di origine iberica in Capitanata (secoli XIII–XIV)," in *Federico II e i cavalieri teutonici in Capitanata: recenti ricerche storiche e archeologiche. Atti del Convegno internazionale, Foggia-Lucera 10–13 giugno 2009*, ed. H. Huben, K. Toomaspeg; "Fulfilling a Mediterranean Vocation: The *Domus Sancte Marie Montis Gaudii de Jerusalem* in North-west Italy," in *Proceedings of the Conference of the Society for the Study of the Crusades and the Latin East, Avignon, 27th–31st August 2009*, ed. H. Nicholson, *Crusades. Subsidia*, Ashgate [2011]; "The Temple, the Hospital and the Towns of North and Central Italy: *Status Quaestionis* and Lines of Future Research," in *Les Ordres religieux militaires dans la ville medievale. 1150–1350*, ed. D. Carraz; "The Spanish Military Orders in Italy: Initial Remarks on Patronage and Settlement (XII–XIV Centuries)," in MO5; "Gerusalemme, la Terrasanta e la crociata nelle memorie agiografiche delle città marinare (1098–c.1135). Le traslazioni dei santi Nicola, Isidoro e Giovanni Battista," *Quaderni di storia religiosa*, 17 (2010) [2011]; "A neglected source for the History of the Hospital: The Letter of Master Jobert (1171/72–1177) to the Citizens of Savona."

BERKOVICH, Ilya, "The Battle of Forbie and the Second Frankish Kingdom of Jerusalem,"

Journal of Military History, 2011; "Templars, Franks, Syrians and the Double Pact of 1244," in MO5.

BIDDLECOMBE, Steven, The *Historia Ierosolimitana* of Baldric of Bourgueil – A New Edition in Latin and an Analysis, Proposal for publication currently with Boydell and Brewer.

BIRD, Jessalyn, Entries on Oliver of Paderborn and his works for *Christian–Muslim Relations: A Bibliographical History*, Brill.

BOMBI, Barbara, "Innocent III and the Baltic Crusade after the Conquest of Constantinople," in I. Fonnesberg Schmidt and T. Nielsen, ed., *A Storm against the Infidel. Crusading in the Iberian Peninsula and the Baltic Region in the Central Middle Ages*, Aldershot, 2012.

BONNEAUD, Pierre, "Success and Failure in the Practice of Power by Pere Ramon Sacosta, Master of the Hospital (1461–1467), in MO5; "Les Hospitaliers Catalans entre Rhodes, l'Italie et la Gascogne (1420–1480), in *Élites et ordres militaires au Moyen Âge*, Madrid, Casa Velasquez.

BREWER, Keagan, *The Prester John Sourcebook*, Ashgate, 2011; with John Pryor and James Kane, edition and translation of the *Libellus de expugnatione terrae sanctae per Saladinum*, Ashgate; for submission: "The Dome of the Rock in the Crusader Kingdom of Jerusalem, 1099–1187."

BUTTIGIEG, Emanuel, *Nobility, Faith and Masculinity: The Order of Malta c.1580–c.1700*, London, Continuum.

CARR, Annemarie, (with Andreas Nicolaides), *Asinou: The Church and Frescoes of the Panagia Phorbiotissa*, Cambridge MA, Harvard University Press, 2011; "The Matter of the Word in an Icon in Houston," in *Festschrift for Alice-Mary Talbot*, ed. Elizabeth Fisher, Stratis Papaioannou, Denis Sullivan, Leiden, Brill; "The Cycle of the Rockefeller McCormick New Testament: Reading Styles of Use," in *Donations et donateurs dans l'empire byzantin*, Réalités byzantines, 14, ed. Jean-Michel Spieser and Elisabeth Yota, Paris: Lethielleux; "Three Illuminated Chrysobulls of Andronikos II?," *Nea Rhomi* 6; "Sinai and Cyprus: Holy Mountain, Holy Isle," in *Holy Image, Hallowed Ground*. Symposium on the exhibition at the J. Paul Getty Museum, Los Angeles.

CARRAZ, Damien, "Templiers et hospitaliers de Terre sainte au temps de Saladin," *Saladin et son temps*, éd. A. Zouache, *Histoire Antique et Médiévale*, HS n° 25, 2011; "*Pro servitio maiestatis nostre*. Templiers et hospitaliers au service de la diplomatie de Charles Iᵉʳ et Charles II," in *La Diplomatie des États Angevins aux XIIIᵉ et XIVᵉ siècles,* actes du colloque de Szeged-Budapest, 13–16 septembre 2007, ed. Z. Kordé and I. Petrovics, Szeged, early 2011; "Structures confraternelles et défense de la foi (XIᵉ–XIIIᵉ siècles)," in *Noblesse et défense de l'orthodoxie (XIIᵉ–XVIIᵉ siècles)*, ed. F. Mercier and A. Boltanski, Rennes, Presses Universitaires de Rennes, march 2011; (with Sophie Aspord-Mercier), "Le programme architectural d'un pôle seigneurial: la commanderie de Montfrin (Gard)," in *Organiser l'enclos, penser l'espace: sacré et topographie dans les maisons hospitalières et templières du Midi de la France, actes de la journée d'étude de Toulouse, 24 avril 2009,* ed. Y. Mattalia, *Archéologie du Midi médiéval*, spring 2011; "La territorialisation de la seigneurie monastique. Les commanderies provençales du Temple (XIIᵉ–XIIIᵉ siècle)," in *Les pouvoirs territoriaux en Italie centrale et dans le Sud de la France. Hiérarchies, institutions et langages (12ᵉ–14ᵉ siècles)*, actes de la table-ronde de Chambéry (4 mai 2007), ed. G. Castelnuovo and A. Zorzi, *Mélanges de l'École française de Rome-Moyen Âge*; "Une commanderie de l'Hôpital dans la capitale des comtes de Provence (XIIᵉ–XIVᵉ siècle)," in *De Saint-Jean-de-Malte au Musée Granet*, ed. N. Nin and S. Claude, Aix-en-Provence (Documents d'Archéologie Aixoise, VI); "La spiritualité de la chevalerie au regard du cartulaire du Temple de Richerenches," in

Le XIIIe siècle entre Provence et Dauphiné, actes du colloque de Lachau, 25–27 septembre 2009, ed. M. Bois, Pont-Saint-Esprit; "Aux origines de la commanderie de Manosque. Le dossier des comtes de Forcalquier dans les archives de l'Hôpital (début XIIe–milieu XIIIe siècle)," in *La mémoire des origines propres chez les ordres religieux militaires au Moyen Âge*, actes du colloque de Göttingen, juin 2009, ed. M. Olivier and Ph. Josserand, Münster, *Vita regularis*; "Le monachisme militaire, laboratoire de la sociogenèse des élites laïques dans l'Occident médiéval?," in *Élites et ordres militaires au Moyen Âge*, actes du colloque de Lyon, 21–23 octobre 2009, ed. N. Bériou, Ph. Josserand and L. F. Oliveira, Madrid, Casa de Velázquez; "Expériences religieuses en contexte urbain. De l'*ordo monasticus* aux *Religiones novæ*: le jalon du monachisme militaire," in *Les ordres religieux militaires dans la ville médiévale (1100–1350)*, actes du colloque de Clermont-Ferrand, 26–28 mai 2010, ed. D. Carraz, Clermont-Ferrand, Presses universitaires Blaise-Pascal; "Églises et cimetières des ordres militaires. Contrôle des lieux sacrés et *dominium* ecclésiastique en Provence (XIIe–XIIIe siècle)," in *Lieux sacrés et espace ecclésial, Cahiers de Fanjeaux*, 46, juillet 2011.

CASSIDY-WELCH, Megan, "Images of Blood in the Historia Albigensis of Pierre of les Vaux-de-Cernay," *Journal of Religious History*, 35:4, 2011; "The medieval refugee: war, displacement and social justice in thirteenth-century France," in Celia Chazelle, Amy Remensnyder and Felice Lifshitz, ed., *Why the Middle Ages Matter*, London, Routledge, 2011; "L'Emprisonnement dans les textes hagiographiques au moyen âge," in Isabelle Heullant-Donat, ed., *Enfermements: Le Cloître et la prison au Moyen Âge*, Paris: Publications de la Sorbonne, 2011.

CHRISSIS, Nikolaos, "The City and the Cross: the image of Constantinople and the Latin Empire in papal crusading rhetoric in the thirteenth century," *Byzantine and Modern Greek Studies*, 35, 2011; *Crusading in Frankish Greece: a Study of Byzantine-Western Relations and Attitudes, 1204–1282*, Turnhout, Brepols, 2012; "Crusades and crusaders in Medieval Greece," in P. Lock and N. Tsougarakis, eds., *A Handbook of Medieval Greece*, Leiden, Brill, 2012; "Gregory IX and the Greek East," in C. Egger and D. Smith, ed., *Pope Gregory IX*, Farnham, Ashgate, 2012.

CHRIST, Georg, *Conflicts at the Intersection of Orient and Occident? A Venetian Consul in Mamluk Alexandria 1418–1420*, The medieval Mediterranean. Leiden: Brill; "Contrebande, vin et révolte: lecture critique d'un conflit inter-culturel à l'ombre des rapports officieux entre Venise et Alexandrie à l'époque medieval," in *Alexandrie médiévale 4*, ed. Christian Décobert, *Études alexandrines*, Le Caire: Imprimerie de l'IFAO; "Quelques observations concernant la navigation vénitienne à Alexandrie à la fin du Moyen Âge," in *Venise et la Méditerranée*, ed. Sandro G Franchini, and Gennaro Toscano, Paris-Venice, INP, Istituto Veneto; "Sliding Legalities: Venetian Slave Trade in Alexandria and the Aegean," in *Slavery and the Slave Trade in the Mediterranean Region During the Medieval Period (1000–1500)*, ed. Christoph Cluse and Reuven Amitai; "Mapping change: A Collaborative GIS-based Cue Card System for the Humanities," in *Proceedings of the SCCH09-Scientific Computing & Cultural Heritage November 16th–18th 2009*, ed. Michael Winckler, and Hubert Mara. Heidelberg, Springer; "Filippo di Malerbi – un spécialiste du transfert clandestin en Égypte au début du 15ème siècle," in *Acteurs des transferts culturels en Méditerranée médiévale*, ed. Daniel König, Yassir Benhima, and Rania Abdellatif, Elisabeth Ruchaud, Paris, DHIP.

CHRISTIE, Niall G. F., *The Book of the Jihad of ʿAli ibn Tahir al-Sulami (d. 1106): Text, Translation and Commentary*, Aldershot: Ashgate, 2011, viii–377 p.; "Paradise and Hell in the *Kitab al-Jihad* of ʿAli b. Tahir al-Sulami (d. 500/1106)," *Roads to Paradise: Eschatology and Concepts of the Hereafter in Islam*, ed. Sebastian Günther and Todd Lawson (Brill);

"'Ali b. Tahir al-Sulami," in *Christian–Muslim Relations: A Bibliographical History, Volume 2 (900–1200)*, ed. David Thomas *et al.,* Leiden, Brill.

CHRISTOFORAKI, Ioanna, "Paving the Road to Sinai: George and Maria Soteriou on the Holy Mountain," in Sharon E. J. Gerstel and Robert S. Nelson, ed., *Approaching the Holy Mountain. Art and Liturgy at St Catherine's Monastery in the Sinai*, Turnhout, Brepols, 2011; "An 'Italo-Byzantine' Icon with the Pietà and Saints from Cyprus," *Cypriot Studies*, 72, 2008 (in Greek) [forthcoming in 2011].

CLAVERIE, Pierre-Vincent, "Mythes et réalités de la présence templière à Famagouste," *Medieval and Renaissance Famagusta: History and Monuments*, ed. P. Edbury, N. Coureas et M. Walsh, Aldershot, 2011; "La contribution des sources diplomatiques à l'histoire ecclésiastique de Tyr sous la latinocratie (XIIᵉ–XIIIᵉ siècles)," *Tyr dans les textes l'Antiquité et du Moyen Âge*, ed. J. Aliquot, P.-L. Gatier et L. Nordiguian, Damas, Institut Français du Proche-Orient, 2011; "L'évolution des réseaux d'information de l'Orient latin durant les croisades (fin XIᵉ–début XIVᵉ siècle)," *Les réseaux à l'épreuve du temps*, ed. Ch. Picard, Paris, 2011; "Un patriarche latin d'Antioche méconnu: Grazia de Florence (1219)," *Le Moyen Age*, CXVII, 2011; Pierre de Blois et la légende dorée de Renaud de Châtillon," in *Egypt and Syria in the Fatimid, Ayyubid and Mamluk Eras, t. VII.*, ed. U. Vermeulen and K. D'hulster, Louvain, 2011; "La politique orientale du Saint-Siège à l'avènement d'Honorius III (1216)," ibidem; "Les relations du Saint-Siège avec les ordres militaires sous le pontificat d'Honorius III (1216–1227)," *Elites et ordres militaires au Moyen Âge. Colloque international de Lyon, 21–23 octobre 2009*, ed. N. Bériou, P. Josserand et Luís Filipe Oliveira, Madrid, 2011.

CONNELL, Charles W., "War or Peace: The Struggle over Public opinion at the Time of the First Crusade," Avignon 2008 SSCLE; "The Voice of the Poor and the Tin Ear of the English Medievalism," in *Poverty and Prosperity: The Rich and the Poor in the Middle Ages and the Renaissance*, Turnhout: Brepols, 2010.

CORRIE, Rebecca W., "Byzantine influence in Western European Art," *Grove Art Online*; "Sinai, Acre, Tripoli, and the 'Backwash of the Levant': where did the Icon Painters work," in Gerstel and Nelson, ed., *Approaching the Holy Mountain*, Turnhout: Brepols, 2010; "Images of the Virgin and Political Power in late Medieval Sina," in Steinhobb and Smith, ed., *Art and Politics*, Ashgate, 2010.

COUREAS, Nicholas S., "A Political History of Nicosia," in *A History of Nicosia*, ed. D. Michaelides (Rimal Publications: Nicosia, 2011); "An Ecclesiastical History of Nicosia," *ibid.;* "The Latin Church and the non-Latin Christians of the City of Famagusta in the Fourteenth and Fifteenth Centuries," in *Medieval Famagusta*, Nicosia, 2012; "Taverns in Medieval Famagusta," in *Medieval and Renaissance Famagusta: History and Monuments*, ed. M. Walsh, N. Coureas and P. Edbury, Aldershot: Ashgate, 2011; "Commercial Relations between Genoese Famagusta and the Mamluk Sultanate, 1374–1464," in *Egypt and Syria in the Fatimid, Ayyubid and Mamluk Eras 7, Proceedings of the 16th,17th and 18th HES*, ed. U. Vermeulen and K. D'hulster,Leuven: Peeters, 2012; "Losing the War but Winning the Peace: Cyprus and Mamluk Egypt in the Fifteenth Century," *ibid.*; "The Tribute Paid to the Mamluk Sultanate, 1426–1517: The Perspective from Lusignan and Venetian Cyprus," ibid.; "The Third Crusade according to Greek Sources from Cyprus," *The Medieval Chronicle*, 8, 2011; "King James II of Cyprus and the Hospitallers: Evidence from the *Livre des Remembrances*," in MO5; "Friend or Foe? The Armenians in Cyprus as others saw them in the Lusignan Period," in *The History of the Armenian Mediterranean 12th to 15th Centuries*, ed. G. Dédéyan and C. Mutafian, Paris, 2012.

CRAWFORD, Paul F., "Malicide not Homicide: The Military Religious Orders" and sidebar on Bernard of Clairvaux's *In Praise of the New Knighthood*" for the *World History Encylopedia* in the medieval volume, ed. Alfred Andrea, ABC-Clio, set publication date: December 2010; "Four Myths about the Crusades," *The Intercollegiate Review*, 46, 2011, pp. 3–11.

CUSHING, Dana, "New Information about Cogs and Medieval Naval Logistics from an Eyewitness Crusader Chronicle: De Itinere Navali," *AVISTA Forum Journal*, 20, 2011; *A German Crusader's Chronicle of the Voyage and Reconquest (Xelb 1189–1197): De Itinere Navali*, History of Warfare Series, Brill, 2012.

DANSETTE, Béatrice, éd., Bernard de Breydenbach, *Voyage en Terre sainte et en Égypte*, transcription, traduction et notes sous la direction du Professeur Jean Meyers, collectif.

DEMPSEY, John A., "From Holy War to Patient Endurance: Henry IV, Matilda of Tuscany and the Evolution of Bonizo of Sutri's Response to Heretical Princes," in *War and Peace: New Perspectives in European History and Literature*, ed. Nadia Margolis and Albrecht Classen, Berlin: De Gruyter.

DICKSON, Gary, *Medieval Revivalism in Medieval Christianity*, vol. 4, ed. Daniel E. Borstein, *People's History of Christianity*, gen. ed. Denis R. Janz, Minneapolis: Augsburg Fortress Press, 2008.

DOSTOURIAN, Ara, *Armenia and the Crusades: The Chronicle of Matthew of Edessa*, 2nd ed., paperback, Armenian Heritage Press, National Association for Armenian Studies and Research, 2012.

DOUROU-ELIOPOULOU, Maria, "The cultural life of the Latins in Romania during the crusades," in *Volume in Honour of Professor Evangelos Chryssos*; "The crusading ideology of the Aragonese in the eastern Mediterranean," ibidem.

EDBURY, Peter, Co-editor with Michael Walsh and Nicholas Coureas: *Medieval and Renaissance Famagusta: Studies in Architecture, Art and History,* (to be published by Ashgate in 2011); Famagusta and the Tradition of History Writing in Frankish Cyprus' for *Medieval and Renaissance Famagusta* (as above); "The Old French Translation of William of Tyre and Templars" for a collection of essays to be entitled *From Holy War to Peaceful Co-habitation* (CEU Budapest); "Famagusta and the Lusignan Kingdom of Cyprus, 1192–1374" for a volume on *Medieval Famagusta*, ed. Chris Schabel, Angel Nicolaou-Konnari, Catherine Otten-Froux and Gilles Grivaud (Brill); "Gerard of Ridefort and the battle of Le Cresson (1 May 1187): the developing narrative tradition" in MO5; "Machaut, Mézières, Makhairas and *Amadi*: Constructing the reign of Peter I (1359–1369)" in *The Age of Philippe de Mézières*, ed. Renate Blumenfeld-Kosinski and Kiril Petkov (Brill); "Cultural Encounters in the Latin East: John of Jaffa and Philip of Novara" in *Cultural Encounters during the Crusades*, ed. Helle Vogt *et al.*; articles for J. Tolan, ed., *Christian–Muslim Relations: A Bibliographical History* (Brill).

EDGINGTON, Susan, "Pagans and Others in the *Chanson de Jérusalem*," in *Languages of Love and Hate*, ed. S. Lambert and E. James, Turnhout, Brepols, 2011; with Carol Sweetenham: *The Chanson d'Antioche: a translation and commentary* (Ashgate Crusade Texts in Translation series, 2011); "Walter the Chancellor," in *Christian–Muslim Relations: A Bibliographical History. Volume Two: 900–1200 CE*, ed. A. Mallett et al., Leiden, Brill, 2011; "Matilda of Canossa (1046–1115)" and "Bouillon, Godfrey de (ca. 1060–1100)," in *The Encyclopedia of War*, ed. G. Martel, Blackwell, 2011.

EHLERS, Axel, "Indulgentia und Historia. Die Bedeutung des Ablasses für die spätmittelalterliche Erinnerung an die Ursprünge des Deutschen Ordens und anderer

Gemeinschaften," in *Actes du colloque "Mémoire des origines dans les ordres religieux-militaires au Moyen Âge"*, ed. P. Josserand and M. Olivier, Münster, Lit, 2011.

FOLDA, Jaroslav, "Picturing the First Crusade and Commemorating the Fall of Jerusalem," in *Acta of the 28th Annual Conference of the Center for Medieval Studies*, Fordham University (2008), Leiden: Brill, 2010–2011, 25 p.; "Sacred Objects with Holy Light: Byzantine Icons with Chrysography," in *Byzantine Religious Culture: Studies in Honor of Alice-Mary Talbot*, Leiden: Brill, 2010–2011, 19 p.; "Melisende of Jerusalem: Queen and Patron of Art and Architecture in the Crusader Kingdom," in *Reassessing the Roles of Women as "Makers" of Medieval Art and Architecture*, ed. Therese Martin, Brill, 2012, 47 p.

FONSECA, Luís Adão da, "The Papacy and the Crusade in Fifteenth Century Portugal" (with Maria Cristina Pimenta and Paula Pinto Costa), in Avignon SSCLE 7; "The Portuguese Military Orders, the Royal Power and the Maritime Expansion (XVth century)," in MO5; "The crusade idea in the Medieval Portugal: political aims and ideological framing," in *A Storm against the Infidel. Crusading in the Iberian Peninsula and the Baltic Region in the Central Middle Ages*, ed. Torben K. Nielsen and Iben Fonnesberg-Schmidt, Turnhout, Brepols, 2011; "As Ordens Militares no século XV" (with Maria Cristina Pimenta and Paula Pinto Costa), in *Historiografia sobre a Idade Média em Portugal*, ed. José Mattoso, Lisbon, 2011

FOREY, Alan J., "Where the Templars Guilty, even if they were not Heretics or Apostates ?," *Viator*, 42, 2011.

FRANKE, Daniel, "War, Crisis, and East Anglia, 1334–1340: Towards a Reassessment," in *The Hundred Years War III*, ed. Donald Kagay and L. J. Andrew Villalon, Leiden, Brill, 2011.

GABRIELE, Matthew, "On the Language of Christian Violence in Contemporary American Society: From Iraq to Virginia Tech," in *Denkmuster christlicher Legitimation von Gewalt*, ed. Theo Riches and Gerd Althoff; "Translation of Charlemagne's Pilgrimage from Benedict of Monte Soratte's *Chronicon*," in *Pilgrimage in the Middle Ages*, ed. Brett Whalen, University of Toronto Press, 2011.

GAPOSCHKIN, Cecilia, "Talking about Kingship when Preaching about Saint Louis," in *Prédication et société politique: depuis l'Antiquité tardive jusqu'à la fin du Moyen Âge*, éd. Franco Morenzoni; "Louis IX and Liturgical Memory," in *Memory in Medieval France*, ed. Elma Brenner.

GEORGIOU, Constantinos, "Richard I of England and Cyprus," in Proceedings of *From Holy War to Peaceful Co-habitation: diversity of Crusading and the military orders'* conference, Budapest: Central European University.

GEORGIOU, Stavros G., "The Anonymous Kamytzes of Pentekontakephalon of Saint Neophytos the Recluse," *Hellenica*, 61, 2011 [in Greek]; "The Atribution of the titles of Sebastohypertatos and Despotes to the Archon of Nafplion Leo Sgouros (ca. 1200–1208)," in *Volume Dedicated to Professor Alkmene Stavridou-Zafraka*, Thessalonica 2011; "The Saved Historical Testimonies for the Foundation of Astromeritis and the honour of Saint Auxibios," in *Volume for Saint Auxibios, Holy Bishopric of Morphou*, 2011; "The Bishopric of Tamasos from its Foundation until Today," in *Volume for the History and the Monuments of the Holy Bishopric of Tamasos and Orinis*, 2011; "The Bishopric of Tamasos," in V. Lysandrou, ed., *Ekklisies and exoklisia tis mitropolitikis periphereias Tamasou, Holy Bishopric of Tamasos and Orinis*, 2011.

GILCHRIST, Marianne, "'The Fugitive: Conrad of Montferrat and the myth of a murder' – an examination of Runciman's misrepresentation of the death of Alexios Vranas, and its perpetuation and embellishment by later popular writers on the Crusades," submitted to SSCLE for *Crusade*.

GOURDIN, Philippe, Direction (with Monique Longerstay), *De Tabarka aux 'Nouvelles Tabarka': Carloforte, Calasetta, Nueva Tabarca. Histoire, environnement, préservation*, Tunis (2011); "De Tabarka aux 'Nouvelles Tabarka': les chemins de l'exil," ibidem.

GRASSO, Christian, "*Ad promovendum negotium crucis*: gestione finanziaria e promozione pubblica della crociata durante il pontificato di Onorio III (1216–1227)," in *Zentralität: Papsttum und Orden im Europa des 12. und 13. Jahrhunderts*, ed. Klaus Herbers-Cristina Andenna-Gert Melville, Munster, LT Verlag.

HALL, Martin, *Caffaro, Genoa and the Twelfth Century Crusades*, jointly with Jonathan Phillips, Ashgate's "Crusader Texts in Translation" Series; publication; an annotated English translation of all Caffaro's works and other texts relevant to Genoa's role in the Crusades and the Holy Land to 1200, with historical introduction.

HAMILTON, Bernard, with Andrew Jotischky, *Latin and Orthodox Monasticism in the Crusader States*, CUP., 2011; "Why did the Crusader States produce so few Saints?," in *Sainthood and Sanctity*, ed. D. D. Clarke and T. Clayton, The Boydel Press, Studies in Church History, 47, 2011; "Latins and Georgians and the Crusader Kingdom," *Al-Masāq*, 23 (ii), 2011.

HESLOP, Michael, co-edition of *Byzantium and Venice, 1204–1453, Collected Studies of Julian Chrysostomides*, Ashgate, 2011.

IRWIN, Robert, *Mameluks and Crusaders*, Ashgate, Variorum Collected studies, June 2010; *Men of the Sword and the Pen: Studies in the Political and Cultural History of the Near East*, Variorum; edition and introduction of *The New Cambridge History of Islam*, vol. 4, *Islamic Cultures and Societies to 1800*.

JACKSON, Peter, "Franciscan Friars as Papal and Royal Envoys to the Tartars (1245–1255)," in *The Cambridge Companion to Francis of Assisi*, ed. Michael Robson, Cambridge UP, 2011.

JASPERT, Nikolas, "Gedenkwesen und Erinnerung des Ordens vom Heiligen Grab," in *Wider das Vergessen und für das Seelenheil. Memoria und Totengedenken im Mittelalter*, ed. Rainer Berndt S.J. / Ursula Vones-Liebenstein (Erudiri Sapientia), Münster 2011; "Die Kreuzzüge – Motivationen, Mythos und Missverständnisse," in *Stauferzeit – Zeit der Kreuzzüge*, ed. Karl-Heinz Rueß, Göppingen, 2011; "Reconquista. Interdependenzen und Tragfähigkeit eines wertekategorialen Deutungsmusters," in *Christlicher Norden – Muslimischer Süden. Die Iberische Halbinsel im Kontext kultureller, religiöser und politischer Veränderungen zwischen dem 11. und 15. Jahrhundert*, ed. Alexander Fidora / Matthias Tischler, Frankfurt am Main, 2011.

JENSEN, Carsten Selch, ed. with M. Tamm, L. Kaljundi, *Crusading and Chronicle Writing on the Medieval Baltic Frontier*, Farnham: Ashgate; "*Verbis non verberibus*, The representation of sermons in the Chronicle of Henry of Livonia," ibidem; "Conquest of Gotland," in *The Encyclopedia of War*, ed. Gordon Martel, Wiley-Blackwell, 2011.

JOSSERAND, Philippe, *La mémoire des origines dans les ordres religieux militaires au Moyen Âge, Actes du colloque de la Mission Historique Française en Allemagne des 25 et 26 juin 2009*, ed. with Mathieu Olivier, Dresde, in *"Vita Regularis." Ordnungen und Deutungen religiosen Lebens im Mittelalter*; "L'ordre de Santiago face au récit de ses origines au tournant du Moyen Âge et de l'époque moderne: variations sur l'espace et le temps," ibid.; *Élites et ordres militaires au Moyen Âge. Rencontre en l'honneur d'Alain Demurger, Actes du colloque international réuni à Lyon les 21, 22 et 23 octobre 2009*, ed. with Nicole Bériou and Luís Filipe Oliveira, 2010; "Les croisades de Terre sainte et les ordres militaires dans les chroniques royales castillano-léonaises (milieu XIIᵉ–milieu XIIIᵉ siècle)," in *Christlicher Norden – Muslimischer Süden. Die iberische Halbinsel im Kontext kultureller, religiöser und politischer Veränderungen zwischen dem 11. und 15. Jahrhundert (Internationale Tagung, 20–23 Juni 2007,Frankfurt am Main)*, ed. Matthias Tischler and Alexandre Fidora, 2010; "Vientos de cambio. Las transformaciones de la orden de Calatrava a partir de finales del siglo XIII a través de la normativa cistercience," in *El nacimiento de la orden de Calatrava. Primeros tiempos de expansión, siglos XII–XIII (Almagro, 14–17 de octubre de 2008)*, ed. L. R. Villegas Díaz), 2010; "Troubles and Tensions before the Trial: the Last Years of the Castilian Templar Province," in MO5, Cardiff, 2009; "*Omne que meior lo pudiese mantener e defender*. The Master and the Islamic Frontier in Mid-Fourteenth Century Castile," in *Late Crusades – Les croisades tardives (Budapest, 15th–17th November 2009)*, ed. J. Laszlovszky; "De l'arrière au front. Perspectives croisées, perspectives compares," introductory rapport to the fifth session "Oriente e Ocidente," in *VI Encontro sobre ordens militares*, directed by Isabel Cristina Ferreira Fernandes (10–13 March 2010); with Carlos de Ayala Martínez, "La actitud de los freiles de las órdenes militares ante el problema de la muerte en Castilla (siglos XII–XIV)," *Miscellanea di studi sugli ordini monastico-cavallereschi*; "Portrait de maître en héros croisé: la chronique perdue de Pelayo Pérez Correa," in *Croisades tardives et noblesse en Europe*, éd. Daniel Baloup et Martin Nejedly; "Frontière et ordres militaires dans le monde latin au Moyen Âge," in *Frontières oubliées, frontières retrouvées. Marches et limites anciennes en France et en Europe* (Châteaubriant, 30 septembre–2 octobre 2010*)*, éd. Michel Catala, Dominique Le Page et Jean-Claude Meuret.

JOTISCHKY, Andrew, "Holy Fire and Holy Sepulchre: Ritual and Space in Jerusalem from the 9th to the 14th Centuries," in Frances Andrews, ed., *Ritual and Space in the Middle Ages*, Donnington, Shaun Tyas, 2011; "Pilgrimage, Procession and Ritual Encounters Between Christians and Muslims in the Holy Land," in Kurt Villads Jensen, ed., *Cultural Contacts in the Crusades*, Copenhagen/Damascus, Danish Institute in Damascus; "Ethnic and Religious Categories in the Treatment of Jews and Muslims in the Crusader States," in J. Renton and B. Giddins, ed., *Antisemitism and Islamophobia,* Bloomington, Indiana University Press, 2012; "Pope Eugenius III and the Latin Church in the Crusader States," in Iben Fonnesberg-Schmidt and Andrew Jotischky, ed., *Pope Eugenius III*, Aldershot: Ashgate, 2012; with Bernard Hamilton, *Monasticism in the Crusader States,* Cambridge, CUP, 2012.

KEDAR, Benjamin Z., "The Latin Hermits of the Frankish Levant Revisited," in a Festschrift; "Emicho of Flonheim and the Apocalyptic Motif in the 1096 Massacres: Between Paul Alphandéry and Alphonse Dupront," in a Festschrift; "Prolegomena to a World History of Harbor and River Chains," in a Festschrift.

KOSTICK, Conor, Review: Malcolm Barber and Keith Bate, "Letters from the East," *Journal of Military History,* 2011.

KRÄMER, Thomas, "Terror, Torture and the Truth – The Testimonies of the Templars revisited," in DTT.

LAPINA, Elizabeth, "Maccabees and the Battle of Antioch (1098)" in *Dying for the Faith, Killing for the Faith: Old-Testament Faith-Warriors (Maccabees 1 and 2) in Cultural Perspective*, ed. Gabriela Signori*, Brill's Studies of Intellectual History.*

LIGATO, Giuseppe*, Il mito della crociata nel frammento di mosaico pavimentale recuperato dalla basilica di S. Maria Maggiore a Vercelli.*

LOUD, Graham A., *The Crusade of Frederic Barbarossa*, Ashgate: Crusader Texts in Translation, 2010; "The papal 'Crusade' against Frederick II, 1228–1230," in Avignon SSCLE 7.

Luchitskaya, Svetlana, *"Homo legens": traditions orale et écrite dans les pratiques de lecture: l'analyse comparée de la littérature médiévale* (book coed. With Marie.-Christine Varol), Brepols, 2011.

Mack, Merav, "A Genoese Perspective of the Third Crusade," *Crusades* 10 (2011); ed., *Captives and Captivity* [in Hebrew] Jerusalem, The Van Leer Jerusalem Institute; "The Mistakes of the Catholic Church in the Middle East," review of Anthony O'Mahony and John Flannery, ed., *The Catholic Church in the Contemporary Middle East: Studies for the Synod for the Middle East*, Melisende, 2010, *Journal of Levantine Studies* 1, 2011.

Madden, Thomas F., *Venice: Islands of Honor and Profit*, Viking-Penguin, 2011; ed., with James L. Naus and Vincent T. Ryan, *Crusades: Medieval Worlds in Conflict: Papers from the First International Symposium on Crusade Studies,* Brookfield, Ashgate Publishers; "Crusades" in *The Oxford Dictionary of the Middle Ages*, Oxford: Oxford University Press; "Alexander III and Venice," in *Pope Alexander III (1159–1181),* Damian Smith, ed., Brookfield: Ashgate Publishing.

Marwin, Laurence W., 7 Entries in *The Encyclopedia of War*, ed. Gordon Martel, Oxford, Blackwell: "Albigensian Crusades (1209–1226)," "Fifth Crusade," "First Crusade," "Fourth Crusade," Grandson, Otto of (ca. 1238–1338)," "Second Crusade," "Philip IV of France ('The Fair', 1268–1314)."

Menache, Sophia, "Papal Attempts at a Commercial boycott of the Muslims during the Crusader Period," *Journal of Ecclesiastical History*, 2012; "When Ideology met Reality: Clement V and the Crusade," *Crusades-Subsidia* 3, ed. M. Balard.

Militzer, Klaus, *Herrschaft, Netzwerke, Brüder. Der Deutsche Orden in Mittelalter und Früher Neuzeit,* Quellen und Studien zur Geschichte des Deutschen Ordens, 2011 or 2012; *Regesten der Urkunden des Deutschordenshauses in Köln*, 2012

Mitchell, Piers D., "The spread of disease with the crusades," in *Between Text and Patient: The Medical Enterprise in Medieval and Early Modern Europe*, ed. B. Nance and E. F. Glaze. Florence: Sismel; "Medical and nursing care in the military orders," in W. T. Reich, and J. S. C. Riley-Smith, ed., *Chivalry, Honor and Care,* Washington, Georgetown University Press; with T. G. Wagner, "The Illnesses of King Richard and King Philippe on the Third Crusade: an Understanding of Leonardie and Arnaldia," *Crusades*, 2011.

Morton, Nicholas, *"In Subsidium*: The declining contribution of Germny and Eastern Europe to the Crusades to the Holy Land, 1187–1291," *German Historical Institute Bulletin*, 2011, pp. 33–66.

Murray, Alan V., "The Capture of Jerusalem in Western Narrative Sources of the First Crusade," in *Jerusalem the Golden: The Conquest of the Dream (From the West to the Holy Land)*, ed. L. Garcia-Guijarro Ramos; "The Saracens of the Baltic: Pagan and Christian Lithuanians in the Perception of English and French Crusaders to Prussia," *Journal of Baltic Studies*; "La construcción de Jerusalén como capital cristiana: Topografía y población de la Ciudad Santa bajo el dominio franco en el siglo XII," in *Construir la ciudad en la Edad media. Encuentros internacionales del Medievo 2009, Nájera*, ed. B. Arizaga Bolumburu and J. Angel Solórzano Telechea, Logroño: Instituto de Estudios Riojanos; "National Identity, Regional Identity and Language in the Crusades to the Holy Land, 1096–1192," in *Conflict and Cohabitation*, ed. C. Kostick; 10 articles: Ager Sanguinis, battle (1119), Antioch, sieges of (1097–98), Ascalon, battle (1099), Bohemond, Clergy, Godfrey of Bouillon, Hab, battle (1119), Hattin, battle (1187), Jerusalem, siege (1099), Nationalism and National Identity, in *Medieval Warfare and Military Technology: An Encyclopedia*, ed. C. Rogers, Oxford: Oxford University Press.

Naus, James L., *Crusades: Medieval Worlds in Conflict*, ed. Thomas F. Madden, James Naus and Vince Ryan, Ashgate.

Nicholson, Helen J., "The Role of Women in the Military Orders," in *Militiae Christi*, 1, 2010, ed. Filip Hooghe and Jan Hosten, pp. 210–229; "Itinerarium peregrinorum et gesta Regis Ricardi," in *The Encyclopedia of the Medieval Chronicle*, ed. Graeme Dunphy, Leiden, Brill.

Nicolaou-Konnari, Angel, "The Crusader Ideology in the Greek Cypriot *Chronicle* of Leontios Makhairas," *Crusades*, 9, 2010; "Apologists or Critics? The Reign of Peter I of Lusignan (1359–1369) viewed by Philippe de Mézières (1327–1405) and Leontios Makhairas (ca. 1360/80–after 1432)," Proceedings of the International Symposium *The Age of Philippe de Mezières: Fourteenth-Century Piety and Politics between France, Venice, and Cyprus* (Nicosia, 11–13 June 2009), ed. Renate Blumenfeld-Kosinski and Kiril Petkov, Leiden, Brill, 2111; "The Fascinating Journey of a Pioneer: Louis de Mas Latrie (1805–1897) and the Medieval History of Cyprus" (in Greek), in *Aspects of Clio: Historiography of Cyprus*, Nicosia, University of Cyprus, 2011; "Cultural Interaction and Ethnic Identity in Lusignan Cyprus," XXIIe Congrès d'Études Byzantines, Table ronde "Chypre entre l'Orient et l'Occident," Sofia, 22–27 August 2011.

Omran, Mahmoud Said, "Coin in Europe during the Middle Ages" [in Arabic], January 2011.

Pastori, Aurelio, "Navigare necesse, vivere non necesse? El estudio de la Historia Medieval en el Uruguay, comparado con los países limítrofes. Balance y desafíos," in *Pasado, Presente y Porvenir de las Humanidades y las Artes*, III. México, Zacatecas, AZECME, Asociación Zacatecana de Estudios Clásicos y Medievales, 2011; "Las Cruzadas, 1095–1291," in *Cuestiones de Historia Medieval*. Buenos Aires, Universidad Católica Argentina, 2011.

Paviot, Jacques, *Les projets de croisade en Europe, XIIIᵉ–XVIIᵉ siècle*, Actes du colloque de Paris, 11–12 juin 2009, éd. avec D. Baloup, Toulouse, 2011; "L'idée de croisade à la fin du Moyen Âge," ibidem; "Les croisades tardives (XIVᵉ–XVIᵉ s.): bilan historiographique et état de la recherche: France et Angleterre," in *Les croisades tardives (XIVᵉ–XVIᵉ s.): bilan historiographique et état de la recherche. Actes du colloque de Toulouse, 22–23 mars 2007*, Toulouse, 2010; "Inciter le roi de France à partir à la croisade: Le sermon *Exaltavi lignum humile* de Pierre de La Palud (1332) et le *Discours du voyage d'outre-mer* de Jean Germain (1451)," in *Croisade et discours de guerre sainte à la fin du Moyen Âge. Légitimation, propagande, prosélytisme*, Actes du colloque de Toulouse, 27–28 mars 2008, Toulouse, 2011.

Perra, Photeine V., "Bibliography for the Peloponnesus (396–1453 A.C.)," in *Lexicon of Byzantine Peloponnesus*, Athens 2010

Petrovskaia, Natalia I., "East and West in *De Principis Instructione* of Giraldus Cambrensis," *Quaestio Insularis*, 10.

Phillips, Jonathan, A Book: *Holy Warriors: A Modern History of the Crusades* will be translated into German (DVA) and Italian (Laterza) in 2011.

Phillips, Simon D., "Hospitaller Relations with the Local Communities on Cyprus," in Proceedings of the Fourth International Congress of Cypriot Studies, Nicosia, 29 April–3 May 2008, The Society of Cypriot Studies, 2011; "Walking a Thin Line: Hospitaller Priors, Politics and Power in Late Medieval England," in MO5.

Piana, Mathias, "A Bulwark Never Conquered: The Fortifications of the Templar Citadel of Tortosa on the Syrian Coast," in *The Architecture and Archaeology of the Military Orders*, ed. Mathias Piana, Christer Carlsson, Aldershot, Ashgate, 2011.

Pimenta, Maria Cristina, "As Ordens Militares de Avis e de Santiago e o Rei D. Manuel I (1495–1521): algumas notas de reflexão," *Revista de las Órdenes Militares*, Madrid: Real

Consejo de las Órdenes Militares, 6, 2010, pp. 1–50; "As Ordens Militares no século XV," *Historiografia sobre a Idade Média em Portugal*, coord. José Mattoso, Lisbon, 2011 (in collaboration).

PINTO COSTA, Paula Maria, "As Ordens Militares no século XV," in *Historiografia sobre a Idade Média em Portugal*, coord. José Mattoso, Lisbon, 2011. (in collaboration); "St. John's Order and its role on the pilgrimage and politics: the case of the North of Portugal," in *Pilgrims and Politics*, Ashgate, 2011.

POLEJOWSKI, Karol, "The counts of Brienne and military orders in the XIII century," in MO5; "The Briennes in the Chronicle of Jean de Joinville," in the book offered Prof Barbara Popielas-Szultka, Słupsk 2011; "Teutonic Order's propaganda in France during the wars against Poland and Lithuania (XV century)," Brno, Czech Republic, 2011, papers from the conference *Die geistlichen Ritterorden in Mitteleuropa*; "The creation of the Teutonic Order and the development of its administrative structure by the end of the XIIIth century," in *Europa, Bulletin of the University of Tumen* (Republic of Russia), 2011; "Gdansk Guild Seals in the Archives Nationales in Paris," in Rocznik Gdański, Gdansk 2011.

POWELL, James, "1291: A Vacuum of Leadership"; "Innocent III and Secular Law."

POWER, Amanda, "Going among the infidels: the Mendicant Orders and Louis IX's first Mediterranan Campaign," *Mediterranean Historical Review*, 25. 2, 2010; *Roger Bacon and the Defence of Christendom*, Cambridge UP, 2011; "The Importance of Greeks in Latin Thought: the Evidence of Roger Bacon," in *The Byzantine and Crusader Mediterranean (6th–14th Centuries): Trade, Cultural Exchange, Warfare and Archaeology*, ed. E. Jeffries and R. Gertwegen, Ashgate; "The Cosmographical Imagination of Roger Bacon," in K. D. Lilley, ed. *Mapping Medieval Geographies: Geographical encounters and cartographic cultures in the Latin West and beyond: 300–1600*, Cambridge UP; "The Remedies for Great Danger: Contemporary Appraisals of Roger Bacon's Expertise," in J. Canning, E. King and M. Staub, ed., *Knowledge, Discipline and Power: Essays in Honour of David Luscombe*, Leiden, Brill.

PRINGLE, Denys, "The Order of St Thomas of Canterbury in Acre," in MO5; Crusader Castles and Fortifications: The Armenian Connection. In G. Dédeyan and C. Mutafian, ed., *La Méditerranée des Arméniens, XIIᵉ–XVᵉ siècle*s, Lisbonne, Fondation Calouste Gulbenkian.

PUJEAU, Emmanuelle, "Preveza in 1538: the Background of a very complex Situation," in Second and international Symposium of Preveza, end of 2010; "Consiglio di Monsignor Giovio al modo di far l'impresa contra infideli," italian edition with presentation and notes, Venice, 2011; "Messer San Marco gonfalonier de la croisade," *Studi Veneziani*, LIX–LX; "La lamentation de Constantinople en vers, la plume contre l'épée?," *Revue de l'université de Ioannina*; "Les croisades et la question turque chez les humanistes italiens," in *Les croisades tardives*, Méridiennes, Toulouse; "Conseils pour l'entreprise contre les Infidèles ou le modus operandi de la croisade," in *Les projets de croisade et leur objectif*, Méridiennes, Toulouse; "Financement et logistique de la croisade," in *Partir en croisade à la fin du Moyen Age: financement et logistique*, Méridiennes, Toulouse.

RICHARD, Jean, "Papacy and Cyprus. Introduction historique," *Bullarium Cyprium*, éd. Ch. Schabel, Centre de recherche de Nicosie, I, 2010.

RIST, Rebecca, (with C. Leglu, C. Taylor), ed., *The Cathars and the Albigensian Crusade: A Sourcebook*, Longman, 2011; "Pope Gregory IX and the Grant of Indulgences for Military Campaigns in Europe in the 1230s: A Study in Papal Rhetoric," *Crusades* 10, 2011; "The Baltic Crusades (11th–15th Century)" in *The Encyclopedia of War*, ed. G. Martel, Blackwell, 2011.

RYAN, Vincent, ed. with Thomas F. Madden and James Naus, *Crusades: Medieval Worlds in Conflict*, Aldershot, Ashgate, 2010.

SHATZMILLER, Maya, "Economic Performance and Economic Growth in the early Islamic World, 700–1000," *Journal of the Economic and Social History of the Orient*, 54, 2, 2010.

SCHENK, Jochen, "Nomadic Violence in the Latin Kingdom of Jerusalem and the Military Orders," *Reading Medieval Studies*, 2010.

SIMSONS, Raitis, *Prūšu nobiles Dusburgas Pētera Chronicon Terrae Prussiae un to loma prūšu sabiedrībā (Prussian nobiles in "Chronicon Terrae Prussiae" by Petri de Dusburg and their probable political role in the Prussian community)*, University of Latvia, Scientific Papers University of Latvia – History, Spring 2011.

STANTCHEV, Stefan, "Inevitable Conflict or Opportunity to Explore? The Mechanics of Venice's Embargo against Mehmed II and the Problem of Western-Ottoman trade after 1453," *Mediaevalia*, 2011.

STAPEL, Rombert, "Power to the educated? Priest-brethren and their education, using data of the Utrecht bailiwick of the Teutonic Order, 1350–1600," in MO 5.

STOHLER, Patrick, "Wahrnehmung und Traditionsbildung in einem Traktat des 14. Jh."; "Das 18. Jahrhundert und 'der Kreuzzug': Genese und Entwicklung eines Konzepts."

TEBRUCK, Stefan, "Der sächsische Fernbesitz der sizilischen Klöster S. Maria Latina und S. Maria in Valle Josaphat," in *Italien-Mitteldeutschland-Polen. Internationale Tagung der Universität Leipzig*, ed. Enno Bünz und Wolfgang Huschner (Schriften zur sächsischen Geschichte und Volkskunde); "Crusades, Crusaders I. Christianity," in *Encyclopedia of the Bible and its Reception*, published by de Gruyter, Berlin/ New York, 2011.

THROOP, Susanna, *Crusading as an Act of Vengeance, 1095–1216*, Ashgate, 2011.

TOUATI, François-Olivier, "Mahomet, Charlemagne et la Corse: quels enjeux entre Francs et Musulmans au haut Moyen Âge?," in *La Corse, la Méditerranée et le monde musulman*, Journées Universitaires de Bonifacio (22–23 mai 2010), Ajaccio, 2011, pp. 9–26; "'Un sale résidu des croisades'? Maladies et médecine en Terre sainte," *L'Émoi de l'Histoire*, 33, 2011, pp. 29–41; "Face-à-face. Médecins des croisades et médecins d'Orient," *L'Histoire*, 2011; "Le récit des origines de Saint-Lazare de Jérusalem: mythe ou réalités ?," in *La mémoire des origines dans les ordres religieux-militaires au Moyen Âge*, éd. Ph. Josserand et M. Olivier, *Vita regularis. Ordnungen und Deutungen religiosen Lebens im Mittelalter*; "*Judicium leprae*. Acteurs et pratiques de l'expertise de lèpre. Du Moyen Âge à la Modernité (Orient-Occident)," in *Expertise et Conseil au Moyen Âge*, 42ᵉ Congrès de la Société des Historiens Médiévistes de l'Enseignement Supérieur public, (Oxford, 31 mars–3 avril 2011); "Orient latin: nouveaux objets, nouvelle histoire?," *Médiévales*.

TYERMAN, Christopher, *The Debate on the Crusades, 1099–2010*, Manchester UP, 2011.

De VAIVRE, Jean-Bernard, Le siège de Rhodes de 1480 (with Laurent Vissière); Note sur la commanderie de Bellecroix aux XIIe–XVe siècles; Les Châteaux de Kos et de Symi.

WEIDENKOPF, Steven A., *The Early Church: an Epic Journey through Church History Time Period Study*, Ascension Press.

5. Work in progress

AMITAI, Reuven, "Ibn Khaldun on Mongol Military Might"; "*Im Westen nichts Neues*? Re-examining Hülegü's Offensive into the Jazīra and Northern Syria in Light of Recent Research"; "Buddhism in Iran under the Mongols."

ANTAKI-MASSON, Patricia, Crusader fortifications of Beirut; Crusader topography and fortifications of Tyre; Medieval sundials of Lebanon; History of the cistercian abbey of Belmont (Tripoli-Lebanon); Cistercian abbeys of Lebanon.

ARBEL, Benjamin, The Venetian *Stato da Mar* in the Early Modern Period; Venetian Cyprus; Venetian Famagusta; Renaissance Attitudes to Animals; Falcons of the Venetian Colonial Empire; Jews in Venetian Crete.

BALARD, Michel, Les épices au Moyen Âge.

BELLOMO, Elena, "Diplomazia e Crociata nel Mediterraneo di inizio Trecento: il Francescano savonese Filippo Brusserio"; "I Sentieri della memoria: crociata e reliquie oltremarine in un'anonima cronaca monferrina medievale"; "Arnau de Villanova and the Recovery of the Holy Land (tentative title)"; "Peter, archbishop of Nazareth and his exile in North Italy" [articles]; The Spanish military Orders in Italy (XIII–XV centuries). Research projects: Italian maritimes cities and the first crusades. A study on motivation and propaganda; Italian military orders and armed confraternities.

BIDDLECOMBE, Steven, Currently engaged as a research fellow at the University of Bristol upgrading my doctoral thesis for publication and working on a translation of the *Historia Ierosolimitana* and additional analysis of the communal and familial aspects of Baldric's narrative.

BINYSH, Betty, in plan for CIHEC Israel 29 May 2011: "Making peace with 'God's enemies'. The dilemma of Frankish–Muslim Treaties in the Latin East from the 11th to 13th centuries"; in plan for IMC Leeds 12 July 2011: "'Rich' Peace or 'Poor' War – the dilemma of Crusader–Muslim Treaties in the Latin East."

BIRD, Jessalyn, Work on a monograph on women and the crusades, articles on prophecy and the crusades and projects as described in previous bulletins. Work on Christian Society and the Crusades, 1198–1274 with Edward Peters and James M. Powell continues.

BISAHA, Nancy, *On Europe*, a translation with introduction and commentary of Aeneas Silvius Piccolomini's *De Europa* (1458), in collaboration with Robert Brown.

BOAS, Adrian J., *Montfort One: History, Early Research and Recent Studies*.

BOM, Myra, *Women in the military orders in the 12th and 13th centuries* [book].

BOMBI, Barbara, Canon law and conversion of non-Christians in the 13th century.

CARR, Annemarie, Monograph: *An Icon in Context: The Virgin of Kykko*.

CARRAZ, Damien, CARRAZ, Damien, "Les Templiers de Provence et la Terre Sainte: mobilité et carrières (XIIIe–XIVe siècles)," in *VI Encontro sobre Ordens Militares. Freires, Guerreiros, Cavaleiros*, Palmela, 10–14 mars 2010, ed. I. C. Ferreira Fernandes; "Pour une approche globale des *novæ religiones*: en Basse-Provence aux XIIe–XIIIe siècles," in Journée d'étude en l'honneur du Professeur D. Le Blévec, Université de Montpellier, 3 février 2011; "Les établissements des ordres militaires dans l'espace urbain au XIIIe siècle. État de la question (Orient/Occident)," in *Espaces monastiques et espaces urbains*, ed. C. Caby, *Mélanges de l'École française de Rome-Moyen Âge*; "Templars and Hospitallers as peacemakers in feudal and princely conflicts in Occitania during the twelfth and thirteenth centuries," in *Military Orders in War and Peace*, Torun conference, 22–25 september 2011; "Paix et trêve entre

X^e et XIIe siècles," *La réforme "grégorienne" dans le Midi (milieu XIe–fin XIIe siècle)*, 48e colloque de Fanjeaux, juillet 2012.

CASSIDY-WELCH, Megan, Imprisonment in the Medieval Religious Imagination; The Medieval Refugee: Memory, Space and the Aftermath of War in thirteenth-century France (supported by an Australia Research Council Grant from 2008–2011).

CATLOS, Brian, *Muslim Societies in Latin Christendom, 1050–1614*, Cambridge: Cambridge University Press.

CHRISSIS, Nikolaos, publication of the proceedings of the conference organized with Mike Carr (RHUL), under the auspices of the SSCLE, entitled: "Contact and conflict in Frankish Greece and the Aegean: crusade, trade and religion amongst Latins, Greeks and Muslims, 1204–1453," 9 July 2010, Institute of Historical Research, London. The volume will include contributions on Byzantine, crusade and Ottoman history, by Prof. Bernard Hamilton (Nottingham), Prof. Peter Lock (York St John), Dr Evrim Binbaş (RHUL), Mike Carr (RHUL), Dr Nikolaos Chrissis (RHUL), Dr Rhoads Murphey (Birmingham), Dr Teresa Shawcross (Amherst), and Dr Judith Ryder (Wolfson College, Oxford).

CHRIST, Georg, ed. with Stefan Burkhardt, *Between Parallel Society and Integration. Diaspora and Transcultural Agency in the Medieval Eastern Mediterranean*, Transcultural Studies, Heidelberg, Springer; "At the Fringe of a Diaspora: Venetian agents between Alexandria and Cairo," Ibidem.

CHRISTIE, Niall G. F., *Preaching Holy War: Crusade and Jihad, 1095–1105*, with Deborah Gerish (to be published by Ashgate).

CIPOLLONE, Giulio, Edition of Proceedings of Congresso internazionale *La partecipazione di Anselmo al processo di costruzione della "nuova" Europa*, Roma, Pontificia Università Gregoriana (25–27 November 2010); ed. of Proceedings of Congresso internazionale *Colori e significati. Una "croce disarmata" tra crociata e gihad*, Roma, Pontificia Università Urbaniana (26–28 June 2011)

COLEMAN, Edward, "Ireland and the Crusades. A survey of the evidence"; "The Italian city communes and the Crusades in the twelfth century" [articles].

CONNELL, Charles W., *Public Opinion in the Middles Ages* [book].

CORRIE, Rebecca W., book on *Arezzo Manuscripts*; book *on Images of Virgin (East and West)*; article on "Palermo Manuscripts and Crusader Iconography."

COUREAS, Nicholas S., The Chronicle of "Amadi": A Translation into English, Cyprus Research Centre; The Life of Peter Thomas by Philippe de Mézières: A Translation into English, Cyprus Research Centre.

CRAWFORD, Paul F., See Bulletin 30, 2010 in vol. 9; also an article on Gregory VII and the idea of a military-religious order.

DANSETTE, Béatrice, La *Peregrinatio in terram sanctam* de Bernhard von Breidenbach, édition critique sous la direction du Pr. Jean Meyers.

DEMURGER, Alain, *Les hospitaliers de Saint-Jean de Jérusalem (XIe–début du XIVe siècle)*, à paraître 2011/2012; *Le peuple templier: prosopographie des Templiers d'après les procès-verbaux des interrogatoires des templiers au cours des process*, Catalogue alphabétique électronique et introduction sous forme de livre.

DICKSON, Gary, Charisma, Medieval and Modern [Essay].

DIVALL, Richard, Music Edition from Archives of Malta and Wignacourt Museum, Works by Michel'Angelo Falosi and Don Michel'Angelo Vella (18th Century).

Dourou-Eliopoulou, Maria, Research program of the University of Athens: The Aragonese policy in Greece in the 14th century based on unpublished archival material from Barcelona.

Edbury, Peter, Critical edition of the Old French Continuations of William of Tyre (with Massimiliano Gaggero); with Nicholas Coureas, *Chronique d'Amadi* (translation), Cyprus Research Centre; paper on the Old French Continuations of William of Tyre for IMC, Leeds 2010; Editor: MO5.

Edgington, Susan, Guido da Vigevano's *Regimen sanitatis*: edition, translation and commentary; Paperback translation of Albert of Aachen's *Historia* (for Ashgate).

van Elst, Toon, From Dover to Damiata: Former *Brabançons* and Flemish mercenaries in the Fifth Crusade.

Favreau-Lilie, Marie-Luise, *Italien und der islamische Orient zur Zeit der Kreuzzüge*; *Merkantile Expansion und historische Selbstdarstellung der itallienischen Seestädte* [book].

Folda, Jaroslav, Study of the Origins and Development of Chrysography in Byzantine, Crusader, and Italian painting.

Fonseca, Luís Adão da, Coordinator of the research project Comendas das Ordens Militares: perfil nacional e inserção internacional (FCT-Portugal-2010–2013) [Commanderies of the Military Orders: national profile and international setting].

Forey, Alan J., The Papacy and the Spanish Reconquest; Western converts to Islam; Paid Troops in the service of the military Orders; Marriage of Westerners and Non-Christians.

Franke, Daniel P., "The Crusade in Fourteenth-century England: A Story of Ebb and Flow, 1268–1420," for the Medieval Society, University of Rochester, Spring 2010; "Crusades Bibliography," Online project at the University of Rochester (Contributor); "The Medium and the Message: Rethinking the Besançon Incident of 1157"; "*Neve malum pro malo redderet*: Engaging the Turks in German Chronicles of the Third Crusade"; "Feeding the Fight: A Comparative Approach to East Anglian participation in late Plantagenet Warfare."

Friedman, Yvonne, Book: *Interludes of Peace*.

Gabriele, Matthew, Prophecy, Apocalypse, and the Intellectual Transformation of the Medieval West; The *Origins of the First Crusade; Reading the World: Ademar of Chabannes and the Intersection of Religion and culture in Medieval Europe*, ed. with Michael Frassetto and John Hosler; *The Legend of Charlemagne in Latin Culture*, ed. with William Purkis, Rochester, NY, Boydell and Brewer; *Exegesis in Practice, Prophecy Come True: Pope Urban II, the Arc of Sacred History, and the Language of Christian Consideration*.

Gaposchkin, Cecilia, Crusade and Liturgy; The rite of taking the cross.

Gilchrist, Marianne M, Biographical research on Conrad of Montferrat.

Grasso, Christian, *Papauté et croisade entre le IVᵉ Concile du Latran et le Iᵉʳ Concile de Lyon (1216–1245)*, thèse de Post-doctorat, École pratique des hautes études, Paris.

Hall, Martin, "An academic call to arms in 1252: John of Garland's crusading epic '*De triumphis Ecclesiae*"; English translation of Jean de Garlande's *De triumphis Ecclesiae*; Genoese texts relating to the Twelfth Century crusades [with Prof. Jonathan Phillips].

Hamilton, Bernard, *The Crusades and the Wider World*, Continuum Books.

Hammad Jahama, Mona, *Reliving the Past, Arab Modern Historiography of the Crusades.*

Harris, Jonathan, Research into the last 150 years before the fall of Constantinople.

Harscheidt, Michael, Intensive studies of the interior rites and endogenic customs of the Order of the Knights Templar during the late period of their history.

Hosten, Jan, Research on Gerard de Ridefort.

HOUSLEY, Norman, *Regenerating the Crusade: the Catholic Church and the Turkisch Treat, 1453–1505*, Oxford University Press.

IRWIN, Robert, Book on Hamilton Gibb and Bernard Lewis; Twelfth-century Arabic poetry with reference to the Crusades; The Mamluk army in thirteenth-century Syria.

JOTISCHKY, Andrew, *The cult of St Katherine of Alexandria across the Norman diaspora*, to be published in a collection of essays co-edited by Keith Stringer as part of the AHRC-funded 'Norman Edge' research project at Lancaster University; a short book for the general reader on the Crusades in the *Beginners Guide* series in 2011/12.

KANGAS, Sini, *Children in Holy War, c. 1100–1300*, Helsinki Collegium for Advanced Studies.

KEDAR, Benjamin Z., *A cultural history of the Kingdom of Jerusalem* [book]; Inventio patriarcharum – part 2 [article]; The battle of Arsuf, 1191[article].

KOLIA-DERMITZAKI, Athina, The captures of cities and their repercussions the cities' development and the lives of citizens in the Balkans, Asia Minor and Palestine (11th–13th centuries); Byzantine State officials int the Historiographers' account. Part II: Civil and Military officials of the 11th and 12th centuries. See also Bulletin of the SSCLE 25, 2005.

KOSTICK, Conor, *Social unrest and the Second Crusade* [Post-Doctoral Research sponsored by the Irish Research Council for the Humanities and Social Sciences]; *The Crusades: Conflict and Cohabitation* [sponsored by the Centre of Mediterranean and Near Eastern Studies at Trinity College Dublin and the Long Room Hub].

LEONARD Jr., Robert D., Gold Coins of the Crusader States.

LIGATO, Giuseppe, The Tower of David in Crusader times [article].

LOUD, Graham A., *Roger II and the Creation of the Kingdom of Sicily* (for Manchester Medieval Translations, to be completed autumn 2010).

LOWER, Michael, "Gregory IX and the Crusades," book chapter for *Pope Gregory IX (1227–1241)*, Ashgate, 2012; *The Tunis Crusade of 1270* [book].

LUCHITSKAYA, Svetlana, Images of Saracens in the *Bibles* moralisées [series of articles].

MACK, Merav, with Steven Kaplan and Merav Mack, ed., *Transnationalism and the Contemporary Christian Communities in the Holy Land*, peer-reviewed proceedings of a conference held at the Van Leer Jerusalem Institute and the CRFJ, in June 2010; *The Palestinian Christian Communities in Israel: A Crucial Minority.*

MADDEN, Thomas F., "The Venetian Version of the Fourth Crusade: Memory and the Conquest of Constantinople in Medieval Venice" [article].

MASÈ, Federica, Histoire urbaine. Les Vénitiens à l'œuvre en métropole et en Méditerranée orientale: acquisition, urbanisation et gestion publique et/ou privée des quartiers et donc du patrimoine foncier et immobilier (choix politiques, religieux, sociaux et économiques).

MENACHE, Sophia, Papal Attempts of Commercial Boycott in the Mediterranean during the Crusader Period.

MESCHINI, Marco, *Percezione dell'idea di crociata nella Cristianità dei secoli XI–XIII.* [Progetto di ricerca finanziato dal Consiglio Nazionale delle Ricerche, Roma, 2008–2009].

MITCHELL, Piers D., Analysis of several crusader period cesspools from the Kingdom of Jerusalem for evidence of human intestinal parasitic worms and dysentery.

MÖHRING, Hannes, *Saladin und seine Nachfolger. Die Geschichte der Aiyubiden* [book].

MORTON, Nicholas, The Defense of the Holy Land and the Memory of the Maccabees; *"In subsidium*: The declining contribution of Germany and Eastern Europe to the crusades to the Holy Land, 1187–291."

MURRAY, Alan V., A study of the crusade of Frederick Barbarossa.

NICHOLSON, Helen J., *The Proceedings Against the Templars in the British Isles*, 2 vols (Farnham: Ashgate) [edition with translation of the surviving testimonies] – as described in bulletin no. 28; *The Knights Templars' English Estates, 1308–11*, a transcription and analysis of the inventories and accounts of the Templars' properties in England during the trial of the Templars – as described in bulletin no. 29; Editing: the papers relating to the Military Orders that were presented at SSCLE Avignon, August 2008 – as described in bulletin no. 29.

NICOLAOU-KONNARI, Angel, *History of Limassol*, co-editor with Chris Schabel, Medochemie Series 2, 2009/10; with C. Schabel, "Frankish and Venetian Limassol," ibidem; *Two Cypriots of the Diaspora: Works and Days of Pietro and Giorgio de Nores* [Cyprus Research Centre] Nicosia, 2010; *The Encounter of Greeks and Franks in Cyprus in the Late Twelfth and Thirteenth Centuries. Phenomena of Acculturation and Ethnic Awareness*, Birmingham University Press, Ashgate, 2010; *Medieval Famagusta*, co-editor with G. Grivaud, C. Otten-Froux, C. Schabel, and A. Weyl Carr, 2010/11; "Women and Family Life (in Lusignan and Venetian Famagusta)," ibidem.

NICOVICH, J. Mark, Venetian involvement in naval leagues against the Turks in the 14th, 15th and 16th centuries; currently against Umur Bey, 1343–1345.

PAVIOT, Jacques, "Inciter le roi de France à partir à la croisade: Le sermon *Exaltavi lignum humile* de Pierre de La Palud (1332) et le *Discours du voyage d'outre-mer* de Jean Germain (1451)," in *Croisade et discours de guerre sainte à la fin du Moyen Âge. Légitimation, propagande, prosélytisme. Actes du colloque de Toulouse, 27–28 mars 2008*, Toulouse, 2010; "Des images pour la croisade? À propos de la Flagellation de Piero della Francesca et de Notre-Dame de Grâce de Cambrai, in *Mémoires, histoires et images des croisades aux derniers siècles du Moyen Âge. Actes du colloque de Prague, 20–21 novembre 2008*, Toulouse, 2011.

PERRY, David M., *Miracles from the Sea: Venice, Stolen Relics, and the Aftermath of the Fourth Crusade*.

PHILLIPS, Christopher Matthew, Book on *Crusade Preaching, Doctrine of Redemption, Devotion to the Cross*.

PHILLIPS, Jonathan, *Caffaro of Genoa and the Crusades*, (a translation, with Martin Hall); *The Crusades, 1095–1204*, second edition of Longman book first published in 2002 (2011/2012); "Eugenius III and the Second Crusade," in *Pope Eugenius III: Essays and Documents*, ed. A. Jotischky and I.Fonnesberg-Schmidt, Farnham, 2011; "The Motivation of Early Crusaders: Caffaro, Genoa and Pisa" (article); A long-term study on the motivation of Italian Crusaders; "The Historical Legacy of Saladin" (article); "Ibn Jubayr, Saladin and the 'Unified' Muslim Near East," in *Cultural Encounters during the Crusades*, ed. K.Villads Jensen, L. P.Visti Hansen, H.Vogt and H-C. Korsholm Nielsen.

PHILLIPS, Simon D., The Hospitallers on Cyprus and Rhodes in the Late Middle Ages; The Hospitaller Priory at Clerkenwell and the local community 1400–1540; The Military Orders and Island History.

POLEJOWSKI, Karol, *The Briennes and the Mediterranean World in the XIIIth and XIVth centuries; The Teutonic Order in the XIIIth and XIVth centuries*.

POWELL, James M., *Christian Society and the Crusades, 1198–1274*, with Edward Peters and Jessalyn Bird.

Power, Amanda, "Roger Bacon's Opus maius and related works," in D. Thomas and B. Roggema, ed., *Christian–Muslim Relations: A Bibliographical History*, vol. 3: 1200–1500, Leiden, Brill, 2011; Roger Bacon and the Jews; The Fears od Adam Marsh.

Pringle, Denys*, Pilgrimage to Jerusalem and the Holy Land, 1187–1291*, Crusade Texts in Translation, Ashgate, Aldershot; *The Mamluk and Ottoman Castle of al-'Aqaba (Jordan)*. Levant Supplementary Series, Oxford; Oxbow; with P. Chomowicz and D. Gammill, The Town Walls of Ascalon in the Byzantine, Early Islamic and Crusader periods; Edition of *Wilbrand of Oldenburg's journey to Cilicia, Cyprus and the Holy Land (1211–1212)*.

Pryor, John H., Crusading by sea: the maritime history of the Crusades, 1095–1291(continuing, previously notified). This is now planned as a two-volume work. The first will be devoted to the maritime technology, the ships and technologies and techniques of navigation and naval warfare; Sea Technologies, in: The Cambridge History of War. Volume two: War and the medieval world, ed. Reuven Amitai, Anne Curry, David Graff; new edition of the *Libellus de expugnatione Terrae Sanctae per Saladinum* with facing translation, commentary, and studies of several themes of the work. [This work is being undertaken together with a group of students, including Keagan Brewer, Deyel Dalziel-Charlier, Jennifer Green, and James Kane].

Pujeau, Emmanuelle, participation to the ANR project *Late crusades*; editions of some italian *Relazione*.

Purkis, William J., "Crusading and the Military Orders in Caesarius of Heisterbach's *Dialogus miraculorum*" (Article), part of an ongoing project on the Cistercians and the crusading movement.

Reynolds, Burnam W., The Prehistory of the Crusades: Missionary War and the Baltic Crusades, London, Continuum Press, 2013.

Richard, Jean, *Bullarium Cyprium*, t. III (Jean XXII–Grégoire XI).

Rist, Rebecca, Book on *The Papacy and the Jews in the Central Middle Ages*.

Rodriguez Garcia, José Manuel*, The Teutonic Order and the Kingdoms of Spain* [book].

Rubenstein, Jay, Holy War and History: The First Crusade at the End of the Time.

Sarnowsky, Juergen, project financed by Deutsche Forschungsgemeinschaft – DFG; 2008–2012, Erschliessung und virtuelle Rekonstruktion der aelteren Register der Hochmeister des Deutschen Ordens (with Sebastian Kubon); this project aims at calendaring the early registers of the Grand Masters of the Teutonic Knights in Prussia, preserved in the Geheimes Staatsarchiv Preussischer Kulturbesitz, Berlin.

Schryver, James G., with Tasha Vorderstrasse, A study of the Port St. Symeon ware from Hama, in the National Museum of Copenhagen.

Sinibaldi, Micaela, Co-direction of excavations at Bayda Medieval Village, Petra: started in summer 2010 and will continue in summer 2011 (Brown University Petra Archaeological Project, co-directed by S. Alcock and C. Tuttle). Occupation includes 12th to 16th century phases and is carried out in conjunctionwith extensive site survey of the Petra area.

Slack, Corliss, British Crusade Sites, a book dedicated to the memory of the crusades, in the British Isles.

Stantchev, Stefan, *Spiritual Rationality: Papal Embargo as Cultural Practice, 1150–1520* (Book); "The Medieval Origins of Embargo as a Policy Tool."

Stohler, Patrick, "Wahrnehmung und Traditionsbildung in einem Traktat des 14. Jh."; "Das 18. Jahrhundert und 'der Kreuzzug': Genese und Entwicklung eines Konzepts."

TEBRUCK, Stefan, "Der Bischof als Kreuzfahrer: Konrad von Halberstadt (†1225) und der Vierte Kreuzzug"; "Von Jerusalem nach Sachsen: Der Fernbesitz von S. Maria Latina und S. Maria in Valle Josaphat in den Harzvorlanden"; *Aufbruch und Heimkehr. Jerusalempilger und Kreuzfahrer aus dem Raum zwischen Harz und Elbe (1100–1300)*, Habilitationsschrift, Universität Jena.

TESSERA, Miriam Rita, Il sogno di re Amalrico, la reliquia della Vera Croce e la canonizzazione di Bernardo di Clairvaux [article]; Melisenda, regina di Gerusalemme [book].

TOUATI, François-Olivier, *Les actes et documents relatifs à Saint-Lazare de Jérusalem (Orient-Occident)*, édition.

TYERMAN, Christopher J., Book on *Crusade*.

De VAIVRE, Jean-Bernard, Rhodes aux XIVe–XVe et début du XVIe siècle; Fortifications des Hospitalliers en Dodécanèse; Chypre, iconographie à la fin du XIVe siècle.

WEBER, Benjamin, Edition and comment of the *Liber Sancte Cruciate*, book of account oft the Pius II's crusade (1464).

6. Theses in progress/ Thèses en cours

ANCKAER, Jan, Belgium and the Ottoman Empire during the reign of Leopold I (1831–1865), PhD.

ANDREI, Filippo, Boccaccio the Philosopher: The Language of Knowledge in the Decameron, PhD, University of California, Berkeley, Department of Italian Studies, program in *Romance Languages and Literatures*, supervised by Prof. S. Botterill; A. R. Ascoli; I. Navarrete.

ANTAKI-MASSON, Patricia, Tyr à l'époque des Croisades: Topographie urbaine d'une ville majeure de Terre sainte, Thèse de Doctorat à l'Université de Poitiers sous la direction de Nicolas Faucherre (Soutenance en 2011)

BALDWIN, Philip B., Pope Gregory X and the Crusades, PhD, Queen Mary, University of London.

BARBÉ, Hervé, Le château de Safed et son territoire durant la période des croisades, PhD, Hebrew University of Jerusalem, supervised by Prof. Benjamin Z. KEDAR co-directed with Prof. Nicolas Faucherre.

BARBU, Diana Cornelia, The Anjou Dynasty, the Order of Saint George and the links with the rulers of Wallachia, PhD, Valahia University of Targoviste, Romania.

BERNER, Alexander, Crusaders from the Lower Rheinland, PhD, Bochum University, supervised by Prof. Nikolas Jaspert.

BINYSH, Betty, Peace-making in the Latin East between 1099 and 1291, Ph.D., Cardiff University, supervised by Dr Helen Nicholson.

BISHOP, Adam, The development of crusader law in the twelfth century, PhD, Centre for Medieval Studies, University of Toronto.

BLEY, Matthias, Purity, Reform and the Other, PhD, Bochum University, supervised by Prof. Nikolas Jaspert.

BRACHTHÄUSER, Urs, The Crusade against Mahdia in 1390, PhD Thesis, Bochum University, supervised by Prof. Nikolas Jaspert.

BREWER, Keagan, M.Phil., on *Marvels in medieval manuscripts*, University of Sydney.

BUCK, Andrew David, A study of the principality of Antioch as a frontier society in the 12th and 13th centuries, MPhil/PhD, Queen Mary, University of London, supervised by Dr Tom Asbridge.

Buckingham, Hannah, Identity and archaeology in everyday life: the material culture of the Crusader states, PhD, Cardiff University, supervised by Denys Pringle.

Carr, Michael, Motivations and Response to Crusades in the Aegean: c. 1302–1348, PhD, Royal Holloway, University of London, supervised by Prof. Jonathan Harris.

Christ, Georg, Trading Secrets: Bans, Customs and Smuggling in the Hanseatic and Venetian Trade Systems (1291–1450), Universität Heidelberg, Habilitation/second book.

Cosgrove, Walker Reid, Clergy and Crusade: the Church of Languedoc during the Albigensian Crusade, PhD, Saint-Louis University, U.S.A.

Cushing, Dana, Critical edition, translation and reconstruction of the Germanic Crusaders' sealift and siege of Almohad Silves (1189–1191) from an eyewitness account.

Durkin, Frances, Crusade Preaching: Origins, Evolution and Impact, PhD, University of Birmingham, supervised by Dr William Purkis.

Franke, Daniel, East Anglia at War: The Conduct and Impacts of the Hundred Years' War in the Reign of Edward III, 1327–1377, PhD, University of Rochester.

Froumin, Robin, Continuation or non-continuation of Pilgrimage in the Holy Land; Churches from the Crusader Period built on the remains of Byzantine Churches, MA, Haifa University, supervised by Professor Adrian Boas.

Gammill, Deborah, Construction materials and techniques in early Islamic Ramla, PhD, Cardiff University, supervised by Professor Denys Pringle.

Georgiou, Constantinos, Crusading preaching during the 14th century, PhD, University of Cyprus, supervised by Christopher Schabel.

Gomez, Miguel, A Cultural and institutional study of the battle of Las Navas de Tolosa and crusading in Iberia in the early thirteenth century, PhD, University of Tennessee, Knoxville.

Gourinard, Henri, Levantine Towns in the *itineraria* of the 14th–17th Centuries, supervised by Prof. Benjamin Z. Kedar.

Gurack, Ditte, The Devotion to the Virgin Mary in the Military Orders (12th – 16th Century), PhD, Bochum University, supervised by Professor Nikolas Jaspert.

Handyside, Philip David, The old French Translation of William of Tyre, PhD., Cardiff University, supervised by Prof. Peter Edbury.

Ikonomopoulos, Konstantinos, Byzantium and Jerusalem, 9th–13th Centuries, PhD, Royal Holloway, University of London, supervised by Prof. Jonathan Harris.

John, Simon, Godfrey of Bouillon: Perceptions of a First Crusader, 1100–c.1350, PhD, Swansea University, supervised by Prof. John France and Prof. Daniel Power.

Kool, Robert, The Circulation and Use of Coins in the Latin kingdom of Jerusalem, 1099–1291, PhD, Hebrew University of Jerusalem, supervised by Prof. Benjamin Z. Kedar and Prof. Michael Metcalf.

Lewis, Kevin James, A study of the internal aspects of the county of Tripoli during the twelfth century, PhD, Oxford University, supervised by Dr Christopher Tyerman.

Morris, April Jehan, Imag[in]ing the "East": The Holy Land as Threat and Desire in the Aquitaine, 1095–1195, PhD, Art History, University of Texas at Austin.

Mylod, Liz, Pilgrimage in the Holy Land in the Thirteenth Century, PhD, Institute for Medieval Studies, University of Leeds.

Naus, James L., Crusading and Capetian Dynastic Ideology: 1099–1226, PhD, Saint Louis University.

ORDMAN, Jilana, Feeling like a Crusader: Crusader Affect and Crusade Theology, 1095–1291, PhD, Loyola University, Chicago.

PARK, Danielle, "Those who were left behind" – Protection of the families and properties of crusaders, c. 1095–1291, PhD, Royal Holloway, University of London.

PARKER, Kenneth Scott, The Impact of the Crusades on the Christian Churches of the Near East, 1291–1402, PhD, Royal Holloway, University of London, supervised by Prof. Jonathan Harris.

PASTORI RAMOS, Aurelio, La idea de guerra santa en la obra de Bernardo de Claraval, PhD, Facultad de Filosofía y Letras, Universidad de Buenos Aires, Argentina.

ROSSI-RIVERA, Shirley, Relationships and interactions between Christian and Muslim Women during the times of the crusades.

PERRY, Guy, The Career and Significance of John of Brienne, king of Jerusalem, emperor of Constantinople, PhD, University of Oxford.

PETRO, Theodore D., Fame on Earth and Glory in Heaven: Returning Crusaders and Twelfth-century Constructs of Honor and Piety, PhD, University of Cincinnati.

PETROVSKAIA, Natalia I., *Medieval Welsh Perception of the Orient*, PhD, University of Cambridge.

POLEJOWSKI, Karol, *The Briennes and the Mediterranean World in the XIIIth and XIVth centuries*, post-PhD (habilitation thesis), University of Gdansk, Department of History, 2011/2012

PONTES, Cleber Da Silva, The Catalan domination in Athens – 1311, PhD, Université de Paris I – Sorbonne, supervised by Michel Balard.

ROACH, Daniel, Orderic Vitalis, crusading Historian, PhD, University of Exeter.

RONEN-RUBIN, Jonathan, Intellectual Activities in Acre, 1191–1291, PhD, Hebrew University of Jerusalem, supervised by Prof. Benjamin Z. Kedar, co-directed with Laura Minervini.

RUSSELL, Eugenia, Encomia to St Demetrius in Late Byzantine Thessalonica, PhD, Royal Holloway, University of London, supervised by Prof. Jonathan Harris.

RYAN, Vincent, The Cult of the Virgin Mary and the Crusading Movement during the High Middle Ages, PhD, Saint Louis University.

SHOTTEN-HALLEL, Vardit, The Churches of the Latin Kingdom of Jerusalem: Medieval Building Technologies and Architecture in the Frankish Levant and in Europe, PhD, Hebrew University of Jerusalem, supervised by Prof. Benjamin Z. Kedar.

SINIBALDI, Micaela, Villages of Crusader Transjordan: Production, circulation and use of ceramics in the 12th century, PhD, Cardiff University, supervised by Professor Denys Pringle.

SIMSONS, Raitis, M.A. at University of Latvia: Senprūšu sabiedrības sociālo struktūru atainojums Elbingas vārdnīcā (The depiction of Old Prussian social structures in Elbing Vocabulary).

SMITH, Thomas, Pope Honorius III and Crusading to Egypt and the Holy Land, 1216–1227, PhD, Royal Holloway, University of London, supervised by Professor Jonathan Phillips.

STAPEL, Rombert, Cronike van der Duytscher Oirden ["Jüngere Hochmeisterchronik"], PhD, Leiden University/Fryske Akademy.

STOHLER, Patrick, Europa: Konflikt, Kontakt, Konstrukt. Europäisierung und Nationenbildung im Mittelalter. Die Kreuzzüge im Spannungsfeld zeitgenössischer Wahrnehmung, PhD, University of Basel, supervised by Prof. Dr Achatz Freiherr von Müller.

TAMMINEN, Miikka, *Ad crucesignatos et crucesignandos*. Constructing "the True Crusader" in the Crusade Model Sermons of the 13th Century, PhD, University of Tampere, Finland.

VANDEBURIE, Jan, Sources and Influence of Jacques de Vitry's *Historia Orientalis*, PhD, University of Kent.

VANDERKERCKHOVE, Dweezil, The Armenian settlement of Cilicia in the 11th and 12 centuries, PhD, Cardiff University, supervised by Denys Pringle and Frank Trombley.

WINTERBOTTOM, Ashley Sarah, Gender identities in William of Tyre's chronicle "A History of Dedds Done beyond the Sea," PhD, University of Huddersfield.

ZELNIK, Joseph, *Silent enim leges inter arma*?: Laws of War in the Latin Kingdom of Jerusalem, PhD, Bar-Ilan University, Israel, supervised by Professor Yvonne Friedman.

7. Fieldwork planned or undertaken recently

In August 2010, Prof. Reuven Amitai with Prof. Michal Biran took a group of students and colleagues on a study tour of Mongolia. This tour placed an emphasis on the Mongol world empire, but also looked at the history and archeology in the centuries before the erection of the empire, as well as subsequent developments, up to the present day. This trip resulted in contact with foreign and Mongolian archeologists, and will hopefully lead to Israeli archeologists working in the country. While this may seem peripheral to Crusading Studies, the role of the Mongols on the history of the Frankish settlement in the East, as well as the Crusading movement as a whole, is not negligible, and in addition, the reports of papal envoys to Mongolia in the mid-thirteenth century contribute greatly to our knowledge of the empire, and especially its capital, Qara Qorum. The explanations and lectures during the tour often touched upon crusading matters.

ANDREI, Filippo, Italian Literature; Romance Philology; Medieval Latin Literature.

ANTAKI MASSON, Patricia, The crusader fortress of Beirut: recent discoveries; Masons' marks of the Cistercian abbey of Belmont (Tripoli); Medieval sundials of the county of Tripoli.

ARBEL, Benjamin, "The *Stato da Mar*," for E. Dursteller ed., *A Handbook of Venetian History*, Leiden: Brill; "Famagusta under Venetian Rule," for G. Grivaud and C. Schabel ed., *Medieval and Renaissance Famagusta; The Animal Renaissance; Falcons in Venice's Stato da Mar*; Jews in Venice's Stato da Mar.

BOAS, Adrian J., Excavations in outer ward of Montfort Castle (Planned for summer of 2011).

CARLSSON, Christer, An archaeological field school at Sandford Templar Preceptory in Oxfordshire, U.K.

CARRAZ, Damien, (with Pascale Chevalier), Archaeological study of the crypt and the monastic church of St Pierre du Mont (9th to 15th c.), Nièvre, France; (with Esther Dehoux); The Military Orders and the Cult of Warrior Saints (in France, twelfth to fifteenth century).

CHRIST, Georg, Palaeography and Archive Workshop in Heidelberg, Venice, including group research in the Archivio di Stato di Venezia.

CHRISTOFORAKI, Ioanna, Recipient of the combined CAORC (Council of American Overseas Research Centers) and Getty Research Exchange Fellowship for the Mediterranean Basin and the Middle East, to carry out research at the Cyprus American Archaeological Research Institute (CAARI) on a project entitled: "The Sacred Landscape of Medieval Cyprus: Village Saints and Popular Piety" (June–July 2011).

CLOVER, David, Medieval churches in, and around L'Aquila, Italy.

CUSHING, Dana, Planning a site visit to the castle of Silves, Portugal, for Summer 2011; the purpose will be to measure the site and visit neighbouring villages along the Arade river, with a view to re-constructing the Crusader/Almohad sieges of 1189–1191, especially the Crusader encampment, town waterworks and harbor areas. Also planning to visit various Maritime Museums with twelfth-century artefacts in Denmark, Germany, the Netherlands and Belgium in 2011 to examine cogs, ship's stores, and harbour artefacts/sites.

KEDAR, Benjamin Z., Coordinating excavations in Acre's Genoese quarter.

MICHAUDEL, Benjamin, June 2010: Syrian-French joint archaeological survey in the Nahr al-Kabir al-Shamali region (Coastal Syria) to locate and study the architectural remains of medieval settlements; October–November 2010: 4rd campaign of the Syrian-French joint archaeological mission on Saladin/Saone/Sahyun Castle (Syria).

PUJEAU, Emmanuelle, "Europe" for the Early Moderns; the Turkish point of view about the late Crusades.

POLEJOWSKI, Karol, History of the French families, especially the Briennes, in the XIII and first half of the XIV century in the Mediterranean region (Outremer, Greece, Italy).

SINIBALDI, Micaela, Shawbak castle, Jordan: fieldwork and study of ceramic artefacts.

TEBRUCK, Stefan, Crusaders in the Holy Roman Empire during 11th to 13th centuries – comparative studies on social, economic, political and spiritual aspects of crusading in different territories – this research is planned to be a project of the Chair of Medieval History at the University of Gießen.

De VAIVRE, Jean-Bernard, Rhodes au temps des Hospitaliers; L'ordre de Saint-Jean de Jérusalem, XIIIe–début XVIe siècles.

WEBER, Benjamin, Ethiopian–Western relations; role of Ethipia in the crusading plans.

8. News of interest to members

a) Conferences and seminars

International conference The Role of Peace in Monotheistic Traditions, org. by Sophia Menache and Yvonne Friedman, Cosponsored by C.I.H.E.C, Bar-Ilan University, Van Leer Institute, Jerusalem and Haifa University, 29 May–2 June 2010, Israel.

Union in Separation. Trading Diasporas in the Eastern Mediterranean (1200–1700), University of Heidelberg, 17–19 February 2011: a three-day international conference hosted by the Transcultural Studies Programme at the University of Heidelberg. The conference focuses on transcultural diasporic communities in the medieval Mediterranean with specific respect to their role in trade between perceived separate cultural areas. http://www.uni-heidelberg.de/transculturality/union_in_separation.html

"L'Occident, la Croisade et l'Éthiopie," Table-ronde, organisée par le CEMAF, Paris, 8 April 2011.

Emanuel Buttigieg and Dr Simon Phillips of the University of Cyprus, organized a conference in Rhodes, 27–29 April 2011 on *Islands and the Military Orders*. The plenary speakers were Anthony Luttrell and Victor Mallia-Milanes.

The "Norman Edge" project (http://www.lancs.ac.uk/normanedge/homepage.htm) will be holding a final conference at Lancaster in December 2011. Further details will be posted on the project website.

The *Crusades Studies Forum* at Saint Louis University is a venue for the presentation of current research, the discussion of recent scholarship, and the exploration of new directions in topics relating to the Crusades. Participants include those local to the Saint Louis region as well as distinguished scholars from across the globe. For the current and past schedules see http://crusades.slu.edu.

On 22 January 2011, the Hebrew University research group "The Formation of Islamic Society in Palestine-Eretz-Israel (ca. 600–1500 C.E.)" held a conference on "Palestine during the Middle Ages (634–1517): Demographic, Social and Cultural Trends" in Jerusalem. The group is sponsored and funded by the Israel Science Foundation, and includes researchers from Ben-Gurion University of Beersheva. For filmed transcripts of the lectures (in Hebrew), go to http://islamization.huji.ac.il/pub.php and see there also for more information about the group's activities.

The East (Near and Far) will be the next theme of *The Rendez-Vous de l'Histoire* at Blois (France) from 13 to 16 October 2011. This large festival is open to the wider public and professionals: it offers a unique occasion of meeting with multiple conferences, round tables, debates, films and a huge gathering of booksellers and authors.

"Écrire l'histoire des croisades (III): L'économie des Croisades et des États latins," Journée d'Étude, org. by Prof. François-Olivier Touati, Université François-Rabelais, Tours, 23 March 2012.

International conference at University of Gießen (june 2012) on *Crusaders in the Holy Roman Empire during 11th to 13th centuries*.

b) Other news

L'Affaire des Templiers. Du Procès au Mythe, an exhibition held in Paris, Archives nationales, 2 March–16 May 2011, shown many documents relative to the trial and the seed of the myth.

Dr Megan Cassidy-Welch has recently been awarded an Australian Research Council Future Fellowship to pursue a 4-year project on war memory in the Middle Ages, with a particular focus on the 12th and 13th century crusades. The project is titled "War and memory in European Culture: A Long Perspective."

Dr Michael Harscheidt has established the website www.templaria.de beyond neo-templarian associations and beyond Masonic based corporations, only for actual scientific information.

Angeliki Lymberopoulou of the Open University in the U.K., has received a large grant from the Leverhulme Foundation to make a full photographic record and interdisciplinary study of the imagery of Hell in the wall painting of Venetian Crete, 13th–17th century, in itself and in comparison with that of other once Byzantine islands under Latin rule. She has a team of nine, including, along with Dr Lymberopoulou herself, Annemarie Carr, Rembrandt Duits, Charalambos Gasparis, Diana Newall, Athanasios Semoglou, Dionysios Stathakopoulos, Vasiliki Tsamakda, Rainer Warland.

9. Members' queries

Dana Cushing is planning a research trip to Silves, Portugal. She would greatly appreciate contact with Portuguese colleagues, and any advice for disabled travel in the Algarve region from members who have visited already.

10. Income and expenditure for the SSCLE from 1 October 2009 to 30 September 2010

This report shows SSCLE assets in separate columns, totaling the amount in each of the three currencies in which these funds are held. Whenever notes that follow refer to the total assets or liabilities of the Society, these are totaled and reported in sterling followed by the equivalent amount in dollars and in euros. In each case these are computed using the prevailing rates as of 30 September 2010 (i.e.: £1 = $1.5711 = €1.1527), rounded to the nearest whole unit.

Using these currency equivalencies, on 1 October 2009, the total of SSCLE funds equaled £21,101 (or $34,723 or €25,476). On 30 September 2010 the Society's assets totaled £26,533 (or $41,685 or €30,584). 354 subscriptions were paid during this reporting period, the majority of which (263) were for membership with the journal (*Crusades* Vol. 9). Additional funds were received for back issues of the journal and as prepayment for future subscriptions. Because the Society is billed for the journal only after it is published, and *Crusades* Vol. 8 was published October 2010, the bill for that volume, which totaled £5,260 (or $8,264 or €6,063), must be considered as pending charges against SSCLE assets. In addition £1,160 (or $1,822 or €1,337) was collected in prepayments for future issues of the journal, and must also be considered as pending charges. These liabilities are roughly equal to 29% of the Society's funds on deposit as of the close of the reporting period. The expenditure of funds for the journal reported above (£5,940) was in payment for *Crusades* Vol. 8 (for 2009), which was mailed out in November 2009, and in payment for various back-issues of *Crusades* during the reporting period.

Notable expenses for this period include £381 ($598, €432) for dues as an Associate Member of the *Le Comité international des sciences historique* (CISH/ICHS). Also of note, interest earned vis-à-vis the prior year has increased slightly, reflecting a return to more normal practices in the banking industry. In addition the use of Paypal, an on-line banking service that allows members to pay their subscriptions using a credit card, continues to increase. Use of this service has lowered banking fees for both the SSCLE and its individual members, but has also resulted in an increase in the proportion of dues payments made in US currency.

In summary, the number of paid memberships has increased slightly, and the Society is fiscally stronger year over year. The resources available to the Society remain modest, however, and additional steps may need to be taken to improve the Society's fiscal health. A particular concern is the complexity of the current dues structure, which demands detailed and time-consuming record keeping. Some scholarly societies, similar in size to the SSCLE but with a more streamlined dues structure, now employ collection services to perform many of the tasks formerly done by volunteer treasurers. Your treasurer will be making recommendations to the Executive Committee to simplify the dues structure of our Society, and, if they are accepted and implemented, the changes will both augment the Society's resources and make it possible for future treasurers to maintain the SSCLE's records with greater ease.

I again express gratitude to the members the SSCLE for their support, encouragement and unfailing courtesy.

Respectfully submitted,

James D. Ryan, Treasurer

U.K. Accounts (£)	U.S. Accounts ($)	Euro Accounts (€)

BALANCES CARRIED FORWARD, 1 OCTOBER 2009

£10,873.2	**$12,444.55**	**€3,824.98**

INCOME

U.K. Accounts (£)		U.S. Accounts ($)		Euro Accounts (€)	
£2379.00	Subs. Etc. received	$8728.80	Subs. Etc. received	€3460.00	Subs. Etc. received
£4.36	Interest received	$23.86	Interest received		
£2,383.36	**Total income**	**$8,752.66**	**Total income**	**€3,460.00**	**Total income**

EXPENDITURES

U.K. Accounts (£)		U.S. Accounts ($)		Euro Accounts (€)	
£5,940.00	Expenditures – journal	$94.82	postage, supplies, etc.	€26.83	bank charges
		$22.61	bank charges		
		$547.84	dues CHIS		
(£5,940.00)	**Total expenditures**	**($715.27)**	**Total expenditures**	**(€26.83)**	**Total expenditures**

SURPLUS OF INCOME OVER EXPENDITURES

(£3,556.64)	**$8,037.39**	**€3,433.17**

TRANSFER OF FUNDS BETWEEN CURRENCIES

U.K. Accounts (£)		U.S. Accounts ($)		Euro Accounts (€)	
£3,059.98	Transferred from US$	($5,000.00)	Transferred to UK£	(€2,250.00)	Transferred to UK£
£1,971.09	Transferred from €				

BALANCES ON HAND, 30 SEPTEMBER 2010

U.K. Accounts (£)	U.S. Accounts ($)	Euro Accounts (€)
£12,347.66	**$15,481.94**	**€5,008.15**

11. List of members and their addresses

(* Recorded as new member)

Dr David S. H. ABULAFIA, Gonville and Caius College, Cambridge, CB2 1TA, ENGLAND, U.K.

*Marianne AILES, Dept of French, School of Modern Languages, University of Bristol, Bristol, BS8 1TE, ENGLAND, U.K.; marianne.ailes@bristol.ac.uk

Brian ALLISON LEWIS, c/o Sabic, P.O. Box 5101, Riyadh 11422, SAUDI ARABIA

Dr Martín ALVIRA CABRER, Universidad Complutense de Madrid, Facultad de Geografía e Historia, Departamento de Historia Medieval, C/Profesor Aranguren, s/n, 28040-Madrid (Spain); malvira@ghis.ucm.es

Prof. Reuven AMITAI, The Eliyahu Elath Chair for the History of the Muslim Peoples, Institute of Asian and African Studies, Hebrew Univ., Jerusalem 91905, ISRAEL; r_amitai@mscc.huji.ac.il

Dr Monique AMOUROUX, 2, Avenue de Montchalette, Cassy, 33138 Lanton, FRANCE; monique.amouroux@aliceadsl.fr

Jan ANCKAER, Rue des Fleuristes 5, B-1082 Brussels, BELGIUM; jananckaer@yahoo.com

Prof. Alfred J. ANDREA, 161 Austin Drive, Apartment 3, Burlington VT 05401, U.S.A.; aandrea@uvm.edu

Dr Filippo ANDREI, 1644 Oxford Street, Apt. 5, Berkeley CA, 94709, U.S.A.; filandrei@berkeley.edu

Patricia ANTAKI-MASSON, Rés. La Palisse Bât B., 5 rue du 21 juin 1940, 64100 Bayonne, Bayonne, France; patriciaantaki@yahoo.com

*Spyridon ANTONOPOULOS, 112 Yarmouth Road, Norwood MA 02062, U.S.A.; spyridonantonopoulos@yahoo.com

Dr Benjamin ARBEL, School of History, Tel-Aviv Univ., Tel-Aviv 69978, ISRAEL; arbel@post.tau.ac.il

Dr Marco AROSIO, Università del Sacro Cuore, Milano, ITALY; marco_arosio@tin.it

Dr Thomas S. ASBRIDGE, Dept. of History, Queen Mary and Westfield College, Univ. of London, Mile End Road, London E1 4NS, ENGLAND, U.K.; t.s.asbridge@qmul.ac.uk

Prof. Zubaida ATTA, 19 Sphinx Building – Sphinx Square, Apartment 85, Muhandessin, Cairo, EGYPT; prof.zatta@yahoo.com

Hussein M. ATTIYA, 20 Ahmed Sidik Street, Sidi Gaber El-Sheik, Alexandria, EGYPT; husseinattiya@hotmail.com

Marc J. AYERS, 2593 Inverness Point Dr., Birmingham, AL 35242, U.S.A.; mayers@babc.com

Prof. Taef Kamal EL-AZHARI, International Affairs Dept., Qatar Univ., Faculty of Arts, 2713 Doho, QATAR; taef@gega.net

Dr Mohammed AZIZ, P.O. Box 135513, Beirut, LEBANON

Dr Xavier BAECKE, Louis-Roelandplein 29, 9000 Gent, BELGIUM; xavierbaecke@hotmail.com

Dr Dan BAHAT, P.O. Box 738, Mevasseret Zion 90805, ISRAEL; danbahat@gmail.com

Archibald BAIN, Dufftown, Banffshire AB55 4AJ, SCOTLAND, U.K.; ArchieBain@aol.co.uk or gilliesbeag@yahoo.co.uk

Prof. Michel Balard, 4, rue des Remparts, 94370 Sucy-en-Brie, FRANCE; Michel.Balard@univ-paris1.fr

Prof. Susan Balderstone, Adjunct Professor in Cultural Heritage, Deakin Univ., Melbourne, AUSTRALIA; susan.balderstone@bigpond.com

Philip B. Baldwin, RR 2, 5738 County Road 1, Consecon, Ontario, K0K 1T0, CANADA; pipbb@yahoo.com

Laura Balletto, Via Orsini 40/B, 16146 Genova, ITALY; Laura.Balletto@lettere.unige.it

Prof. Malcolm Barber, Dept. of History, Univ. of Reading, P.O. Box 218, Whiteknights, Reading RG6 6AA, ENGLAND, U.K.; m.c.barber@reading.ac.uk

Diana Cornelia Barbu, Calea Martirilor no.60, sc.A, Apt.32, Timisoara 300719, ROMANIA; dia.704@gmail.com

Dr Michael Bardot, Dept. Behavioral and Social Sciences, Lincoln Univ., 820 Chestnut Street, Room 310 Founders Hall, Jefferson City MO 65102, U.S.A.; Bardotm@lincolnu.edu

Prof. John W. Barker, 5611 Longford Terrace, Madison, WI 53711, U.S.A.; jwbarker@wisc.edu

Dr Sebastian Bartos, 319 Oak Center Place, Valdosta GA 31602, U.S.A.; sebartos@hotmail.com

Prof. George Beech, 1745 Hillshire Drive, Kalamazoo, MI 49008, U.S.A.; george.beech@wmich.edu

Dr Gregory D. Bell, Duke Univ., History Dept., Durham NC 27708, U.S.A.; gdb@duke.edu

Dr Elena Bellomo, via dei Rospigliosi 1, 20151 Milano, ITALY; elena.bellomo@libero.it

Cadet Colin Bennett, PO Box 0408, United States Military Academy, West Point, NY 10997-0408, U.S.A.; colin.bennett@usma.edu

Matthew Bennett, 58 Mitchell Avenue, Hartley Wintney, Hampshire RG27 8HG, ENGLAND, U.K.; mattbennett@waitrose.com

Stephen Bennett, 1 Kelvin Court, 24–26 Marlborough Road, Richmond, Surrey TW10 6JS, ENGLAND, U.K.; bennett_stephen876@btinternet.com

Dr Nora Berend, St Catharine's College, Cambridge CB2 1RL, ENGLAND, U.K.; nb213@cam.ac.uk

Ilya Berkovich, Peterhouse, Cambridge CB2 1RD, ENGLAND, U.K.; ib275@cam.ac.uk

Dr Steven Biddlecombe, 65 Conybeare Road, Canton, Cardiff CF5 1GB, WALES, U.K.; hisjb@bristol.ac.uk

*Betty Binysh, 1 The Paddock, Cowbridge, Vale of Glamorgan, CF71 7EJ, WALES, U.K.; binyshe@cardiff.ac.uk

Jessalynn Bird, 1514 Cortland Drive, Naperville IL 60565, U.S.A.; jessalynn.bird@iname.com

Prof. Nancy Bisaha, Vassar College, History Department, Box 711, 124 Raymond Avenue, Poughkeepsie NY 12604, U.S.A.; nabisaha@vassar.edu

Adam Bishop, 53-3400 Rhonda Valley, Mississauga, Ontario L5A 3L9, CANADA; adam.bishop@utoronto.ca

Charl Blignaut, P.O. Box 566, Ventersdorp 2710, North-West Province, SOUTH AFRICA; charlblignaut777@yahoo.com

Prof. John R. E. Bliese, Communication Studies Dept., Texas Tech Univ., Lubbock TX 79409, U.S.A.

Prof. Adrian J. Boas, Dept. of Archaeology, University of Haifa, Mount Carmel, Haifa 31095, ISRAEL; adrianjboas@yahoo.com

Prof. Mark S. Bocija, Columbus State Community College, 550 E. Spring Street, Columbus OH 43216-1609, U.S.A.; mbocija@cscc.edu

Louis Boisset, Université Saint-Joseph de Beyrouth, BP 166 778, Achrafieh, Beirut, LEBANON; lboisset@usj.edu.lb

Brenda M. Bolton, 8 Watling Street, St Albans AL1 2PT, ENGLAND, U.K.; brenda@bolton.vianw.co.uk

Dr Barbara Bombi, School of History, Rutheford College, Univ. of Kent, Canterbury CT2 7NX, ENGLAND, U.K.; bb55@kent.ac.uk

*Myra Bom, 306 Glade Street, Chapel Hill, NC 27516, U.S.A.; myrambom@gmail.com

Pierre Bonneaud, Chemin des chênes verts, Pont des Charrettes, 30700 Uzès, FRANCE; pierre.bonneaud@orange.fr

Prof. Karl Borchardt, c/o Monumenta Germaniae Historica, Ludwigstraße 16, 80539 München, for letters: Postfach 34 02 23, 80099 München, GERMANY; karl.borchardt@mgh.de

Prof. Charles R. Bowlus, History Dept., Univ. of Arkansas, 8081 Mabelvale Pike, Little Rock AR 72209-1099, U.S.A.; Haymannstraße 2A, 85764 Oberschleißheim, GERMANY; crbowlus@ualr.edu

Prof. Charles M. Brand, 180 South 38th Street, Boulder, CO 80305, U.S.A.; cmbrand@indra.com

Dr Cristian Bratu, Baylor University, One Bear Place #97392, Waco, TX 76798-7392, U.S.A.; Cristian_Bratu@baylor.edu

Dr Michael Brett, School of Oriental and African Studies, Univ. of London, Malet Street, London WC1E 7HP, ENGLAND, U.K.

*Keagan Brewer, 3/51–55 Frances St, Lidcombe, NSW, 2144, AUSTRALIA; keaganjoelbrewer@hotmail.com

Heidi Bridger, The Old Station House, Kedington Road, Sturmer, Essex CB9 7XR, ENGLAND, U.K.; hbridger@hotmail.com

Robert Brodie, Saint Agnes Lodge, 16 High Saint Agnesgate, Ripon, North Yorkshire HG4 1QR, ENGLAND, U.K.; robertbrodie@btinternet.com

Dr Judith Bronstein, Ilanot 29/2, Haifa 34324, ISRAEL; Judith_bronstein@hotmail.com

Prof. Elizabeth A. R. Brown, 160 West 86th Street PH4, New York NY 10024, U.S.A.; earbrown160@aol.com

Prof. James A. Brundage, 1102 Sunset Drive, Lawrence KS 66044-4548, U.S.A.; jabrun@ku.edu

David Bryson, 1935 Westview Drive, North Vancouver, B.C., Canada V7M3B1; dbryson1935@telus.net

Andrew David Buck, Hartley Corner, 6a Old Lodge Lane, Purley, Surrey, CR8 4DE, ENGLAND, U.K.; ledzep_4_ever_69@hotmail

Dr Marcus G. Bull, Dept. of Historical Studies, Univ. of Bristol, 13–15 Woodland Road, Clifton, Bristol BS8 1TB, ENGLAND, U.K.; m.g.bull@bris.ac.uk

Prof. Jochen Burgtorf, California State Univ., Dept. of History, 800 North State College Boulevard, Fullerton CA 92834, U.S.A.; jburgtorf@fullerton.edu

Prof. Charles Burnett, The Warburg Institute, Univ. of London, Woburn Square, London WC1H 0AB, ENGLAND, U.K.; charles.burnett@sas.ac.uk

The Rev. Prof. Robert I. Burns, 300 College Avenue, Los Gatos CA 95030, U.S.A.

Dr Peter Burridge, Harmer Mill, Millington, York YO4 2TX, ENGLAND, U.K.

Dr Emanuel Buttigieg, 110, Palm Street, Paola, PLA 1412, MALTA; emanuel_buttigieg@yahoo.co.uk

Ane Lise Bysted, Dept. of History, Univ. of Southern Denmark, Campusvej 55, 5230 Odense M, DENMARK; bysted@hist.sdu.dk

Christer Carlsson, Litsbyvägen 66, 18746 Täby, SWEDEN; cc-archaeologist@yahoo.se

Dr Annemarie Weyl Carr, 608 Apple Road, Newark DE 19711, U.S.A.; acarr@smu.edu

Michael Carr, Flat 4, 11 Rochester Terrace, Camden, London, NW1 9JN, ENGLAND, U.K.; m.carr@rhul.ac.uk

Dr Damien Carraz, 14, rue François Arago, 84000 Avignon, FRANCE; damien.carraz@wanadoo.fr

Marc Carrier, 1038 Péladeau, St-Jean-sur-Richelieu, Québec, J3A 2A2, CANADA; marctcarrier@yahoo.ca

Dr Megan Cassidy-Welch, School of Historical, Philosophical and International Studies, Monash University, Victoria 3800, AUSTRALIA; megan.cassidy-welch@monash.edu

Prof. Brian A. Catlos, Dept. of History, Univ. of California Santa Cruz, Stevenson Academic Center, 1156 High Street, Santa Cruz CA 95064-1077, U.S.A.; bcatlos@ucsc.edu

Prof. Fred A. Cazel Jr., 309 Gurleyville Road, Storrs Mansfield CT 06268-1403, U.S.A.

Dr Simonetta Cerrini, Via Carducci 68A, 15076 Ovada (Alessandria), ITALY; alloisiocerrini@inwind.it

William Chapman, 68 Carisbrooke Gardens, Yeovil, Somerset BA20 1BY, ENGLAND, U.K.; bill-chapman@pilgrim-env.co.uk

Dr Martin Chasin, 1125 Church Hill Road, Fairfield CT 06432-1371, U.S.A.; mchasin@att.net

Dr Nikolaos G. Chrissis, Flat 16, Victoria House, South Lambeth Road, SW8 1QT, London, U.K.; N.Chrissis@rhul.ac.uk or nchrissis@yahoo.co.uk

Georg Christ, Friedrich-Ebert-Anlage 39, 69117 Heidelberg, GERMANY; georgchrist@gmail.com

Dr Katherine Christensen, CPO 1756 Berea College, Berea KY 40404, U.S.A.; katherine_christensen@berea.edu

Dr Niall G. F. Christie, Corpus Christi College, 5935 Iona Drive, Vancouver, BC, V6T 1J7, CANADA; niallchristie@yahoo.com

Ioanna Christoforaki, Centre for Byzantine and Post-byzantine Art, Academy of Athens, Anagnostopouloy 14, GR-106 73 Athens, GREECE or Heracleous 6, GR-152 34 Halandri, Athens, GREECE; ichristoforaki@yahoo.co.uk

Prof. Giulio Cipollone, Piazza S. Maria alle Fornaci 30, 00165 Roma, ITALY; cipolloneunigre6009@fastwebnet.it

Dr G. H. M. Claassens, Departement Literatuurwetenschap, Katholieke Universiteit Leuven, Blijde Inkomststraat 21, Postbus 33, 3000 Leuven, BELGIUM

Pierre-Vincent Claverie, 9 rue du Bois-Rondel, 35700 Rennes, FRANCE; pvclaverie@yahoo.fr

David J. CLOVER, 5460 Ocean View Drive, Oakland CA 94618, U.S.A.; rollsroyceggm24@yahoo.com

Paul M. COBB, Dept. of Near Eastern Languages and Civilizations, University of Pennsylvania, Philadelphia, PA 19104, U.S.A.; pmcobb@sas.upenn.edu

Dr Penny J. COLE, Trinity College, 6 Hoskin Avenue, Toronto, Ontario M5S 1HB, CANADA; pjcole@trinity.utoronto.ca

Dr Edward COLEMAN, Dept. of History and Archives, Faculty of Arts and Celtic Studies, University College Dublin, Belfield, Dublin 4, IRELAND; Email: edward.coleman@ucd.ie

Prof. Eleanor A. CONGDON, Dept. of History, Youngstown State Univ., 1 University Plaza, Youngstown OH 44555, U.S.A.; eacongdon@ysu.edu

Prof. Charles W. CONNELL, P.O. Box 6023, Dept. of History, Northern Arizona Univ., Flagstaff AZ 86011-6023, U.S.A.; charles.connell@nau.edu

Prof. Robert CONNOR, Triton College, River Grove IL; 53 Lakebreez Ct, Lake Zurich, IL 60047, U.S.A.; rconnor1@triton.edu

Prof. Giles CONSTABLE, Institute for Advanced Study, 506 Quaker Road, Princeton NJ 085 40, U.S.A.

Prof. Olivia Remie CONSTABLE, Dept. of History, Univ. of Notre Dame, Notre Dame, IN 46556-0368, U.S.A.; constable.1@nd.edu

James CONWAY, 30 Park Drive, Little Paxton, St. Neots, Cambridgeshire, PE19 6NT, ENGLAND, U.K.; penny.conway@ntlworld.com

Prof. Robert F. COOK, French Language and General Linguistics Dept., Univ. of Virginia, 302 Cabell Hall, Charlottesville, VA 22903, U.S.A.

Barry COOPER, Director of Studies, Loretto School, Linkfield Road, Musselburgh, East Lothian EH21 7RE, SCOTLAND, U.K.; bcooper@loretto.com

Prof. Rebecca W. CORRIE, Phillips Professor of Art, Bates College, Lewiston ME 04240, U.S.A.; rcorrie@bates.edu

Walker Reid COSGROVE, History Dept., Saint Louis Univ., 3800 Lindell Boulevard, Saint Louis MO 63108, U.S.A.; cosgrowr@slu.edu

Dr Nicholas S. COUREAS, P.O. Box 26619, Lykarittos, 1640 Nicosia, CYPRUS; ncoureas@moec.gov.cy or ncoureas@hotmail.com

The Rev. H. E. J. COWDREY, 19 Church Lane, Old Marston, Oxford OX3 0NZ, ENGLAND, U.K.; fax (0)1865 279090

Prof. Paul F. CRAWFORD, 5 Mum Drive, Washington PA 15301, U.S.A.; crawford_p@calu.edu or paul.f.crawford@gmail.com

Dana CUSHING, 201 N Garden Avenue, Sierra Vista AZ 85635, U.S.A.; dana.cushing@alumni.utoronto.ca

*David M. CVET, 822-18 Concorde Pl., Toronto, ON, M3C 3T9, CANADA; david.cvet@gmail.com

Charles DALLI, Dept. of History, Faculty of Arts, Univ. of Malta, Msida MSD06, MALTA; cdalli@arts.um.edu.mt

Philip Louis DANIEL, Archivist, Equestrian Order of the Holy Sepuchre of Jerusalem, 37 Somerset Road, Meadvale, Redhill, Surrey RH1 6LT, ENGLAND, U.K.; fax 01737-240722

Dr Béatrice DANSETTE, 175, Boulevard Malesherbes, 75017 Paris, FRANCE; beatricedansette@orange.fr

Americo DE SANTIS, 88 East Main Street, Box Number 141, Mendham NJ 07945, U.S.A.; ricodesantis@hotmail.com

Prof. Bernhard DEMEL O.T., Leiter des Deutschordenszentralarchivs, Singerstraße 7, 1010 Wien, AUSTRIA; tel. 513 70 14

John A. DEMPSEY, 218 Edgehill Road, Milton MA 02186-5310, U.S.A.; jdempsey@wsc.ma.edu

Dr Alain DEMURGER, 5, rue de l'Abricotier, 95000 Cergy, FRANCE; ademurger@orange.fr

Prof. George T. DENNIS, S.H. Jesuit Center, 300 College Avenue, Los Gatos, CA 95031, U.S.A.; gdennis@calprov.org

Eugene DE RASS, Po Box 35043, Ottawa ON K1Z 1A2, Canada; eugene959@gmail.com

Kelly DEVRIES, Department of History, Loyola College, 4501 N Charles Street, Bltimore, MD 21210-2699, U.S.A.; kdevries@loyola.edu

Dr Gary DICKSON, School of History, Classics and Archaeology, University of Edinburgh, Doorway 4, Teviot Place, Edinburgh EH8 9AG, SCOTLAND, U.K.; garydickson1212@blueyonder.co.uk

Prof. Richard DIVALL, 301 / 228 The Avenue, Parkville, Melbourne 3052, AUSTRALIA; maestro@spin.net.au

Dr Erica Cruikshank DODD, 4208 Wakefield Place, Victoria, B.C. V8N 6E5, CANADA; edodd@uvic.ca

César DOMÍNGUEZ, Universidad de Santiago de Compostela, Facultad de Filologia, Avda. Castealo s/n, 15704 Santiago (La Coruna), ESPAÑA

Cristina DONDI, 128 Berkeley Court, Glentworth Street, London NW1 5NE, ENGLAND, U.K.; christina.dondi@history.ox.ac.uk

Dr John DORAN, Dept of History and Archaeology, University of Chester, Parkgate Road, Chester, CH1 4BJ, ENGLAND, U.K.; j.doran@chester.ac.uk

Ara DOSTOURIAN, Box 420, Harmony, RI 02829, U.S.A.

Maria DOUROU-ELIOPOULOU, Kephallenias 24, Althea 19400, Attiki, GREECE; mdourou@arch.uoa.gr

*Janet DRAHEIM, 732 W Happfield Dr., Arlington Heights, IL 60004-7100, U.S.A.; jandra818@comcast.net

Andrew DUNN, 229 W 60th Street, Apt. 4T, New York, NY 10023, U.S.A.; aggdunn@yahoo.com

John DURANT, 32 Maple Street, P.O. Box 373, West Newbury MA 01985, U.S.A.

Frances DURKIN, 16 Billington Road, Leighton Buzzard, Bedfordshire, LU7 4TH, ENGLAND, U.K.; frankie_durkin@hotmail.com

Dr Valerie EADS, 308 West 97th Street, New York NY 10025, U.S.A.

Prof. Richard EALES, School of History, Univ. of Kent, Canterbury CT2 7NX, ENGLAND, U.K.; r.eales1@btinternet.com

Ana ECHEVARRÍA ARSUAGA, Facultad de Geografía e Historia, Departimento de Historia Medieval, Av. Conde de Aranda 1, 3° E, 28200 San Lorenzo del Escorial (Madrid), ESPAÑA; anaevjosem@hotmail.com

Prof. Peter W. EDBURY, School of History and Archaeology, Cardiff University, Humanities Building, Colum Drive, Cardiff CF10 3EU, WALES, U.K.; edbury@cf.ac.uk

Dr Susan B. EDGINGTON, 3 West Street, Huntingdon, Cambs., PE29 1WT, ENGLAND, U.K.; s.b.edgington@btinternet.com

Dr Axel EHLERS, Gehägestraße 20 N, 30655 Hannover, GERMANY; aehlers1@gwdg.de

Prof. Sven EKDAHL, Sponholzstraße 38, 12159 Berlin, GERMANY; Sven.Ekdahl@t-online.de

Dr Ronnie ELLENBLUM, 13 Reuven Street, Jerusalem 93510, ISRAEL; msronni@pluto.mscc. huji.ac.il

Prof. Steven A. EPSTEIN, History Dept., Univ. of Kansas, Lawrence KS 66045-7590, U.S.A.; sae@ku.edu

Dr Helen C. EVANS, The Medieval Dept., The Metropolitan Museum of Art, 1000 Fifth Avenue, New York NY 10028, U.S.A.; helen.evans@metmuseum.org

Michael EVANS, 301 West Broomfield, Kewardin 10-03, Mount Pleasant MI 48858, U.S.A.; evans2m@cmich.edu

Prof. Theodore EVERGATES, 146 West Main Street, Westminster MD 21157, U.S.A.

Nicolas FAUCHERRE, 4, rue de l'Hôtel de Ville, 44000 Nantes, FRANCE; n.faucherre@ wanadoo.fr

Prof. Marie-Luise FAVREAU-LILIE, Kaiser-Friedrich-Straße 106, 10585 Berlin, GERMANY; mlfavre@zedat.fu-berlin.de

Gil FISHHOF, Dept. of Art History, Tel Aviv Univ., Tel Aviv 69978, ISRAEL; fishhofg@post. tau.ac.il

Dr Jean FLORI, 69, rue Saint Cornély, 56340 Carnac, FRANCE; flori.jean@wanadoo.fr

Prof. Jaroslav FOLDA, 112a Hanes Art Center, Dept. of Art, Univ. of North Carolina, Chapel Hill NC 27599-3405, U.S.A.; jfolda@email.unc.edu

Dr Michelle FOLTZ, M.D., PMB 33, P.O. Box 1226, Columbus MT 59019, U.S.A.; mfoltz@ imt.net

Dr Iben FONNESBERG SCHMIDT, Dept. of History, Aalborg Univ., Fibgerstraede 5, 9220 Aalborg, DENMARK; imfs@ihis.aau.dk

Luis Adão DA FONSECA, Rua do Revilão 521, 4100-427 Porto, PORTUGAL; luisadaofonseca@ netcabo.pt

Harold FORD, P.O. Box 871009, Stone Mountain GA 30087, U.S.A.; tsh212511@aol.com

Dr Alan J. FOREY, The Bell House, Church Lane, Kirtlington, Oxon. OX5 3HJ, ENGLAND, U.K.; foreys@somail.it

Edith FORMAN, 38 Burnham Hill, Westport CT 06880, U.S.A.

Barbara FRALE, via A. Gramsci 17, 01028 Orte (VT), ITALY; barbara-frale@libero.it

Dr John FRANCE, Department of History and Classics, Swansea University, SA2 8PP, WALES, U.K.; j.france@swansea.ac.uk

Daniel FRANKE, University of Rochester, Department of History, 364 Rush Rhees Library, Rochester, NY 14627, U.S.A.; danielfranke79@gmail.com

Prof. Yvonne FRIEDMAN, Department of General History, Department of Land of Israel Studies and Archeology, Bar-Ilan University, Ramat-Gan 52900, ISRAEL; yfried36@gmail.com

Robin FROUMIN, P.O. Box 9713, Hadera 38541, ISRAEL; robin_fr@zahav.net.il

Michael and Neathery FULLER, 13530 Clayton Road, St Louis MO 63141, U.S.A.

*Michael S. FULTON, 272 Sydenham St., Kingston, Ontario, CANADA; michael.fulton@ tricolour.queensu.ca

Prof. Matthew GABRIELE, Dept. of Interdisciplinary Studies, Virginia Tech, 342 Lane Hall (0227), Blacksburg VA 24061-0227, U.S.A.; mgabriele@vt.edu

Cecilia GAPOSCHKIN, 6107 Carson Hall, History Department, Dartmouth College, Hanover NH 03755, U.S.A.; m.c.gaposchkin@dartmouth.edu

Prof. Luis GARCÍA-GUIJARRO, Facultad de Ciencias Humanas, Plaza de la Constitución s/n, 22001 Huesca, SPAIN; luguijar@unizar.es

Sabine GELDSETZER, M.A., Westheide 6, 44892 Bochum, GERMANY; sabine.geldsetzer@ruhr-uni-bochum.de

Constantinos GEORGIOU, 3 Thessalonikis Street, Flat 201, Strovolos, 2020, Nicosia, CYPRUS; grconsta@hotmail.com

Dr Stavros G. GEORGIOU, P.O. Box 25729, 1311 Strovolos, CYPRUS; stggeorgiou@yahoo.gr

Dr Ruthy GERTWAGEN, 30 Ranans Street, P.O. Box 117, Qiryat Motzkin 26317, ISRAEL; ruger@macam.ac.il

Dr Marianne McLeod GILCHRIST, Flat 10, 13 Kelvin Drive, Glasgow G20 8QG, SCOTLAND, U.K.; docm@silverwhistle.free-online.co.uk

Prof. John B. GILLINGHAM, 49 Old Shoreham Road, Brighton, Sussex BN1 5DQ, ENGLAND, U.K.; johnbgilli@gmail.com

Prof. Anne GILMOUR-BRYSON, 1935 Westview Drive, North Vancouver, B.C. V7M 3B1, CANADA; annegb@telus.net

Charles R. GLASHEEN, 4300 Yacht Club Road, Jacksonville FL 32210, U.S.A.; rglashee@comcast.net

Prof. Dorothy F. GLASS, 11 Riverside Drive, Apartment 6-OW, New York NY 10023, U.S.A.; dglass1@att.net

Miguel GOMEZ, Department of History, 6th Floor Dunford Hall, University of Tennessee, Knoxville, TN, 37996, U.S.A.; Mgomez3@utk.edu

Prof. Philippe GOURDIN, 11, avenue du général de Gaulle, 91000 Évry, FRANCE; philgourdin@yahoo.fr

Dr Christian GRASSO, via Colucci 30, 83048 Montella, ITALY; CHRISGRASSO@IOL.IT

Ciham-UMR 5648 Université Louis-Lumière-Lyon 2, 18 Quai Claude Bernard, 69365 Lyon Cedex 07, FRANCE; chrisgrasso@iol.it

Prof. Gilles GRIVAUD, 8, rue du Général de Miribel, 69007 Lyon, FRANCE

The Rev. Joseph J. GROSS, Holy Trinity Monastery, 8400 Park Heights Avenue, P.O. Box 5742, Baltimore, MD 21282, U.S.A.; jjgross@trinitarianhistory.org

Dr Darius von GUETTNER, School of Historical Studies, Univ. of Melbourne, Victoria 3010, AUSTRALIA; d.guttner@unimelb.edu.au

Prof. Klaus GUTH, Greiffenbergstraße 35, 96052 Bamberg, GERMANY; klaus.guth@uni-bamberg.de

Rachel HADDAD, 5 avenue de Verdun, Mont de Gif, 95200 Sarcelles, FRANCE; haddadrachel@yahoo.fr

*Dr Brian J. HALE, 4228 Nebel Street, Stevens Point, WI 54481, U.S.A.; bhaleuwsp.edu

Martin HALL, 8 Stanhope Place, London, W2 2HB, ENGLAND, U.K.; martin.allan.hall@gmail.com

Benjamin HALLIBURTON, 4020 Lindell Blvd. #216, St. Louis, MO 63108, U.S.A.; bhallibu@slu.edu

Adina HAMILTON, 469 Albert Street, Brunswick, West Victoria 3055, AUSTRALIA or History Dept., Univ. of Melbourne, Parkville, Victoria 3052, AUSTRALIA

Prof. Bernard HAMILTON, 7 Lenton Avenue, The Park, Nottingham NG7 IDX, ENGLAND, U.K.; bernhamilt@yahoo.com

Dr Mona HAMMAD JAHAMA, Hollins University, Box 9586, Roanoke, VA 24020, U.S.A.; monahammad@hotmail.com

Philip David HANDYSIDE, School of History and Archaeology, Cardiff University, Humanities Building, Colum road, Cardiff, CF10 3EU, WALES, U.K.; handysidepd@cardiff.ac.uk

Peter HARITATOS Jr., 1500 North George Street, Rome NY 13440, U.S.A.

Jonathan HARRIS, Dept. of History, Royal Holloway, Univ. of London, Egham, Surrey TW20 0EX, ENGLAND, U.K.; jonathan.harris@rhul.ac.uk

Kathryn D. HARRIS, 6 Gallows Hill, Saffron Walden, Essex CB11 4DA, ENGLAND, U.K.; lfiddock@ntlworld.com

Dr Michael HARSCHEIDT, Dellbusch 229, D-42279 Wuppertal, GERMANY; office@harscheidt.de

Jeff HASS, Ave Maria University, 2395 Naples Trace Creek # 3, Naples, FL 34109, U.S.A.; jeffrey.hass@avemaria.edu, or jd-hass@yahoo.com

Prof. Eva HAVERKAMP, Rice Univ., History Dept. MS 42, for letters P.O. Box 1892, Houston TX 77251-1892 or for packages 6100 Main Street, Houston TX 77005, U.S.A.; haver@rice.edu

David HAY, 164 McCaul Street, Apartment 1, Toronto, Ontario M5T 1WA, CANADA.

Prof. Thérèse de HEMPTINNE, Universiteit Gent, Faculteit van de Letteren, Vakgroep Middeleeuwse Geschiedenis, Blandijnberg 2, 9000 Gent, BELGIUM

Michael HESLOP, The Old Vicarage, 1 Church Street, Lower Sunbury, Middlesex TW16 6RQ, ENGLAND, U.K.; michaelheslop@ntlworld.com

Dr Paul HETHERINGTON, 15 Luttrell Avenue, London SW15 6PD, ENGLAND, U.K.; phetherington@ukonline.co.uk

Prof. Rudolf HIESTAND, Brehmstraße 76, 40239 Düsseldorf, GERMANY

Charles A. HILKEN, P.O. Box 4825, St Mary's College, Moraga CA 94575, U.S.A.; chilken@stmarys-ca.edu

Dr George HINTLIAN, Armenian Patriarchate, P.O. Box, Jerusalem 14001, ISRAEL

Dr Martin HOCH, Konrad-Adenauer-Stiftung, Rathausallee 12, 53757 Sankt Augustin, GERMANY; Lobebaer@gmail.com

Dr Natasha HODGSON, Dept. of History, Heritage and Geography, Nottingham Trent Univ., Clifton Campus, Nottingham NG11 8NS, ENGLAND, U.K.; natasha.hodgson@ntu.ac.uk

Laura H. HOLLENGREEN; Univ. of Arizona, School of Architecture, 1040 North Olive, P.O. Box 210075, Tucson AZ 85721-0075, U.S.A.; laurah@u.arizona.edu

Dr Catherine HOLMES, University College, Oxford OX1 4BH, ENGLAND, U.K.; catherine.holmes@univ.ox.ac.uk

John D. HOSLER, Dept. of History and Geography, Morgan State University, 325 Holmes Hall, Baltimore, MD 21251, U.S.A.; john.hosler@morgan.edu

Jan HOSTEN, Kaaistraat 12, 8900 Ieper, BELGIUM; jan.hosten@leicon.be

Dr C. Patrick HOTLE, Culver-Stockton Coll., N° 1 College Hill, Canton, MO 63435, U.S.A.; photle@culver.edu

Prof. Norman J. Housley, School of Historical Studies, The Univ. of Leicester, Leicester LE1 7RH, ENGLAND, U.K.; hou@le.ac.uk

Prof. John Howe, Texas Tech Univ., Dept. of History, Box 41013, Lubbock TX 79409-1013, U.S.A.; John.Howe@ttu.edu

Lubos Hradsky, Svermova 23, 97404 Banska Bystrica, SLOVAK REPUBLIC; lubohradsky@centrum.sk

Prof. Lucy-Anne Hunt, Head of Art, School of Art, Manchester Metropolitan University, Righton Building, Cavendish Street, Manchester M1 5 6BG, ENGLAND, U.K.; l.a.hunt@mmu.ac.uk

Dr Zsolt Hunyadi, 27 Szekeres u., 6725 Szeged, HUNGARY; hunyadiz@hist.u-szeged.hu

Prof. Robert B. C. Huygens, Witte Singel 28, 2311 BH Leiden, THE NETHERLANDS

Sheldon Ibbotson, P.O. Box 258, Rimbey, Alberta T0C 2JO, CANADA; bronwen@telusplanet.net

Robert Irwin, 39 Harleyford Road, London SE11 5AX, ENGLAND, U.K.; irwin960@btinternet.com

John E. Isles, 10575 Darrel Drive, Hanover MI 49241, U.S.A.; jisles@hughes.net

Prof. Peter Jackson, Department of History, University of Keele, Keele, Staffs. ST5 5BG, ENGLAND, U.K.; p.jackson@his.keele.ac.uk

Martin Jacobowitz, The Towers of Windsor Park, 3005 Chapel Avenue — 11P, Cherry Hill NJ 08002, U.S.A.

Prof. David Jacoby, Dept. of History, The Hebrew Univ., Jerusalem 91905 ISRAEL; jacobgab@mscc.huji.ac.il

*Colin Wheldon James, 30 Hendrefoilan Avenue, Sketty, Swansea, SA2 7LZ, WALES, U.K.; col.james@ymail.com

Prof. Nikolas Jaspert, Ruhr-Univ. Bochum, Historisches Institut – Lehrstuhl Mittelalter II, Universitätsstraße 150 (GA 4/31), 44801 Bochum, GERMANY; nikolas.jaspert@rub.de

Carsten Selch Jensen, Department of Church History, Faculty of Theology, University of Copenhagen, Koebmagergade 44–46, 1150 DK-Copenhagen, DENMARK; csj@teol.ku.dk

Dr Janus Møller Jensen, Dept. of History and Civilization, Univ. of Southern Denmark, Campusvej 55, 5230 Odense M, DENMARK; jamj@hist.sdu.dk or: mailto:jamj@hist.sdu.dk

Prof. Kurt Villads Jensen, Dept. of History and Civilization, Univ. of Southern Denmark, Campusvej 55, 5230 Odense M, DENMARK; kvj@hist.sdu.dk

Lady Jill, Duchess of Hamilton, 52, Elm Park Gardens, Chelsea, London, SW10 9PA, ENGLAND, U.K.

*Luc Jocqué, c/o Corpus Christianorum, Sint-Annaconvent, Begijnhof 39, B-2300 Turnhout, Belgium

Simon A. John, 68 Abernethy Quay, The Marina, Swansea, SA1 1UL, WALES, U.K.; 308858@swan.ac.uk

Prof. William Chester Jordan, Dept. of History, Princeton Univ., Princeton NJ 08544, U.S.A.; wchester@princeton.edu

Dr Philippe Josserand, 14, rue du roi Albert, 44000 Nantes, FRANCE; ph.josserand@wanadoo.fr

Dr Andrew Jotischky, Dept. of History, Lancaster Univ., Lancaster LA1 4YG, ENGLAND, U.K.; a.jotischky@lancaster.ac.uk

Dr Margaret A. Jubb, Dept. of French, Taylor Building, Univ. of Aberdeen, Old Aberdeen, AB15 9NU, SCOTLAND, U.K.; m.jubb@abdn.ac.uk

Elena Kaffa, 2B Thiron Kaimakli, 1026 Nicosia, CYPRUS; niryida@yahoo.com

Prof. Sophia Kalopissi-Verti, Kronou 30, Palaio Faliro, GR-175 61 Athens, Greece; skalop@arch.uoa.gr

Dr Sini Kangas, Dept. of History, PL 4 (Porthania 384), 00014 Univ. of Helsinki, FINLAND; shkangas@mappi.helsinki.fi

Dr Fotini Karassava-Tsilingiri, Th. Kairi 14, Nea Smyrni, Athens 17122, GREECE; ptsiling@teiath.gr

Tatiana Kartseva, 73-50 Vavilova Street, Ap. 50, Moscow 117335, RUSSIA; tvkartseva@hotmail.com

Anna-Maria Kasdagli, 59 Stockholmis Street, 85100 Rhodes, GREECE.

Prof. Benjamin Z. Kedar, Dept. of History, The Hebrew Univ., Jerusalem 91905, ISRAEL; fax (home) 972-8-970-0802, bzkedar@huji.ac.il

Alexander Kempton, Skøyenveien 30, 0375 Oslo, NORWAY; alexansk@student.hf.uio.no

Prof. Nurith Kenaan-Kedar, Dept. of Art History, Tel-Aviv Univ., Tel-Aviv 69978, ISRAEL; kenaank@post.tau.ac.il

Prof. Sharon Kinoshita, Associate Professor of Literature, Humanities Academic Services, Univ. of California Santa Cruz, Santa Cruz CA 95064, U.S.A.; sakinosh@ucsc.edu

Dr Klaus-Peter Kirstein, Frankenstraße 251, 45134 Essen, GERMANY; k.kirstein@r25.de

David Kloster, 7914 7th Street, Downey CA 90241, U.S.A.; jesushunter22@yahoo.com

Dr Michael A. Koehler, Hertogenlaan 14, 1970 Wezembeek-Oppem, BELGIUM; koehler.family@pandora.be

Prof. Athina Kolia-Dermitzaki, Plateia Kalliga 3, Athens 11253, GREECE; akolia@arch.uoa.gr

Miha Kosi, Zgodovinski institut ZRC SAZU, Novi trg 2, p.p. 306, 1000 Ljubljana, SLOVENIA; kosi@zrc-sazu.si

*Philip Koski, 1310 Jersey Avenue N, Golden Valley, MN 55427, U.S.A.; pkoski@slu.edu

Dr Conor Kostick, 31, Ashington Gardens, Navan Road, Dublin 7, IRELAND; kosticc@tcd.ie

Thomas Krämer, Friedrich-Franz-Straße 18, 12103 Berlin, GERMANY; thomas_kraemer@yahoo.com

*Dr James G. Kroemer, 9440 N. Bethanne Dr Browne Deer, WI 53223, U.S.A.; jameskroemer@gmail.com

Prof. Jürgen Krüger, Steinbügelstraße 22, 76228 Karlsruhe, GERMANY; krueger-kunstgeschichte@t-online.de

Suha Kudsieh, Box: 19027, 360 A Bloor Street W., Toronto, ON., M5S 3C9 CANADA; kudsieh@gmail.com

*Türk Tarih Kurumu, Kizilay Sokak, no. 1, Sihhiye 06100, Ankara, TURKEY.

*Dr Malcolm David Lambert, Flat 3, 3 Queens Road, Worthing, BN11 3LX, ENGLAND, U.K.

Mark Lambert, 515, North High, Kirksville, MO 63501, U.S.A.; mml184@truman.edu, or marklambert@gmail.com

Sarah LAMBERT, 35 Cromer Road, London SW17 9JN, ENGLAND, U.K.; slambert@gold.ac.uk

The Rev. William LANE, Brooke Hall, Charterhouse, Godalming, Surrey GU7 2DX, ENGLAND, U.K.; wjl@charterhouse.org.uk

Elizabeth LAPINA, Department of History, 43 North Bailey, Durham, DH1 3EX, ENGLAND, U.K.; ealapina@yahoo.com

Stephen LAY, c/o Dept. of History, Monash Univ., Melbourne, AUSTRALIA

Armelle LECLERCQ, 36, rue de l'Orillen, 75011 Paris, FRANCE; armelle73@yahoo.com

Eric LEGG, PSC 98 Box 36, Apo AE 09830, U.S.A.; ericlegg@hotmail.com

Robert D. LEONARD Jr., 1065 Spruce Street, Winnetka IL 60093, U.S.A.; rlwinnetka@aol.com

Richard A. LESON, 2720 St Paul Street, Apartment 2FF, Baltimore MD 21218, U.S.A.; ral2@jhunix.hef.jhu.edu

Dr Yaacov LEV, P.O. Box 167, Holon 58101, ISRAEL; yglev@actcom.net.il

*Kevin James LEWIS, Merton College, Merton Street, Oxford, OX1 4JD, ENGLAND, U.K.; kevin.lewis@history.ox.ac.uk or kevin.j.lewis@hotmail.co.uk

Dr Christopher G. LIBERTINI, Dominican College, 470 Western Highway, Orangeburg, NY 10962, U.S.A.; christopher.libertini@de

Dr Tom LICENCE, Magdalene College, Cambridge, CB3 0AG, ENGLAND, U.K.; tol21@cam.ac.uk

Laura S. LIEBER, Dept. of Religion, Middlebury College, Middlebury VT 05753, U.S.A.; llieber@middlebury.edu

Dr Giuseppe LIGATO, Viale San Gimignano 18, 20146 Milano, ITALY; giuseppeligato@virgilio.it

Prof. Ralph-Johannes LILIE, Kaiser-Friedrich-Straße 106, 10585 Berlin, GERMANY; liliefavreau@arcor.de

Dr Ora LIMOR, 5b Elroey Street, Jerusalem 92108, ISRAEL; orali@openu.ac.il

Prof. Guy LOBRICHON, 4, Impasse Caillod, 84000 Avignon, FRANCE; guy.lobrichon@univ-avignon.fr

Prof. Peter W. LOCK, 9 Straylands Grove, Stockton Lane, York YO31 1EB, ENGLAND, U.K.; ptrlock425@googlemail.com

Scott LONEY, 4153 Wendell Road, West Bloomfield, MI 48323, U.S.A.; scottloney@live.com

*Albert G. LOPEZ, 277 Patterson Avenue, Stratford, CT 06614, U.S.A.; aglopez46@snet.net

Prof. Graham A. LOUD, School of History, Univ. of Leeds, Leeds LS2 9JT, ENGLAND, U.K.; g.a.loud@leeds.ac.uk

Prof. Michael LOWER, 1814 N. Lincoln Park West, # 1, Chicago, IL 60614, U.S.A.; mlower@umn.edu

Zoyd R. LUCE, 2441 Creekside Court, Hayward CA 94542, U.S.A.; zluce1@earthlink.net

Dr Svetlana LUCHITSKAYA, Institute of General History, Leninski pr. 89-346, Moscow 119313, RUSSIA; svetlana-luchitskaya@yandex.ru

Andrew John LUFF, Flat 3, The Hermitage, St Dunstans Road, Lower Feltham, Middlesex TW13 4HR, ENGLAND, U.K.; andrew@luffa.freeserve.co.uk

Dr Anthony LUTTRELL, 20 Richmond Place, Bath BA1 5PZ, ENGLAND, U.K.; margaretluttrell@gmail.com

Christopher MacEVITT, Dumbarton Oaks, 1703 32nd Street NW, Washington DC 20007, U.S.A.

Dr James B. MacGREGOR, Dept. of History, Philosophy, and Geography, Missouri Western State Univ., 4525 Downs Drive, Saint Joseph MO 64501, U.S.A.; macgregor@missouriwestern.edu

Dr Merav MACK, The Van Leer Jerusalem Institute, 43 Jabotinsky Street, Jerusalem, 91040, ISRAEL; merav.mack@gmail.com

Dr Alan D. MacQUARRIE, 173 Queen Victoria Drive, Glasgow G14 7BP, SCOTLAND, U.K. [See also Mc]

Prof. Thomas F. MADDEN, Dept. of History, Saint Louis Univ., 3800 Lindell Boulevard, P.O. Box 56907, Saint Louis MO 63108, U.S.A.; maddentf@slu.edu

Ben MAHONEY, 131 High Street, Doncaster, Victoria 3181, AUSTRALIA; bmahoney@abl.com.au

Dr Christoph T. MAIER, Sommergasse 20, 4056 Basel, SWITZERLAND; ctmaier@hist.uzh.ch

Christie MAJOROS, 215 W. 7th St., #14, Long Beach, CA 90813, U.S.A.; c_majoros@yahoo.com

Prof. Lucy DER MANUELIAN, 10 Garfield Road, Belmont MA 02478, U.S.A.; lucy.manuelian@tufts.edu

Roben McDonald MARLOW, 36 Burton Old Road West, Lichfield, Staffordshire, WS13 6EN, ENGLAND, U.K.; roben@mac.com

Prof. Laurence W. MARVIN, History Dept., Evans School of Humanities, Berry College, Mount Berry GA 30149-5010, U.S.A.; lmarvin@berry.edu

Dr Federica MASÈ, 100 rue de la Roquette, 75011 Paris, FRANCE; f.mase@free.fr

Prof. Hans Eberhard MAYER, Historisches Seminar der Universität Kiel, 24098 Kiel, GERMANY

Robert MAYNARD, The Old Dairy, 95 Church Road, Bishopsworth, Bristol BS13 8JU, ENGLAND, U.K.; maynard966@btinternet.com

Brian C. MAZUR, 718 W. Webster, Royal Oak MI 48073, U.S.A.; bcmazur1066@yahoo.com

Roben McDONALD MARLOW: see to Roben McDonald MARLOW

Dr Marianne McLeod GILCHRIST: see to Dr Marianne M. GILCHRIST

M. McNAUGHTON, The Old Rectory, River Street, Pewsey SN9 5DB, ENGLAND, U.K.; pewsey_books@hotmail.com

Gerald P. McOSKER, Salve Regina Univ., 100 Ochre Point Avenue, Newport, RI 06240, U.S.A.; gerald.mcosker@salve.edu

Sean Robert MARTIN, 74 Electric Avenue, West Seneca, NY 14206, U.S.A.; Seanmart32482@gmail.com

Prof. Sophia MENACHE, Department of History, University of Haifa, Haifa 31905, ISRAEL; menache@research.haifa.ac.il

Marco MESCHINI, Via alle Cascine 37/B, 21100 Varese, ITALY; marco.meschini@unicatt.it

Dr Benjamin MICHAUDEL, IFPO, P.O.Box 344, Damascus, SYRIA; benjamin_michaudel@hotmail.com

Prof. Klaus MILITZER, Winckelmannstraße 32, 50825 Köln, GERMANY; klaus.militzer@uni-koeln.de

Greg MILLER, 105 Valley Street, Burlington IA 52601, U.S.A.; greg.miller@lpl.com

Jane MILLIKEN, 26 Emmetts Farm Road, Rossmore NSW 2557, AUSTRALIA; jane.milliken@swahs.health.nsw.gov.au

Dr Paul Richard MILLIMAN, 107 E Custis Avenue, Alexandria, VA 22301; U.S.A.; prmilliman@gmail.com

Peter John MILLS, 3 Huxley Road, Leyton, London E10 5QT, ENGLAND, U.K.; petermills@lireone.net

Prof. Laura MINERVINI, Dipartimento di Filologia Moderna, Università di Napoli Federico II, Via Porta di Massa 1, 80133 Napoli, ITALY; laura.minervini@unina.it

*Vincenzo Felice MIRIZIO, Via Manzoni nr.5, 73039 Tricase, Province of Lecce, ITALY; vincenzomirizio@email.it

Dr Piers D. MITCHELL, Leverhulme Centre for Human Evolutionary Studies, University of Cambridge, The Henry Wellcome Building, Fitzwilliam Street, Cambridge CB2 1QH, ENGLAND, U.K.; pdm39@cam.ac.uk

PD Dr Hannes MÖHRING, Wilhelm-Bode-Straße 11, 38104 Braunschweig, GERMANY; hannes_moehring@web.de

Prof. Johannes A. (Hans) MOL, Grote Dijlakker 29, 8701 KW Bolsward, THE NETHERLANDS; hmol@fryske-akademy.nl

Dr Kristian MOLIN, 38 Vessey Terrace, Newcastle-under-Lyme, Staffordshire ST5 1LS, ENGLAND, U.K.; kristian.molin@nottingham.ac.uk

Dauvergne C. MORGAN, 235 Tooronga Road, Glen Iris, Melbourne, Victoria 3142, AUSTRALIA

Jonathan C. MORGAN, 19 Elia Street, Islington, London N1 8DE, ENGLAND, U.K.; jonathan.morgan@whb.co.uk

J. Diana MORGAN, 64 Victoria Avenue, Swanage, Dorset BH19 1AR, ENGLAND, U.K.

Hiroki MORITAKE, Kami-Ono 371, Hiyoshi-mura, Kitauwa-gun, Ehime-ken 798-1503, JAPAN; jerus@hiroshima-u.ac.jp

April Jehan MORRIS, 1114 Camino La Costa, Apt. 2075, Austin, Texas 78752, U.S.A.; ajehanmorris@gmail.com

The Rev. Prof. Colin MORRIS, 12 Bassett Crescent East, Southampton SO16 7PB, ENGLAND, U.K.; cm5@soton.ac.uk

Dr Rosemary MORRIS, Dept. of History, Univ. of York, York YO10 5DD, ENGLAND, U.K.; rm22@york.ac.uk

Michael MORTON, 19 Bruce Street, Even Swindon, Swindon, Wiltshire SN2 2El, ENGLAND, U.K.; michaelmorton37@hotmail.co.uk

Dr Nicholas MORTON, School of Arts and Humanities, Nottingham Trent University, Clifton Lane, Nottingham, NG11 8NS, ENGLAND, U.K.; nicholas.morton@ntu.ac.uk

Suleiman Ali MOURAD, Smith College, Dept. of Religion, Wright Hall 114, Northampton MA 01063, U.S.A.; smourad@smith.edu

Dr Alan V. MURRAY, International Medieval Institute, The University of Leeds, Parkinson 103, Leeds LS2 9JT, ENGLAND, U.K.; a.v.murray@leeds.ac.uk

Stephen R. A. MURRAY, Apartment 351, 176 The Esplanade, Toronto, Ontario M5A 4H2, CANADA; sramurray@hotmail.com

286 SOCIETY FOR THE STUDY OF THE CRUSADES
Claude Mutafian, 216, rue Saint-Jacques, 75005 Paris, FRANCE; claude.mutafian@wanadoo.fr

Liz Mylod, Liz Mylod, Institute for Medieval Studies, Parkinson 4.06, University of Leeds, Leeds, LS2 9JT, ENGLAND, U.K.; e.j.mylod@leeds.ac.uk

Dr Abdollah Naseri Taheri, P.O Box 19935-581, Tehran, IRAN; a.naseri@tarikhnevesht.com and naseri_na@yahoo.com

James Naus, Dept. of History, Saint Louis Univ., 3800 Lindell Boulevard, Saint Louis MO 63108, U.S.A.; nausjl@slu.edu

Alan Neill, 13 Chesham Crescent, Belfast BT6 8GW, NORTHERN IRELAND, U.K.; neilla@rescueteam.com

Dr Helen J. Nicholson, Cardiff School of History, Archaeology and Religion, Cardiff University, Humanities Building, Colum Drive, Cardiff CF10 3EU, WALES, U.K.; nicholsonhj@cardiff.ac.uk

Angel Nicolaou-Konnari, P.O. Box 54106, 3721 Limassol, CYPRUS; an.konnaris@cytanet.com.cy

Dr David Nicolle, 67 Maplewell Road, Woodhouse Eaves, Leicestershire LE12 8RG, ENGLAND, U.K.; david.c.nicolle@btinternet.com

J. Mark Nicovich, 119 Short Bay Street, Hattiesburg MS 39401, U.S.A.; mnicovich@wmcarey.edu

Prof. Torben Kjersgaard Nielsen, Institute for History, International and Social Studies, Aalborg Univ., Fibigerstraede 5, 9220 Aalborg OE, DENMARK; tkn@ihis.aau.dk

Yoav Nitzen, 4 H'Adereth Street, Jerusalem 92343, ISRAEL; raem@bezeqint.net

Leila Norako, 1415 Clover St., Rochester, NY 14610, U.S.A.; lknorako@gmail.

Dr Randall L. Norstrem, 28822 Pacific Highway S., Federal Way WA 98003, U.S.A.; templariidvm@yahoo.com

Elvor Andersen Oftestad, Faculty of Theology, Postboks 1023 Blindern, 0315 Oslo, NORWAY; e.a.oftestad@teologi.uio.no

Dr Gregory O'Malley, 4 Holly Bank, Hugglescote, Leicestershire LE67 2FR, ENGLAND, U.K.; gregoryomalley@btinternet.com

Prof. Mahmoud Said Omran, History Dept., Faculty of Arts, Univ. of Alexandria, Alexandria, EGYPT; msomran@dataxprs.com.eg; Web Site: www.msomran.com

Col. Erhard (Erik) Opsahl, 5303 Dennis Drive, McFarland WI 53558, U.S.A.; epopsahlw@aol.com

Jilana Ordman, 2525 W Cortex St., Apartment 2, Chicago IL 60622, U.S.A.; jordman@luc.edu

Rhiain O'Sullivan, Second Floor Flat, 116-117 Saffron Hill, London EC1N 8QS, ENGLAND, U.K.; rhiainaroundtheworld@hotmail.com

Catherine Otten, 9, rue de Londres, 67000 Strasbourg, FRANCE; otten@umb.u-strasbg.fr.

Marcello Pacifico, Corso Pisani 274, 90120 Palermo, ITALY; marcellopacifico@unipa.it

Barbara Packard, 35 Marnham Crecent, Greenford, Middlesex UB6 9SW, ENGLAND, U.K.; bcpackard@yahoo.co.uk

Dr Johannes Pahlitzsch, Parallelstraße 12, 12209 Berlin, GERMANY; pahlitz@zedat.fu-berlin.de

Dr Aphrodite Papayianni, 40 Inverness Terrace, London W2 3JB, ENGLAND, U.K.; aphroditepapayianni@hotmail.com

Danielle Park, 2 Blagrave Rise, Tilehurst, Reading, Berks RG31 4SF, ENGLAND, U.K.; D.Park@rhul.ac.uk

Kenneth Scott Parker, History Dept., Royal Holloway, Univ. of London, Egham, Surrey TW20 0EX, ENGLAND, U.K.; kscottparker@gmail.com

Dr Peter D. Partner, Murhill Farmhouse, Murhill, Limpley Stoke, Bath BA2 7FH, ENGLAND, U.K.; pdp4@aol.com

Aurelio Pastori Ramos, 8424 NW 56th. Street, Suite MVD 05249, Miami, FL 33166, U.S.A.; apastori@correo.um.edu.uy; or: Ejido 1365/802, 11100 Montevideo, URUGUAY; apastori@um.edu.uy

Martin Patail, 2211 South West First Avenue Unit 102, Portland OR 97210, U.S.A.; patailm@pdx.edu

Dr Nicholas L. Paul, Department of History, Fordham University, Dealy Hall, 441 E. Fordham Road, Bronx, NY 10458, U.S.A.; npaul@fordham.edu

Prof. Jacques Paviot, Faculté des Lettres et Sciences humaines, Université de Paris XII – Val de Marne, 61, avenue du Général de Gaulle, F-94010 Créteil Cedex, FRANCE; paviot@u-pec.fr

Michael J. Peixoto, 168 East 82nd Street, Apartment 5B, New York NY 10028-2214, U.S.A.

Peter Shlomo Peleg, 2 Mordhai Street, Kiryat Tivon 36023, ISRAEL; fax 972 4 9931 122; ppeleg@netvision.net.il

*Stelios Vasilis Perdios, 1344 Walton Dr, app. 206, Ames, IA 50014, U.S.A.; sperdios3@gmail.com

Christopher Perkins, 137 Adrian Drive, Stockbridge, GA 30281, U.S.A.; gop7384@yahoo.com

Dr Photeine V. Perra, Hexamilia Corinth, Corinth 201 00, GREECE; fperra@hol.gr

Prof. David M. Perry, Assistant Professor, Dept. of History, Dominican Univ., 7900 Division Street, River Forest IL 60305, U.S.A.; dperry@dom.edu

Guy Perry, Lincoln College, Oxford, OXI 3DR, England, U.K.; guy.perry@lincoln.ox.ac.uk

Nicholas J. Perry, P.O. Box 389, La Mesa NM 88044, U.S.A.; nicholasperry@earthlink.net

James Petre, The Old Barn, 8A Church Road, Stevington, Bedfordshire MK43 7QB, ENGLAND, U.K.; jamespetre@btinternet.com

Theodore D. Petro, New England College, 98 Bridge Street, P.O. Box 74, Henniker NH 03242, U.S.A.; tpetro@nec.edu

*Natalia I. Petrovskaia, Peterhouse, Cambridge, CB2 1RD, ENGLAND, U.K.; np272@cam.ac.uk

Dr Christopher Matthew Phillips, Social Science Dept., Concordia Univ., 800 N. Columbia Avenue, Seward NE 68434, U.S.A.; Matthew.Phillips@cune.edu

Prof. Jonathan P. Phillips, Dept. of History, Royal Holloway Univ. of London, Egham, Surrey TW20 0EX, ENGLAND, U.K.; j.p.phillips@rhul.ac.uk

Dr Simon D. Phillips, 15 Parthenonos Street, Apt. 202, Strovolos 2020, CYPRUS; simondph@ucy.ac.cy

Dr Mathias Piana, Benzstraße 9, 86420 Diedorf, GERMANY; mathias.piana@phil.uni-augsburg.de

Dr Maria Cristina PIMENTA, Rua Costa Cabral, 1791 1º, 4200-228 Porto, PORTUGAL; cristina_pimenta@sapo.pt

Marion PINCEMAILLE, 15 rue des Rossignols, 67320 Ottwiller, FRANCE; marion.pincemaille@gmail.com

Paula Maria de Carvalho PINTO COSTA, Faculdade de Letras da Universidade do Porto, Via Panorâmica, s/n, 4150-564 Porto, PORTUGAL; ppinto@letras.up.pt

Dr Karol POLEJOWSKI, Ul. Wadowicka, 1B/12, 80-180 Gdansk, POLAND; k.polejowski@univ.gda.pl

Cleber Da Silva PONTES, Rua Silva Rosa, nº 261/ apt. 402, Maria da Graça, Rio de Janeiro – RJ 21050-650, BRASIL; cl-pontes@hotmail.com

Jon PORTER, Global Historical Program, Butler University, 4600 Sunset Avenue, Indianapolis IN 46208, U.S.A.; jporter1@butler.edu

Valentin PORTNYCKH, 2 Pigorov Street, 630090, Novosibirsk, RUSSIA; valport@list.ru

Prof. James M. POWELL, 5100 Highbridge Street, Apartment 18D, Fayetteville NY 13066, U.S.A.; mpowell@dreamscape.com

Dr Amanda POWER, Department of History, University of Sheffield, Sheffield, S 10 2TN, U.K.; a.power@sheffield.ac.uk

Prof. R. Denys PRINGLE, School of History and Archaeology, Cardiff Univ., P.O. Box 909, Cardiff CF10 3EU, WALES, U.K.; pringlerd@cardiff.ac.uk

Dragan PROKIC, M.A., Rubensallee 47, 55127 Mainz, GERMANY; dragan.prokic@o2online.de

Prof. John H. PRYOR, Centre for Medieval Studies, Univ. of Sydney, John Wolley Building A20, Sydney, New South Wales 2006, AUSTRALIA; john.pryor@usyd.edu.au

Dr Emmanuelle PUJEAU, Ca Antica d'En Duras, Chemin de Fregouville, 32200 Maurens, France; emmanuelle.pujeau@wanadoo.fr

Dr William J. PURKIS, School of History and Cultures, Univ. of Birmingham, Edgbaston, Birmingham B15 2TT, ENGLAND, U.K.; w.j.purkis@bham.ac.uk

Rachael PYMM, 4 Beechtree Avenue, Englefield Green, Egham, Surrey TW20 0SR, ENGLAND, U.K.; peruvian_explorer@hotmail.com

Gary RAMSELL, 25 Kings Road, East Sheen, London, SW148PF, ENGLAND, U.K.; gary@ramsell.com

Prof. Pierre RACINE, 8, rue Traversière, 67201 Eckbolsheim, FRANCE; racine.p@evc.net

Yevgeniy / Eugene RASSKAZOV, Worth Avenue Station, P.O. Box 3497, Palm Beach FL 33480-3497, U.S.A.; medievaleurope@apexmail.com

Burnam W. REYNOLDS, P.O. Box 51, 400 McCauley Pike, Wilmore, KY 40390, U.S.A.; burnam.reynolds@asbury.edu

Prof. Jean RICHARD, 12, rue Pelletier de Chambure, 21000 Dijon, FRANCE

Maurice RILEY Esq., 2 Swallow Court, Winsford, Cheshire CW7 1SR, ENGLAND, U.K.; rileymaurice@yahoo.com

Prof. Jonathan S. C. RILEY-SMITH, The Downs, Croxton, St Neots, Cambridgeshire PE19 4SX, ENGLAND, U.K.; jonathan.rileysmith@btinternet.com

Dr Rebecca RIST, Department of History, University of Reading, Reading, RG6 6AH, ENGLAND, U.K.; r.a.c.rist@reading.ac.uk

Daniel ROACH, 7 Waverley Avenue, Exeter, Devon EX4 4NL, ENGLAND, U.K.; dr229@ex.ac.uk

Prof. Louise Buenger ROBBERT, 709 South Skinker Boulevard Apartment 701, St Louis MO 63105, U.S.A.; lrobbert@mindspring.com

Jason T. ROCHE, Seaview, Kings Highway, Largoward, Fife KY9 1HX, SCOTLAND, U.K.; jtr@st-andrews.ac.uk

José Manuel RODRÍGUEZ-GARCÍA, Av. Conde de Aranda 1, 3° E, 28200 San Lorenzo del Escorial (Madrid), ESPAÑA; anaevjosem@hotmail.com

*Keoen ROELANDTS, 2393 Spring Mill Estates Dr, Saint Charles, MO 63303, U.S.A.; kroeland@slu.edu

Jean-Marc ROGER, 14 rue Jean Jaurès, 86000 Poitiers, FRANCE; j-m.roger@wanadoo.fr

Prof. Manuel ROJAS, Departamento de Historia, Facultad de Filosofia y Lettras, Universidad de Extremadura, 10071- Càceres, SPAIN; mrojas@unex.es

*Anne ROMINE, 5537 Dugan Avenue, Saint Louis MO 63110, U.S.A.

Prof. Myriam ROSEN-AYALON, Institute of Asian and African Studies, The Hebrew Univ., Jerusalem 91905, ISRAEL

Prof. John ROSSER, Dept. of History, Boston College, Chestnut Hill MA 02467, U.S.A.; rosserj@bc.edu

*Shirley ROSSI-RIVERA, 2205 Roslyn Ln, Lakeland, FL 33812, U.S.A.; rossirivera@rocketmail.com

Jesse S. ROUSE, 8001 160th Ave, Bristol, WI 53104, U.S.A.; sikkibahm@hotmail.com

Prof. Jay RUBENSTEIN, Dept. of History, Univ. of Tennessee, 6th Floor, Dunford Hall, Knoxville TN 37996-4065, U.S.A.; jrubens1@utk.edu

Jonathan RUBIN, Elazar Hamodai 12, Jerusalem 93671, ISRAEL; yonigali@gmail.com

Prof. Frederick H. RUSSELL, Dept. of History, Conklin Hall, Rutgers Univ., Newark NJ 07102, U.S.A.; frussell@andromeda.rutgers.edu

Prof. James D. RYAN, 100 West 94th Street, Apartment 26M, New York, NY 10025, U.S.A.; james.d.ryan@verizon.net

Vincent RYAN, Dept. of History, Saint Louis Univ., 3800 Lindell Boulevard, Saint Louis MO 63108, U.S.A.; ryanvt@slu.edu

Sebastian SALVADO, 308 Gateway Drive, Apt. 236, Pacifica CA 94044, U.S.A.

Dr Andrew J. SARGENT, 33 Coborn Street, Bow, London E3 2AB, ENGLAND, U.K.; asargent164@gtinternet.com

Prof. Juergen SARNOWSKY, Historisches Seminar, Universität Hamburg, Von-Melle-Park 6, 20146 Hamburg, GERMANY; juergen.sarnowsky@uni-hamburg.de

Christopher J. SAUNDERS OBE, Watery Hey, Springvale Road, Hayfield, High Peak SK22 2LD, ENGLAND, U.K.; christopher.saunders@savoyim.com

Prof. Alexios G. C. SAVVIDES, Aegean Univ., Dept. of Mediterranean Studies, Rhodes, GREECE; or: 7 Tralleon Street, Nea Smyrne, Athens 17121, GREECE; savvides@rhodes.aegean.gr

Christopher SCHABEL, Dept. of History and Archaeology, Univ. of Cyprus, P.O. Box 20537, 1678 Nicosia, CYPRUS; schabel@ucy.ac.cy

Dr Jochen SCHENK, German Historical Institute London, 17 Bloomsbury Square, London WC1A 2NJ, ENGLAND, U.K.; schenk@ghil.ac.uk

Dr James G. SCHRYVER, Univ. of Minnesota Morris, HUM 104, 600 East 4th Street, Morris MN 56267, U.S.A.; schryver@morris.umn.edu

Warren C. SCHULZ, De Paul Univ., Dept. of History, 2320 Kenmore, Chicago, IL 60614, U.S.A.; wschultz@depaul.edu

Dr Beate SCHUSTER, 19, rue Vauban, 67000 Strasbourg, FRANCE; beaschu@compuserve. com

Prof. Rainer C. SCHWINGES, Historisches Institut der Universität Bern, Unitobler – Länggass-Straße 49, 3000 Bern 9, SWITZERLAND; rainer.schwinges@hist.unibe.ch

Einat SEGAL, 20 Neve Rehim Street, Ramat Hasharon, ISRAEL; eisegal@netvision.net.il

Iris SHAGRIR, Dept. of History, The Open Univ. of Israel, P.O. Box 808, Ra'anana 43107, ISRAEL; irissh@openu.ac.il

*Joseph SHANNON, 269 Lawson Street, Saline, MI 48176, U.S.A.; salinecett@yahoo.com

Prof. Maya SHATZMILLER, 19 King Street, London, Ontario N6A 5N8, CANADA; maya@ uwo.ca

Dr Teresa SHAWCROSS, Trinity Hall, Cambridge CB2 1TJ, ENGLAND, U.K.; teresa. shawcross@googlemail.com

Dr Jonathan SHEPARD, Box 483, 266 Banbury Road, Oxford OX2 7DL, ENGLAND, U.K.; nshepard@easynet.co.uk

Vardit SHOTTEN-HALLEL, 12 Dan Street, P.O. Box 1404, Ramat Hasharon 47100, ISRAEL; shotten-hallel@012.net.il

William SHULL, 481 Barham Avenue, Henderson, TN 38340, U.S.A.; wshull@gmail.com

Dr Elizabeth J. SIBERRY, 28 The Mall, Surbiton, Surrey KT6 4E9, ENGLAND, U.K.; sibersealyham@totalise.co.uk

Kaare Seeberg SIDSELRUD, Granebakken 9, 1284 Oslo, NORWAY; kss@sidselrud.net

Raitis SIMSONS, Konsula 15A-1, Riga 1007, LATVIA; raitiss@btv.lv

Micaela SINIBALDI, School of History, Archaeology and Religion, Cardiff University, Humanities Building, Colum Drive, Cardiff CF 10 3EU, WALES, U.K.; sinibaldim@cardiff. ac.uk

Dr Corliss K. SLACK, Department of History, Apartment 1103, Whitworth University, Spokane WA 99251, U.S.A.; cslack@whitworth.edu

Rima E. SMINE, 25541 Altamont Road, Los Altos Hills CA 94022, U.S.A.

Dr Caroline SMITH, 551, 47th Road, 3L, Long Island City, NY 11101, U.S.A.; caroline.a.smith@ gmail.com

Thomas SMITH, Connaught Hall, 36-45 Tavistock Square, London, WC1H 9EX, U.K.; Thomas.Smith.2009@live.rhul.ac.uk

Simon SONNAK, 658 Canning Street, North Carlton, 3054 Victoria, AUSTRALIA; ssonnak@ bigpond.net.au

Arnold SPAER, 8 King David Street, Jerusalem 94104, ISRAEL; hui@spaersitton.co.il

Dr Alan M. STAHL, 11 Fairview Place, Ossining NY 10562, U.S.A.; amstahl@optonline.net

*Stefan STANTCHEV, 18007 N 88th Dr, Peoria, AZ 85382, U.S.A.; stefan.stantchev@asu.edu

Rombert STAPEL, Fryske Akademy, Postbus 54, 8900AB, Leeuwarden, The Netherlands / home: Koolgracht 33, 2312PD, Leiden, The Netherlands; rstapel@fryske-akademy.nl / r.j.stapel@hum.leidenuniv.nl

Rodney STARK, 170 Camino Rayo del Sol, Corales NM 87048, U.S.A.; rs@rodneystark.com

Patrick Stohler, Oetlingerstraße 192, 4057 Basel, SWITZERLAND; Patrick.Stohler@unibas.ch

Dr Myra Struckmeyer, 171 North Hamilton Road, Chapel Hill NC 27517, U.S.A.; struckme@alumni.unc.edu

Jace Stuckey, Louisiana Tech Univ., History Dept., P.O. Box 8548, Rushton, LA 71272, U.S.A.; jace@latech.edu

Miikka Tamminen, University of Tampere, Department of History and Philosophy, Kanslerinrinne 133014, B2067, FINLAND; miikka.tamminen@uta.fi

Prof. Dr Stefan Tebruck, Historisches Institut der Justus-Liebig-Universität Gießen, Otto-Behaghel-Str. 10 C 2, D-35394 Gießen, Germany; Stefan.Tebruck@geschichte.uni-giessen.de

Miriam Rita Tessera, via Moncalvo 16, 20146 Milano, ITALY; monachus_it@yahoo.it

Prof. Peter Thorau, Historisches Institut, Univ. des Saarlandes, for letters Postfach 15 11 50, 66041 Saarbrücken, for packages Im Stadtwald, 66123 Saarbrücken, GERMANY; p.thorau@mx.uni-saarland.de

*Susanna Throop, Ursinus College, History Department, PO Box 1000, Collegeville, PA 19426-1000, U.S.A.; sthroop@ursinus.edu

Dr Steven Tibble, Copsewood, Deadhearn Lane, Chalfont St Giles, Buckinghamshire HP8 4HG, ENGLAND, U.K.; steve.tibble@btinternet.com

Prof. Hirofumi Toko, 605-3 Kogasaka, Machida, Tokyo 194-0014, JAPAN; htoko@mtd.biglobe.ne.jp

Prof. John Victor Tolan, Département d'Histoire, Université de Nantes, B.P. 81227, 44312 Nantes, FRANCE, or: 2, rue de la Chevalerie, 44300 Nantes, FRANCE; john.tolan@univ-nantes.fr

Ignacio de la Torre, Saxifraga 9, 28036 Madrid, ESPAÑA; ide@profesor.ie.edu

Prof. François-Olivier Touati, Département d'Histoire et d'Archéologie, Université François-Rabelais, 3 rue des Tanneurs, B.P. 4103, F-37041 Tours Cedex 1, or: La Croix Saint-Jérôme, 11, allée Émile Bouchut, 77123 Noisy-sur-École, FRANCE; francoistouati@aol.com

Dr Christopher J. Tyerman, Hertford College, Oxford, Catte Street, Oxford OX1 3BW, ENGLAND, U.K.; christopher.tyerman@hertford.ox.ac.uk

Dr Judith M. Upton-Ward, 6 Haywood Court, Reading, Berks., RG1 3QF, ENGLAND, U.K.; juptonward@btopenworld.com

*Jean-Bernard de Vaivre, Vieux Château, Le Bourg, 71800 Amanze, FRANCE; jbv@100cibles.fr

*Theresa Van, Hill Museum & Manuscript Library, Saint John's University, Collegeville, MN 56321, U.S.A.; tvann@csbsju.edu

*Jan Vandeburie, De Gribovalstraat 9, 8550 Zwevegem, BELGIUM; jv68@kent.ac.uk

*Øyvind Fossum Vangberg, Engveien 10, 1920 Sørumsand, NORWAY; ofvangberg@live.no

*Dweezil Vandekerckhove, Talybont South, Trotman Dickinson Place, House 20/0/1-4, Cardiff C14 3UU, WALES, U.K.; vandekerckhoved@cardiff.ac.uk

Toon Van Elst, Prof. Piccardlaan 32, 2610 Wilrijk, BELGIUM; toonvanelst@hotmail.com

Theresa M. Vann, Hill Monastic Manuscript Library, St John's Univ., Collegeville MN 56321, U.S.A.; tvann@csbsju.edu

Rafael Velázquez Parejo, c/ Villa de Rota, nº2, 4º F, 14005 Córdoba, ESPAÑA; mariceli50@hotmail.com

Dr Lucas VILLEGAS-ARISTIZABAL, 286 Queens Road East, Beeston, Nottingham, Nottinghamshire, NG9 1JA, ENGLAND, U.K.; lucasvillegasa@gmail.com

Fiona Weir WALMSLEY, 41 Broomley Street, Kangaroo Point, Queensland 4169, AUSTRALIA; f.walmsley@optusnet.com.au

Laura WANGERIN, 811 W. Belden Avenue, Chicago, IL 60614, U.S.A.; lwangerin@latinschool. org

Dr Marie-Louise VON WARTBURG MAIER, Paphosprojekt der Universität Zürich, Karl Schmid-Strasse 4, CH-8006 Zürich; ml.v.wartburg@access.uzh.ch

Michael WASSON, P.O. box 940, Randwick PO Randwick N.S.W. 2031, AUSTRALIA; mwasson7@bigpond.com

Benjamin WEBER, 31, avenue Étienne Billières, 31300 Toulouse, FRANCE; benji.tigrou@gmail.com

Steven A. WEIDENKOPF, 6814 Barnack Drive, Springfield, VA 22152, U.S.A.; the. weidenkopfs@verizon.net

Dr Mark WHITTOW, St Peter's College, Oxford OX1 2DL, ENGLAND, U.K.; mark.whittow@st-peters.oxford.ac.uk

Raymond WIESNER, 1725 Graham Avenue, Apartment 409, St. Paul MN 55116-3280, U.S.A.; raymondwiesner@yahoo.com

Timothy WILKES, A. H. Baldwin & Sons Ltd., 11 Adelphi Terrace, London WC2N 6BJ, ENGLAND, U.K.; timwilkes@baldwin.sh

The Rev. Dr John D. WILKINSON, 7 Tenniel Close, London W2 3LE, ENGLAND, U.K.; johnwilkinson@globalnet.co.uk

Dr Ann WILLIAMS, 40 Greenwich South Street, London SE10 8UN, ENGLAND, U.K.; ann. williams@talk21.com

Prof. Steven James WILLIAMS, Dept. of History, New Mexico Highlands Univ., P.O. Box 9000, Las Vegas NM 87701, U.S.A.; stevenjameswilliams@yahoo.com

Ian James WILSON, 1 Freeman Close, Hadleigh, Suffolk, IP7 6HH, England, U.K.; ian. wilson@btopenworld.com

Peter van WINDEKENS, Kleine Ganzendries 38, 3212 Pellenberg, BELGIUM; wit.hus@skynet.be

Prof. Johanna Maria VAN WINTER, Keizerstraat 35 A, NL-3512 EA Utrecht, NETHERLANDS; j.m.vanwinter@uu.nl

Ashley Sarah WINTERBOTTOM, 158 Broadway, Chadderton, Oldham. OL9 0JY, ENGLAND, U.K.; ashley.winterbottom@hud.ac.uk

Dr Noah WOLFSON, 13 Avuqa Street, Tel-Aviv 69086, ISRAEL; noah@meteo-tech.co.il

Prof. Shunji YATSUZUKA, 10–22 Matsumoto 2 chome, Otsu-shi, Shiga 520, JAPAN; shunchan@mub.biglobe.ne.jp

William G. ZAJAC, 9 Station Terrace, Pen-y-rheal, Caerphilly, CF83 2RH, WALES, U.K.

Prof. Ossama Zaki ZEID, 189 Abd al-Salam Aref Tharwat, Alexandria, EGYPT; ossama_zeid@hotmail.com

Joseph ZELNIK, 25 Wingate Street, Ra'anana 43587, ISRAEL; jzelnik@galilcol.ac.il

Ann ZIMO, 2809 Pleasant Avenue, Apt. 106, Minneapolis, MN 55408, U.S.A.; zimox001@umn.edu

Institutions subscribing to the SSCLE

Bibliothécaire Guy Cobolet, Le Bibliothécaire, École Française d'Athènes, 6, Didotou 10680 Athènes, GREECE

Centre de Recherches d'histoire et civilisation de Byzance et du Proche-Orient Chétien, Université de Paris 1, 17, rue de la Sorbonne, 75231 Paris Cedex, FRANCE

Centre for Byzantine, Ottoman and Modern Greek Studies, Univ. of Birmingham, Edgbaston, Birmingham B15 2TT, ENGLAND, U.K.

Corpus Christianoru, Brepols Publishers, Sint-Annaconvent, Begijnhof 39, 2300 Turnhout, BELGIUM

Couvent des Pères Dominicains, Saint-Étienne, Bibliotèque, P.O. Box 19053, 91 190, Jerusalem, ISRAEL

Deutsches Historisches Institut in Rom, Via Aurelia Antica 391, 00165 Roma, ITALY

Deutschordenszentralarchiv (DOZA), Singerstraße 7, 1010 Wien, AUSTRIA

Dumbarton Oaks Research Library, 1703 32nd Street North West, Washington D.C. 20007, U.S.A.

Europäisches Burgeninstitut, Schlossstraße 5, 56338 Braubach, GERMANY; ebi@deutsche-burgen.org

Germanisches Nationalmuseum, Bibliothek, Kornmarkt 1, 90402 Nürnberg, GERMANY

History Department, Campbell College, Belfast, BT4 2 ND, NORTHERN IRELAND, U.K.

The Jewish National and University Library, P.O. Box 34165, Jerusalem 91341, ISRAEL

The Library, The Priory of Scotland of the Most Venerable Order of St John, 21 St John Street, Edinburgh EH8 8DG, SCOTLAND, U.K.

The National Library of Israel, Periodical Department, P.O. Box 39105, 91390 Jerusalem, ISRAEL

The Stephen Chan Library, Institute of Fine Arts, New York Univ., 1 East 78th Street, New York NY 10021-0102, U.S.A.

Metropolitan Museum of Art, Thomas J. Watson Library, Serials Dept., 1000 Fifth Avenue, New York NY 10028-0198, U.S.A.

Museum and Library of the Order of St John, St John's Gate, Clerkenwell, London EC1M 4DA, ENGLAND, U.K.

Order of the Temple of Jerusalem, Priory of England and Wales, c/o Mr. John Reddington, 2 Alberta Gardens, Coggeshall, Coldchester, Essex CO6 1UA, ENGLAND, U.K.

Serials Department, 11717 Young Research Library, Univ. of California, Box 951575, Los Angeles CA 90095-1575, U.S.A.

Sourasky Library, Tel-Aviv Univ., Periodical Dept., P.O. Box 39038, Tel-Aviv, ISRAEL

Teutonic Order Bailiwick of Utrecht, Dr John J. Quarles van Ufford, Secretary of the Bailliwick, Springweg 25, 3511 VJ Utrecht, THE NETHERLANDS

Türk Tarih Kurumu [Turkish Historical Society], Kizilay Sokak No. 1, Sihhiye 06100 Ankara, TURKEY

Eberhard-Karls-Universität Tübingen, Orientalisches Seminar, Münzgasse 30, 72072 Tübingen, GERMANY

University of California Los Angeles Serials Dept. / YRL, 11717 Young Research Library, Box 951575, Los Angeles CA 90095-1575, U.S.A.

*University of California, Los Angeles Serials Dept. / YRL, 11020 Kinross, Box 957230, Los Angeles CA 90 095-723, U.S.A.

University of London Library, Periodicals Section, Senate House, Malet Street, London, WC1E 7HU, ENGLAND, U.K.

University of North Carolina, Davis Library CB 3938, Periodicals and Serials Dept., Chapel Hill NC 27514-8890, U.S.A.

Universitätsbibliothek Tübingen, Wilhelmstraße 32, Postfach 26 20, 72016 Tübingen, GERMANY

University of Reading, Graduate Centre for Medieval Studies, Whiteknights, P.O. Box 218, Reading, Berks., RG6 6AA, ENGLAND, U.K

University of Washington, Libraries, Serials Division, P.O. Box 352900, Seattle WA 98195, U.S.A.

University of Western Ontario Library, Acquisitions Dept., Room M1, D. B. Weldon Library, London, Ontario N6A 3K7, CANADA

The Warburg Institute, Univ. of London, Woburn Square, London WC1H 0AB, ENGLAND, U.K. [John Perkins, Deputy Librarian, jperkins@a1.sas.ac.uk]

W. F. Albright Institute of Archaeological Research, 26 Salah ed-Din Street, P.O. Box 19096, Jerusalem 91190, ISRAEL

12. Officers of the Society

President: Professor Bernard Hamilton.

Honorary Vice-Presidents: Professor Jean Richard, Professor Jonathan Riley-Smith, Professor Benjamin Z. Kedar, Professor Michel Balard.

Secretary: Professor Luis García-Guijarro Ramos.

Assistant Secretary: Professor Adrian Boas.

Conference Secretary: Professor Manuel Rojas

Editor of the Bulletin: Professor François-Olivier Touati.

Treasurer: Professor James D. Ryan.

Website: Dr Zsolt Hunyadi.

Officer for Postgraduate Members: Professor Jonathan Phillips.

Committee of the Society: Professor Antonio Carile (Bologna), Professor Robert Huygens (Leiden), Professor Hans Eberhard Mayer (Kiel).

Guidelines for the Submission of Papers

The editors ask contributors to adhere to the following guidelines. Failure to do so will result in the article being returned to the author for amendment, or may result in its having to be excluded from the volume.

1. Submissions. Submissions should be sent as email attachments to one of the editors. Papers should be formatted using MS Word, double-spaced and with wide margins. Times New Roman (12 pt) is preferred. Remember to include your name and contact details (both postal and email addresses) on your paper.

2. Peer Review. All submissions will be peer reviewed. They will be scrutinized by the editors and sent to at least one outside reader before a decision on acceptance is made.

3. Length. Normally, the maximum length of articles should not exceed 6,000 words, not including notes. The editors reserve the right to edit papers that exceed these limits.

4. Notes. Normally, notes should be REFERENCE ONLY and placed at the end of the paper. Number continuously.

5. Style sheet. Please use the most recent *Speculum* style sheet (currently *Speculum* 75 (2000), 547–52). This sets out the format to be used for notes. Please note that this is not necessarily the same format as has been used by other edited volumes on the crusades and/or the Military Orders. Failure to follow the Speculum format will result in accepted articles being returned to the author for amendment. In the main body of the paper you may adhere to either British or American spelling, but it must be consistent throughout the article.

6. Language. Papers will be published in English, French, German, Italian and Spanish.

7. Abbreviations. Please use the abbreviation list on pp. vii–ix of this journal.

8. Diagrams and Maps should be referred to as figures and photographs as plates. Please keep illustrations to the essential minimum, since it will be possible to include only a limited number. All illustrations must be supplied by the contributor in camera-ready copy, and free from all copyright restrictions.

9. Italics. Words to be printed in italics should be italicized if possible. Failing this they should be underlined.

10. Capitals. Please take every care to ensure consistency in your use of capitals and lower case letters. Use initial capitals to distinguish the general from the specific (for example, "the count of Flanders" but "Count Philip of Flanders").

11. Summary of Article. Contributors will be required to provide a 250 words summary of their paper at the start of each article. This will be accompanied by the author's email address. The summary of the paper is to be in English, regardless of the language of the main article.

Editors

Prof. Benjamin Z. Kedar
Department of History
The Hebrew University of Jerusalem
Jerusalem 91905, Israel
bzkedar@huji.ac.il

Prof. Jonathan Phillips
Department of History
Royal Holloway, University of London
Egham
Surrey TW20 0EX
U.K.
J.P.Phillips@rhul.ac.uk

SOCIETY FOR THE STUDY OF THE CRUSADES AND THE LATIN EAST
MEMBERSHIP INFORMATION

The primary function of the Society for the Study of the Crusades and the Latin East is to enable members to learn about current work being done in the field of crusading history, and to contact members who share research interests through the information in the Society's Bulletin. There are currently 467 members of the SSCLE from 41 countries. The Society also organizes a major international conference every four years, as well as sections on crusading history at other conferences where appropriate.

The committee of the SSCLE consists of:
Prof. Bernard Hamilton, *President*
Prof. Jean Richard, Prof. Jonathan Riley-Smith, Prof. Benjamin Z. Kedar and Prof. Michel Balard, *Honorary Vice-presidents*
Prof. Luis García-Guijarro Ramos, *Secretary*
Dr Adrian Boas, *Assistant Secretary*
Prof. Manuel Rojas, *Conference Secretary*
Prof. James D. Ryan, *Treasurer*
Prof. Jonathan Phillips, *Officer for Postgraduate Members*
Prof. François-Olivier Touati, *Bulletin Editor*
Dr Zsolt Hunyadi, *Website*

Current subscription fees are as follows:
* Membership and Bulletin of the Society: Single £10, $20 or €15;
* Student £6, $12 or €9;
* Joint membership £15, $30 or €21;
* Membership and the journal *Crusades*, including the Bulletin: £25, $46 or €32.